BASIC
COMMUNITY
LAWS

FOURTH EDITION

EDITED BY

BERNARD RUDDEN

AND

DERRICK WYATT

CLARENDON PRESS · OXFORD

1993

Oxford University Press, Walton Street, Oxford OX2 6DP

Oxford New York Toronto
Delhi Bombay Calcutta Madras Karachi
Petaling Jaya Singapore Hong Kong Tokyo
Nairobi Dar es Salaam Cape Town
Melbourne Auckland
and associated companies in
Berlin Ibadan

Oxford is a trade mark of Oxford University Press

Published in the United States
by Oxford University Press, New York

First published 1980
Second edition 1986
Third edition 1992
Fourth Edition 1993

British Library Cataloguing in Publication Data
Data available

Library of Congress Cataloging in Publication Data
Data available
ISBN 0–19–876326–3 (cloth)
ISBN 0–19–876327–1 (pbk)

Set by Hope Services (Abingdon) Ltd
Printed in Great Britain by
Biddles Ltd, Guildford and King's Lynn

PREFACE TO THE FOURTH EDITION

Our aim as always is to provide a handy collection of the basic primary and secondary legislation of the European Community. Unfortunately events conspire to make each edition longer than its predecessors. The Treaty on European Union signed at Maastricht on 7 February 1992 was first rejected by the Danes, and the UK Parliament is taking a very long time to approve ratification. Designed to lead the Member States to economic and monetary union, the new Treaty makes basic changes to the founding documents—above all to the Treaty establishing the EEC. Furthermore, it subsumes in treaty form developments which were earlier brought about by means of other instruments such as the Single European Act, Council Decisions, and Joint Declarations.

It has also faced the editors of this work with a dilemma. One alternative was to print the whole new Treaty separately, although most of its text consists of amendments to existing Treaties. A second possibility was to give only the latest amended version of the founding Treaties. The third alternative was to attempt a composite text, presenting both the old and the new versions of the law. We selected this last option, and give the new law in square, and the old in curly, brackets. The main arguments against this choice are that it increases the length of the work, and results in a text whose form is typographically unpleasing. The following considerations, however, prompted our decision: it seems a more scholarly way of presenting the new text for the first time, for it enables the reader accustomed to the old law to see at once what changes have been made; and the Court of Justice is seised of a number of references on the interpretation of provisions whose form or substance is altered only for the period after the TEU takes effect—consequently the old text will still be important for some years to come.

The problem of keeping this edition within a reasonable compass has been tackled as follows. Part I contains extracts from the ECSC Treaty; the EC Treaty with related acts; the TEU with related acts; the Denmark documents; and, at the suggestion of practitioners, the Court's Statute and Rules of Procedure. Several instruments which appeared in earlier editions have been omitted. Such texts are of two types. Firstly, there are those whose substance reappears in the TEU—such as the 1965 Merger Treaty, the 1977 Human Rights Declaration, and the 1985 Own Resources Decision. Secondly, there are the Accessions documents, which by their very nature, have not been amended. As a replacement for these, we have compiled a historical table of significant developments which, where appropriate, refers the reader to the relevant pages in the earlier editions of this work. A brief Introduction tries to explain the main changes made by the Treaty of Maastricht to the structure of the Treaty of Rome.

Unless otherwise stated, the old Treaty texts are taken from those presented to the UK Parliament. The new Treaty provisions are in the form brought out by the Council and Commission and published by the Office for Official Publications of the European Communities. The same is true of the Declaration of 1 May 1992 on Protocol 17 (on the Irish Constitution's provision on abortion) and that of 12 December 1992 on Denmark. Secondary legislation is taken from the Official Journal of the European Communities. Obvious printing errors have been corrected without comment.

We are pleased to record our gratitude for the help given by Ms Barbara Tearle, Ms Elizabeth Martin, and by all the learned staff of the Bodleian Law Library, and for the patience and skill of the Oxford University Press and its printers. For errors of judgment, and for plain mistakes, we continue to accept joint and several liability.

BR
DW

Oxford, Midsummer 1993

CONTENTS

PART II SECONDARY LEGISLATION AND OTHER DOCUMENTS

The Free Movement of Goods

Freedom of Movement for Workers

The Right of Establishment and the Freedom to Provide Services

Competition

INTRODUCTION

A. European Union

The main, and modest, purpose of these paragraphs is to assist the reader accustomed to the old version of the community texts. The 1992 Treaty on European Union achieves its several aims partly by its own provisions (which are lettered, not numbered), partly by amending the existing Treaties, partly through Protocols, and perhaps partly through Declarations. Admittedly the articles of the EEC Treaty dealing with the four freedoms, with agriculture, and with competition remain basically the same. Yet the language, the location, and in many cases the substance of several key institutional, economic, and monetary provisions are much altered. Some of the TEU provisions and some of the amendments simply embody the substance of earlier instruments like the Merger Treaty, the Court of First Instance Decision, and the decisions of the ECJ in the cases involving the Parliament (e.g. 294/83 *Greens* [1986] ECR 1339, 34/86 *Council* v *Parliament* [1986] ECR 2155, C-70/88 *Chernobyl* [1990] ECR I-2041). Others go far beyond this.

We deal first with the changes, both in form and substance, to the EEC Treaty. Most of these are effected by amendments to that Treaty, but in a few cases articles are repealed and replaced by provisions of the TEU. As a preliminary, we note that the adjective 'economic' is dropped from the name of the Community, that article 6 is excised, and that articles 7 and 8 become 6 and 7. As a guide to the main alterations, we offer the following simplified grouping.

1. Constitutional amendments

(a) *European Union citizenship*. A new EC article 8 establishes Union citizenship together with the right to vote in local and European elections, and article 100c empowers the Council to determine the third countries whose nationals will require a visa to enter the Community.

(b) *Subsidiarity* is introduced by the TEU preamble and enacted by EC article 3b. This permits the Community, in areas not falling within its exclusive competence, to act only where what needs to be done cannot be sufficiently achieved by Member States but, because of its scale or effects, can be better done by the Community. A Committee of the

Regions, with advisory status, is set up by article 198a-c. It is intended to give a voice to representatives of regional and local bodies, of whom the most obvious current examples are the German *Länder* and the Spanish *Communidades autonomas*.

(c) *Human rights*, as guaranteed by the European Convention of 1950, are the subject of a Treaty commitment in TEU arts. F.2, J.1 (2) last para., and K.2.

(d) *Treaty amendments and the admission of new Member States* are dealt with by TEU arts. N and O. EEC arts.236 and 237 are repealed, but their substance is retained.

2. Institutional amendments

(a) *The European Parliament* is acknowledged to have legal, and not merely consultative, powers (EC art.137) and is given powers of co-decision on the internal market, education, consumer affairs and other sectors. It may be defendant and (within limits) plaintiff under EC art.173, and is directed to appoint an Ombudsman (art.138e). From 1995 the Parliament must approve nominations for appointment to the Commission (EC art.158(2)).

(b) *The European Council* (of Heads of State or Government) has its functions and composition set out in TEU art. D.

(c) *The Commission* will be appointed for the two years 1993-4, and will thereafter have a five-year term of office (EC art.158).

(d) *The Court of Justice* is empowered, at the suit of the Commission, to fine a Member State which fails to respect a judgment (EC art.171). Essentially, however, its jurisdiction remains confined to existing areas: TEU art.L.

(e) *The Court of Auditors* becomes a fifth Institution (EC art.4), and its powers are set out in arts.188a-c.

(f) *Banking entities* appear in EC art.4a-b. Although not given the name of institution, the European Central Bank (ECB) will be accorded law-making powers and other prerogatives (see EC arts.105-9, 180(d)), and will be subject to judicial review and legal liability (arts.173, 175-177, 215). A separate Protocol 3 enacts its statute and that of the European System of Central Banks. From 1994 until the ECB is established, the European Monetary Institute will hold a similar legal position (EC art.109f.(9) and Protocol 4).

(g) *The law-making interrelationship* among Council, Commission and Parliament is taken out of EC art.149 (repealed) and inserted in a new art.189a-c. Consequently, familiar phrases ('the Council, on a pro-posal from the Commission, in co-operation with the European

Parliament') are deleted from numerous provisions, to be replaced by a reference to the appropriate procedure under EC 189b (co-decision) or 189c.

3. Economic and Monetary Union.

Of this extremely complex sector, the following points seem worthy of immediate note. From 1994 there will be free movement of capital (EC art.73b-g). Monetary policy envisages that the deadline for currency union among those States which satisfy certain convergence criteria will be 1999 (EC art. 109j.(4)). The ecu rate will then be conclusively fixed, and the ECB will have the exclusive right to authorize the issue of bank-notes (EC arts.105a, 109g.). The revised provisions on economic policy will give the Council power to police and ultimately to fine a Member State whose government debt is too high (EC art.104c and Protocol 5)). The UK may, and Denmark will, remain outside the final stage of economic and monetary union (Protocols 11 and 12; Decision on Denmark of 12 December 1992).

4. Scope of the EC Treaty.

Additions to EC art.3 list a number of areas of Community activity, including education, culture, consumer protection, and tourism. Most of these fields are developed in new or amended articles of the EC Treaty.

5. Other Policies.

Two major areas fall outside the EC Treaties, but share the same institutional framework (TEU art.C). The provisions on a common foreign and security policy (TEU art.J) enable the European Council to lay down guidelines, and the Council to take decisions, on joint action. As to the decision-making procedure, the Council will be able (unanimously) to define matters on which decisions can be taken by qualified majority. Under the title of justice and home affairs, TEU art.K deals with immigration into the Community, asylum, and co-operation among judicial, customs, and police authorities. Subject to the subsidiarity principle, the Council has certain powers of decision by qualified majority.

6. Protocols.

Annexed to the EC Treaty are 17 protocols covering a number of subjects ranging from second homes in Denmark through the Statute of the

ECB, to the implementation of the Social Charter. Two are of particular
juridical interest. Protocol 2 tackles the decision in Case C-262/88 Barber
[1990] ECR I-1989 (which held that certain pension schemes fell under
EEC art.119) and limits its effect to periods after the decision was handed
down. Protocol 14 on social policy empowers 11 Member States to use
the Community institutions in order to adopt the legal acts and decisions
needed to implement the 1989 Social Charter. Unless measures are
adopted by all 12 Member States acting under the existing, and amended,
articles of the EC Treaty, the United Kingdom is to play no part in the
deliberative or legislative processes in this field.

7. Declarations.

The Intergovernmental Conferences added a number of Declarations.
From a purely legal point of view, the following are worthy of note. No.
2 states that, whenever the EC Treaty refers to 'nationals of Member
States', it is the State concerned (and not the EC) which decides who
counts as its national (this is reinforced in the Denmark Decision sect.A).
No. 10 expresses the view that the principles of Case 22/70 ERTA [1970]
ECR 263 are not affected by those articles which refer to the power of
Member States to conclude international agreements. No. 16 commits the
1996 Intergovernmental Conference to an examination and classification
of the different types of community juridical act.

   The Edinburgh Summit of December 1992 saw a Decision and
Declaration on Denmark, taken not by the Council on a proposal from
the Commission, but by the Heads of State and Government meeting
within the European Council.

B. Significant Dates and Developments

This table aims to give a swift, if superficial, overview, without detail or
punctilious dating. References to 1E, 2E or 3E indicate where relevant
documents will be found in those editions of this work.

1945 End of War in Europe

1949 Council of Europe created with consultative Assembly, and
Committee of Ministers. UK joins.

1950 Declaration of Robert Schuman (French Foreign Minister): Franco-
German coal and steel to be under a common 'higher authority'.

1952 ECSC established by Treaty of Paris, signed by the Six: France,
Germany, Italy, Belgium, Netherlands, Luxembourg. Has Assembly,
High Authority, Council, and Court. UK declines to join.

1953 Council of Europe's European Convention on Human Rights (ECHR) comes into force, with Commission on Human Rights.

1954 The Six fail to set up a European Defence Community.

1955 Intergovernmental Conference of the Six to prepare for the EEC. UK sends observers but declines to participate.

1958 EEC and Euratom Treaties come into force (signed 25/3/57). They share Assembly ('Parliament') and Court with ECSC.

1959 European Court of Human Rights (established under 1950 ECHR) comes into operation.

1960 European Free Trade Area (EFTA) set up.

1961 Negotiations begin on UK membership of EC.

1962 Start of Common Agricultural Policy.

1963 UK's application to EC fails.

1964 First Yaoundé Convention associates 17 African States with EEC.

1965 Merger Treaty: ECSC and EEC share High Authority/Commission and Council (1E/111).
Deadlock on CAP and majority voting. France boycotts Council.

1966 Luxembourg Accords break political deadlock (1E/71, 2E/79).

1967 UK, Ireland, Denmark, Norway apply for membership of EC.

1970 Council Decision on Own Resources (1E/120).

1971 Start of Common Fisheries Policy.
Second Yaoundé Convention in force.

1972 UK, Ireland, Denmark, Norway sign Accession Treaty. Norway (by referendum) rejects ratification.

1973 UK, Ireland, Denmark members of EC (2E/153).
Judgments Convention in force for Six.

1974 EC gains observer status at UNO.

1975 Budget Treaty. Joint Declaration on Conciliation Procedure (1E/124, 2E/131).
UK referendum on continued membership.

1976 First Lomé Convention (EEC and 46 African, Caribbean, Pacific countries).
Direct Elections decision (1E/126, 2E/133).

1977 Fishery limits extended to 200 miles.
Joint Declaration on Fundamental Rights (1E/131, 2E/138, 3E/158)

1978 European Monetary System (EMS) and exchange rate mechanism (ERM) set up by Council Resolution.

1979 First Direct Elections to EC Parliament.

1981 Greece joins EC (2E/163).
Second Lomé Convention in force.

1984 Second direct elections to European Parliament.

1985 Greenland leaves EC, remains associated territory (2E/172). Second Council Decision on Own Resources (2E/142).

1986 Spain and Portugal join EC (2E/175).
Third Lomé Convention in force.

1987 Single European Act in force (2E/147).
Turkey applies to join EC.

1988 EC Court of First Instance established.

1989 Third direct elections to European Parliament.
Austria applies to join EC.

1990 Germany united. UK joins ERM.
Fourth Lomé Convention in force.
Cyprus and Malta apply to join EC.

1991 Intergovernmental Conferences on Economic and Monetary Union and on Political Union: Maastricht accords.
Agreement on European Economic Area signed by EEC and EFTA ; ECJ holds it incompatible with community law.
Rome Convention (1980) on the law applicable to contractual obligations enters into force.
Soviet Union dies.
Sweden applies to join EC.

1992 TEU signed. Denmark (by June referendum) rejects ratification; European Council December Decision on Denmark. Amended Agreement on European Economic Area signed by EEC and EFTA (Austria, Finland, Iceland, Liechtenstein, Norway, Sweden, Switzerland); ECJ holds it compatible with community law; Switzerland (by December referendum) rejects ratification.
UK and Italy leave ERM
Finland and Switzerland apply to join EC.

1993 Deadline for internal market. Second Danish referendum on TEU ratification.

1999 Deadline for monetary union.

2001 ECSC Treaty due to expire.

PART I
THE TREATIES
AND
RELATED ACTS

Treaty Establishing the European Coal and Steel Community as Amended by Subsequent Treaties.
Paris, 18 April 1951

[*NB Amendments occasioned by the 1992 Treaty on European Union are in square brackets. Adjacent text in curly brackets will be deleted when the TEU enters into force.*]

[EXTRACTS]

The President of the Federal Republic of Germany, His Royal Highness The Prince Royal of Belgium, the President of the French Republic, the President of the Italian Republic, Her Royal Highness The Grand Duchess of Luxembourg, Her Majesty The Queen of the Netherlands,

Considering that world peace can be safeguarded only by creative efforts commensurate with the dangers that threaten it,

Convinced that the contribution which an organised and vital Europe can make to civilisation is indispensable to the maintenance of peaceful relations,

Recognising that Europe can be built only through practical achievements which will first of all create real solidarity, and through the establishment of common bases for economic development,

Anxious to help, by expanding their basic production, to raise the standard of living and further the works of peace,

Resolved to substitute for age-old rivalries the merging of their essential interests; to create, by establishing an economic community, the basis for a broader and deeper community among peoples long divided by bloody conflicts; and to lay the foundations for institutions which will give direction to a destiny henceforward shared,

Having decided to create a European Coal and Steel Community and to this end have designated as their plenipotentiaries: . . .

who, having exchanged their full powers, found in good and due form, have agreed as follows:

TITLE I. THE EUROPEAN COAL AND STEEL COMMUNITY

Article 1. By this Treaty, the High Contracting Parties establish among themselves a European Coal and Steel Community, founded upon a common market, common objectives and common institutions.

Article 2. The European Coal and Steel Community shall have as its task to contribute, in harmony with the general economy of the Member States and through the establishment of a common market as provided in Art. 4, to economic expansion, growth of employment and a rising standard of living in the Member States.

The Community shall progressively bring about conditions which will of themselves ensure the most rational distribution of production at the highest possible level of productivity, while safeguarding continuity of employment and taking care not to provoke fundamental and persistent disturbances in the economies of Member States.

Article 3. The institutions of the Community shall, within the limits of their respective powers, in the common interest:

(a) ensure an orderly supply to the common market, taking into account the needs of third countries;

(b) ensure that all comparably placed consumers in the common market have equal access to the sources of production;

(c) ensure the establishment of the lowest prices under such conditions that these prices do not result in higher prices charged by the same undertakings in other transactions or in a higher general price level at another time, while allowing necessary amortization and normal return on invested capital;

(d) ensure the maintenance of conditions which will encourage undertakings to expand and improve their production potential and to promote a policy of using natural resources rationally and avoiding their unconsidered exhaustion;

(e) promote improved working conditions and an improved standard of living for the workers in each of the industries for which it is responsible, so as to make possible their harmonisation while the improvement is being maintained;

(f) promote the growth of international trade and ensure that equitable limits are observed in export pricing;

(g) promote the orderly expansion and modernisation of production, and the improvement of quality, with no protection against competing industries that is not justified by improper action on their part or in their favour.

Article 4. The following are recognised as incompatible with the common market for coal and steel and shall accordingly be abolished and prohibited within the Community, as provided in this Treaty:

(a) import and export duties, or charges having equivalent effect, and quantitative restrictions on the movement of products;

(b) measures or practices which discriminate between producers, between purchasers or between consumers, especially in prices and delivery terms or transport rates and conditions, and measures or practices which interfere with the purchaser's free choice of supplier;

(c) subsidies or aids granted by States, or special charges imposed by States, in any form whatsoever;

(d) restrictive practices which tend towards the sharing or exploiting of markets.

Article 5. The Community shall carry out its task in accordance with this Treaty, with a limited measure of intervention.
To this end the Community shall:

provide guidance and assistance for the parties concerned, by obtaining information, organising consultations and laying down general objectives;

– place financial resources at the disposal of undertakings for their investment and bear part of the cost of readaptation;

– ensure the establishment, maintenance and observance of normal competitive conditions and exert direct influence upon production or upon the market only when circumstances so require;

– publish the reasons for its actions and take the necessary measures to ensure the observance of the rules laid down in this Treaty.

The institutions of the Community shall carry out these activities with a minimum of administrative machinery and in close co-operation with the parties concerned.

Article 6. The Community shall have legal personality.
In international relations, the Community shall enjoy the legal capacity it requires to perform its functions and attain its objectives.
In each of the Member States, the Community shall enjoy the most extensive legal capacity accorded to legal persons constituted in that State; it may, in particular, acquire or dispose of movable and immovable property and may be a party to legal proceedings.
The community shall be represented by its institutions, each within the limits of its powers.

Article 7. The Institutions of the Community shall be a High Authority {assisted by a Consultative Committee} [hereinafter referred to as 'the Commission';]
a Common Assembly (hereinafter {called} [referred to as] the {'Assembly'} [European Parliament;]

a Special Council of Ministers (hereinafter {called} [referred to as] the 'Council';)

a Court of Justice {(hereinafter called the 'Court';)}

[a Court of Auditors]

[The Commission shall be assisted by a Consultative Committee.] {The audit shall be carried out by a Court of Auditors acting within the limits of the powers conferred upon it by this Treaty.}

CHAPTER I. THE [COMMISSION] {HIGH AUTHORITY}

Article 8. It shall be the duty of the [Commission] {High Authority} to ensure that the objectives set out in this Treaty are attained in accordance with the provisions thereof.

Articles 9–13. [The same, mutatis mutandis, as E{E}C arts. 156–63]

Article 14. In order to carry out the tasks assigned to it the [Commission] {High Authority} shall, in accordance with the provisions of this Treaty, take decisions, make recommendations or deliver opinions.

Decisions shall be binding in their entirety.

Recommendations shall be binding as to the aims to be pursued but shall leave the choice of the appropriate methods for achieving these aims to those to whom the recommendations are addressed.

Opinions shall have no binding force.

In cases where the [Commission] {High Authority} is empowered to take a decision, it may confine itself to making a recommendation.

Article 15. Decisions, recommendations and opinions of the [Commission[{High Authority} shall state the reasons on which they are based and shall refer to any opinions which were required to be obtained.

Where decisions and recommendations are individual in character, they shall become binding upon being notified to the party concerned.

In all other cases, they shall take effect by the mere fact of publication.

The [Commission] {High Authority} shall determine the matter in which this Article is to be implemented.

Article 18. A consultative Committee shall be attached to the [Commission] {High Authority}. It shall consist of not less than 72 and not more than 96 members and shall comprise equal numbers of producers, of workers, and of consumers and dealers.

The members of the Consultative Committee shall be appointed by the Council.

In the case of the producers and workers, the Council shall designate representative organisations among which it shall allocate the seats to be filled. Each organisation shall be required to draw up a list containing twice as many names as there are seats allotted to it. Appointments shall be made from this list.

The members of the Consultative Committee shall be appointed in their personal capacity for two years. They shall not be bound by any mandate or instructions from the organisations which nominated them.

The Consultative Committee shall elect its chairman and officers from among its members for a term of one year. The Committee shall adopt its rules of procedure.

Article 19. The [Commission] {High Authority} may consult the Consultative Committee in all cases in which it considers this appropriate. It must do so whenever such consultation is prescribed by this Treaty.

The [Commission] {High Authority} shall submit to the Consultative Committee the general objectives and the programmes drawn up under Art. 46 and shall keep the Committee informed of the broad lines of its action under Arts. 54, 65 and 66.

Should the [Commission] {High Authority} consider it necessary, it may set the Consultative Committee a time limit for the submission of its opinion. The period allowed may not be less than ten days from the date on which the chairman receives notification to this effect.

The Consultative Committee shall be convened by its chairman, either at the request of the [Commission] {High Authority} or at the request of a majority of its members, for the purpose of discussing a specific question.

The minutes of the proceedings shall be forwarded to the [Commission] {High Authority} and to the Council at the same time as the opinions of the Committee.

CHAPTER 2. THE [EUROPEAN PARLIAMENT] {ASSEMBLY}

Article 20. The [European Parliament] {Assembly} which shall consist of representatives of the peoples of the States brought together in the Community, shall exercise the supervisory powers which are conferred upon it by this Treaty.

Articles 21–25. [The same, mutatis mutandis, as E{E}C arts. 138–44]

CHAPTER 3. THE COUNCIL

Article 26. The Council shall exercise its powers in the cases provided for and in the manner set out in this Treaty, in particular in order to harmonise the action of the [Commission] {High Authority} and that of the

Governments, which are responsible for the general economic policies of their countries.

To this end, the Council and the [Commission] {High Authority} shall exchange information and consult each other.

The Council may request the [Commission] {High Authority} to examine any proposals or measures which the Council may consider appropriate or necessary for the attainment of the common objectives.

Article 28. When the Council is consulted by the [Commission] {High Authority}, it shall consider the matter without necessarily taking a vote. The minutes of its proceedings shall be forwarded to the [Commission] {High Authority}.

Wherever this Treaty requires that the assent of the Council be given, that assent shall be considered to have been given if the proposal submitted by the [Commission] {High Authority} receives the approval:

– of an absolute majority of the representatives of the Member States, including the votes of the representatives of two Member States which each produce at least one ninth of the total value of the coal and steel output of the Community; or
– in the event of an equal division of votes and if the [Commission] {High Authority} maintains its proposal after a second discussion, of the representatives of three Member States which each produce at least one ninth of the total value of the coal and steel output of the Community.

Wherever this Treaty requires a unanimous decision or unanimous assent, such decision or assent shall have been duly given if all the members of the Council vote in favour. However, for the purpose of applying Arts. 21, 32, 32a, 78e and 78h of this Treaty, and Art. 16, the third paragraph of Art. 20, the fifth paragraph of Art. 28 and Art. 44 of the Protocol on the Statute of the Court of Justice, abstention by members present in person or represented shall not prevent the adoption by the Council of acts which require unanimity.

Decisions of the Council, other than those for which a qualified majority or unanimity is required, shall be taken by a vote of the majority of its members; this majority shall be considered to be attained if it represents an absolute majority of the representatives of the Member States, including the votes of the representatives of two Member States which each produce at least one ninth of the total value of the coal and steel output of the Community. However, for the purpose of applying those provisions of Arts. 78, 78b and 78d of this Treaty which require a qualified majority, the votes of the members of the Council are weighted as follows: Belgium 5, Denmark 3, Germany 10, Greece 5, Spain 8,

France 10, Ireland 3, Italy 10, Luxembourg 2, Netherlands 5, Portugal 5, United Kingdom 10. For their adoption, acts shall require at least 54 votes in favour, cast by not less than eight members.

Where a vote is taken, any member of the Council may act on behalf of not more than one other member.

The Council shall deal with the Member States through its President.

The acts of the Council shall be published in such a manner as it may decide.

CHAPTER 4. THE COURT

Article 31. The Court shall ensure that in the interpretation and application of this Treaty, and of rules laid down for the implementation thereof, the law is observed.

Article 32. [The same, *mutatis mutandis*, as E{E}C arts. 165–8.]

Article 33. The Court [of Justice] shall have jurisdiction in actions brought by a Member State or by the Council to have decisions or recommendations of the [Commission] {High Authority} declared void on grounds of lack of competence, infringement of an essential procedural requirement, infringement of this Treaty or of any rule of law relating to its application, or misuse of powers. The Court [of Justice] may not, however, examine the evaluation of the situation, resulting from economic facts or circumstances, in the light of which the [Commission] {High Authority} took its decisions or made its recommendations, save where the [Commission] {High Authority} is alleged to have misused its powers or to have manifestly failed to observe the provisions of this Treaty or any rule of law relating to its application.

Undertakings or the associations referred to in Art. 48 may, under the same conditions, institute proceedings against decisions or recommendations concerning them which are individual in character or against general decisions or recommendations which they consider to involve a misuse of powers affecting them.

The proceedings provided for in the first two paragraphs of this Article shall be instituted within one month of the notification or publication, as the case may be, of the decision or recommendation.

[The Court of Justice shall have jurisdiction under the same conditions in actions brought by the European Parliament for the purpose of protecting its prerogatives.]

Article 34. If the Court [of Justice] declares a decision or recommendation void, it shall refer the matter back to the [Commission] {High Authority}. The [Commission] {High Authority} shall take the necessary steps to comply with the judgment. If direct and special harm is suffered by an undertaking or group of undertakings by reason of a decision or recommendations held by the Court [of Justice] to involve a fault of such a nature as to render the Community liable, the [Commission] {High Authority} shall, using the powers conferred upon it by this Treaty, take steps to ensure equitable redress for the harm resulting directly from the decision or recommendation declared void and, where necessary, pay appropriate damages.

If the [Commission] {High Authority} fails to take within a reasonable time the necessary steps to comply with the judgment, proceedings for damages may be instituted before the Court [of Justice].

Article 35. Wherever the [Commission] {High Authority} is required by this Treaty, or by rules laid down for the implementation thereof, to take a decision or make a recommendation and fails to fulfil this obligation, it shall be for States, the Council, undertakings or associations, as the case may be, to raise the matter with the [Commission] {High Authority}.

The same shall apply if the [Commission] {High Authority}, where empowered by this Treaty, or by rules laid down for the implementation thereof, to take a decision or make a recommendation, abstains from doing so and such abstention constitutes a misuse of powers.

If at the end of two months the [Commission] {High Authority} has not taken any decision or made any recommendation, proceedings may be instituted before the Court [of Justice] within one month against the implied decision of refusal which is to be inferred from the silence of the [Commission] {High Authority} on the matter.

Article 36. Before imposing a pecuniary sanction or ordering a periodic penalty payment as provided for in this Treaty, the [Commission] {High Authority} must give the party concerned the opportunity to submit its comments.

The Court [of Justice] shall have unlimited jurisdiction in appeals against pecuniary sanctions and periodic penalty payments imposed under this Treaty.

In support of its appeal, a party may, under the same conditions as in the first paragraph of Art. 33 of this Treaty, contest the legality of the decision or recommendation which that party is alleged not to have observed.

Article 37. If a Member State considers that in a given case action or failure to act on the part of the [Commission] {High Authority} is of such a nature as to provoke fundamental and persistent disturbances in its economy, it may raise the matter with the [Commission] {High Authority}.

The [Commission] {High Authority}, after consulting the Council, shall, if there are grounds for so doing, recognise the existence of such a situation and decide on the measures to be taken to end it, in accordance with the provisions of this Treaty, while at the same time safeguarding the essential interests of the Community.

When proceedings are instituted in the Court [of Justice] under this Article against such a decision or against an express or implied decision refusing to recognise the existence of the situation referred to above, it shall be for the Court [of Justice] to determine whether it is well founded.

If the Court [of Justice] declares the decision void, the [Commission] {High Authority} shall, within the terms of the judgment of the Court [of Justice], decide on the measures to be taken for the purposes indicated in the second paragraph of this Article.

Article 38. The Court [of Justice] may, on application by a Member State or the [Commission] {High Authority} declare an act of the [European Parliament] {Assembly} or of the Council to be void.

Application shall be made within one month of the publication of the act of the [European Parliament] {Assembly} or the notification of the act of the Council to the Member States or to the [Commission] {High Authority}.

The only grounds for such an application shall be lack of competence or infringement of an essential procedural requirement.

Article 39. Actions brought before the Court [of Justice] shall not have suspensory effect.

The Court [of Justice] may, however, if it considers that circumstances so require, order that application of the contested decision or recommendation be suspended.

The Court [of Justice] may prescribe any other necessary interim measures.

Article 40. Without prejudice to the first paragraph of Art. 34, the Court [of Justice] shall have jurisdiction to order pecuniary reparation from the Community, on application by the injured party, to make good any injury caused in carrying out this Treaty by a wrongful act or omission on the part of the Community in the performance of its functions.

The Court [of Justice] shall also have jurisdiction to order the Community to make good any injury caused by a personal wrong by a servant of the Community in the performance of his duties. The personal liability of its servants towards the Community shall be governed by the provisions laid down in their Staff Regulations or the Conditions of Employment applicable to them.

All other disputes between the Community and persons other than its servants to which the provisions of this Treaty or the rules laid down for the implementation thereof do not apply shall be brought before national courts or tribunals.

Article 41. The Court [of Justice] shall have sole jurisdiction to give preliminary rulings on the validity of acts of the [Commission] {High Authority} and of the Council where such validity is in issue in proceedings brought before a national court or tribunal.

Article 42. The Court [of Justice] shall have jurisdiction to give judgment pursuant to any arbitration clause contained in a contract concluded by or on behalf of the Community, whether that contract be governed by public or private law.

Article 43. The Court [of Justice] shall have jurisdiction in any other case provided for by a provision supplementing this Treaty.
It may also rule in all cases which relate to the subject matter of this Treaty where jurisdiction is conferred upon it by the law of a Member State.

Article 44. The judgments of the Court [of Justice] shall be enforceable in the territory of Member States under the conditions laid down in Article 92.

Article 45. The Statute of the Court [of Justice] is laid down in a Protocol annexed to this treaty.
The Council may, acting unanimously at the request of the Court of Justice and after consulting the Commission and the European Parliament, amend the provisions of Title III of the Statute.

TITLE III. ECONOMIC AND SOCIAL PROVISIONS

[Articles 46–56 and 59–75 are omitted.]

Article 57. In the sphere of production, the [Commission] {High Authority} shall give preference to the indirect means of action at its disposal, such as:

– co-operation with Governments to regularise or influence general consumption, particularly that of the public services;
– intervention in regard to prices and commercial policy as provided for in this Treaty.

Article 58. 1.   In the event of a decline in demand, if the [Commission] {High Authority} considers that the Community is confronted with a period of manifest crisis and that the means of action provided for in Art. 57 are not suffcient to deal with this, it shall, after consulting the Consultative Committee and with the assent of the Council, establish a system of production quotas, accompanied to the necessary extent by the measures provided for in Art. 74.

If the [Commission] {High Authority} fails to act, a Member State may bring the matter before the Council, which may, acting unanimously, require the [Commission] {High Authority} to establish a system of quotas.

2.   The [Commission] {High Authority} shall, on the basis of studies made jointly with undertakings and associations of undertakings, deter mine the quotas on an equitable basis, taking account of the principles set out in Arts 2, 3 and 4. It may in particular regulate the level of activity of undertakings by appropriate levies on tonnages exceeding a reference level set by a general decision.

The funds thus obtained shall be used to support undertakings whose rate of production has fallen below that envisaged, in order, in particular, to maintain employment in these undertakings as far as possible.

3.   The system of quotas shall be ended on a proposal made to the Council by the [Commission] {High Authority} after consulting the Consultative Committee, or by the Government of a Member State, unless the Council decides otherwise, acting unanimously if the proposal emanates from the [Commission] {High Authority} or by a simple majority if the proposal emanates from a Government. An announcement on the ending of the quota system shall be made by the [Commission] {High Authority}.

4.   The [Commission] {High Authority} may impose upon undertakings which do not comply with decisions taken by it under this Article fines not exceeding the value of the tonnages produced in disregard thereof.

TITLE IV. GENERAL PROVISIONS

[Articles 76–82, 84 and 85 are omitted.]

Article 83.   The establishment of the Community shall in no way prejudice the system of ownership of undertakings to which this Treaty applies.

Article 86.   Member States undertake to take all appropriate measures, whether general or particular, to ensure fulfilment of the obligations resulting from decisions and recommendations of the institutions of the Community and to facilitate the performance of the Community's tasks.

Member States undertake to refrain from any measures incompatible with the common market referred to in Arts. 1 and 4.

They shall make all appropriate arrangements, as far as lies within their powers, for the settlement of international accounts arising out of trade in coal and steel within the common market and shall afford each other mutual assistance to facilitate such settlements.

Officials of the [Commission] {High Authority} entrusted by it with tasks of inspection shall enjoy in the territories of Member States, to the full extent required for the performance of their duties, such rights and powers as are granted by the laws of these States to their own revenue officials. Forthcoming visits of inspection and the status of the officials shall be duly notified to the State concerned. Officials of that State may, at its request or at that of the [Commission] {High Authority}, assist the [Commission] {High Authority}'s officials in the performance of their task.

Article 87. The High Contracting Parties undertake not to avail themselves of any treaties, conventions or declarations made between them for the purpose of submitting a dispute concerning the interpretation or application of this Treaty to any method of settlement other than those provided for therein.

Article 88. If the [Commission] {High Authority} considers that a State has failed to fulfil an obligation under this Treaty, it shall record this failure in a reasoned decision after giving the State concerned the opportunity to submit its comments. It shall set the State a time limit for the fulfilment of its obligation.

The State may institute proceedings before the Court [of Justice] within two months of notification of the decision; the Court [of Justice] shall have unlimited jurisdiction in such cases.

If the State has not fulfilled its obligation by the time limit set by the [Commission] {High Authority} or if it brings an action which is dismissed, the [Commission] {High Authority} may, with the assent of the Council acting by a two-thirds majority:

(a) suspend the payment of any sums which it may be liable to pay to the State in question under this Treaty;
(b) take measures, or authorise the other Member States to make measures, by way of derogation from the provisions of Art. 4, in order to correct the effects of the infringement of the obligation.

Proceedings may be instituted before the Court [of Justice] against decisions taken under subparagraphs (a) and (b) within two months of their notification; the Court [of Justice] shall have unlimited jurisdiction in such cases.

If these measures prove ineffective, the [Commission] {High Authority} shall bring the matter before the Council.

Article 89. Any dispute between Member States concerning the application of this Treaty which cannot be settled by another procedure provided for in this Treaty may be submitted to the Court [of Justice] on application by one of the States which are parties to the dispute.

The Court [of Justice] shall also have jurisdiction in any dispute between member States which relates to the subject matter of this Treaty, if the dispute is submitted to it under a special agreement between the parties.

Article 90. If failure to fulfil an obligation under this Treaty on the part of an undertaking also constitutes an infringement of its obligations under the law of its State and judicial or administrative action is being taken under that law against the undertaking, the State in question shall so inform the [Commission] {High Authority}, which may defer its decision.

If the [Commission] {High Authority} defers its decision, it shall be kept informed of the progress of the action taken by national authorities and shall be permitted to produce all relevant documents and expert and other evidence. It shall also be informed of the final decision on the case and shall take account of this decision in determining any penalty it may itself impose.

Article 91. If an undertaking does not pay by the time limit set a sum which it is liable to pay to the [Commission] {High Authority} either under this Treaty or rules laid down for the implementation thereof or in discharge of a pecuniary sanction or periodic penalty payment imposed by the [Commission] {High Authority} the [Commission] {High Authority} may suspend payment of sums which it is liable to pay to that undertaking, up to the amount of the outstanding payment.

Article 92. Decisions of the [Commission] {High Authority} which impose a pecuniary obligation shall be enforceable.

Enforcement in the territory of Member States shall be carried out by means of the legal procedure in force in each State, after the order for enforcement in the form in use in the State in whose territory the decision is to be enforced has been appended to the decision, without other formality than verification of the authenticity of the decision. This formality shall be carried out at the instance of a Minister designated for this purpose by each of the Governments.

Enforcement may be suspended only by a decision of the Court [of Justice].

Article 95. In all cases not provided for in this Treaty where it becomes apparent that a decision or recommendation of the [Commission] {High Authority} is necessary to attain, within the common market in coal and steel and in accordance with Art. 5, one of the objectives of the Community set out in Arts. 2, 3 and 4, the decision may be taken or the recommendation made with the unanimous assent of the Council and after the Consultative Committee has been consulted.

Any decision so taken or recommendation so made shall determine what penalties, if any, may be imposed.

If, after the end of the transitional period provided in the Convention on the Transitional Provisions, unforeseen difficulties emerging in the light of experience in the application of this Treaty, or fundamental economic or technical changes directly affecting the common market in coal and steel, make it necessary to adapt the rules for the [Commission] {High Authority}'s exercise of its powers, appropriate amendments may be made; they must not, however, conflict with the provisions of Arts. 2, 3 and 4 or interfere with the relationship between the powers of the [Commission] {High Authority} and those of the other institutions of the Community.

These amendments shall be proposed jointly by the [Commission] {High Authority} and the Council, acting by a ten-twelfths majority of its members, and shall be submitted to the Court [of Justice] for its opinion. In considering them, the Court [of Justice] shall have full power to assess all points of fact and of law. If as a result of such consideration it finds the proposals compatible with the provisions of the preceding paragraph, they shall be forwarded to the [European Parliament] {Assembly} and shall enter into force if approved by a majority of three-quarters of the votes cast and two-thirds of the members of the [European Parliament] {Assembly}.

Article 96. After the end of the transitional period, the Government of any Member State or the [Commission] {High Authority} may propose amendments to this Treaty. Such proposals shall be submitted to the Council. If the Council, acting by a two-thirds majority, delivers an opinion in favour of calling a conference of representatives of the Governments of the Member States, the conference shall be convened forthwith by the President of the Council for the purpose of determining by common accord the amendments to be made to the Treaty.

Such amendments shall enter into force after being ratified by all the Member States in accordance with their respective constitutional requirements.

Article 97. This Treaty is concluded for a period of fifty years from its entry into force.

Article 98. Any European State may apply to accede to this Treaty. It shall address its application to the Council, which shall act unanimously after obtaining the opinion of the [Commission] {High Authority}, the Council shall also determine the terms of accession, likewise acting unanimously. Accession shall take effect on the day when the instrument of accession is received by the Government acting as depository of this Treaty.

Article 99. This Treaty shall be ratified by all the Member States in accordance with their respective constitutional requirements; the instruments of ratification shall be deposited with the Government of the French Republic.

  This Treaty shall enter into force in the date of deposit of the instrument of ratifiction by the last signatory State to take this step.*

  If all the instruments of ratification have not been deposited within six months of the signature of this Treaty, the Governments of the States which have deposited their instruments shall consult each other on the measures to be taken.

Article 100. This Treaty, drawn up in a single original, shall be deposited in the archives of the Government of the French Republic, which shall transmit a certified copy thereof to each of the Governments of the other signatory States.

In witness whereof, the undersigned plenipotentiaries have signed this Treaty and affixed thereto their seals.

  Done at Paris this eighteenth day of April in the year one thousand nine hundred and fifty-one.
[Here follow the signatures.]

*The Treaty entered into force on 23 July 1952

Treaty Establishing the
European {Economic} Community
as Amended by Subsequent Treaties
Rome, 25 March, 1957

[*NB. Amendments occasioned by the 1992 Treaty on European Union (TEU) are in square brackets. Adjacent text in curly brackets will be deleted when the TEU enters into force.*]

His Majesty The King of the Belgians, the President of the Federal Republic of Germany, the President of the French Republic, the President of the Italian Republic, Her Royal Highness The Grand Duchess of Luxembourg, Her Majesty The Queen of the Netherlands,

Determined to lay the foundations of an ever closer union among the peoples of Europe,

Resolved to ensure the economic and social progress of their countries by common action to eliminate the barriers which divide Europe,

Affirming as the essential objective of their efforts the constant improvement of the living and working conditions of their peoples,

Recognising that the removal of existing obstacles calls for concerted action in order to guarantee steady expansion, balanced trade and fair competition,

Anxious to strengthen the unity of their economies and to ensure their harmonious development by reducing the differences existing between the various regions and the backwardness of the less favoured regions,

Desiring to contribute, by means of a common commercial policy, to the progressive abolition of restrictions on international trade,

Intending to confirm the solidarity which binds Europe and the overseas countries and desiring to ensure the development of their prosperity, in accordance with the principles of the Charter of the United Nations,

Resolved by thus pooling their resources to preserve and strengthen peace and liberty, and calling upon the other peoples of Europe who share their ideal to join in their efforts,

Have decided to create a European Economic Community and to this end have designated as their Plenipotentiaries:

His Majesty The King of the Belgians: Mr. Paul-Henri Spaak, Minister for Foreign Affairs, Baron J. Ch. Snoy et d'Oppuers, Secretary-General of the Ministry of Economic Affairs, Head of the Belgian Delegation to the Intergovernmental Conference;

The President of the Federal Republic of Germany: Dr. Konrad

Adenauer, Federal Chancellor, Professor Dr. Walter Hallstein, State
Secretary of the Federal Foreign Office;

The President of the French Republic: Mr. Christian Pineau, Minister
for Foreign Affairs, Mr. Maurice Faure, Under-Secretary of State for
Foreign Affairs;

The President of the Italian Republic: Mr. Antonio Segni, President of
the Council of Ministers, Professor Gaetano Martino, Minister for
Foreign Affairs;

Her Royal Highness The Grand Duchess of Luxembourg: Mr. Joseph
Bech, President of the Government, Minister for Foreign Affairs, Mr.
Lambert Schaus, Ambassador, Head of the Luxembourg Delegation to
the Intergovernmental Conference;

Her Majesty The Queen of the Netherlands: Mr. Joseph Luns, Minister
for Foreign Affairs, Mr. J. Linthorst Homan, Head of the Netherlands
Delegation to the Intergovernmental Conference;

Who, having exchanged their full powers, found in good and due form,
Have agreed as follows:

Part One. Principles

Article 1.   By this Treaty, the High Contracting Parties establish among
themselves a European {Economic} Community.

Article 2.   The Community shall have as its task, by establishing a common market and [an economic and monetary union and by implementing
the common policies or activities referred to in Articles 3 and 3a] {pro-
gressively approximating the economic policies of the Member States}, to
promote throughout the Community a harmonious [and balanced] development of economic activities, [sustainable and non-inflationary growth
respecting the environment, a high degree of convergence of economic
performance, a high level of employment and of social protection, the
raising of the standard of living and quality of life, and economic and
social cohesion and solidarity among Member States] {a continuous and
balanced expansion, an increase in stability, an accelerated raising of the
standard of living and closer relations between the States belonging to it.}

Article 3.   For the purposes set out in Article 2, the activities of the
Community shall include, as provided by this Treaty and in accordance
with the timetable set out therein:

(a)   the elimination as between Member States, of customs duties
           and quantitative restrictions on the import and export of goods,
           and of all other measures having equivalent effect;

(b)   [a common commercial policy;] {the establishment of a common customs tariff and of a common commercial policy towards third countries;}

(c)   [an internal market characterized by] the abolition, as between Member States, of obstacles to the free movement of [goods], persons, services and capital;

[(d)   Measures concerning the entry and movement of persons in the internal market as provided for in Article 100c;]

[(e)] {(d) the adoption of} a common policy in the sphere of agriculture [and fisheries;]

[(f)] {(e) the adoption of} a common policy in the sphere of transport;

[(g)]{(f) the institution of} a system ensuring that competition in the common market is not distorted;

{(g)   the application of procedures by which the economic policies of Member States can be co-ordinated and disequilibria in their balances of payments remedied;}

(h)   the approximation of the laws of the Member States to the extent required for the {proper} functioning of the common market;

(i)   [a policy in the social sphere comprising] {the creation of} a European Social Fund {in order to improve employment opportunities for workers and to contribute to the raising of their standard of living;}

[(j)   the strengthening of economic and social cohesion;] {the establishment of a European Investment Bank to facilitate the economic expansion of the Community by opening up fresh resources;}

[(k)   a policy in the sphere of the environment;] {the association of the overseas countries and territories in order to increase trade and to promote jointly economic and social development.}

[(l)   the strengthening of the competitiveness of Community industry;

(m)   the promotion of research and technological development;

(n)   encouragement for the establishment and development of trans-European networks;

(o)   a contribution to the attainment of a high level of health protection;

(p)   a contribution to education and training of quality and to the flowering of the cultures of the Member States;

(q)   a policy in the sphere of development cooperation;

(r)   the association of the overseas countries and territories in order to increase trade and promote jointly economic and social development;

(s)   a contribution to the strengthening of consumer protection;
(t)   measures in the spheres of energy, civil protection and tourism.]

[*Article 3a.*   1. For the purposes set out in Article 2, the activities of the Member States and the Community shall include, as provided in this Treaty and in accordance with the timetable set out therein, the adoption of an economic policy which is based on the close coordination of Member States' economic policies, on the internal market and on the definition of common objectives, and conducted in accordance with the principle of an open market economy with free competition.

2. Concurrently with the foregoing, and as provided in this Treaty and in accordance with the timetable and the procedures set out therein, these activities shall include the irrevocable fixing of exchange rates leading to the introduction of a single currency, the ecu, and the definition and conduct of a single monetary policy and exchange rate policy the primary objective of both of which shall be to maintain price stability and, without prejudice to this objective, to support the general economic policies in the Community, in accordance with the principle of an open market economy with free competition.

3. These activities of the Member States and the Community shall entail compliance with the following guiding principles: stable prices, sound public finances and monetary conditions and a sustainable balance of payments.]

[*Article 3b.*   The Community shall act within the limits of the powers conferred upon it by this Treaty and of the objectives assigned to it therein.

In areas which do not fall within its exclusive competence, the Community shall take action, in accordance with the principle of subsidiarity, only if and in so far as the objectives of the proposed action cannot be sufficiently achieved by the Member States and can therefore, by reason of the scale or effects of the proposed action, be better achieved by the Community.

Any action by the Community shall not go beyond what is necessary to achieve the objectives of this Treaty.]

Article 4.   1. The tasks entrusted to the Community shall be carried out by the following institutions:

– an Assembly,
– a Council,
– a Commission,
– a Court of Justice.
[– a Court of Auditors]

Each institution shall act within the limits of the powers conferred upon it by this Treaty.

2. The Council and the Commission shall be assisted by an Economic and Social Committee [and a Committee of the Regions] acting in an advisory capacity.

{3. The audit shall be carried out by a Court of Auditors acting within the limits of the powers conferred upon it by this Treaty.}

[*Article 4a.* A European System of Central Banks (hereinafter referred to as 'ESCB') and a European Central Bank (hereinafter referred to as 'ECB') shall be established in accordance with the procedures laid down in this Treaty; they shall act within the limits of the powers conferred upon them by this Treaty and by the Statute of the ESCB and of the ECB (hereinafter referred to as 'Statute of the ESCB') annexed thereto.]

[*Article 4b.* A European Investment Bank is hereby established, which shall act within the limits of the powers conferred upon it by this Treaty and the Statute annexed thereto.]

Article 5. Member States shall take all appropriate measures, whether general or particular, to ensure fulfilment of the obligations arising out of this Treaty or resulting from action taken by the institutions of the Community. They shall facilitate the achievement of the Community's tasks.

They shall abstain from any measure which could jeopardise the attainment of the objectives of this Treaty.

{*Article 6.* 1. Member States shall, in close co-operation with the institutions of the Community, co-ordinate their respective economic policies to the extent necessary to attain the objectives of this Treaty.

2. The institutions of the Community shall take care not to prejudice the internal and external financial stability of the Member States.}

Article [6.] {7.} Within the scope of application of this Treaty, and without prejudice to any special provisions contained therein, any discrimination on the grounds of nationality shall be prohibited.

[The Council, acting in accordance with the procedure referred to in Article 189c] {on a proposal from the Commission and in co-operation with the European Parliament} may adopt {by a qualified majority} rules designed to prohibit such discrimination.

Article [7.] {8.} 1. The common market shall be progressively established during a transitional period of twelve years.

This transitional period shall be divided into three stages of four years each; the length of each stage may be altered in accordance with the provisions set out below.

2. To each stage there shall be assigned a set of actions to be initiated and carried through concurrently.

3. Transition from the first to the second stage shall be conditional upon a finding that the objectives specifically laid down in this Treaty for the first stage have in fact been attained in substance and that, subject to the exceptions and procedures provided for in this Treaty, the obligations have been fulfilled.

This finding shall be made at the end of the fourth year by the Council, acting unanimously on a report from the Commission. A Member State may not, however, prevent unanimity by relying upon the non-fulfilment of its own obligations. Failing unanimity, the first stage shall automatically be extended for one year.

At the end of the fifth year, the Council shall make its finding under the same conditions. Failing unanimity, the first stage shall automatically be extended for a further year.

At the end of the sixth year, the Council shall make its finding, acting by a qualified majority on a report form the Commission.

4. Within one month of the last-mentioned vote any Member State which voted with the minority or, if the required majority was not obtained, any Member State shall be entitled to call upon the Council to appoint an arbitration board whose decision shall be binding upon all Member States and upon the institutions of the Community. The arbitration board shall consist of three members appointed by the Council acting unanimously on a proposal from the Commission.

If the Council has not appointed the members of the arbitration board within one month of being called upon to do so, they shall be appointed by the Court of Justice within a further period of one month.

The arbitration board shall elect its own Chairman.

The board shall make its award within six months of the date of the Council vote referred to in the last subparagraph of paragraph 3.

5. The second and third stages may not be extended or curtailed except by a decision of the Council, acting unanimously on a proposal from the Commission.

6. Nothing in the preceding paragraphs shall cause the transitional period to last more than fifteen years after the entry into force of this Treaty.

7. Save for the exceptions or derogations provided for in this Treaty, the expiry of the transitional period shall constitute the latest date by which all the rules laid down must enter into force and all the measures required for establishing the common market must be implemented.

Article [7a] {8a}. The Community shall adopt measures with the aim of progressively establishing the internal market over a period expiring on 31 December 1992, in accordance with the provisions of this Article and of Articles 8b, 8c, 28, 57(2), 59, 70(1), 84, 99, 100a and 100b and without prejudice to the other provisions of this Treaty.

The internal market shall comprise an area without internal frontiers in which the free movement of goods, persons, services and capital is ensured in accordance with the provisions of this Treaty.

Article [7b] {8b}. The Commission shall report to the Council before 31 December 1988 and again before 31 December 1990 on the progress made towards achieving the internal market within the time limit fixed in Article 8a.

The Council, acting by a qualified majority on a proposal from the Commission, shall determine the guidelines and conditions necessary to ensure balanced progress in all the sectors concerned.

Article [7c] {8c}. When drawing up its proposals with a view to achieving the objectives set out in Article 8a, the Commission shall take into account the extent of the effort that certain economies showing differences in developments will have to sustain during the period of establishment the internal market and it may propose appropriate provisions.

If these provisions take the form of derogations, they must be of a temporary nature and must cause the least possible disturbance to the functioning of the common market.

[Part Two. Citizenship of the Union]

[*Article 8.* 1. Citizenship of the Union is hereby established.

Every person holding the nationality of a Member State shall be a citizen of the Union.

2. Citizens of the Union shall enjoy the rights conferred by this Treaty and shall be subject to the duties imposed thereby.]

[*Article 8a.* 1. Every citizen of the Union shall have the right to move and reside freely within the territory of the Member States, subject to the limitations and conditions laid down in this Treaty and by the measures adopted to give it effect.

2. The Council may adopt provisions with a view to facilitating the exercise of the rights referred to in paragraph 1; save as otherwise provided in this Treaty, the Council shall act unanimously on a proposal

from the Commission and after obtaining the assent of the European Parliament.]

[*Article 8b.* 1. Every citizen of the Union residing in a Member State of which he is not a national shall have the right to vote and to stand as a candidate at municipal elections in the Member State in which he resides, under the same conditions as nationals of that State. This right shall be exercised subject to detailed arrangements to be adopted before 31 December 1994 by the Council, acting unanimously on a proposal from the Commission and after consulting the European Parliament; these arrangements may provide for derogations where warranted by problems specific to a Member State.

2. Without prejudice to Article 138(3) and to the provisions adopted for its implementation, every citizen of the Union residing in a Member State of which he is not a national shall have the right to vote and to stand as a candidate in elections to the European Parliament in the Member State in which he resides, under the same conditions as nationals of that State. This right shall be exercised subject to detailed arrangements to be adopted before 31 December 1993 by the Council, acting unanimously on a proposal from the Commission and after consulting the European Parliament; these arrangements may provide for derogations where warranted by problems specific to a Member State.]

[*Article 8c.* Every citizen of the Union shall, in the territory of a third country in which the Member State of which he is a national is not represented, be entitled to protection by the diplomatic or consular authorities of any Member State, on the same conditions as the nationals of that State. Before 31 December 1993, Member States shall establish the necessary rules among themselves and start the international negotiations required to secure this protection.]

[*Article 8d.* Every citizen of the Union shall have the right to petition the European Parliament in accordance with Article 138d.

Every citizen of the Union may apply to the Ombudsman established in accordance with Article 138e.]

[*Article 8e.* The Commission shall report to the European Parliament, to the Council and to the Economic and Social Committee before 31 December 1993 and then every three years on the application of the provisions of this Part. This report shall take account of the development of the Union.

On this basis, and without prejudice to the other provisions of this Treaty, the Council, acting unanimously on a proposal from the

Commission and after consulting the European Parliament, may adopt provisions to strengthen or to add to the rights laid down in this Part, which it shall recommend to the Member States for adoption in accordance with their respective constitutional requirements.]

[Part Three. Community Policies]

{Part Two. Foundations of the Community}

TITLE I. FREE MOVEMENT OF GOODS

Article 9.   1. The Community shall be based upon a customs union which shall cover all trade in goods and which shall involve the prohibition between Member States of customs duties on imports and exports and of all charges having equivalent effect, and the adoption of a common customs tariff in their relations with third countries.

2. The provisions of Chapter 1, Section 1, and of Chapter 2 of this Title shall apply to products originating in Member States and to products coming from third countries which are in free circulation in Member States.

Article 10.   1. Products coming from a third country shall be considered to be in free circulation in a Member State if the import formalities have been complied with and any customs duties or charges having equivalent effect which are payable have been levied in that Member State, and if they have not benefited from a total or partial drawback of such duties or charges.

2. The Commission shall, before the end of the first year after the entry into force of this Treaty, determine the methods of administrative co-operation to be adopted for the purpose of applying Art. 9(2), taking into account the need to reduce as much as possible formalities imposed on trade.

Before the end of the first year after the entry into force of this Treaty, the Commission shall lay down the provisions applicable, as regards trade between Member States, to goods originating in another Member State in whose manufacture products have been used on which the exporting Member State has not levied the appropriate customs duties or charges having equivalent effect, or which have benefited from a total or partial drawback of such duties or charges.

In adopting these provisions, the Commission shall take into account the rules for the elimination of customs duties within the Community and for the progressive application of the common customs tariff.

Article 11.   Member States shall take all appropriate measures to enable Governments to carry out, within the periods of time laid down, the obligations with regard to customs duties which devolve upon them pursuant to this Treaty.

CHAPTER I. THE CUSTOMS UNION

Section 1. Elimination of Customs Duties Between Member States

Article 12.   Member States shall refrain from introducing between themselves any new customs duties on imports or exports or any charges having equivalent effect, and from increasing those which they already apply in their trade with each other.

Article 13.   1. Customs duties on imports in force between Member States shall be progressively abolished by them during the transnational period in accordance with Arts. 14 and 15.

2. Charges having an effect equivalent to customs duties on imports, in force between Member States, shall be progressively abolished by them during the transitional period. The Commission shall determine by means of directives the timetable for such abolition. It shall be guided by the rules contained in Art. 14(2) and (3) and by the directives issued by the Council pursuant to Art. 14(2).

Article 14.   1. For each product, the basic duty to which the successive reductions shall be applied shall be the duty applied on 1 January 1957.

2. The timetable for the reductions shall be determined as follows:

(a) during the first stage, the first reduction shall be made one year after the date when this Treaty enters into force; the second reduction, eighteen months later; the third reduction, at the end of the fourth year after the date when this Treaty enters into force;
(b) during the second stage, a reduction shall be made eighteen months after that stage begins; a second reduction, eighteen months after the preceding one; a third reduction, one year later;
(c) any remaining reductions shall be made during the third stage; the Council shall, acting by a qualified majority on a proposal from the Commission, determine the timetable therefore by means of directives.

3.   At the time of the first reduction, Member States shall introduce between themselves a duty on each product equal to the basic duty minus 10 per cent.

At the time of each subsequent reduction, each Member State shall reduce its customs duties as a whole in such manner as to lower by 10 per cent its total customs receipts as defined in paragraph 43 and to reduce the duty on each product by at least 5 per cent of the basic duty.

In the case, however, of products on which the duty is still in excess of 30 per cent, each reduction must be at least 10 per cent of the basic duty.

4. The total customs receipts of each Member State, as referred to in paragraph 3, shall be calculated by multiplying the value of imports from other Member States during 1956 by the basic duties.

5. Any special problems raised in applying paragraphs 1 to 4 shall be settled by directives issued by the Council acting by a qualified majority on a proposal from the Commission.

6. Member States shall report to the Commission on the manner in which effect has been given to the preceding rules for the reduction of duties. They shall endeavour to ensure that the reduction made in the duties of each product shall amount:

– at the end of the first stage, to at least 25 per cent of the basic duty;
– at the end of the second stage, to at least 50 per cent of the basic duty.

If the Commission finds that there is a risk that the objectives laid down in Art. 13, and the percentages laid down in this paragraph, cannot be attained, it shall make all appropriate recommendations to Member States.

7. The provisions of this Article may be amended by the Council, acting unanimously on a proposal from the Commission and after consulting the Assembly.

Article 15. 1. Irrespective of the provisions of Art. 14, any Member State may, in the course of the transitional period, suspend in whole or in part the collection of duties applied by it to products imported from other Member States. It shall inform the other Member States and the Commission thereof.

2. The Member States declare their readiness to reduce customs duties against the other Member States more rapidly than is provided for in Art. 14 if their general economic situation and the situation of the economic sector concerned so permit.

To this end, the Commission shall make recommendations to the Member States concerned.

Article 16. Member States shall abolish between themselves customs duties on exports and charges having equivalent effect by the end of the first stage at the latest.

Article 17. 1. The provisions of Arts. 9 to 15 (1) shall also apply to customs duties of a fiscal nature. Such duties shall not, however, be taken into consideration for the purpose of calculating either total customs receipts or the reduction of customs duties as a whole as referred to in Art. 14 (3) and (4).

Such duties shall, at each reduction, be lowered by not less than 10 per cent of the basic duty. Member States may reduce such duties more rapidly than is provided for in Art. 14.

2. Member States shall, before the end of the first year after the entry into force of this Treaty, inform the Commission of their customs duties of a fiscal nature.

3. Member States shall retain the right to substitute for these duties an internal tax which complies with the provisions of Art. 95.

4. If the Commission finds that substitution for any customs duty of a fiscal nature meets with serious difficulties in a Member State, it shall authorise that State to retain the duty on condition that it shall abolish it not later than six years after the entry into force of this Treaty. Such authorisation must be applied for before the end of the first year after the entry into force of this Treaty.

Section 2. Setting up of the Common Customs Tariff

Article 18. The Member States declare their readiness to contribute to the development of international trade and the lowering of barriers to trade by entering into agreements designed, on a basis of reciprocity and mutual advantage, to reduce customs duties below the general level of which they could avail themselves as a result of the establishment of a customs union between them.

Article 19. 1. Subject to the conditions and within the limits provided for hereinafter, duties in the common customs tariff shall be at the level of the arithmetical average of the duties applied in the four customs territories comprised in the Community.

2. The duties taken as the basis for calculating this average shall be those applied by Member States on 1 January 1957.

In the case of the Italian tariff, however, the duty applied shall be that without the temporary 10 per cent reduction. Furthermore, with respect to items on which the Italian tariff contains a conventional duty, this duty shall be substituted for the duty applied as defined above, provided that it does not exceed the latter by more than 10 per cent. Where the conventional duty exceeds the duty applied as defined above by more than 10 per cent, the latter duty plus 10 per cent shall be taken as the basis for calculating the arithmetical average.

With regard to the tariff headings in List A, the duties shown in that List shall, for the purpose of calculating the arithmetical average, be substituted for the duties applied.

3. The duties in the common customs tariff shall not exceed:

(a) 3 per cent for products within the tariff headings in List B;
(b) 10 per cent for products within the tariff headings in List C;
(c) 15 per cent for products within the tariff headings in List D;
(d) 25 per cent for products within the tariff headings in List E; where, in respect of such products, the tariff of the Benelux countries contains a duty not exceeding 3 per cent, such duty shall, for the purpose of calculating the arithmetical average, be raised to 12 per cent.

4. List F prescribes the duties applicable to the products listed therein.

5. The Lists of tariff headings referred to in this Article and in Art. 20 are set out in Annex I to this Treaty.

Article 20. The duties applicable to the products in List G shall be determined by negotiation between the Member States. Each Member State may add further products to this List to a value not exceeding 2 per cent of the total value of its imports from third countries in the course of the year 1956.

The Commission shall take all appropriate steps to ensure that such negotiations shall be undertaken before the end of the second year after the entry into force of this Treaty and be concluded before the end of the first stage.

If, for certain products, no agreement can be reached within these periods, the Council shall, on a proposal from the Commission, acting unanimously until the end of the second stage and by a qualified majority thereafter, determine the duties in the common customs tariff.

Article 21. 1. Technical difficulties which may arise in applying Arts. 19 and 20 shall be resolved, within two years of the entry into force of this Treaty, by directives issued by the Council acting by a qualified majority on a proposal from the Commission.

2. Before the end of the first stage, or at latest when the duties are determined, the Council shall, acting by a qualified majority on a proposal from the Commission, decide on any adjustments required in the interests of the internal consistency of the common customs tariff as a result of applying the rules set out in Arts. 19 and 20, taking into account in particular of the degree of processing undergone by various goods to which the common tariff applies.

Article 22. The Commission shall, within two years of the entry into force of this Treaty, determine the extent to which the customs duties of a fiscal nature referred to in Art. 17 (2) shall be taken into account in calculating the arithmetical average provided for in Art. 19 (1). The Commission shall take account of any protective character which such duties may have.

Within six months of such determination, any Member State may request that the procedure provided for in Art. 20 should be applied to the product in question, but in this event the percentage limit provided in that Article shall not be applicable to that State.

Article 23. 1. For the purpose of the progressive introduction of the common customs tariff, Member States shall amend their tariffs applicable to third countries as follows:

(a) in the case of tariff headings on which the duties applied in practice on 1 January 1957 do not differ by more than 15 per cent in either direction from the duties in the common customs tariff, the latter duties shall be applied at the end of the fourth year after the entry into force of this Treaty;

(b) in any other case, each Member State shall, as from the same date, apply a duty reducing by 30 per cent the difference between the duty applied in practice on 1 January 1957 and the duty in the common customs tariff;

(c) at the end of the second stage this difference shall again be reduced by 30 per cent;

(d) in the case of tariff headings for which the duties in the common customs tariff are not yet available at the end of the first stage, each Member State shall, within six months of the Council's action in accordance with Art. 20, apply such duties as would result from application of the rules contained in this paragraph.

2. Where a Member State has been granted an authorisation under Art. 17 (4), it need not, for as long as that authorisation remains valid, apply the preceding provisions to the tariff headings to which the authorisation applies. When such authorisation expires, the Member State concerned shall apply such duty as would have resulted from application of the rules contained in paragraph 1.

3. The common customs tariff shall be applied in its entirety by the end of the transitional period at the latest.

Article 24. Member States shall remain free to change their duties more rapidly than is provided for in Art. 23 in order to bring them into line with the common customs tariff.

Article 25. 1. If the Commission finds that the production in Member States of particular products contained in Lists B, C and D is insufficient to supply the demands of one of the Member States, and that such supply traditionally depends to a considerable extent on imports from third countries, the Council shall, acting by a qualified majority on a proposal from the Commission, grant the Member State concerned tariff quotas at a reduced rate of duty or duty free.

Such quotas may not exceed the limits beyond which the risk might arise of activities being transferred to the detriment of other Member States.

2. In the case of the products in List E, and of those in List G for which the rates of duty have been determined in accordance with the procedure provided for in the third paragraph of Art. 20, the Commission shall, where a change in sources of supply or a shortage of supplies within the Community is such as to entail harmful consequences for the processing industries of a Member State, at the request of that Member State, grant it tariff quotas at a reduced rate of duty or duty free.

Such quotas may not exceed the limits beyond which the risk might arise of activities being transferred to the detriment of other Member States.

3. In the case of the products listed in Annex II to this Treaty, the Commission may authorise any Member State to suspend, in whole or in part, collection of the duties applicable or may grant such Member State tariff quotas at a reduced rate of duty or duty free, provided that no serious disturbance of the market or the products concerned results therefrom.

4. The Commission shall periodically examine tariff quotas granted pursuant to this Article

Article 26.   The Commission may authorise any Member State encountering special difficulties to postpone the lowering or raising of duties provided for in Art. 23 in respect of particular headings in its tariff.

Such authorisation may only be granted for a limited period and in respect of tariff headings which, taken together, represent for such State not more than 5 per cent of the value of its imports from third countries in the course of the latest year for which statistical data are available.

Article 27.   Before the end of the first stage, Member States shall, in so far as may be necessary, take steps to approximate their provisions laid down by law, regulation or administrative action in respect of customs matters. To this end, the Commission shall make all appropriate recommendations to Member States.

Article 28.   Any autonomous alteration or suspension of duties in the common customs tariff shall be decided by the Council, acting by a qualified majority on a proposal from the Commission.

Article 29.   In carrying out the tasks entrusted to it under this Section the Commission shall be guided by:

(a) the need to promote trade between Member States and third countries;
(b) developments in conditions of competition within the Community in so far as they lead to an improvement in the competitive capacity of undertakings;
(c) the requirements of the Community as regards the supply of raw materials and semi-finished goods; in this connection the Commission shall take care to avoid distorting conditions of competition between Member States in respect of finished goods;
(d) the need to avoid serious disturbances in the economies of Member States and to ensure rational development of production and an expansion of consumption within the Community.

CHAPTER 2. ELIMINATION OF QUANTITATIVE RESTRICTIONS BETWEEN MEMBER STATES

Article 30.   Quantitative restrictions on imports and all measures having equivalent effect shall, without prejudice to the following provisions, be prohibited between Member States.

[For Dir. 70/50 on the abolition of measures which have an effect equivalent to quantitative restrictions, see p. 285]

Article 31.   Member States shall refrain from introducing between themselves any new quantitative restrictions or measures having equivalent effect.

This obligation shall, however, relate only to the degree of liberalisation attained in pursuance of the decisions of the Council of the Organisation for European Economic Co-operation of 14 January 1955. Member States shall supply the Commission, not later than six months after the entry into force of this Treaty, with lists of the products liberalised by them in pursuance of these decisions. These lists shall be consolidated between Member States.

Article 32.   In their trade with one another Member States shall refrain from making more restrictive the quotas and measures having equivalent effect existing at the date of the entry into force of this Treaty.

These quotas shall be abolished by the end of the transitional period at the latest. During that period, they shall be progressively abolished in accordance with the following provisions.

Article 33.   1. One year after the entry into force of this Treaty, each Member State shall convert any bilateral quotas open to any other

Member States into global quotas open without discrimination to all other Member States.

On the same date, Member States shall increase the aggregate of the global quotas so established in such a manner as to bring about an increase of not less than 20 per cent in their total value as compared with the preceding year. The global quota for each product, however, shall be increased by not less than 10 per cent.

The quotas shall be increased annually in accordance with the same rules and in the same proportions in relation to the preceding year.

The fourth increase shall take place at the end of the fourth year after the entry into force of this Treaty; the fifth, one year after the beginning of the second stage.

2. Where, in the case of a product which has not been liberalised, the global quota does not amount to 3 per cent of the national production of the State concerned, a quota equal to not less than 3 per cent of such national production shall be introduced not later than one year after the entry into force of this Treaty. This quota shall be raised to 4 per cent at the end of the second year, and to 5 per cent at the end of the third. Thereafter, the Member State concerned shall increase the quota by not less than 15 per cent annually.

Where there is no such national production, the Commission shall take a decision establishing an appropriate quota.

3. At the end of the tenth year, each quota shall be equal to not less than 20 per cent of the national production.

4. If the Commission finds by means of a decision that during two successive years the imports of any product have been below the level of the quota opened, this global quota shall not be taken into account in calculating the total value of the global quotas. In such case, the Member State shall abolish quota restrictions on the product concerned.

5. In the case of quotas representing more than 20 per cent of the national production of the product concerned, the Council may, acting by a qualified majority on a proposal from the Commission, reduce the minimum percentage of 10 per cent laid down in paragraph 1. This alteration shall not however, affect the obligation to increase the total value of global quotas by 20 per cent annually.

6. Member States which have exceeded their obligations as regards the degree of liberalisation attained in pursuance of the decisions of the Council of the Organisation for European Economic Co-operation of 14 January 1955 shall be entitled, when calculating the annual total increase of 20 per cent provided for in paragraph 1, to take into account the amount of imports liberalised by autonomous action. Such calculation shall be submitted to the Commission for its prior approval.

7. The Commission shall issue directives establishing the procedure and

timetable in accordance with which Member States shall abolish, as between themselves, any measures in existence when this Treaty enters into force which have an effect equivalent to quotas.

8. If the Commission finds that the application of the provisions of this Article, and in particular of the provisions concerning percentages, makes it impossible to ensure that the abolition of quotas provided for in the second paragraph of Art. 32 is carried out progressively, the Council may, on a proposal from the Commission, acting unanimously during the first stage and by a qualified majority thereafter, amend the procedure laid down in this Article and may, in particular, increase the percentages fixed.

Article 34.   1. Quantitative restrictions on exports, and all measures having equivalent effect, shall be prohibited between Member States.

2. Member States shall, by the end of the first stage at the latest, abolish all quantitative restrictions on exports and any measures having equivalent effect which are in existence when this Treaty enters into force.

Article 35.   The Member States declare their readiness to abolish quantitative restrictions on imports from and exports to other Member States more rapidly than is provided for in the preceding Articles, if their general economic situation of the economic sector concerned so permit.

To this end, the Commission shall make recommendations to the States concerned.

Article 36.   The provisions of Arts. 30 to 34 shall not preclude prohibitions or restrictions on imports, exports or goods in transit justified on grounds of public morality, public policy or public security; the protection of health and life of humans, animals or plants; the protection of national treasures possessing artistic, historic or archaeological value; or the protection of industrial and commercial property. Such prohibitions or restrictions shall not, however, constitute a means of arbitrary discrimination or a disguised restriction on trade between Member States.

Article 37.   1. Member States shall progressively adjust any State monopolies of a commercial character so as to ensure that when the transitional period has ended no discrimination regarding the conditions under which goods are procured and marketed exists between nationals of Member States.

The provisions of this Article shall apply to any body through which a Member State, in law or in fact, either directly or indirectly supervises, determines or appreciably influences imports or exports between Member States. These provisions shall likewise apply to monopolies delegated by the State to others.

2. Member States shall refrain from introducing any new measure which is contrary to the principles laid down. in paragraph 1 or which restricts the scope of the Articles dealing with the abolition of customs duties and quantitative restrictions between Member States.

3. The timetable for the measures referred to in paragraph 1 shall be harmonised with the abolition of quantitative restrictions on the same products provided for in Arts. 30 to 34.

If a product is subject to a State monopoly of a commercial character in only one or some Member States, the Commission may authorise the other Member States to apply protective measures until the adjustment provided for in paragraph 1 has been effected; the Commission shall determine the conditions and details of such measures.

4. If a State monopoly of a commercial character has rules which are designed to make it easier to dispose of agricultural products or obtain for them the best return, steps should be taken in applying the rules contained in this Article to ensure equivalent safeguards for the employment and standard of living of the producers concerned, account being taken of the adjustments that will be possible and the specialisation that will be needed with the passage of time.

5. The obligations on Member States shall be binding only in so far as they are compatible with existing international agreements.

6. With effect from the first stage the Commission shall make recommendations as to the manner in which and the timetable according to which the adjustment provided for in this Article shall be carried out.

TITLE II. AGRICULTURE

Article 38. 1. The common market shall extend to agriculture and trade in agricultural products 'Agricultural products' means the products of the soil, of stock-farming and of fisheries and products of first-stage processing directly related to these products.

2. Save as otherwise provided in Arts. 39 to 46, the rules laid down for the establishment of the common market shall apply to agricultural products.

3. The products subject to the provisions of Arts. 39 to 46 are listed in Annex II to this Treaty. Within two years of the entry into force of this Treaty, however, the Council shall, acting by a qualified majority on a proposal from the Commission, decide what products are to be added to this list.

4. The operation and development of the common market for agricultural products must be accompanied by the establishment of a common agricultural policy among the Member States.

Article 39. 1. The objectives of the common agricultural policy shall be:

(a) to increase agricultural productivity by promoting technical progress and by ensuring the rational development of agricultural production and the optimum utilisation of the factors of production, in particular labour;

(b) thus to ensure a fair standard of living for the agricultural community, in particular by increasing the individual earnings of persons engaged in agriculture;

(c) to stabilise markets;

(d) to assure the availability of supplies;

(e) to ensure that supplies reach consumers at reasonable prices.

2. In working out the common agricultural policy and the special methods for its application, account shall be taken of:

(a) the particular nature of agricultural activity, which results from the social structure of agriculture and from structural and natural disparities between the various agricultural regions;

(b) the need to effect the appropriate adjustments by degrees;

(c) the fact that in the Member States agriculture constitutes a sector closely linked with the economy as a whole.

Article 40. 1. Member States shall develop the common agricultural policy by degrees during the transitional period and shall bring it into force by the end of that period at the latest.

2. In order to attain the objectives set out in Art. 39 a common organisation of agricultural markets shall be established.

This organisation shall take one of the following forms, depending on the product concerned;

(a) common rules on competition;

(b) compulsory co-ordination of the various national market organisations;

(c) a European market organisation.

3. The common organisation established in accordance with paragraph 2 may include all measures required to attain the objectives set out in Art. 39, in particular regulation of prices, aids for the production and marketing of the various products, storage and carry-over arrangements and common machinery for stabilising imports or exports.

The common organisation shall be limited to pursuit of the objectives set out in Art. 39 and shall exclude any discrimination between producers or consumers within the Community.

Any common price policy shall be based on common criteria and uniform methods of calculation.

E C

4. In order to enable the common organisation referred to in paragraph 2 to attain its objectives, one or more agricultural guidance and guarantee funds may be set up.

Article 41. To enable the objectives set out in Art. 39 to be attained, provision may be made within the framework of the common agricultural policy for measures such as:

(a) an effective co-ordination of efforts in the spheres of vocational training, of research and of the dissemination of agricultural knowledge; this may include joint financing of projects or institutions;
(b) joint measures to promote consumption of certain products.

Article 42. The provisions of the Chapter relating to rules on competition shall apply to production of and trade in agricultural products only to the extent determined by the Council within the framework of Art. 43 (2) and (3) and in accordance with the procedure laid down therein, account being taken of the objectives set out in Art. 39.

The Council may, in particular, authorise the granting of aid:

(a) for the protection of enterprises handicapped by structural or natural conditions;
(b) within the framework of economic development programmes.

Article 43. 1. In order to evolve the broad lines of a common agricultural policy, the Commission shall, immediately this Treaty enters into force, convene a conference of the Member States with a view to making a comparison of their agricultural policies, in particular by producing a statement of their resources and needs.

2. Having taken into account the work of the conference provided for in paragraph 1, after consulting the Economic and Social Committee and within two years of the entry into force of this Treaty, the Commission shall submit proposals for working out and implementing the common agricultural policy, including the replacement of the national organisations by one of the forms of common organisation provided for in Art. 40 (2), and for implementing the measures specified in this Title.

These proposals shall take account of the interdependence of the agricultural matters mentioned in this Title.

The Council shall, on a proposal from the Commission and after consulting the Assembly, acting unanimously during the first two stages and by a qualified majority thereafter, make regulations, issue directives, or take decisions, without prejudice to any recommendations it may also make.

3. The Council may, acting by a qualified majority and in accordance

with paragraph 2, replace the national market organisations by the common organisation provided for in Art. 40 (2) if:

(a) the common organisation offers Member States which are opposed to this measure and which have an organisation of their own for the production in question equivalent safeguards for the employment and standard of living of the producers concerned, account being taken of the adjustments that will be possible and the specialisation that will be needed with the passage of time;
(b) such an organisation ensures conditions for trade within the Community similar to those existing in a national market.

4. If a common organisation for certain raw materials is established before a common organisation exists for the corresponding processed products, such raw materials as are used for processed products intended for export to third countries may be imported from outside the Community.

Article 44. 1. In so far as progressive abolition of customs duties and quantitative restrictions, between Member States may result in prices likely to jeopardise the attainment of the objectives set out in Art. 39, each Member State shall, during the transitional period, be entitled to apply to particular products, in a non-discriminatory manner and in substitution for quotas and to such an extent as shall not impede the expansion of the volume of trade provided for in Art. 45 (2), a system of minimum prices below which imports may be either:

– temporarily suspended or reduced; or
  allowed, but subjected to the condition that they are made at a price higher than the minimum price for the product concerned.

In the latter case the minimum prices shall not include customs duties.

2. Minimum prices shall neither cause a reduction of the trade existing between Member States when this Treaty enters into force nor form an obstacle to progressive expansion of this trade. Minimum prices shall not be applied so as to form an obstacle to the development of a natural preference between Member States.

3. As soon as this Treaty enters into force the Council shall, on a proposal from the Commission, determine objective criteria for the establishment of minimum price systems and for the fixing of such prices.

These criteria shall in particular take account of the average national production costs in the Member State applying the minimum price, of the position of the various undertakings concerned in relation to such average production costs, and of the need to promote both the progressive improvement of agricultural practice and the adjustments and specialisation needed within the common market.

The Commission shall further propose a procedure for revising these criteria in order to allow for and speed up technical progress and to approximate prices progressively within the common market.

These criteria and the procedure for revising them shall be determined by the Council acting unanimously within three years of the entry into force of this Treaty.

4. Until the decision of the Council takes effect, Member States may fix minimum prices on condition that these are communicated before hand to the Commission and to the other Member States so that they may submit their comments.

Once the Council has taken its decision, Member States shall fix minimum prices on the basis of the criteria determined as above.

The Council may, acting by a qualified majority on a proposal from the Commission, rectify any decisions taken by Member States which do not conform to the criteria defined above.

5. If it does not prove possible to determine the said objective criteria for certain products by the beginning of the third stage, the Council may, acting by a qualified majority on a proposal from the Commission, vary the minimum prices applied to these products.

6. At the end of the transitional period, a table of minimum prices still in force shall be drawn up. The Council shall, acting on a proposal from the Commission and by a majority of nine votes in accordance with the weighting laid down in the first subparagraph of Art. 148 (2), determine the system to be applied within the framework of the common agricultural policy.

Article 45. 1. Until national market organisations have been replaced by one of the forms of common organisation referred to in Art. 40 (2), trade in products in respect of which certain Member States:

– have arrangements designed to guarantee national producers a market for their products; and
– are in need of imports,

shall be developed by the conclusion of long-term agreements or contracts between importing and exporting Member States.

These agreements or contracts shall be directed towards the progressive abolition of any discrimination in the application of these arrangements to the various producers within the Community.

Such agreements or contracts shall be concluded during the first stage; account shall be taken of the principle of reciprocity.

2. As regards quantities, these agreements or contracts shall be based on the average volume of trade between Member States in the products concerned during the three years before the entry into force of this Treaty

and shall provide for an increase in the volume of trade within the limits of existing requirements, account being taken of traditional patterns of trade.

As regards prices, these agreements or contracts shall enable producers to dispose of the agreed quantities at prices which shall be progressively approximated to those paid to national producers on the domestic market of the purchasing country.

This approximation shall proceed as steadily as possible and shall be completed by the end of the transitional period at the latest.

Prices shall be negotiated between the parties concerned within the framework of directives issued by the Commission for the purpose of implementing the two preceding subparagraphs.

If the first stage is extended, these agreements or contracts shall continue to be carried out in accordance with the conditions applicable at the end of the fourth year after the entry into force of this Treaty, the obligation to increase quantities and to approximate prices being suspended until the transition to the second stage.

Member States shall avail themselves of any opportunity open to them under their legislation, particularly in respect of import policy, to ensure the conclusion and carrying out of these agreements or contracts.

3. To the extent that Member States require raw materials for the manufacture of products to be exported outside the Community in competition with products of third countries, the above agreements or contracts shall not form an obstacle to the importation of raw materials for this purpose from third countries. This provision shall not, however, apply if the Council unanimously decides to make provision for payments required to compensate for the higher price paid on goods imported for this purpose on the basis of these agreements or contracts in relation to the delivered price of the same goods purchased on the world market.

Article 46.   Where in a Member State a product is subject to a national market organisation or to internal rules having equivalent effect which affect the competitive position of similar production in another Member State, a countervailing charge shall be applied by Member States to imports of this product coming from the Member State where such organisations or rules exist, unless that State applies a countervailing charge on export.

The Commission shall fix the amount of these charges at the level required to redress the balance; it may also authorise other measures, the conditions and details of which it shall determine.

Article 47.   As to the functions to be performed by the Economic and Social Committee in pursuance of this Title, its agricultural section shall hold itself at the disposal of the Commission to prepare, in accordance with the provisions of Arts. 197 and 198, the deliberations of the Committee.

TITLE III. FREE MOVEMENT OF PERSONS, SERVICES AND CAPITAL

CHAPTER I. WORKERS

Article 48. 1. Freedom of movement for workers shall be secured within the Community by the end of the transitional period at the latest.

2. Such freedom of movement shall entail the abolition of any discrimination based on nationality between workers of the Member States as regards employment, remuneration and other conditions of work and employment.

3. It shall entail the right, subject to limitations justified on grounds of public policy, public security or public health:

(a) to accept offers of employment actually made;
(b) to move freely within the territory of Member States for this purpose;
(c) to stay in a Member State for the purpose of employment in accordance with the provisions governing the employment of nationals of that State laid down by law, regulation or administrative action;
(d) to remain in the territory of a Member State after having been employed in that State, subject to conditions which shall be embodied in implementing regulations to be drawn up by the Commission.

4. The provisions of this Article shall not apply to employment in the public service.

Article 49. As soon as this Treaty enters into force, the Council shall, acting [in accordance with the procedure referred to in Article 189b] {by a qualified majority on a proposal from the Commission, in co-operation with the European Parliament} and after consulting the Economic and Social Committee, issue directives or make regulations setting out the measures required to bring about, by progressive stages, freedom of movement for workers, as defined in Article 48, in particular:

(a) by ensuring close co-operation between national employment services;
(b) by systematically and progressively abolishing those administrative procedures and practices and those qualifying periods in respect of eligibility for available employment, whether resulting from national legislation or from agreements previously concluded between Member States, the maintenance of which would form an obstacle to liberalisation of the movement of workers;
(c) by systematically and progressively abolishing all such qualifying peri-

ods and other restrictions provided for either under national legislation or under agreements previously concluded between Member States as impose on workers of other Member States conditions regarding the free choice of employment other than those imposed on workers of the State concerned;

(d) by setting up appropriate machinery to bring offers of employment into touch with applications for employment and to facilitate the achievement of a balance between supply and demand in the employment market in such a way as to avoid serious threats to the standard of living and level of employment in the various regions and industries.

[For secondary legislation on entry and residence, equality of treatment, the public policy proviso, and residence after retirement, see pp. 290 ff.].

Article 50. Member States shall, within the framework of a joint programme, encourage the exchange of young workers.

Article 51. The Council shall, acting unanimously on a proposal from the Commission, adopt such measures in the field of social security as are necessary to provide freedom of movement for workers; to this end, it shall make arrangements to secure for migrant workers and their dependants:

(a) aggregation, for the purpose of acquiring and retaining the right to benefit and of calculating the amount of benefit, of all periods taken into account under the laws of the several countries;

(b) payment of benefits to persons resident in the territories of Member States.

[For secondary legislation providing for the co-ordination of the national social security rules, see pp. 376 ff.]

CHAPTER 2. RIGHT OF ESTABLISHMENT

Article 52. Within the framework of the provisions set out below, restrictions on the freedom of establishment of nationals of a Member State in the territory of another Member State shall be abolished by progressive stages in the course of the transitional period. Such progressive abolition shall also apply to restrictions on the setting up of agencies, branches, or subsidiaries by nationals of any Member State established in the territory of any Member State.

Freedom of establishment shall include the right to take up and pursue activities as self-employed persons and to set up and manage undertakings, in particular companies or firms within the meaning of the second paragraph of Art. 58, under the conditions laid down for its own nationals by the law of the country where such establishment is effected, subject to the provisions of the Chapter relating to capital.

[For a secondary legislation on the entry and residence of non-wage-earners, and their residence in Member States after retirement, see pp. 300 and 406 ff.]

Article 53.   Member States shall not introduce any new restrictions on the right of establishment in their territories of nationals of other Member States, save as otherwise provided in this Treaty.

Article 54.   1. Before the end of the first stage, the Council shall, acting unanimously on a proposal from the Commission and after consulting the Economic and Social Committee and the Assembly, draw up a general programme for the abolition of existing restrictions on freedom of establishment within the Community. The Commission shall submit its proposal to the Council during the first two years of the first stage.

The programme shall set out the general conditions under which freedom of establishment is to be attained in the case of each type of activity and in particular the stages by which it is to be attained.

2. In order to implement this general programme or, in the absence of such programme, in order to achieve a stage in attaining freedom of establishment as regards a particular activity, the Council, acting [in accordance with the procedure referred to in Article 189b] {on a proposal from the Commission in co-operation with the European Parliament} and after consulting the Economic and Social Committee, [shall act by means of directives.] {shall issue directives, acting unanimously until the end of the first stage and by a qualified majority thereafter.}

3. The Council and the Commission shall carry out the duties developing upon them under the preceding provisions, in particular:

(a) by according, as a general rule, priority treatment to activities where freedom of establishment makes a particularly valuable contribution to the development of production and trade;

(b) by ensuring close co-operation between the competent authorities in the Member States in order to ascertain the particular situation within the Community of the various activities concerned;

(c) by abolishing those administrative procedures and practices, whether resulting from national legislation or from agreements previously concluded between Member States, the maintenance of which would form an obstacle to freedom of establishment;

(d) by ensuring that workers of one Member State employed in the territory of another Member State may remain in that territory for the purpose of taking up activities therein as self-employed persons, where they satisfy the conditions which they would be required to satisfy if they were entering that State at the time when they intended to take up such activities;

(e) by enabling a national of one Member State to acquire and use land and buildings situated in the territory of another Member State, in so far as this does not conflict with the principles laid down in Art. 39 (2);

(f) by effecting the progressive abolition of restrictions on freedom of establishment in every branch of activity under consideration, both as regards the conditions for setting up agencies, branches or subsidiaries in the territory of a Member State and as regards the conditions governing the entry of personnel belonging to the main establishment into managerial or supervisory posts in such agencies, branches or subsidiaries;

(g) by co-ordinating to the necessary extent the safeguards which, for the protection of the interests of members and others, are required by Member States of companies or firms within the meaning of the second paragraph of Art. 58 with a view to making such safeguards equivalent throughout the Community;

(h) by satisfying themselves that the conditions of establishment are not distorted by aids granted by Member States.

[For the General Programme on the Abolition of Restrictions and the Right of Establishment, see pp. 310 ff.]

Article 55. The provisions of this Chapter shall not apply, so far as any given Member State is concerned, to activities in which that State are connected, even occasionally, with the exercise of official authority.

The Council may, acting by a qualified majority on a proposal from the Commission, rule that the provisions of this Chapter shall not apply to certain activities.

Article 56. 1. The provisions of this Chapter and measures taken in pursuance thereof shall not prejudice the applicability of provisions laid down by law, regulation or administrative action providing for special treatment for foreign nationals on grounds of public policy, public security or public health.

2. Before the end of the transitional period the Council shall, acting unanimously on a proposal from the Commission and after consulting the European Parliament, issue directives for the co-ordination of the above mentioned provisions laid down by law, regulation or administrative action. After the end of the second stage, however, the Council shall, acting [in accordance with the provisions referred to in Article 189b,] {by

a qualified majority on a proposal from the Commission with the European Parliament,} issue directives for the co-ordination of such provisions as, in each Member State, are a matter for regulation or administrative action.

[For secondary legislation, see pp. 304 ff.]

Article 57. 1. In order to make it easier for persons to take up and pursue activities as self-employed persons, the Council shall, acting [in accordance with the procedure referred to in Article 189b,] {on a proposal from the Commission and in co-operation with the European Parliament, acting unanimously during the first stage and by a qualified majority thereafter,} issue directives for the mutual recognition of diplomas, certificates and other evidence of formal qualifications.

2. For the same purpose, the Council shall, before the end of the transitional period, {acting on a proposal from the Commission and after consulting the Assembly,} issue directives for the co-ordination of the provisions laid down by law, regulation or administrative action in Member States concerning the taking up and pursuit of activities as self-employed persons. [The Council, acting unanimously on a proposal from the Commission and after consulting the European Parliament, shall decide on] {Unanimity shall be required for} directives the implementation of which involves in at least one Member State amendment of the existing principles laid down by law governing the professions with respect to training and conditions of access for natural persons. [In other cases the Council shall act in accordance with the procedure referred to in Article 189b.] {In other cases the Council shall act by a qualified majority in co-operation with the European Parliament.}

3. In the case of the medical and allied and pharmaceutical professions, the progressive abolition of restrictions shall be dependent upon coordination of the conditions for their exercise in the various Member States.

Article 58. Companies or firms formed in accordance with the law of a Member State and having their registered office, central administration or principal place of business within the Community shall, for the purposes of this Chapter, be treated in the same way as natural persons who are nationals of Member States.

'Companies or firms' means companies or firms constituted under civil or commercial law, including co-operative societies, and other legal persons governed by public or private law, save for those which are non-profit making.

CHAPTER 3. SERVICES

Article 59. Within the framework of the provisions set out below, restrictions on freedom to provide services within the Community shall be progressively abolished during the transitional period in respect of nationals of Member States who are established in a State of the Community other than that of the person for whom the services are intended.

The Council may, acting by a qualified majority on a proposal from the Commission, extend the provisions of this Chapter to nationals of a third country who provide services and who are established within the Community.

[For the entry and residence of persons providing services, and of persons in receipt of services, see pp. 316 ff.]

Article 60. Services shall be considered to be 'services' within the meaning of this Treaty where they are normally provided for remuneration, in so far as they are not governed by the provisions relating to freedom of movement for goods, capital and persons.

'Services' shall in particular include:

(a) activities of an industrial character;
(b) activities of a commercial character;
(c) activities of craftsmen;
(d) activities of the professions.

Without prejudice to the provisions of the Chapter relating to the right of establishment, the person providing a service may, in order to do so, temporarily pursue his activity in the State where the service is provided, under the same conditions as are imposed by that State on its own nationals.

Article 61. 1. Freedom to provide services in the field of transport shall be governed by the provisions of the Title relating to transport.

2. The liberalisation of banking and insurance services connected with movements of capital shall be effected in step with the progressive liberalisation of movement of capital.

Article 62. Save as otherwise provided in this Treaty, Member States shall not introduce any new restrictions on the freedom to provide services which has in fact been attained at the date of the entry into force of this Treaty.

Article 63. 1. Before the end of the first stage, the Council shall, acting unanimously on a proposal from the Commission and after consulting the Economic and Social Committee and the Assembly, draw up a general programme for the abolition of existing restrictions on freedom to provide services within the Community. The Commission shall submit its proposal to the Council during the first two years of the first stage.

The programme shall set out the general conditions under which and the stages by which each type of service is to be liberalised.

2. In order to implement this general programme or, in the absence of such programme, in order to achieve a stage in the liberalisation of a specific service, the Council shall, on a proposal from the Commission and after consulting the Economic and Social Committee and the Assembly, issue directives, acting unanimously until the end of the first stage and by a qualified majority thereafter.

3. As regards the proposals and decisions referred to in paragraphs 1 and 2, priority shall as a general rule be given to those services which directly affect production costs or the liberalisation of which helps to promote trade in goods.

[For the General Programme on the Abolition of Restrictions on the Freedom to Provide Services, see pp. 313.]

Article 64. The Member States declare their readiness to undertake the liberalisation of services beyond the extent required by the directives issued pursuant to Art. 63 (2), if their general economic situation and the situation of the economic sector concerned so permit.

To this end, the Commission shall make recommendations to the Member States concerned.

Article 65. As long as restrictions on freedom to provide services have not been abolished, each Member State shall apply such restrictions without distinction on grounds of nationality or residence to all persons providing services within the meaning of the first paragraph of Art. 59.

Article 66. The provisions of Arts. 55 to 58 shall apply to the matters covered by this Chapter.

CHAPTER 4. CAPITAL [AND PAYMENTS]

Article 67. 1. During the transitional period and to the extent necessary to ensure the proper functioning of the common market, Member States shall progressively abolish between themselves all restrictions on the movement of capital belonging to persons resident in Member States and any discrimination based on the nationality or on the place of residence of the parties or on the place where such capital is invested.

2. Current payments connected with the movement of capital between Member States shall be freed from all restrictions by the end of the first stage at the latest.

Article 68. 1. Member States shall, as regards the matters dealt with in this Chapter, be as liberal as possible in granting such exchange authorisations as are still necessary after the entry into force of this Treaty.

2. Where a Member State applies to the movements of capital liberalised in accordance with the provisions of this Chapter the domestic rules governing the capital market and the credit system, it shall do so in a non-discriminatory manner.

3. Loans for the direct or indirect financing of a Member State or its regional or local authorities shall not be issued or placed in other Member States unless the States concerned have reached agreement thereon. This provision shall not preclude the application of Art. 22 of the Protocol on the Statute of the European Investment Bank.

Article 69. The Council shall, on a proposal from the Commission, which for this purpose shall consult the Monetary Committee provided for in Art. 105, issue the necessary directives for the progressive implementation of the provisions of Art. 67, acting unanimously during the first two stages and by a qualified majority thereafter.

Article 70. 1. The Commission shall propose to the Council measures for the progressive co-ordination of the exchange policies of Member States in respect of the movement of capital between those States and third countries. For this purpose the Council shall issue directives, acting by a qualified majority. It shall endeavour to attain the highest possible degree of liberalisation. Unanimity shall be required for measures which constitute a step back as regards the liberalisation of capital movements.

2. Where the measures taken in accordance with paragraph 1 do not permit the elimination of differences between the exchange rules of Member States and where such differences could lead persons resident in one of the Member States to use the freer transfer facilities within the Community which are provided for in Art. 67 in order to evade the rules of one of the Member States concerning the movement of capital to or from third countries, that State may, after consulting the other Member States and the Commission, take appropriate measures to overcome these difficulties.

Should the Council find that these measures are restricting the free movement of capital within the Community to a greater extent than is required for the purpose of overcoming the difficulties, it may, acting by a qualified majority on a proposal from the Commission, decide that the State concerned shall amend or abolish these measures.

Article 71. Member States shall endeavour to avoid introducing within the Community any new exchange restrictions on the movement of capital and current payments connected with such movements, and shall endeavour not to make existing rules more restrictive.

They declare their readiness to go beyond the degree of liberalisation of capital movements provided for in the preceding Articles in so far as their economic situation, in particular the situation of their balance of payments, so permits.

The Commission may, after consulting the Monetary Committee, make recommendations to Member States on this subject.

Article 72. Member States shall keep the Commission informed of any movements of capital to and from third countries which come to their knowledge. The Commission may deliver to Member States any opinions which it considers appropriate on this subject.

Article 73. 1. If movements of capital lead to disturbances in the functioning of the capital market in any Member State, the Commission shall, after consulting the Monetary Committee, authorise that State to take protective measures in the field of capital movements, the conditions and details of which the Commission shall determine.

The Council may, acting by a qualified majority, revoke this authorisation or amend the conditions or details thereof.

2. A Member State which is in difficulties may, however, on grounds of secrecy or urgency, take the measures mentioned above, where this proves necessary, on its own initiative. The Commission and the other Member States shall be informed of such measures by the date of their entry into force at the latest. In this event the Commission may, after consulting the Monetary Committee, decide that the State concerned shall amend or abolish the measures.

[*Article 73a.* As from 1 January 1994, Articles 67 to 73 shall be replaced by Articles 73b, c, d, e, f and g.]

[*Article 73b.* 1. Within the framework of the provisions set out in this Chapter, all restrictions on the movement of capital between Member States and between Member States and third countries shall be prohibited.

2. Within the framework of the provisions set out in this Chapter, all restrictions on payments between Member States and between Member States and third countries shall be prohibited.]

[*Article 73c.*   1. The provisions of Article 73b shall be without prejudice
to the application to third countries of any restrictions which exist on 31
December 1993 under national or Community law adopted in respect of
the movement of capital to or from third countries involving direct
investment—including investment in real estate—establishment, the provision of financial services or the admission of securities to capital markets.

2. Whilst endeavouring to achieve the objective of free movement of
capital between Member States and third countries to the greatest extent
possible and without prejudice to the other Chapters of this Treaty, the
Council may, acting by a qualified majority on a proposal from the
Commission, adopt measures on the movement of capital to or from third
countries involving direct investment—including investment in real estate—
establishment, the provision of financial services or the admission of securities to capital markets. Unanimity shall be required for measures under
this paragraph which constitute a step back in Community law as regards
the liberalization of the movement of capital to or from third countries.]

[*Article 73d.*   1. The provisions of Article 73b shall be without prejudice
to the right of Member States:

(a) to apply the relevant provisions of their tax law which distinguish
    between tax-payers who are not in the same situation with regard to
    their place of residence or with regard to the place where their capital
    is invested;
(b) to take all requisite measures to prevent infringements of national law
    and regulations, in particular in the field of taxation and the pruden-
    tial supervision of financial institutions, or to lay down procedures
    for the declaration of capital movements for purposes of administra-
    tive or statistical information, or to take measures which are justified
    on grounds of public policy or public security.

2. The provisions of this Chapter shall be without prejudice to the
applicability of restrictions on the right of establishment which are compatible with this Treaty.

3. The measures and procedures referred to in paragraphs 1 and 2
shall not constitute a means of arbitrary discrimination or a disguised
restriction on the free movement of capital and payments as defined in
Article 73b.]

[*Article 73e.*   By way of derogation from Article 73b, Member States
which, on 31 December 1993, enjoy a derogation on the basis of existing
Community law, shall be entitled to maintain, until 31 December 1994 at
the latest, restrictions on movements of capital authorized by such derogations as exist on that date.]

[*Article 73f*. Where, in exceptional circumstances, movements of capital to or from third countries cause, or threaten to cause, serious difficulties for the operation of economic and monetary union, the Council, acting by a qualified majority on a proposal from the Commission and after consulting the ECB, may take safeguard measures with regard to third countries for a period not exceeding six months if such measures are strictly necessary.]

[*Article 73g*. 1. If, in the case envisaged in Article 228a, action by the Community is deemed necessary, the Council may, in accordance with the procedure provided for in Article 228a, take the necessary urgent measures on the movement of capital and on payments as regards the third countries concerned.

2. Without prejudice to Article 224 and as long as the Council has not taken measures pursuant to paragraph 1, a Member State may, for serious political reasons and on grounds of urgency, take unilateral measures against a third country with regard to capital movements and payments. The Commission and the other Member States shall be informed of such measures by the date of their entry into force at the latest.

The Council may, acting by a qualified majority on a proposal from the Commission, decide that the Member State concerned shall amend or abolish such measures. The President of the Council shall inform the European Parliament of any such decision taken by the Council.]

[*Article 73h*. Until 1 January 1994, the following provisions shall be applicable:

(1) Each Member State undertakes to authorize, in the currency of the Member State in which the creditor or the beneficiary resides, any payments connected with the movement of goods, services or capital, and any transfers of capital and earnings, to the extent that the movement of goods, services, capital and persons between Member States has been liberalized pursuant to this Treaty.

The Member States declare their readiness to undertake the liberalization of payments beyond the extent provided in the preceding subparagraph, in so far as their economic situation in general and the state of their balance of payments in particular so permit.

(2) In so far as movements of goods, services and capital are limited only by restrictions on payments connected therewith, these restrictions shall be progressively abolished by applying, mutatis mutandis, the provisions of this Chapter and the Chapters relating to the abolition of quantitative restrictions and to the liberalization of services.

(3) Member States undertake not to introduce between themselves any

new restrictions on transfers connected with the invisible transactions listed in Annex III to this Treaty.

The progressive abolition of existing restrictions shall be effected in accordance with the provisions of Articles 63 to 65, in so far as such abolition is not governed by the provisions contained in paragraphs 1 and 2 or by the other provisions of this Chapter.

(4) If need be, Member States shall consult each other on the measures to be taken to enable the payments and transfers mentioned in this Article to be effected; such measures shall not prejudice the attainment of the objectives set out in this Treaty.]

TITLE IV. TRANSPORT

Article 74. The objectives of this Treaty shall, in matters governed by this Title, be pursued by Member States within the framework of a common transport policy.

Article 75. For the purpose of implementing Article 74, and taking into account the distinctive features of transport, the Council shall, acting [in accordance with the procedure referred to in Article 189c and after consulting the Economic and Social Committee,] {unanimously until the second stage and by a qualified majority thereafter,} lay down {, on a proposal from the Commission and after consulting the Economic and Social Committee and the Assembly:}

(a)   common rules applicable to international transport to or from the territory of a Member State or passing across the territory of one or more Member States;

(b)   the conditions under which non-resident carriers may operate transport services within a Member State;

[(c)   measures to improve transport safety;]

[(d)] {(c)} any other appropriate provisions.

2. The provisions referred to in (a) and (b) of paragraph 1 shall be laid down during the transitional period.

3. By way of derogation from the procedure provided for in paragraph 1, where the application of provisions concerning the principles of the regulatory system for transport would be liable to have a serious effect on the standard of living and on employment in certain areas and on the operation of transport facilities, they shall be laid down by the Council acting unanimously [on a proposal from the Commission, after consulting the European Parliament and the Economic and Social Committee]. In so doing, the Council shall take into account the need for adaptation to the economic development which will result from establishing the common market.

Article 76. Until the provisions referred to in Art. 75 (1) have been laid down, no Member State may, without the unanimous approval of the Council, make the various provisions governing the subject when this Treaty enters into force less favourable in their direct or indirect effect on carriers of other Member States as compared with carriers who are nationals of that State.

Article 77. Aids shall be compatible with this Treaty if they meet the needs of co-ordination of transport or if they represent reimbursement for the discharge of certain obligations inherent in the concept of a public service.

Article 78. Any measures taken within the framework of this Treaty in respect of transport rates and conditions shall take account of the economic circumstances of carriers.

Article 79. 1. In the case of transport within the Community, discrimination which takes the form of carriers charging different rates and imposing different conditions for the carriage of the same goods over the same transport links on grounds of the country of origin or of destination of the goods in question, shall be abolished, at the latest, before the end of the second stage.

2. Paragraph 1 shall not prevent the Council from adopting other measures in pursuance of Art. 75 (1).

3. Within two years of the entry into force of this Treaty, the Council shall, acting by a qualified majority on a proposal from the Commission and after consulting the Economic and Social Committee, lay down rules for implementing the provisions of paragraph 1.

The Council may in particular lay down the provisions needed to enable the institutions of the Community to secure compliance with the rule laid down in paragraph 1 and to ensure that users benefit from it to the full.

4. The Commission shall, acting on its own initiative or on application by a Member State, investigate any cases of discrimination falling within paragraph 1 and, after consulting any Member State concerned, shall take the necessary decisions within the framework of the rules laid down in accordance with the provisions of paragraph 3.

Article 80. 1. The imposition by a Member State, in respect of transport operations carried out within the Community, of rates and conditions involving any element of support or protection in the interest of one or more particular undertakings or industries shall be prohibited as from the beginning of the second stage, unless authorised by the Commission.

2. The Commission shall, acting on its own initiative or an application by a Member State, examine the rates and conditions referred to in paragraph 1, taking account in particular of the requirements of an appropriate regional economic policy, the needs of underdeveloped areas and the problems of areas seriously affected by political circumstances on the one hand, and of the effects of such rates and conditions on competition between the different modes of transport on the other.

After consulting each Member State concerned, the Commission shall take the necessary decisions.

3. The prohibition provided for in paragraph 1 shall not apply to tariffs fixed to meet competition.

Article 81. Charges or dues in respect of the crossing of frontiers which are charged by a carrier in addition to the transport rates shall not exceed a reasonable level after taking the costs actually incurred thereby into account.

Member States shall endeavour to reduce these costs progressively.

The Commission may make recommendations to Member States for the application of this Article.

Article 82. The provisions of this Title shall not form an obstacle to the application of measures taken in the Federal Republic of Germany to the extent that such measures are required in order to compensate for the economic disadvantages caused by the division of Germany to the economy of certain areas of the Federal Republic affected by that division.

Article 83. An Advisory Committee consisting of experts designated by the Governments of Member States, shall be attached to the Commission. The Commission, whenever it considers it desirable, shall consult the Committee on transport matters without prejudice to the powers of the transport section of the Economic and Social Committee.

Article 84. 1. The provisions of this Title shall apply to transport by rail, road and inland waterway.

2. The Council may, acting by a qualified majority, decide whether, to what extent and by what procedure appropriate provisions may be laid down for sea and air transport.

The procedural provisions of Article 75(i) and 3 shall apply.

{Part Three. Policy of the Community}

TITLE [V] {I}. COMMON RULES [ON COMPETITION, TAXATION AND
APPROXIMATION OF LAWS]

CHAPTER I. RULES ON COMPETITION

Section 1. Rules Applying to Undertakings

Article 85. 1. The following shall be prohibited as incompatible with the
common market; all agreements between undertakings, decisions by associations of undertakings and concerted practices which may affect trade
between Member States and which have as their object or effect the prevention restriction or distortion of competition within the common market, and in particular those which:

(a) directly or indirectly fix purchase or selling prices or any other trad-
    ing conditions;
(b) limit or control production, markets, technical development, or
    investment;
(c) share markets or sources of supply;
(d) apply dissimilar conditions to equivalent transactions with other trad-
    ing parties, thereby placing them at a competitive disadvantage;
(e) make the conclusion of contracts subject to acceptance by the other
    parties of supplementary obligations which, by their nature or accord-
    ing to commercial usage, have no connection with the subject of such
    contracts.

    2. Any agreements or decisions prohibited pursuant to this Article
shall be automatically void.
    3. The provisions of paragraph 1 may, however, be declared inapplica-
ble in the case of:

– any agreement or category of agreements between undertakings;
– any decision or category of decisions by associations of undertakings;
– any concerted practice or category of concerted practices;

which contributes to improving the production or distribution of goods
or to promoting technical or economic progress, while allowing consumers a fair share of the resulting benefit, and which does not:

(a) impose on the undertakings concerned restrictions which are not
    indispensable to the attainment of these objectives;

(b) afford such undertakings the possibility of eliminating competition in respect of a substantial part of the products in question.

Article 86. Any abuse by one or more undertakings of a dominant position within the common market or in a substantial part of it shall be prohibited as incompatible with the common market in so far as it may affect trade between Member States. Such abuse may, in particular, consist in:

(a) directly or indirectly imposing unfair purchase or selling prices or unfair trading conditions;
(b) limiting production, markets or technical development to the prejudice of consumers;
(c) applying dissimilar conditions to equivalent transactions with other trading parties, thereby placing them at a competitive disadvantage;
(d) making the conclusion of contracts subject to acceptance by the other parties of supplementary obligations which, by their nature or according to commercial usage, have no connection with the subject of such contracts.

Article 87. 1. Within three years of the entry into force of this Treaty the Council shall, acting unanimously on a proposal from the Commission and after consulting the Assembly, adopt any appropriate regulations or directives to give effect to the principles set out in Arts. 85 and 86.

If such provisions have not been adopted within the period mentioned, they shall be laid down by the Council, acting by a qualified majority on a proposal from the Commission and after consulting the Assembly.

2. The regulations or directives referred to in paragraph 1 shall be designed, in particular:

(a) to ensure compliance with the prohibitions laid down in Art. 85 (1) and in Art. 86 by making provision for fines and periodic penalty payments;
(b) to lay down detailed rules for the application of Art. 85 (3), taking into account the need to ensure effective supervision on the one hand, and to simplify administration to the greatest possible extent on the other;
(c) to define, if need be, in the various branches of the economy, the scope of the provisions of Arts. 85 and 86;
(d) to define the respective functions of the Commission and of the Court of Justice in applying the provisions laid down in this paragraph;
(e) to determine the relationship between national laws and the provisions contained in this Section or adopted pursuant to this Article

[For secondary legislation implementing Arts. 85 and 86, see pp. 452 ff.]

Article 88.   Until the entry into force of the provisions adopted in pursuance of Art 87, the authorities in Member States shall rule on the admissibility of agreements, decisions and concerted practices and on abuse of a dominant position in the common market in accordance with the law of their country and with the provisions of Art. 85, in particular paragraph 3, and of Art. 86.

Article 89.   1. Without prejudice to Art. 88, the Commission shall, as soon as it takes up its duties, ensure the application of the principles laid down in Arts. 85 and 86. On application by a Member State or on its own initiative, and in co-operation with the competent authorities in the Member States, who shall give it their assistance, the Commission shall investigate cases of suspected infringement of these principles. If it finds that there has been an infringement, it shall propose appropriate measures to bring it to an end.

2. If the infringement is not brought to an end, the Commission shall record such infringement of the principles in a reasoned decision. The Commission may publish its decision and authorise Member States to take the measures, the conditions and details of which it shall determine, needed to remedy the situation.

Article 90.   1. In the case of public undertakings and undertakings to which Member States grant special or exclusive rights, Member States shall neither enact nor maintain in force any measure contrary to the rules contained in this Treaty, in particular to those rules provided for in Art. 7 and Arts. 85 to 94.

2. Undertakings entrusted with the operation of services of general economic interest or having the character of a revenue-producing monopoly shall be subject to the rules contained in this Treaty, in particular to the rules on competition, in so far as the application of such rules does not obstruct the performance, in law or in fact, of the particular tasks assigned to them. The development of trade must not be affected to such an extent as would be contrary to the interests of the Community.

3. The Commission shall ensure the application of the provisions of this Article and shall, where necessary, address appropriate directives or decisions to Member States.

Section 2. Dumping

Article 91.   1. If, during the transitional period, the Commission, on application by a Member State or by any other interested party, finds that dumping is being practised within the common market, it shall address recommendations to the person or persons with whom such practices originate for the purpose of putting an end to them.

Should the practices continue, the Commission shall authorise the injured Member State to take protective measures, the conditions and details of which the Commission shall determine.

2. As soon as this Treaty enters into force, products which originate in or are in free circulation in one Member State and which have been exported to another Member State shall, on reimportation be admitted into the territory of the first-mentioned State free of all customs duties, quantitative restrictions or measures having equivalent effect. The Commission shall lay down appropriate rules for the application of this paragraph.

Section 3. Aids Granted by States

Article 92. 1. Save as otherwise provided in this Treaty, any aid granted by a Member State or through State resources in any form whatsoever which distorts or threatens to distort competition by favouring certain undertakings or the production of certain goods shall, in so far as it affects trade between Member States, be incompatible with the common market.

2. The following shall be compatible with the common market:

(a)   aid having a social character, granted to individual consumers, provided that such aid is granted without discrimination related to the origin of the products concerned;

(b)   aid to make good the damage caused by natural disasters or other exceptional occurrences;

(c)   aid granted to the economy of certain areas of the Federal Republic of Germany affected by the division of Germany, in so far as such aid is required in order to compensate for the economic disadvantages caused by that division.

3. The following may be considered to be compatible with the common market:

(a)   aid to promote the economic development of areas where the standard of living is abnormally low or where there is serious underemployment;

(b)   aid to promote the execution of an important project of common European interest or to remedy a serious disturbance in the economy of a Member State;

(c)   aid to facilitate the development of certain economic activities or of certain economic areas, where such aid does not adversely affect trading conditions to an extent contrary to the common interest.However, the aids granted to shipbuilding as of 1 January 1957 shall, in so far as they serve only to compensate for the absence of customs protection, be progressively reduced under the same conditions as apply to the elimination of customs duties, subject to the provisions of this Treaty concerning common commercial policy towards third countries;

[(d)   aid to promote culture and heritage conservation where such aid does not affect trading conditions and competition in the Community to an extent that is contrary to the common interest.]

[(e)] {(d)} such other categories of aid as may be specified by decision of the Council acting by a qualified majority on a proposal from the Commission.

Article 93. 1. The Commission shall, in co-operation with Member States, keep under constant review all systems of aid existing in those States. It shall propose to the latter any appropriate measures required by the progressive development or by the functioning of the common market.

2. If, after having given notice to the parties concerned to submit their comments, the Commission finds that aid granted by a State or through State resources is not compatible with the common market having regard to Art. 92, or that such aid is being misused, it shall decide that the State concerned shall abolish or alter such aid within a period of time to be determined by the Commission.

If the State concerned does not comply with this decision within the prescribed time, the Commission or any other interested State may, in derogation from the provisions of Arts. 169 and 170, refer the matter to the Court of Justice direct.

On application by a Member State, the Council may, acting unanimously, decide that aid which that State is granting or intends to grant shall be considered to be compatible with the common market, in derogation from the provisions of Art. 92 or from the regulations provided for in Art. 94, if such a decision is justified by exceptional circumstances. If, as regards the aid in question, the Commission has already initiated the procedure provided for in the first subparagraph of this paragraph, the fact that the State concerned has made its application to the Council shall have the effect of suspending that procedure until the Council has made its attitude known.

If, however, the Council has not made its attitude known within three months of the said application being made, the Commission shall give its decision on the case.

3. The Commission shall be informed, in sufficient time to enable it to submit its comments, of any plans to grant or alter aid. If it considers

that any such plan is not compatible with the common market having regard to Art. 92, it shall without delay initiate the procedure provided for in paragraph 2. The Member State concerned shall not put its proposed measures into effect until this procedure has resulted in a final decision.

Article 94. The Council, acting by a qualified majority on a proposal from the Commission, [and after consulting the European Parliament,] may make any appropriate regulations for the application of Articles 92 and 93 and may in particular determine the conditions under which Article 93 (3) shall apply and the categories of aid exempted from this procedure.

CHAPTER 2, TAX PROVISIONS

Article 95. No Member State shall impose, directly or indirectly, on the products of other Member States any internal taxation of any kind in excess of that imposed directly or indirectly on similar domestic products.

Furthermore, no Member State shall impose on the products of other Member States any internal taxation of such a nature as to afford indirect protection to other products.

Member States shall, not later than at the beginning of the second stage, repeal or amend any provisions existing when this Treaty enters into force which conflict with the preceding rules.

Article 96. Where products are exported to the territory of any Member State, any repayment of internal taxation shall not exceed the internal taxation imposed on them, whether directly or indirectly.

Article 97. Member States which levy a turnover tax calculated on a cumulative multi-stage tax system may, in the case of internal taxation imposed by them on imported products or of repayments allowed by them on exported products, establish average rates for products or groups of products, provided that there is no infringement of the principles laid down in Arts. 95 and 96.

Where the average rates established by a Member State do not conform to these principles, the Commission shall address appropriate directives or decisions to the State concerned.

Article 98. In the case of charges other than turnover taxes, excise duties and other forms of indirect taxation, remissions and repayments in respect of exports to other Member States may not be granted and countervailing charges in respect of imports from Member States may not be imposed unless the measures contemplated have been previously approved for a limited period by the Council acting by a qualified majority on a proposal from the Commission.

Article 99. The Council shall, acting unanimously on a proposal from the Commission and after consulting the European Parliament [and the Economic and Social Committee] adopt provisions for the harmonisation of legislation concerning turnover taxes, excise duties and other forms of indirect taxation to the extent that such harmonisation is necessary to ensure the establishment and the functioning of the internal market within the time-limit laid down in Article [7a] {8a}.

CHAPTER 3. APPROXIMATION OF LAWS]

Article 100. The Council shall, acting unanimously on a proposal from the Commission [and after consulting the European Parliament and the Economic and Social Committee], issue directives for the approximation of such laws, regulations or administrative provisions of the Member States as directly affect the establishment or functioning of the common market.

{The Assembly and the Economic and Social Committee shall be consulted in the case of directives whose implementation would, in one or more Member States, involve the amendment of legislation.}

[For the 1985 Products Liability Directive, see below, p. 583]

Article 100a. 1. By way of derogation from Article 100 and save where otherwise provided in this Treaty, the following provisions shall apply for the achievement of the objectives set out in Article [7a] {8a}. The Council shall, acting [in accordance with the procedure referred to in Article 189b] {by a qualified majority on a proposal from the Commission in co-operation with the European Parliament} and after consulting the Economic and Social Committee, adopt the measures for the approximation of the provisions laid down by law, regulation or administrative action in Member States which have as their object the establishing and functioning of the internal market.

2. Paragraph 1 shall not apply to fiscal provisions, to those relating to the free movement of persons nor to those relating to the rights and interests of employed persons.

3. The Commission, in its proposals envisaged in paragraph 1 concerning health, safety, environmental protection and consumer protection, will take as a base a high level of protection.

4. If, after the adoption of a harmonisation measure by the Council acting by a qualified majority, a Member State deems it necessary to

apply national provisions on grounds of major needs referred to in Article 36, or relating to protection of the environment or the working environment, it shall notify the Commission of these provisions.

The Commission shall confirm the provisions involved after having verified that they are not a means of arbitrary discrimination or a disguised restriction on trade between Member States.

By way of derogation from the procedure laid down in Articles 169 and 170, the Commission or any Member State may bring the matter directly before the Court of Justice if it considers that another Member State is making improper use of the powers provided for in this Article .

5. The harmonisation measures referred to above shall, in appropriate cases, include a safeguard clause authorising the Member States to take, for one or more of the non-economic reasons referred to in Article 36, provisional measures subject to a Community control procedure.

Article 100b.   1. During 1992, the Commission shall, together with each Member State, draw up an inventory of national laws, regulations and administrative provisions which fall under Article 100a and which have not been harmonised pursuant to that Article .

The Council, acting in accordance with the provisions of Article 100a, may decide that the provisions in force in a Member State must be recognised as being equivalent to those applied by another Member State.

2. The provisions of Article 100a(4) shall apply by analogy.

3. The Commission shall draw up the inventory referred to in the first subparagraph of paragraph 1 and shall submit appropriate proposals in good time to allow the Council to act before the end of 1992.

[*Article 100c.*   1. The Council, acting unanimously on a proposal from the Commission and after consulting the European Parliament, shall determine the third countries whose nationals must be in possession of a visa when crossing the external borders of the Member States.

2. However, in the event of an emergency situation in a third country posing a threat of a sudden inflow of nationals from that country into the Community, the Council, acting by a qualified majority on a recommendation from the Commission, may introduce, for a period not exceeding six months, a visa requirement for nationals from the country in question. The visa requirement established under this paragraph may be extended in accordance with the procedure referred to in paragraph 1.

3. From 1 January 1996, the Council shall act by a qualified majority on the decisions referred to in paragraph 1. The Council shall, before that date, acting by a qualified majority on a proposal from the Commission and after consulting the European Parliament, adopt measures relating to a uniform format for visas.

4. In the matters referred to in this Article, the Commission shall examine any request made by a Member State that it submit a proposal to the Council.

5. This Article shall be without prejudice to the exercise of the responsibilities incumbent upon the Member States with regard to the maintenance of law and order and the safeguarding of internal security.

6. This Article shall apply to other matters if so decided pursuant to Article K.9 of the provisions of the Treaty on European Union which relate to cooperation in the fields of justice and home affairs, subject to the voting conditions determined at the same time.

7. The provisions of the conventions in force between the Member States governing matters covered by this Article shall remain in force until their content has been replaced by directives or measures adopted pursuant to this Article.]

[*Article 100d.* The Coordinating Committee consisting of senior officials set up by Article K.4 of the Treaty on European Union shall contribute, without prejudice to the provisions of Article 151, to the preparation of the proceedings of the Council in the fields referred to in Article 100c.]

Article 101. Where the Commission finds that a difference between the provisions laid down by law, regulation or administrative action in Member States is distorting the conditions of competition in the common market and that the resultant distortion needs to be eliminated, it shall consult the Member States concerned.

If such consultation does not result in an agreement eliminating the distortion in question, the Council shall, on a proposal from the Commission, acting unanimously during the first stage and by a qualified majority thereafter, issue the necessary directives. The Commission and the Council may take any other appropriate measures provided for in this Treaty.

Article 102. 1. Where there is reason to fear that the adoption or amendment of a provision laid down by law, regulation or administrative action may cause distortion within the meaning of Art. 101, a Member State desiring to proceed therewith shall consult the Commission. After consulting the Member States, the Commission shall recommend to the States concerned such measures as may be appropriate to avoid the distortion in question.

2. If a State desiring to introduce or amend its own provisions does not comply with the recommendation addressed to it by the Commission, other Member States shall not be required, in pursuance of Art. 101, to amend their own provisions in order to eliminate such distortion. If the

Member State which has ignored the recommendation of the Commission causes distortion detrimental only to itself, the provisions of Art. 101 shall not apply.

TITLE VI. ECONOMIC AND MONETARY POLICY

[NB The articles which will be replaced by this title are printed after Article 109m]

CHAPTER I. ECONOMIC POLICY]

[Article 102a.　Member States shall conduct their economic policies with a view to contributing to the achievement of the objectives of the Community, as defined in Article 2, and in the context of the broad guidelines referred to in Article 103(2). The Member States and the Community shall act in accordance with the principle of an open market economy with free competition, favouring an efficient allocation of resources, and in compliance with the principles set out in Article 3a.]

[Article 103.　1. Member States shall regard their economic policies as a matter of common concern and shall coordinate them within the Council, in accordance with the provisions of Article 102a.

2. The Council shall, acting by a qualified majority on a recommendation from the Commission, formulate a draft for the broad guidelines of the economic policies of the Member States and of the Community, and shall report its findings to the European Council.

The European Council shall, acting on the basis of this report from the Council, discuss a conclusion on the broad guidelines of the economic policies of the Member States and of the Community.

On the basis of this conclusion, the Council shall, acting by a qualified majority, adopt a recommendation setting out these broad guidelines. The Council shall inform the European Parliament of its recommendation.

3. In order to ensure closer coordination of economic policies and sustained convergence of the economic performances of the Member States, the Council shall, on the basis of reports submitted by the Commission, monitor economic developments in each of the Member States and in the Community as well as the consistency of economic policies with the broad guidelines referred to in paragraph 2, and regularly carry out an overall assessment.

For the purpose of this multilateral surveillance, Member States shall forward information to the Commission about important measures taken by them in the field of their economic policy and such other information as they deem necessary.

4. Where it is established, under the procedure referred to in paragraph 3, that the economic policies of a Member State are not consistent with the broad guidelines referred to in paragraph 2 or that they risk jeopardizing the proper functioning of economic and monetary union, the Council may, acting by a qualified majority on a recommendation from the Commission, make the necessary recommendations to the Member State concerned. The Council may, acting by a qualified majority on a proposal from the Commission, decide to make its recommendations public.

The President of the Council and the Commission shall report to the European Parliament on the results of multilateral surveillance. The President of the Council may be invited to appear before the competent Committee of the European Parliament if the Council has made its recommendations public.

5. The Council, acting in accordance with the procedure referred to in Article 189c, may adopt detailed rules for the multilateral surveillance procedure referred to in paragraphs 3 and 4 of this Article.]

[*Article 103a.* 1. Without prejudice to any other procedures provided for in this Treaty, the Council may, acting unanimously on a proposal from the Commission, decide upon the measures appropriate to the economic situation, in particular if severe difficulties arise in the supply of certain products.

2. Where a Member State is in difficulties or is seriously threatened with severe difficulties caused by exceptional occurrences beyond its control, the Council may, acting unanimously on a proposal from the Commission, grant, under certain conditions, Community financial assistance to the Member State concerned. Where the severe difficulties are caused by natural disasters, the Council shall act by qualified majority. The President of the Council shall inform the European Parliament of the decision taken.]

[*Article 104.* 1. Overdraft facilities or any other type of credit facility with the ECB or with the central banks of the Member States (hereinafter referred to as 'national central banks') in favour of Community institutions or bodies, central governments, regional, local or other public authorities, other bodies governed by public law or public undertakings of Member States shall be prohibited, as shall the purchase directly from them by the ECB or national central banks of debt instruments.

2. The provisions of paragraph 1 shall not apply to publicly-owned credit institutions, which in the context of the supply of reserves by central banks shall be given the same treatment by national central banks and the ECB as private credit institutions.]

[*Article 104a*.   1. Any measure, not based on prudential considerations, establishing privileged access by Community institutions or bodies, central governments, regional, local or other public authorities, other bodies governed by public law or public undertakings of Member States to financial institutions shall be prohibited.

2. The Council, acting in accordance with the procedure referred to in Article 189c, shall, before 1 January 1994, specify definitions for the application of the prohibition referred to in paragraph 1.]

[*Article 104b*.   1. The Community shall not be liable for or assume the commitments of central governments, regional, local or other public authorities, other bodies governed by public law, or public undertakings of any Member State, without prejudice to mutual financial guarantees for the joint execution of a specific project. A Member State shall not be liable for or assume the commitments of central governments, regional, local or other public authorities, other bodies governed by public law or public undertakings of another Member State, without prejudice to mutual financial guarantees for the joint execution of a specific project.

2. If necessary, the Council, acting in accordance with the procedure referred to in Article 189c, may specify definitions for the application of the prohibitions referred to in Article 104 and in this Article.]

[*Article 104c*.   1. Member States shall avoid excessive government deficits.

2. The Commission shall monitor the development of the budgetary situation and of the stock of government debt in the Member States with a view to identifying gross errors. In particular it shall examine compliance with budgetary discipline on the basis of the following two criteria:

(a) whether the ratio of the planned or actual government deficit to gross domestic product exceeds a reference value, unless
    – either the ratio has declined substantially and continuously and reached a level that comes close to the reference value;
    – or, alternatively, the excess over the reference value is only exceptional and temporary and the ratio remains close to the reference value;
(b) whether the ratio of government debt to gross domestic product exceeds a reference value, unless the ratio is sufficiently diminishing and approaching the reference value at a satisfactory pace.

The reference values are specified in the Protocol on the excessive deficit procedure annexed to this Treaty.

3. If a Member State does not fulfil the requirements under one or both of these criteria, the Commission shall prepare a report. The report

of the Commission shall also take into account whether the government deficit exceeds government investment expenditure and take into account all other relevant factors, including the medium term economic and budgetary position of the Member State.

The Commission may also prepare a report if, notwithstanding the fulfilment of the requirements under the criteria, it is of the opinion that there is a risk of an excessive deficit in a Member State.

4. The Committee provided for in Article 109c shall formulate an opinion on the report of the Commission.

5. If the Commission considers that an excessive deficit in a Member State exists or may occur, the Commission shall address an opinion to the Council.

6. The Council shall, acting by a qualified majority on a recommendation from the Commission, and having considered any observations which the Member State concerned may wish to make, decide after an overall assessment whether an excessive deficit exists.

7. Where the existence of an excessive deficit is decided according to paragraph 6, the Council shall make recommendations to the Member State concerned with a view to bringing that situation to an end within a given period. Subject to the provisions of paragraph 8, these recommendations shall not be made public.

8. Where it establishes that there has been no effective action in response to its recommendations within the period laid down, the Council may make its recommendations public.

9. If a Member State persists in failing to put into practice the recommendations of the Council, the Council may decide to give notice to the Member State to take, within a specified time limit, measures for the deficit reduction which is judged necessary by the Council in order to remedy the situation.

In such a case, the Council may request the Member State concerned to submit reports in accordance with a specific timetable in order to examine the adjustment efforts of that Member State.

10. The rights to bring actions provided for in Articles 169 and 170 may not be exercised within the framework of paragraphs 1 to 9 of this Article.

11. As long as a Member State fails to comply with a decision taken in accordance with paragraph 9, the Council may decide to apply or, as the case may be, intensify one or more of the following measures:

– to require that the Member State concerned shall publish additional information, to be specified by the Council, before issuing bonds and securities;
– to invite the European Investment Bank to reconsider its lending policy towards the Member State concerned;

- to require that the Member State concerned makes a non-interest-bearing deposit of an appropriate size with the Community until the excessive deficit has, in the view of the Council, been corrected;
- to impose fines of an appropriate size.

The President of the Council shall inform the European Parliament of the decisions taken.

12. The Council shall abrogate some or all of its decisions as referred to in paragraphs 6 to 9 and 11 to the extent that the excessive deficit in the Member State concerned has, in the view of the Council, been corrected. If the Council previously has made public recommendations, it shall, as soon as the decision under paragraph 8 has been abrogated, make a public statement that an excessive deficit in the Member State concerned no longer exists.

13. When taking the decisions referred to in paragraphs 7 to 9, 11 and 12, the Council shall act on a recommendation from the Commission by a majority of two thirds of the votes of its members weighted in accordance with Article 148(2) and excluding the votes of the representative of the Member State concerned.

14. Further provisions relating to the implementation of the procedure described in this Article are set out in the Protocol on the excessive deficit procedure annexed to this Treaty.

The Council shall, acting unanimously on a proposal from the Commission and after consulting the European Parliament and the ECB, adopt the appropriate provisions which shall then replace the said Protocol.

Subject to the other provisions of this paragraph the Council shall, before 1 January 1994, acting by a qualified majority on a proposal from the Commission and after consulting the European Parliament, lay down detailed rules and definitions for the application of the provisions of the said Protocol.]

[CHAPTER 2. MONETARY POLICY]

[*Article 105*. 1. The primary objective of the ESCB shall be to maintain price stability. Without prejudice to the objective of price stability, the ESCB shall support the general economic policies in the Community with a view to contributing to the achievement of the objectives of the Community as laid down in Article 2. The ESCB shall act in accordance with the principle of an open market economy with free competition, favouring an efficient allocation of resources, and in compliance with the principles set out in Article 3a.

2. The basic tasks to be carried out through the ESCB shall be:

- to define and implement the monetary policy of the Community;
- to conduct foreign exchange operations consistent with the provisions of Article 109;
- to hold and manage the official foreign reserves of the Member States;
- to promote the smooth operation of payment systems.

3. The third indent of paragraph 2 shall be without prejudice to the holding and management by the governments of Member States of foreign exchange working balances.

4. The ECB shall be consulted:

- on any proposed Community act in its fields of competence;
- by national authorities regarding any draft legislative provision in its fields of competence, but within the limits and under the conditions set out by the Council in accordance with the procedure laid down in Article 106(6).

The ECB may submit opinions to the appropriate Community institutions or bodies or to national authorities on matters within its fields of competence.

5. The ESCB shall contribute to the smooth conduct of policies pursued by the competent authorities relating to the prudential supervision of credit institutions and the stability of the financial system.

6. The Council may, acting unanimously on a proposal from the Commission and after consulting the ECB and after receiving the assent of the European Parliament, confer upon the ECB specific tasks concerning policies relating to the prudential supervision of credit institutions and other financial institutions with the exception of insurance undertakings.]

[*Article 105a.* 1. The ECB shall have the exclusive right to authorize the issue of bank notes within the Community. The ECB and the national central banks may issue such notes. The bank notes issued by the ECB and the national central banks shall be the only such notes to have the status of legal tender within the Community.

2. Member States may issue coins subject to approval by the ECB of the volume of the issue. The Council may, acting in accordance with the procedure referred to in Article 189c and after consulting the ECB, adopt measures to harmonize the denominations and technical specifications of all coins intended for circulation to the extent necessary to permit their smooth circulation within the Community.]

[*Article 106.* 1. The ESCB shall be composed of the ECB and of the national central banks.

2. The ECB shall have legal personality.

3. The ESCB shall be governed by the decision-making bodies of the ECB which shall be the Governing Council and the Executive Board.

4. The Statute of the ESCB is laid down in a Protocol annexed to this Treaty.

5. Articles 5.1, 5.2, 5.3, 17. 18, 19.1, 22, 23, 24, 26, 32.2, 32.3, 32.4, 32.6, 33.1(a) and 36 of the Statute of the ESCB may be amended by the Council, acting either by a qualified majority on a recommendation from the ECB and after consulting the Commission or unanimously on a proposal from the Commission and after consulting the ECB. In either case, the assent of the European Parliament shall be required.

6. The Council, acting by a qualified majority either on a proposal from the Commission and after consulting the European Parliament and the ECB, or on a recommendation from the ECB and after consulting the European Parliament and the Commission, shall adopt the provisions referred to in Articles 4, 5.4, 19.2, 20, 28.1, 29.2, 30.4 and 34.3 of the Statute of the ESCB.]

[*Article 107.* When exercising the powers and carrying out the tasks and duties conferred upon them by this Treaty and the Statute of the ESCB, neither the ECB, nor a national central bank, nor any member of their decision-making bodies shall seek or take instructions from Community institutions or bodies, from any government of a Member State or from any other body. The Community institutions and bodies and the governments of the Member States undertake to respect this principle and not to seek to influence the members of the decision-making bodies of the ECB or of the national central banks in the performance of their tasks.]

[*Article 108.* Each Member State shall ensure, at the latest at the date of the establishment of the ESCB, that its national legislation including the statutes of its national central bank is compatible with this Treaty and the Statute of the ESCB.]

[*Article 108a.* 1. In order to carry out the tasks entrusted to the ESCB, the ECB shall, in accordance with the provisions of this Treaty and under the conditions laid down in the Statute of the ESCB:

- make regulations to the extent necessary to implement the tasks defined in Article 3.1, first indent, Articles 19.1, 22 or 25.2 of the Statute of the ESCB and in cases which shall be laid down in the acts of the Council referred to in Article 106(6);
- take decisions necessary for carrying out the tasks entrusted to the ESCB under this Treaty and the Statute of the ESCB;
- make recommendations and deliver opinions.

2. A regulation shall have general application. It shall be binding in its entirety and directly applicable in all Member States.

Recommendations and opinions shall have no binding force.

A decision shall be binding in its entirety upon those to whom it is addressed.

Article 190 to 192 shall apply to regulations and decisions adopted by the ECB.

The ECB may decide to publish its decisions, recommendations and opinions.

3. Within the limits and under the conditions adopted by the Council under the procedure laid down in Article 106(6), the ECB shall be entitled to impose fines or periodic penalty payments on undertakings for failure to comply with obligations under its regulations and decisions.]

[*Article 109*. 1. By way of derogation from Article 228, the Council may, acting unanimously on a recommendation from the ECB or from the Commission, and after consulting the ECB in an endeavour to reach a consensus consistent with the objective of price stability, after consulting the European Parliament, in accordance with the procedure in paragraph 3 for determining the arrangements, conclude formal agreements on an exchange rate system for the ECU in relation to non-Community currencies. The Council may, acting by a qualified majority on a recommendation from the ECB or from the Commission, and after consulting the ECB in an endeavour to reach a consensus consistent with the objective of price stability, adopt, adjust or abandon the central rates of the ECU within the exchange rate system. The President of the Council shall inform the European Parliament of the adoption, adjustment or abandonment of the ECU central rates.

2. In the absence of an exchange rate system in relation to one or more non-Community currencies as referred to in paragraph 1, the Council, acting by a qualified majority either on a recommendation from the Commission and after consulting the ECB, or on a recommendation from the ECB, may formulate general orientations for exchange rate policy in relation to these currencies. These general orientations shall be without prejudice to the primary objective of the ESCB to maintain price stability.

3. By way of derogation from Article 228, where agreements concerning monetary or foreign exchange regime matters need to be negotiated by the Community with one or more States or international organizations, the Council, acting by a qualified majority on a recommendation from the Commission and after consulting the ECB, shall decide the arrangements for the negotiation and for the conclusion of such agreements. These arrangements shall ensure that the Community expresses a

single position. The Commission shall be fully associated with the negotiation.

Agreements concluded in accordance with this paragraph shall be binding on the institutions of the Community, on the ECB and on Member States.

4. Subject to paragraph 1, the Council shall, on a proposal from the Commission and after consulting the ECB, acting by a qualified majority decide on the position of the Community at international level as regards issues of particular relevance to economic and monetary union and, acting unanimously, decide its representation in compliance with the allocation of powers laid down in Articles 103 and 105.

5. Without prejudice to Community competence and Community agreements as regards Economic and Monetary Union, Member States may negotiate in international bodies and conclude international agreements.]

[CHAPTER 3. INSTITUTIONAL PROVISIONS]

[*Article 109a.* 1. The Governing Council of the ECB shall comprise the members of the Executive Board of the ECB and the Governors of the national central banks.

2. (a) The Executive Board shall comprise the President, the Vice President and four other members.

    (b) The President, the Vice-President and the other members of the Executive Board shall be appointed from among persons of recognized standing and professional experience in monetary or banking matters by common accord of the Governments of the Member States at the level of Heads of State or of Government, on a recommendation from the Council, after it has consulted the European Parliament and the Governing Council of the ECB.

        Their term of office shall be eight years and shall not be renewable.

        Only nationals of Member States may be members of the Executive Board.]

[*Article 109b.* 1. The President of the Council and a member of the Commission may participate, without having the right to vote, in meetings of the Governing Council of the ECB.

The President of the Council may submit a motion for deliberation to the Governing Council of the ECB.

2. The President of the ECB shall be invited to participate in Council meetings when the Council is discussing matters relating to the objectives and tasks of the ESCB.

3. The ECB shall address an annual report on the activities of the ESCB and on the monetary policy of both the previous and current year to the European Parliament, the Council and the Commission, and also to the European Council. The President of the ECB shall present this report to the Council and to the European Parliament, which may hold a general debate on that basis.

The President of the ECB and the other members of the Executive Board may, at the request of the European Parliament or on their own initiative, be heard by the competent Committees of the European Parliament.]

[*Article 109c.* 1. In order to promote coordination of the policies of Member States to the full extent needed for the functioning of the internal market, a Monetary Committee with advisory status is hereby set up.

It shall have the following tasks:

- to keep under review the monetary and financial situation of the Member States and of the Community and the general payments system of the Member States and to report regularly thereon to the Council and to the Commission;
- to deliver opinions at the request of the Council or of the Commission, or on its own initiative for submission to those institutions;
- without prejudice to Article 151, to contribute to the preparation of the work of the Council referred to in Articles 73f, 73g, 103(2), (3), (4) and (5), 103a, 104a, 104b, 104c, 109e(2), 109f(6), 109h, 109i, 109j(2) and 109k(1);
- to examine, at least once a year, the situation regarding the movement of capital and the freedom of payments, as they result from the application of this Treaty and of measures adopted by the Council; the examination shall cover all measures relating to capital movements and payments; the Committee shall report to the Commission and to the Council on the outcome of this examination.

The Member States and the Commission shall each appoint two members of the Monetary Committee.

2. At the start of the third stage, an Economic and Financial Committee shall be set up. The Monetary Committee provided for in paragraph 1 shall be dissolved.

The Economic and Financial Committee shall have the following tasks:

- to deliver opinions at the request of the Council or of the Commission, or on its own initiative for submission to those institutions;
- to keep under review the economic and financial situation of the Member States and of the Community and to report regularly thereon

to the Council and to the Commission, in particular on financial relations with third countries and international institutions;

– without prejudice to Article 151, to contribute to the preparation of the work of the Council referred to in Articles 73f, 73g, 103(2), (3), (4) and (5), 103a, 104a, 104b, 104c, 105(6), 105a(2), 106(5) and (6), 109, 109h, 109i(2) and (3), 109k(2), 109l(4) and (5), and to carry out other advisory and preparatory tasks assigned to it by the Council;

– to examine, at least once a year, the situation regarding the movement of capital and the freedom of payments, as they result from the application of this Treaty and of measures adopted by the Council; the examination shall cover all measures relating to capital movements and payments; the Committee shall report to the Commission and to the Council on the outcome of this examination.

The Member States, the Commission and the ECB shall each appoint no more than two members of the Committee.

3. The Council shall, acting by a qualified majority on a proposal from the Commission and after consulting the ECB and the Committee referred to in this Article, lay down detailed provisions concerning the composition of the Economic and Financial Committee. The President of the Council shall inform the European Parliament of such a decision.

4. In addition to the tasks set out in paragraph 2, if and as long as there are Member States with a derogation as referred to in Articles 109k and 109l, the Committee shall keep under review the monetary and financial situation and the general payments system of those Member States and report regularly thereon to the Council and to the Commission.]

[*Article 109d.* For matters within the scope of Articles 103(4), 104c with the exception of paragraph 14, 109, 109j, 109k and 109l(4) and (5), the Council or a Member State may request the Commission to make a recommendation or a proposal, as appropriate. The Commission shall examine this request and submit its conclusions to the Council without delay.]

[CHAPTER 4. TRANSITIONAL PROVISIONS]

[*Article 109e.* 1. The second stage for achieving economic and monetary union shall begin on 1 January 1994.

2. Before that date

(a) each Member State shall:
– adopt, where necessary, appropriate measures to comply with the obligations laid down in Article 73b, without prejudice to Article 73e, and in Articles 104 and 104a(1);
– adopt, if necessary, with a view to permitting the assessment

provided for in subparagraph (b), multiannual programmes intended to ensure the lasting convergence necessary for the achievement of economic and monetary union, in particular with regard to price stability and sound public finances;

(b) the Council shall, on the basis of a report from the Commission, assess the progress made with regard to economic and monetary convergence, in particular with regard to price stability and sound public finances, and the progress made with the implementation of Community law concerning the internal market.

3. The provisions of Articles 104, 104a(1), 104b(1) and 104c with the exception of paragraphs 1, 9, 11 and 14 shall apply from the beginning of the second stage.

The provisions of Articles 103a(2), 104c(1), (9) and (11), 105, 105a, 107, 109, 109a, 109b and 109c(2) and (4) shall apply from the beginning of the third stage.

4. In the second stage, Member States shall endeavour to avoid excessive government deficits.

5. During the second stage, each Member State shall, as appropriate, start the process leading to the independence of its central bank, in accordance with Article 108.]

[*Article 109f.*   1. At the start of the second stage, a European Monetary Institute (hereinafter referred to as 'EMI') shall be established and take up its duties; it shall have legal personality and be directed and managed by a Council, consisting of a President and the Governors of the national central banks, one of whom shall be Vice-President.

The President shall be appointed by common accord of the Governments of the Member States at the level of Heads of State or of Government, on a recommendation from, as the case may be, the Committee of Governors of the central banks of the Member States (hereinafter referred to as 'Committee of Governors') or the Council of the EMI, and after consulting the European Parliament and the Council. The President shall be selected from among persons of recognized standing and professional experience in monetary or banking matters. Only nationals of Member States may be President of the EMI. The Council of the EMI shall appoint the Vice-President.

The Statute of the EMI is laid down in a Protocol annexed to this Treaty.

The Committee of Governors shall be dissolved at the start of the second stage.

2. The EMI shall:

– strengthen cooperation between the national central banks;

- strengthen the coordination of the monetary policies of the Member States, with the aim of ensuring price stability;
- monitor the functioning of the European Monetary System;
- hold consultations concerning issues falling within the competence of the national central banks and affecting the stability of financial institutions and markets;
- take over the tasks of the European Monetary Cooperation Fund, which shall be dissolved; the modalities of dissolution are laid down in the Statute of the EMI;
- facilitate the use of the ecu and oversee its development, including the smooth functioning of the ecu clearing system.

3. For the preparation of the third stage, the EMI shall:

- prepare the instruments and the procedures necessary for carrying out a single monetary policy in the third stage;
- promote the harmonization, where necessary, of the rules and practices governing the collection, compilation and distribution of statistics in the areas within its field of competence;
- prepare the rules for operations to be undertaken by the national central banks in the framework of the ESCB;
- promote the efficiency of cross-border payments;
- supervise the technical preparation of ecu bank notes.

At the latest by 31 December 1996, the EMI shall specify the regulatory, organizational and logistical framework necessary for the ESCB to perform its tasks in the third stage. This framework shall be submitted for decision to the ECB at the date of its establishment.

4. The EMI, acting by a majority of two thirds of the members of its Council may:

- formulate opinions or recommendations on the overall orientation of monetary policy and exchange rate policy as well as on related measures introduced in each Member State:
- submit opinions or recommendations to Governments and to the Council on policies which might affect the internal or external monetary situation in the Community and, in particular, the functioning of the European Monetary System;
- make recommendations to the monetary authorities of the Member States concerning the conduct of their monetary policy.

5. The EMI, acting unanimously, may decide to publish its opinions and its recommendations.

6. The EMI shall be consulted by the Council regarding any proposed Community act within its field of competence.

Within the limits and under the conditions set out by the Council, acting by a qualified majority on a proposal from the Commission and after consulting the European Parliament and the EMI, the EMI shall be consulted by the authorities of the Member States on any draft legislative provision within its field of competence.

7. The Council may, acting unanimously on a proposal from the Commission and after consulting the European Parliament and the EMI, confer upon the EMI other tasks for the preparation of the third stage.

8. Where this Treaty provides for a consultative role for the ECB, references to the ECB shall be read as referring to the EMI before the establishment of the ECB.

Where this Treaty provides for a consultative role for the EMI, references to the EMI shall be read, before 1 January 1994, as referring to the Committee of Governors.

9. During the second stage, the term 'ECB' used in Articles 173, 175, 176, 177, 180 and 215 shall be read as referring to the EMI.]

[*Article 109g.* The currency composition of the ecu basket shall not be changed.

From the start of the third stage, the value of the ecu shall be irrevocably fixed in accordance with Article 109l(4).]

[*Article 109h.* 1. Where a Member State is in difficulties or is seriously threatened with difficulties as regards its balance of payments either as a result of an overall disequilibrium in its balance of payments, or as a result of the type of currency at its disposal, and where such difficulties are liable in particular to jeopardize the functioning of the common market or the progressive implementation of the common commercial policy, the Commission shall immediately investigate the position of the State in question and the action which, making use of all the means at its disposal, that State has taken or may take in accordance with the provisions of this Treaty. The Commission shall state what measures it recommends the State concerned to take.

If the action taken by a Member State and the measures suggested by the Commission do not prove sufficient to overcome the difficulties which have arisen or which threaten, the Commission shall, after consulting the Committee referred to in Article 109c, recommend to the Council the granting of mutual assistance and appropriate methods therefor.

The Commission shall keep the Council regularly informed of the situation and of how it is developing.

2. The Council, acting by a qualified majority, shall grant such mutual assistance; it shall adopt directives or decisions laying down the conditions and details of such assistance, which may take such forms as:

(a) a concerted approach to or within any other international organizations to which Member States may have recourse;
(b) measures needed to avoid deflection of trade where the State which is in difficulties maintains or reintroduces quantitative restrictions against third countries;
(c) the granting of limited credits by other Member States, subject to their agreement.

3. If the mutual assistance recommended by the Commission is not granted by the Council or if the mutual assistance granted and the measures taken are insufficient, the Commission shall authorize the State which is in difficulties to take protective measures, the conditions and details of which the Commission shall determine.

Such authorization may be revoked and such conditions and details may be changed by the Council acting by a qualified majority.

4. Subject to Article 109k(6), this Article shall cease to apply from the beginning of the third stage.]

[*Article 109i.* 1. Where a sudden crisis in the balance of payments occurs and a decision within the meaning of Article 109h(2) is not immediately taken, the Member State concerned may, as a precaution, take the necessary protective measures. Such measures must cause the least possible disturbance in the functioning of the common market and must not be wider in scope than is strictly necessary to remedy the sudden difficulties which have arisen.

2. The Commission and the other Member States shall be informed of such protective measures not later than when they enter into force. The Commission may recommend to the Council the granting of mutual assistance under Article 109h.

3. After the Commission has delivered an opinion and the Committee referred to in Article 109c has been consulted, the Council may, acting by a qualified majority, decide that the State concerned shall amend, suspend or abolish the protective measures referred to above.

4. Subject to Article 109k(6), this Article shall cease to apply from the beginning of the third stage.]

[*Article 109j.* 1. The Commission and the EMI shall report to the Council on the progress made in the fulfilment by the Member States of their obligations regarding the achievement of economic and monetary union. These reports shall include an examination of the compatibility between each Member State's national legislation, including the statutes of its national central bank, and Articles 107 and 108 of this Treaty and the Statute of the ESCB. The reports shall also examine the achievement of a high degree of sustainable convergence by reference to the fulfilment by each Member State of the following criteria:

- the achievement of a high degree of price stability; this will be apparent from a rate of inflation which is close to that of, at most, the three best performing Member States in terms of price stability;
- the sustainability of the government financial position; this will be apparent from having achieved a government budgetary position without a deficit that is excessive as determined in accordance with Article 104c(6);
- the observance of the normal fluctuation margins provided for by the Exchange Rate Mechanism of the European Monetary System, for at least two years, without devaluing against the currency of any other Member State;
- the durability of convergence achieved by the Member State and of its participation in the Exchange Rate Mechanism of the European Monetary System being reflected in the long-term interest rate levels.

The four criteria mentioned in this paragraph and the relevant periods over which they are to be respected are developed further in a Protocol annexed to this Treaty. The reports of the Commission and the EMI shall also take account of the development of the balances of payments on current account and an examination of the development of unit labour costs and other price indices.

2. On the basis of these reports, the Council, acting by a qualified majority on a recommendation from the Commission, shall assess:

- for each Member State, whether it fulfils the necessary conditions for the adoption of a single currency;
- whether a majority of the Member States fulfil the necessary conditions for the adoption of a single currency,

and recommend its findings to the Council, meeting in the composition of the Heads of State or of Government. The European Parliament shall be consulted and forward its opinion to the Council meeting in the composition of the Heads of State or of Government.

3. Taking due account of the reports referred to in paragraph 1 and the opinion of the European Parliament referred to in paragraph 2, the Council, meeting in the composition of Heads of State or of Government, shall, acting by a qualified majority, not later than 31 December 1996:

- decide, on the basis of the recommendations of the Council referred to in paragraph 2, whether a majority of the Member States fulfil the necessary conditions for the adoption of a single currency;
- decide whether it is appropriate for the Community to enter the third stage,

and if so

– set the date for the beginning of the third stage.

4. If by the end of 1997 the date for the beginning of the third stage has not been set, the third stage shall start on 1 January 1999. Before 1 July 1998, the Council, meeting in the composition of Heads of State or of Government, after a repetition of the procedure provided for in paragraphs 1 and 2, with the exception of the second indent of paragraph 2, taking into account the reports referred to in paragraph 1 and the opinion of the European Parliament, shall, acting by a qualified majority and on the basis of the recommendations of the Council referred to in paragraph 2, confirm which Member States fulfil the necessary conditions for the adoption of a single currency.]

[Article 109k. 1. If the decision has been taken to set the date in accordance with Article 109j(3), the Council shall, on the basis of its recommendations as referred to in Article 109j(2), acting by a qualified majority on a recommendation from the Commission, decide whether any, and if so which, Member States shall have a derogation as defined in paragraph 3 of this Article. Such Member States shall in this Treaty be referred to as 'Member States with a derogation'.

If the Council has confirmed which Member States fulfil the necessary conditions for the adoption of a single currency, in accordance with Article 109j(4), those Member States which do not fulfil the conditions shall have a derogation as defined in paragraph 3 of this Article. Such Member States shall in this Treaty be referred to as 'Member States with a derogation'.

2. At least once every two years, or at the request of a Member State with a derogation the Commission and the ECB shall report to the Council in accordance with the procedure laid down in Article 109j(1). After consulting the European Parliament and after discussion in the Council, meeting in the composition of the Heads of State or of Government, the Council shall, acting by a qualified majority on a proposal from the Commission, decide which Member States with a derogation fulfil the necessary conditions on the basis of the criteria set out in Article 109j(1), and abrogate the derogations of the Member States concerned.

3. A derogation referred to in paragraph 1 shall entail that the following Articles do not apply to the Member State concerned: Articles 104c(9) and (11), 105(1), (2), (3) and (5), 105a, 108a, 109, and 109a(2)(b). The exclusion of such a Member State and its national central bank from rights and obligations within the ESCB is laid down in Chapter IX of the Statute of the ESCB.

4. In Articles 105(1), (2) and (3), 105a, 108a, 109 and 109a(2)(b), 'Member States' shall be read as 'Member States without a derogation'.

5. The voting rights of the Member States with a derogation shall be suspended for the Council decisions referred to in the Articles of this Treaty mentioned in paragraph 3. In that case, by way of derogation from Articles 148 and 189a(1), a qualified majority shall be defined as two thirds of the votes of the representatives of the Member States without a derogation weighted in accordance with Article 148(2), and unanimity of those Member States shall be required for an act requiring unanimity.

6. Articles 109h and 109i shall continue to apply to a Member State with a derogation.]

[*Article 109l.*   1. Immediately after the decision on the date for the beginning of the third stage has been taken in accordance with Article 109j(3), or, as the case may be, immediately after 1 July 1998:

– the Council shall adopt the provisions referred to in Article 106(6);
– the governments of the Member States without a derogation shall appoint, in accordance with the procedure set out in Article 50 of the Statute of the ESCB, the President, the Vice-President and the other members of the Executive Board of the ECB. If there are Member States with a derogation, the number of members of the Executive Board may be smaller than provided for in Article 11.1 of the Statute of the ESCB, but in no circumstances shall it be less than four.

As soon as the Executive Board is appointed, the ESCB and the ECB shall be established and shall prepare for their full operation as described in this Treaty and the Statute of the ESCB. The full exercise of their powers shall start from the first day of the third stage.

2. As soon as the ECB is established, it shall, if necessary, take over functions of the EMI. The EMI shall go into liquidation upon the establishment of the ECB; the modalities of liquidation are laid down in the Statute of the EMI.

3. If and as long as there are Member States with a derogation, and without prejudice to Article 106(3) of this Treaty, the General Council of the ECB referred to in Article 45 of the Statute of the ESCB shall be constituted as a third decision-making body of the ECB.

4. At the starting date of the third stage, the Council shall, acting with the unanimity of the Members States without a derogation, on a proposal from the Commission and after consulting the ECB, adopt the conversion rates at which their currencies shall be irrevocably fixed and at which irrevocably fixed rate the ecu shall be substituted for these currencies, and the ecu will become a currency in its own right. This measure shall by itself not

modify the external value of the ecu. The Council shall, acting according to the same procedure, also take the other measures necessary for the rapid introduction of the ecu as the single currency of those Member States.

5. If it is decided, according to the procedure set out in Article 109k(2), to abrogate a derogation, the Council shall, acting with the unanimity of the Member States without a derogation and the Member State concerned, on a proposal from the Commission and after consulting the ECB, adopt the rate at which the ecu shall be substituted for the currency of the Member State concerned, and take the other measures necessary for the introduction of the ecu as the single currency in the Member State concerned.]

[*Article 109m.* 1. Until the beginning of the third stage, each Member State shall treat its exchange rate policy as a matter of common interest. In so doing, Member States shall take account of the experience acquired in cooperation within the framework of the European Monetary System (EMS) and in developing the ecu, and shall respect existing powers in this field.

2. From the beginning of the third stage and for as long as a Member State has a derogation, paragraph 1 shall apply by analogy to the exchange rate policy of that Member State.]

{CHAPTER 1. CO-OPERATION IN ECONOMIC AND MONETARY POLICY

Article 102A. 1. In order to ensure the convergence of economic and monetary policies which is necessary for the further development of the Community, Member States shall co-operate in accordance with the objectives of Article 104. In so doing, they shall take account of the experience acquired in co-operation within the framework of the European Monetary System (EMS) and in developing the ecu, and shall respect existing powers in this field.

2. Insofar as further development in the field of economic and monetary policy necessitates institutional changes, the provisions of Article 236 shall be applicable. The Monetary Committee and the Committee of Governors the Central Banks shall also be consulted regarding institutional changes in the monetary area.}

{CHAPTER 2. CONJUNCTURAL POLICY

Article 103. 1. Member States shall regard their conjunctural policies as a matter of common concern. They shall consult each other and the Commission on the measures to be taken in the light of the prevailing circumstances.

2. Without prejudice to any other procedures provided for in this Treaty, the Council may, acting unanimously on a proposal from the Commission, decide upon the measures appropriate to the situation.

3. Acting by a qualified majority on a proposal from the Commission, the Council shall, where required, issue any directive needed to give effect to the measures decided upon under paragraph 2.

4. The procedures provided for in this Article shall also apply if any difficulty should arise in the supply of certain products.}

{CHAPTER 3. BALANCE OF PAYMENTS

Article 104. Each Member State shall pursue the economic policy needed to ensure the equilibrium of its overall balance of payments and to maintain confidence in its currency, while taking care to ensure a high level of employment and a stable level of prices.}

{*Article 105.* 1. In order to facilitate attainment of the objectives set out in Art. 104, Member States shall co-ordinate their economic policies. They shall for this purpose provide for co-operation between their appropriate administrative departments and between their central banks.

The Commission shall submit to the Council recommendations on how to achieve such co-operation.

2. In order to promote co-ordination of the policies of Member States in the monetary field to the full extent needed for the functioning of the common market, a Monetary Committee with advisory status is hereby set up. It shall have the following tasks:

– to keep under review the monetary and financial situation of the Member States and of the Community and the general payments system of the Member States and to report regularly thereon to the Council and to the Commission;
– to deliver opinions at the request of the Council or of the Commission or on its own initiative, for submission to these institutions.

The Member States and the Commission shall each appoint two members of the Monetary Committee.}

{*Article 106.* 1. Each Member State undertakes to authorise, in the currency of the Member State in which the creditor or the beneficiary resides, any payments connected with the movement of goods, services or capital, and any transfers of capital and earnings, to the extent that the movement of goods, services, capital and persons between Member States has been liberalised pursuant to this Treaty.

The Member States declare their readiness to undertake the liberalisation of payments beyond the extent provided in the preceding subparagraph, in so far as their economic situation in general and the state of their balance of payments in particular so permit.

2. In so far as movements of goods, services, and capital are limited only by restrictions on payments connected therewith, these restrictions shall be progressively abolished by applying, *mutatis mutandis*, the provisions of the Chapters relating to the abolition of quantitative restrictions, to the liberalisation of services and to the free movement of capital.

3. Member States undertake not to introduce between themselves any new restrictions on transfers connected with the invisible transactions listed in Annex III to this Treaty.

The progressive abolition of existing restrictions shall be effected in accordance with the provisions of Arts. 63 to 65, in so far as such abolition is not governed by the provisions contained in paragraphs 1 and 2 or by the Chapter relating to the free movement of capital.

4. If need be, Member States shall consult each other on the measures to be taken to enable the payments and transfers mentioned in this Article to be effected; such measures shall not prejudice the attainment of the objectives set out in this Chapter.}

{*Article 107.*   1. Each Member State shall treat its policy with regard to rates of exchange as a matter of common concern.

2. If a Member State makes an alteration in its rate of exchange which is inconsistent with the objectives set out in Art. 104 and which seriously distorts conditions of competition, the Commission may, after consulting the Monetary Committee, authorise other Member States to take for a strictly limited period the necessary measures, the conditions and details of which it shall determine, in order to counter the consequences of such alteration.}

{*Article 108.*   1. Where a Member State is in difficulties or is seriously threatened with difficulties as regards its balance of payments either as a result of an overall disequilibrium in its balance of payments, or as a result of the type of currency at its disposal, and where such difficulties are liable in particular to jeopardise the functioning of the common market or the progressive implementation of the common commercial policy, the Commission shall immediately investigate the position of the State in question and the action which, making use of all the means at its disposal, that State has taken or may take in accordance with the provisions of Art. 104. The Commission shall state what measures it recommends the State concerned to take.

If the action taken by a Member State and the measures suggested by the Commission do not prove sufficient to overcome the difficulties which have arisen or which threaten, the Commission shall, after consulting the

Monetary Committee, recommend to the Council the granting of mutual assistance and appropriate methods therefore.

The Commission shall keep the Council regularly informed of the situation and of how it is developing.

2. The Council, acting by a qualified majority, shall grant such mutual assistance; it shall adopt directives or decisions laying down the conditions and details of such assistance, which may take such forms as:

(a) a concerted approach to or within any other international organisations to which Member States may have recourse;
(b) measures needed to avoid deflection of trade where the State which is in difficulties maintains or reintroduces quantitative restrictions against third countries;
(c) the granting of limited credits by other Member States, subject to their agreement.

During the transitional period, mutual assistance may also take the form of special reductions in customs duties or enlargements of quotas in order to facilitate an increase in imports from the State which is in difficulties, subject to the agreement of the States by which such measures would have to be taken.

3. If the mutual assistance recommended by the Commission is not granted by the Council or if the mutual assistance granted and the measures taken are insufficient, the Commission shall authorise the State which is in difficulties to take protective measures, the conditions and details of which the Commission shall determine.

Such authorisation may be revoked and such conditions and details may be changed by the Council acting by a qualified majority.}

{*Article 109.* 1. Where a sudden crisis in the balance of payments occurs and a decision within the meaning of Art. 108 (2) is not immediately taken, the Member State concerned may, as a precaution, take the necessary protective measures. Such measures must cause the least possible disturbance in the functioning of the common market and must not be wider in scope than is strictly necessary to remedy the sudden difficulties which have arisen.

2. The Commission and the other Member States shall be informed of such protective measures not later than when they enter into force. The Commission may also recommend to the Council the granting of mutual assistance under Art. 108.

3. After the Commission has delivered an opinion and the Monetary Committee has been consulted, the Council may, acting by a qualified majority, decide that the State concerned shall amend, suspend or abolish the protective measures referred to above.}

TITLE VII. COMMON COMMERCIAL POLICY

{CHAPTER 4. COMMERCIAL POLICY}

Article 110. By establishing a customs union between themselves Member States aim to contribute, in the common interest, to the harmonious development of world trade, the progressive abolition of restrictions on international trade and the lowering of customs barriers.

The common commercial policy shall take into account the favourable effect which the abolition of customs duties between Member States may have on the increase in the competitive strength of undertakings in those States.

{*Article 111.* The following provisions shall, without prejudice to Arts. 115 and 116, apply during the transitional period:

1. Member States shall co-ordinate their trade relations with third countries so as to bring about, by the end of the transitional period, the conditions needed for implementing a common policy in the field of external trade.

The Commission shall submit to the Council proposals regarding the procedure for common action to be followed during the transitional period and regarding the achievement of uniformity in their commercial policies.

2. The Commission shall submit to the Council recommendations for tariff negotiations with third countries in respect of the common customs tariff.

The Council shall authorise the Commission to open such negotiations.

The Commission shall conduct these negotiations in consultation with a special committee appointed by the Council to assist the Commission in this task and within the framework of such directives as the Council may issue to it.

3. In exercising the powers conferred upon it by this Article , the Council shall act unanimously during the first two stages and by a qualified majority thereafter.

4. Member States shall, in consultation with the Commission, take all necessary measures, particularly those designed to bring about an adjustment of tariff agreements in force with third countries, in order that the entry into force of the common customs tariff shall not be delayed.

5. Member States shall aim at securing as high a level of uniformity as possible between themselves as regards their liberalisation lists in relation to third countries or groups of third countries. To this end, the Commission shall make all appropriate recommendations to Member States.

If Member States abolish or reduce quantitative restrictions in relation to third countries, they shall inform the Commission beforehand and shall accord the same treatment to other Member States.}

Article 112. 1. Without prejudice to obligations undertaken by them within the framework of other international organisations, Member States shall, before the end of the transitional period, progressively harmonise the systems whereby they grant aid for exports to third countries, to the extent necessary to ensure that competition between undertakings of the Community is not distorted.

On a proposal from the Commission, the Council shall, acting unanimously until the end of the second stage and by a qualified majority thereafter, issue any directives needed for this purpose.

2. The preceding provisions shall not apply to such drawback of customs duties or charges having equivalent effect nor to such repayment of indirect taxation including turnover taxes, excise duties and other indirect taxes as is allowed when goods are exported from a Member State to a third country, in so far as such drawback or repayment does not exceed the amount imposed, directly or indirectly, on the products exported.

Article 113. 1. {After the transitional period has ended,} the common commercial policy shall be based on uniform principles, particularly in regard to changes in tariff rates, the conclusion of tariff and trade agreements, the achievement of uniformity in measures of liberalisation, export policy and measures to protect trade such as those to be taken in case of dumping or subsidies.

2. The Commission shall submit proposals to the Council for implementing the common commercial policy.

3. Where agreements with [one or more States or international organizations] {third countries} need to be negotiated, the Commission shall make recommendations to the Council, which shall authorize the Commission to open the necessary negotiations.

The Commission shall conduct these negotiations in consultation with a special committee appointed by the Council to assist the Commission in this task and within the framework of such directives as the Council may issue to it.

[The relevant provisions of Article 228 shall apply.]

4. In exercising the powers conferred upon it by this Article, the Council shall act by a qualified majority.

{*Article 114.* The agreements referred to in Art. 111 (2) and in Art. 113 shall be concluded by the Council on behalf of the Community, acting unanimously during the first two stages and by a qualified majority thereafter.}

Article 115. In order to ensure that the execution of measures of commercial policy taken in accordance with this Treaty by any Member State is not obstructed by deflection of trade, or where differences between such measures lead to economic difficulties in one or more of the Member States, the Commission shall recommend the methods for the requisite co-operation between Member States. Failing this, the Commission shall authorise Member States to take the necessary protective measures, the conditions and details of which it shall determine.

In cases of urgency, {during the transitional period,} Member States [shall request authorization to take the necessary measures from the Commission, which shall take a decision as soon as possible; the Member States concerned shall then notify the measure to the other Member States. The Commission may at any time decide that the Member States concerned shall amend or abolish the measures in question.] {may themselves take the necessary measures, and shall notify them to the other Member States and to the Commission, which may decide that the States concerned shall amend or abolish such measures.}

In the selection of such measures, priority shall be given to those which cause the least disturbance to the functioning of the common market {and which take into account the need to expedite, as far as possible, the introduction of the common customs tariff.}

{*Article 116.* From the end of the transitional period onwards, Member States shall, in respect of all matters of particular interest to the common market, proceed within the framework of international organisations of an economic character only by common action. To this end, the Commission shall submit to the Council, which shall act by a qualified majority, proposals concerning the scope and implementation of such common action.

During the transitional period, Member States shall consult each other for the purpose of concerting the action they take and adopting as far as possible a uniform attitude.}

TITLE [VIII] {III} SOCIAL POLICY [, EDUCATION, VOCATIONAL TRAINING AND YOUTH]

CHAPTER I. SOCIAL PROVISIONS

Article 117. Member States agree upon the need to promote improved working conditions and an improved standard of living for workers, so as to make possible their harmonisation while the improvement is being maintained.

They believe that such a development will ensue not only from the functioning of the common market, which will favour the harmonisation of social systems, but also from the procedures provided for in this Treaty and from the approximation of provisions laid down by law, regulation or administrative action.

Article 118. Without prejudice to the other provisions of this Treaty and in conformity with its general objectives, the Commission shall have the task of promoting close co-operation between Member States in the social field, particularly in matters relating to:

– employment;
– labour law and working conditions;
– basic and advanced vocational training;
– social security;
– prevention of occupational accidents and diseases;
– occupational hygiene; the right of association, and collective bargaining between employers and workers.

To this end, the Commission shall act in close contact with Member States by making studies, delivering opinions and arranging consultations both on problems arising at national level and on those of concern to international organisations.

Before delivering the opinions provided for in this Article, the Commission shall consult the Economic and Social Committee.

Article 118a. 1. Member States shall pay particular attention to encouraging improvements, especially in the working environment, as regards the health and safety of workers, and shall set as their objective the harmonisation of conditions in this area, while maintaining the improvements made.

2. In order to help achieve the objective laid down in the first paragraph, the Council, acting [in accordance with the procedure referred to in Article 189c] {by a qualified majority on a proposal from the Commission, in co-operation with the European Parliament} and after consulting the Economic and Social Committee, shall adopt, by means of directives, minimum requirements for gradual implementation, having regard to the conditions and technical rules obtaining in each of the Member States.

Such directives shall avoid imposing administrative, financial and legal constraints in a way which would hold back the creation and development of small and medium-sized undertakings.

3. The provisions adopted pursuant to this Article shall not prevent any Member State from maintaining or introducing more stringent measures for the protection of working conditions compatible with this Treaty.

Article 118b. The Commission shall endeavour to develop the dialogue between management and labour at European level which could, if the two sides consider it desirable, lead to relations based on agreement.

Article 119. Each Member State shall during the first stage ensure and subsequently maintain the application of the principle that men and women should receive equal pay for equal work.

For the purpose of this Article , 'pay' means the ordinary basic or minimum wage or salary and any other consideration, whether in cash or in kind, which the worker receives, directly or indirectly, in respect of his employment from his employer.

Equal pay without discrimination based on sex means:

(a) that pay for the same work at piece rates shall be calculated on the basis of the same unit of measurement,
(b) that pay for work at time rates shall be the same for the same job.

[For secondary legislation on equal pay, and equal opportunities for men and women in employment, see pp. 591 ff.]

Article 120. Member States shall endeavour to maintain the existing equivalence between paid holiday schemes.

Article 121. The Council may, acting unanimously and after consulting the Economic and Social Committee, assign to the Commission tasks in connection with the implementation of common measures, particularly as regards social security for the migrant workers referred to in Arts. 48 to 51.

Article 122. The Commission shall include a separate chapter on social developments within the Community in its annual report to the Assembly.

The Assembly may invite the Commission to draw up reports on any particular problems concerning social conditions.

CHAPTER 2. THE EUROPEAN SOCIAL FUND

Article 123. In order to improve employment opportunities for workers in the [internal] {common} market and to contribute thereby to raising the standard of living, a European Social Fund is hereby established in accordance with the provisions set out below: it shall [aim to render] {have the task of rendering} the employment of workers easier and [to increase] {of increasing} their geographical and occupational mobility within the Community, [and to facilitate their adaption to industrial changes and to changes in production systems, in particular through vocational training and retraining].

Article 124. The Fund shall be administered by the Commission.

The Commission shall be assisted in this task by a Committee presided over by a member of the Commission and composed of representatives of Governments, trade unions and employers' organisations.

[*Article 125.* The Council, acting in accordance with the procedure referred to in Article 189c and after consulting the Economic and Social Committee, shall adopt implementing decisions relating to the European Social Fund.]

{1. On application by a Member State the Fund shall, within the framework of the rules provided for in Art. 127, meet 50 per cent of the expenditure incurred after the entry into force of this Treaty by that State or by a body governed by public law for the purposes of:

(a) ensuring productive re-employment of workers by means of:vocational retraining;
   resettlement allowances;
(b) granting aid for the benefit of workers whose employment is reduced or temporarily suspended, in whole or in part, as a result of the conversion of an undertaking to other production, in order that they may retain the same wage level pending their full re-employment.

2. Assistance granted by the Fund towards the cost of vocational retraining shall be granted only if the unemployed workers could not be found employment except in a new occupation and only if they have been in productive employment for at least six months in the occupation for which they have been retrained.

Assistance towards resettlement allowances shall be granted only if the unemployed workers have been caused to change their home within the Community and have been in productive employment for at least six months in their new place of residence.

Assistance for workers in the case of the conversion of an undertaking shall be granted only if:

(a) the workers concerned have again been fully employed in that undertaking for at least six months;
(b) the Government concerned has submitted a plan beforehand, drawn up by the undertaking in question, for that particular conversion and for financing it;
(c) the Commission has given its prior approval to the conversion plan.}

[CHAPTER 3. EDUCATION, VOCATIONAL TRAINING AND YOUTH]

[*NB The articles which will be replaced by this Chapter are printed after Article 128*]

[*Article 126.* 1. The Community shall contribute to the development of quality education by encouraging cooperation between Member States and, if necessary, by supporting and supplementing their action, while fully respecting the responsibility of the Member States for the content of teaching and the organization of education systems and their cultural and linguistic diversity.

2. Community action shall be aimed at:

– developing the European dimension in education, particularly through the teaching and dissemination of the languages of the Member States;
– encouraging mobility of students and teachers, inter alia by encouraging the academic recognition of diplomas and periods of study;
– promoting cooperation between educational establishments;
– developing exchanges of information and experience on issues common to the education systems of the Member States;
– encouraging the development of youth exchanges and of exchanges of socio-educational instructors;
– encouraging the development of distance education.

3. The Community and the Member States shall foster co-operation with third countries and the competent international organizations in the sphere of education, in particular the Council of Europe.

4. In order to contribute to the achievement of the objectives referred to in this Article, the Council:

– acting in accordance with the procedure referred to in Article 189b, after consulting the Economic and Social Committee and the Committee of the Regions, shall adopt incentive measures, excluding any harmonization of the laws and regulations of the Member States;
– acting by qualified majority on a proposal from the Commission, shall adopt recommendations.]

[*Article 127.* 1. The Community shall implement a vocational training policy which shall support and supplement the action of the Member States, while fully respecting the responsibility of the Member States for the content and organization of vocational training.

2. Community action shall aim to:

– facilitate adaptation to industrial changes, in particular through vocational training and retraining;

– improve initial and continuing vocational training in order to facilitate vocational integration and reintegration into the labour market;
– facilitate access to vocational training and encourage mobility of instructors and trainees and particularly young people;
– stimulate cooperation on training between educational or training establishments and firms;
– develop exchanges of information and experience on issues common to the training systems of the Member States.

3. The Community and the Member States shall foster cooperation with third countries and the competent international organizations in the sphere of vocational training.

4. The Council, acting in accordance with the procedure referred to in Article 189c and after consulting the Economic and Social Committee, shall adopt measures to contribute to the achievement of the objectives referred to in this Article, excluding any harmonization of the laws and regulations of the Member States.]

[TITLE IX. CULTURE]

[*Article 128.* 1. The Community shall contribute to the flowering of the cultures of the Member States, while respecting their national and regional diversity and at the same time bringing the common cultural heritage to the fore.

2. Action by the Community shall be aimed at encouraging cooperation between Member States and, if necessary, supporting and supplementing their action in the following areas:

– improvement of the knowledge and dissemination of the culture and history of the European peoples;
– conservation and safeguarding of cultural heritage of European significance;
– non-commercial cultural exchanges;
– artistic and literary creation, including in the audiovisual sector.

3. The Community and the Member States shall foster cooperation with third countries and the competent international organizations in the sphere of culture, in particular the Council of Europe.

4. The Community shall take cultural aspects into account in its action under other provisions of this Treaty.

5. In order to contribute to the achievement of the objectives referred to in this Article, the Council:

– acting in accordance with the procedure referred to in Article 189b and after consulting the Committee of the Regions, shall adopt incentive

measures, excluding any harmonization of the laws and regulations of the Member States. The Council shall act unanimously throughout the procedures referred to in Article 189b;
– acting unanimously on a proposal from the Commission, shall adopt recommendations.]

{*Article 126.* When the transitional period has ended, the Council, after receiving the opinion of the Commission and after consulting the Economic and Social Committee and the Assembly, may;

(a) rule, by a qualified majority, that all or part of the assistance referred to in Art. 125 shall no longer be granted; or
(b) unanimously determine what new tasks may be entrusted to the Fund within the framework of its terms of reference as laid down in Art. 123.}

{*Article 127.* The Council shall, acting by a qualified majority on a proposal from the Commission and after consulting the Economic and Social Committee and the Assembly, lay down the provisions required to implement Arts. 124 to 126; in particular it shall determine in detail the conditions under which assistance shall be granted by the Fund in accordance with Art. 125 and the classes of undertakings whose workers shall benefit from the assistance provided for in Art. 125 (1) (b).}

{*Article 128.* The Council shall, acting on a proposal from the Commission and after consulting the Economic and Social Committee, lay down general principles for implementing a common vocational training policy capable of contributing to the harmonious development both of the national economies and of the common market.}

[TITLE X. PUBLIC HEALTH]

[*Article 129.* 1. The Community shall contribute towards ensuring a high level of human health protection by encouraging cooperation between the Member States and, if necessary, lending support to their action.

Community action shall be directed towards the prevention of diseases, in particular the major health scourges, including drug dependence, by promoting research into their causes and their transmission, as well as health information and education.

Health protection requirements shall form a constituent part of the Community's other policies.

2. Member States shall, in liaison with the Commission, coordinate

among themselves their policies and programmes in the areas referred to in paragraph 1. The Commission may, in close contact with the Member States, take any useful initiative to promote such coordination.

3. The Community and the Member States shall foster cooperation with third countries and the competent international organizations in the sphere of public health.

4. In order to contribute to the achievement of the objectives referred to in this Article, the Council:

– acting in accordance with the procedure referred to in Article 189b, after consulting the Economic and Social Committee and the Committee of the Regions, shall adopt incentive measures, excluding any harmonization of the laws and regulations of the Member States;
– acting by a qualified majority on a proposal from the Commission, shall adopt recommendations.]

[TITLE XI. CONSUMER PROTECTION]

[*Article 129a.*   1. The Community shall contribute to the attainment of a high level of consumer protection through:

(a) measures adopted pursuant to Article 100a in the context of the completion of the internal market;
(b) specific action which supports and supplements the policy pursued by the Member States to protect the health, safety and economic interests of consumers and to provide adequate information to consumers.

2. The Council, acting in accordance with the procedure referred to in Article 189b and after consulting the Economic and Social Committee, shall adopt the specific action referred to in paragraph 1(b).

3. Action adopted pursuant to paragraph 2 shall not prevent any Member State from maintaining or introducing more stringent protective measures. Such measures must be compatible with this Treaty. The Commission shall be notified of them.]

[TITLE XII. TRANS-EUROPEAN NETWORKS]

[*Article 129b.*   1. To help achieve the objectives referred to in Articles 7a and 130 a and to enable citizens of the Union, economic operators and regional and local communities to derive full benefit from the setting up of an area without internal frontiers, the Community shall contribute to the establishment and development of trans-European networks in the areas of transport, telecommunications and energy infrastructures.

2. Within the framework of a system of open and competitive markets, action by the Community shall aim at promoting the interconnection and

inter-operability of national networks as well as access to such networks. It shall take account in particular of the need to link island, landlocked and peripheral regions with the central regions of the Community.]

[*Article 129c.*   1. In order to achieve the objectives referred to in Article 129b, the Community:

- shall establish a series of guidelines covering the objectives, priorities and broad lines of measures envisaged in the sphere of trans-European networks; these guidelines shall identify projects of common interest;
- shall implement any measures that may prove necessary to ensure the inter-operability of the networks, in particular in the field of technical standardization;
- may support the financial efforts made by the Member States for projects of common interest financed by Member States, which are identified in the framework of the guidelines referred to in the first indent, particularly through feasibility studies, loan guarantees or interest rate subsidies; the Community may also contribute, through the Cohesion Fund to be set up no later than 31 December 1993 pursuant to Article 130d, to the financing of specific projects in Member States in the area of transport infrastructure.

The Community's activities shall take into account the potential economic viability of the projects.

2. Member States shall, in liaison with the Commission, coordinate among themselves the policies pursued at national level which may have a significant impact on the achievement of the objectives referred to in Article 129b. The Commission may, in close cooperation with the Member States, take any useful initiative to promote such coordination.

3. The Community may decide to cooperate with third countries to promote projects of mutual interest and to ensure the inter-operability of networks.]

[*Article 129d.*   The guidelines referred to in Article 129c(1) shall be adopted by the Council, acting in accordance with the procedure referred to in Article 189b and after consulting the Economic and Social Committee and the Committee of the Regions.

Guidelines and projects of common interest which relate to the territory of a Member States shall require the approval of the Member State concerned.

The Council, acting in accordance with the procedure referred to in Article 189c and after consulting the Economic and Social Committee and the Committee of the Regions, shall adopt the other measures provided for in Article 129c(1).]

[TITLE XIII. INDUSTRY]

[*Article 130.*   1. The Community and the Member States shall ensure that the conditions necessary for the competitiveness of the Community's industry exist.

For that purpose, in accordance with a system of open and competitive markets, their action shall be aimed at:

- speeding up the adjustment of industry to structural changes;
- encouraging an environment favourable to initiative and to the development of undertakings throughout the Community, particularly small and medium-sized undertakings;
- encouraging an environment favourable to cooperation between undertakings;
- fostering better exploitation of the industrial potential of policies of innovation, research and technological development.

2. The Member States shall consult each other in liaison with the Commission and, where necessary, shall coordinate their action. The Commission may take any useful initiative to promote such coordination.

3. The Community shall contribute to the achievement of the objectives set out in paragraph 1 through the policies and activities it pursues under other provisions of this Treaty. The Council, acting unanimously on a proposal from the Commission, after consulting the European Parliament and the Economic and Social Committee, may decide on specific measures in support of action taken in the Member States to achieve the objectives set out in paragraph 1.

This Title shall not provide a basis for the introduction by the Community of any measure which could lead to a distortion of competition.]

{TITLE IV. THE EUROPEAN INVESTMENT BANK}

{*Article 129.*   A European Investment Bank is hereby established; it shall have legal personality.

The members of the European Investment Bank shall be the Member States.

The Statute of the European Investment Bank is laid down in a Protocol annexed to this Treaty.}

{*Article 130.*   The task of the European Investment Bank shall be to contribute, by having recourse to the capital market and utilising its own resources, to the balanced and steady development of the common market in the interest of the Community. For this purpose the Bank shall, operating on a non-profit making basis, grant loans and give guarantees which facilitate the financing of the following projects in all sectors of the economy:

(a) projects for developing less developed regions;
(b) projects for modernising or converting undertakings or for developing fresh activities called for by the progressive establishment of the common market, where these projects are of such a size or nature that they cannot be entirely financed by the various means available in the individual Member States;
(c) projects of common interest to several Member States which are of such a size or nature that they cannot be entirely financed by the various means available in the individual Member States.]

TITLE [XIV] {V}. ECONOMIC AND SOCIAL COHESION

Article 130a. In order to promote its overall harmonious development, the Community shall develop and pursue its actions leading to the strengthening of its economic and social cohesion.

In particular, the Community shall aim at reducing disparities between the levels of development of the various regions and the backwardness of the least-favoured regions, [including rural areas].

Article 130b. Member States shall conduct their economic policies and shall coordinate them in such a way as, in addition, to attain the objectives set out in Article 130a. The [formulation and] implementation of the [Community's policies and actions] {common policies} and [the implementation] of the internal market shall take into account the objectives set out in Article 130a {and in Article 130c} and shall contribute to their achievement. The Community shall [also] support the achievement of these objectives by the action it takes through the Structural Funds (European Agricultural Guidance and Guarantee Fund, Guidance Section; European Social Fund; European Regional Development Fund), the European Investment Bank and the other existing financial instruments.

[The Commission shall submit a report to the European Parliament, the Council, the Economic and Social Committee and the Committee of the Regions every three years on the progress made towards achieving economic and social cohesion and on the manner in which the various means provided for in this Article have contributed to it. This report shall, if necessary, be accompanied by appropriate proposals.

If specific actions prove necessary outside the Funds and without prejudice to the measures decided upon within the framework of the other Community policies, such actions may be adopted by the Council acting unanimously on a proposal from the Commission and after consulting the European Parliament, the Economic and Social Committee and the Committee of the Regions.]

[*Article 130c.* The European Regional Development Fund is intended to help to redress the main regional imbalances in the Community through participation in the development and structural adjustment of regions whose development is lagging behind and in the conversion of declining industrial regions.

[*Article 130d.* Without prejudice to Article 130e, the Council, acting unanimously on a proposal from the Commission and after obtaining the assent of the European Parliament and consulting the Economic and Social Committee and the Committee of the Regions, shall define the tasks, priority objectives and the organization of the Structural Funds, which may involve grouping the Funds. The Council, acting by the same procedure, shall also define the general rules applicable to them and the provisions necessary to ensure their effectiveness and the coordination of the Funds with one another and with the other existing financial instruments.

The Council, acting in accordance with the same procedure, shall before 31 December 1993 set up a Cohesion Fund to provide a financial contribution to projects in the fields of environment and trans-European networks in the area of transport infrastructure.]

{*Article 130d.* Once the Single European Act enters into force the Commission shall submit a comprehensive proposal to the Council, the purpose of which will be to make such amendments to the structure and operational rules of the existing structural Funds (European Agricultural Guidance and Guarantee Fund, Guidance Section, European Social Fund, European Regional Development Fund) as are necessary to clarify and rationalise their tasks in order to contribute to the achievement of the objectives set out in Article 130a and Article 130c, to increase their efficiency and to co-ordinate their activities between themselves and with the operations of the existing financial instruments. The Council shall act unanimously on this proposal within a period of one year, after consulting the European Parliament and the Economic and Social Committee.}

Article 130e. {After adoption of the decision referred to in Article 130d,} [I]mplementing decisions relating to the ‚European Regional Development Fund shall be taken by the Council, acting [in accordance with the procedure referred to in Article 189c and after consulting the Economic and Social Committee and the Committee of the Regions] {by a qualified majority on a proposal from the Commission and in co-operation with the European Parliament.}

With regard to the European Agricultural Guidance and Guarantee Fund, Guidance Section and the European Social Fund, Articles 43 [and 125 respectively shall continue to apply] {126 and 127 remain applicable respectively.}

TITLE [XV] {VI}. RESEARCH AND TECHNOLOGICAL DEVELOPMENT

Article 130f.   1. The [Community shall have the objective of strengthening] {Community's aim shall be to strengthen} the scientific and technological basis of European industry and [encouraging] {to encourage} it to become more competitive at international level [, while promoting all the research activities deemed necessary by virtue of other Chapters of this Treaty].

2. [For this purpose the Community shall, throughout the Community] {In order to achieve this, it shall} encourage undertakings, including small and medium-sized undertakings, research centres and universities in their research and technological development activities [of high quality]; it shall support their efforts to co-operate with one another, aiming notably at enabling undertakings to exploit the {Community's} internal market potential to the full, in particular through the opening up of national public contracts, the definition of common standards and the removal of legal and fiscal [obstacles] {barriers} to that co-operation.

3. [All Community activities under this Treaty in the area of research and technological development, including demonstration projects, shall be decided on and implemented in accordance with the provisions of this Title.] {In the achievement of these aims, special account shall be taken of the connection between the common research and technological development effort, the establishment of the internal market and the implementation of common policies, particularly as regards competition and trade.}

Article 130g.   In pursuing these objectives the Community shall carry out the following activities, complementing the activities carried out in the Member States:

(a) implementation of research, technological development and demonstration programmes by promoting co-operation with undertakings, research centres and universities;
(b) promotion of co-operation in the field of Community research,

technological development and demonstration with third countries
and international organizations;
(c) dissemination and optimisation of the results of activities in
Community research, technological development and demonstration;
(d) stimulation of the training and mobility of researchers in the
Community.

Article 130h. [1. The Community and the Member States shall coordinate their research and technological development activities so as to
ensure that national policies and Community policy are mutually consistent.

2. In close cooperation with the Member States, the Commission may
take any useful initiative to promote the coordination referred to in paragraph 1.]

{Member States shall, in liaison with the Commission, co-ordinate
among themselves the policies and programmes carried out at national
level. In close contact with the Member States, the Commission may take
any useful initiative to promote such co-ordination.}

Article 130i. [1. A multiannual framework programme, setting out all
the activities of the Community, shall be adopted by the Council, acting
in accordance with the procedure referred to in Article 189b after consulting the Economic and Social Committee. The Council shall act unanimously throughout the procedures referred to in Article 189b.

The framework programme shall:

– establish the scientific and technological objectives to be achieved by
the activities provided for in Article 130g and fix the relevant priorities;
– indicate the broad lines of such activities;
– fix the maximum overall amount and the detailed rules for Community
financial participation in the framework programme and the respective
shares in each of the activities provided for.

2. The framework programme shall be adapted or supplemented as the
situation changes.

3. The framework programme shall be implemented through specific
programmes developed within each activity. Each specific programme
shall define the detailed rules for implementing it, fix its duration and
provide for the means deemed necessary. The sum of the amounts
deemed necessary, fixed in the specific programmes, may not exceed the
overall maximum amount fixed for the framework programme and each
activity.

4. The Council, acting by a qualified majority on a proposal from the

Commission and after consulting the European Parliament and the Economic and Social Committee, shall adopt the specific programmes.]

{1. The Community shall adopt a multiannual framework programme setting out all its activities. The framework programme shall lay down the scientific and technical objectives, define their respective priorities, set out the main lines of the activities envisaged and fix the amount deemed necessary, the detailed rules for financial participation by the Community in the programme as a whole and the breakdown of this amount between the various activities envisaged.

2. The framework programme may be adapted or supplemented, as the situation changes.}

[*Article 130j.* For the implementation of the multiannual framework programme the Council shall:

- determine the rules for the participation of undertakings, research centres and universities;
- lay down the rules governing the dissemination of research results.]

{*Article 130k.* The framework programme shall be implemented through specific programmes developed within each activity. Each specific programme shall define the detailed rules for implementing it, fix its duration and provide for the means deemed necessary.

The Council shall define the detailed arrangements for the dissemination of knowledge resulting from the specific programmes.}

Article [130k] {*130l*} In implementing the multiannual framework programme, supplementary programmes may be decided on involving the participation of certain Member States only, which shall finance them subject to possible Community participation.

The Council shall adopt the rules applicable to supplementary programmes, particularly as regards the dissemination of knowledge and access by other Member States.

Article [130l] {*130m*}. In implementing the multiannual framework programme the Community may make provision, in agreement with the Member States concerned, for participation in research and development programmes undertaken by several Member States, including participation in the structures created for the execution of those programmes.

Article [130m] {*130n*}. In implementing the multiannual framework programme, the Community may make provision for co-operation in Community research, technological development and demonstration with third countries or international organisations.

The detailed arrangements for such co-operation may be the subject of international agreements between the Community and the third parties concerned which shall be negotiated and concluded in accordance with Article 228.

Article [130n] {*1300*}.   The Community may set up joint undertakings or any other structure necessary for the efficient execution of Community research, technological development and demonstration programmes.

[*Article 1300*.   The Council, acting unanimously on a proposal from the Commission and after consulting the European Parliament and the Economic and Social Committee, shall adopt the provisions referred to in Article 130n.

The Council, acting in accordance with the procedure referred to in Article 189c and after consulting the Economic and Social Committee, shall adopt the provisions referred to in Articles 130j to l. Adoption of the supplementary programmes shall require the agreement of the Member States concerned.]

{*Article 130p*.   1. The detailed arrangements for financing each programme, including any Community contribution, shall be established at the time of the adoption of the programme.

2. The amount of the Community's annual contribution shall be laid down under the budgetary procedure, without prejudice to other possible methods of Community financing. The estimated cost of the specific programmes must not in aggregate exceed the financial provision in the framework programme.}

[*Article 130p*.   At the beginning of each year the Commission shall send a report to the European Parliament and the Council. The report shall include information on research and technological development activities and the dissemination of results during the previous year, and the work programme for the current year.]

{*Article 130q*.   1. The Council shall, acting unanimously on a proposal from the Commission and after consulting the European Parliament and the Economic and Social Committee, adopt the provisions referred to in Articles 130i and 1300.

2. The Council shall, acting by a qualified majority on a proposal from the Commission, after consulting the Economic and Social Committee, and in co-operation with the European Parliament, adopt the provisions referred to in Articles 130k, 130l, 130m, 130n and 130p(1). The adoption of these supplementary programmes shall also require the agreement of the Member States concerned.}

TITLE [XVI.] {VII.} ENVIRONMENT

Article 130r.   1. [Community policy on the environment shall contribute to pursuit of] {Action by the Community relating to the environment shall have} the following objectives:

- [preserving, protecting and improving] {to preserve, protect and improve} the quality of the environment;
- {to contribute towards} protecting human health;
- {to ensure a} prudent and rational utilization of natural resources.
- [promoting measures at international level to deal with regional or worldwide environmental problems].

2. [Community policy on the environment shall aim at a high level of protection taking into account the diversity of situations in the various regions of the Community. It shall be based on the precautionary principle and] {Action by the Community relating to the environment shall be based} on the principles that preventive action should be taken, that environmental damage should as a priority be rectified at source and that the polluter should pay. Environmental protection requirements [must be integrated into {shall be a component of} the Community's other policies.

[In this context, harmonization measures answering these requirements shall include, where appropriate, a safeguard clause allowing Member States to take provisional measures, for non-economic environmental reasons, subject to a Community inspection procedure.]

3. In preparing its action relating to the environment, the Community shall take account of:

- available scientific and technical data;
- environmental conditions in the various regions of the community;
- the potential benefits and costs of action or of lack of action;
- the economic and social development of the Community as a whole and the balanced development of its regions.

{4. The Community shall take action relating to the environment to the extent to which the objectives referred to in paragraph 1 can be attained better at Community level than at the level of the individual Member States. Without prejudice to certain measures of a Community nature, the Member States shall finance and implement the other measures.}

[4.] {5.} Within their respective spheres of competence, the Community and the Member States shall co-operate with third countries and with the [competent] {relevant} international organizations. The arrangements for

Community co-operation may be the subject of agreements between the Community and the third parties concerned, which shall be negotiated and concluded in accordance with Article 228.

The previous [sub-]paragraph shall be without prejudice to Member States' competence to negotiate in international bodies and to conclude international agreements.

Article 130s. 1. The Council, acting [in accordance with the procedure referred to in Article 189c] {unanimously on a proposal from the Commission} and after consulting {the European Parliament and} the Economic and Social Committee, shall decide what action is to be taken by the Community [in order to achieve the objectives referred to in Article 130r].

[2. By way of derogation from the decision-making procedure provided for in paragraph 1 and without prejudice to Article 100a, the Council, acting unanimously on a proposal from the Commission and after consulting the European Parliament and the Economic and Social Committee, shall adopt:

- provisions primarily of a fiscal nature; .
- measures concerning town and country planning, land use with the exception of waste management and measures of a general nature, and management of water resources;
- measures significantly affecting a Member State's choice between different energy sources and the general structure of its energy supply.]

The Council [may] {shall} under the conditions laid down in the preceding subparagraph, define those matters [referred to in this paragraph] on which decisions are to be taken by a qualified majority.

[3. In other areas, general action programmes setting out priority objectives to be attained shall be adopted by the Council, acting in accordance with the procedure referred to in Article 189b and after consulting the Economic and Social Committee.

The Council, acting under the terms of paragraph 1 or paragraph 2 according to the case, shall adopt the measures necessary for the implementation of these programmes.

4. Without prejudice to certain measures of a Community nature, the Member States shall finance and implement the environment policy.

5. Without prejudice to the principle that the polluter should pay, if a measure based on the provisions of paragraph 1 involves costs deemed disproportionate for the public authorities of a Member State, the Council shall, in the act adopting that measure, lay down appropriate provisions in the form of:

- temporary derogations and/or

– financial support from the Cohesion Fund to be set up no later than 31
   December 1993 pursuant to Article 130d.]

Article 130t.   The protective measures adopted pursuant to Article 130s
shall not prevent any Member State from maintaining or introducing
more stringent protective measures. [Such measures must be] compatible
with this Treaty. [They shall be notified to the Commission.]

[TITLE XVII. DEVELOPMENT COOPERATION]

[*Article 130u.*   1. Community policy in the sphere of development cooperation, which shall be complementary to the policies pursued by the
Member States, shall foster:

– the sustainable economic and social development of the developing
   countries, and more particularly the most disadvantaged among them;
– the smooth and gradual integration of the developing countries into the
   world economy;
– the campaign against poverty in the developing countries.

   2. Community policy in this area shall contribute to the general objective of developing and consolidating democracy and the rule of law, and
to that of respecting human rights and fundamental freedoms.
   3. The Community and the Member States shall comply with the commitments and take account of the objectives they have approved in the
context of the United Nations and other competent international organizations.]

[*Article 130v.*   The Community shall take account of the objectives
referred to in Article 130u in the policies that it implements which are
likely to affect developing countries.

[*Article 130w.*   1. Without prejudice to the other provisions of this
Treaty the Council, acting in accordance with the procedure referred to in
Article 189c, shall adopt the measures necessary to further the objectives
referred to in Article 130u. Such measures may take the form of multiannual programmes.
   2. The European Investment Bank shall contribute, under the terms
laid down in its Statute, to the implementation of the measures referred
to in paragraph 1.
   3. The provisions of this Article shall not affect cooperation with the
African, Caribbean and Pacific countries in the framework of the ACP-
EEC Convention.]

[*Article 130x.* 1. The Community and the Member States shall coordinate their policies on development cooperation and shall consult each other on their aid programmes, including in international organizations and during international conferences. They may undertake joint action. Member States shall contribute if necessary to the implementation of Community aid programmes.

2. The Commission may take any useful initiative to promote the coordination referred to in paragraph 1.]

[*Article 130y.* Within their respective spheres of competence, the Community and the Member States shall cooperate with third countries and with the competent international organizations. The arrangements for Community cooperation may be the subject of agreements between the Community and the third parties concerned, which shall be negotiated and concluded in accordance with Article 228.

The previous paragraph shall be without prejudice to Member States' competence to negotiate in international bodies and to conclude international agreements.]

Part Four. Association of the Overseas Countries and Territories

Article 131. The Member States agree to associate with the Community the non-European countries and territories which have special relations with Belgium, Denmark, France, Italy, the Netherlands and the United Kingdom. These countries and territories (hereinafter called the 'countries and territories') are listed in Annex IV to this Treaty.

The purpose of association shall be to promote the economic and social development of the countries and territories and to establish close economic relations between them and the Community as a whole.

In accordance with the principles set out in the Preamble to this Treaty, association shall serve primarily to further the interests and prosperity of the inhabitants of these countries and territories in order to lead them to the economic, social and cultural development to which they aspire.

Article 132. Association shall have the following objectives:

1. Member States shall apply to their trade with the countries and territories the same treatment as they accord each other pursuant to this Treaty.

2. Each country or territory shall apply to its trade with Member States and with the other countries and territories the same treatment as

that which it applies to the European State with which it has special relations.

3. The Member States shall contribute to the investments required for the progressive development of these countries and territories.

4. For investments financed by the Community, participation in tenders and supplies shall be open on equal terms to all natural and legal persons who are nationals of a Member State or of one of the countries and territories.

5. In relations between Member States and the countries and territories the right of establishment of nationals and companies or firms shall be regulated in accordance with the provisions and procedures laid down in the Chapter relating to the right of establishment and on a non-discriminatory basis, subject to any special provisions laid down pursuant to Art. 136.

Article 133. 1. Customs duties on imports into the Member States of goods originating in the countries and territories shall be completely abolished in conformity with the progressive abolition of customs duties between Member States in accordance with the provisions of this Treaty.

2. Customs duties on imports into each country or territory from Member States or from the other countries or territories shall be progressively abolished in accordance with the provisions of Arts. 12, 13, 14, 15 and 17.

3. The countries and territories may, however, levy customs duties which meet the needs of their development and industrialisation or produce revenue for their budgets.

The duties referred to in the preceding subparagraph shall nevertheless be progressively reduced to the level of those imposed on imports of products from the Member State with which each country or territory has special relations. The percentages and the timetable of the reductions provided for under this Treaty shall apply to the differences between the duty imposed on a product coming from the Member State which has special relations with the country or territory concerned and the duty imposed on the same product coming from within the Community on entry into the importing country or territory.

4. Paragraph 2 shall not apply to countries and territories which, by reason of the particular international obligations by which they are bound, already apply a non-discriminatory customs tariff when this Treaty enters into force.

5. The introduction of or any change in customs duties imposed on goods imported into the countries and territories shall not, either in law or in fact, give rise to any direct or indirect discrimination between imports from the various Member States.

Article 134. If the level of the duties applicable to goods from a third country on entry into a country or territory is liable, when the provisions of Art. 133 (1) have been applied, to cause deflections of trade to the detriment of any Member State, the latter may request the Commission to propose to the other Member States the measures needed to remedy the situation.

Article 135. Subject to the provisions relating to public health, public security or public policy, freedom of movement within Member States for workers from the countries and territories, and within the countries and territories for workers from Member States, shall be governed by agreements to be concluded subsequently with the unanimous approval of Member States.

Article 136. For an initial period of five years after the entry into force of this Treaty, the details of and procedure for the association of the countries and territories with the Community shall be determined by an Implementing Convention annexed to this Treaty.

Before the Convention referred to in the preceding paragraph expires, the Council shall, acting unanimously, lay down provisions for a further period, on the basis of the experience acquired and of the principles set out in this Treaty.

Article 136a. The provisions of Arts. 130 to 136 shall apply to Greenland subject to the special provisions for Greenland set out in the Protocol on special arrangements for Greenland, annexed to this Treaty.

Part Five. Institutions of the Community

TITLE I. PROVISIONS GOVERNING THE INSTITUTIONS

CHAPTER I. THE INSTITUTIONS

Section 1. The [European Parliament] {Assembly}

Article 137. The [European Parliament] {Assembly}, which shall consist of representatives of the peoples of the States brought together in the Community, shall exercise the {advisory and supervisory} powers {which are} conferred upon it by this Treaty.

Article 138. 1. The Assembly shall consist of delegates who shall be designated by the respective Parliaments from among their members in accordance with the procedure laid down by each Member State.

2. The number of these delegates shall be as follows:

Belgium	14
Denmark	10
Germany	36
France	36
Ireland	10
Italy	36
Luxembourg	6
The Netherlands	14
United Kingdom	36

3. The [European Parliament] {Assembly} shall draw up proposals for elections by direct universal suffrage in accordance with a uniform procedure in all Member States.

The Council shall, acting unanimously [after obtaining the assent of the European Parliament which shall act by a majority of its component members], lay down the appropriate provisions, which it shall recommend to Member States for adoption in accordance with their respective constitutional requirements.

[NB. Article 138(1) and (2) lapsed on 17 July 1979 in accordance with the Council Decision and Act of 20 September 1976 on Direct Elections. Articles 1 and 2 as amended are as follows]

Council Decision and Act of 20 September 1976 on Direct Elections

Article 1. The representatives in the Assembly of the peoples of the State brought together in the Community shall be elected by direct universal suffrage.

Article 2. The number of representatives elected in each Member State shall be as follows:

Belgium	25
Denmark	16
Germany	99
Greece	25
Spain	64
France	87
Ireland	15
Italy	87
Luxembourg	6

The Netherlands   31
Portugal   25
United Kingdom   87

[*Article 138a.* Political parties at European level are important as a factor for integration within the Union. They contribute to forming a European awareness and to expressing the political will of the citizens of the Union.]

[*Article 138b.* In so far as provided in this Treaty, the European Parliament shall participate in the process leading up to the adoption of Community acts by exercising its powers under the procedures laid down in Articles 189b and 189c and by giving its assent or delivering advisory opinions.

The European Parliament may, acting by a majority of its members, request the Commission to submit any appropriate proposal on matters on which it considers that a Community act is required for the purpose of implementing this Treaty.]

[*Article 138c.* In the course of its duties, the European Parliament may, at the request of a quarter of its members, set up a temporary Committee of Inquiry to investigate, without prejudice to the powers conferred by this Treaty on other institutions or bodies, alleged contraventions or maladministration in the implementation of Community law, except where the alleged facts are being examined before a court and while the case is still subject to legal proceedings.

The temporary Committee of Inquiry shall cease to exist on the submission of its report.

The detailed provisions governing the exercise of the right of inquiry shall be determined by common accord of the European Parliament, the Council and the Commission.]

[*Article 138d.* Any citizen of the Union, and any natural or legal person residing or having its registered office in a Member State, shall have the right to address, individually or in association with other citizens or persons, a petition to the European Parliament on a matter which comes within the Community's fields of activity and which affects him, her or it directly.]

[*Article 138e.* 1. The European Parliament shall appoint an Ombudsman empowered to receive complaints from any citizen of the Union or any natural or legal person residing or having its registered office in a Member State concerning instances of maladministration in the activities of the Community institutions or bodies, with the exception of the Court of Justice and the Court of First Instance acting in their judicial role.

In accordance with his duties, the Ombudsman shall conduct inquiries for which he finds grounds, either on his own initiative or on the basis of complaints submitted to him direct or through a member of the European Parliament, except where the alleged facts are or have been the subject of legal proceedings. Where the Ombudsman establishes an instance of maladministration, he shall refer the matter to the institution concerned, which shall have a period of three months in which to inform him of its views. The Ombudsman shall then forward a report to the European Parliament and the institution concerned. The person lodging the complaint shall be informed of the outcome of such inquiries.

The Ombudsman shall submit an annual report to the European Parliament on the outcome of his inquiries.

2. The Ombudsman shall be appointed after each election of the European Parliament for the duration of its term of office. The Ombudsman shall be eligible for reappointment.

The Ombudsman may be dismissed by the Court of Justice at the request of the European Parliament if he no longer fulfils the conditions required for the performance of his duties or if he is guilty of serious misconduct.

3. The Ombudsman shall be completely independent in the performance of his duties. In the performance of those duties he shall neither seek nor take instructions from any body. The Ombudsman may not, during his term of office, engage in any other occupation, whether gainful or not.

4. The European Parliament shall, after seeking an opinion from the Commission and with the approval of the Council acting by a qualified majority, lay down the regulations and general conditions governing the performance of the Ombudsman's duties.]

Article 139. The Assembly shall hold an annual session. It shall meet, without requiring to be convened, on the second Tuesday in March.

The Assembly may meet in extraordinary session at the request of a majority of its members or at the request of the Council or of the Commission.

Article 140. The Assembly shall elect its President and its officers from among its members.

Members of the Commission may attend all meetings and shall, at their request, be heard on behalf of the Commission.

The Commission shall reply orally or in writing to questions put to it by the Assembly or by its members.

The Council shall be heard by the Assembly in accordance with the conditions laid down by the Council in its rules of procedure.

Article 141. Save as otherwise provided in this Treaty, the Assembly shall act by an absolute majority of the votes cast.

The rules of procedure shall determine the quorum.

Article 142. The Assembly shall adopt its rules of procedure, acting by a majority of its members.

The proceedings of the Assembly shall be published in the manner laid down in its rules of procedure.

Article 143. The Assembly shall discuss in open session the annual general report submitted to it by the Commission.

Article 144. If a motion of censure on the activities of the Commission is tabled before it, the Assembly shall not vote thereon until at least three days after the motion has been tabled and only by open vote.

If the motion of censure is carried by a two-thirds majority of the votes cast, representing a majority of the members of the Assembly, the members of the Commission shall resign as a body. They shall continue to deal with current business until they are replaced in accordance with Art. 158. [In this case, the term of office of the members of the Commission appointed to replace them shall expire on the date on which the term of office of the members of the Commission obliged to resign as a body would have expired.]

Section 2. The Council

Merger Treaty

Article 1. A Council of the European Communities (hereinafter called the 'Council') is hereby established. This Council shall take the place of the Special Council of Ministers of the European Coal and Steel Community, the Council of the European Economic Community and the Council of the European Atomic Energy Community.

It shall exercise the powers and jurisdiction conferred on those institutions in accordance with the provisions of the Treaties established in the European Coal and Steel Community, the European Economic Community and the European Atomic Energy Community, and of this Treaty.

Article 145. To ensure that the objectives set out in this Treaty are attained, the Council shall, in accordance with the provisions of this Treaty:

- ensure co-ordination of the general economic policies of the Member States;
- have power to take decisions.
- confer on the Commission, in the acts which the Council adopts, powers for the implementation of the rules which the Council lays down. The Council may impose certain requirements in respect of the exercise of these powers. The Council may also reserve the right, in specific cases, to exercise directly implementing powers itself. The procedures referred to above must be consonant with principles and rules to be laid down in advance by the Council, acting unanimously on a proposal from the Commission and after obtaining the opinion of the European Parliament.

[*Article 146.* The Council shall consist of a representative of each Member State at ministerial level, authorized to commit the government of that Member State.

The office of President shall be held in turn by each Member State in the Council for a term of six months, in the following order of Member States:

- for a first cycle of six years: Belgium, Denmark, Germany, Greece, Spain, France, Ireland, Italy, Luxembourg, Netherlands, Portugal, United Kingdom;
- for the following cycle of six years: Denmark, Belgium, Greece, Germany, France, Spain, Italy, Ireland, Netherlands, Luxembourg, United Kingdom, Portugal.]

[*Article 147.* The Council shall meet when convened by its President on his own initiative or at the request of one of its members or of the Commission.]

Article 148. Save as otherwise provided in this Treaty, the Council shall act by a majority of its members.

2. Where the Council is required to act by a qualified majority, the votes of its members shall be weighted as follows:

Belgium	5
Denmark	3
Germany	10
Greece	5
Spain	8

France	10
Ireland	3
Italy	10
Luxembourg	2
The Netherlands	5
Portugal	5
United Kingdom	10

For their adoption, acts of the Council shall require at least:

54 votes in favour where this Treaty requires them to be adopted on a proposal from the commission.

54 votes in favour, cast by at least eight members, in other cases.

3. Abstentions by members present in person or represented shall not prevent the adoption by the Council of acts which require unanimity.

*{*Article 149*. 1. Where, in pursuance of this Treaty, the Council acts on a proposal from the Commission, unanimity shall be required for an act constituting an amendment to that proposal.

2. Where, in pursuance of this Treaty, the Council acts in co-operation with the European Parliament, the following procedure shall apply:

(a) The Council, acting by a qualified majority under the conditions of paragraph 1, on a proposal from the Commission and after obtaining the opinion of the European Parliament, shall adopt a common position.

(b) The Council's common position shall be communicated to the European Parliament. The Council and the Commission shall inform the European Parliament fully of the reasons which led the Council to adopt its common position and also of the Commission's position.

   If, within three months of such communication, the European Parliament approves this common position or has not taken a decision within that period, the Council shall definitively adopt the act in question in accordance with the common position.

(c) The European Parliament may within the period of three months referred to in point (b), by an absolute majority of its component members, propose amendments to the Council's common position. The European Parliament may also, by the same majority, reject the Council's common position. The result of the proceedings shall be transmitted to the Council and the Commission.

   If the European Parliament has rejected the Council's common position, unanimity shall be required for the Council to act on a second reading.

(d) The Commission shall, within a period of one month, re-examine the

* See art. 189(a)–(c).

proposal on the basis of which the Council adopted its common position, by taking into account the amendments proposed by the European Parliament.

The Commission shall forward to the Council, at the same time as its re-examined proposal, the amendments of the European Parliament which it has not accepted, and shall express its opinion on them. The Council may adopt these amendments unanimously.

(e) The Council, acting by a qualified majority, shall adopt the proposal as re-examined by the Commission.

Unanimity shall be required for the Council to amend the proposal as re-examined by the Commission.

(f) In the cases referred to in points (c), (d) and (e), the Council shall be required to act within a period of three months. If no decision is taken within this period, the Commission proposal shall be deemed not to have been adopted.

(g) The periods referred to in points (b) and (f) may be extended by a maximum of one month by common accord between the Council and the European Parliament.

3. As long as the Council has not acted, the Commission may alter its proposal at any time during the procedures mentioned in paragraphs 1 and 2.}

Article 150. Where a vote is taken, any member of the Council may also act on behalf of not more than one other member.

[*Article 151.* 1. A committee consisting of the Permanent Representatives of the Member States shall be responsible for preparing the work of the Council and for carrying out the tasks assigned to it by the Council.

2. The Council shall be assisted by a General Secretariat, under the direction of a Secretary-General. The Secretary-General shall be appointed by the Council acting unanimously.

The Council shall decide on the organization of the General Secretariat.

3. The Council shall adopt its rules of procedure.]

Article 152. The Council may request the Commission to undertake any studies which the Council considers desirable for the attainment of the common objectives, and to submit to it any appropriate proposals.

Article 153. The Council shall, after receiving an opinion from the Commission, determine the rules governing the committees provided for in this Treaty.

Merger Treaty

Article 9. A Commission of the European Communities (hereinafter called the 'Commission') is hereby established. This Commission shall take the place of the High Authority of the European Coal and Steel Community, the Commission of the European Community and the Commission of the European Atomic Energy Community.

It shall exercise the powers and jurisdiction conferred on those institutions in accordance with the provisions of the Treaties establishing the European Coal and Steel Community, the European Economic Community and the European Atomic Energy Community, and of this Treaty.

[*Article 154.* The Council shall, acting by a qualified majority, determine the salaries, allowances and pensions of the President and members of the Commission, and of the President, Judges, Advocates-General and Registrar of the Court of Justice. It shall also, again by a qualified majority, determine any payment to be made instead of remuneration.]

Article 155. In order to ensure the proper functioning and development of the common market, the Commission shall:

– ensure that the provisions of this Treaty and the measures taken by the institutions pursuant thereto are applied;
– formulate recommendations or deliver opinions on matters dealt with in this Treaty, if it expressly so provides or if the Commission considers it necessary;
– have its power of decision and participate in the shaping of measures taken by the Council and by the Assembly in the manner provided for in this Treaty;
– exercise the powers conferred on it by the Council for the implementation of the rules laid down by the latter.

[*Article 156.* The Commission shall publish annually, not later than one month before the opening of the session of the European Parliament, a general report on the activities of the Community.]

[*Article 157.* 1. The Commission shall consist of seventeen members, who shall be chosen on the grounds of their general competence and whose independence is beyond doubt.

The number of members of the Commission may be altered by the Council, acting unanimously.

Only nationals of Member States may be members of the Commission.

The Commission must include at least one national of each of the Member States, but may not include more than two members having the nationality of the same State.

2. The members of the Commission shall, in the general interest of the Community, be completely independent in the performance of their duties.

In the performance of these duties, they shall neither seek nor take instructions from any government or from any other body. They shall refrain from any action incompatible with their duties. Each Member State undertakes to respect this principle and not to seek to influence the members of the Commission in the performance of their tasks.

The members of the Commission may not, during their term of office, engage in any other occupation, whether gainful or not. When entering upon their duties they shall give a solemn undertaking that, both during and after their term of office, they will respect the obligations arising therefrom and in particular their duty to behave with integrity and discretion as regards the acceptance, after they have ceased to hold office, of certain appointments or benefits. In the event of any breach of these obligations, the Court of Justice may, on application by the Council or the Commission, rule that the member concerned be, according to the circumstances, either compulsorily retired in accordance with Article 160 or deprived of his right to a pension or other benefits in its stead.]

[*Article 158.* 1. The members of the Commission shall be appointed, in accordance with the procedure referred to in paragraph 2, for a period of five years, subject, if need be, to Article 144.

Their term of office shall be renewable.

2. The governments of the Member States shall nominate by common accord, after consulting the European Parliament, the person they intend to appoint as President of the Commission.

The governments of the Member States shall, in consultation with the nominee for President, nominate the other persons whom they intend to appoint as members of the Commission.

The President and the other members of the Commission thus nominated shall be subject as a body to a vote of approval by the European Parliament. After approval by the European Parliament, the President and the other members of the Commission shall be appointed by common accord of the governments of the Member States.

3. Paragraphs 1 and 2 shall be applied for the first time to the President and the other members of the Commission whose term of office begins on 7 January 1995.

The President and the other members of the Commission whose term of office begins on 7 January 1993 shall be appointed by common accord of the governments of the Member States. Their term of office shall expire on 6 January 1995.]

[*Article 159.* Apart from normal replacement, or death, the duties of a member of the Commission shall end when he resigns or is compulsorily retired.

The vacancy thus caused shall be filled for the remainder of the member's term of office by a new member appointed by common accord of the governments of the Member States. The Council may, acting unanimously, decide that such a vacancy need not be filled.

In the event of resignation, compulsory retirement or death, the President shall be replaced for the remainder of his term of office. The procedure laid down in Article 158(2) shall be applicable for the replacement of the President.

Save in the case of compulsory retirement under Article 160, members of the Commission shall remain in office until they have been replaced.]

[*Article 160.* If any member of the Commission no longer fulfils the conditions required for the performance of his duties or if he has been guilty of serious misconduct, the Court of Justice may, on application by the Council or the Commission, compulsorily retire him.]

[*Article 161.* The Commission may appoint a Vice-President or two Vice-Presidents from among its members.]

[*Article 162.* 1. The Council and the Commission shall consult each other and shall settle by common accord their methods of cooperation.

2. The Commission shall adopt its rules of procedure so as to ensure that both it and its departments operate in accordance with the provisions of this Treaty. It shall ensure that these rules are published.]

[*Article 163.* The Commission shall act by a majority of the number of members provided for in Article 157.

A meeting of the Commission shall be valid only if the number of members laid down in its rules of procedure is present.]

Section 4. The Court of Justice

Article 164. The Court of Justice shall ensure that in the interpretation and application of this Treaty the law is observed.

Article 165. The Court of Justice shall consist of 13 Judges.

The Court of Justice shall sit in plenary session. It may, however, form chambers, each consisting of three or five Judges, either to undertake certain preparatory inquiries or to adjudicate on particular categories of cases in accordance with rules laid down for these purposes.

[The Court of Justice shall sit in plenary session when a Member State or a Community institution that is a party to the proceedings so requests.[{Whenever the Court of Justice hears cases brought before it by a Member State or by one of the institutions of the Community or, to the extent that the chambers of the Court do not have the requisite jurisdiction under the Rules of Procedure, has to give preliminary rulings on questions submitted to it pursuant to Article 177, it shall sit in plenary session.}

Should the Court of Justice so request, the Council may, acting unanimously, increase the number of judges and make the necessary adjustments to the second and third paragraphs of this Article and to the second paragraph of Article 167.

Article 166.   The Court of Justice shall be assisted by six Advocates-General.

It shall be the duty of the Advocate-General, acting with complete impartiality and independence, to make, in open court, reasoned submissions on cases brought before the Court of Justice, in order to assist the Court in the performance of the task assigned to it in Art. 164.

Should the Court of Justice so request, the Council may, acting unanimously, increase the number of Advocates-General and make the necessary adjustments to the third paragraph of Art. 167.

Article 167.   The Judges and Advocates-General shall be chosen from persons whose independence is beyond doubt and who possess the qualifications required for appointment to the highest judicial offices in their respective countries or who are juriconsults of recognised competence; they shall be appointed by common accord of the Governments of the Member States for a term of six years.

Every three years there shall be a partial replacement of the Judges. Seven and six Judges shall be replaced alternately.

Every three years there shall be a partial replacement of the Advocates-General. Three Advocates-General shall be replaced on each occasion.

Retiring Judges and Advocates-General shall be eligible for re-appointment.

The Judges shall elect the President of the Court of Justice from among their number for a term of three years. He may be re-elected.

Article 168.   The Court of Justice shall appoint its Registrar and lay down the rules governing his service.

[*Article 168a.*   1. A Court of First Instance shall be attached to the Court of Justice with jurisdiction to hear and determine at first instance, subject to a right of appeal to the Court of Justice on points of law only and in accordance with the conditions laid down by the Statute, certain classes of action or proceeding defined in accordance with the conditions laid down in paragraph 2. The Court of First Instance shall not be competent to hear and determine questions referred for a preliminary ruling under Article 177.

2. At the request of the Court of Justice and after consulting the European Parliament and the Commission, the Council, acting unanimously, shall determine the classes of action or proceeding referred to in paragraph 1 and the composition of the Court of First Instance and shall adopt the necessary adjustments and additional provisions to the Statute of the Court of Justice. Unless the Council decides otherwise, the provisions of this Treaty relating to the Court of Justice, in particular the provisions of the Protocol on the Statute of the Court of Justice, shall apply to the Court of First Instance.

3. The members of the Court of First Instance shall be chosen from persons whose independence is beyond doubt and who possess the ability required for appointment to judicial office; they shall be appointed by common accord of the governments of the Member States for a term of six years. The membership shall be partially renewed every three years. Retiring members shall be eligible for re-appointment.

4. The Court of First Instance shall establish its rules of procedure in agreement with the Court of Justice. Those rules shall require the unanimous approval of the Council.]

{*Article 168a.*   At the request of the Court of Justice and after consulting the Commission and the European Parliament, the Council may, acting unanimously, attach to the Court of Justice a court with jurisdiction to hear and determine at first instance, subject to a right of appeal to the Court of Justice on points of law only and in accordance with the conditions laid down by the Statute, certain classes of action or proceeding brought by natural or legal persons. That court shall not be competent to hear and determine actions brought by Member States or by Community Institutions or questions referred for a preliminary ruling under Article 177.

2. The Council following the procedure laid down in paragraph 1, shall determine the composition of that court and adopt the necessary adjustments and additional provisions to the Statute of the Court of Justice. Unless the Council decide otherwise, the provisions of this Treaty relating to the Court of Justice, in particular the provisions of the Protocol on the Statute of the Court of Justice, shall apply to that court.

3. The members of that court shall be chosen from persons whose

independence is beyond doubt and who possess the ability required for appointment to judicial office; they shall be appointed by common accord of the Governments of the Member States for a term of six years. The membership shall be partially renewed every three years. Retiring members shall be eligible for reappointment.

4. That court shall establish its rules of procedure in agreement with the Court of Justice. Those rules shall require the unanimous approval of the Council.}

[For rules of procedure etc. see p. 236 ff.]

Article 169. If the Commission considers that a Member State has failed to fulfil an obligation under this Treaty, it shall deliver a reasoned opinion on the matter after giving the State concerned the opportunity to submit its observations.

If the State concerned does not comply with the opinion within the period laid down by the Commission the latter may bring the matter before the Court of Justice.

Article 170. A Member State which considers that another Member State has failed to fulfil an obligation under this Treaty may bring the matter before the Court of Justice.

Before a Member State brings an action against another Member State for an alleged infringement of an obligation under this Treaty, it shall bring the matter before the Commission.

The Commission shall deliver a reasoned opinion after each of the States concerned has been given the opportunity to submit its own case and its observations on the other party's case both orally and in writing.

If the Commission has not delivered an opinion within three months of the date on which the matter was brought before it, the absence of such opinion shall not prevent the matter from being brought before the Court of Justice.

Article 171. [1.] If the Court of Justice finds that a Member State has failed to fulfil an obligation under this Treaty, the State shall be required to take the necessary measures to comply with the judgment of the Court of Justice.

[2. If the Commission considers that the Member State concerned has not taken such measures it shall, after giving that State the opportunity to submit its observations, issue a reasoned opinion specifying the points on which the Member State concerned has not complied with the judgement of the Court of Justice.

If the Member State concerned fails to take the necessary measures to comply with the Court's judgment within the time-limit laid down by the Commission, the latter may bring the case before the Court of Justice. In so doing it shall specify the amount of the lump sum or penalty payment to be paid by the Member State concerned which it considers appropriate in the circumstances.

If the Court of Justice finds that the Member State concerned has not complied with its judgment it may impose a lump sum or penalty payment on it.

This procedure shall be without prejudice to Article 170.]

Article 172. Regulations [adopted jointly by the European Parliament and the Council, and] {made} by the Council pursuant to the provisions of this Treaty, may give the Court of Justice unlimited jurisdiction in regard to the penalties provided for in such regulations.

Article 173. The Court of Justice shall review the legality of acts [adopted jointly by the European Parliament and the Council, of acts] of the Council, [of] {and} the Commission [, and of the ECB] other than recommendations and opinions [, and of acts of the European Parliament intended to produce legal effects vis-à-vis third parties].

It shall for this purpose have jurisdiction in actions brought by a Member State, the Council or the Commission on grounds of lack of competence, infringement of an essential procedural requirement, infringement of this Treaty or of any rule of law relating to its application, or misuse of powers.

[The Court shall have jurisdiction under the same conditions in actions brought by the European Parliament and by the ECB for the purpose of protecting their prerogatives.]

Any natural or legal person may, under the same conditions, institute proceedings against a decision addressed to that person or against a decision which, although in the form of a regulation or a decision addressed to another person, is of direct and individual concern to the former.

The proceedings provided for in this Article shall be instituted within two months of the publication of the measure, or of its notification to the plaintiff, or, in the absence thereof, of the day on which it came to the knowledge of the latter, as the case may be.

Article 174. If the action is well founded, the Court of Justice shall declare the act concerned to be void.

In the case of a regulation, however, the Court of Justice shall, if it considers this necessary, state which of the effects of the regulation which it has declared void shall be considered as definitive.

Article 175. Should the [European Parliament,] the Council or the Commission, in infringement of this Treaty, fail to act, the Member

States and the other institutions of the Community may bring an action before the Court of Justice to have the infringement established.

The action shall be admissible only if the institution concerned has first been called upon to act. If, within two months of being so called upon, the institution concerned has not defined its position, the action may be brought within a further period of two months.

Any natural or legal person may, under the conditions laid down in the preceding paragraphs, complain to the Court of Justice that an institution of the Community has failed to address to that person any act other than a recommendation or an opinion.

[The Court of Justice shall have jurisdiction, under the same conditions, in actions or proceedings brought by the ECB in the areas falling within the latter's field of competence and in actions or proceedings brought against the latter.]

Article 176. The institution or institutions whose act has been declared void or whose failure to act has been declared contrary to this Treaty shall be required to take the necessary measures to comply with the judgment of the Court of Justice.

This obligation shall not affect any obligation which may result from the application of the second paragraph of Article 215.

[This Article shall also apply to the ECB.]

Article 177. The Court of Justice shall have jurisdiction to give preliminary rulings concerning:

(a) the interpretation of this Treaty;
(b) the validity and interpretation of acts of the institutions of the Community [and of the ECB];
(c) the interpretation of the statutes of bodies established by an act of the Council, where those statutes so provide.

Where such a question is raised before any court or tribunal of a Member State, that court or tribunal may, if it considers that a decision on the question is necessary to enable it to give judgment, request the Court of Justice to give a ruling thereon.

Where any such question is raised in a case pending before a court or tribunal of a Member State, against whose decisions there is no judicial remedy under national law, that court or tribunal shall bring the matter before the Court of Justice.

Article 178. The Court of Justice shall have jurisdiction in disputes relating to the compensation for damage provided for in the second paragraph of Art. 215.

Article 179. The Court of Justice shall have jurisdiction in any dispute between the Community and its servants within the limits and under the conditions laid down in the Staff Regulations or the Conditions of Employment.

Article 180. The Court of Justice shall, within the limits hereinafter laid down, have jurisdiction in disputes concerning:

(a) the fulfilment by Member States of obligations under the Statute of the European Investment Bank. In this connection, the Board of Directors of the Bank shall enjoy the powers conferred upon the Commission by Article 169;

(b) measures adopted by the Board of Governors of the [European Investment] Bank. In this connection, any Member State, the Commission or the Board of Directors of the Bank may institute proceedings under the conditions laid down in Article 173;

(c) measures adopted by the Board of Directors of the [European Investment] Bank. Proceedings against such measures may be instituted only by Member States or by the Commission, under the conditions laid down in Article 173, and solely on the grounds of non-compliance with the procedure provided for in Article 21(2), (5), (6) and (7) of the Statute of the Bank;

[(d) the fulfilment by national central banks of obligations under this Treaty and the Statute of the ESCB. In this connection the powers of the Council of the ECB in respect of national central banks shall be the same at those conferred upon the Commission in respect of Member States by Article 169. If the Court of Justice finds that a national central bank has failed to fulfil an obligation under this Treaty, that bank shall be required to take the necessary measures to comply with the judgment of the Court of Justice.]

Article 181. The Court of Justice shall have jurisdiction to give judgment pursuant to any arbitration clause contained in a contract concluded by or on behalf of the Community, whether that contract be governed by public or private law.

Article 182. The Court of Justice shall have jurisdiction in any dispute between Member States which relates to the subject matter of this Treaty if the dispute is submitted to it under a special agreement between the parties.

Article 183. Save where jurisdiction is conferred on the Court by this Treaty, disputes to which the Community is a party shall not on that

ground be excluded from the jurisdiction of the courts or tribunals of the Member States.

Article 184. Notwithstanding the expiry of the period laid down in the [fifth] {third} paragraph of Article 173, any party may, in proceedings in which a regulation of the Council, of the Commission [or of the ECB] is at issue, plead the grounds specified in the [second] {first} paragraph of Article 173 in order to invoke before the Court of Justice the inapplicability of that regulation.

Article 185. Actions brought before the Court of Justice shall not have suspensory effect. The Court of Justice may, however, if it considers that circumstances so require, order that application of the contested act be suspended.

Article 186. The Court of Justice may in any cases before it prescribe any necessary interim measures.

Article 187. The judgments of the Court of Justice shall be enforceable under the conditions laid down in Art. 192.

Article 188. The Statute of the Court of Justice is laid down in a separate Protocol.

The Council may, acting unanimously at the request of the Court of Justice and after consulting the Commission and the European Parliament, amend the provisions of Title III of the Statute.

The Court of Justice shall adopt its rules of procedure. These shall require the unanimous approval of the Council.

[*Section 5. The Court of Auditors*]

[*Article 188a.* The Court of Auditors shall carry out the audit.]

[*Article 188b.* 1. The Court of Auditors shall consist of twelve members.

2. The members of the Court of Auditors shall be chosen from among persons who belong or have belonged in their respective countries to external audit bodies or who are especially qualified for this office. Their independence must be beyond doubt.

3. The members of the Court of Auditors shall be appointed for a term of six years by the Council, acting unanimously after consulting the European Parliament.

However, when the first appointments are made, four members of the

Court of Auditors, chosen by lot, shall be appointed for a term of office of four years only.

The members of the Court of Auditors shall be eligible for reappointment.

They shall elect the President of the Court of Auditors from among their number for a term of three years. The President may be re-elected.

4. The members of the Court of Auditors shall, in the general interest of the Community, be completely independent in the performance of their duties.

In the performance of these duties, they shall neither seek nor take instructions from any government or from any other body. They shall refrain from any action incompatible with their duties.

5. The members of the Court of Auditors may not, during their term of office, engage in any other occupation, whether gainful or not. When entering upon their duties they shall give a solemn undertaking that, both during and after their term of office, they will respect the obligations arising therefrom and in particular their duty to behave with integrity and discretion as regards the acceptance, after they have ceased to hold office, of certain appointments or benefits.

6. Apart from normal replacement, or death, the duties of a member of the Court of Auditors shall end when he resigns, or is compulsorily retired by a ruling of the Court of Justice pursuant to paragraph 7.

The vacancy thus caused shall be filled for the remainder of the member's term of office.

Save in the case of compulsory retirement, members of the Court of Auditors shall remain in office until they have been replaced.

7. A member of the Court of Auditors may be deprived of his office or of his right to a pension or other benefits in its stead only if the Court of Justice, at the request of the Court of Auditors, finds that he no longer fulfils the requisite conditions or meets the obligations arising from his office.

8. The Council, acting by a qualified majority, shall determine the conditions of employment of the President and the members of the Court of Auditors and in particular their salaries, allowances and pensions. It shall also, by the same majority, determine any payment to be made instead of remuneration.

9. The provisions of the Protocol on the Privileges and Immunities of the European Communities applicable to the Judges of the Court of Justice shall also apply to the members of the Court of Auditors.]

[*Article 188c.* 1. The Court of Auditors shall examine the accounts of all revenue and expenditure of the Community. It shall also examine the accounts of all revenue and expenditure of all bodies set up by the

Community in so far as the relevant constituent instrument does not preclude such examination.

The Court of Auditors shall provide the European Parliament and the Council with a statement of assurance as to the reliability of the accounts and the legality and regularity of the underlying transactions.

2. The Court of Auditors shall examine whether all revenue has been received and all expenditure incurred in a lawful and regular manner and whether the financial management has been sound.

The audit of revenue shall be carried out on the basis both of the amounts established as due and the amounts actually paid to the Community.

The audit of expenditure shall be carried out on the basis both of commitments undertaken and payments made.

These audits may be carried out before the closure of accounts for the financial year in question.

3. The audit shall be based on records and, if necessary, performed on the spot in the other institutions of the Community and in the Member States. In the Member States the audit shall be carried out in liaison with the national audit bodies or, if these do not have the necessary powers, with the competent national departments. These bodies or departments shall inform the Court of Auditors whether they intend to take part in the audit.

The other institutions of the Community and the national audit bodies or, if these do not have the necessary powers, the competent national departments, shall forward to the Court of Auditors, at its request, any document or information necessary to carry out its task.

4. The Court of Auditors shall draw up an annual report after the close of each financial year. It shall be forwarded to the other institutions of the Community and shall be published, together with the replies of these institutions to the observations of the Court of Auditors, in the Official Journal of the European Communities.

The Court of Auditors may also, at any time, submit observations, particularly in the form of special reports, on specific questions and deliver opinions at the request of one of the other institutions of the Community.

It shall adopt its annual reports, special reports or opinions by a majority of its members.

It shall assist the European Parliament and the Council in exercising their powers of control over the implementation of the budget.]

CHAPTER 2. PROVISIONS COMMON TO SEVERAL INSTITUTIONS

Article 189. In order to carry out their task and in accordance with the provisions of this Treaty, [the European Parliament acting jointly with the Council,] the Council and the Commission shall make regulations and issue directives, take decisions, make recommendations or deliver opinions.

A regulation shall have general application. It shall be binding in its entirety and directly applicable in all Member States.

A directive shall be binding, as to the result to be achieved, upon each Member State to which it is addressed, but shall leave to the national authorities the choice of form and methods.

A decision shall be binding in its entirety upon those to whom it is addressed.

Recommendations and opinions shall have no binding force.

[*Article 189a.* 1. Where, in pursuance of this Treaty, the Council acts on a proposal from the Commission, unanimity shall be required for an act constituting an amendment to that proposal, subject to Article 189b(4) and (5).

2. As long as the Council has not acted, the Commission may alter its proposal at any time during the procedures leading to the adoption of a Community act.]

[*Article 189b.* 1. Where reference is made in this Treaty to this Article for the adoption of an act, the following procedure shall apply.

2. The Commission shall submit a proposal to the European Parliament and the Council.

The Council, acting by a qualified majority after obtaining the Opinion of the European Parliament, shall adopt a common position. The common position shall be communicated to the European Parliament. The Council shall inform the European Parliament fully of the reasons which led it to adopt its common position. The Commission shall inform the European Parliament fully of its position.

If, within three months of such communication, the European Parliament:

(a) approves the common position, the Council shall definitively adopt the act in question in accordance with that common position;
(b) has not taken a decision, the Council shall adopt the act in question in accordance with its common position;
(c) indicates, by an absolute majority of its component members, that it intends to reject the common position, it shall immediately inform the Council. The Council may convene a meeting of the Conciliation Committee referred to in paragraph 4 to explain further its position. The European Parliament shall thereafter either confirm, by an absolute majority of its component members, its rejection of the com-

mon position, in which event the proposed act shall be deemed not to
have been adopted, or propose amendments in accordance with subparagraph (d) of this paragraph;

(d) proposes amendments to the common position by an absolute majority of its component members, the amended text shall be forwarded
to the Council and to the Commission, which shall deliver an opinion
on those amendments.

3. If, within three months of the matter being referred to it, the
Council, acting by a qualified majority, approves all the amendments of
the European Parliament, it shall amend its common position accordingly
and adopt the act in question; however, the Council shall act unanimously on the amendments on which the Commission has delivered a
negative opinion. If the Council does not approve the act in question, the
President of the Council, in agreement with the President of the
European Parliament, shall forthwith convene a meeting of the
Conciliation Committee.

4. The Conciliation Committee, which shall be composed of the members of the Council or their representatives and an equal number of representatives of the European Parliament, shall have the task of reaching
agreement on a joint text, by a qualified majority of the members of the
Council or their representatives and by a majority of the representatives
of the European Parliament. The Commission shall take part in the
Conciliation Committee's proceedings and shall take all the necessary initiatives with a view to reconciling the positions of the European
Parliament and the Council.

5. If, within six weeks of its being convened, the Conciliation
Committee approves a joint text, the European Parliament, acting by an
absolute majority of the votes cast, and the Council, acting by a qualified
majority, shall have a period of six weeks from that approval in which to
adopt the act in question in accordance with the joint text. If one of the
two institutions fails to approve the proposed act, it shall be deemed not
to have been adopted.

6. Where the Conciliation Committee does not approve a joint text,
the proposed act shall be deemed not not have been adopted unless the
Council, acting by a qualified majority within six weeks of expiry of the
period granted to the Conciliation Committee, confirms the common
position to which it agreed before the conciliation procedure was initiated, possibly with amendments proposed by the European Parliament.
In this case, the act in question shall be finally adopted unless the
European Parliament, within six weeks of the date of confirmation by the
Council, rejects the text by an absolute majority of its component members, in which case the proposed act shall be deemed not to have been
adopted.

7. The periods of three months and six weeks referred to in this Article may be extended by a maximum of one month and two weeks respectively by common accord of the European Parliament and the Council. The period of three months referred to in paragraph 2 shall be automatically extended by two months where paragraph 2(c) applies.

8. The scope of the procedure under this Article may be widened, in accordance with the procedure provided for in Article N(2) of the Treaty on European Union, on the basis of a report to be submitted to the Council by the Commission by 1996 at the latest.]

[*Article 189c.*   Where reference is made in this Treaty to this Article for the adoption of an act, the following procedure shall apply:

(a) The Council, acting by a qualified majority on a proposal from the Commission and after obtaining the Opinion of the European Parliament, shall adopt a common position.

(b) The Council's common position shall be communicated to the European Parliament. The Council and the Commission shall inform the European Parliament fully of the reasons which led to the Council to adopt its common position and also of the Commission's position.

   If, within three months of such communication, the European Parliament approves this common position or has not taken a decision within that period, the Council shall definitively adopt the act in question in accordance with the common position.

(c) The European Parliament may, within the period of three months referred to in point (b), by an absolute majority of its component members, propose amendments to the Council's common position. The European Parliament may also, by the same majority, reject the Council's common position. The result of the proceedings shall be transmitted to the Council and the Commission.

   If the European Parliament has rejected the Council's common position, unanimity shall be required for the Council to act on a second reading.

(d) The Commission shall, within a period of one month, re-examine the proposal on the basis of which the Council adopted its common position, by taking into account the amendments proposed by the European Parliament.

   The Commission shall forward to the Council, at the same time as its re-examined proposal, the amendments of the European Parliament which it has not accepted, and shall express its opinion on them. The Council may adopt these amendments unanimously.

(e) The Council, acting by a qualified majority, shall adopt the proposal as re-examined by the Commission.

Unanimity shall be required for the Council to amend the proposal as re-examined by the Commission.

(f) In the cases referred to in points (c), (d) and (e), the Council shall be required to act within a period of three months. If no decision is taken within this period, the Commission proposal shall be deemed not to have been adopted.

(g) The periods referred to in points (b) and (f) may be extended by a maximum of one month by common accord between the Council and the European Parliament.]

Article 190. Regulations, directives and decisions [adopted jointly by the European Parliament and the Council, and such acts adopted by] {of} the Council or the Commission, shall state the reasons on which they are based and shall refer to any proposals or opinions which were required to be obtained pursuant to this Treaty.

Article 191. [1. Regulations, directives and decisions adopted in accordance with the procedure referred to in Article 189b shall be signed by the President of the European Parliament and by the President of the Council and shall be published in the Official Journal of the Community. They shall enter into force on the date specified in them or, in the absence thereof, on the twentieth day following that of their publication.

2.] Regulations [of the Council and of the Commission, as well as directives of those institutions which are addressed to all Member States] shall be published in the Official Journal of the Community. They shall enter into force on the date specified in them or, in the absence thereof, on the twentieth day following that of their publication.

[3. Other] directives and decisions shall be notified to those to whom they are addressed and shall take effect upon such notification.

Article 192. Decisions of the Council or of the Commission which impose a pecuniary obligation on persons other than States shall be enforceable.

Enforcement shall be governed by the rules of civil procedure in force in the State in the territory of which it is carried out. The order for its enforcement shall be appended to the decision, without other formality than verification of the authenticity of the decision, by the national authority which the Government of each Member State shall designate for this purpose and shall make known to the Commission and to the Court of Justice.

When these formalities have been completed on application by the party concerned, the latter may proceed to enforcement in accordance with the national law, by bringing the matter directly before the competent authority.

Enforcement may be suspended only by a decision of the Court of Justice. However, the courts of the country concerned shall have jurisdiction over complaints that enforcement is being carried out in an irregular manner.

CHAPTER 3. THE ECONOMIC AND SOCIAL COMMITTEE

Article 193. An Economic and Social Committee is hereby established. It shall have advisory status.

The Committee shall consist of representatives of the various categories of economic and social activity, in particular, representatives of producers, farmers, carriers, workers, dealers, craftsmen, professional occupations and representatives of the general public.

Article 194. The number of members of the Committee shall be as follows:

Belgium	12
Denmark	9
Germany	24
Greece	12
Spain	21
France	24
Ireland	9
Italy	24
Luxembourg	[6] {5}
The Netherlands	12
Portugal	12
United Kingdom	24

The members of the Committee shall be appointed by the Council, acting unanimously, for four years. Their appointments shall be renewable.

[The members of the Committee may not be bound by any mandatory instructions. They shall be completely independent in the performance of their duties, in the general interest of the Community.

The Council, acting by a qualified majority, shall determine the allowances of members of the Committee.]

{The members of the Committee shall be appointed in their personal capacity and may not be bound by any mandatory instructions.}

Article 195. 1. For the appointment of the members of the Committee, each Member State shall provide the Council with a list containing twice as many candidates as there are seats allotted to its nationals.

The composition of the Committee shall take account of the need to ensure adequate representation of the various categories of economic and social activity.

2. The Council shall consult the Commission. It may obtain the opinion of European bodies which are representative of the various economic and social sectors to which the activities of the Community are of concern.

Article 196. The Committee shall elect its chairman and officers from among its members for a term of two years.

It shall adopt its rules of procedure {and shall submit them to the Council for its approval, which must be unanimous.}

The Committee shall be convened by its chairman at the request of the Council or of the Commission. [It may also meet on its own initiative.]

Article 197. The Committee shall include specialised sections for the principal fields covered by this Treaty.

In particular, it shall contain an agricultural section and a transport section, which are the subject of special provisions in the Titles relating to agriculture and transport.

These specialised sections shall operate within the general terms of reference of the Committee. They may not be consulted independently of the Committee.

Sub-committees may also be established within the Committee to prepare, on specific questions or in specific fields, draft opinions to be submitted to the Committee for its consideration.

The rules of procedure shall lay down the methods of composition and the terms of reference of the specialised sections and of the sub-committees.

Article 198. The Committee must be consulted by the Council or by the Commission where this Treaty so provides. The Committee may be consulted by these institutions in all cases in which they consider it appropriate. [It may take the initiative of issuing an opinion in cases in which it considers such action appropriate.]

The Council or the Commission shall, if it considers it necessary, set the Committee, for the submission of its opinion, a time limit which may not be less than one month {ten days} from the date on which the chairman receives notification to this effect. Upon expiry of the time limit, the absence of an opinion shall not prevent further action.

The opinion of the Committee and that of the specialised section, together with a record of the proceedings, shall be forwarded to the Council and to the Commission.

[CHAPTER 4. THE COMMITTEE OF THE REGIONS]

[*Article 198a.* A Committee consisting of representatives of regional and local bodies, hereinafter referred to as the 'Committee of the Regions', is hereby established with advisory status.

The number of members of the Committee of the Regions shall be as follows:

Belgium	12
Denmark	9
Germany	24
Greece	12
Spain	21
France	24
Ireland	9
Italy	24
Luxembourg	6
Netherlands	12
Portugal	12
United Kingdom	24

The members of the Committee and an equal number of alternate members shall be appointed for four years by the Council acting unanimously on proposals from the respective Member States. Their term of office shall be renewable.

The members of the Committee may not be bound by any mandatory instructions. They shall be completely independent in the performance of their duties, in the general interest of the Community.]

[*Article 198b.* The Committee of the Regions shall elect its chairman and officers from among its members for a term of two years.

It shall adopt its rules of procedure and shall submit them for approval to the Council, acting unanimously.

The Committee shall be convened by its chairman at the request of the Council or of the Commission. It may also meet on its own initiative.]

[*Article 198c.* The Committee of the Regions shall be consulted by the Council or by the Commission where this Treaty so provides and in all other cases in which one of these two institutions considers it appropriate.

The Council or the Commission shall, if it considers it necessary, set the Committee, for the submission of its opinion, a time-limit which may not be less than one month from the date on which the chairman receives notification to this effect. Upon expiry of the time-limit, the absence of an opinion shall not prevent further action.

Where the Economic and Social Committee is consulted pursuant to Article 198, the Committee of the Regions shall be informed by the Council or the Commission of the request for an opinion. Where it considers that specific regions interests are involved, the Committee of the Regions may issue an opinion on the matter.

It may take the initiative of issuing an opinion in cases in which it considers such action appropriate.

The opinion of the Committee, together with a record of the proceedings, shall be forwarded to the Council and to the Commission.]

[CHAPTER 5. EUROPEAN INVESTMENT BANK]

[*Article 198d.* The European Investment Bank shall have legal personality.

The members of the European Investment Bank shall be the Member States.

The Statute of the European Investment Bank is laid down in a Protocol annexed to this Treaty.]

[*Article 198e.* The task of the European Investment Bank shall be to contribute, by having recourse to the capital market and utilizing its own resources, to the balanced and steady development of the common market in the interest of the Community. For this purpose the Bank shall, operating on a non-profit-making basis, grant loans and give guarantees which facilitate the financing of the following projects in all sectors of the economy:

(a) projects for developing less-developed regions;
(b) projects for modernizing or converting undertakings or for developing fresh activities called for by the progressive establishment of the common market, where these projects are of such a size or nature that they cannot be entirely financed by the various means available in the individual Member States;
(c) projects of common interest to several Member States which are of such a size or nature that they cannot be entirely financed by the various means available in the individual Member States.

In carrying out its task, the Bank shall facilitate the financing of investment programmes in conjunction with assistance from the structural Funds and other Community financial instruments.]

TITLE II. FINANCIAL PROVISIONS

Article 199. All items of revenue and expenditure of the Community, including those relating to the European Social Fund, shall be included in estimates to be drawn up for each financial year and shall be shown in the budget.

[The administrative expenditure occasioned for the institutions by the provisions of the Treaty on European Unity relating to common foreign and security policy and to co-operation in the sphere of justice and home affairs shall be charged to the budget. The operational expenditure occasioned by the implementation of the said provisions may, under the conditions referred to therein, be charged to the budget.]

The revenue and expenditure shown in the budget shall be in balance.

{*Article 200.* 1. The budget revenue shall include, irrespective of any other revenue, financial contributions of Member States on the following scale:

Belgium	7.9
Germany	28
France	28
Italy	28
Luxembourg	0.2
The Netherlands	7.9

2. The financial contributions of Member States to cover the expenditure of the European Social Fund, however, shall be determined on the following scale:

Belgium	8.8
Germany	32
France	32
Italy	20
Luxembourg	0.2
The Netherlands	7

3. The scales may be modified by the Council, acting unanimously.}

Article 201. [Without prejudice to other revenue, the budget shall be financed wholly from own resources.

The Council, acting unanimously on a proposal from the Commission and after consulting the European Parliament, shall lay down provisions relating to the system of own resources of the Community, which it shall recommend to the Member States for adoption in accordance with their respective constitutional requirements.]

{The Commission shall examine the conditions under which the financial contributions of Member States provided for in Art. 200 could be replaced by the Community's own resources, in particular by revenue accruing from the common customs tariff when it has been finally introduced.

To this end, the Commission shall submit proposals to the Council.

After consulting the Assembly on these proposals the Council may, acting unanimously, lay down the appropriate provisions, which it shall recommend to the Member States for adoption in accordance with their respective constitutional requirements.}

[*Article 201a.* With a view to maintaining budgetary discipline, the Commission shall not make any proposal for a Community act, or alter its proposals, or adopt any implementing measure which is likely to have appreciable implications for the budget without providing the assurance that that proposal or that measure is capable of being financed within the limit of the Community's own resources arising under provisions laid down by the Council pursuant to Article 201.]

Article 202. The expenditure shown in the budget shall be authorised for one financial year, unless the regulations made pursuant to Art. 209 provide otherwise.

In accordance with conditions to be laid down pursuant to Art. 209, any appropriations, other than those relating to staff expenditure, that are unexpended at the end of the financial year may be carried forward to the next financial year only.

Appropriations shall be classified under different chapters grouping items of expenditure according to their nature or purpose and subdivided, as far as may be necessary, in accordance with the regulations made pursuant to Art. 209.

The expenditure of the Assembly, the Council, the Commission and the Court of Justice shall be set out in separate parts of the budget, without prejudice to special arrangements for certain common items of expenditure.

Article 203. 1. The financial year shall run from 1 January to 31 December.

2. Each institution of the Community shall, before 1 July, draw up estimates of its expenditure. The Commission shall consolidate these estimates in a preliminary draft budget. It shall attach thereto an opinion which may contain different estimates.

The preliminary draft budget shall contain an estimate of revenue and an estimate of expenditure.

3. The Commission shall place the preliminary draft budget before the Council not later than 1 September of the year preceding that in which the budget is to be implemented.

The Council shall consult the Commission and, where appropriate, the other institutions concerned whenever it intends to depart from the preliminary draft budget.

The Council acting by a qualified majority, shall establish the draft budget and forward it to the Assembly.

4. The draft budget shall be placed before the Assembly not later than 5 October of the year preceding that in which the budget is to be implemented.

The Assembly shall have the right to amend the draft budget, acting by a majority of its members, and to propose to the Council, acting by an absolute majority of the votes cast, modifications to the draft budget relating to expenditure necessarily resulting from this Treaty or from acts adopted in accordance therewith.

If, within forty-five days of the draft budget being placed before it, the Assembly has given its approval, the budget shall stand as finally adopted. If within this period the Assembly has not amended the draft budget nor proposed any modifications thereto, the budget shall be deemed to be finally adopted.

If within this period the Assembly has adopted amendments or proposed modifications, the draft budget together with the amendments or proposed modifications shall be forwarded to the Council.

5. After discussing the draft budget with the Commission and, where appropriate, with the other institutions concerned, the Council shall act under the following conditions:

(a) The Council may, acting by a qualified majority, modify any of the amendments adopted by the Assembly;

(b) With regard to the proposed modifications:

- where a modification proposed by the Assembly does not have the effect of increasing the total amount of the expenditure of an institution, owing in particular to the fact that the increase in expenditure which it would involve would be expressly compensated by one or more proposed modifications correspondingly reducing expenditure, the Council may, acting by a qualified majority, reject the proposed modification. In the absence of a decision to reject it, the proposed modification shall stand as accepted;

- where a modification proposed by the Assembly has the effect of increasing the total amount of the expenditure of an institution, the Council may, acting by a qualified majority, accept this proposed modification. In the absence of a decision to accept it, the proposed modification shall stand as rejected; where in pursuance of one of the two preceding sub-paragraphs, the Council has rejected a proposed modification, it may, acting by a qualified majority, either retain the amount shown in the draft budget or fix another amount.

The draft budget shall be modified on the basis of the proposed modifications accepted by the Council.

If, within fifteen days of the draft budget being placed before it, the Council has not modified any of the amendments adopted by the Assembly and if the modifications proposed by the latter have been accepted, the budget shall be deemed to be finally adopted. The Council shall inform the Assembly that it has not modified any of the amendments and that the proposed modifications have been accepted.

If, within this period the Council has modified one or more of the amendments adopted by the Assembly or if the modifications proposed by the later have been rejected or modified, the modified draft budget shall again be forwarded to the Assembly. The Council shall inform the Assembly of the results of its deliberations.

6. Within fifteen days of the draft budget being placed before it, the Assembly, which shall have been notified of the action taken on its proposed modifications, may, acting by a majority of its members and three-fifths of the votes cast, amend or reject the modifications to its amendments made by the Council and shall adopt the budget accordingly. If, within this period the Assembly has not acted, the budget shall be deemed to be finally adopted.

7. When the procedure provided for in this Article has been completed, the President of the Assembly shall declare that the budget has been finally adopted.

8. However, the Assembly, acting by a majority of its members and two-thirds of the votes cast, may if there are important reasons reject the draft budget and ask for a new draft to be submitted to it.

9. A maximum rate of increase in relation to the expenditure of the same type to be incurred during the current year shall be fixed annually for the total expenditure other than that necessarily resulting from this Treaty or from acts adopted in accordance therewith.

The Commission shall, after consulting the Economic Policy Committee, declare what this maximum rate is as it results from:

- the trend, in terms of volume, of the gross national products within the Community;
- the average variation in the budgets of the Member States; and
- the trend of the cost of living during the preceding financial year.

The maximum rate shall be communicated, before 1 May, to all the institutions of the Community. The latter shall be required to conform to this during the budgetary procedure, subject to the provisions of the fourth and fifth subparagraphs of this paragraph.

If, in respect of expenditure other than that necessarily resulting from this Treaty or from acts adopted in accordance therewith, the actual rate of increase in the draft budget established by the Council is over half the maximum rate, the Assembly may, exercising its right of amendment, further increase the total amount of that expenditure to a limit not exceeding half the maximum rate.

Where the Assembly, the Council or the Commission consider that the activities of the Communities require that the rate determined according to the procedure laid down in this paragraph should be exceeded, another rate may be fixed by agreement between the Council, acting by a qualified majority, and the Assembly, acting by a majority of its members and three-fifths of the votes cast.

10. Each institution shall exercise the powers conferred upon it by this Article , with due regard for the provisions of the Treaty and for acts adopted in accordance therewith, in particular those relating to the Communities' own resources and to the balance between revenue and expenditure.

Article 204. If, at the beginning of a financial year, the budget has not yet been voted, a sum equivalent to not more than one-twelfth of the budget appropriations for the preceding financial year may be spent each month in respect of any chapter or other subdivision of the budget in accordance with the provisions of the regulations made pursuant to Art. 209; this arrangement shall not, however, have the effect of placing at the disposal of the Commission appropriations in excess of one-twelfth of those provided for in the draft budget in course of preparation.

The Council may, acting by a qualified majority, provided that the other conditions laid down in the first subparagraph are observed, authorise expenditure in excess of one-twelfth.

If the decision relates to expenditure which does not necessarily result from this Treaty or from acts adopted in accordance therewith, the Council shall forward it immediately to the Assembly; within thirty days the Assembly, acting by a majority of its members and three-fifths of the votes cast, may adopt a different decision on the expenditure in excess of the one-twelfth referred to in the first subparagraph. This part of the decision of the Council shall be suspended until the Assembly has taken its decision. If within the period the Assembly has not taken a decision which differs from the decision of the Council, the latter shall be deemed to be finally adopted.

The decisions referred to in the second and third subparagraphs shall lay down the necessary measures relating to resources to ensure application of this Article .

Article 205. The Commission shall implement the budget, in accordance with the provisions of the regulations made pursuant to Article 209, on its own responsibility and within the limits of the appropriations, [having regard to the principles of sound financial management].

The regulations shall lay down detailed rules for each institution concerning its part in effecting its own expenditure.

Within the budget, the Commission may, subject to the limits and conditions laid down in the regulations made pursuant to Article 209, transfer appropriations from one chapter to another or from one subdivision to another.

Article 205a. The Commission shall submit annually to the Council and to the Assembly the accounts of the preceding financial year relating to the implementation of the budget. The Commission shall also forward to them a financial statement of the assets and liabilities of the Community.

Article 206. [1. The European Parliament, acting on a recommendation from the Council which shall act by a qualified majority, shall give a discharge to the Commission in respect of the implementation of the budget. To this end, the Council and the European Parliament in turn shall examine the accounts and the financial statement referred to in Article 205a, the annual report by the Court of Auditors together with the replies of the institutions under audit to the observations of the Court of Auditors and any relevant special reports by the Court of Auditors.

2. Before giving a discharge to the Commission, or for any other purpose in connection with the exercise of its powers over the implementation of the budget, the European Parliament may ask to hear the Commission give evidence with regard to the execution of expenditure or the operation of financial control systems. The Commission shall submit any necessary information to the European Parliament at the latter's request.

3. The Commission shall take all appropriate steps to act on the observations in the decisions giving discharge and on other observations by the European Parliament relating to the execution of expenditure, as well as on comments accompanying the recommendations on discharge adopted by the Council.

At the request of the European Parliament or the Council, the Commission shall report on the measures taken in the light of these observations and comments and in particular on the instructions given to the departments which are responsible for the implementation of the budget. These reports shall also be forwarded to the Court of Auditors.]

{*Article 206.* 1. A Court of Auditors is hereby established.*

2. The Court of Auditors shall consist of 12 members.

3. The members of the Court of Auditors shall be chosen from among persons who belong or have belonged in their respective countries to external audit bodies or who are especially qualified for this office. Their independence must be beyond doubt.

* See art. 188a–c]

4. The members of the Court of Auditors shall be appointed for a term of six years by the Council, acting unanimously after consulting the Assembly.

However, when the first appointments are made, four members of the Court of Auditors, chosen by lot, shall be appointed for a term of office of four years only.

The members of the Court of Auditors shall be eligible for re-appointment.

They shall elect the President of the Court of Auditors from among their number for a term of three years. The President may be re-elected.

5. The members of the Court of Auditors shall, in the general interest of the Community, be completely independent in the performance of their duties.

In the performance of these duties, they shall neither seek nor take instructions from any Government or from any other body. They shall refrain from any action incompatible with their duties.

6. The members of the Court of Auditors may not, during their term of office, engage in any other occupation, whether gainful or not. When entering upon their duties they shall give a solemn undertaking that, both during and after their term of office, they will respect the obligations arising therefrom and in particular their duty to behave with integrity and discretion as regards the acceptance, after they have ceased to hold office, of certain appointments or benefits.

7. Apart from normal replacement, or death, the duties of a member of the Court of Auditors shall end when he resigns, or is compulsorily retired by a ruling of the Court of Justice pursuant to paragraph 8.

The vacancy thus caused shall be filled for the remainder of the member's term of office.

Save in the case of compulsory retirement, members of the Court of Auditors shall remain in office until they have been replaced.

8. A member of the Court of Auditors may be deprived of his office or of his right to a pension or other benefits in its stead only if the Court of Justice, at the request of the Court of Auditors, finds that he no longer fulfils the requisite conditions or meets the obligations arising from his office.

9. The Council, acting by a qualified majority, shall determine the conditions of employment of the President and the members of the Court of Auditors and in particular their salaries, allowances and pensions. It shall also, by the same majority, determine any payment to be made instead of remuneration.

10. The provisions of the Protocol on the Privileges and Immunities of the European Communities applicable to the Judges of the Court of Justice shall also apply to the members of the Court of Auditors.}

{*Article 206a.*   1. The Court of Auditors shall examine the accounts of all revenue and expenditure of the Community. It shall also examine the accounts of all revenue and expenditure of all bodies set up by the Community insofar as the relevant constituent instrument does not preclude such examination.

2. The Court of Auditors shall examine whether all revenue has been received and all expenditure incurred in a lawful and regular manner and whether the financial management has been sound.

The audit of revenue shall be carried out on the basis both of the amounts established as due and the amounts actually paid to the Community.

The audit of expenditure shall be carried out on the basis both of commitments undertaken and payments made.

These audits may be carried out before the closure of accounts for the financial year in question.

3. The audit shall be based on records and, if necessary, performed on the spot in the institutions of the Community and in the Member States. In the Member States the audit shall be carried out in liaison with the national audit bodies or, if these do not have the necessary powers, with the competent national departments. These bodies or departments shall inform the Court of Auditors whether they intend to take part in the audit.

The institutions of the Community and the national audit bodies or, if these do not have the necessary powers, the competent national departments, shall forward to the Court of Auditors, at its request, any document or information necessary to carry out its task.

4. The Court of Auditors shall draw up an annual report after the close of each financial year. It shall be forwarded to the institutions of the Community and shall be published, together with the replies of these institutions to the observations of the Court of Auditors, in the Official Journal of the European Communities.

The Court of Auditors may also, at any time, submit observations on specific questions and deliver opinions at the request of one of the institutions of the Community.

It shall adopt its annual reports or opinions by a majority of its members.

It shall assist the Assembly and the Council in exercising their powers of control over the implementation of the budget.}

{*Article 206b.*   The Assembly, acting on a recommendation from the Council which shall act by a qualified majority, shall give a discharge to the Commission in respect of the implementation of the budget. To this end, the Council and the Assembly in turn shall examine the accounts and the financial statement referred to in Art. 205a and the annual report by the Court of Auditors together with the replies of the institutions under audit to the observations of the Court of Auditors.}

Article 207. The budget shall be drawn up in the unit of account determined in accordance with the provisions of the regulations made pursuant to Art. 209.

The financial contributions provided for in Art. 200(1) shall be placed at the disposal of the Community by the Member States in their national currencies.

The available balances of these contributions shall be deposited with the Treasuries of Member States or with bodies designated by them. While on deposit, such funds shall retain the value corresponding to the parity, at the date of deposit, in relation to the unit of account referred to in the first paragraph.

The balances may be invested on terms to be agreed between the Commission and the Member State concerned.

The regulations made pursuant to Art. 209 shall lay down the technical conditions under which financial operations relating to the European Social Fund shall be carried out.

Article 208. The Commission may, provided it notifies the competent authorities of the Member States concerned, transfer into the currency of one of the Member States its holdings in the currency of another Member State, to the extent necessary to enable them to be used for purposes which come within the scope of this Treaty. The Commission shall as far as possible avoid making such transfers if it possesses cash or liquid assets in the currencies which it needs.

The Commission shall deal with each Member State through the authority designated by the State concerned. In carrying out financial operations the Commission shall employ the services of the bank of issue of the Member State concerned or of any other financial institution approved by that State.

Article 209. The Council, acting unanimously on a proposal from the Commission and after consulting the [European Parliament] {Assembly} and obtaining the opinion of the Court of Auditors, shall:

(a) make financial regulations specifying in particular the procedure to be adopted for establishing and implementing the budget and for presenting and auditing accounts;

(b) determine the methods and procedures whereby the budget revenue provided under the arrangements relating to the Communities' own resources shall be made available to the Commission, and determine the measures to be applied, if need be, to meet cash requirements;

(c) lay down rules concerning the responsibility of [financial controllers,] authorising officers and accounting officers and concerning appropriate arrangements for inspection.

[*Article 209a.* Member States shall take the same measures to counter fraud affecting the financial interests of the Community as they take to counter fraud affecting their own financial interests.

Without prejudice to other provisions of this Treaty, Member States shall co-ordinate their action aimed at protecting the financial interests of the Community against fraud. To this end they shall organize, with the help of the Commission, close and regular co-operation between the competent departments of their administrations.]

Part Six. General and Final Provisions

Article 210. The Community shall have legal personality.

Article 211. In each of the Member States, the Community shall enjoy the most extensive legal capacity accorded to legal persons under their laws; it may, in particular, acquire or dispose of movable and immovable property and may be a party to legal proceedings. To this end, the Community shall be represented by the Commission.

[Article 212 was repealed by the Merger Treaty.]

Article 213. The Commission may, within the limits and under the conditions laid down by the Council in accordance with the provisions of this Treaty, collect any information and carry out any checks required for the performance of the tasks entrusted to it.

Article 214. The members of the institutions of the Community, the members of committees and the officials and other servants of the Community shall be required, even after their duties have ceased, not to disclose information of the kind covered by the obligation of professional secrecy, in particular information about undertakings, their business relations or their cost components.

Article 215. The contractual liability of the Community shall be governed by the law applicable to the contract in question.

In the case of non-contractual liability, the Community shall, in accordance with the general principles common to the laws of the Member States, make good any damage caused by its institutions or by its servants in the performance of their duties.

[The preceding paragraph shall apply under the same conditions to damage caused by the ECB or by its servants in the performance of their duties.]

The personal liability of its servants towards the Community shall be governed by the provisions laid down in their Staff Regulations or in the Conditions of Employment applicable to them.

Article 216. The seat of the institutions of the Community shall be determined by common accord of the Governments of the Member States.

Article 217. The rules governing the languages of the institutions of the Community shall, without prejudice to the provisions contained in the rules of procedure of the Court of Justice, be determined by the Council, acting unanimously.

[Article 218 was repealed by the Merger Treaty.]

Merger Treaty

Article 28. The European Communities shall enjoy in the territories of the Member States such privileges and immunities as are necessary for the performance of their tasks, under the conditions laid down in the Protocol annexed to this Treaty. The same shall apply to the European Investment Bank.

Article 219. Member States undertake not to submit a dispute concerning the interpretation or application of this Treaty to any method of settlement other than those provided for therein.

Article 220. Member States shall, so far as is necessary, enter into negotiations with each other with a view to securing for the benefit of their nationals:

– the protection of persons and the enjoyment and protection of rights under the same conditions as those accorded by each State to its own nationals;
– the abolition of double taxation within the Community;
– the mutual recognition of companies or firms within the meaning of the

second paragraph of Art. 58, the retention of legal personality in the event of transfer of their seat from one country to another, and the possibility of mergers between companies or firms governed by the laws of different countries;

– the simplification of formalities governing the reciprocal recognition and enforcement of judgments of courts or tribunals and of arbitration awards.

Article 221. Within three years of the entry into force of this Treaty, Member States shall accord nationals of the other Member States the same treatment as their own nationals as regards participation in the capital of companies or firms within the meaning of Art. 58, without prejudice to the application of the other provisions of this Treaty.

Article 222. This Treaty shall in no way prejudice the rules in Member States governing the system of property ownership.

Article 223. 1. The provisions of this Treaty shall not preclude the application of the following rules:

(a) No Member State shall be obliged to supply information the disclosure of which it considers contrary to the essential interests of its security;

(b) Any Member State may take such measures as it considers necessary for the protection of the essential interests of its security which are connected with the production of or trade in arms, munitions and war material; such measures shall not, however, adversely affect the conditions of competition in the common market regarding products which are not intended for specifically military purposes.

2. During the first year after the entry into force of this Treaty, the Council shall, acting unanimously, draw up a list of products to which the provisions of paragraph 1 (b) shall apply.

3. The Council may, acting unanimously on a proposal from the Commission, make changes in this list.

Article 224. Member States shall consult each other with a view to taking together the steps needed to prevent the functioning of the common market being affected by measures which a Member State may be called upon to take in the event of serious internal disturbance affecting the maintenance of law and order, in the event of war or serious international tension constituting a threat of war, or in order to carry out obligations it has accepted for the purpose of maintaining peace and international security.

Article 225. If measures taken in the circumstances referred to in Arts. 223 and 224 have the effect of distorting the conditions of competition in the common market, the Commission shall, together with the State concerned, examine how these measures can be adjusted to the rules laid down in this Treaty.

By way of derogation from the procedure laid down in Arts. 169 and 170, the Commission or any Member State may bring the matter directly before the Court of Justice if it considers that another Member State is making improper use of the powers provided for in Arts. 223 and 224. The Court of Justice shall give its ruling *in camera.*

Article 226. 1. If, during the transitional period, difficulties arise which are serious and liable to persist in any sector of the economy or which could bring about serious deterioration in the economic situation of a given area, a Member State may apply for authorisation to take protective measures in order to rectify the situation and adjust the sector concerned to the economy of the common market.

2. On application by the State concerned, the Commission shall, by emergency procedure, determine without delay the protective measures which it considers necessary, specifying the circumstances and the manner in which they are to be put into effect.

3. The measures authorised under paragraph 2 may involve derogations from the rules of this Treaty, to such an extent and for such periods as are strictly necessary in order to attain the objectives referred to in paragraph 1. Priority shall be given to such measures as will least disturb the functioning of the common market.

Article 227. 1. This Treaty shall apply to the Kingdom of Belgium, the Kingdom of Denmark, the Federal Republic of Germany, the Hellenic Republic, the Kingdom of Spain, the French Republic, Ireland, the Italian Republic, the Grand Duchy of Luxembourg, the Kingdom of the Netherlands, the Portuguese Republic and the United Kingdom of Great Britain and Northern Ireland.

2. With regard to {Algeria and} the French overseas departments, the general and particular provisions of this Treaty relating to:

- the free movement of goods;
- agriculture, save for Art. 40 (4);
- the liberalisation of services;
- the rules on competition;
- the protective measures provided for in Arts. 108[h], 109[i] and 226;
- the institutions;

shall apply as soon as this Treaty enters into force.

The conditions under which the other provisions of this Treaty are to apply shall be determined, within two years of the entry into force of this Treaty, by decisions of the Council, acting unanimously on a proposal from the Commission.

The institutions of the Community will, within the framework of the procedures provided for in this Treaty, in particular Art. 226, take care that the economic and social development of these areas is made possible.

3. The special arrangements for association set out in Part Four of this Treaty shall apply to the overseas countries and territories listed in Annex IV to this Treaty.

This Treaty shall not apply to those overseas countries and territories having special relations with the United Kingdom of Great Britain and Northern Ireland which are not included in the aforementioned list.

4. The provisions of this Treaty shall apply to the European territories for whose external relations a Member State is responsible.

5. Notwithstanding the preceding paragraphs:

(a) This Treaty shall not apply to the Faroe Islands. {The Government of the Kingdom of Denmark may, however, give notice, by a declaration deposited by 31 December 1975 at the latest with the Government of the Italian Republic, which shall transmit a certified copy thereof to each of the Governments of the other Member States, that this Treaty shall apply to those Islands. In that event, this Treaty shall apply to those Islands from the first day of the second month following the deposit of the declaration.}

(b) This Treaty shall not apply to the Sovereign Base Areas of the United Kingdom of Great Britain and Northern Ireland in Cyprus.

(c) This Treaty shall apply to the Channel Islands and the Isle of Man only to the extent necessary to ensure the implementation of the arrangements for those islands set out in the Treaty concerning the accession of new Member States to the European {Economic} Community and to the European Atomic Energy Community signed on 22 January 1972.

Article 228. [1. Where this Treaty provides for the conclusion of agreements between the Community and one or more States or international organizations, the Commission shall make recommendations to the Council, which shall authorize the Commission to open the necessary negotiations. The Commission shall conduct these negotiations in consultation with special committees appointed by the Council to assist it in this task and within the framework of such directives as the Council may issue to it.

In exercising the powers conferred upon it by this paragraph, the Council shall act by a qualified majority, except in the cases provided for in the second sentence of paragraph 2, for which it shall act unanimously.

2. Subject to the powers vested in the Commission in this field, the agreements shall be concluded by the Council, acting by a qualified majority on a proposal from the Commission. The Council shall act unanimously when the agreement covers a field for which unanimity is required for the adoption of internal rules, and for the agreements referred to in Article 238.

3. The Council shall conclude agreements after consulting the European Parliament, except for the agreements referred to in Article 113(3), including cases where the agreement covers a field for which the procedure referred to in Article 189b or that referred to in Article 189c is required for the adoption of internal rules. The European Parliament shall deliver its Opinion within a time limit which the Council may lay down according to the urgency of the matter. In the absence of an Opinion within that time limit, the Council may act.

By way of derogation from the previous subparagraph, agreements referred to in Article 238, other agreements establishing a specific institutional framework by organizing cooperation procedures, agreements having important budgetary implications for the Community and agreements entailing amendment of an act adopted under the procedure referred to in Article 189b shall be concluded after the assent of the European Parliament has been obtained.

The Council and the European Parliament may, in an urgent situation, agree upon a time limit for the assent.

4. When concluding an agreement, the Council may, by way of derogation from paragraph 2, empower the Commission to approve modifications on behalf of the Community where the agreement provides for them to be adopted by a simplified procedure or by a body set up by the agreement; it may attach specific conditions to such empowerment.

5. When the Council envisages concluding an agreement which calls for amendments to this Treaty, the amendments must first be adopted in accordance with the procedure laid down in Article N of the Treaty on European Union.

6. The Council, the Commission or a Member State may obtain the opinion of the Court of Justice as to whether an agreement envisaged is compatible with the provisions of this Treaty. Where the opinion of the Court of Justice is adverse, the agreement may enter into force only in accordance with Article N of the Treaty on European Union.

7. Agreements concluded under the conditions set out in this Article shall be binding on the institutions of the Community and on Member States.]

{1. Where this Treaty provides for the conclusion of agreements between the Community and one or more States or an international organisation, such agreements shall be negotiated by the Commission.

Subject to the powers vested in the Commission in this field, such agreements shall be concluded by the Council, after consulting the Assembly where required by this Treaty.

The Council, the Commission or a Member State may obtain beforehand the opinion of the Court of Justice as to whether an agreement envisaged is compatible with the provisions of this Treaty. Where the opinion of the Court of Justice is adverse, the agreement may enter into force only in accordance with Art. 236.

2. Agreements concluded under these conditions shall be binding on the institutions of the Community and on Member States.}

[*Article 228a.*   Where it is provided, in a common position or in a joint action adopted according to the provisions of the Treaty on European Union relating to the common foreign and security policy, for an action by the Community to interrupt or to reduce, in part or completely, economic relations with one or more third countries, the Council shall take the necessary urgent measures. The Council shall act by a qualified majority on a proposal from the Commission.]

Article 229.   It shall be for the Commission to ensure the maintenance of all appropriate relations with the organs of the United Nations, of its specialised agencies and of the General Agreement on Tariffs and Trade.

The Commission shall also maintain such relations as are appropriate with all international organisations.

Article 230.   The Community shall establish all appropriate forms of co-operation with the Council of Europe.

Article 231.   The Community shall establish close co-operation with the Organisation for {European} Economic Co-operation [and Development], the details [of which shall be] {to} be determined by common accord.

Article 232.   1. The provisions of this Treaty shall not affect the provisions of the Treaty establishing the European Coal and Steel Community, in particular as regards the rights and obligations of Member States, the powers of the institutions of that Community and the rules laid down by that Treaty for the functioning of the common market in coal and steel.

2. The provisions of this Treaty shall not derogate from those of the Treaty establishing the European Atomic Energy Community.

Article 233.   The provisions of this Treaty shall not preclude the existence or completion of regional unions between Belgium, Luxembourg and the Netherlands, to the extent that the objectives of these regional unions are not attained by application of this Treaty.

Article 234. The rights and obligations arising from agreements concluded before the entry into force of this Treaty between one or more Member States on the one hand, and one or more third countries on the other, shall not be affected by the provisions of this Treaty.

To the extent that such agreements are not compatible with this Treaty, the Member State or States concerned shall take all appropriate steps to eliminate the incompatibilities established. Member States shall, where necessary, assist each other to this end and shall, where appropriate, adopt a common attitude.

In applying the agreements referred to in the first paragraph, Member States shall take into account the fact that the advantages accorded under this Treaty by each Member State form an integral part of the establishment of the Community and are thereby inseparably linked with the creation of common institutions, the conferring of powers upon them and the granting of the same advantages by all the other Member States.

Article 235. If action by the Community should prove necessary to attain, in the course of the operation of the common market, one of the objectives of the Community and this Treaty has not provided the necessary powers, the Council shall, acting unanimously on a proposal from the Commission and after consulting the Assembly, take the appropriate measures.

{*Article 236.* The Government of any Member State or the Commission may submit to the Council proposals for the amendment of this Treaty.

If the Council, after consulting the Assembly and, where appropriate, the Commission, delivers an opinion in favour of calling a conference of representatives of the Governments of the Member States, the conference shall be convened by the President of the Council for the purpose of determining by common accord the amendments to be made to this Treaty.

The amendments shall enter into force after being ratified by all the Member States in accordance with their respective constitutional requirements.}

[For amendment procedures, see TEU, art. N p. 224]

{*Article 237.* Any European State may apply to become a member of the Community. It shall address its application to the Council, which shall act unanimously after consulting the Commission and after receiving the assent of the European Parliament which shall act by an absolute majority of its component members.

The conditions of admission and the adjustments to this Treaty necessitated thereby shall be the subject of an agreement between the Member States and the applicant State. This agreement shall be submitted for ratification by all the contracting States in accordance with their respective constitutional requirements.}

[For membership applications, see TEU, art. O p. 225]

Article 238. The Community may conclude with [one or more States or international organizations] {a third State, a union of States or an international organization} agreements establishing an association involving reciprocal rights and obligations, common action and special procedures.

{These agreements shall be concluded by the Council, acting unanimously and after receiving the assent of the European Parliament which shall act by an absolute majority of its component members.

Where such agreements call for amendments to this Treaty, these amendments shall first be adopted in accordance with the procedure laid down in Art. 236.}

Article 239. The Protocols annexed to this Treaty by common accord of the Member States shall form an integral part thereof.

Article 240. This Treaty is concluded for an unlimited period.

SETTING UP OF THE INSTITUTIONS

Article 241. The Council shall meet within one month of the entry into force of this Treaty.

Article 242. The Council shall, within three months of its first meeting, take all appropriate measures to constitute the Economic and Social Committee.

Article 243. The Assembly shall meet within two months of the first meeting of the Council, having been convened by the President of the Council, in order to elect its officers and draw up its rules of procedure. Pending the election of its officers, the oldest member shall take the chair.

Article 244. The Court of Justice shall take up its duties as soon as its members have been appointed. Its first President shall be appointed for three years in the same manner as its members.

The Court of Justice shall adopt its rules of procedure within three months of taking up its duties.

No matter may be brought before the Court of Justice until its rules of procedure have been published. The time within which an action must be brought shall run only from the date of this publication.

Upon his appointment, the President of the Court of Justice shall exercise the powers conferred upon him by this Treaty.

Article 245. The Commission shall take up its duties and assume the responsibilities conferred upon it by this Treaty as soon as its members have been appointed.

Upon taking up its duties, the Commission shall undertake the studies and arrange the contacts needed for making an overall survey of the economic situation of the Community.

Article 246. 1. The first financial year shall run from the date on which this Treaty enters into force until 31 December following. Should this Treaty, however, enter into force during the second half of the year, the first financial year shall run until 31 December of the following year.

2. Until the budget for the first financial year has been established, Member States shall make the Community interest-free advances which shall be deducted from their financial contributions to the implementation of the budget.

3. Until the Staff Regulations of officials and the Conditions of Employment of other servants of the Community provided for in Art. 212 have been laid down, each institution shall recruit the staff it needs and to this end conclude contracts of limited duration.

Each institution shall examine together with the Council any question concerning the number, remuneration and distribution of posts.

FINAL PROVISIONS

Article 247. This Treaty shall be ratified by the High Contracting Parties in accordance with their respective constitutional requirements. The instruments of ratification shall be deposited with the Government of the Italian Republic.

This Treaty shall enter into force on the first day of the month following the deposit of the instrument of ratification by the last signatory State to take this step. If, however, such deposit is made less than fifteen days before the beginning of the following month, this Treaty shall not enter into force until the first day of the second month after the date of such deposit.

Article 248. This Treaty, drawn up in a single original in the Dutch, French, German and Italian languages, all four texts being equally authentic, shall be deposited in the archives of the Government of the Italian Republic, which shall transmit a certified copy to each of the Governments of the other signatory States.

In witness whereof, the undersigned Plenipotentiaries have signed this Treaty.

Done at Rome this twenty-fifth day of March in the year one thousand nine hundred and fifty-seven.

[Here follow the signatures.]

Annexes

[EXTRACTS]

ANNEX IV. OVERSEAS COUNTRIES AND TERRITORIES
to which the provisions of Part Four of this Treaty apply.

French West Africa: Senegal, French Sudan, French Guinea, Ivory Coast, Dahomey, Mauritania, Niger and Upper Volta;

French Equatorial Africa: Middle Congo, Ubangi-Shari, Chad and Gabon;

Saint Pierre and Miquelon, the Comoro Archipelago, Madagascar and dependencies, French Somaliland, New Caledonian and dependencies, French Settlements in Oceania, Southern and Antarctic Territories;

The Autonomous Republic of Togoland;
The Trust Territory of the Cameroons under French administration;
The Belgian Congo and Ruanda-Urundi;
The Trust Territory of Somaliland under Italian administration;
The Netherlands New Guinea;
The Netherlands Antilles;
Anglo-French Condominium of the New Hebrides;
The Bahamas;
Bermuda;
British Antarctic Territory;
British Honduras;
British Indian Ocean Territory;
British Solomon Islands;
British Virgin Islands;
Brunei.

Associated States in the Caribbean: Antigua, Dominica, Grenada, St. Lucia, St. Vincent, St. Kitts-Nevis-Anguilla;

Cayman Islands;
Central and Southern Line Islands;
Falkland Islands and Dependencies;
Gilbert and Ellice Islands;
Montserrat;
Pitcairn;
St. Helena and Dependencies;
The Seychelles;
Turks and Caicos Islands;
Greenland.

Protocol on the Privileges and Immunities of the European Communities

The High Contracting Parties,

Considering that, in accordance with Art. 28 of the Treaty establishing a Single Council and a Single Commission of the European Communities, these Communities and the European Investment Bank shall enjoy in the territories of the Member States such privileges and immunities as are necessary for the performance of their tasks,

Have agreed upon the following provisions, which shall be annexed to this Treaty:

CHAPTER I. PROPERTY, FUNDS, ASSETS AND OPERATIONS OF THE EUROPEAN COMMUNITIES

Article 1. The premises and buildings of the Communities shall be inviolable. They shall be exempt from search, requisition, confiscation or expropriation. The property and assets of the Communities shall not be the subject of any administrative or legal measure of constraint without the authorisation of the Court of Justice.

Article 2. The archives of the Communities shall be inviolable.

Article 3. The Communities, their assets, revenues and other property shall be exempt from all direct taxes.

The Governments of the Member States shall, wherever possible, take the appropriate measures to remit or refund the amount of indirect taxes or sales taxes included in the price of movable or immovable property, where the Communities make, for their official use, substantial purchases the price of which includes taxes of this kind. These provisions shall not be applied, however, so as to have the effect of distorting competition within the Communities.

No exemption shall be granted in respect of taxes and dues which amount merely to charges for public utility services.

Article 4. The Communities shall be exempt from all customs duties, prohibitions and restrictions on imports and exports in respect of articles intended for their official use; articles so imported shall not be disposed of, whether or not in return for payment, in the territory of the country into which they have been imported, except under conditions approved by the Government of that country.

The Communities shall also be exempt from any customs duties and any prohibitions and restrictions on imports and exports in respect of their publications.

Article 5. The European Coal and Steel Community may hold currency of any kind and operate accounts in any currency.

CHAPTER II. COMMUNICATIONS AND LAISSEZ-PASSER

Article 6. For their official communications and the transmission of all their documents, the institutions of the Communities shall enjoy in the territory of each Member State the treatment accorded by that State to diplomatic missions.

Official correspondence and other official communications of the institutions of the Communities shall not be subject to censorship.

Article 7. 1. *Laissez-passer* in a form to be prescribed by the Council, which shall be recognised as valid travel documents by the authorities of the Member States, may be issued to members and servants of the institutions of the Communities by the Presidents of these institutions. These *laissez-passer* shall be issued to officials and other servants under conditions laid down in the Staff Regulations of officials and the Conditions of Employment of other servants of the Communities.

The Commission may conclude agreements for these *laissez-passer* to be recognised as valid travel documents within the territory of third countries.

2. The provisions of Art. 6 of the Protocol on the Privileges and Immunities of the European Coal and Steel Community shall, however, remain applicable to members and servants of the institutions who are at the date of entry into force of this Treaty in possession of the

laissez-passer provided for in that Article, until the provisions of paragraph 1 of this Article are applied.

CHAPTER III. MEMBERS OF THE ASSEMBLY

Article 8.   No administrative or other restriction shall be imposed on the free movement of members of the Assembly travelling to or from the place of meeting of the Assembly.

Members of the Assembly shall, in respect of customs and exchange control, be accorded:

(a) by their own Government, the same facilities as those accorded to senior officials travelling abroad on temporary official missions;
(b) by the Governments of other Member States, the same facilities as those accorded to representatives of foreign Governments on temporary official missions.

Article 9.   Members of the Assembly shall not be subject to any form of inquiry, detention or legal proceedings in respect of opinions expressed or votes cast by them in the performance of their duties.

Article 10.   During the sessions of the Assembly, its members shall enjoy:

(a) in the territory of their own State, the immunities accorded to members of their parliament;
(b) in the territory of any other Member State, immunity from any measure of detention and from legal proceedings.

Immunity shall likewise apply to members while they are travelling to and from the place of meeting of the Assembly.

Immunity cannot be claimed when a member is found in the act of committing an offence and shall not prevent the Assembly from exercising its right to waive the immunity of one of its members.

CHAPTER IV. REPRESENTATIVES OF MEMBER STATES TAKING PART IN THE WORK OF THE INSTITUTIONS OF THE EUROPEAN COMMUNITIES

Article 11.   Representatives of Member States taking part in the work of the institutions of the Communities, their advisers and technical experts shall, in the performance of their duties and during their travel to and from the place of meeting, enjoy the customary privileges, immunities and facilities.

This Article shall also apply to members of the advisory bodies of the Communities.

CHAPTER V. OFFICIALS AND OTHER SERVANTS OF THE EUROPEAN COMMUNITIES

Article 12. In the territory of each Member State and whatever their nationality, officials and other servants of the Communities shall:

(a) subject to the provisions of the Treaties relating, on the one hand, to the rules on the liability of officials and other servants towards the Communities and, on the other hand, to the jurisdiction of the Court in disputes between the Communities and their officials and other servants, shall be immune from legal proceedings in respect of acts performed by them in their official capacity, including their words spoken or written. They shall continue to enjoy this immunity after they have ceased to hold office;

(b) together with their spouses and dependent members of their families, not be subject to immigration restrictions or to formalities for registration of aliens;

(c) in respect of currency or exchange regulations, be accorded the same facilities as are customarily accorded to officials of international organisations;

(d) enjoy the right to import free of duty their furniture and effects at the time of first taking up their post in the country concerned, and the right to re-export free of duty their furniture and effects, on termination of their duties in that country, subject in either case to the conditions considered to be necessary by the Government of the country in which this right is exercised;

(e) have the right to import free of duty a motor car for their personal use, acquired either in the country of their last residence or in the country of which they are nationals on the terms ruling in the home market in that country, and to re-export it free of duty, subject in either case to the conditions considered to be necessary by the Government of the country concerned.

Article 13. Officials and other servants of the Communities shall be liable to a tax for the benefit of the Communities on salaries, wages and emoluments paid to them by the Communities, in accordance with the conditions and procedure laid down by the Council, acting on a proposal from the Commission.

They shall be exempt from national taxes on salaries, wages and emoluments paid by the Communities.

Article 14. In the application of income tax, wealth tax and death duties and in the application of conventions on the avoidance of double taxation concluded between Member States of the Communities, officials and other servants of the Communities who, solely by reason of the performance of their duties in the services of the Communities, establish their residence in the territory of a Member State other than their country of domicile for tax purposes at the time of entering the service of the Communities, shall be considered, both in the country of their actual residence and in the country of domicile for tax purposes, as having maintained their domicile in the latter country provided that it is a member of the Communities. This provision shall also apply to a spouse to the extent that the latter is not separately engaged in a gainful occupation, and to children dependent on and in the care of the persons referred to in this Article .

Movable property belonging to persons referred to in the first paragraph and situated in the territory of the country where they are staying shall be exempt from death duties in that country; such property shall, for the assessment of such duty, be considered as being in the country of domicile for tax purposes, subject to the rights of third countries and to the possible application of provisions of international conventions on double taxation.

Any domicile acquired solely by reason of the performance of duties in the service of other international organisations shall not be taken into consideration in applying the provisions of this Article.

Article 15. The Council shall, acting unanimously on a proposal from the Commission, lay down the scheme of social security benefits for officials and other servants of the Communities.

Article 16. The Council shall, acting on a proposal from the Commission and after consulting the other institutions concerned, determine the categories of officials and other servants of the Communities to whom the provisions of Art. 12, the second paragraph of Art. 13, and Art. 14 shall apply, in whole or in part.

The names, grades and addresses of officials and other servants included in such categories shall be communicated periodically to the Governments of the Member States.

CHAPTER VI. PRIVILEGES AND IMMUNITIES OF MISSIONS OF THIRD COUNTRIES ACCREDITED TO THE EUROPEAN COMMUNITIES

Article 17. The Member State in whose territory the Communities have their seat shall accord the customary diplomatic immunities and privileges to missions of third countries accredited to the Communities.

CHAPTER VII. GENERAL PROVISIONS

Article 18. Privileges, immunities and facilities shall be accorded to officials and other servants of the Communities solely in the interests of the Communities.

Each institution of the Communities shall be required to waive the immunity accorded to an official or other servant wherever that institution considers that the waiver of such immunity is not contrary to the interests of the Communities.

Article 19. The institutions of the Communities shall, for the purpose of applying this Protocol, co-operate with the responsible authorities of the Member States concerned.

Article 20 Arts. 12 to 15 and Art. 18 shall apply to members of the Commission.

Article 21. Arts. 12 to 15 and Art. 18 shall apply to the Judges, the Advocates-General, the Registrar and the Assistant Rapporteurs of the Court of Justice, without prejudice to the provisions of Art. 3 of the Protocols on the Statute of the Court of Justice concerning immunity from legal proceedings of Judges and Advocates-General.

Article 22. This Protocol shall also apply to the European Investment Bank, to the members of its organs, to its staff and to the representatives of the Member States taking part in its activities, without prejudice to the provisions of the Protocol on the Statute of the Bank.

The European Investment Bank shall in addition be exempt from any form of taxation or imposition of a like nature on the occasion of any increase in its capital and from the various formalities which may be connected therewith in the State where the Bank has its seat. Similarly, its dissolution or liquidation shall not give rise to any imposition. Finally, the activities of the Bank and of its organs carried on in accordance with its Statute shall not be subject to any turnover tax.

In witness whereof, the undersigned Plenipotentiaries have signed this Protocol.

Done at Brussels this 8 April 1965.

[Here follow the signatures.]

[*Article 23.* This Protocol shall also apply to the European Central Bank, to the members of its organs and to its staff, without prejudice to the provisions of the Protocol on the Statute of the European System of Central Banks and the European Central Bank.

The European Central Bank shall, in addition, be exempt from any form of taxation or imposition of a like nature on the occasion of any increase in its capital and from the various formalities which may be connected therewith in the State where the bank has its seat. The activities of the Bank and of its organs carried on in accordance with the Statute of the European System of Central Banks and of the European Central Bank shall not be subject to any turnover tax.

The above provisions shall also apply to the European Monetary Institute. Its dissolution or liquidation shall not give rise to any imposition.]

[Added by TEU Protocol 7]

Protocols

Annexed by the Treaty on European Union to the Treaty Establishing the European Community

[NB The formal clauses have been omitted, the titles shortened, and the texts numbered.]

1 Property in Denmark Notwithstanding the provisions of this Treaty, Denmark may maintain the existing legislation on the acquisition of second homes.

2 Article 119 For the purposes of Article 119 of this Treaty, benefits under occupational social security schemes shall not be considered as remuneration if and in so far as they are attributable to periods of employment prior to 17 May 1990, except in the case of workers or those claiming under them who have before that date intitiated legal proceedings or introduced an equivalent claim under the applicable national law.

3 ESCB and ECB Statute

CHAPTER I. CONSTITUTION OF THE ESCB

Article 1. The European System of Central Banks.

1.1. The European System of Central Banks (ESCB) and the European Central Bank (ECB) shall be established in accordance with Article 4a of this Treaty; they shall perform their tasks and carry on their activities in accordance with the provisions of this Treaty and of this Statute.

1.2. In accordance with Article 106(1) on this Treaty, the ESCB shall be composed of the ECB and of the central banks of the Member States ('national central banks'). The Insitut monétaire luxembourgeois will be the central bank of Luxembourg.

CHAPTER II. OBJECTIVES AND TASKS OF THE ESCB

Article 2. Objectives
In accordance with Article 105(1) of this Treaty, the primary objective of the ESCB shall be to maintain price stability. Without prejudice to the objective of price stability, it shall support the general economic policies in the Community with a view to contributing to the achievement of the objectives of the Community as laid down in Article 2 of this Treaty. The ESCB shall act in accordance with the principle of an open market economy with free competition, favouring an efficient allocation of resources, and in compliance with the principles set out in Article 3a of this Treaty.

Article 3. Tasks
3.1. In accordance with Article 105(2) of this Treaty, the basic tasks to be carried out through the ESCB shall be:

- to define and implement the monetary policy of the Community;
- to conduct foreign exchange operations consistent with the provisions of Article 109 of this Treaty;
- to hold and manage the official foreign reserves of the Member States;
- to promote the smooth operation on payment systems.

3.2. In accordance with Article 105(3) of this Treaty, the third indent of Article 3.1 shall be without prejudice to the holding and management by the governments of Member States of foreign exchange working balances.
3.3. In accordance with Article 105(5) of this Treaty, the ESCB shall contribute to the smooth conduct of policies pursued by the competent authorities relating to the prudential supervision of credit institutions and the stability of the financial system.

Article 4. Advisory functions
In accordance with Article 105(4) of this Treaty:
(a) the ECB shall be consulted:
   - on any proposed Community act in its fields of competence;
   - by national authorities regarding any draft legislative provision in its fields of competence, but within the limits and under the conditions set out by the Council in accordance with the procedure laid down in Article 42;

(b) the ECB may submit opinions to the appropriate Community institutions or bodies or to national authorities on matters in its fields of competence.

Article 5. Collection of statistical information

5.1. In order to undertake the tasks of the ESCB, the ECB, assisted by the national central banks, shall collect the necessary statistical information either from the competent national authorities or directly from economic agents. For these purposes it shall co-operate with the Community institutions or bodies and with the competent authorities of the Member States or third countries and with international organizations.

5.2. The national central banks shall carry out, to the extent possible, the tasks described in Article 5.1.

5.3. The ECB shall contribute to the harmonization, where necessary, of the rules and practices governing the collection, compilation and distribution of statistics in the areas within its fields of competence.

5.4. The Council, in accordance with the procedure laid down in Article 42, shall define the natural and legal persons subject to reporting requirements, the confidentiality regime and the appropriate provisions for enforcement.

Article 6. International co-operation

6.1. In the field of international co-operation involving the tasks entrusted to the ESCB, the ECB shall decide how the ESCB shall be represented.

6.2. The ECB and, subject to its approval, the national central banks may participate in international monetary institutions.

6.3. Articles 6.1 and 6.2 shall be without prejudice to Article 109(4) of this Treaty.

CHAPTER III. ORGANIZATION OF THE ESCB

Article 7. Independence

In accordance with Article 107 of this Treaty, when exercising the powers and carrying out the tasks and duties conferred upon them by this Treaty and this Statute, neither the ECB, nor a national central bank, nor any member of their decision-making bodies shall seek or take instructions from Community institutions or bodies, from any government of a Member State or from any other body. The Community institutions and bodies and the governments of the Member States undertake to respect this principle and not to seek to influence the members of the decision-making bodies of the ECB or of the national central banks in the performance of their tasks.

Article 8.   General principle
The ESCB shall be governed by the decision-making bodies of the ECB.

Article 9.   The European Central Bank
9.1. The ECB which, in accordance with Article 106(2) of this Treaty, shall have legal personality, shall enjoy in each of the Member States the most extensive legal capacity accorded to legal persons under its law; it may, in particular, acquire or dispose of movable and immovable property and may be a party to legal proceedings.
9.2. The ECB shall ensure that the tasks conferred upon the ESCB under Article 105(2), (3) and (5) of this Treaty are implemented either by its own activities pursuant to this Statute or through the national central bank pursuant to Articles 12.1 and 14.
9.3. In accordance with Article 106(3) of this Treaty, the decision-making bodies of the ECB shall be the Governing Council and the Executive Board.

Article 10.   The Governing Council
10.1. In accordance with Article 109a(1) of this Treaty, the Governing Council shall comprise the members of the Executive Board of the ECB and the Governors of the national central banks.
10.2. Subject to Article 10.3, only members of the Governing Council present in person shall have the right to vote. By way of derogation from this rule, the Rules of Procedure referred to in Article 12.3 may lay down that members of the Governing Council may cast their vote by means of teleconferencing. These rules shall also provide that a member of the Governing Council who is prevented from voting for a prolonged period may appoint an alternate as a member of the Governing Council.

   Subject to Articles 10.3 and 11.3, each member of the Governing Council shall have one vote. Save as otherwise provided for in this Statue, the Governing Council shall act by a simple majority. In the event of a tie the President shall have the casting vote.

   In order for the Governing Council to vote, there shall be quorum of two-thirds of the members. If the quorum is not met, the President may convene and extraordinary meeting at which decisions may be taken without regard to the quorum.
10.3. For any decisions to be taken under Articles 28, 29, 30, 32, 33 and 51, the votes in the Governing Council shall be weighted according to the national central banks' shares in the subscribed capital of the

ECB. The weight of the votes of the members of the Executive Board shall be zero. A decision requiring a qualified majority shall be adopted if the votes cast in favour represent at least two thirds of the subscribed capital of the ECB and represent at least half of the shareholders. If a Governor in unable to be present, he may nominate an alternate to cast his weighted vote.

10.4. The proceedings of the meetings shall be confidential. The Governing Council may decide to make the outcome of its deliberations public.

10.5. The Governing Council shall meet at least ten times a year.

Article 11.   The Executive Board

11.1. In accordance with Article 109a(2)(a) of this Treaty, the Executive Board shall comprise the President, the Vice-President and four other members.

The members shall perform their duties on a full-time basis. No member shall engage in any occupation, whether gainful or not, unless exemption is exceptionally granted by the Governing Council.

11.2. In accordance with Article 109a(2)(b) of this Treaty, the President, the Vice-President and the other Members of the Executive Board shall be appointed from among persons of recognized standing and professional experience in monetary or banking matters by common accord of the governments of the Member States at the level of the Heads of State or of government, on a recommendation from the Council after it has consulted the European Parliament and the Governing Council.

Their term of office shall be 8 years and shall not be renewable.

Only nationals of Member States may be members of the Executive Board.

11.3. The terms and conditions of employment of the members of the Executive Board, in particular their salaries, pensions and other social security benefits shall be the subject of contracts with the ECB and shall be fixed by the Governing Council on a proposal from a Committee comprising three members appointed by the Governing Council and three members appointed by the Council. The members of the Executive Board shall not have the right to vote on matters referred to in this paragraph.

11.4. If a member of the Executive Board no longer fulfils the conditions required for the performance of his duties or if he has been guilty of serious misconduct, the Court of Justice may, on application by the Governing Council or the Executive Board, compulsorily retire him.

11.5. Each member of the Executive Board present in person shall have the right to vote and shall have, for that purpose, one vote. Save as otherwise provided, the Executive Board shall act by a simple majority of the votes cast. In the event of a tie, the President shall have the casting vote. The voting arrangements shall be specified in the Rules of Procedure referred to in Article 12.3.

11.6. The Executive Board shall be responsible for the current business of the ECB.

11.7. Any vacancy on the Executive Board shall be filled by the appointment of a new member in accordance with Article 11.2.

Article 12. Responsibilities of the decision-making bodies

12.1. The Governing Council shall adopt the guidelines and take the decisions necessary to ensure the performance of the tasks entrusted to the ESCB under this Treaty and this Statute. The Governing Council shall formulate the monetary policy of the Community including, as appropriate, decisions relating to intermediate monetary objectives, key interest rates and the supply of reserves in the ESCB and shall establish the necessary guidelines for their implementation.

The Executive Board shall implement monetary policy in accordance with the guidelines and decisions laid down by the Governing Council. In doing so the Executive Board shall give the necessary instructions to national central banks. In addition the Executive Board may have certain powers delegated to it where the Governing Council so decides.

To the extent deemed possible and appropriate and without prejudice to the provisions of this Article, the ECB shall have recourse to the national central banks to carry out operations which form part of the tasks of the ESCB.

12.2. The Executive Board shall have the responsibility for the preparation of meetings of the Governing Council.

12.3. The Governing Council shall adopt Rules of Procedure which determine the internal organization of the ECB and its decision-making bodies.

12.4. The Governing Council shall exercise the advisory functions referred to Article 4.

12.5. The Governing Council shall take the decisions referred to Article 6.

Article 13. The President

13.1. The President or, in his absence, the Vice-President shall chair the governing Council and the Executive Board of the ECB.

13.2. Without prejudice to Article 39, the President or his nominee shall represent the ECB externally.

Article 14.   National Central Banks

14.1. In accordance with Article 108 of this Treaty, each Member State shall ensure, at the latest at the date of the establishment of the ESCB, that its national legislation, including the statues of its national central bank, is compatible with this Treaty and this Statute.

14.2. The statutes of the national central banks shall, in particular, provide that the term of office of a Governor of a national central bank shall be no less than 5 years.

A Governor may be relieved from office only if he no longer fulfils the conditions required for the performance of his duties or if he has been guilty of serious misconduct. A decision to this effect may be referred to the Court of Justice by the Governor concerned or the Governing Council on grounds of infringement of this Treaty or of any rule of law relating to its application. Such proceedings shall be instituted within two months of the publication of the decision or of its notification to the plaintiff or, in the absence thereof, of the day on which it came to knowledge of the latter, as the case may be.

14.3. The national central banks are an integral part of the ESCB and shall act in accordance with the guidelines and instructions of ECB. The Governing Council shall take the necessary steps to ensure compliance with the guidelines and instructions of the ECB, and shall require that any necessary information be given to it.

14.4. National central banks may perform functions other than those specified in this Statute unless the Governing Council finds, by a majority of two thirds of the votes cast, that these interfere with the objectives and tasks of the ESCB. Such functions shall be performed on the responsibility and liability of national central banks and shall not be regarded as being part of the functions of the ESCB.

Article 15.   Reporting commitments.

15.1. The ECB shall draw up and publish reports on the activities of the ESCB at least quarterly.

15.2. A consolidated financial statement of the ESCB shall be published each week.

15.3. In accordance with Article 109b(3) of this Treaty, the ECB shall address an annual report on the activities of the ESCB and on the monetary policy of both the previous and the current year to the European Parliament, the Council and the Commission, and also the European Council.

15.4. The reports and statements referred to in this Article shall be made available to interested parties free of charge.

Article 16. Bank notes.
In accordance with Article 105a(1) of this Treaty, the Governing Council shall have the exclusive right to authorize the issue of bank notes within the Community. The ECB and the national central banks may issue such notes. The bank notes issued by the ECB and the national central banks shall be the only such notes to have the status of legal tender within the Community.

The ECB shall respect as far as possible existing practices regarding the issue and design of bank notes.

CHAPTER IV. MONETARY FUNCTIONS AND OPERATIONS OF THE ESCB

Article 17. Accounts with the ECB and the national central banks.
In order to conduct their operations, the ECB and the national central banks may open accounts for credit institutions, public entities and other market participants and accept assets, including book-entry securities, as collateral.

Article 18. Open market and credit operations.
18.1. In order to achieve the objectives of the ESCB and to carry out its tasks, the ECB and the national central banks may:

  – operate in the financial markets by buying and selling outright (spot or forward) or under repurchase agreement and by lending or borrowing claims and marketable instruments, whether in Community or in non-Community currencies, as well as precious metals;
  – conduct credit operations with credit institutions and other market participants, with lending being based on adequate collateral.

18.2. The ECB shall establish general principles for open market and credit operations carried out by itself or the national central banks, including for the announcement of conditions under which they stand ready to enter into such transactions.

Article 19. Minimum reserves
19.1. Subject to Article 2, the ECB may require credit institutions established in Member States to hold minimum reserves on accounts with the ECB and national central banks in pursuance of monetary policy objectives. Regulations concerning the calculation and determination of the required minimum reserves may be established by the Governing Council. In cases of non-compliance the ECB shall

be entitled to levy penalty interest and to impose other sanctions with comparable effect.

19.2. For the application of this Article, the Council shall, in accordance with the procedure laid down in Article 42, define the basis for minimum reserves and the maximum reserves and the maximum permissible ratios between those reserves and their basis, as well as the appropriate sanctions in cases of non-compliance.

Article 20.   Other instruments of monetary control

The Governing Council may, by a majority of two thirds of the votes cast, decide upon the use of such other operational methods of monetary control as it sees fit, respecting Article 2.

The Council shall, in accordance with the procedure laid down in Article 42, define the scope of such methods if they impose obligations on third parties.

Article 21.   Operations with public entities.

21.1. In accordance with Article 104 of the Treaty, overdrafts or any other type of credit facility with the ECB or with the national central banks in favour of Community institutions or bodies, central governments, regional, local or other public authorities, other bodies governed by public law, or public undertakings of Member States shall be prohibited, as shall the purchase directly from them by the ECB or national central banks of debt instruments.

21.2. The ECB and national central banks may act as fiscal agents for the entities referred to in 21.1.

21.3. The provisions of this Article shall not apply to publicly-owned credit institutions which, in the context of the supply of reserves by central banks, shall be given the same treatment by national central banks and the ECB as private credit institutions.

Article 22.   Clearing and payment systems

The ECB and national central banks may provide facilities, and the ECB may make regulations, to ensure efficient and sound clearing and payment systems within the Community and with other countries.

Article 23.   External operations

The ECB and national central banks may:

– establish relations with central banks and financial institutions in other countries and, where appropriate, with international organizations;
– acquire and sell spot and forward all types of foreign exchange assets and precious metals; the term 'foreign exchange asset' shall include

securities and all other assets in the currency of any country or units of account in whatever form held;
- hold and manage the assets referred to in this Article;
- conduct all types of banking transactions in relations with third countries and international organizations, including borrowing and lending operations.

Article 24. Other operations

In addition to operations arising from their tasks, the ECB and national central banks may enter into operations for their administrative purposes or for their staff.

CHAPTER V. PRUDENTIAL SUPERVISION

Article 25. Prudential supervision

25.1. The ECB may offer advice to and be consulted by the Council, the Commission and the competent authorities of the Member States on the scope and implementation of Community legislation relating to the prudential supervision of credit institutions and to the stability of the financial system.

25.2. In accordance with any decision of the Council under Article 105(6) of this Treaty, the ECB may perform specific tasks concerning policies relating to the prudential supervision of credit institutions and other financial institutions with the exception of insurance undertakings.

CHAPTER VI. FINANCIAL PROVISIONS OF THE ESCB

Article 26. Financial accounts

26.1. The financial year of the ECB and national central banks shall begin on the first day of January and end on the last day of December.

26.2. The annual accounts of the ECB shall be drawn up by the Executive Board, in accordance with the principles established by the Governing Council. The accounts shall be approved by the Governing Council and shall thereafter be published.

26.3. For analytical and operational purposes, the Executive Board shall draw up a consolidated balance sheet of the ESCB, comprising those assets and liabilities of the national central banks that fall within the ESCB.

26.4. For the application of this Article, the Governing Council shall establish the necessary rules for standardizing the accounting and reporting of operations undertaken by the national central banks.

Article 27. Auditing

27.1. The account of the ECB and national central banks shall be audited by independent external auditors recommended by the Governing Council and approved by the Council. The auditors shall have full power to examine all books and accounts of the ECB and national central banks and obtain full information about their transactions.

27.2. The provisions of Article 188c of this Treaty shall only apply to an examination of the operational efficiency of the management of the ECB.

Article 28. Capital of the ECB

28.1. The capital of the ECB, which shall become operational upon its establishment, shall be ECU 5 000 million. The capital may be increased by such amounts as may be decided by the Governing Council acting by the qualified majority provided for in Article 10.3, within the limits and under the conditions set by the Council under the procedure laid down in Article 42.

28.2. The national central banks shall be the sole subscribers to and holders of the capital of the ECB. The subscription of capital shall be according to the key established in accordance with Article 29.

28.3. The Governing Council, acting by the qualified majority provided for in Article 10.3, shall determine the extent to which and the form in which the capital shall be paid up.

28.4. Subject to Article 28.5, the shares of the national central banks in the subscribed capital of the ECB may not be transferred, pledged or attached.

28.5. If the key referred to in Article 29 is adjusted, the national central banks shall transfer among themselves capital shares to the extent necessary to ensure that the distribution of capital shares corresponds to the adjusted key. The Governing Council shall determine the terms and conditions of such transfers.

Article 29. Key for capital subscription

29.1. When in accordance with the procedure referred to in Article 109l(1) of this Treaty the ESCB and the ECB have been established, the key for subscription of the ECB's capital shall be established. Each national central bank shall be assigned a weighting in this key which shall be equal to the sum of:

- 50% of the share of its respective Member State in the population of the Community in the penultimate year preceding the establishment of the ESCB;

– 50% of the share of its respective Member State in the gross domestic product at market prices of the Community as recorded in the last five years preceding the penultimate year before the establishment of the ESCB;

The percentages shall be rounded up to the nearest multiple 0.05 percentage points.

29.2. The statistical data to be used for the application of this Article shall be provided by the Commission in accordance with the rules adopted by the Council under the procedure provided for in Article 42.

29.3. The weighting assigned to the national central banks shall be adjusted every five years after the establishment of the ESCB by analogy with the provisions laid down in Article 29.1. The adjusted key shall apply with effect from the first day of the following year.

29.4. The Governing Council shall take all other measures necessary for the application of this Article.

Article 30.   Transfer of foreign reserve assets to the ECB

30.1. Without prejudice to Article 28, the ECB shall be provided by the national central banks with foreign reserve assets, other than Member States' currencies, ECUs, IMF reserve positions and SDRs, up to an amount equivalent to ECU 50 000 million. The Governing Council shall decide upon the proportion to be called up by the ECB following its establishment and the amounts called up at later dates. The ECB shall have the full right to hold and manage the foreign reserves that are transferred to it and to use them for the purposes set out in this Statute.

30.2. The contributions of each national central bank shall be fixed in proportion to its share in the subscribed capital of the ECB.

30.3. Each national central bank shall be credited by the ECB with a claim equivalent to its contribution. The Governing Council shall determine the denomination and remuneration of such claims.

30.4. Further calls of foreign reserve assets beyond the limit set in Article 30.1. may be effected by the ECB, in accordance with Article 30.2, within the limits and under the conditions set by the Council in accordance with the procedure laid down in Article 42.

30.5. The ECB may hold and manage IMF reserve positions and SDRs and provide for the pooling of such assets.

30.6. The Governing Council shall take all other measures necessary for the application of this Article.

Article 31.   Foreign reserve assets held by national central banks

31.1. The national central banks shall be allowed to perform transactions in fulfilment of their obligations towards international organizations in accordance with Article 23.

31.2. All other operations in foreign reserve assets remaining with the national central banks after the transfers referred to in Article 30, and Member States' transactions with their foreign exchange working balances shall, above a certain limit to be established within the framework of Article 31.3, be subject to approval by the ECB in order to ensure consistency with the exchange rate and monetary policies of the Community.

31.3. The Governing Council shall issue guidelines with a view to facilitating such operations.

Article 32.   Allocation of monetary income of national central banks.

32.1. The income accruing to the national central banks in the performance of the ESCB's monetary policy function (hereinafter referred to as 'monetary income') shall be allocated at the end of each financial year in accordance with the provisions of this Article.

32.2. Subject to Article 32.3, the amount of each national central bank's monetary income shall be equal to its annual income derived from its assets held against notes in circulation and deposit liabilities to credit institutions. These assets shall be earmarked by national central banks in accordance with guidelines to be established by the Governing Council.

32.3. If, after the start of the third stage, the balance sheet structures of the national central banks do not, in the judgment of the Governing Council, permit the application of Article 32.2, the Governing Council, acting by a qualified majority, may decide that, by way of derogation form Article 32.2, monetary income shall be measured according to an alternative method for a period of not more than five years.

32.4. The amount of each national central bank's monetary income shall be reduced by an amount equivalent to any interest paid by that central bank on its deposit liabilities to credit institutions in accordance with Article 19.

The Governing Council may decide that national central banks shall be indemnified against costs incurred in connection with the issue of bank notes or in exceptional circumstances for specific losses arising from monetary policy operations undertaken for the ESCB. Indemnification shall be in a form deemed appropriate in the judgment of the Governing Council; these amounts may be offset against the national central banks' monetary income.

32.5. The sum of the national central banks' monetary income shall be allocated to the national central banks in proportion to their paid-up shares in the capital of the ECB, subject to any decision taken by the Governing Council pursuant to Article 33.2.

32.6. The clearing and settlement of the balances arising from the allocation of monetary income shall be carried out by the ECB in accordance with guidelines established by the Governing Council.

32.7. The Governing Council shall take all other measures necessary for the application of this Article.

Article 33. Allocation of net profits and losses of the ECB

33.1. The net profit of the ECB shall be transferred in the following order:

(a) an amount to be determined by the Governing Council, which may not exceed 20% of the net profit, shall be transferred to the general reserve fund subject to a limit equal to a 100% of the capital;

(b) the remaining net profit shall be distributed to the shareholders of the ECB in proportion to their paid-up shares.

33.2. In the event of a loss incurred by the ECB, the shortfall may be offset against the general reserve fund of the ECB and, if necessary, following a decision by the Governing Council, against the monetary income of the relevant financial year in proportion and up to the amounts allocated to the national central banks in accordance with Article 32.5.

CHAPTER VII. GENERAL PROVISIONS

Article 34. Legal acts

34.1. In accordance with Article 108a of this Treaty, the ECB shall:

– make regulations to the extent necessary to implement the tasks defined in Article 3.1., first indent, Articles 19.1, 22 or 25.2 and in cases which shall be laid down in the acts of the Council referred to in Article 42;

– take decisions necessary for carrying out the tasks entrusted to the ESCB under this Treaty and this Statute;

– make recommendations and deliver opinions.

34.2. A regulation shall have general application. It shall be binding in its entirety and directly applicable in all Member States.

Recommendations and opinions shall have no binding force.

A decision shall be binding in its entirety upon those to whom it is addressed.

Articles 190 to 192 of this Treaty shall apply to regulations and decisions adopted by the ECB.

The ECB may decide to publish its decisions, recommendations and opinions.

34.3. Within the limits and under the conditions adopted by the Council under the procedure laid down in Article 42, the ECB shall be entitled to impose fines or periodic penalty payments on undertakings for failure to comply with obligations under its regulations and decisions.

Article 35.   Judicial control and related matters

35.1. The acts or omissions of the ECB shall be open to review or interpretation by the Court of Justice in the cases and under the conditions laid down in this Treaty. The ECB may institute proceedings in the cases and under the conditions laid down in this Treaty.

35.2. Disputes between the ECB, on the one hand, and its creditors, debtors or any other person, on the other, shall be decided by the competent national courts, save where jurisdiction has been conferred upon the Court of Justice.

35.3. The ECB shall be subject to the liability regime provided for in Article 215 of this Treaty. The national central banks shall be liable according to their respective national laws.

35.4. The Court of Justice shall have jurisdiction to give judgment pursuant to any arbitration clause contained in a contract concluded by or on behalf of the ECB, whether that contract be governed by public or private law.

35.5. A decision of the ECB to bring an action before the Court of Justice shall be taken by the Governing Council.

35.6. The Court of Justice shall have jurisdiction in disputes concerning the fulfillment by a national central bank of obligations under this Statute. If the ECB considers that a national central bank has failed to fulfill an obligation under this Statute, it shall deliver a reasoned opinion on the matter after giving the national central bank concerned the opportunity to submit its observations. If the national central bank concerned does not comply with the opinion within the period laid down by the ECB, the latter may bring the matter before the Court of Justice.

Article 36.   Staff

36.1. The Governing Council, on a proposal from the Executive Board, shall lay down the conditions of employment of the staff of the ECB.

36.2. The Court of Justice shall have jurisdiction in any dispute between the ECB and its servants within the limits and under the conditions laid down in the conditions of employment.

Article 37.   Seat
Before the end of 1992, the decision as to where the seat of the ECB will be established shall be taken by common accord of the governments of the Member States at the level of Heads of State or of Government.

Article 38.   Professional secrecy
38.1. Members of the governing bodies and the staff of the ECB and the national central banks shall be required, even after their duties have ceased, not to disclose information of the kind covered by the obligation of professional secrecy.
38.2. Persons having access to data covered by Community legislation imposing an obligation of secrecy shall be subject to such legislation.

Article 39.   Signatories
The ECB shall be legally committed to third parties by the President or by two members of the Executive Board or by the signatures of two members of the staff of the ECB who have been duly authorized by the President to sign on behalf of the ECB.

Article 40.   Privileges and immunities.
The ECB shall enjoy in the territories of the Member States such privileges and immunities as are necessary for the performance of its tasks, under the conditions laid down in the Protocol on the Privileges and Immunities of the European Communities annexed to the Treaty establishing a Single Council and a Single Commission of the European Communities.

CHAPTER VIII. AMENDMENT OF THE STATUTE AND COMPLEMENTARY LEGISLATION

Article 41.   Simplified amendment procedure
41.1. In accordance with Article 106(5) of this Treaty, Articles 5.1, 5.2, 5.3, 17, 18, 19.1, 22, 23, 24, 26, 32.2, 32.3, 32.4, 32.6, 33.1(a) and 36 of this Statute may be amended by the Council, acting either by a qualified majority on a recommendation from the ECB and after consulting the Commission, or unanimously on a proposal from the Commission and after consulting the ECB. In either case the assent of the European Parliament shall be required.
41.2. A recommendation made by the ECB under this Article shall require a unanimous decision by the Governing Council.

Article 42. Complementary legislation
In accordance with Article 106(6) of this Treaty, immediately after the decision on the date for the beginning of the third stage, the Council, acting by a qualified majority either on a proposal from the Commission and after consulting the European Parliament and the ECB or on a recommendation from the ECB and after consulting the European Parliament and the Commission, shall adopt the provisions referred to in Articles 4, 5.4, 19.2, 20, 28.1, 29.2, 30.4, and 34.3. of this Statute.

CHAPTER IX. TRANSITIONAL AND OTHER PROVISIONS FOR THE ESCB

Article 43. General Provisions
43.1. A derogation as referred to in Article 109k(1) of this Treaty shall entail that the following Articles of this Statue shall not confer any rights or impose any obligations on the Member State concerned: 3, 6, 9.2, 12.1, 14.3, 16, 18, 19, 20, 22, 23, 26.2, 27, 30, 31, 32, 33, 34, 50 and 52.
43.2. The central banks of Member States with derogation as specified in Article 109k(1) of this Treaty shall retain their powers in the field of monetary policy according to national law.
43.3. In accordance with Article 109k(4) of this Treaty, 'Member States' shall be read as 'Member States without derogation' in the following Articles of this Statute: 3, 11.2, 19, 34.2 and 50.
43.4. 'National central banks' shall be read as central banks of Member States without a derogation' in the following Articles of this Statute: 9.2, 10.1, 10.3, 12.1, 16, 17, 18, 22, 23, 27, 30, 31, 32, 33.2 and 52.
43.5. 'Shareholders' shall be read as 'central banks of Member States without a derogation' in Articles 10.3 and 33.1.
43.6. 'Subscribed capital of the ECB' shall be read as 'capital of the ECB subscribed by the central banks of Member States without a derogation' in Articles 10.3 and 30.2.

Article 44. Transitional tasks of the ECB
The ECB shall take over those tasks of the EMI which, because of the derogations of one or more Member States, still have to be performed in the third stage.
The ECB shall give advice in the preparations for the abrogation of the derogations specified in Article 109k of this Treaty.

Article 45. The General Council of the ECB
45.1. Without prejudice to Article 106(3) of this Treaty, the General

Council shall be constituted as a third decision-making body of the ECB.

45.2. The General Council shall compromise the President and Vice-President of the ECB and the Governors of the national central banks. The others members of the Executive Board may participate, without having the right to vote, in meetings of the General Council.

45.3. The responsibilities of the General Council are listed in full in Article 47 of this Statute.

Article 46. Rules of procedure of the General Council

46.1. The President or, in his absence, the Vice President of the ECB shall chair the General Council of the ECB.

46.2. The President of the Council and a member of the Commission may participate, without having to right to vote, meetings of the General Council.

46.3. The President shall prepare the meetings of the General Council.

46.4. By way of derogation from Article 12.3, the General Council shall adopt its Rules of Procedure.

46.5. The Secretariat of the General Council shall be provided by the ECB.

Article 47. Responsibilities of the General Council

47.1. The General Council shall:
  – perform the tasks referred to in Article 44;
  – contribute to the advisory functions referred to in Articles 4 and 25.1.

47.2. The General Council shall contribute to:

  – the collection of statistical information as referred to in Article 5;
  – the reporting activities of the ECB as referred to in Article 15;
  – the establishment of the necessary rules for the application of Article 26 as referred to in Article 26.4;
  – the taking of all other measures necessary for the application of Article 29 as referred to Article 29.4;
  – the laying down of the conditions of employment of the staff of the ECB as referred to in Article 36.

47.3. The General Council shall contribute to the necessary preparations for irrevocably fixing the exchange rates of the currencies of Member States with a derogations against the currencies, or the single currency, of the Member States without a derogation, as referred to in Article 109(5) of this Treaty.

47.4. The General Council shall be informed by the President of the ECB of decisions of the Governing Council.

Article 48.   Transitional provisions for the capital of the ECB
In accordance with Article 29.1 each national central bank shall be assigned a weighting in the key for subscription of the ECB's capital. By way of derogation from Article 28.3, central banks of Member States with a derogation shall not pay up their subscribed capital unless the General Council, acting by as majority representing at least two thirds of the subscribed capital of the ECB and at least half of the shareholders, decides that a minimal percentage has to be paid up as a contribution to the operational costs of the ECB.

Article 49.   Deferred payment of capital, reserves and provisions of the ECB
49.1. The central bank of a Member State whose derogation has been abrogated shall pay up its subscribed share of the capital of the ECB to the same extent as the central banks of other Member States without a derogation, and shall transfer to the ECB foreign reserve assets in accordance with Article 30.1. The sum to be transferred shall be determined by multiplying the ECU value at current exchange rates of the foreign reserve assets which have already been transferred to the ECB in accordance with Article 30.1, by the ratio between the number of shares subscribed by the national central bank concerned and the number of shares already paid up by the other national central banks.

49.2. In addition to the payment to be made in accordance with Article 49.1, the central bank concerned shall contribute to the reserves of the ECB, to those provisions equivalent to reserves, and to the amount still to be appropriated to the reserves and provisions corresponding to the balance of the profit and loss account as at 31 December of the year prior to the abrogation of the derogation. The sum to be contributed shall be determined by multiplying the amount of the reserves, as defined above and as stated in the approved balance sheet of the ECB, by the ratio between the number of shares subscribed by the central bank concerned and the number of shares already paid up the other central banks.

Article 50.   Initial appointment of the members of the Executive Board.
When the Executive Board of the ECB is being established, the President, the Vice-President and the other members of the Executive Board shall be appointed by common accord of the governments of the Member States at the level of Heads of State or of Government, on a recommendation

from the Council and after consulting the European Parliament and the Council of the EMI. The President of the Executive Board shall be appointed for 8 years. By way of derogation from Article 11.2, the Vice-President shall be appointed for 4 years and the other members of the Executive Board for terms of office of between 5 and 8 years. No term of office shall be renewable. The number of members of the Executive Board may be smaller than provided for in Article 11.1, but in no circumstance shall it be less than four.

Article 51.   Derogation from Article 32
51.1. If, after the start of the third stage, the Governing Council decides that the application of Article 32 results in significant changes in national central banks' relative income positions, the amount of income to allocated pursuant to Article 32 shall be reduced by a uniform percentage which shall not exceed 60% in the first financial year after the start of the third stage and which shall decrease by at least 12 percentage points in each subsequent financial year.
51.2. Article 51.1. shall be applicable for not more than five financial years after the start of the third stage.

Article 52.   Exchange of bank notes in Community currencies.
Following the irrevocable fixing of exchange rates, the Governing Council shall take the necessary measures to ensure that bank notes denominated in currencies with irrevocably fixed exchange rates are exchanged by the national central banks at their respective par values.

Article 53.   Applicability of the transitional provisions
If and as long as there are Member States with a derogation Articles 43 to 48 shall be applicable.

4   *EMI Statute*

Article 1.   Constitution and name
1.1. The European Monetary Institute (EMI) shall be established in accordance with Article 109f of this Treaty; it shall perform its functions and carry out its activities in accordance with the provisions of this Treaty and of this Statute.
1.2. The members of the EMI shall be the central banks of the Member States ('national central banks'). For the purposes of the Statute, the Institut monetaire luxembourgeois shall be regarded as the central bank of Luxembourg.

1.3. Pursuant to Article 109f of this Treaty, both the Committee of Governors and the European Monetary Co-operation Fund (EMCF) shall be dissolved. All assets and liabilities of the EMCF shall pass automatically to the EMI.

Article 2. Objectives

The EMI shall contribute to the realization of the conditions necessary for the transition to the third stage of Economic and Monetary Union, in particular by:

- strengthening the co-ordination of monetary policies with a view to ensuring price stability;
- making the preparations required for the establishment of the European System of Central Banks (ESCB), and for the conduct of a single monetary policy and the creation of a single currency in the third stage;
- overseeing the development of the ecu.

Article 3. General principles

3.1. The EMI shall carry out the tasks and functions conferred upon it by this Treaty and this Statute without prejudice to the responsibility of the competent authorities for the conduct of the monetary policy within the respective Member States.

3.2. The EMI shall act in accordance with the objectives and principles stated in Article 2 of the Statute of the ESCB.

Article 4. Primary tasks

4.1. In accordance with Article 109f(2) of this Treaty, the EMI shall:

- strengthen co-operation between the national central banks;
- strengthen the co-ordination of the monetary policies of the Member States with the aim of ensuring price stability;
- monitor the functioning of the European Monetary System (EMS);
- hold consultations concerning issues falling within the competence of the national central banks and affecting the stability of financial institutions and markets;
- take over the tasks of the EMCF; in particular it shall perform the functions referred to in Articles 6.1, 6.2 and 6.3;
- facilitate the use of the ecu and oversee its development, including the smooth functioning of the ecu clearing system.

The EMI shall also:

- hold regular consultations concerning the course of monetary policies and the use of monetary policy instruments;
- normally be consulted by the national monetary authorities before they take decisions on the course of monetary policy in the context of the common framework for ex ante co-ordination.

4.2. At the latest by 31 December 1996, the EMI shall specify the regulatory, organizational and logistical framework necessary for the ESCB to perform its tasks in the third stage, in accordance with the principle of an open market economy with free competition. This framework shall be submitted by the Council of the EMI for decision to the ECB at the date of its establishment.

In accordance with Article 109f(3) of this Treaty, the EMI shall in particular:

- prepare the instruments and the procedures necessary for carrying out a single monetary policy in the third stage;
- promote the harmonization, where necessary, of the rules and practices governing the collection, compilation and distribution of statistics in the areas within its field of competence;
- prepare the rules for operations to be undertaken by the national central banks in the framework of the ESCB;
- promote the efficiency of cross-border payments;
- supervise the technical preparation of ecu bank notes.

Article 5. Advisory functions.
5.1 In accordance with Article 109f(4) of this Treaty, the Council of the EMI may formulate opinions or recommendations on the overall orientation of monetary policy and exchange rate policy as well as on related measures introduced in each Member State. The EMI may submit opinions or recommendations to governments and to the Council on policies which might affect the internal or external monetary situation in the Community and, in particular, the functioning of the EMS.
5.2. The Council of the EMI may also make recommendations to the monetary authorities of the Member States concerning the conduct of their monetary policy.
5.3. In accordance with Article 109f(6) of this Treaty, the EMI shall be consulted by the Council regarding any proposed Community act within its field of competence.

Within the limits and under the conditions set out by the Council acting by a qualified majority on a proposal from the Commission and after consulting the European Parliament and the EMI shall be consulted by the authorities of the Member States on any draft legislative provision within its field of competence, in particular with regard to Article 4.2.

5.4. In accordance with Article 109f(5) of this Treaty, the EMI may decide to publish its opinions and its recommendations.

Article 6.   Operational and technical functions

6.1. The EMI shall;

- provide for the multilateralization of positions resulting from interventions by the national central banks in Community currencies and the multilateralization of intra-Community settlements;
- administer the very short-term financing mechanism provided for by the Agreement of 13 March 1979 between the central banks of the Member States of the European Economic Community laying down the operating procedures for the European Monetary System (hereinafter referred to as 'EMS Agreement') and the short-term monetary support mechanism provided for in the Agreement between the central banks of the Member States of the European Economic Community of 9 February 1970, as amended;
- perform the functions referred to in Article 11 of Council Regulation (EEC) No 1969/88 of 24 June 1988 establishing a single facility providing medium-term financial assistance for Member States' balances of payments.

6.2. The EMI may receive monetary reserves from the national central banks and issue ecus against such assets for the purpose of implementing the EMS Agreement. These ecus may be used by the EMI and the national central banks as a means of settlement and for transactions between them and the EMI. The EMI shall take the necessary administrative measures for the implementation of this paragraph.

6.3. The EMI may grant to the monetary authorities of third countries and to international monetary institutions the status of 'Other Holders' of ecus and fix the terms and conditions under which such ecus may be acquired, held or used by Other Holders.

6.4. The EMI shall be entitled to hold and manage foreign exchange reserves as an agent for and at the request of national central banks. Profits and losses regarding these reserves shall be for the account of the national central bank depositing the reserves. The EMI shall perform this function on the basis of bilateral contracts in accordance with rules laid down in a decision of the EMI. These rules shall ensure that transactions with these reserves shall not interfere with the monetary policy and exchange rate policy of the competent monetary authority of any Member State and shall be consistent with the objectives of the EMI and the proper functioning of the Exchange Rate Mechanism of the EMS.

Article 7. Other tasks

7.1. Once a year the EMI shall address a report to the Council on the state of the preparations for the third stage. These reports shall include an assessment of the progress towards convergence in the Community, and cover in particular the adaptation of monetary policy instruments and the preparation of the procedures necessary for carrying out a single monetary policy in the third stage, as well as the statutory requirements to be fulfilled for national central banks to become an integral part of the ESCB.

7.2. In accordance with the Council decisions referred to in Article 109f(7) of this Treaty, the EMI may perform other tasks for the preparation of the third stage.

Article 8. Independence

The members of the Council of the EMI who are the representatives of their institutions shall, with respect to their activities, act according to their own responsibilities. In exercising the powers and performing the tasks and duties conferred upon them by this Treaty and this Statute, the Council of the EMI may not seek or take any instructions from Community institutions or bodies or governments of Member States. The Community institutions and bodies as well as the governments of the Member States undertake to respect this principle and not seek to influence the Council of the EMI in the performance of its tasks.

Article 9. Administration

9.1. In accordance with Article 109f(1) of this Treaty, the EMI shall be directed and managed by the Council of the EMI.

9.2. The Council of the EMI shall consist of a President and the Governors of the national central banks, on of whom shall be Vice-President. If a Governor is prevented from attending a meeting, he may nominate another representative of his institution.

9.3. The President shall be appointed by common accord of the governments of the Member States at the level of Heads of State or of Government, on a recommendation from, as the case may be, the Committee of Governors or the Council of the EMI, and after consulting the European Parliament and the Council. The President shall be selected from among persons of recognized standing and professional experience in monetary or banking matters. Only nationals of Member States may be President of the EMI. The Council of the EMI shall appoint the Vice-President. The President and Vice-President shall be appointed for a period of three years.

9.4. The President shall perform his duties on a full-time basis. He shall not engage in any occupation, whether gainful or not, unless exemption is exceptionally granted by the Council of the EMI.

9.5. The President shall

- prepare and chair meetings of the Council of the EMI;
- without prejudice to Article 22, present the views of the EMI externally;
- be responsible for the day-to-day management of the EMI.

   In the absence of the President, his duties shall be performed by the Vice-President.

9.6. The terms and conditions of employment of the President, in particular his salary, pension and other social security benefits, shall be the subject of a contract with the EMI and shall be fixed by the Council of the EMI on a proposal from a Committee comprising three members appointed by the Committee of Governors or the Council of the EMI, as the case may be, and three members appointed by the Council. The President shall not have the right to vote on matters referred to in this paragraph.

9.7. If the President no longer fulfils the conditions required for the performance of his duties or if he has been guilty of serious misconduct, the Court of Justice may, on application by the Council of the EMI, compulsorily retire him.

9.8. The Rules of Procedure of the EMI shall be adopted by the Council of the EMI.

Article 10.   Meetings of the Council of the EMI and voting procedures

10.1. The Council of the EMI shall meet at least ten times a year. The proceedings of Council meetings shall be confidential. The Council of the EMI may, acting unanimously, decide to make the outcome of its deliberations public.

10.2. Each member of the Council of the EMI or his nominee shall have one vote.

10.3. Save as otherwise provided for in this Statute, the Council of the EMI shall act by a simple majority of its members.

10.4. Decisions to be taken in the context of Articles 4.2, 5.4, 6.2, and 6.3 shall require unanimity of the members of the Council of the EMI.

   The adoption of opinions and recommendations under Articles 5.1 and 5.2, the adoption of decisions under Articles 6.4, 16 and

23.6 and the adoption of guidelines under Article 15.3 shall require a qualified majority of two thirds of the members of the Council of the EMI.

Article 11.   Interinstitutional co-operation and reporting requirements
11.1. The President of the Council and a member of the Commission may participate, without having the right to vote, in meetings of the Council of the EMI.
11.2. The President of the EMI shall be invited to participate in Council meetings when the Council is discussing matters relating to the objectives and tasks of the EMI.
11.3. At a date to be established in the Rules of Procedure, the EMI shall prepare an annual report on its activities and on monetary and financial conditions in the Community. The annual report, together with the annual accounts of the EMI, shall be addressed to the European Parliament, the Council and the Commission and also to the European Council.
   The President of the EMI may, at the request of the European Parliament or on his own initiative, be heard by the competent Committees of the European Parliament.
11.4. Reports published by the EMI shall be made available to interested parties free of charge.

Article 12.   Currency denomination
The operations of the EMI shall be expressed in ecus.

Article 13.   Seat
Before the end of 1992, the decision as to where the seat of the EMI will be established shall be taken by common accord of the governments of the Member States at the level of Heads of State or of Government.

Article 14.   Legal capacity
The EMI, which in accordance with Article 109f(1) of this Treaty shall have legal personality, shall enjoy in each of the Member States the most extensive legal capacity accorded to legal persons under their law; it may, in particular, acquire or dispose of movable or immovable property and may be a party to legal proceedings.

Article 15.   Legal acts
15.1. In the performance of its tasks, and under the conditions laid down in this Statute, the EMI shall:

   – deliver opinions
   – make recommendations;

   – adopt guidelines, and take decisions, which shall be addressed to the national central banks.

15.2. Opinions and recommendations of the EMI shall have no binding force

15.3. The Council of the EMI may adopt guidelines laying down the methods for the implementation of the conditions necessary for the ESCB to perform its functions in the third stage. EMI guidelines shall have no binding force; they shall be submitted for decision to the ECB.

15.4. Without prejudice to Article 3.1, a decision of the EMI shall be binding in its entirety upon those to whom it is addressed. Articles 190 and 191 of this Treaty shall apply to these decisions.

Article 16.   Financial resources

16.1. The EMI shall be endowed with its own resources. The size of the resources of the EMI shall be determined by the Council of the EMI with a view to ensuring the income deemed necessary to cover the administrative expenditure incurred in the performance of the tasks and functions of the EMI.

16.2. The resources of the EMI determined in accordance with Article 16.1 shall be provided out of contributions by the national central banks in accordance with the key referred to in Article 29.1 of the Statute of the ESCB and be paid up at the establishment of the EMI. For this purpose, the statistical data to be used for the determination of the key shall be provided by the Commission, in accordance with the rules adopted by the Council, acting by a qualified majority on a proposal from the Commission and after consulting the European Parliament, the Committee of Governors and the Committee referred to in Article 109c of this Treaty.

16.3. The Council of the EMI shall determine the form in which contributions shall be paid up.

Article 17.   Annual accounts and auditing

17.1. The financial year of the EMI shall begin on the first day of January and end on the last day of December.

17.2. The Council of the EMI shall adopt an annual budget before the beginning of each financial year.

17.3. The annual accounts shall be drawn up in accordance with the principles established by the Council of the EMI. The annual accounts shall be approved by the Council of the EMI and shall thereafter be published.

17.4. The annual accounts shall be audited by independent external auditors approved by the Council of the EMI. The auditors shall have full power to examine all books and accounts of the EMI and to obtain full information about its transactions.

The provisions of Article 188c of this Treaty shall only apply to an examination of the operational efficiency of the management of the EMI.

17.5. Any surplus of the EMI shall be transferred in the following order

(a) an amount to be determined by the Council of the EMI shall be transferred to the general reserve fund of the EMI.

(b) any remaining surplus shall be distributed to the national central banks in accordance with the key referred to in Article 16.2.

17.6 In the event of a loss incurred by the EMI, the shortfall shall be offset against the general reserve fund of the EMI. Any remaining shortfall shall be made good by contributions from the national central banks, in accordance with the key as referred to in Article 16.2.

Article 18. Staff

18.1. The Council of the EMI shall lay down the conditions of employment of the staff of the EMI.

18.2. The Court of Justice shall have jurisdiction in any dispute between the EMI and its servants within the limits and under the conditions laid down in the conditions of employment.

Article 19. Judicial control and related matters.

19.1. The acts or omissions of the EMI shall be open to review or interpretation by the Court of Justice in the cases and under the conditions laid down in this Treaty. The EMI may institute proceedings in the cases and under the conditions laid down in this Treaty.

19.2. Disputes between the EMI, on the one hand, and its creditors, debtors or any other person, on the other, shall fall within the jurisdiction of the competent national courts, save where jurisdiction has been conferred upon the Court of Justice.

19.3. The EMI shall be subject to the liability regime provided for in Article 215 of this Treaty.

19.4. The Court of Justice shall have jurisdiction to give judgment pursuant to any arbitration clause contained in a contract concluded by or on behalf of the EMI, whether that contract be governed by public or private law.

19.5. A decision of the EMI to bring an action before the Court of Justice shall be taken by the Council of the EMI.

Article 20. Professional Secrecy

20.1. Members of the Council of the EMI and the staff of the EMI shall be required, even after their duties have ceased, not to disclose information of the kind covered by the obligation of professional secrecy.

20.2. Persons having access to data covered by Community legislation imposing and obligation of secrecy shall be subject to such legislation.

Article 21. Privileges and immunities

The EMI shall enjoy in the territories of the Member States such privileges and immunities as are necessary for the performance of its tasks, under the conditions laid down in the Protocol on the Privileges and Immunities of the European Communities annexed to the Treaty establishing a Single Council and a Single Commission of the European Communities.

Article 22. Signatories

The EMI shall be legally committed to third parties by the President or the Vice-President or by the signatures of two members of the staff of the EMI who have been duly authorized by the President to sign on behalf of the EMI.

Article 23. Liquidation of the EMI

23.1. In accordance with Article 109l of this Treaty, the EMI shall go into liquidation on the establishment of the ECB. All assets and liabilities of the EMI shall then pass automatically to the ECB. The latter shall liquidate the EMI according to the provisions of this Article. The liquidation shall be completed by the beginning of the third stage.

23.2. The mechanism for the creation of ECUs against gold and US dollars as provided for by Article 17 of the EMS agreement shall be unwound by the first day of the third stage in accordance with Article 20 of the said Agreement.

23.3. All claims and liabilities arising from the very short-term financing mechanism and the short-term monetary support mechanism, under the Agreements referred to in Article 6.1, shall be settled by the first day of the third stage.

23.4. All remaining assets of the EMI shall be disposed of and all remaining liabilities of the EMI shall be settled.

23.5. The proceeds of the liquidation described in Article 23.4. shall be distributed to the national central banks in accordance with the key referred to in Article 16.2

23.6. The Council of the EMI may take the measures necessary for the application of Articles 23.4. and 23.5.

23.7. Upon the establishment of the ECB, the President of the EMI shall relinquish his office.

5   Excessive deficit procedure

Article 1.   The reference values referred to in Article 104c(2) of this Treaty are:

- 3% for the ratio of the planned or actual government deficit to gross domestic product at market prices;
- 60% for the ratio of government debt to gross domestic product at market prices.

Article 2.   In Article 104c of this Treaty and in this Protocol:

- government means general government, that is central government, regional or local government and social security funds, to the exclusion of commercial operations, as defined in the European System of Integrated Economic Accounts;
- deficit means net borrowing as defined in the European System of Integrated Economic Accounts;
- investment means gross fixed capital formation as defined in the European System of Integrated Economic Accounts;
- debt means total gross debt at nominal value outstanding at the end of the year and consolidated between and within the sectors of general government as defined in the first indent.

Article 3.   In order to ensure the effectiveness of the excessive deficit procedure, the governments of the Member States shall be responsible under this procedure for the deficits of general government as defined in the first indent of Article 2. The Member States shall ensure that national procedures in the Budgetary area enable them to meet their obligations in this area deriving from this Treaty. The Member States shall report their planned and actual deficits and the levels of their debt promptly and regularly to the Commission.

Article 4.   The statistical data to be used for the application of this Protocol shall be provided by the Commission.

6 Convergence criteria

Article 1.   The criterion on price stability referred to in the first indent of Article 109j(1) of this Treaty shall mean that a Member State has a price performance that is sustainable and an average rate of inflation, observed over a period of one year before the examination, that does not exceed by more than 1 1/2 percentage points that of, at most, the three best performing Member States in terms of price stability. Inflation shall be measured by means of the consumer price index on a comparable basis, taking into account differences in national definitions.

Article 2.   The criterion on the government budgetary position referred to in the second indent of Article 109j(1) of this treaty shall mean that at the time of the examination the Member State is not the subject of a Council decision under Article 104c(6) of this Treaty that an excessive deficit exists.

Article 3.   The criterion on participation in the Exchange Rate mechanism of the European Monetary System referred to in the third indent of Article 109j(1) of this Treaty shall mean that a Member State has respected the normal fluctuation margins provided for by the Exchange Rate Mechanism of the European Monetary System without severe tensions for at least the last two years before the examination. In particular, the Member State shall not have devalued its currency's bilateral central rate against any other Member State's currency on its own initiative for the same period.

Article 4.   The criterion on the convergence of interest rates referred to in the fourth indent of Article 109j(1) of this Treaty shall mean that, observed over a period of one year before the examination, a Member State has had an average nominal long-term interest rate that does not exceed by more than 2 percentage points that of, at most, the three best performing Member States in terms of price stability. Interest rates shall be measured on the basis of long term government bonds or comparable securities, taking into account differences in national definitions.

Article 5.   The statistical data to be used for the application of this protocol shall be provided by the Commission.

Article 6.   The Council shall, acting unanimously on a proposal from the Commission and after consulting the European Parliament, the EMI or the ECB as the case may be, and the Committee referred to in Article 109c, adopt appropriate provisions to lay down the details of the convergence criteria referred to Article 109j of this Treaty, which shall then replace this Protocol.

7 ECB Privileges and Immunities (see art. 23 of the Protocol on the Privileges and Immunities of the EC.)

8 Denmark

The provisions of Article 14 of the Protocol on the Statute of the European System of Central Banks and of the European System of Central Banks and of the European Central Bank shall not affect the right of the National Bank of Denmark to carry out its existing tasks concerning those parts of the Kingdom of Denmark which are not part of the Community

9 Portugal

1. Portugal is hereby authorized to maintain the facility afforded to the Autonomous Regions of Azores and Madeira to benefit from an interest-free credit facility with the Banco de Portugal under the terms established by existing Portuguese law.
2. Portugal commits itself to pursue its best endeavors in order to put an end to the above mentioned facility as soon as possible.

10 EMU third stage

THE HIGH CONTRACTING PARTIES,
Declare the irreversible character of the Community's movement to the third stage of Economic and Monetary Union by signing the new Treaty provisions on Economic and Monetary Union.

Therefore all Member States shall, whether they fulfil the necessary conditions for the adoption of a single currency or not, respect the will for the Community to enter swiftly into the third stage, and therefore no Member State shall prevent the entering into the third stage.

If by the end of 1997 the date of the beginning of the third stage has not been set, the Member States concerned, the Community institutions and other bodies involved shall expedite all preparatory work during 1998, in order to enable the Community to enter the third stage irrevocably on 1 January 1999 and to enable the ECB and ESCB to start their full functioning from this date.

This Protocol shall be annexed to the Treaty establishing the European Community.

11 EMU and UK

THE HIGH CONTRACTING PARTIES,
RECOGNIZING that the United Kingdom shall not be obliged or committed to move to the third stage of economic and monetary union without a separate decision to do so by its government and Parliament,
NOTING the practice of the government of the United Kingdom to fund its borrowing requirement by the sale of debt to the private sector.
HAVE AGREED the following provisions, which shall be annexed to the Treaty establishing the European Community:

1. The United Kingdom shall notify the Council whether it intends to move to the third stage before the Council makes its assessment under Article 109j(2) of this Treaty;
   Unless the United Kingdom notifies the Council that it intends to move to the third stage, it shall be under no obligation to do so.
   If no date is set for the beginning of the third stage under Article 109j(3) of this Treaty, the United Kingdom may notify its intention to move to the third stage before 1 January 1998.
2. Paragraphs 3 to 9 shall have effect if the United Kingdom notifies the Council that it does not intend to move to the third stage.
3. The United Kingdom shall not be included among the majority of Member States which fulfil the necessary conditions referred to in the second indent of Article 109j(2) and the first indent of Article 109j(3) of this Treaty.
4. The United Kingdom shall retain its powers in the field of monetary policy according to national law.
5. Articles 3a(2), 104c(1), (9) and (11), 105(1) to (5), 105a, 107, 108, 108a, 109, 109a(1) and (2)(b) and 109l(4) and (5) of this Treaty shall not apply to the United Kingdom. In these provisions references to the Community or the Member States shall not include the United Kingdom and references to national central banks shall not include the Bank of England.
6. Articles 109e(4) and 109h and i of this Treaty shall continue to apply to the United Kingdom. Articles 109c(4) and 109m shall apply to the united Kingdom as if it had a derogation.
7. The voting rights of the United Kingdom shall be suspended in respect of acts of the Council referred to in Articles listed in paragraph 5. For this purpose the weighted votes of the United Kingdom shall be excluded form any calculation of a qualified majority under Article 109k(5) of this Treaty.
   The United Kingdom shall also have no right to participate in the appointment of the President, the Vice-President and the other mem-

bers of the Executive Board of the ECB under Articles 109a(2)(b) and 109l(1) of this Treaty.

8. Articles 3, 4, 6, 7, 9.2, 10.1, 10.3, 11.2, 12.1, 14, 16, 18 to 20, 22, 23, 26, 27, 30 to 34, 50 and 52 of the Protocol on the Statute of the European System of Central Banks and of the European Central Bank ('the Statute') shall not apply to the United Kingdom.

   In those Articles, references to the Community or the Member States shall not include the United Kingdom and references to national central banks or shareholders shall not include the Bank of England.

   References in Articles 10.3 and 30.2. of the Statute to 'subscribed capital of the ECB' shall not include capital subscribed by the Bank of England.

9. Article 109(3) of this Treaty and Articles 44 to 48 of the Statute shall have effect, whether or not there is any Member State with a derogation, subject to the following amendments:

   (a) References in Article 44 ot the tasks of the ECB and the EMI shall include those tasks that still need to be performed in the third stage owing to any decision of the United kingdom not to move to that Stage.

   (b) In addition to the tasks referred to in Article 47 the ECB shall also give advice in relation to and contribute to the preparation of any decision of the Council with regard to the United Kingdom taken in accordance with paragraphs 10(a) and 10(c).

   (c) The Bank of England shall pay up its subscription to the capital of the ECB as a contribution of its operational costs on the same basis as national central banks of Member States with a derogation.

10. If the United Kingdom does not move to the third stage, it may change its notification at any time after the beginning of that stage. In that event:

    (a) The United Kingdom shall have the right to move to the third stage provided only that it satisfies the necessary conditions. The Council, acting at the request of the United Kingdom and under the conditions and in accordance with the procedure laid down in Article 109k(2) of this Treaty, shall decide whether it fulfills the necessary conditions.

    (b) The Bank of England shall pay up its subscribed capital, transfer to the ECB foreign reserve assets and contribute to its reserves on the same basis as the national central bank of a Member State whose derogation has been abrogated.

(c) The Council, acting under the conditions and in accordance with the procedure laid down in Article 109(5) of this Treaty, shall take all other necessary decisions to enable the United Kingdom to move to the third stage.

If the United Kingdom moves to the third stage pursuant to the provisions of this protocol, paragraphs 3 to 9 shall cease to have effect.

11. Notwithstanding Articles 104 and 109e(3) of this Treaty and Article 21.1. of the Statute, the government of the United Kingdom may maintain its ways and means facility with the Bank of England if and so long as the United Kingdom does not move to the third stage.

12 *EMU and Denmark*

THE HIGH CONTRACTING PARTIES,
DESIRING to settle, in accordance with the general objectives of the Treaty establishing the European Community, certain particular problems existing at the present time,
TAKING INTO ACCOUNT that the Danish Constitution contains provisions which may imply a referendum in Denmark prior to Danish participation in the third stage of Economic and Monetary Union,
HAVE AGREED on the following provisions, which shall be annexed to the Treaty establishing the European Community:

1. The Danish Government shall notify the Council of its position concerning participation in the third stage before the Council makes its assessment under Article 109j(2) of this Treaty.
2. In the event of a notification that Denmark will not participate in the third stage, Denmark shall have an exemption. The effect of the exemption shall be that all Articles and provisions of this Treaty and the Statute of the ESCB referring to a derogation shall be applicable to Denmark.
3. In such case, Denmark shall not be included among the majority of Member States which fulfil the necessary conditions referred to in the second indent of Article 109j(2) and the first indent of Article 109j(3) of this Treaty.
4. As for the abrogation of the exemption, the procedure referred to in Article 109k(2) shall only be initiated at the request of Denmark.
5. In the event of abrogation of the exemption status, the provisions of this Protocol shall cease to apply.

13 *France*

France will keep the privilege of monetary emission in its overseas territories under the terms established by its national laws, and will be solely entitled to determine the parity of the CFP franc.

14 *Social Policy*

THE HIGH CONTRACTING PARTIES,

NOTING that eleven Member States, that is to say the Kingdom of Belgium, the Kingdom of Denmark and Federal Republic of Germany, the Hellenic Republic, the Kingdom of Spain, the French Republic, Ireland, the Italian Republic, the Grand Duchy of Luxembourg, the Kingdom of the Netherlands and the Portuguese Republic, wish to continue along the path laid down in the 1989 Social Charter; that they have adopted among themselves an Agreement to this end; that this Agreement is annexed to this Protocol; that this Protocol and the said Agreement are without prejudice to the provisions of this Treaty, particularly those relating to social policy which constitute an integral part of the 'acquis communautaire':

1. Agree to authorize those eleven Member States to have recourse to the institutions, procedures and mechanisms of the Treaty for the purposes of taking among themselves and applying as far as they are concerned the acts and decisions required for giving effect to the abovementioned Agreement.

2. The United Kingdom of Great Britain and Northern Ireland shall not take part in the deliberations and the adoption by the Council of Commission proposals made on the basis of the Protocol and the above mentioned Agreement.

    By way of derogation from Article 148(2) of the Treaty, acts of the Council which are made pursuant to this Protocol and which must be adopted by a qualified majority shall be deemed to be so adopted if they have received at least forty-four votes in favour. The unanimity of the members of the Council, with the exception of the United Kingdom of Great Britain and Northern Ireland, shall be necessary for acts of the Council which must be adopted unanimously and for those amending the Commission proposal.

    Acts adopted by the Council and any financial consequences other than administrative costs entailed for the institutions shall not be applicable to the United Kingdom of Great Britain and Northern Ireland.

3. This Protocol shall be annexed to the Treaty establishing the European Community.

AGREEMENT ON SOCIAL POLICY

The undersigned eleven HIGH CONTRACTING PARTIES, that is to say, the Kingdom of Belgium, the Kingdom of Denmark, the Federal Republic of Germany, the Hellenic Republic, the Grand Duchy of Luxembourg, the Kingdom of the Netherlands and the Portuguese Republic (hereinafter referred to the 'the Member States'),

WISHING TO implement to the 1989 Social Charter on the basis of the 'acquis communautaire',
CONSIDERING the Protocol on social policy,
HAVE AGREED as follows:

Article 1. The Community and the Member States shall have as their objectives the promotion of employment, improved living and working conditions, proper social protection, dialogue between management and labour, the development of human resources with a view to lasting high employment and the combating of exclusion. To this end the Community and Member States shall implement measures which take account of the diverse forms of national practices, in particular in the field of contractual relations, and the need to maintain the competitiveness of the Community economy.

Article 2.
1. With a view to achieving the objectives of Article 1, the Community shall support and complement the activities of the Member States in the following fields:
   - improvement in particular of the working environment to protect workers' health and safety;
   - working conditions;
   - the information and consultation of workers;
   - equality between men and women with regard to labour market opportunities and treatment at work;
   - the integration of persons excluded from the labour market, without prejudice to Article 127 of the Treaty establishing the European Community (hereinafter referred to as 'the Treaty').

2. To this end, the Council may adopt, by means of directives, minimum requirements for gradual implementation, having regard to the conditions and technical rules obtaining in each of the Member States. Such directives shall avoid imposing administrative, financial and legal constraints in a way which would hold back the creation and development of small and medium-sized undertakings.
   The Council shall act in accordance with the procedure referred to in Article 189c of the Treaty after consulting the Economic and Social Committee.
3. However, the Council shall act unanimously on a proposal from the Commission, after consulting the European Parliament and the Economic and Social Committee, in following areas:
   - social security and social protection of workers;
   - protection of workers where their employment contract is terminated;

- representation and collective defence of the interests of worker and employers, including co-determination, subject to paragraph 6;
- conditions of employment for third-country nationals legally residing in Community territory;
- financial contributions for promotion of employment and job-creation, without prejudice to the provisions relating to the Social Fund.

4. A Member State may entrust management and labour, at their joint request, with the implementation of directives adopted pursuant to paragraphs 2 and 3.

In this case, it shall ensure that, no later than the date on which a directive must be transposed in accordance with Article 189, management and labour have introduced the necessary measures by agreement, the Member State concerned being required to take any necessary measure enabling it at any time to be in a position to guarantee the results imposed by that directive.

5. The provisions adopted pursuant to this Article shall not prevent any Member State from maintaining or introducing more stringent protective measures compatible with the Treaty.

6. The provisions of this Article shall not apply to pay, the right of association, the right to strike or the right to impose lock-outs.

Article 3.

1. The Commission shall have the task of promoting the consultation of management and labour at Community level and shall take any relevant measure to facilitate their dialogue by ensuring balanced support for the parties.

2. To this end, before submitting proposals in the social policy field, the Commission shall consult management and labour on the possible direction of Community action.

3. If, after such consultation, the Commission considers Community action advisable, it shall consult management and labour on the content of the envisaged proposal. Management and labour shall forward to the Commission an opinion or, where appropriate, a recommendation.

4. On the occasion of such consultation, management and labour may inform the Commission of their wish to initiate the process provided for in Article 4. The duration of the procedure shall not exceed nine months, unless the management and labour concerned and the Commission decide jointly to extend it.

Article 4.

1. Should management and labour so desire, the dialogue between them at Community level may lead to contractual relations, including agreements.

2. Agreements concluded at Community level shall be implemented either in accordance with the procedures and practices specific to management and labour and the Member States or, in matters covered by Article 2, at the joint request of the signatory parties, by a Council decision on a proposal from the Commission.

The Council shall act by qualified majority, except where the agreement in question contains one or more provisions relating to one of the areas referred to in Article 2(3), in which case it shall act unanimously.

Article 5.

With a view to achieving the objectives of Article 1 and without prejudice to the other provisions of the Treaty, the Commission shall encourage co-operation between the Member States and facilitate the co-ordination of their action in all social policy fields under this Agreement.

Article 6.

1. Each Member State shall ensure that the principle of equal pay for male and female workers for equal work is applied.
2. For the purpose of this Article, 'pay' means the ordinary basic or minimum wage or salary and any other consideration, whether in cash or in kind, which the worker receives directly or indirectly, in respect of his employment, from his employer.

Equal pay without discrimination based on sex means:

(a) that pay for the same work at piece rates shall be calculated on the basis of the same unit of measurement.
(b) that pay for work at time rates shall be the same for the same job.

3. This Article shall not prevent any Member State from maintaining or adopting measures providing for specific advantages in order to make it easier for women to pursue a vocational activity or to prevent or compensate for disadvantages in their professional careers.

Article 7.

The Commission shall draw up a report each year on progress in achieving the objective of Article 1, including the demographic situation in the Community. It shall forward the report to the European Parliament, the Council and the Economic and Social Committee.

The European Parliament may invite the Commission to draw up reports on particular problems concerning the social situation.

DECLARATIONS

1. Declaration on Article 2(2)

The eleven High Contracting Parties note that in the discussions on Article 2(2) of the Agreement it was agreed that the Community does not intend, in laying down minimum requirements for the protection of the safety and health of employees, to discriminate in a manner unjustified by the circumstances against employees in small and medium-sized undertakings.

2. Declaration on Article 4(2)

The eleven High Contracting Parties declare that the first of the arrangements for application of the agreements between management and labour at Community level – referred to in Article 4(2) – will consist in developing, by collective bargaining according to the rules of each Member State, the content of the agreements, and that consequently this arrangement implies no obligation on the Member States to apply the agreements directly or to work out rules for their transposition, or any obligation to amend national legislation in force to facilitate their implementation.

15 *Economic and social cohesion*

THE HIGH CONTRACTING PARTIES,

RECALLING that the Union has set itself the objective of promoting economic and social progress, inter alia, through the strengthening of economic and social cohesion;

RECALLING that Article 2 of the Treaty establishing the European Community includes the task of promoting economic and social cohesion and solidarity between Member States and that the strengthening of economic and social cohesion figures among the activities of the Community listed in Article 3;

RECALLING that the provisions of Part Three, Title XIV, on economic and social cohesion as a whole provide the legal basis for consolidating and further developing the Community's action in the field of economic and social cohesion, including the creation of a new fund;

RECALLING that the provisions of Part Three, Title XII on trans-European networks and Title XVI on environment envisage a Cohesion Fund to be set up before 31 December 1993;

STATING their belief that progress towards Economic and Monetary Union will contribute to the economic growth of all Member States;

NOTING that the Community's Structural Funds are being doubled in real terms between 1987 and 1993, implying large transfers, especially as a proportion of GDP of the less prosperous Member States;

NOTING that the European Investment Bank is lending large and increasing amounts for the benefit of the poorer regions;

NOTING the desire for greater flexibility in the arrangements for allocation from the Structural Funds;

NOTING the desire for modulation of the levels of Community participation in programmes and projects in certain countries;

NOTING the proposal to take greater account of the relative prosperity of Member States in the system of own resources,

REAFFIRM that the promotion of economic and social cohesion is vital to the full development and enduring success of the Community, and underline the importance of the inclusion of economic and social cohesion in Articles 2 and 3 of this Treaty;

REAFFIRM their conviction that the Structural Funds should continue to play a considerable part in the achievement of Community objectives in the field of cohesion;

REAFFIRM their conviction that the European Investment Bank should continue to devote the majority of its resources to the promotion of economic and social cohesion, and declare their willingness to review the capital needs of the European Investment Bank as soon as this is necessary for that purpose;

REAFFIRM the need for a thorough evaluation of the operation and effectiveness of the Structural Funds in 1992, and the need to review, on that occasion, the appropriate size of these Funds in the light of the tasks of the Community in the area of economic and social cohesion;

AGREE that the Cohesion Fund to be set up before 31 December 1993 will provide Community financial contributions to projects in the fields of environment and trans-European networks in Member States with a per capita GNP of less than 90% of the Community average which have a programme leading to the fulfilment of the conditions of economic convergence as set out in Article 104c;

DECLARE their intention of allowing a greater margin of flexibility in allocating financing from the Structural Funds to specific needs not covered under the present Structural Funds regulations;

DECLARE their willingness to modulate the levels of Community participation in the context of programmes and projects of the Structural Funds, with a view to avoiding excessive increases in budgetary expenditure in the less prosperous Member States;

RECOGNIZE the need to monitor regularly the progress made towards achieving economic and social cohesion and state their willingness to study all necessary measures in this respect;

DECLARE their intention of taking greater account of the contributive capacity of individual Member States in the system of own resources, and of examining means of correcting, for the less prosperous Member States, regressive elements existing in the present own resources system;

AGREE to annex this Protocol to the Treaty establishing the European Community.

16 *Economic and Social Committee: Committee of the Regions*
The Economic and Social Committee and the Committee of the Regions shall have a common organizational structure.

17 *Irish Constitution*
Nothing in the Treaty on European Union, or in the Treaties establishing the European Communities, or in the Treaties or Acts modifying or supplementing those Treaties, shall affect the application in Ireland of Article 40.3.3 of the Constitution of Ireland.

Declaration on Protocol 17
On 1 May 1992, in Guimaraes (Portugal), the High Contracting Parties to the Treaty on European Union adopted the following Declaration:

The High Contracting Parties to the Treaty on European Union signed at Maastricht on the seventh day of February 1992,
Having considereed the terms of Protocol No 17 to the said Treaty on European Union which is annexed to that Treaty and to the Treaties establishing the European Communities,
Hereby give the following legal interpretation:

That it was and is their intention that the Protocol shall not limit freedom to travel between Member States or, in accordance with conditions which may be laid down, in conformity with Community law, by Irish legislation, to obtain or make available in Ireland information relating to services lawfully available in Member States.

At the same time the High Contracting Parties solemly declare that, in the event of a future constitutional amendment in Ireland which concerns the subject matter of Article 40.3.3. of the Constitution of Ireland and which does not conflict with the intention of the High Contracting Parties hereinbefore expressed, they will, following the entry into force of the Treaty on European Union, be favourably disposed to amending the said Protocol so as to extend its application to such constitutional amendment if Ireland so requests.

TREATY ON EUROPEAN UNION

Maastricht, 7 February 1992

[*NB. Formal provisions are abbreviated; amendments to the EEC and ECSC Treaties occasioned by Titles II and III are inserted in the texts of those Treaties; Title IV on Euratom is omitted.*]

[The Heads of State of the Kingdom of Belgium, the Kingdom of Denmark, the Federal Republic of Germany, the Hellenic Republic, the Kingdom of Spain, the French Republic, Ireland, the Italian Republic, the Grand Duchy of Luxembourg, the Kingdom of the Netherlands, the Portuguese Republic, the United Kingdom of Great Britain and Northern Ireland]

RESOLVED to mark a new stage in the process of European integration undertaken with the establishment of the European Communities,

RECALLING the historic importance of the ending of the division of the European continent and the need to create firm bases for the construction of the future Europe,

CONFIRMING their attachment to the principles of liberty, democracy and respect for human rights and fundamental freedoms and of the rule of law,

DESIRING to deepen the solidarity between their peoples while respecting their history, their culture and their traditions,

DESIRING to enhance further the democratic and efficient functioning of the institutions so as to enable them better to carry out, within a single institutional framework, the tasks entrusted to them,

RESOLVED to achieve the strengthening and the convergence of their economies and to establish an economic and monetary union including, in accordance with the provisions of this Treaty, a single and stable currency,

DETERMINED to promote economic and social progress for their peoples, within the context of the accomplishment of the internal market and of reinforced cohesion and environmental protection, and to implement policies ensuring that advances in economic integration are accompanied by parallel progress in other fields,

RESOLVED to establish a citizenship common to the nationals of their countries,

RESOLVED to implement a common foreign and security policy including the eventual framing of a common defence policy, which might in time lead to a common defence, thereby reinforcing the European identity and its independence in order to promote peace, security and progress in Europe and in the world,

REAFFIRMING their objective to facilitate the free movement of persons while ensuring the safety and security of their peoples, by including provisions on justice and home affairs in this Treaty,

RESOLVED to continue the process of creating an ever closer union among the peoples of Europe, in which decisions are taken as closely as possible to the citizen in accordance with the principle of subsidiarity,

IN VIEW of further steps to be taken in order to advance European integration,

HAVE DECIDED to establish a European Union and to this end have designated as their plenipotentiaries [names omitted]:

WHO, having exchanged their full powers, found in good and due form, have agreed as follows:

TITLE I. COMMON PROVISIONS

Article A.   By this Treaty, the High Contracting Parties establish among themselves a European Union, hereinafter called 'the Union'.
This Treaty marks a new stage in the process of creating an ever closer union among the peoples of Europe, in which decisions are taken as closely as possible to the citizen.
   The Union shall be founded on the European Communities, supplemented by the policies and forms of cooperation established by this Treaty. Its task shall be to organize, in a manner demonstrating consistency and solidarity, relations between the Member States and between their peoples.

Article B.   The Union shall set itself the following objectives:

– to promote economic and social progress which is balanced and sustainable, in particular through the creation of an area without internal frontiers, through the strengthening of economic and social cohesion and through the establishment of economic and monetary union, ultimately including a single currency in accordance with the provisions of this Treaty;

- to assert its identity on the international scene, in particular through the implementation of a common foreign and security policy including the eventual framing of a common defence policy, which might in time lead to a common defence;
- to strengthen the protection of the rights and interests of the nationals of its Member States through the introduction of a citizenship of the Union;
- to develop close cooperation on justice and home affairs;
- to maintain in full the 'acquis communautaire' and build on it with a view to considering, through the procedure referred to in Article N(2), to what extent the policies and forms of cooperation introduced by this Treaty may need to be revised with the aim of ensuring the effectiveness of the mechanisms and the institutions of the Community.

The objectives of the Union shall be achieved as provided in this Treaty and in accordance with the conditions and the timetable set out therein while respecting the principle of subsidiarity as defined in Article 3b of the Treaty establishing the European Community.

Article C. The Union shall be served by a single institutional framework which shall ensure the consistency and the continuity of the activities carried out in order to attain its objectives while respecting and building upon the 'acquis communautaire'.

The Union shall in particular ensure the consistency of its external activities as a whole in the context of its external relations, security, economic and development policies. The Council and the Commission shall be responsible for ensuring such consistency. They shall ensure the implementation of these policies, each in accordance with its respective powers.

Article D. The European Council shall provide the Union with the necessary impetus for its development and shall define the general political guidelines thereof.

The European Council shall bring together the Heads of State or of Government of the Member States and the President of the Commission. They shall be assisted by the Ministers for Foreign Affairs of the Member States and by a Member of the Commission. The European Council shall meet at least twice a year, under the chairmanship of the Head of State or of Government of the Member State which holds the Presidency of the Council.

The European Council shall submit to the European Parliament a report after each of its meetings and a yearly written report on the progress achieved by the Union.

Article E.   The European Parliament, the Council, the Commission and the Court of Justice shall exercise their powers under the conditions and for the purposes provided for, on the one hand, by the provisions of the Treaties establishing the European Communities and of the subsequent Treaties and Acts modifying and supplementing them and, on the other hand, by the other provisions of this Treaty.

Article F.

1. The Union shall respect the national identities of its Member States, whose systems of government are founded on the principles of democracy.

2. The Union shall respect fundamental rights, as guaranteed by the European Convention for the Protection of Human Rights and Fundamental Freedoms signed in Rome on 4 November 1950 and as they result from the constitutional traditions common to the Member States, as general principles of Community law.

3. The Union shall provide itself with the means necessary to attain its objectives and carry through its policies.

TITLE V. PROVISIONS ON A COMMON FOREIGN AND SECURITY POLICY

Article J.   A common foreign and security policy is hereby established which shall be governed by the following provisions.

Article J.1.

1. The union and its Member States shall define and implement a common foreign and security policy, governed by the provisions of the Title and covering all areas of foreign and security policy.

2. The objectives of the common foreign and security policy shall be:

    - to safeguard the common values, fundamental interests and independence of the Union;
    - to strengthen the security of the Union and its Member States in all ways;
    - to preserve peace and strengthen international security, in accordance with the principles of the United Nations Charter as well as the principles of the Helsinki Final Act and the objectives of the Paris Charter;
    - to promote international co-operation;

- to develop and consolidate democracy and the rule of law, and respect for human rights and fundamental freedoms.

3. The Union shall pursue these objectives;

   - by establishing systematic co-operation between Member States in the conduct of policy, in accordance with Article J.2;
   - by gradually implementing, in accordance with Article J.3, joint action in the areas in which the Member States have important interests in common.

4. The Member States shall support the Union's external and security policy actively and unreservedly in a spirit of loyalty and mutual solidarity. They shall refrain from any action which is contrary to the interests of the Union or likely to impair its effectiveness as a cohesive force in international relations. The Council shall ensure that these principles are complied with.

Article J.2.

1. Member States shall inform and consult one another within the Council on any matter of foreign and security policy of general interest in order to ensure that their combined influence is exerted as effectively as possible by means of concerted and convergent action.

2. Whenever it deems it necessary, the Council shall define a common position.

   Member States shall ensure that their national policies conform on the common positions.

3. Member States shall co-ordinate their action in international organizations and at international conferences. They shall uphold the common positions in such fora.

   In international organizations and at international conferences where not all the Member States participate, those which do take part shall uphold the common positions.

Article J.3. The procedure for adopting joint action in matters covered by foreign and security policy shall be the following:

1. The Council shall decide, on the basis of general guidelines from the European Council, that a matter should be the subject of joint action.

   Whenever the Council decides on the principle of joint action, it shall lay down the specific scope, the Union's general and specific objectives in carrying out such action, if necessary its duration, and the means, procedures and conditions for its implementation.

2. The Council shall, when adopting the joint action and at any stage during its development, define those matters on which decisions are to be taken by a qualified majority.

   Where the Council is required to act by a qualified majority pursuant to the preceding subparagraph, the votes of its members shall be weighted in accordance with Article 148(2) of the Treaty establishing the European Community, and for their adoption, acts of the Council shall require at least fifty-four votes in favour, cast by at least eight members.

3. If there is a change in circumstances having a substantial effect on a question subject to joint action, the Council shall review the principles and objectives of that action and take the necessary decisions. As long as the Council has not acted, the joint action shall stand.

4. Joint actions shall commit the Member States in the positions they adopt and in the conduct of their activity.

5. Whenever there is any plan to adopt a national position or take national action pursuant to a joint action, information shall be provided in time to allow, if necessary, for prior consultations within the Council. The obligation to provide prior information shall not apply to measures which are merely a national transposition of Council decisions.

6. In cases of imperative need arising from changes in the situation and failing a Council decision, Member States may take the necessary measures as a matter of urgency having regard to the general objectives of the joint action. The Member State concerned shall inform the Council immediately of any such measures.

7. Should there be any major difficulties in implementing a joint action, a Member State shall refer them to the Council which shall discuss them and seek appropriate solutions. Such solutions shall not run counter to the objectives of the joint action or impair its effectiveness.

Article J.4.

1. The common foreign and security policy shall include all questions related to the security of the Union, including the eventual framing of a common defence policy, which might in time lead to a common defence.

2. The union requests the Western European Union (WEU), which is an integral part of the development of the Union, to elaborate and implement decisions and actions of the Union which have defence

implications. The Council shall, in agreement with the institutions of the WEU, adopt the necessary practical arrangements.

3. Issues having defence implications dealt with under this Article shall not be subject to the procedures set out in Article J.3.

4. The policy of the Union in accordance with this Article shall not prejudice the specific character of the security and defence policy of certain Member States and shall respect the obligations of certain Member States under the North Atlantic Treaty and be compatible with the common security and defence policy established within that framework.

5. The provisions of this Article shall not prevent the development of closer co-operation between two or more Member States on a bilateral level, in the framework of the WEU and the Atlantic Alliance, provided such co-operation does not run counter to or impede that provided for in this Title.

6. With a view to furthering the objective of this Treaty, and having in view the date of 1998 in the context of Article XII of the Brussels Treaty, the provisions of this Article may be revised as provided for in Article N(2) on the basis of a report to be presented in 1996 by the Council to the European Council, which shall include an evaluation of the progress made and the experience gained until then.

Article J.5.

1. The Presidency shall represent the Union in matters coming within the common foreign and security policy.

2. The Presidency shall be responsible for the implementation of common measures; in that capacity it shall in principle express the position of the Union in international organizations and international conferences.

3. In the tasks referred to in paragraphs 1 and 2, the presidency shall be assisted if needs be by the previous and next Member States to hold the Presidency. The Commission shall be fully associated in these tasks.

4. Without prejudice to Article J.2(3) and Article J.3(4), Member States represented in international organizations or international conferences where not all the Member States participate shall keep the latter informed of any matter of common interest.

    Member States which are also members of the United Nations Security Council will concert and keep the other Member States fully informed. Member States which are permanent members of the

Security Council will, in the execution of their functions, ensure the defence of the positions and the interests of the union, without prejudice to their responsibilities under the provisions of the United Nations Charter.

Article J.6. The diplomatic and consular missions of the Member States and the Commission Delegations in third countries and international conferences, and their representations to international organizations, shall cooperate in ensuring that the common positions and common measures adopted by the Council are complied with and implemented.

They shall step up co-operation by exchanging information, carrying out joint assessments and contributing to the implementation of the provisions referred to in Article 8c of the Treaty establishing the European Community.

Article J.7. The Presidency shall consult the European Parliament on the main aspects and the basic choices of the common foreign and security policy and shall ensure that the views of the European Parliament are duly taken into consideration. The European Parliament shall be kept regularly informed by the Presidency and the Commission of the development of the Union's foreign and security policy.

The European Parliament may ask questions of the Councils or make recommendations to it. It shall hold an annual debate on progress in implementing the common foreign and security policy.

Article J.8.

1. The European Council shall define the principles of and general guidelines for the common foreign and security policy.

2. The Council shall take the decisions necessary for defining and implementing the common foreign and security policy on the basis of the general guidelines adopted by the European Council. It shall ensure the unity, consistency and effectiveness of action by the Union.

   The Council shall act unanimously, except for procedural questions and in the case referred to in Article J.3(2).

3. Any Member State or the Commission may refer to the Council any question relating to the common foreign policy and may submit proposals to the Council.

4. In cases requiring a rapid decision, the Presidency, of its own motion, or at the request of the Commission or a Member State, shall convene an extraordinary Council meeting within forty-eight hours or, in an emergency, within a shorter period.

5. Without prejudice to Article 151 of the Treaty establishing the European Community, a Political Committee consisting of Political Directors shall monitor the international situation in the areas covered by common foreign and security policy and contribute to the definition of policies by delivering opinions to the Council at the request of the Council or on its own initiative. It shall also monitor the implementation of agreed policies, without prejudice to the responsibility of the Presidency and the Commission.

Article J.9.   The Commission shall be fully associated with the work carried out in the common foreign and security policy field.

Article J.10.   On the occasion of any review of the security provisions under Article J.4, the Conference which is convened to that effect shall also examine whether any other amendments need to be made to provisions relating to the common foreign and security policy.

Article J.11.

1. The provisions referred to in Articles 137, 138, 139 to 142, 146, 147, 150 to 153, 157 to 163 and 217 of the Treaty establishing the European Community shall apply to the provisions relating to the areas referred to in this Title.

2. Administrative expenditure which the provisions relating to the areas referred to in this Title entail for the institutions shall be charged to the budget of the European Communities.
    The Council may also:

    – either decide unanimously that operational expenditure to which the implementation of those provisions gives rise is to be charged to the budget of the European Communities; in that event, the budgetary procedure laid down in the Treaty establishing the European Community shall be applicable;
    – or determine that such expenditure shall be charged to the Member States, where appropriate in accordance with a scale to be decided.

TITLE VI. PROVISIONS ON COOPERATION IN THE FIELD OF JUSTICE AND HOME AFFAIRS

Article K.   Co-operation in the fields of justice and home affairs shall be governed by the following provisions.

Article K.1.   For the purposes of achieving the objectives of the Union, in particular the free movement of persons, and without prejudice to the powers of the European Community, Member States shall regard the following areas as matters of common interest:

1. asylum policy;
2. rules governing the crossing by persons of the external borders of the Member States and the exercise of controls thereon;
3. immigration policy and policy regarding nationals of third countries;
    (a) conditions of entry and movement by nationals of third countries on the territory of Member States;
    (b) conditions of residence by nationals of third countries on the territory of Member States, including family reunion and access to employment;
    (c) combatting unauthorized immigration, residence and work by nationals of third countries on the territory of Member States;
4. combating drug addiction in so far as this is not covered by 7 to 9;
5. combating fraud on an international scale in so far as this is not covered by 7 to 9;
6. judicial co-operation in civil matters;
7. judicial co-operation in criminal matters;
8. customs co-operation;
9. police co-operation for the purposes of preventing and combating terrorism, unlawful drug trafficking and other serious forms of international crime, including if necessary certain aspects of customs co-operation, in connection with the organization of a Union-wide system for exchanging information within a European Police Office (Europol).

Article K.2.

1. The matters referred to in Article K.1 shall be dealt with in compliance with the European Convention for the Protection of Human Rights and Fundamental Freedoms of 4 November 1950 and the Convention relating to the Status of Refugees of 28 July 1951 and having regard to the protection afforded by Member States to persons persecuted on political grounds.

2. This Title shall not affect the exercise of the responsibilities incumbent upon Member States with regard to the maintenance of law and order and the safeguarding of internal security.

Article K.3.

1. In the areas referred to in Article K.1, Member States shall inform and consult one another within the Council with a view to co-

ordinating their action. To that end, they shall establish collaboration between the relevant departments of their administrations.

2. The Council may:

- on the initiative of any Member State or of the Commission, in the areas referred to in Article K.1(1) to (6);
- on the initiative of any Member State, in the areas referred to Article K1(7) to (9):
  (a) adopt joint positions and promote, using the appropriate form and procedures, any co-operation contributing to the pursuit of the objectives of the Union;
  (b) adopt joint action in so far as the objectives of the Union can be attained better by joint action than by the Member States acting individually on account of the scale or effects of the action envisaged; it may decide that measures implementing joint action are to be adopted by a qualified majority;
  (c) without prejudice to Article 220 of the Treaty establishing the European Community, draw up conventions which it shall recommend to the Member States for adoption in accordance with their respective constitutional requirements.

    Unless otherwise provided by such conventions, measures implementing them shall be adopted within the Council by a majority of two-thirds of the High Contracting Parties.

    Such conventions may stipulate that the Court of Justice shall have jurisdiction to interpret their provisions and to rule on any disputes regarding their application, in accordance with such arrangements as they may lay down.

Article K.4.

1. A Co-ordinating Committee shall be set up consisting of senior officials. In additions to its co-ordinating role, it shall be the task of the Committee to;

- give opinions for the attention of the Council, either at the Council's request or on its own initiative;
- contribute, without prejudice to Article 151 of the Treaty establishing the European Community, to the preparation of the Council's discussions in the areas referred to in Article K.1 and, in accordance with the conditions laid down in Article 100d of the Treaty establishing the European Community, in the areas referred to in Article 100c of that Treaty.

2. The Commission shall be fully associated with the work in the areas referred to in this Title.

3. The Council shall act unanimously, except on matters of procedure and in cases where Article K.3 expressly provides for other voting rules.

Where the Council is required to act by a qualified majority, the votes of its members shall be weighted as laid down in Article 148(2) of the Treaty establishing the European Community, and for their adoption, acts of the Council shall require at least fifty-four votes in favour, cast by at least eight members.

Article K.5. Within international organizations and at international conferences in which they take part, Member States shall defend the common positions adopted under the provisions of this Title.

Article K.6. The Presidency and the Commission shall regularly inform the European Parliament of discussions in the areas covered by this Title.

The Presidency shall consult the European Parliament on the principal aspects of activities in the areas referred to in this Title and shall ensure that the views of the European Parliament are duly taken into consideration.

The European Parliament may ask questions of the Council or make recommendations to it. Each year, it shall hold a debate on the progress made in implementation of the areas referred to in this Title.

Article K.7. The provisions of this Title shall not prevent the establishment or development of closer co-operation between two or more Member States in so far as such co-operation does not conflict with, or impede, that provided for in this Title.

Article K.8.

1. The provisions referred to in Article 137, 138, 139 to 142, 146, 147, 150 to 153, 157 to 163 and 217 of the Treaty establishing the European Community shall apply to the provisions relating to the areas referred to in this Title.

2. Administrative expenditure which the provisions relating to the areas referred to in this Title entail for the institutions shall be charged to the budget of European Communities.

   The Council may also:

   − either decide unanimously that operational expenditure to which the implementation of those provisions gives rise is to be charged to the budget of the European Communities; in that event, the budgetary

procedure laid down in the treaty establishing the European Community shall be applicable;
- or determine that such expenditure shall be charged to the Member States, where appropriate in accordance with a scale to be decided.

Article K.9. The Council, acting unanimously on the initiative of the Commission or a Member State, may decide to apply Article 100c of the Treaty establishing the European Community to action in areas referred to in Article K.1(1) to (6), and at the same time determine the relevant voting conditions relating to it. It shall recommend the Member States to adopt that decision in accordance with their respective constitutional requirements.

TITLE VII. FINAL PROVISIONS

Article L. The provisions of the Treaty establishing the European Community, the Treaty establishing the European Coal and Steel Community and the Treaty establishing the European Atomic Energy Community concerning the powers of the Court of Justice of the European Communities and the exercise of those powers shall apply only to the following provisions of this Treaty:

(a) provisions amending the Treaty establishing the European Economic Community, the Treaty establishing the European Coal and Steel Community and the Treaty establishing the European Atomic Energy Community;
(b) the third subparagraph of Article K.3(2)(c);
(c) articles L to S.

Article M. Subject to the provisions amending the Treaty establishing the European Economic Community with a view to establishing the European Community, the Treaty establishing the European Coal and Steel Community and the Treaty establishing the European Atomic Energy Community, and to these final provisions, nothing in this Treaty shall effect the Treaties establishing the European Communities or the subsequent Treaties and Acts modifying or supplementing them.

Article N.

1. The government of any Member State or the Commission may submit to the Council proposals for the amendment of the Treaties on which the Union is founded.
   If the Council, after consulting the European Parliament and, where appropriate, the Commission, delivers an opinion in favour of calling a

conference of representatives of the governments of the Member States, the conference shall be convened by the President of the Council for the purpose of determining by common accord the amendments to be made to those Treaties. The European Central Bank shall also be consulted in the case of institutional changes in the monetary area.

The amendments shall enter into force after being ratified by all the Member States in accordance with their respective constitutional requirements.

2. A conference of representatives of the governments of the Member States shall be convened in 1996 to examine those provisions of this Treaty for which revision is provided, in accordance with the objectives set out in Articles A and B.

Article O. Any European State may apply to become a Member of the Union. It shall address its application to the Council, which shall act unanimously after consulting the Commission and after receiving the assent of the European Parliament, which shall act by an absolute majority of its component members.

The conditions of admission and the adjustments to the Treaties on which the Union is founded which such admission entails shall be the subject of an agreement between the Member States and the applicant State. This agreement shall be submitted for ratification by all the contracting States in accordance with their respective constitutional requirements.

Article P.

1. Articles 2 to 7 and 10 to 19 of the Treaty establishing a single Council and a single Commission of the European Communities, signed in Brussels on 8 April 1965, are hereby repealed.

2. Article 2, Article 3(2) and Title III of the Single European Act signed in Luxembourg on 17 February 1986 and in the Hague on February 1986 are hereby repealed.

Article Q. This Treaty is concluded for an unlimited period.

Article R.

1. This Treaty shall be ratified by the High Contracting Parties in accordance with their respective constitutional requirements. The instruments of ratification shall be deposited with the government of the Italian Republic.

2. This Treaty shall enter into force on 1 January 1993, provided that all the instruments of ratification have been deposited, or, failing that, on the first day of the month following the deposit of the instrument of ratification by the last signatory State to take this step.

Article S. This Treaty, drawn up in a single original in the Danish, Dutch, English, French, German, Greek, Irish, Italian, Portuguese and Spanish languages, the texts in each of these languages being equally authentic, shall be deposited in the archives of the government of the Italian Republic, which will transmit a certified copy to each of the governments of the other signatory States.

IN WITNESS WHEREOF, the undersigned Plenipotentiaries have signed this Treaty.

Done at Maastricht, on 7 February 1992.

[Here follow the signatures]

PROTOCOL on the Irish Constitution
[See Protocol 17 annexed to the EC Treaty]

DECLARATIONS OF THE INTERGOVERNMENTAL CONFERENCE WHICH LED TO THE TREATY ON EUROPEAN UNION

[*NB Only selected Declarations are printed here. Their numbers as given in the Final Act have been retained, but their titles have been shortened.*]

2 *Nationality*
The Conference declares that, wherever in the Treaty establishing the European Community reference is made to nationals of the Member States, the question whether an individual possesses the nationality of a Member State shall be settled solely by reference to the national law of the Member State concerned. Member States may declare, for information, who are to be considered their nationals for Community purposes by way of declaration lodged with the Presidency and may amend any such declarations when necessary.

6 *Monetary relations*: San Marino, Vatican, Monaco
The Conference agrees that the existing monetary relations between Italy
and San Marino and the Vatican City and between France and Monaco
remain unaffected by the Treaty establishing the European Community
until the introduction of the ecu as the single currency of the Community.

The Community undertakes to facilitate such renegotiations of existing
arrangements as might become necessary as a result of the introduction
of the ecu as a single currency.

7 *Article 73d EC*
The Conference affirms that the right of Member States to apply the relevant provisions of their tax law as referred to in Article 73d(1)(a) of this
Treaty will apply only with respect to the relevant provisions which exist
at the end of 1993. However, this Declaration shall apply only to capital
movements between Member States and to payments effected between
Member States.

8 *Article 109*
The Conference emphasizes that use of the term 'formal agreements' in
Article 109(1) is not intended to create a new category of international
agreement within the meaning of Community law.

10 *Case 22/70*
The Conference considers that the provisions of Article 109(5), Article
130r(4), second subparagraph, and Article 130y do not affect the principles resulting from the judgment handed down by the Court of Justice in
the AETR case.

13 *National Parliaments*
The Conference considers that it is important to encourage greater
involvement of national Parliaments in the activities of the European
Union.

To this end, the exchange of information between the national
Parliaments and the European Parliament should be stepped up. In this
context, the governments of the Member States will ensure, inter alia,
that national Parliaments receive Commission proposals for legislation in
good time for information or possible examination.

Similarly, the Conference considers that it is important for contacts
between the national Parliaments and the European Parliament to be
stepped up, in particular through the granting of appropriate reciprocal
facilities and regular meetings between members of Parliament interested
in the same issues.

14 *Conference of the Parliaments*

The Conference invites the European Parliament and the national Parliaments to meet as necessary as a Conference of the Parliaments (or 'Assises')

The Conference of the Parliaments will be consulted on the main features of the European Union, without prejudice to the powers of the European Parliament and the rights of the national Parliaments. The President of the European Council and the President of the Commission will report to each session of the Conference of the Parliaments on the state of the Union.

16 *Hierarchy of Community acts*

The Conference agrees that the Intergovernmental Conference to be convened in 1996 will examine to what extent it might be possible to review the classification of Community acts with a view to establishing an appropriate hierarchy between the different categories of act.

17 *Freedom of information*

The Conference considers that transparency of the decision-making process strengthens the democratic nature of the institutions and the public's confidence in the administration. The Conference accordingly recommends that the Commission submit to the Council no later than 1993 a report on measures designed to improve public access to the information available to the institutions.

19 *Implementation of Community law*

1. The Conference stresses that it is central to the coherence and unity of the process of European construction that each Member State should fully and accurately transpose into national law the Community Directives addressed to it within the deadlines laid down therein.

    Moreover, the Conference, while recognizing that it must be for each Member State to determine how the provisions of Community law can best be enforced in the light of its own particular institutions, legal system and other circumstances, but in any event in compliance with Article 189 of the Treaty establishing the European Community, considers it essential for the proper functioning of the Community that the measures taken by the different Member States should result in Community law being applied with the same effectiveness and rigour as in the application of their national law.

2. The Conference calls on the Commission to ensure, in exercising its powers under Article 155 of this Treaty, that Member States fulfill their obligations. It asks the Commission to publish periodically a full report for the Member States and the European Parliament.

25   *Overseas countries and territories*
The Conference, noting that in exceptional circumstances divergences
may arise between the interests of the Union and those of the overseas
countries and territories referred to in Article 227(3) and (5)(a) and (b),
agrees that the Council will seek to reach a solution which accords with
the position of the Union. However, in the event that this proves impossible, the Conference agrees that the Member State concerned may act separately in the interests of the said overseas countries and territories,
without this affecting the Community's interests. The Member State concerned will give notice to the Council and the Commission where such a
divergence of interests is likely to occur and, when separate action proves
unavoidable, make it clear that it is acting in the interests of overseas territory mentioned above.
   This declaration also applies to Macao and East Timor.

26   *Outermost regions*
The Conference acknowledges that the outermost regions of the
Community (the French overseas departments, Azores and Madeira and
Canary Islands) suffer from major structural backwardness compounded
by several phenomena (remoteness, island status, small size, difficult
topography and climate, economic dependence on a few products), the
permanence and combination of which severely restrain their economic
and social development.
   It considers that, while the provisions of the Treaty establishing the
European Community and secondary legislation apply automatically to
outermost regions, it is nonetheless possible to adopt specific measures to
assist them inasmuch and as long as there is an objective need to take
such measures with a view to the economic and social development of
those regions. Such measures should have their aim both the completion
of the internal market and a recognition of the regional reality to enable
the outermost regions to achieve the average economic and social level of
the Community.

27   *Council voting*
The Conference agrees that, with regard to Council decisions requiring
unanimity, Member States will, to the extent possible, avoid preventing a
unanimous decision where a qualified majority exists in favour of that
decision.

29   *Languages*
The Conference agrees that the use of languages shall be in accordance
with the rules of the European Communities.

For COREU communications, the current practice of European political co-operation will serve as a guide for the time being.

All common foreign and security policy texts which are submitted to or adopted at meeting of the European Council and of the Council as well as all texts which are to be published are immediately and simultaneously translated into all the official Community languages.

31 *Asylum*

1. The Conference agrees that, in the context of the proceedings provided for in Articles K.1 and K.3 of the provisions on co-operation in the fields of justice and home affairs, the Council will consider as a matter of priority questions concerning Member States' asylum policies, with the aim of adoption by the beginning of 1993, common action to harmonize aspects of them, in the light of the work programme and timetable contained in the report on asylum drawn up at the request of the European Council meeting in Luxembourg on 28 and 29 June 1991.

2. In this connection, the Council will also consider, by the end of 1993, on the basis of a report, the possibility of applying Article K.9 to such matters.

Done at Maastricht on the 7th day of February 1992
[Here follow the signatures]

Decision of the Heads of State and Government, Meeting within the European Council, Concerning Certain Problems Raised by Denmark on the Treaty on European Union
Edinburgh 12 December 1992

The Heads of State and Government, meeting within the European Council, whose Governments are signatories of the Treaty on European Union, which involves independent and sovereign States having freely decided, in accordance with the existing Treaties, to exercise in common some of their competences, desiring to settle, in conformity with the Treaty on European Union, particular problems existing at the present time specifically for Denmark and raised in its memorandum 'Denmark in Europe' of 30 October 1992,

– having regard to the conclusions of the Edinburgh European Council on subsidiarity and transparency,
– noting the declarations of the Edinburgh European Council relating to Denmark,
  taking cognizance of the unilateral declarations of Denmark made on the same occasion which will be associated with its act of ratification,
– noting that Denmark does not intend to make use of the following provisions in such a way as to prevent closer cooperation with the Treaty and within the framework of the Union and its objectives,

Have agreed on the following decision:

SECTION A. CITIZENSHIP

The provisions of Part Two of the Treaty establishing the European Community relating to citizenship of the Union give nationals of the Member States additional rights and protection as specified in that Part. They do not in any way take the place of national citizenship. The question whether an individual possesses the nationality of a Member State will be settled solely by reference to the national law of the Member State concerned.

SECTION B. ECONOMIC AND MONETARY UNION

1. The Protocol on certain provisions relating to Denmark attached to the Treaty establishing the European Community gives Denmark the right to notify the Council of the European Communities of its position concerning participation in the third stage of Economic and Monetary Union. Denmark has given notification that it will not participate in the third stage. This notification will take effect upon the coming into effect of this decision.

2. As a consequence, Denmark will not participate in the single currency, will not be bound by the rules concerning economic policy which apply only to the Member States participating in the third stage of Economic and Monetary Union, and will retain its existing powers in the field of monetary policy according to its national laws and regulations, including powers of the National Bank of Denmark in the field of monetary policy.

3. Denmark will participate fully in the second stage of Economic and

Monetary Union and will continue to participate in exchange-rate co-operation within the European Monetary System (EMS).

SECTION C. DEFENCE POLICY

The Heads of State and Government note that, in response to the invitation from the Western European Union (WEU), Denmark has become an observer to that organization. They also note that nothing in the Treaty on European Union commits Denmark to become a member of the WEU. Accordingly, Denmark does not participate in the elaboration and the implementation of decisions and actions of the Union which have defence implications, but will not prevent the development of closer co-operation between Member States in this area.

SECTION D. JUSTICE AND HOME AFFAIRS

Denmark will participate fully in cooperation on Justice and Home Affairs on the basis of the provisions of Title VI of the Treaty on European Union.

SECTION E. FINAL PROVISIONS

1. This decision will take effect on the date of entry into force of the Treaty on European Union; its duration shall be governed by Articles Q and N(2) of that Treaty.

2. At any time Denmark may, in accordance with its constitutional requirements, inform other Member States that it no longer wishes to avail itself of all or part of this decision. In that event, Denmark will apply in full all relevant measures then in force taken within the framework of the European Union.

Declarations of the European Council

DECLARATION ON SOCIAL POLICY, CONSUMERS, ENVIRONMENT, DISTRIBUTION OF INCOME

1. The Treaty on European Union does not prevent any Member State from maintaining or introducing more stringent protection measures compatible with the EC Treaty:

– in the field of working conditions and in social policy (Article 118a(3) of the EC Treaty and Article 2(5) of the Agreement on social policy concluded between the Member States of the European Community

with the exception of the United Kingdom),
- in order to attain a high level of consumer protection (Article 129a(3) of the EC Treaty),
- in order to pursue the objectives of protection of the environment (Article 130t of the EC Treaty).

2. The provisions introduced by the Treaty on European Union, including the provisions on Economic and Monetary Union, permit each Member State to pursue its own policy with regard to distribution of income and maintain or improve social welfare benefits.

DECLARATION ON DEFENCE

The European Council takes note that Denmark will renounce its right to exercise the Presidency of the Union in each case involving the elaboration and the implementation of decisions and actions of the Union which have defence implications. The normal rules for replacing the President, in the case of the President being indisposed, shall apply. These rules will also apply with regard to the representation of the Union in international organizations, international conferences and with third countries.

Unilateral Declarations of Denmark, to be Associated to the Danish Act of Ratification of the Treaty on European Union and of which the Eleven Other Member States will take Cognizance

DECLARATION ON CITIZENSHIP OF THE UNION

1. Citizenship of the Union is a political and legal concept which is entirely different from the concept of citizenship within the meaning of the Constitution of the Kingdom of Denmark and of the Danish legal system. Nothing in the Treaty on European Union implies or foresees an undertaking to create a citizenship of the Union in the sense of citizenship of a nation-state. The question of Denmark participating in any such development does, therefore, not arise.

2. Citizenship of the Union in no way in itself gives a national of another Member State the right to obtain Danish citizenship or any of the rights, duties, privileges or advantages that are inherent in Danish citizenship by virtue of Denmark's constitutional, legal and administrative rules.

Denmark will fully respect all specific rights expressly provided for in the Treaty and applying to nationals of the Member States.

3. Nationals of the other Member States of the European Community enjoy in Denmark the right to vote and to stand as a candidate at municipal elections, foreseen in Article 8b of the European Community Treaty. Denmark intends to introduce legislation granting nationals of the other Member States the right to vote and to stand as a candidate for elections to the European Parliament in good time before the next elections in 1994. Denmark has no intention of accepting that the detailed arrangements foreseen in paragraphs 1 and 2 of this Article could lead to rules detracting from the rights already given in Denmark in that matter.

4. Without prejudice to the other provisions of the Treaty establishing the European Community, Article 8e requires the unanimity of all the Members of the Council of the European Communities, i.e. all Member States, for the adoption of any provision to strengthen or to add to the rights laid down in Part Two of the EC Treaty. Moreover, any unanimous decision of the Council, before coming into force, will have to be adopted in each Member State, in accordance with its constitutional requirements. In Denmark, such adoption will, in the case of a transfer of sovereignty, as defined in the Danish Constitution, require either a majority of $5/6$ of Members of the Folketing or both a majority of the Members of the Folketing and a majority of voters in a referendum.

DECLARATION ON COOPERATION IN THE FIELDS OF JUSTICE AND HOME AFFAIRS

Article K9 of the Treaty on European Union requires the unanimity of all the Members of the Council of the European Union, i.e. all Member States, to the adoption of any decision to apply Article 100c of the Treaty establishing the European Community to action in areas referred to in Article K1(1) to (6). Moreover, any unanimous decision of the Council, before coming into force, will have to be adopted in each Member State, in accordance with its constitutional requirements. In Denmark, such adoption will, in the case of a transfer of sovereignty, as defined in the Danish Constitution, require either a majority of 5/6 of Members of the Folketing or both a majority of the Members of the Folketing and a majority of voters in a referendum.

FINAL DECLARATION

The Decision and Declarations above are a response to the result of the Danish referendum of 2 June 1992 on ratification of the Maastricht

Treaty, As far as Denmark is concerned, the objectives of that Treaty in the four areas mentioned in sections A to D of the Decision are to be seen in the light of these documents, which are compatible with the Treaty and do not call its objectives into question.

Protocol on the Statute of the Court of Justice of the European Economic Community as amended by Council Decision of 24 October 1988 establishing a Court of First Instance

The High Contracting parties to the Treaty establishing the European Economic Community:

Desiring to lay down the Statute of the Court provided for in Art. 188 of this Treaty,

Have designated . . . their Plenipotentiaries for this purpose: . . .

Who, having exchanged their Full Powers, found in good and due form,

Have agreed upon the following provisions, which shall be annexed to the Treaty establishing the European Economic Community:

Article 1. The Court established by Art. 4 of this Treaty shall be constituted and shall function in accordance with the provisions of this Treaty and of this Statute.

TITLE I. JUDGES AND ADOVOCATES-GENERAL

Article 2. Before taking up his duties each Judge shall, in open court, take an oath to perform his duties impartially and conscientiously and to preserve the secrecy of the deliberations of the Court.

Article 3. The Judges shall be immune from legal proceedings. After they have ceased to hold office, they shall continue to enjoy immunity in respect of acts performed by them in their legal capacity, including words spoken or written.

The Court, sitting in plenary session, may waive the immunity.

Where immunity has been waived and criminal proceedings are instituted against a Judge, he shall be tried, in any of the Member States, only by the Court competent to judge the members of the highest national judiciary.

Article 4. The Judges may not hold any political or administrative office.

They may not engage in any occupation, whether gainful or not, unless exemption is exceptionally granted by the Council.

When taking up their duties, they shall give a solemn undertaking that, both during and after their term of office, they will respect the obligations arising thereform, in particular the duty to behave with integrity and discretion as regards the acceptance, after they have ceased to hold office, of certain appointments or benefits.

Any doubts on this point shall be settled by decision of the Court.

Article 5. Apart from normal replacement, or death, the duties of a Judge shall end when he resigns.

Where a Judge resigns, his letter of resignation shall be addressed to the President of the Court for transmission to the President of the Council. Upon this notification a vacancy shall arise on the bench.

Save where Art. 6 applies, a Judge shall continue to hold office until his successor takes up his duties.

Article 6. A Judge may be deprived of his office or of his right to a pension or other benefits in its stead only if, in the unanimous opinion of the Judges and Advocates-General of the Court, he no longer fulfils the requisite conditions or meets the obligations arising from his office. The Judge concerned shall not take part in any such deliberations.

The Registrar of the Court shall communicate the decision of the Court to the President of the Assembly and to the President of the Commission and shall notify it to the President of the Council.

In the case of a decision depriving a Judge of his office, a vacancy shall arise on the bench upon this latter notification.

Article 7. A Judge who is to replace a member of the Court whose term of office has not expired shall be appointed for the remainder of his predecessor's term.

Article 8. The provisions of Arts. 2 to 7 shall apply to the Advocates-General.

TITLE II. ORGANISATION

Article 9. The Registrar shall take an oath before the Court to perform his duties impartially and conscientiously and to preserve the secrecy of the deliberations of the Court.

Article 10. The Court shall arrange for replacement of the Registrar on occasions when he is prevented from attending the Court.

Article 11. Officials and other servants shall be attached to the Court to enable it to function. They shall be responsible to the Registrar under the authority of the President.

Article 12. On a proposal from the Court, the Council may, acting unanimously, provide for the appointment of Assistant Rapporteurs and lay down the rules governing their service. The Assistant Rapporteurs may be required, under conditions laid down in the rules of procedure, to participate in preparatory inquiries in cases pending before the Court and to co-operate with the Judge who acts as Rapporteur.

The Assistant Rapporteurs shall be chosen from persons whose independence is beyond doubt and who possess the necessary legal qualifications; they shall be appointed by the Council. They shall take an oath before the Court to perform their duties impartially and conscientiously and to preserve the secrecy of the deliberations of the Court.

Article 13. The Judges, the Advocates-General and the Registrar shall be required to reside at the place where the Court has its seat.

Article 14. The Court shall remain permanently in session. The duration of the judicial vacations shall be determined by the Court with due regard to the needs of its business.

Article 15. Decisions of the Court shall be valid only when an uneven number of its members is sitting in the deliberations. Decisions of the full Court shall be valid if seven members are sitting. Decisions of the Chambers shall be valid only if three Judges are sitting; in the event of one of the Judges of a Chamber being prevented from attending, a Judge of another Chamber may be called upon to sit in accordance with conditions laid down in the rules of procedure.

Article 16. No Judge or Advocate-General may take part in the disposal of any case in which he has previously taken part as agent or adviser or has acted for one of the parties, or on which he has been called upon to pronounce as a member of a court or tribunal, of a commission of inquiry or in any other capacity.

If, for some special reason, any Judge or Advocate-General considers that he should not take part in the judgment or examination of a particular case, he shall so inform the President. If, for some special reason, the President considers that any Judge or Advocate-General should not sit or make submissions in a particular case, he shall notify him accordingly. Any difficulty arising as to the application of this Article shall be settled by decision of the Court.

A party may not apply for a change in the composition of the Court or of one of its Chambers on the grounds of either the nationality of a Judge or the absence from the Court or from the Chamber of a Judge of the nationality of that party.

TITLE III. PROCEDURE

Article 17. The States and the institutions of the Community shall be represented before the Court by an agent appointed for each case; the agent may be assisted by an adviser or by a lawyer entitled to practise before a court of a Member State.

Other parties must be represented by a lawyer entitled to practise before a court of a Member State.

Such agents, advisers and lawyers shall, when they appear before the Court, enjoy the rights and immunities necessary to the independent exercise of their duties, under conditions laid down in the rules of procedure.

As regards such advisers and lawyers who appear before it, the Court shall have the powers normally accorded to Courts of law, under conditions laid down in the rules of procedure.

University teachers being nationals of a Member State whose law accords them a right of audience shall have the same rights before the Court as are accorded by this Article to lawyers entitled to practise before a court of a Member State.

Article 18. The procedure before the Court shall consist of two parts: written and oral.

The written procedure shall consist of the communication to the parties and to the institutions of the Community whose decisions are in dispute of applications, statements of case, defences and observations, and of replies, if any, as well as of all papers and documents in support of or certified copies of them.

Communications shall be made by the Registrar in the order and within the time laid down in the rules of procedure.

The oral procedure shall consist of the reading of the report presented by a Judge acting as Rapporteur, the hearing by the Court of agents, advisers and lawyers entitled to practise before a court of a Member State and of the submissions of the Advocate-General, as well as the hearing, if any, of witnesses and experts.

Article 19. A case shall be brought before the Court by a written application addressed to the Registrar. The application shall contain the applicant's name and permanent address and the description of the signatory, the name of the party against whom the application is made, the subject matter of the dispute, the submissions and a brief statement of the grounds on which the application is based.

The application shall be accompanied, where appropriate, by the measure the annulment of which is sought or, in the circumstances referred to in Art. 175 of this Treaty, by documentary evidence of the date on which an institution was, in accordance with that Article, requested to act. If the documents are not submitted with the application, the Registrar shall ask the party concerned to produce them within a reasonable period, but in that event the rights of the party shall not lapse even if such documents are produced after the time limit for bringing proceedings.

Article 20.   In the cases governed by Art. 177 of this Treaty, the decision of the court or tribunal of a Member State which suspends its proceedings and refers a case to the Court shall be notified to the Court by the court or tribunal concerned. The decision shall then be notified by the Registrar of the Court to the parties, to the Member States and to the Commission, and also to the Council if the act the validity or interpretation of which is in dispute originates from the Council.

Within two months of this notification, the parties, the Member States, the Commission and, where appropriate, the Council, shall be entitled to submit statements of case or written observations to the Court.

Article 21.   The Court may require the parties to produce all documents and to supply all information which the Court considers desirable. Formal note shall be taken of any refusal.

The Court may also require the Member States and institutions not being parties to the case to supply all information which the Court considers necessary for the proceedings.

Article 22.   The Court may at any time entrust any individual, body, authority, committee or other organisation it chooses with the task of giving an expert opinion.

Article 23.   Witnesses may be heard under conditions laid down in the rules of procedure.

Article 24.   With respect to defaulting witnesses the Court shall have the powers generally granted to courts and tribunals and may impose pecuniary penalties under conditions laid down in the rules of procedure.

Article 25.   Witnesses and experts may be heard on oath taken in the form laid down in the rules of procedure or in the manner laid down by the law of the country of the witness or expert.

Article 26.   The Court may order that a witness or expert be heard by the judicial authority of his place of permanent residence.

The order shall be sent for implementation to the competent judicial authority under conditions laid down in the rules of procedure. The documents drawn up in compliance with the letters rogatory shall be returned to the Court under the same conditions.

The Court shall defray the expenses, without prejudice to the right to charge them, where appropriate, to the parties.

Article 27. A Member State shall treat any violation of an oath by a witness or expert in the same manner as if the offence had been committed before one of its courts with jurisdiction in civil proceedings. At the instance of the Court, the Member State concerned shall prosecute the offender before its competent court.

Article 28. The hearing in court shall be public, unless the Court, of its own motion or on application by the parties, decides otherwise for serious reasons.

Article 29. During the hearings the Court may examine the experts, the witnesses and the parties themselves. The latter, however, may address the Court only through their representatives.

Article 30. Minutes shall be made of each hearing and signed by the President and the Registrar.

Article 31. The cause list shall be established by the President.

Article 32. The deliberations of the Court shall be and shall remain secret.

Article 33. Judgments shall state the reasons on which they are based. They shall contain the names of the Judges who took part in the deliberations.

Article 34. Judgments shall be signed by the President and the Registrar. They shall be read in open court.

Article 35. The Court shall adjudicate upon costs.

Article 36. The President of the Court may, by way of summary procedure, which may, in so far as necessary, differ from some of the rules contained in this Statute and which shall be laid down in the rules of procedure, adjudicate upon applications to suspend execution, as provided for in Art. 185 of this Treaty, or to prescribe interim measures in pursuance of Art. 186, or to suspend enforcement in accordance with the last paragraph of Art. 192.

Should the President be prevented from attending, his place shall be taken by another Judge under conditions laid down in the rules of procedure.

The ruling of the President or of the Judge replacing him shall be provisional and shall in no way prejudice the decision of the Court on the substance of the case.

Article 37.   Member States and institutions of the Community may intervene in cases before the Court.

The same right shall be open to any other person establishing an interest in the result of any case submitted to the Court, save in cases between Member States, between institutions of the Community or between Member States and institutions of the Community.

Submissions made in an application to intervene shall be limited to supporting the submissions of one of the parties.

Article 38.   Where the defending party, after having been duly summoned, fails to file written submissions in defence, judgment shall be given against that party by default. An objection may be lodged against the judgment within one month of it being notified. The objection shall not have the effect of staying enforcement of the judgment by default unless the Court decides otherwise.

Article 39.   Member States, institutions of the Community and any other natural or legal persons may, in cases and under conditions to be determined by the rules of procedure, institute third-party proceedings to contest a judgment rendered without their being heard, where the judgment is prejudicial to their rights.

Article 40.   If the meaning or scope of a judgment is in doubt, the Court shall construe it on application by any party or any institution of the Community establishing an interest therein.

Article 41.   An application for revision of a judgment may be made to the Court only on discovery of a fact which is of such a nature as to be a decisive factor, and which, when the judgment was given, was unknown to the Court and to the party claiming the revision.

The revision shall be opened by a judgment of the Court expressly recording the existence of a new fact, recognising that it is of such a character as to lay the case open to revision and declaring the application admissible on this ground.

No application for revision may be made after the lapse of ten years from the date of the judgment.

Article 42.   Periods of grace based on considerations of distance shall be determined by the rules of procedure.

No right shall be prejudiced in consequence of the expiry of a time limit if the party concerned proves the existence of unforeseeable circumstances or of *force majeure*.

Article 43. Proceedings against the Community in matters arising from non-contractual liability shall be barred after a period of five years from the occurrence of the event giving rise thereto. The period of limitation shall be interrupted if proceedings are instituted before the Court or if prior to such proceedings an application is made by the aggrieved party to the relevant institution of the Community. In the latter event the proceedings must be instituted within the period of two months provided for in Art. 173; the provisions of the second paragraph of Art. 175 shall apply where appropriate.

TITLE IV. THE COURT OF FIRST INSTANCE OF THE EUROPEAN COMMUNITIES

Article 44. Articles 2 to 8, and 13 to 16 of this Statute shall apply to the Court of First Instance and its members. The oath referred to in Article 2 shall be taken before the Court of Justice and the decisions referred to in Articles 3, 4 and 6 shall be adopted by that Court after hearing the Court of First Instance.

Article 45. The Court of First Instance shall appoint its Registrar and lay down the rules governing his service. Articles 9, 10 and 13 of this Statute shall apply to the Registrar of the Court of First Instance *mutatis mutandis*.

The President of the Court of Justice and the President of the Court of First Insance shall determine, by common accord, the conditions under which officials and other servants attached to the Court of Justice shall render their services to the Court of First Instance to enable it to function. Certain officials or other servants shall be responsible to the Registrar of the Court of First Instance under the authority of the President of the Court of First Instance.

Article 46. The procedure before the Court of First Instance shall be governed by Title III of this Statute, with the exception of Article 20.

Such further and more detailed provisions as may be necessary shall be laid down in the Rules of Procedure established in accordance with Article 168a (4) of this Treaty.

Notwithstanding the fourth paragraph of Article 18 of this Statute, the Advocate-General may make his reasoned submissions in writing.

Article 47. Where an application or other procedural document addressed to the Court of First Instance is lodged by mistake with the Registrar of the Court of Justice it shall be transmitted immediately by that Registrar to the Registrar of the Court of First Instance; likewise, where an application or other procedural document addressed to the Court of Justice is lodged by mistake with the Registrar of the Court of First Instance, it shall be transmitted immediately by that Registrar to the Registrar of the Court of Justice.

Where the Court of First Instance finds that it does not have jurisdiction to hear and determine an action in respect of which the Court of Justice has jurisdiction, it shall refer that action to the Court of Justice; likewise, where the Court of Justice finds that an action falls within the jurisdiction of the Court of First Instance, it shall refer that action to the Court of First Instance, whereupon that Court may not decline jurisdiction.

Where the Court of Justice and the Court of First Instance are seised of cases in which the same relief is sought, the same issue of interpretation is raised or the validity of the same act is called in question, the Court of First Instance may, after hearing the parties, stay the proceedings before it until such time as the Court of Justice shall have delivered judgment. Where applications are made for the same act to be declared void, the Court of First Instance may also decline jurisdiction in order that the Court of Justice may rule on such applications. In the cases referred to in this subparagraph, the Court of Justice may also decide to stay the proceedings before it; in that event, the proceedings before the Court of First Instance shall continue.

Article 48. Final decisions of the Court of First Instance, decisions disposing of the substantive issues in part only or disposing of a procedural issue concerning a plea of lack of competence or inadmissibility, shall be notified by the Registrar of the Court of First Instance to all parties as well as all Member States and the Community institutions even if they did not intervene in the case before the Court of First Instance.

Article 49. An appeal may be brought before the Court of Justice, within two months of the notification of the decision appealed against, against final decisions of the Court of First Instance and decisions of that Court disposing of the substantive issues in part only or disposing of a procedural issue concerning a plea of lack of competence or inadmissibility.

Such an appeal may be brought by any party which has been unsuccessful, in whole or in part, in its submissions. However, interveners other than the Member States and the Community institutions may bring such an appeal only where the decision of the Court of First Instance directly affects them.

With the exception of cases relating to disputes between the Community and its servants, an appeal may also be brought by Member States and Community institutions which did not intervene in the proceedings before the Court of First Instance. Such Member States and institutions shall be in the same position as Member States or institutions which intervened at first instance.

Article 50. Any person whose application to intervene has been dismissed by the Court of First Instance may appeal to the Court of Justice within two weeks of the notification of the decision dismissing the application.

The parties to the proceedings may appeal to the Court of Justice against any decision of the Court of First Instance made pursuant to Article 185 or 186 or the fourth paragraph of Article 192 of this Treaty within two months from their notification.

The appeal referred to in the first two paragraphs of this Article shall be heard and determined under the procedure referred to in Article 36 of this Statute.

Article 51. An appeal to the Court of Justice shall be limited to points of law. It shall lie on the grounds of lack of competence of the Court of First Instance, a breach of procedure before it which adversely affects the interests of the appellant as well as the infringement of Community law by the Court of First Instance.

No appeal shall lie regarding only the amount of the costs or the party ordered to pay them.

Article 52. Where an appeal is brought against a decision of the Court of First Instance, the procedure before the Court of Justice shall consist of a written part and an oral part. In accordance with conditions laid down in the Rules of Procedure the Court of Justice, having heard the Advocate-General and the parties, may dispense with the oral procedure.

Article 53. Without prejudice to Articles 185 and 186 of this Treaty, an appeal shall not have suspensory effect.

By way of derogation from Article 187 of this Treaty, decisions of the Court of First Instance declaring a regulation to be void shall take effect only as from the date of expiry of the period referred to in the first paragraph of Article 49 of this Statute or, if an appeal shall have been brought within that period, as from the date of dismissal of the appeal, without prejudice, however, to the right of a party to apply to the Court of Justice, pursuant to Articles 185 and 186 of this Treaty, for the suspension of the effects of the regulation which has been declared void or for the prescription of any other interim measure.

Article 54. If the appeal is well founded, the Court of Justice shall quash the decision of the Court of First Instance. It may itself give final judgment in the matter, where the state of the proceedings so permits, or refer the case back to the Court of First Instance for judgment.

Where a case is referred back to the Court of First Instance, that Court shall be bound by the decision of the Court of Justice on points of law.

When an appeal brought by a Member State or a Community institution, which did not intervene in the proceedings before the Court of First Instance, is well founded the Court of Justice may, if it considers this necessary, state which of the effects of the decision of the Court of First Instance which has been quashed shall be considered as definitive in respect of the parties to the litigation.

Article 55. The rules of procedure of the Court provided for in Art. 188 of this Treaty shall contain, apart from the provisions contemplated by this Statute, any other provisions necessary for applying and, where required, supplementing it.

Article 56. The Council may, acting unanimously, make such further adjustments to the provisions of this Statute as may be required by reason of measures taken by the Council in accordance with the last paragraph of Art. 165 of this Treaty.

Article 57. Immediately after the oath has been taken, the President of the Council shall proceed to choose by lot the Judges and the Advocates-General whose terms of office are to expire at the end of the first three years in accordance with the second and third paragraphs of Art. 167 of this Treaty.

In witness whereof, the undersigned Plenipotentiaries have signed this Protocol.

Done at Brussels this 17 April 1957.

[Here follow the signatures.]

COUNCIL DECISION OF 24 OCTOBER 1988 ESTABLISHING A COURT OF FIRST INSTANCE (EXTRACTS) (88/591/ ECSC, EEC, EURATOM)

Article 1. A Court, to be called the Court of First Instance of the European Communities, shall be attached to the Court of Justice of the European Communities. Its seat shall be at the Court of Justice.

Article 2. 1. The Court of First Instance shall consist of 12 members.

2. The members shall elect the President of the Court of First Instance from among their number for a term of three years. He may be re-elected.

3. The members of the Court of First Instance may be called upon to perform the task of an Advocate-General.

It shall be the duty of the Advocate-General, acting with complete impartiality and independence, to make, in open court, reasoned submissions on certain cases brought before the Court of First Instance in order to assist the Court of First Instance in the performance of its task.

The criteria for selecting such cases, as well as the procedures for designating the Advocates-General, shall be laid down in the Rules of Procedure of the Court of First Instance.

A member called upon to perform the task of Advocate-General in a case may not take part in the judgment of the case.

4. The Court of First Instance shall sit in chambers of three or five judges. The composition of the chambers and the assignment of cases to them shall be governed by the Rules of Procedure. In certain cases governed by the Rules of Procedure the Court of First Instance may sit in plenary session.

5. Article 21 of the Protocol on Privileges and Immunities of the European Communities and Article 6 of the Treaty establishing a Single Council and a Single Commission of the European Communities shall apply to the members of the Court of First Instance and to its Registrar.

Article 3. 1. The Court of First Instance shall exercise at first instance the jurisdiction conferred on the Court of Justice by the Treaties establishing the Communities and by the acts adopted in implementation thereof:

(a) in disputes between the Communities and their servants referred to in Article 179 of the EEC Treaty and in Article 152 of the EAEC Treaty;

(b) in actions brought against the Commission pursuant to the second paragraph of Article 33 and Article 35 of the ECSC Treaty by under

takings or by associations of undertakings referred to in Article 48 of that Treaty, and which concern individual acts relating to the application of Article 50 and Articles 57 to 66 of the said Treaty;
(c) in actions brought against an institution of the Communities by natural or legal persons pursuant to the second paragraph of Article 173 and the third paragraph of Article 175 of the EEC Treaty relating to the implementation of the competition rules applicable to undertakings.

2. Where the same natural or legal person brings an action which the Court of First Instance has jurisdiction to hear by virtue of paragraph 1 of this Article and an action referred to in the first and second paragraphs of Article 40 of the ECSC Treaty, Article 178 of the EEC Treaty, or Article 151 of the EAEC Treaty, for compensation for damage caused by a Community institution through the act or failure to act which is the subject of the first action, the Court of First Instance shall also have jurisdiction to hear and determine the action for compensation for that damage.

3. The Council will, in the light of experience, including the development of jurisprudence, and after two years of operation of the Court of First Instance, re-examine the proposal by the Court of Justice to give the Court of First Instance competence to exercise jurisdiction in actions brought against the Commission pursuant to the second paragraph of Articles 33 and 35 of the ECSC Treaty by undertakings or by associations of undertakings referred to in Article 48 of that Treaty, and which concern acts relating to the application of Article 74 of the said Treaty as well as in actions brought against an institution of the Communities by natural or legal persons pursuant to the second paragraph of Article 173 and the third paragraph of Article 175 of the EEC Treaty and relating to measures to protect trade within the meaning of Article 113 of that Treaty in the case of dumping and subsidies.

Article 4.   Save as hereinafter provided, Articles 34, 36, 39, 44 and 92 of the ECSC Treaty, Articles 172, 174, 176, 184 to 187 and 192 of the EEC Treaty, and Articles 147, 149, 156 to 159 and 164 of the EAEC Treaty shall apply to the Court of First Instance.

RULES OF PROCEDURE OF THE COURT OF JUSTICE
19 JUNE 1991

[NB. Omitted from this version of the text are: the formal parts; the provisions on the Judges, Advocates-General, Registrar, and Assistant Rapporteurs; and the special procedures under Euratom arts. 103–5. As a guide to the provisions printed, see Table of Contents. The full text is at OJ 1991 L 176/7.]

TITLE I. ORGANIZATION OF THE COURT

CHAPTER 2. PRESIDENCY OF THE COURT AND CONSTITUTION OF THE CHAMBERS

Article 7.   1. The Judges shall, immediately after the partial replacement provided for in Article 32b of the ECSC Treaty, Article 167 of the EEC Treaty and Article 139 of the Euratom Treaty, elect one of their number as President of the Court for a term of three years.

2. If the office of the President of the Court falls vacant before the normal date of expiry thereof, the Court shall elect a successor for the remainder of the term.

3. The elections provided for in this Article shall be by secret ballot. If a Judge obtains an absolute majority he shall be elected. If no Judge obtains an absolute majority, a second ballot shall be held and the Judge obtaining the most votes shall be elected. Where two or more Judges obtain an equal number of votes the oldest of them shall be deemed elected.

Article 8.   The President shall direct the judicial business and the administration of the Court; he shall preside at hearings and deliberations.

Article 9.   1. The Court shall set up Chambers in accordance with the provisions of the second paragraph of Article 32 of the ECSC Treaty, the second paragraph of Article 165 of the EEC Treaty and the second paragraph of Article 137 of the Euratom Treaty and shall decide which Judges shall be attached to them.

The composition of the Chambers shall be published in the *Official Journal of the European Communities.*

2. As soon as an application initiating proceedings has been lodged, the President shall assign the case to one of the Chambers for any preparatory inquiries and shall designate a Judge from that Chamber to act as Rapporteur.

3. The Court shall lay down criteria by which, as a rule, cases are to be assigned to Chambers.

4. These Rules shall apply to proceedings before the Chambers.
In cases assigned to a Chamber the powers of the President of the Court shall be exercised by the President of the Chamber.

Article 10.   1. The Court shall appoint for a period of one year the Presidents of the Chambers and the First Advocate-General.

The provisions of Article 7 (2) and (3) shall apply.
Appointments made in pursuance of this paragraph shall be published in the *Official Journal of the European Communities.*

The First Advocate-General shall assign each case to an Advocate-General as soon as the Judge-Rapporteur has been designated by the President. He shall take the necessary steps if an Advocate-General is absent or prevented from attending.

Article 11. When the President of the Court is absent or prevented from attending or when the office of President is vacant, the actions of President shall be exercised by a President of a Chamber according to the order of precedence laid down in Article 6 of these Rules.

If the President of the Court and the President of the Chambers are all prevented from attending at the same time, or their posts are vacant at the same time, the functions of President shall be exercised by one of the other Judges according to the order of precedence laid down in Article 6 of these Rules.

CHAPTER 5. THE WORKING OF THE COURT

Article 25. 1. The dates and times of the sittings of the Court shall be fixed by the President.

2. The dates and times of the sittings of the Chambers shall be fixed by their respective Presidents.

3. The Court and the Chambers may choose to hold one or more sittings in a place other than that in which the Court has its seat.

Article 26. 1. Where, by reason of a Judge being absent or prevented from attending, there is an even number of Judges, the most junior Judge within the meaning of Article 6 of these Rules shall abstain from taking part in the deliberations unless he is the Judge-Rapporteur. In that case the Judge immediately senior to him shall abstain from taking part in the deliberations.

2. If after the Court has been convened it is found that the quorum of seven Judges has not been attained, the President shall adjourn the sitting until there is a quorum.

3. If in any Chamber the quorum of three Judges has not been attained, the President of that Chamber shall so inform the President of the Court who shall designate another Judge to complete the Chamber.

Article 27. 1. The Court and Chambers shall deliberate in closed session.

2. Only those Judges who were present at the oral proceedings and the Assistant Rapporteur, if any, entrusted with the consideration of the case may take part in the deliberations.

3. Every Judge taking part in the deliberations shall state his opinion and the reasons for it.

4. Any Judge may require that any questions be formulated in the language of his choice and communicated in writing to the Court or Chamber before being put to the vote.

5. The conclusions reached by the majority of the Judges after final discussion shall determine the decision of the Court. Votes shall be cast in reverse order to the order to precedence laid down in Article 6 of these Rules.

6. Differences of view on the substance, wording or order of questions, or on the interpretation of the voting shall be settled by decision of the Court or Chamber.

7. Where the deliberations of the Court concern questions of its own administration, the Advocates-General shall take part and have a vote. The Registrar shall be present, unless the Court decides to the contrary.

8. Where the court sits without the Registrar being present it shall, if necessary, instruct the most senior Judge within the meaning of Article 6 of these rules to draw up minutes. The minutes shall be signed by this Judge and by the President.

Article 28. 1. Subject to any special decision of the Court, its vacations shall be as follows:

- from 18 December to 10 January,
- from the Sunday before Easter to the second Sunday after Easter,
- from 15 July to 15 September.

During the vacations, the functions of President shall be exercised at the place where the Court has its seat either by the President himself, keeping in touch with the Registrar, or by a President of Chamber or other Judge invited by the President to take his place.

2. In a case of urgency, the President may convene the Judges and the Advocates-General during the vacations.

3. The Court shall observe the official holidays of the place where it has its seat.

4. The Court may, in proper circumstances, grant leave of absence to any Judge or Advocate-General.

CHAPTER 6. LANGUAGES

Article 29. 1. The language of a case shall be Danish, Dutch, English, French, German, Greek, Irish, Italian, Portuguese or Spanish.

2. The language of a case shall be chosen by the applicant, except that:

(a) where the defendant is a Member State or a natural or legal person having the nationality of a Member State, the language of the case shall be the official language of that State; where that State has more than one official language, the applicant may choose between them;

(b) at the joint request of the parties the Court may authorise another of
    the languages mentioned in paragraph (1) of this Article to be used as
    the language of the case for all or part of the proceedings;
(c) at the request of one of the parties, and after the opposite party and
    the Advocate-General have been heard, the Court, may, by way of
    derogation from subparagraphs (a) and (b), authorise another of the
    languages mentioned in paragraph (1) of this Article to be used as the
    language of the case for all or part of the proceedings; such a request
    may not be submitted by an institution of the European Com-
    munities.

In cases to which Article 103 of these Rules applies, the language of
the case shall be the language of the national court or tribunal which
refers the matter to the Court.

3. The language of the case shall be used in the written and oral pleadings of the parties and in supporting documents, and also in the minutes
and decisions of the Court.

Any supporting documents expressed in another language must be
accompanied by a translation into the languages of the case.

In the case of lengthy documents, translations may be confined to
extracts. However, the Court or Chamber may, of its own motion or at
the request of a party, at any time call for a complete or fuller translation.

Notwithstanding the foregoing provisions, a Member State shall be
entitled to use its official language when intervening in a case before the
Court or when taking part in any reference of a kind mentioned in
Article 103. This provision shall apply both to written statements and to
oral addresses. The Registrar shall cause any such statement or address
to be translated into the language of the case.

4. Where a witness or expert states that he is unable adequately to
express himself in one of the languages refered to in paragraph (1) of this
Article, the Court or Chamber may authorise him to give his evidence in
another language. The Registrar shall arrange for translation into the language of the case.

5. The President of the Court and the Presidents of Chambers in conducting oral proceedings, the Judge-Rapporteur both in his preliminary
report and in his report for the hearing, Judges and Advocates-General in
putting questions and Advocates-General in delivering their opinions may
use one of the languages referred to in paragraph (1) of this Article other
than the language of the case. The Registrar shall arrange for translation
into the language of the case.

Article 30.   1. The Registrar shall, at the request of any Judge, of the
Advocate-General or of a party, arrange for anything said or written in

the course of the proceedings before the Court or a Chamber to be translated into the languages he chooses from those refered to in Article 29 (1).

2. Publications of the Court shall be issued in the languages referred to in Article 1 of Council Regulation No. 1.

Article 31. The texts of documents drawn up in the language of the case or in any other language authorised by the Court pursuant to Article 29 of these rules shall be authentic.

CHAPTER 7. RIGHTS AND OBLIGATIONS OF AGENTS, ADVISERS AND LAWYERS

Article 32. 1. Agents representing a State or an institution, as well as advisers and lawyers, appearing before the Court or before any judicial authority to which the Court has addressed letters rogatory, shall enjoy immunity in respect of words spoken or written by them concerning the case or the parties.

2. Agents, advisers and lawyers shall enjoy the following further privileges and facilities:

(a) papers and documents relating to the proceedings shall be exempt from both search and seizure; in the event of a dispute the customs officials or police may seal those papers and documents;

(b) they shall then be immediately forwarded to the Court for inspection in the presence of the Registrar and of the person concerned; agents, advisers and lawyers shall be entitled to such allocation of foreign currency as may be necessary for the performance of their duties;

(c) agents, advisers and lawyers shall be entitled to travel in the course of duty without hindrance.

Article 33. In order to qualify for the privileges, immunities and facilities specified in Article 32, persons entitled to them shall furnish proof of their status as follows:

(a) agents shall produce an official document issued by the State or institution which they represent; a copy of this document shall be forwarded without delay to the Registrar by the State or institution concerned;

(b) advisers and lawyers shall produce a certificate signed by the Registrar. The validity of this certificate shall be limited to a specified period, which may be extended or curtailed according to the length of the proceedings.

Article 34. The privileges, immunities and facilities specified in Article 32 of these Rules are granted exclusively in the interests of the proper conduct of proceedings.

The Court may waive the immunity where it considers that the proper conduct of proceedings will not be hindered thereby.

Article 35. 1. Any adviser or lawyer whose conduct towards the Court, a Chamber, a Judge, an Advocate-General or the Registrar is incompatible with the dignity of the Court, or who uses his rights for purposes other than those for which they were granted, may at any time be excluded from the proceedings by an order of the Court or Chamber, after the Advocate-General has been heard; the person concerned shall be given an opportunity to defend himself.

The order shall have immediate effect.

2. Where an adviser or lawyer is excluded from the proceedings, the proceedings shall be suspended for a period fixed by the President in order to allow the party concerned to appoint another adviser or lawyer.

3. Decisions taken under this Article may be rescinded.

Article 36. The provisions of this Chapter shall apply to university teachers who have a right of audience before the Court in accordance with Article 20 of the ECSC Statute and Article 17 of the EEC and Euratom Statutes.

TITLE II. PROCEDURE

CHAPTER I. WRITTEN PROCEDURE

Article 37. 1. The original of every pleading must be signed by the party's agent or lawyer.

The original, accompanied by all annexes referred to therein, shall be lodged together with five copies for the Court and a copy for every other party to the proceedings. Copies shall be certified by the party lodging them.

2. Institutions shall in addition produce, within time-limits laid down by the Court, translations of all pleadings into the other languages provided for by Article 1 of Council Regulation No 1. The second subparagraph of paragraph (1) of this Article shall apply.

3. All pleadings shall bear a date. In the reckoning of time-limits for taking steps in proceedings, only the date of lodgment at the Registry shall be taken into account.

4. To every pleading there shall be annexed a file containing the documents relied on in support of it, together with a schedule listing them.

5. Where in view of the length of a document only extracts from it are annexed to the pleading, the whole document or a full copy of it shall be lodged at the Registry.

Article 38. 1. An application of the kind referred to in Article 22 of the ECSC Statute and Article 19 of the EEC and Euratom Statutes shall state:

(a) the name and address of the applicant;
(b) the designation of the party against whom the application is made;
    the subject-matter of the proceedings and a summary of the pleas in law on which the application is based;
(c) the form of order sought by the applicant;
(d) where appropriate, the nature of any evidence offered in support.

2. For the purpose of the proceedings, the application shall state an address for service in the place where the Court has its seat and the name of the person who is authorised and has expressed willingness to accept service.

If the application does not comply with these requirements, all service on the party concerned for the purpose of the proceedings shall be effected, for so long as the defect has not been cured, by registered letter addressed to the agent or laywer of that party. By way of derogation from Article 79, service shall then be deemed to be duly effected by the lodging of the registered letter at the post office of the place where the Court has its seat.

3. The lawyer acting for a party must lodge at the Registry appropriate, by the documents specified in the second paragraph of Article 22 of the ECSC Statute and in the second paragraph of Article 19 of the EEC and Euratom Statutes.

5. An application made by a legal person governed by private law shall be accompanied by:

(a) the instrument or instruments constituting or regulating that legal person or a recent extract from the register of companies, firms or associations or any other proof of its existence in law;
(b) proof that the authority granted to the applicant's lawyer has been properly conferred on him by someone authorized for the purpose.

6. An application submitted under Articles 42 and 89 of the ECSC Treaty, Articles 181 and 182 of the EEC Treaty and Articles 153 and 154 of the Euratom Treaty shall be accompanied by a copy of the arbitration clause contained in the contract governed by private or public law entered into by the Communities or on their behalf, or, as the case may be, by a copy of the special agreement concluded between the Member States concerned.

7. If an application does not comply with the requirements set out in paragraphs (3) to (6) of this Article, the Registrar shall prescribe a reasonable period within which the applicant is to comply with them

whether by putting the application itself in order or by producing any of the above mentioned documents. If the application fails to put the application in order or to produce the required documents within the time prescribed, the Court shall, after hearing the Advocate-General, decide whether the non-compliance with these conditions renders the application formally inadmissible.

Article 39.   The application shall be served on the defendant. In a case where Article 38 (7) applies, service shall be effected as soon as the application has been put in order or the Court has declared it admissible notwithstanding the failure to observe the formal requirements set out in that Article.

Article 40.   1. Within one month after service on him of the application, the defendant shall lodge a defence, stating:

(a) the name and address of the defendant;
(b) the arguments of fact and law relied on;
(c) the form of order sought by the defendant;
(d) he nature of any evidence offered by him.

The provisions of Article 38 (2) to (5) of these Rules shall apply to the defence.

2. The time-limit laid down in paragraph (1) of this Article may be extended by the President on a reasoned application by the defendant.

Article 41.   1. The application initiating the proceedings and the defence may be supplemented by a reply from the applicant and by a rejoinder from the defendant.

2. The President shall fix the time-limits within which these pleadings are to be lodged.

Article 42.   1. In reply or rejoinder a party may offer further evidence. The party must, however, give reasons for the delay in offering it.

2. No new plea in law may be introduced in the course of proceedings unless it is based on matters of law or of fact which come to light in the course of the procedure.

If in the course of the procedure one of the parties puts forward a new plea in law which is so based, the President may, even after the expiry of the normal procedural time-limits, acting on a report of the Judge-Rapporteur and after hearing the Advocate-General, allow the other party time to answer on that plea.

The decision on the admissibility of the plea shall be reserved for the final judgment.

Article 43. The Court may, at any time, after hearing the parties and the Advocate-General, if the assignment referred to in Article 10 (2) has taken place, order that two or more cases concerning the same subject-matter shall, on account of the connection between them, be joined for the purposes of the written or oral procedure or of the final judgment. The cases may subsequently be disjoined.

Article 44. 1. After the rejoinder provided for in Article 41 (1) of these Rules has been lodged, the President shall fix a date on which the Judge-Rapporteur is to present his preliminary report to the Court. The report shall contain recommendations as to whether a preparatory inquiry or any other preparatory step should be undertaken and whether the case should be referred to the Chamber to which it has been assigned under Article 9 (2).

The Court shall decide, after hearing the Advocate-General, what action to take upon the recommendations of the Judge-Rapporteur.

The same procedure shall apply:

(a) where no reply or no rejoinder has been lodged within the time-limit fixed in accordance with Article 41 (2) of these Rules;
(b) where the party concerned waives his right to lodge a reply or rejoinder.

2. Where the Court orders a preparatory inquiry and does not undertake it itself, it shall assign the inquiry to the Chamber.

Where the Court decides to open the oral procedure without an inquiry, the President shall fix the opening date.

Article 44(a). Without prejudice to any special provisions laid down in these Rules, and except in the specific cases in which, after the pleadings referred to in Article 40 (1) and, as the case may be, in Article 41 (1) have been lodged, the Court, acting on a report from the Judge-Rapporteur, after hearing the Advocate-General and with the express consent of the parties, decides otherwise, the procedure before the Court shall also include an oral part.

CHAPTER 2. PREPARATORY INQUIRIES

Section 1. Measures of inquiry

Article 45. 1. The Court, after hearing the Advocate-General, shall prescribe the measures of inquiry that it considers appropriate by means of an order setting out the facts to be proved. Before the Court decides on the measures of inquiry referred to in paragraph (2) (c), (d) and (e) the parties shall be heard.

The order shall be served on the parties.

2. Without prejudice to Articles 24 and 25 of the ECSC Statute, Articles 21 and 22 of the EEC Statute or Articles 22 and 23 of the Euratom Statute, the following measures of inquiry may be adopted:

(a) the personal appearance of the parties;
(b) a request for information and production of documents;
(c) oral testimony;
(d) the commissioning of an expert's report;
(e) an inspection of the place or thing in question.

3. The measures of inquiry which the Court has ordered may be conducted by the Court itself, or be assigned to the Judge-Rapporteur.

The Advocate-General shall take part in the measures of inquiry.

4. Evidence may be submitted in rebuttal and previus evidence may be amplified.

Article 46. 1. A Chamber to which a preparatory inquiry has been assigned may exercise the powers vested in the Court by Articles 45 and 47 to 53 of these Rules; the powers vested in the President of the Court may be exercised by the President of the Chamber.

2. Articles 56 and 57 of the Rules shall apply in a corresponding manner to proceedings before the Chamber.

3. The parties shall be entitled to attend the measures of inquiry.

Section 2. The summoning and examination of witnesses and experts

Article 47. 1. The Court may, either of its own motion or an application by a party, and after hearing the Advocate-General, order that certain facts be proved by witnesses. The order of the Court shall set out the facts to be established.

The Court may summon a witness of its own motion or on application by a party or at the instance of the Advocate-General.

An application by a party for the examination of a witness shall state precisely about what facts and for what reasons the witness should be examined.

2. The witness shall be summoned by an order of the Court containing the following information:

(a) the surname, forenames, description and address of the witness;
(b) an indication of the facts about which the witness is to be examined;
(c) where appropriate, particulars of the arrangements made by the Court for reimbursement of expenses incurred by the witness, and of the penalties which may be imposed on defaulting witnesses.

The order shall be served on the parties and the witnesses.

3. The Court may make the summoning of a witness for whose examination a party has applied conditional upon the deposit with the cashier of the Court of a sum sufficient to cover the taxed costs· thereof; the Court shall fix the amount of the payment.

The cashier shall advance the funds necessary in connection with the examination of any witness summoned by the Court of its own motion.

4. After the identity of the witness has been established, the President shall inform him that he will be required to vouch the truth of his evidence in the manner laid down in these Rules.

The witness shall give his evidence to the Court, the parties having been given notice to attend. After the witness has given his main evidence the President may, at the request of a party or of his own motion, put questions to him.

The other Judges and the Advocate-General may do likewise.

Subject to the control of the President, questions may be put to witnesses by the representatives of the parties.

5. After giving evidence, the witness shall take the following oath:

'I swear that I have spoken the truth, the whole truth and nothing but the truth.'

The Court may, after hearing the parties, exempt a witness from taking the oath.

6. The Registrar shall draw up minutes in which the evidence of each witness is reproduced.

The minutes shall be signed by the President or by the Judge-Rapporteur responsible for conducting the examination of the witness, and by the Registrar. Before the minutes are thus signed, witnesses must be given an opportunity to check the content of the minutes and to sign them.

The minutes shall constitute an official record.

Article 48. 1. Witnesses who have been duly summoned shall obey the summons and attend for examination.

2. If a witness who has been duly summoned fails to appear before the Court, the Court may impose upon him a pecuniary penalty not exceeding ECU 5000 and may order that a further summons be served on the witness at his own expense.

The same penalty may be imposed upon a witness who, without good reason, refuses to give evidence or to take the oath or where appropriate to make a solemn affirmation equivalent thereto.

3. If the witness proffers a valid excuse to the Court, the pecuniary penalty imposed on him may be cancelled. The pecuniary penalty

imposed may be reduced at the request of the witness where he established that it is disproportionate to his income.

4. Penalties imposed and other measures ordered under this Article shall be enforced in accordance with Articles 44 and 92 of the ECSC Treaty, Articles 187 and 192 of the EEC Treaty and Articles 159 and 164 of the Euratom Treaty.

Article 49. 1. The Court may order that an expert's report be obtained. The order appointing the expert shall define his task and set a time-limit within which he is to make his report.

2. The expert shall receive a copy of the order, together with all the documents necessary for carrying out his task. He shall be under the supervision of the Judge-Rapporteur, who may be present during his investigation and who shall be kept informed of his progress in carrying out his task.

The Court may request the parties or one of them to lodge security for the costs of the expert's report.

3. At the request of the expert, the Court may order the examination of witnesses. Their examination shall be carried out in accordance with Article 47 of these Rules.

4. The expert may give his opinion only on points which have been expressly referred to him.

5. After the expert has made his report, the Court may order that he be examined, the parties having been given notice to attend.

Subject to the control of the President, questions may be put to the expert by the representatives of the parties.

6. After making his report, the expert shall take the following oath before the Court:

'I swear that I have conscientiously and impartially carried out my task.'

The Court may, after hearing the parties, exempt the expert from taking the oath.

Article 50. 1. If one of the parties objects to a witness or to an expert on the ground that he is not a competent or a proper person to act as witness or expert or for any other reason, or if a witness or expert refuses to give evidence, to take the oath or to make a solemn affirmation equivalent thereto, the matter shall be resolved by the Court.

2. An objection to a witness or to an expert shall be raised within two weeks after service of the order summoning the witness or appointing the expert; the statement of objection must set out the grounds of objection and indicate the nature of any evidence offered.

Article 51. 1. Witnesses and experts shall be entitled to reimbursement of their travel and subsistence expenses. The cashier of the Court may make a payment to them towards these expenses in advance.

2. Witnesses shall be entitled to compensation for loss of earnings, and experts to fees for their services. The cashier of the Court shall pay witnesses and experts their compenstion or fees after they have carried out their respective duties or tasks.

Article 52. The Court may, on application by a party or of its own motion, issue letters rogatory for the examination of witnesses or experts, as provided for in the supplementary rules mentioned in Article 125 of these Rules.

Article 53. 1. The Registrar shall draw up minutes of every hearing. The minutes shall be signed by the President and by the Registrar and shall constitute an official record.

2. The parties may inspect the minutes and any expert's report at the Registry and obtain copies at their own expense.

Section 3. Closure of the preparatory inquiry

Article 54. Unless the Court prescribes a period within which the parties may lodge written observations, the President shall fix the date for the opening of the oral procedure after the preparatory inquiry has been completed.

Where a period had been prescribed for the lodging of written observations, the President shall fix the date for the opening of the oral procedure after that period has expired.

CHAPTER 3. ORAL PROCEDURE

Article 55. 1. Subject to the priority of decisions provided for in Article 85 of these Rules, the Court shall deal with the cases before it in the order in which the preparatory inquiries in them have been completed. Where the preparatory inquiries in several cases are completed simultaneously, the order in which they are to be dealt with shall be determined by the dates of entry in the register of the applications initiating them respectively.

2. The President may in special circumstances order that a case be given priority over others.

The President may in special circumstances, after hearing the parties and the Advocate-General, either on his own initiative or at the request of one of the parties, defer a case to be dealt with at a later date. On a joint application by the parties the President may order that a case be deferred.

Article 56. 1. The proceedings shall be opened and directed by the President, who shall be responsible for the proper conduct of the hearing.

2. The oral proceedings in cases heard *in camera* shall not be published.

Article 57. The President may in the course of the hearing put questions to the agents, advisers or lawyers of the parties.

The other Judges and the Advocate-General may do likewise.

Article 58. A party may address the Court only through his agent, adviser or lawyer.

Article 59. 1. The Advocate-General shall deliver his opinion orally at the end of the oral procedure.

2. After the Advocate-General has delivered his opinion, the President shall declare the oral procedure closed.

Article 60. The Court may at any time, in accordance with Article 45 (1), after hearing the Advocate-General, order any measure of inquiry to be taken or that a previous inquiry be repeated or expanded. The Court may direct the Chamber or the Judge-Rapporteur to carry out the measures so ordered.

Article 61. The Court may after hearing the Advocate-General order the reopening of the oral procedure.

Article 62. 1. The Registrar shall draw up minutes of every hearing. The minutes shall be signed by the President and by the Registrar and shall constitute an official record.

2. The parties may inspect the minutes at the Registry and obtain copies at their own expense.

CHAPTER 4. JUDGMENTS

Article 63. The judgment shall contain:

– a statement that it is the judgment of the Court,
– the date of its delivery,
– the names of the President and of the Judges taking part in it,
– the name of the Advocate-General,
– the name of the Registrar,
– the description of the parties,
– the names of the agents, advisers and lawyers of the parties,
– a statement of the forms of order sought by the parties,

- a statement that the Advocate-General has been heard, a summary of the facts,
- the grounds for the decision,
- the operative part of the judgment, including the decision as to costs.

Article 64. 1. The judgment shall be delivered in open court; the parties shall be given notice to attend to hear it.

2. The original of the judgment, signed by the President, by the Judges who took part in the deliberations and by the Registrar, shall be sealed and deposited at the Registry; the parties shall be served with certified copies of the judgment.

3. The Registrar shall record on the original of the judgment the date on which it was delivered.

Article 65. The judgment shall be binding from the date of its delivery.

Article 66. 1. Without prejudice to the provisions relating to the interpretation of judgments the Court may, of its own motion or on application by a party made within two weeks after the delivery of a judgment, rectify clerical mistakes, errors in calculation and obvious slips in it.

2. The parties, whom the Registrar shall duly notify, may lodge written observations within a period prescribed by the President.

3. The Court shall take its decision in closed session after hearing the Advocate-General.

4. The original of the rectification order shall be annexed to the original of the rectified judgment. A note of this order shall be made in the margin of the original of the rectified judgment.

Article 67. If the Court should omit to give a decision on a specific head of claim or on costs, any party may within a month after service of the judgment apply to the Court to supplement its judgment.

The application shall be served on the opposite party and the President shall prescribe a period within which that party may lodge written observations.

After these observations have been lodged, the Court shall, after hearing the Advocate-General, decide both on the admissibility and on the substance of the application.

Article 68. The Registrar shall arrange for the publication of reports of cases before the Court.

CHAPTER 5. COSTS

Article 69.   1. A decision as to costs shall be given in the final judgment or in the order which closes the proceedings.

2. The unsuccessful party shall be ordered to pay the costs if they have been applied for in the successful party's pleadings.

Where there are several unsuccessful parties the Court shall decide how the costs are to be shared.

3. Where each party succeeds on some and fails on other heads, or where the circumstances are exceptional, the Court may order that the costs be shared or that the parties bear their own costs.

The Court may order a party, even if successful, to pay costs which the Court considers that party to have unreasonably or vexatiously caused the opposite party to incur.

4. The Member States and institutions which intervene in the proceedings shall bear their own costs.

The Court may order an intervener other than those mentioned in the preceding subparagraph to bear his own costs.

5. A party who discontinues or withdraws from proceedings may be ordered to pay the costs if they have been applied for in the other party's pleadings. However, upon application by the party who discontinues or withdraws from proceedings, the costs shall be borne by the other party if this appears justified by the conduct of that party.

Where the parties have come to an agreement on costs, the decision as to costs shall be in accordance with that agreement.

If costs are not claimed, the parties shall bear their own costs.

6. Where a case does not proceed to judgment the costs shall be in the discretion of the Court.

Article 70.   Without prejudice to the second subparagraph of Article 69 (3) of these Rules, in proceedings between the Communities and their servants the institutions shall bear their own costs.

Article 71.   Costs necessarily incurred by a party in enforcing a judgment or order of the Court shall be refunded by the opposite party on the scale in force in the State where the enforcement takes place.

Article 72.   Proceedings before the Court shall be free of charge, except that:

(a)   where a party has caused the Court to incur avoidable costs the Court may, after hearing the Advocate-General, order that party to refund them;

(b)   where copying or translation work is carried out at the request of a party, the cost shall, in so far as the Registrar considers it excessive, be paid for by that party on the scale of charges referred to in Article 16 (5) of these Rules.

Article 73. Without prejudice to the preceding Article, the following shall be regarded as recoverable costs:

(a) sums payable to witnesses and experts under Article 51 of these Rules;
(b) expenses necessarily incurred by the parties for the purpose of the proceedings, in particular the travel and subsistence expenses and the remuneration of agents, advisers or lawyers.

Article 74. 1. If there is a dispute concerning the costs to be recovered, the Chamber to which the case has been assigned shall, on application by the party concerned and after hearing the opposite party and the Advocate General, make an order, from which no appeal shall lie.

2. The parties may, for the purposes of enforcement, apply for an authenticated copy of the order.

Article 75. 1. Sums due from the cashier of the Court shall be paid in the currency of the country where the Court has its seat.
At the request of the person entitled to any sum, it shall be paid in the currency of the country where the expenses to be refunded were incurred or where the steps in respect of which payment is due were taken.

2. Other debtors shall make payment in the currency of their country of origin.

3. Conversions of currency shall be made at the official rates of exchange ruling on the day of payment in the country where the Court has its seat.

CHAPTER 6. LEGAL AID

Article 76. 1. A party who is wholly or in part unable to meet the costs of the proceedings may at any time apply for legal aid.

The application shall be accompanied by evidence of the applicant's need of assistance, and in particular by a document from the competent authority certifying his lack of means.

2. If the application is made prior to proceedings which the applicant wishes to commence, it shall briefly state the subject of such proceedings.

The application need not be made through a lawyer.

3. The President shall designate a Judge to act as Rapporteur. The Chamber to which the latter belongs shall, after considering the written observations of the opposite party and after hearing the Advocate-General, decide whether legal aid should be granted in full or in part, or

whether it should be refused. The Chamber shall consider where there is manifestly no cause of action.

The Chamber shall make an order without giving reasons, and no appeal shall lie therefrom.

4. The Chamber may at any time, either of its own motion or on application, withdraw legal aid if the circumstances which led to its being granted alter during the proceedings.

5. Where legal aid is granted, the cashier of the Court shall advance the funds necessary to meet the expenses.

In its decision as to costs the Court may order the payment to the cashier of the Court of the whole or any part of amounts advanced as legal aid.

The Registrar shall take steps to obtain the recovery of these sums from the party ordered to pay them.

CHAPTER 7. DISCONTINUANCE

Article 77. If, before the Court has given its decision, the parties reach a settlement of their dispute and intimate to the Court the abandonment of their claims, the President shall order the case to be removed from the register and shall give a decision as to costs in accordance with Article 69 (5), having regard to any proposals made by the parties on the matter.

This provision shall not apply to proceedings under Articles 33 and 35 of the ECSC Treaty, Articles 173 and 175 of the EEC Treaty or Articles 146 and 148 of the Euratom Treaty.

Article 78. If the applicant informs the Court in writing that he wishes to discontinue the proceedings, the President shall order the case to be removed from the register and shall give a decision as to costs in accordance with Article 69 (5).

CHAPTER 8. SERVICE

Article 79. Where these Rules require that a document be served on a person, the Registrar shall ensure that service is effected at that person's address for service either by the dispatch of a copy of the document by registered post with a form for acknowledgement of receipt or by personal delivery of the copy against a receipt.

The Registrar shall prepare and certify the copies of documents to be served, save where the parties themselves supply the copies in accordance with Article 37 (1) of these Rules.

CHAPTER 9. TIME LIMITS

Article 80. 1. Any period of time prescribed by the ECSC, EEC or Euratom Treaties, the Statutes of the Court or these Rules for the taking of any procedural step shall be reckoned as follows:

(a) where a period expressed in days, weeks, months or years is to be calculated from the moment at which an event occurs or an action takes place, the day during which that event occurs or that action takes place shall not be counted as falling within the period in question;

(b) a period expressed in weeks, months or in years shall end with the expiry of whichever day in the last week, month or year is the same day of the week, or falls on the same date, as the day during which the event or action from which the period is to be calculated occurred or took place. If, in a period expressed in months or in years, the day on which it should expire does not occur in the last month, the period shall end with the expiry of the last day of that month;

(c) where a period is expressed in months and days, it shall first be reckoned in whole months, then in days;

(d) periods shall include official holidays, Sundays and Saturdays;

(e) periods shall not be suspended during the judicial vacations.

2. If the period would otherwise end on a Saturday, Sunday or an official holiday, it shall be extended until the end of the first following working day.

A list of official holidays drawn up by the Court shall be published in the *Official Journal of the European Communities.*

Article 81. 1. The period of time allowed for commencing proceedings against a measure adopted by an institution shall run from the day following the receipt by the person concerned of notification of the measure or, where the measure is published, from the 15th day after publication thereof in the *Official Journal of the European Communities.*

2. The extensions, on account of distance, of prescribed time limits shall be provided for in a decision of the Court which shall be published in the *Official Journal of the European Communities.*

Article 82. Any time limit prescribed pursuant to these Rules may be extended by whoever prescribed it.

The President and the Presidents of Chambers may delegate to the Registrar power of signature for the purpose of fixing time limits which, pursuant to these Rules, it falls to them to prescribe or of extending such time limits.

CHAPTER 10. STAY OF PROCEEDINGS

Article 82a. 1. The proceedings may be stayed:

(a) in the circumstances specified in the third paragraph of Article 47 of the ECSC Statute, the third paragraph of Article 47 of the EEC Statute and the third paragraph of Article 48 of the Euratom Statute, by order of the Court or of the Chamber to which the case has been assigned, made after hearing the Advocate-General;

(b) in all other cases, by decision of the President adopted after hearing the Advocate-General and, save in the case of references for a preliminary ruling as referred to in Article 103, the parties.

The proceedings may be resumed by order or decision, following the same procedure.

The orders or decisions referred to in this paragraph shall be served on the parties.

2. The stay of proceedings shall take effect on the date indicated in the order or decision of stay or, in the absence of such indication, on the date of that order or decision.

While proceedings are stayed time shall cease to run for the purposes of prescribed time limits for all parties.

Where the order or decision of stay does not fix the length of stay, it shall end on the date indicated in the order or decision of resumption or, in the absence of such indication, on the date of the order or decision of resumption.

From the date of resumption time shall begin to run afresh for the purposes of the time limits.

TITLE III. SPECIAL FORMS OF PROCEDURE

CHAPTER 1. SUSPENSION OF OPERATION OR ENFORCEMENT AND OTHER INTERIM MEASURES

Article 83. An application to suspend the operation of any measure adopted by an institution, made pursuant to the second paragraph of Article 39 of the ECSC Treaty, Article 185 of the EEC Treaty or Article 157 of the Euratom Treaty, shall be admissible only if the applicant is challenging that measure in proceedings before the Court.

An application for the adoption of any other interim measure referred to in the third paragraph of Article 39 of the ECSC Treaty, Article 186 of the EEC Treaty or Article 158 of the Euratom Treaty shall be admissible only if it is made by a party to a case before the Court and relates to that case.

2. An application of a kind referred to in paragraph (1) of this Article

shall state the subject-matter of the proceedings, the circumstances giving rise to urgency and the pleas of fact and law establishing a *prima facie* case for the interim measures applied for.

3. The application shall be made by a separate document and in accordance with the provisions of Articles 37 and 38 of these Rules.

Article 84. 1. The application shall be served on the opposite party, and the President shall prescribe a short period within which that party may submit written or oral observations.

2. The President may order a preparatory inquiry.

The President may grant the application even before the observations of the opposite party have been submitted. This decision may be varied or cancelled even without any application being made to any party.

Where the application is referred to it, the Court shall postpone all other cases, and shall give a decision after hearing the Advocate-General. Article 84 shall apply.

Article 86. 1. The decision on the application shall take the form of a reasoned order, from which no appeal shall lie. The order shall be served on the parties forthwith.

2. The enforcement of order may be made conditional on the lodging by the applicant of security, of an amount and nature to be fixed in the light of the circumstances.

3. Unless the order fixes the date on which the interim measure is to lapse, the measure shall lapse when final judgment is delivered.

4. The order shall have only an interim effect, and shall be without prejudice to the decision of the Court on the substance of the case.

Article 87. On application by a party, the order may at any time be varied or cancelled on account of a change in circumstances.

Article 88. Rejection of an application for an interim measure shall not bar the party who made it from making a further application on the basis of new facts.

Article 89. The provisions of this Chapter shall apply to applications to suspend the enforcement of a decision of the Court or of any measure adopted by another institution, submitted pursuant to Articles 44 and 92 of the ECSC Treaty, Articles 187 and 192 of the EEC Treaty or Articles 159 and 164 of the Euratom Treaty.

The order granting the application shall fix, where appropriate, a date on which interim measure is to lapse.

CHAPTER 2. PRELIMINARY ISSUES

Article 91. 1. A party applying to the Court for a decision on a preliminary objection or other preliminary plea not going to the substance of the case shall make the application by a separate document.

The application must state the pleas of fact and law relied on and the form of order sought by the applicant; any supporting documents must be annexed to it.

2. As soon as the application has been lodged, the President shall prescribe a period within which the opposite party may lodge a document containing a statement of the form of order sought by that party and its pleas in law.

3. Unless the Court decides otherwise, the remainder of the proceedings shall be oral.

4. The Court shall, after hearing the Advocate-General, decide on the application or reserve its decision for the final judgment.

If the Court refuses the application or reserves its decision, the President shall prescribe new time-limits for the further steps in the proceedings.

Article 92. 1. Where it is clear that the Court has no jurisdiction to take cognizance of an action or where the action is manifestly inadmissible, the Court may, by reasoned order, after hearing the Advocate-General and without taking further steps in the proceedings, give a decision on the action.

2. The Court may at any time of its own motion consider whether there exists any absolute bar to proceeding with a case, and shall give a decision in accordance with Article 91 (3) and (4) of these Rules.

CHAPTER 3. INTERVENTION

Article 93. 1. An application to intervene must be made within three months of the publication of the notice referred to in Article 16 (6) of these Rules.

The application shall contain:

(a) the description of the case;
(b) the description of the parties;
(c) the name and address of the intervener;
(d) the intervener's address for service at the place where the Court has its set;
(e) the form of order sought, by one or more of the parties, in support of which the intervener is applying for leave to intervene;
(f) except in the case of applications to intervene made by Member States or institutions, a statement of the reasons establishing the intervener's interest in the result of the case.

The intervener shall be represented in accordance with the first and second paragraphs of Article 20 of the ECSC Statute and with Article 17 of the EEC and Euratom Statutes.

Articles 37 and 38 of these Rules shall apply.

2. The application shall be served on the parties.

The President shall give the parties an opportunity to submit their written or oral observations before deciding on the application.

The President shall decide on the application by order or shall refer the application to the Court.

3. If the President allows the intervention, the intervener shall receive a copy of every document served on the parties. The President may, however, on application by one of the parties, omit secret or confidential documents.

4. The intervener must accept the case as he finds it at the time of his intervention.

5. The President shall prescribe a period within which the intervener may submit a statement in intervention.

The statement in intervention shall contain:

(a) a statement of the form of order sought by the intervener in support of or opposing, in whole or in part, the form of order sought by one of the parties;
(b) the pleas in law and arguments relied on by the intervener;
(c) where appropriate, the nature of any evidence offered.

6. After the statement in intervention has been lodged, the President shall, where necessary, prescribe a time-limit within which the parties may reply to that statement.

CHAPTER 4. JUDGMENTS BY DEFAULT AND APPLICATIONS TO SET THEM ASIDE

Article 94. 1. If a defendant on whom an application initiating proceedings has been duly served fails to lodge a defence to the application in the proper form within the time prescribed, the applicant may apply for judgment by default.

The application shall be served on the defendant. The President shall fix a date for the opening of the oral procedure.

2. Before giving judgment by default the Court shall, after hearing the Advocate-General, consider whether the application initiating proceedings is admissible, whether the appropriate formalities have been complied with, and whether the application appears well founded. The Court may order a preparatory inquiry.

3. A judgment by default shall be enforceable. The Court may, however, grant a stay of execution until the Court has given its decision on

any application under paragraph (4) to set aside the judgment, or it may make execution subject to the provision of security of an amount and nature to be fixed in the light of the circumstances; this security shall be released if no such application is made or if the application fails.

4. Application may be made to set aside a judgment by default.

The application to set aside the judgment must be made within one month from the date of service of the judgment and must be lodged in the form prescribed by Articles 37 and 38 of these Rules.

5. After the application has been served, the President shall prescribe a period within which the other party may submit his written observations.

The proceedings shall be conducted in accordance with Articles 44 *et seq.* of these Rules.

6. The Court shall decide by way of a judgment which may not be set aside. The original of this judgment shall be annexed to the original of the judgment by default. A note of the judgment on the application to set aside shall be made in the margin of the original of the judgment by default.

CHAPTER 5. CASES ASSIGNED TO CHAMBERS

Article 95. 1. The Court may assign to a Chamber any appeal brought against a decision of the Court of First Instance pursuant to Article 49 of the ECSC Statute, Article 49 of the EEC Statute and Article 50 of the Euratom Statute, any reference for a preliminary ruling of a kind mentioned in Article 103 of these Rules and any other case, with the exception of those brought by a Member State or an institution, in so far as the difficulty or the importance of the case or particular circumstances are not such as to require that the Court decide it in plenary session.

2. The decision so to assign a case shall be taken by the Court at the end of the written procedure upon consideration of the preliminary report presented by the Judge-Rapporteur and after the Advocate-General has been heard.

However, a case may not be so assigned if a Member State or an institution, being a party to the proceedings, has requested that the case be decided in plenary session. In this subparagraph the expression 'party to the proceedings' means any Member State or any institution which is a party to or an intervener in the proceedings or which has submitted written observations in any reference of a kind mentioned in Article 103 of these Rules.

The request referred to in the preceding subparagraph may not be made in proceedings between the Communities and their servants.

3. A Chamber may at any stage refer a case back to the Court.

Article 96. (repealed)

CHAPTER 6. EXCEPTIONAL REVIEW PROCEDURES

Section 1. Third-party proceedings

Article 97. 1. Articles 37 and 38 of these Rules shall apply to an application initiating third-party proceedings. In addition such an application shall:

(a) specify the judgment contested;
(b) state how that judgment is prejudicial to the rights of the third party;
(c) indicate the reasons for which the third party was unable to take part in the original case.

The application must be made against all the parties to the original case.

Where the judgment has been published in the *Official Journal of the European Communities*, the application must be lodged within two months of the publication.

2. The Court may, on application by the third party, order a stay of execution of the judgment. The provisions of Title III, Chapter 1, of these Rules shall apply.

3. The contested judgment shall be varied on the points on which the submissions of the third party are upheld.

The original of the judgment in the third-party proceedings shall be annexed to the original of the contested judgment. A note of the judgment in the third-party proceedings shall be made in the margin of the original of the contested judgment.

Section 2. Revision

Article 98. An application for revision of a judgment shall be made within three months of the date on which the facts on which the application is based came to the applicant's knowledge.

Article 99. 1. Articles 37 and 38 of these Rules shall apply to an application for revision. In addition such an application shall:

(a) specify the judgment contested;
(b) indicate the points on which the judgment is contested;
(c) set out the facts on which the application is based;
(d) indicate the nature of the evidence to show that there are facts justifying revision of the judgment, and that the time-limit laid down in Article 98 has been observed.

2. The application must be made against all parties to the case in which the contested judgment was given.

Article 100.   1. Without prejudice to its decision on the substance, the Court, in closed session, shall, after hearing the Advocate-General and having regard to the written observations of the parties, give in the form of a judgment its decision on the admissibility of the application.

2.   If the Court finds the application admissible, it shall proceed to consider the substance of the application and shall give its decision in the form of a judgment in accordance with these Rules.

3.   The original of the revising judgment shall be annexed to the original of the judgment revised. A note of the revising judgment shall be made in the margin of the original of the judgment revised.

CHAPTER 7. [EURATOM]

CHAPTER 8. INTERPRETATION OF JUDGMENTS

Article 102.   1. An application for interpretation of a judgment shall be made in accordance with Articles 37 and 38 of these Rules. In addition it shall specify:

(a)   the judgment in question;
(b)   the passages of which interpretation is sought.

The application must be made against all the parties to the case in which the judgment was given.

2. The Court shall give its decision in the form of a judgment after having given the parties an opportunity to submit their observations and after hearing the Advocate-General.

The original of the interpreting judgment shall be annexed to the original of the judgment interpreted. A note of the interpreting judgment shall be made in the margin of the original of the judgment interpreted.

CHAPTER 9. PRELIMINARY RULINGS AND OTHER REFERENCES FOR INTERPRETATION

Article 103.   1. In cases governed by Article 20 of the EEC Statute and Article 21 of the Euratom Statute, the procedure shall be governed by the provisions of these Rules, subject to adaptations necessitated by the nature of the reference for a preliminary ruling.

2. The provisions of paragraph (1) shall apply to the references for a preliminary ruling provided for in the Protocol concerning the interpretation by the Court of Justice of the Convention of 29 February 1968 on the mutual recognition of companies and legal persons and the Protocol concerning the interpretation by the Court of Justice of the Convention of 27 September 1968 on jurisdiction and the enforcement of judgments in civil and commercial matters, signed at Luxembourg on 3 June 1971, and to the references provided for by Article 4 of the latter Protocol.

The provisions of paragraph (1) shall apply also to references for interpretation provided for by other existing or future agreements.

3. In cases provided for in Article 41 of the ECSC Treaty, the text of the decision to refer the matter shall be served on the parties in the case, the Member States, the Commission and the Council.

These parties, States and institutions may, within two months from the date of such service, lodge written statements of case or written observations.

The provisions of paragraph (1) shall apply.

Article 104. 1. The decisions of national courts or tribunals referred to in Article 103 shall be communicated to the Member States in the original version, accompanied by a translation into the official language of the State to which they are addressed.

2. As regards the representation and attendance of the parties to the main proceedings in the preliminary ruling procedure the Court shall take account of the rules of procedure of the national court or tribunal which made the reference.

3. Where a question referred to the Court for a preliminary ruling is manifestly identical to a question on which the Court has already ruled, the Court may, after informing the court or tribunal which referred the question to it, hearing any observations submitted by the persons referred to in Article 20 of the EEC Statute, Article 21 of the Euratom Statute and Article 103 (3) of these Rules and hearing the Advocate-General, give its decision by reasoned order in which reference is made to its previous judgment.

4. Without prejudice to paragraph (3) of this Article, the procedure before the Court in the case of a reference for a preliminary ruling shall also include an oral part. However, after the statements of case or written observations referred to in Article 20 of the EEC Statute, Article 21 of the Euratom Statute and Article 103 (3) of these Rules have been submitted, the Court, acting on a report from the Judge-Rapporteur, after informing the persons who under the aforementioned provisions are entitled to submit such statements or observations, may, after hearing the Advocate-General, decide otherwise, provided that none of those persons has asked to present oral judgment.

5. It shall be for the national court or tribunal to decide as to the costs of the reference.

In special circumstances the Court may grant, by way of legal aid, assistance for the purpose of facilitating the representation or attendance of a party.

CHAPTER 10. [EURATOM]

CHAPTER II. OPINIONS

Article 107. A request by the Council for an Opinion under Article 228 of the EEC Treaty shall be served on the Commission. Such a request by the Commission shall be served on the Council and on the Member States. Such a request by a Member State shall be served on the Council, the Commission and the other Member States.

The President shall prescribe a period within which the institutions and Member States which have been served with a request may submit their written observations.

2. The Opinion may deal not only with the question whether the envisaged agreement is compatible which the provisions of the EEC Treaty but also with the question whether the Community or any Community institution has the power to enter into that agreement.

Article 108. 1. As soon as the request for an Opinion has been lodged, the President shall designate a Judge to act as Rapporteur.

2. The Court sitting in closed session shall, after hearing the Advocates-General, deliver a reasoned Opinion.

3. The Opinion, signed by the President, by the Judges who took part in the deliberations and by the Registrar, shall be served on the Council, the Commission and the Member States.

Article 109. Requests for the Opinion of the Court under the fourth paragraph of Article 95 of the ECSC Treaty shall be submitted jointly by the Commission and the Council.

The Opinion shall be delivered in accordance with the provisions of the preceding Article. It shall be communicated to the Commission, the Council and the European Parliament.

TITLE IV. APPEALS AGAINST DECISIONS OF THE COURT OF FIRST INSTANCE

Article 110. Without prejudice to the arrangements laid down in Article 29 (2) (b) and (c) and the fourth subparagraph of Article 29 (3) of these Rules, in appeals against decisions of the Court of First Instance as referred to in Articles 49 and 50 of the ECSC Statute, Articles 49 and 50 of the EEC Statute and Articles 50 and 51 of the Euratom Statute, the language of the case shall be the language of the decision of the Court of First Instance against which the appeal is brought.

Article 111. 1. An appeal shall be brought by lodging an application at the Registry of the Court of Justice or of the Court of First Instance.

2. The Registry of the Court of First Instance shall immediately transmit to the Registry of the Court of Justice the papers in the case at first instance and, where necessary, the appeal.

Article 112. 1. An appeal shall contain:

(a)   the name and address of the appellant;
(b)   the names of the other parties to the proceedings before the Court of First Instance;
(b)   the pleas in law and legal arguments relied on;
(c)   the form or order sought by the appellant.

Article 37 and Article 38 (2) and (3) of these Rules shall apply to appeals.

2.   The decision of the Court of First Instance appealed against shall be attached to the appeal. The appeal shall state the date on which the decision appealed against was notified to the appellant.

3.   If an appeal does not comply with Article 38 (3) or with paragraph (2) of this Article, Article 38 (7) of these Rules shall apply.

Article 113. 1. An appeal may seek:

– to set aside, in whole or in part, the decision of the Court of First Instance;
– the same form of order, in whole or in part, as that sought at first instance and shall not seek a different form of order.

2. The subject-matter of the proceedings before the Court of First Instance may not be changed in the appeal.

Article 114.   Notice of the appeal shall be served on all the parties to the proceedings before the Court of First Instance. Article 39 of these Rules shall apply.

Article 115. 1. Any party to the proceedings before the Court of First Instance may lodge a response within two months after service on him of notice of the appeal. The time-limit for lodging a response shall not be extended.

2. A response shall contain:

(a)   the name and address of the party lodging it;
(b)   the date on which notice of the appeal was served on him;
(c)   the pleas in law and legal arguments relied on;
(d)   the form of order sought by the respondent.

Article 38 (2) and (3) of these Rules shall apply.

Article 116. 1. A response may seek:

– to dismiss, in whole or in part, the appeal or to set aside, in whole or in part, the decision of the Court of First Instance;
– the same form of order, in whole or in part, as that sought at first instance and shall not seek a different form of order.

2. The subject-matter of the proceedings before the Court of First Instance may not be changed in the response.

Article 117. 1. The appeal and the response may be supplemented by a reply and a rejoinder or any other pleading, where the President expressly, on application made within seven days of service of the response or of the reply, considers such further pleading necessary and expressly allows it in order to enable the party concerned to put forward its point of view or in order to provide a basis for the decision on the appeal.

2. Where the response seeks to set aside, in whole or in part, the decision of the Court of First Instance on a plea in law which was not raised in the appeal, the appellant or any other party may submit a reply on that plea alone within two months of the service of the response in question. Paragraph (1) shall apply to any further pleading following such a reply.

3. Where the President allows the lodging of a reply and a rejoinder, or any other pleading, he shall prescribe the period within which they are to be submitted.

Article 118. Subject to the following provisions, Articles 42 (2), 43, 44, 55 to 90, 93, 95 to 100 and 102 of these Rules shall apply to the procedure before the Court of Justice on appeal from a decision of the Court of First Instance.

Article 119. Where the appeal is, in whole or in part, clearly inadmissible or clearly unfounded, the Court may at any time, acting on a report from the Judge-Rapporteur and after hearing the Advocate-General, by reasoned order dismiss the appeal in whole or in part.

Article 120. After the submission of pleadings as provided for in Articles 115 (1) and, if any, Article 117 (1) and (2) of these Rules, the Court may, acting on a report from the Judge-Rapporteur and after hearing the Advocate-General and the parties, decide to dispense with the oral part of the procedure unless one of the parties objects on the ground that the written procedure did not enable him fully to defend his point of view.

Article 121. The report referred to in Article 44 (1) shall be presented to the Court after the pleadings provided for in Article 115 (1) and Article 117 (1) and (2) of these Rules have been lodged. The report shall contain, in addition to the recommendations provided for in Article 44 (1), a recommendation as to whether Article 120 of these Rules should be applied. Where no such pleadings are lodged, the same procedure shall apply after the expiry of the period prescribed for lodging them.

Article 122. Where the appeal is unfounded or where the appeal is well founded and the Court itself gives final judgment in the case, the Court shall make a decision as to costs.

In proceedings between the Communities and their servants:

- Article 70 of these Rules shall apply only to appeals brought by institutions;
- by way of derogation from Article 69 (2) of these Rules, the Court may, in appeals brought by officials or other servants of an institution, order the parties to share the costs where equity so requires.

If the appeal is withdrawn Article 69 (5) shall apply.

When an appeal brought by a Member State or an institution which did not intervene in the proceedings before the Court of First Instance is well founded, the Court of Justice may order that the parties share the costs or that the successful appellant pay the costs which the appeal has caused an unsuccessful party to incur.

Article 123. An application to intervene made to the Court in appeal proceedings shall be lodged before the expiry of a period of three months running from the date on which the appeal was lodged. The Court shall, after hearing the Advocate-General, give its decision in the form of an order on whether or not the intervention is allowed.

MISCELLANEOUS PROVISIONS

Article 124. 1. The President shall instruct any person who is required to take an oath before the Court, as witness or expert, to tell the truth or to carry out his task conscientiously and impartially, as the case may be, and shall warn him of the criminal liability provided for in his national law in the event of any breach of this duty.

2. The witness shall take the oath either in accordance with the first subparagraph of Article 47 (5) of these Rules or in the manner laid down by his national law.

Where his national law provides the opportunity to make, in judicial proceedings, a solemn affirmation equivalent to an oath as well as or instead of taking an oath, the witness may make such an affirmation under the conditions and in the form prescribed in his national law.

Where his national law provides neither for taking an oath nor for making a solemn affirmation, the procedure described in paragraph (1) shall be followed.

3. Paragraph (2) shall apply *mutatis mutandis* to experts, a reference to the first subparagraph of Article 49 (6) replacing in this case the reference to the first subparagraph of Article 47 (5) of these Rules.

Article 125. Subject to the provisions of Article 188 of the EEC Treaty and Article 160 of the Euratom Treaty and after consultation with the Governments concerned, the Court shall adopt supplementary rules concerning its practice in relation to:

(a) letters rogatory;
(b) applications for legal aid;
(c) reports or perjury by witnesses or experts, delivered pursuant to Article 28 of the ECSC and Euratom Statutes and Article 27 of the EEC Statute.

Article 126. These Rules replace the Rules of Procedure of the Court of Justice of the European Communities adopted on 4 December 1974 (*Official Journal of the European Communities No* L 350 of 28 December 1974, p. 1), as last amended on 15 May 1991.

Article 127. These Rules, which are authentic in the languages mentioned in Article 29 (1) of these Rules, shall be published in the *Official Journal of the European Communities* and shall enter into force on the first day of the second month following their publication.

Done at Luxembourg, 19 June 1991.

ANNEX II. DECISION ON EXTENSION OF TIME-LIMITS ON ACCOUNT OF DISTANCE

Article 1. In order to take account of distance, procedural time-limits for all parties save those habitually resident in the Grand Duchy of Luxembourg shall be extended as follows:

– for the Kingdom of Belgium: two days,
– for the Federal Republic of Germany, the European territory of the French Republic and the European territory of the Kingdom of the Netherlands: six days,
– for the European territory of the Kingdom of Denmark, for the Hellenic Republic, for Ireland, for the Italian Republic, for the Kingdom of Spain, for the Portuguese Republic (with the exception of the Azores and Madeira) and for the United Kingdom: 10 days,
– for other European countries and territories: two weeks,
– for the autonomous regions of the Azores and Madeira of the Portuguese Republic: three weeks,
– for other countries, departments and territories: one month.

Done at Luxembourg, 19 June 1991.

Fundamental Rights: Joint Declaration by the European Parliament, The Council and the Commission of 5 April 1977

The European Parliament, the Council and the Commission,

Whereas the Treaties establishing the European Communities are based on the principle of respect for the law;

Whereas, as the Court of Justice has recognized, that law comprises, over and above the rules embodied in the treaties and secondary Community legislation, the general principles of law and in particular the fundamental rights, principles and rights on which the constitutional law of the Member States is based;

Whereas, in particular, all the Member States are Contracting Parties to the European Convention for the Protection of Human Rights and Fundamental Freedoms signed in Rome on 4 November 1950,

Have adopted the following declaration;

1. The European Parliament, the Council and the Commission stress the prime importance they attach to the protection of fundamental rights, as derived in particular from the constitutions of the Member States and the European Convention for the Protection of Human Rights and Fundamental Freedoms.

2. In the exercise of their powers and in pursuance of the aims of the European Communities they respect and will continue to respect these rights.

Done at Luxembourg on 5 April 1977.
[Here follow the signatures.]

PART II

SECONDARY LEGISLATION
AND
OTHER DOCUMENTS

The Free Movement of Goods

Commission Directive of 22 December 1969 based on the provisions of Art. 33 (7), on the abolition of measures which have an effect equivalent to quantitative restrictions on imports and are not covered by other provisions adopted in pursuance of the EEC Treaty (70/50/EEC)[1]

The Commission of the European Communities,

Having regard to the provisions of the Treaty establishing the European Economic Community, and in particular Art. 33 (7) thereof;

Whereas for the purpose of Art. 30 *et seq.* 'measures' means laws, regulations, administrative provisions, administrative practices, and all instruments issuing from a public authority, including recommendations;

Whereas for the purposes of this Directive 'administrative practices' means any standard and regularly followed procedure of a public authority; whereas 'recommendations' means any instruments issuing from a public authority which, while not legally binding on the addressees thereof, cause them to pursue a certain conduct;

Whereas the formalities to which imports are subject do not as a general rule have an effect equivalent to that of quantitative restrictions and, consequently, are not covered by this Directive;

Whereas certain measures adopted by Member States, other than those applicable equally to domestic and imported products, which were operative at the date of entry into force of the Treaty and are not covered by other provisions adopted in pursuance of the Treaty, either preclude importation or make it more difficult or costly than the disposal of domestic production;

Whereas such measures must be considered to include those which make access of imported products to the domestic market, at any marketing stage, subject to a condition which is not laid down for domestic products or to a condition differing from that laid down for domestic products, and more difficult to satisfy, so that a burden is thus placed on imported products only;

[1] OJ Sp. Ed., 1970 (I), p. 17.

Whereas such measures must also be considered to include those which, at any marketing stage, grant to domestic products a preference, other than an aid, to which conditions may or may not be attached, and where such measures totally or partially preclude the disposal of imported products;

Whereas such measures hinder imports which could otherwise take place, and thus have an effect equivalent to quantitative restrictions on imports;

Whereas effects on the free movement of goods of measures which relate to the marketing of products and which apply equally to domestic and imported products are not as a general rule equivalent to those of quantitative restrictions, since such effects are normally inherent in the disparities between rules applied by Member States in this respect;

Whereas, however, such measures may have a restrictive effect on the free movement of goods over and above that which is intrinsic to such rules;

Whereas such is the case where imports are either precluded or made more difficult or costly than the disposal of domestic production and where such effect is not necessary for the attainment of an objective within the scope of the powers for the regulation of trade left to member states by the Treaty; whereas such is in particular the case where the said objective can be attained just as effectively by other means which are less of a hindrance to trade; whereas such is also the case where the restrictive effect of these provisions on the free movement of goods is out of proportion to their purpose;

Whereas these measures accordingly have an effect equivalent to that of quantitative restrictions on imports;

Wheres the customs union cannot be achieved without the abolition of such measures having an equivalent effect to quantitative restrictions on imports;

Whereas Member States must abolish all measures having equivalent effect by the end of the transitional period at the latest, even if no Commission Directive expressly requires them to do so;

Whereas the provisions concerning the abolition of quantitative restrictions and measures having equivalent effect between Member States apply both to products originating in and exported by Member States and to products originating in third countries and put into free circulation in the other Member States;

Whereas Art. 33 (7) does not apply to measures of the kind referred to which fall under other provisions of the Treaty, and in particular those which fall under Arts. 37 (1) and 44 of the Treaty or form an integral part of a national organisation of an agricultural market;

Whereas Art. 33 (7) does not apply to the charges and taxation referred to in Art. 12 *et seq.* and Art. 95 *et seq.* or to the aids mentioned in Art. 92;

Whereas the provisions of Art. 33 (7) do not prevent the application, in particular, of Arts. 36 and 233;

Has adopted this directive:

Article 1. The purpose of this Directive is to abolish the measures referred to in Arts. 2 and 3, which were operative at the date of entry into force of the EEC Treaty.

Article 2. 1. This Directive covers measures, other than those applicable equally to domestic or imported products, which hinder imports which could otherwise take place including measures which make importation more difficult or costly than the disposal of domestic production

2. In particular, it covers measures which make imports or the disposal, at any marketing stage, of imported products subject to a condition—other than a formality—which is required in respect of imported products only, or a condition differing from that required for domestic products and more difficult to satisfy. Equally, it covers, in particular, measures which favour domestic products or grant them a preference, other than an aid, to which conditions may or may not be attached.

3. The measures refered to must be taken to include those measures which:

(a) lay down, for imported products only, minimum or maximum prices below or above which imports are prohibited, reduced or made sub ject to conditions liable to hinder importation;

(b) lay down less favourable prices for imported products than for domestic products;

(c) fix profit margins or any other price components for imported products only or fix these differently for domestic products and for imported products, to the detriment of the latter;

(d) preclude any increase in the price of the imported product corresponding to the supplementary costs and charges inherent in importation;

(e) fix the prices of products solely on the basis of the cost price or the quality of domestic products at such a level as to create a hindrance to importation;

(f) lower the value of an imported product, in particular by causing a reduction in its intrinsic value, or increase its costs;

(g) make access of imported products to the domestic market conditional upon having an agent or representative in the territory of the importing Member State;

(h) lay down conditions of payment in respect of imported products only, or subject imported products to conditions which are different from those laid down for domestic products and more difficult to satisfy;

(i) require, for imports only, the giving of guarantees or making of payments on account;

(j) subject imported products only to conditions, in respect, in particular of shape, size, weight, composition, presentation, identification or putting up, or subject imported products to conditions which are different from those for domestic products and more difficult to satisfy;

(k) hinder the purchase by private individuals of imported products only, or encourage, require or give preference to the purchase of domestic products only;

(l) totally or partially preclude the use of national facilities or equipment in respect of imported products only, or totally or partially confine the use of such facilities or equipment to domestic products only;

(m) prohibit or limit publicity in respect of imported products only, or totally or partially confine publicity to domestic products only;

(n) prohibit, limit or require stocking in respect of imported products only; totally or partially confine the use of stocking facilities to domestic products only, or make the stocking of imported products subject to conditions which are different from those required for domestic products and more difficult to satisfy;

(o) make importation subject to the granting of reciprocity by one or more Member States;

(p) prescribe that imported products are to conform, totally or partially, to rules other than those of the importing country;

(q) specify time limits for imported products which are insufficient or excessive in relation to the normal course of the various transactions to which these time limits apply;

(r) subject imported products to controls, other than those inherent in the customs clearance procedure, to which domestic products are not subject or which are stricter in respect of imported products than they are in respect of domestic products, without this being necessary in order to ensure equivalent protection;

(s) confine names which are not indicative of origin or source to domestic products only.

Article 3. This Directive also covers measures governing the marketing of products which deal, in particular, with shape, size, weight, composition, presentation, identification or putting up and which are equally applicable to domestic and imported products, where the restrictive effect of such measures on the free movement of goods exceeds the effects intrinsic to trade rules.

This is the case, in particular, where:

– the restrictive effects on the free movement of goods are out of proportion to their purpose;
– the same objective can be attained by other means which are less of a hindrance to trade.

Article 4.   1. Member States shall take all necessary steps in respect of products which must be allowed to enjoy free movement pursuant to Arts. 9 and 10 of the Treaty to abolish measures having an effect equivalent to quantitative restrictions on imports and covered by this Directive.

2. Member States shall inform the Commission of measures taken pursuant to this Directive.

Article 5.   1. This Directive does not apply to measures:

(a) which fall under Art. 37 (1) of the EEC Treaty;
(b) which are referred to in Art. 44 of the EEC Treaty or form an integral part of a national organisation of an agricultural market not yet replaced by a common organisation.

2. This Directive shall apply without prejudice to the application, in particular, of Arts. 36 and 223 of the EEC Treaty.

[Final provisions omitted.]

Freedom of Movement for Workers

Regulation (EEC) No 1612/68 of the Council of 15 October 1968 on freedom of movement for workers within the Community[1]

The Council of the European Communitites,

Having regard to the Treaty establishing the European Economic Community, and in particular Art. 49 thereof;

Having regard to the proposal from the Commission;

Having regard to the Opinion of the European Parliament;

Having regard to the Opinion of the Economic and Social Committee;

Whereas freedom of movement for workers should be secured within the Community by the end of the transitional period at the latest; whereas the attainment of this objective entails the abolition of any discrimination based on nationality between workers of the Member States as regards employment, remuneration and other conditions of work and employment, as well as the right of such workers to move freely within the Community in order to pursue activities as employed persons subject to any limitations justified on grounds of public policy, public security or public health;

Whereas by reason in particular of the early establishment of the customs union and in order to ensure the simultaneous completion of the principal foundations of the Community, provisions should be adopted to enable the objectives laid down in Arts. 48 and 49 of the Treaty in the field of freedom of movement to be achieved and to perfect measures adopted successively under Regulation No 15 on the first steps for attainment of freedom of movement and under Council Regulation No 38/54/EEC of 25 March 1964 on freedom of movement for workers within the Community;

Whereas freedom of movement constitutes a fundamental right of workers and their families; whereas mobility of labour within the Community must be one of the means by which the worker is guaranteed the possibility of improving his living and working conditions and promoting his social advancement, while helping to satisfy the requirements of the economies of the Member States; whereas the right of all workers

---

Text not reproduced amended by Reg. 2434/92, OJ 1992 L 245/1.

[1] OJ Sp. Ed., 1968 (II), p. 475. As last amended by Reg. 312/76, OJ 1976, L 39/2.

in the Member States to pursue the activity of their choice within the Community should be affirmed,

Whereas such right must be enjoyed without discrimination by permanent, seasonal and frontier workers and by those who pursue their activities for the purpose of providing services;

Whereas the right of freedom of movement, in order that it may be exercised, by objective standards, in freedom and dignity, requires that equality of treatment shall be ensured in fact and in law in respect of all matters relating to the actual pursuit of activities as employed persons and to eligibility for housing, and also that obstacles to the mobility of workers shall be eliminated, in particular as regards the worker's right to be joined by his family and the conditions for the integration of that family into the host country;

Whereas the principle of non-discrimination between Community workers entails that all nationals of Member States have the same priority as regards employment as is enjoyed by national workers;

[Recitals omitted.]

Has adopted this Regulation:

Part One. Employment and Workers' Families

TITLE I. ELIGIBILITY FOR EMPLOYMENT

Article 1.   1. Any national of a Member State, shall, irrespective of his place of residence, have the right to take up a activity as an employed person, and to pursue such activity, within the territory of another Member State in accordance with the provisions laid down by law, regulation or administrative action governing the employment of nationals of that State.

2. He shall, in particular, have the right to take up available employment in the territory of another Member State with the same priority as nationals of that State.

Article 2.   Any national of a Member State and any employer pursuing an activity in the territory of a Member State may exchange their applications for and offers of employment, and may conclude and perform contracts of employment in accordance with the provisions in force laid down by law, regulation or administrative action, without any discrimination resulting therefrom.

Article 3.   1. Under this Regulation, provisions laid down by law, regulation or administrative action or administrative practices of a Member State shall not apply:

– where they limit application for and offers of employment, or the right of foreign nationals to take up and pursue employment or subject these to conditions not applicable in respect of their own nationals; or
– where, though applicable irrespective of nationality, their exclusive or principal aim or effect is to keep nationals of other Member States away from the employment offered.

This provision shall not apply to conditions relating to linguistic knowledge required by reason of the nature of the post to be filled.

2. There shall be included in particular among the provisions or practices of a Member State referred to in the first subparagraph of paragraph 1 those which:

(a) prescribe a special recruitment procedure for foreign nationals;
(b) limit or restrict the advertising of vacancies in the press or through any other medium or subject it to conditions other than those applicable in respect of employers pursuing their activities in the territory of that Member State;
(c) subject eligibility for employment to conditions of registration with employment offices or impede recruitment of individual workers, where persons who do not reside in the territory of that State are concerned.

Article 4. 1. Provisions laid down by law, regulation or administrative action of the Member States which restrict by number or percentage the employment of foreign nationals in any undertaking, branch of activity or region, or at a national level, shall not apply to nationals of the other Member States.

2. When in a Member State the granting of any benefit to undertakings is subject to a minimum percentage of national workers being employed, nationals of the other Member States shall be counted as national workers, subject to the provisions of the Council Directive of 15 October 1963.[2]

Article 5. A national of a Member State who seeks employment in the territory of another Member State shall receive the same assistance there as that afforded by the employment offices in that State to their own nationals seeking employment.

Article 6. 1. The engagement and recruitment of a national of one Member State for a post in another Member State shall not depend on medical, vocational or other criteria which are discriminatory on grounds

---

[2] Dir. 63/607, OJ Sp. Ed. 1963-4, p. 52.

of nationality by comparison with those applied to nationals of the other Member State who wish to pursue the same activity.

2. Nevertheless, a national who holds an offer in his name from an employer in a Member State other than that of which he is a national may have to undergo a vocational test, if the employer expressly requests this when making his offer of employment.

TITLE II. EMPLOYMENT AND EQUALITY OF TREATMENT

Article 7. 1. A worker who is a national of a Member State may not, in the territory of another Member State, be treated differently from national workers by reason of his nationality in respect of any conditions of employment and work, in particular as regards remuneration, dismissal, and should he become unemployed, reinstatement or re employ ment.

2. He shall enjoy the same social and tax advantages as national workers.

3. He shall also, by virtue of the same right and under the same conditions as national workers, have access to training in vocational schools and retraining centres.

4. Any clause of a collective or individual agreement or of any other collective regulation concerning eligibility for employment, employment, remuneration and other conditions of work or dismissal shall be null and void in so far as it lays down or authorises discriminatory conditions in respect of workers who are nationals of the other Member States.

Article 8. 1. A worker who is a national of a Member State and who is employed in the territory of another Member State shall enjoy equality of treatment as regards membership of trade unions and the exercise of rights attaching thereto, including the right to vote and to be eligible for the administration and management of bodies governed by public law and from holding an office governed by public law. Furthermore, he shall have the right of eligibility for workers' representative bodies in the undertaking. The provisions of this Article shall not affect laws or regulations in certain Member States which grant more extensive rights to workers coming from the other Member States.

Article 9. 1. A worker who is a national of a Member State and who is employed in the territory of another Member State shall enjoy all the rights and benefits accorded to national workers in matters of housing, including ownership of the housing he needs.

2. Such worker may, with the same right as nationals, put his name down on the housing lists in the region in which he is employed, where such lists exist; he shall enjoy the resultant benefits and priorities.

If his family has remained in the country whence he came, they shall be considered for this purpose as residing in the said region, where national workers benefit from a similar presumption.

TITLE III. WORKERS' FAMILIES

Article 10. 1. The following shall, irrespective of their nationality, have the right to install themselves with a worker who is a national of one Member State and who is employed in the territory of another Member State:

(a) his spouse and their descendants who are under the age of 21 years or are dependants;
(b) dependent relatives in the ascending line of the worker and his spouse.

2. Member States shall facilitate the admission of any member of the family not coming within the provisions of paragraph 1 if dependent on the worker referred to above or living under his roof in the country whence he comes.

3. For the purposes of paragraphs 1 and 2, the worker must have available for his family housing considered as normal for national workers in the region where he is employed; this provision, however must not give rise to discrimination between national workers and workers from the other Member States.

Article 11. Where a national of a Member State is pursuing an activity as an employed or self-employed person in the territory of another Member State, his spouse and those of the children who are under the age of 21 years or dependent on him shall have the right to take up any activity as an employed person throughout the territory of that same State, even if they are not nationals of any Member State.

Article 12. The children of a national of a Member State who is or has been employed in the territory of another Member State shall be admitted to that State's general educational, apprenticeship and vocational training courses under the same conditions as the nationals of that State, if such children are residing in its territory.

Member States shall encourage all efforts to enable such children to attend these courses under the best possible conditions.

[The remainder of the Regulation is omitted.]

Council Directive of 15 October 1968 on the abolition of
restrictions on movement and residence within the
Community for workers of Member States and their families
(68/360/EEC)[3]

The Council of the European Communities,

Having regard to the Treaty establishing the European Economic
Community, and in particular Art. 49 thereof;

Having regard to the proposal from the Commission;

Having regard to the Opinion of the European Parliament;

Having regard to the Opinion of the Economic and Social Committee;

Whereas Council Regulation (EEC) No 1612/68 fixed the provisions
governing freedom of movement for workers within the Community;
whereas, consequently, measures should be adopted for the abolition of
restrictions which still exist concerning movement and residence within
the Community, which conform to the rights and privileges accorded by
the said Regulation to nationals of any Member State who move in order
to pursue activities as employed persons and to members of their families;

Whereas the rules applicable to residence should, as far as possible,
bring the position of workers from other Member States and members of
their families into line with that of nationals;

Whereas the co-ordination of special measures relating to the movement and residence of foreign nationals, justified on grounds of public
policy, public security or public health, is the subject of the Council
Directive of 25 February 1964, adopted in application of Art. 56 (2) of
the Treaty;

Has adopted this Directive:

Article 1. Member States shall, acting as provided in this Directive,
abolish restrictions on the movement and residence of nationals of the
said States and of members of their families to whom Regulation (EEC)
No 1612/68 applies.

Article 2. 1. Member States shall grant the nationals referred to in Art 1
the right to leave their territory in order to take up activities as employed
persons and to pursue such activities in the territory of another Member
State. Such right shall be exercised simply on production of a valid identity card or passport. Members of the family shall enjoy the same right as
the national on whom they are dependent.

[3] OJ Sp. Ed., 1968 (II), p. 485. As last amended by the 1985 Act of Accession, Annex II,
VIII, 8.

2. Member States shall, acting in accordance with their laws, issue to such nationals, or renew, an identity card or passport, which shall state in particular the holder's nationality.

3. The passport must be valid at least for all Member States and for countries through which the holder must pass when travelling between Member States. Where a passport is the only document on which the holder may lawfully leave the country, its period of validity shall be not less than five years.

4. Member States may not demand from the nationals referred to in Art. 1 any exit visa or any equivalent document.

Article 3. 1. Member States shall allow the persons referred to in Art. 1 to enter their territory simply on production of a valid identity card or passport.

2. No entry visa or equivalent document may be demanded save from members of the family who are not nationals of a Member State. Member States shall accord to such persons every facility for obtaining any necessary visas.

Article 4. 1. Member States shall grant the right of residence in their territory to the persons referred to in Art. 1 who are able to produce the documents listed in paragraph 3.

2. As proof of the right of residence, a document entitled 'Residence Permit for a National of a Member State of the EEC' shall be issued. This document must include a statement that it has been issued pursuant to Regulation (EEC) No 1612/68 and to the measures taken by the Member States for the implementation of the present Directive. The text of such statement is given in the Annex to this Directive.

3. For the issue of a Residence Permit for a National of a Member State of the EEC, Member States may require only the production of the following documents;
– by the worker:

(a) the document with which he entered their territory;
(b) a confirmation of engagement from the employer or a certificate of employment;

– by the members of the worker's family:

(c) the document with which they entered the territory;
(d) a document issued by the competent authority of the State of origin or the State whence they came, proving their relationship;
(e) in the cases referred to in Art. 10 (1) and (2) of Regulation (EEC) No 1612/68, a document issued by the competent authority of the State

of origin or the State whence they came, testifying that they are dependent on the worker or that they live under his roof in such country.

4. A member of the family who is not a national of a Member State shall be issued with a residence document which shall have the same validity as that issued to the worker on whom he is dependent.

Article 5. Completion of the formalities for obtaining a residence permit shall not hinder the immediate beginning of employment under a contract concluded by the applicants.

Article 6. 1. The residence permit:

(a) must be valid throughout the territory of the Member State which issued it;
(b) must be valid for at least five years from the date of issue and be automatically renewable.

2. Breaks in residence not exceeding six consecutive months and absence on military service shall not affect the validity of a residence permit.

3. Where a worker is employed for a period exceeding three months but not exceeding a year in the service of an employer in the host State or in the employ of a person providing services, the host Member State shall issue him a temporary residence permit, the validity of which may be limited to the expected period of the employment.

Subject to the provisions of Art. 8 (1) (c), a temporary residence permit shall be issued also to a seasonal worker employed for a period of more than three months. The period of employment must be shown in the documents referred to in paragraph 4 (3) (b).

Article 7. 1. A valid residence permit may not be withdrawn from a worker solely on the ground that he is no longer in employment, either because he is temporarily incapable of work as a result of illness or accident, or because he is involuntarily unemployed, this being duly confirmed by the competent employment office.

2. When the residence permit is renewed for the first time, the period of residence may be restricted, but not to less than twelve months, where the worker has been involuntarily unemployed in the Member State for more than twelve consecutive months.

Article 8. 1. Member States shall, without issuing a residence permit, recognise the right of residence in their territory of:

(a) a worker pursuing an activity as an employed person, where the activity is not expected to last for more than three months. The document with which the person concerned entered the territory and a statement by the employer on the expected duration of the employment shall be sufficient to cover his stay; a statement by the employer shall not, however, be required in the case of workers coming within the provisions of the Council Directive of 25 February 1964[4] on the attainment of freedom of establishment and freedom to provide services in respect of the activities of intermediaries in commerce, industry and small craft industries.

(b) a worker who, while having his residence in the territory of a Member State to which he returns as a rule, each day or at least once a week, is employed in the territory of another Member State. The competent authority of the State where he is employed may issue such worker with a special permit valid for five years and automatically renewable;

(c) a seasonal worker who holds a contract of employment stamped by the competent authority of the Member State on whose territory he has come to pursue his activity.

2. In all cases referred to in paragraph 1, the competent authorities of the host Member State may require the worker to report his presence in the territory.

Article 9. 1. The residence documents granted to nationals of a Member State of the EEC referred to in this Directive shall be issued and renewed free of charge or on payment of an amount not exceeding the dues and taxes charged for the issue of identity cards to nationals.

2. The visa referred to in Art. 3 (2) and the stamp referred to in Art. 8 (1) (c) shall be free of charge.

3. Member States shall take the necessary steps to simplify as much as possible the formalities and procedure for obtaining the documents mentioned in paragraph 1.

Article 10. Member States shall not derogate from the provisions of this Directive save on grounds of public policy, public security or public health.

Article 11. 1. This Directive shall not affect the provisions of the Treaty establishing the European Coal and Steel Community which relate to workers with recognised skills in coal mining and steel making, or the provisions of the Treaty establishing the European Atomic Energy

[4] Dir. 64/224, OJ Sp. Ed. 1963–4, p. 126.

Community which deal with the right to take up skilled employment in the field of nuclear energy, or any measures taken in implementation of those Treaties.

2. Nevertheless, this Directive shall apply to the categories of workers referred to in paragraph 1, and to members of their families, in so far as their legal position is not governed by the abovementioned Treaties or measures.

Article 12. 1. Member States shall, within nine months of notification of this Directive, bring into force the measures necessary to comply with its provisions and shall forthwith inform the Commission thereof.

2. They shall notify the Commission of amendments made to provisions imposed by law, regulation or administrative action for the simplification of the formalities and procedure for issuing such documents as are still necessary for the entry, exit and residence of workers and members of their familites.

Article 13. 1. The Council Directive of 25 March 1964[5] on the abolition of restrictions on movement and on residence within the Community of workers and their families shall continue to have effect until this Directive is implemented by the Member States.

2. Residence permits issued pursuant to the Directive referred to in Paragraph 1 shall remain valid until the date on which they next expire.

[Final provisions omitted.]

ANNEX

Test of the statement referred to in Art. 4 (2):
'This permit is issued pursuant to Regulation (EEC) No 1612/68 of the Council of the European Communities of 15 October 1968 and to the measures taken in implementation of the Council Directive of 15 October 1968.
In accordance with the provisions of the above-mentioned Regulation, the holder of this permit has the right to take up and pursue an activity as an employed person in . . . .* territory under the same conditions as . . . .* workers.'

* Belgian, Danish, German, Greek, Spanish, French, Irish, Italian, Luxembourg, Dutch, Portuguese, United Kingdom, depending on which country issues the card.
[5] OJ No. 62, 17.4. 1964, p. 981/64

Regulation (EEC) No 1251/70 of the
Commission of 29 June 1970 on the right of
workers to remain in the territory of a
Member State after having been
employed in that State[6]

The Commission of the European Communities,

Having regard to the Treaty establishing the European Economic Community, and in particular Art. 48 (3) (d) thereof, and Art. 2 of the Protocol on the Grand Duchy of Luxembourg;

Having regard to the Opinion of the European Parliament;

Whereas Council Regulation (EEC) No 1612/68 of 15 October 1968 and Council Directive No 68/360/EEC of 15 October 1968 enabled freedom of movement for workers to be secured at the end of a series of measures to be achieved progressively; whereas the right of residence acquired by workers in active employment has as a corollary the right, granted by the Treaty to such workers, to remain in the territory of a Member State after having been employed in that State; whereas it is important to lay down the conditions for the exercise of such right,

Whereas the said Council Regulation and Council Directive contain the appropriate provisions concerning the right of workers to reside in the territory of a Member State for the purposes of employment; whereas the right to remain, referred to in Art. 48 (3) (d) of the Treaty, is interpreted therefore as the right of the worker to maintain his residence in the territory of a Member State when he ceases to be employed there;

Whereas the mobility of labour in the Community requires that workers may be employed successively in several Member States without thereby being placed at a disadvantage;

Whereas it is important, in the first place, to guarantee to the worker residing in the territory of a Member State the right to remain in that territory when he ceases to be employed in that State because he has reached retirement age or by reason of permanent incapacity to work; whereas, however, it is equally important to ensure that right for the worker who, after a period of employment and residence in the territory of a Member State, works as an employed person in the territory of another Member State, while still retaining his residence in the territory of the first State;

Whereas, to determine the conditions under which the right to remain arises, account should be taken of the reasons which have led to the

---

[6] OJ Sp. Ed., 1970 (II), p. 402; HMSO Subject Ed., Vol. 10, p. 23.

termination of employment in the territory of the Member State concerned and, in particular, of the difference between retirement, the normal and foreseeable end of working life, and incapacity to work which leads to a premature and unforeseeable termination of activity; whereas special conditions must be laid down where termination of activity is the result of an accident at work or occupational disease, or where the worker's spouse is or was a national of the Member State concerned;

Whereas the worker who has reached the end of his working life should have sufficient time in which to decide where he wishes to establish his final residence;

Whereas the exercise by the worker of the right to remain entails that such right shall be extended to members of his family; whereas in the case of the death of the worker during his working life, maintenance of the right of residence of the members of his family must also be recognised and be the subject of special conditions;

Whereas persons to whom the right to remain applies must enjoy equality of treatment with national workers who have ceased their working lives;

Has adopted this Regulation:

Article 1. The provisions of this Regulation shall apply to nationals of a Member State who have worked as employed persons in the territory of another Member State and to members of their families, as defined in Art. 10 of Council Regulation (EEC) No 1612/68 on freedom of movement for workers within the Community.

Article 2. 1. The following shall have the right to remain permanently in the territory of a Member State:

(a) a worker who, at the time of termination of his activity, has reached the age laid down by the law of that Member State for entitlement to an old-age pension and who has been employed in that State for at least the last twelve months and has resided there continuously for more than three years;

(b) a worker who, having resided continuously in the territory of that State for more than two years, ceases to work there as an employed person as a result of permanent incapacity to work. If such incapacity is the result of an accident at work or an occupational disease entitling him to a pension for which an institution of that State is entirely or partially responsible, no condition shall be imposed as to length of residence;

(c) a worker who, after three years' continuous employment and residence in the territory of that State, works as an employed person in the territory of another Member State, while retaining his residence in the territory of the first State, to which he returns, as a rule, each day or at least once a week.

Periods of employment completed in this way in the territory of the other Member State shall, for the purposes of entitlement to the rights referred to in subparagraphs (a) and (b), be considered as having been completed in the territory of the State of residence.

2. The conditions as to length of residence and employment laid down in paragraph 1 (a) and the condition as to length of residence laid down in paragraph 1 (b) shall not apply if the worker's spouse is a national of the Member State concerned or has lost the nationality of that State by marriage to that worker.

Article 3.   1. The members of a worker's family referred to in Art. 1 of this Regulation who are residing with him in the territory of a Member State shall be entitled to remain there permanently if the worker has acquired the right to remain in the territory of that State in accordance with Art. 2, and to do so even after his death.

2. If, however, the worker dies during his working life and before having acquired the right to remain in the territory of the State concerned, members of his family shall be entitled to remain there permanently on condition that:

- the worker, on the date of his decease, had resided continuously in the territory of that Member State for at least 2 years; or
- his death resulted from an accident at work or an occupational disease; or
- the surviving spouse is a national of the State of residence or lost the nationality of that State by marriage to that worker.

Article 4.   1. Continuity of residence as provided for in Arts. 2 (1) and 3 (2) may be attested by any means of proof in use in the country of residence. It shall not be affected by temporary absences not exceeding a total of three months per year, nor by longer absences due to compliance with the obligations of military service.

2. Periods of involuntary unemployment, duly recorded by the competent employment office, and absences due to illness or accident shall be considered as periods of employment within the meaning of Art. 2 (1).

Article 5.   1. The person entitled to the right to remain shall be allowed to exercise it within two years from the time of becoming entitled to such right pursuant to Art. 2 (1) (a) and (b) and Art. 3. During such period he may leave the territory of the Member State without adversely affecting such right.

2. No formality shall be required on the part of the person concerned in respect of the exercise of the right to remain.

Article 6. 1. Persons coming under the provisions of this Regulation shall be entitled to a residence permit which:

(a) shall be issued and renewed free of charge or on payment of a sum not exceeding the dues and taxes payable by nationals for the issue or renewal of identity documents;
(b) must be valid throughout the territory of the Member State issuing it; must be valid for at least five years and be renewable automatically.

2. Periods of non-residence not exceeding six consecutive months shall not affect the validity of the residence permit.

Article 7. The right to equality of treatment, established by Council Regulation (EEC) No 1612/68, shall apply also to persons coming under the provisions of this Regulation.

Article 8. 1. This Regulation shall not affect any provisions laid down by law, regulation or administrative action of one Member State which would be more favourable to nationals of other Member States.

2. Member States shall facilitate re-admission to their territories of workers who have left those territories after having resided there permanently for a long period and having been employed there and who wish to return there when they have reached retirement age or are permanently incapacitated for work.

Article 9. 1. The Commission may, taking account of developments in the demographic situation of the Grand Duchy of Luxembourg, lay down, at the request of that State, different conditions from those provided for in this Regulation, in respect of the exercise of the right to remain in Luxembourg territory.

2. Within two months after the request supplying all appropriate details has been put before it, the Commission shall take a decision, stating the reasons on which it is based.

It shall notify the Grand Duchy of Luxembourg of such decision and inform the other Member States thereof;

[Final provisions omitted.]

Council Directive of 25 February 1964 on the co-ordination of special measures concerning the movement and residence of foreign nationals which are justified on grounds of public policy, public security or public health (64/221/EEC)[7]

The Council of the European Economic Community,

Having regard to the Treaty establishing the European Economic Community, and in particular Art. 56 (2) thereof;

Having regard to Council Regulation No 15 of 16 August 1961 on initial measures to bring about free movement of workers within the Community, and in particular Art. 47 thereof;

Having regard to Council Directive of 16 August 1961 on administrative procedures and practices governing the entry into and employment and residence in a Member State of workers and their families from other Member States of the Community;

Having regard to the General Programmes for the abolition of restrictions on freedom of establishment and on freedom to provide services, and in particular Title II of each such programme;

Having regard to the Council Directive of 25 February 1964 on the abolition of restrictions on movement and residence within the Community for nationals of Member States with regard to establishment and the provision of services;

Having regard to the proposal from the Commission;

Having regard to the Opinion of the European Parliament;

Having regard to the Opinion of the Economic and Social Committee;

Whereas co-ordination of provisions laid down by law, regulation or administrative action which provide for special treatment for foreign nationals on grounds of public policy, public security or public health should in the first place deal with the conditions for entry and residence of nationals of Member States moving within the Community either in order to pursue activities as employed or self-employed persons, or as recipients of services;

Whereas such co-ordination presupposes in particular an approximation of the procedures followed in each Member State when invoking grounds of public policy, public security or public health in matters connected with the movement or residence of foreign nationals;

Whereas, in each Member State, nationals of other Member States should have adequate legal remedies available to them in respect of the decisions of the administration in such matters;

[7] OJ Sp. Ed., 1963–4, p. 117.

Whereas it would be of little practical use to compile a list of diseases and disabilities which might endanger public health, public policy or public security and it would be difficult to make such a list exhaustive; whereas it is sufficient to classify such diseases and disabilities in groups;

Has adopted this Directive:

Article 1.   1. The provisions of this Directive shall apply to any national of a Member State who resides in or travels to another Member State of the Community, either in order to pursue an activity as an employed or self-employed person, or as a recipient of services.

2. These provisions shall apply also to the spouse and to members of the family who come within the provisions of the regulations and directives adopted in this field in pursuance of the Treaty.

Article 2.   1. This Directive relates to all measures concerning entry into their territory, issue or renewal of residence permits, or expulsion from their territory, taken by Member States on grounds of public policy, public security or public health.

2. Such grounds shall not be invoked to service economic ends.

Article 3.   1. Measures taken on grounds of public policy or of public security shall be based exclusively on the personal conduct of the individual concerned.

2. Previous criminal convictions shall not in themselves constitute grounds for the taking of such measures.

3. Expiry of the identity card or passport used by the person concerned to enter the host country and to obtain a residence permit shall not justify expulsion from the territory.

4. The State which issued the identity card or passport shall allow the holder of such docuent to re-enter its territory without any formality even if the document is no longer valid or the nationality of the holder is in dispute.

Article 4.   1. The only diseases or disabilities justifying refusal of entry into a territory or refusal to issue a first residence permit shall be those listed in the Annex to this Directive.

2. Diseases or disabilities occurring after a first residence permit has been issued shall not justify refusal to renew the residence permit or expulsion from the territory.

3. Member States shall not introduce new provisions or practices which are more restrictive than those in force at the date of notification of this Directive.

Article 5. 1. A decision to grant or to refuse a first residence permit shall be taken as soon as possible and in any event not later than six months from the date of application for the permit.

The person concerned shall be allowed to remain temporarily in the territory pending a decision either to grant or to refuse a residence permit.

2. The host country may, in cases where this is considered essential, request the Member State of origin of the applicant, and if need be other Member States, to provide information concerning any previous police record. Such enquiries shall not be made as a matter of routine. The Member State consulted shall give its reply within two months.

Article 6. The person concerned shall be informed of the grounds of public policy, public security, or public health upon which the decision taken in his case is based, unless this is contrary to the interests of the security of the State involved.

Article 7. The person concerned shall be officially notified of any decision to refuse the issue or renewal of a residence permit or to expel him from the territory. The period allowed for leaving the territory shall be stated in this notification. Save in cases of urgency, this period shall not be less than fifteen days if the person concerned has not yet been granted a residence permit and not less than one month in all other cases.

Article 8. The person concerned shall have the same legal remedies in respect of any decision concerning entry, or refusing the issue or renewal of a residence permit, or ordering expulsion from the territory, as are available to nationals of the State concerned in respect of acts of the administration.

Article 9. 1. Where there is no right of appeal to a court of law, or where such appeal may be only in respect of the legal validity of the decision, or where the appeal cannot have suspensory effect, a decision refusing renewal of a residence permit or ordering the expulsion of the holder of a residence permit from the territory shall not be taken by the administrative authority, save in cases of urgency, until an opinion has been obtained from a competent authority of the host country before which the person concerned enjoys such rights of defence and of assistance or representation as the domestic law of that country provides for.

This authority shall not be the same as that empowered to take the decision refusing renewal of the residence permit or ordering expulsion.

2. Any decision refusing the issue of a first residence permit or ordering expulsion of the person concerned before the issue of the permit shall,

where that person so requests, be referred for consideration to the authority whose prior opinion is required under paragraph 1. The person concerned shall then be entitled to submit his defence in person, except where this would be contrary to the interests of national security.

Article 10.   1. Member States shall within six months of notification of this Directive put into force the measures necessary to comply with its provisions and shall forthwith inform the Commission thereof.

2. Member States shall ensure that the texts of the main provisions of national law which they adopt in the field governed by this Directive are communicated to the Commission.

[Final provisions omitted.]

ANNEX

A. Diseases which might endanger public health:
1. Diseases subject to quarantine listed in International Health Regulation No 2 of the World Health Organisation of 25 May 1951; Tuberculosis of the respiratory system in an active state or showing a tendency to develop;
2. Syphilis;
3. Other infectious diseases or contagious parasitic diseases if they are the subject of provisions for the protection of nationals of the host country.

B. Diseases and disabilities which might threaten public policy or public security:
1. Drug addition;
2. Profound mental disturbance; manifest conditions of psychotic disturbance with agitation, delirium, hallucinations or confusion.

Council Directive of 25 July 1977
on the education of the children of migrant workers
(77/486/EEC)

The Council of the European Communities,

Having regard to the Treaty establishing the European Economic Community, and in particular Article 49 thereof,

Having regard to the proposal from the Commission,

Having regard to the opinion of the European Parliament,

Having regard to the opinion of the Economic and Social Committee,

Whereas in its resolution of 21 January 1974 concerning a social action programme,[8] the Council included in its priority actions those designed to improve the conditions of freedom of movement for workers relating in particular to reception and to the education of their children;

Whereas in order to permit the integration of such children into the educational environment and the school system of the host State, they should be able to receive suitable tuition including teaching of the language of the host State;

Whereas host Member States should also take, in conjunction with the Member States of origin, appropriate measures to promote the teaching of the mother tongue and of the culture of the country of origin of the abovementioned children, with a view principally to facilitating their possible reintegration into the Member State of origin,

Has adopted this directive:

Article 1. This Directive shall apply to children for whom school attendance is compulsory under the laws of the host State, who are dependants of any worker who is a national of another Member State, where such children are resident in the territory of the Member State in which that national carries on or has carried on an activity as an employed person.

Article 2. Member States shall, in accordance with their national circumstances and legal systems, take appropriate measures to ensure that free tuition to facilitate initial reception is offered in their territory to the children referred to in Article 1, including, in particular, the teaching— adapted to the specific needs of such children—of the official language or one of the official languages of the host State.

Member States shall take the measures necessary for the training and further training of the teachers who are to provide this tuition.

[8] OJ No C 13, 12. 2. 1974, p. 1.

Article 3. Member States shall, in accordance with their national circumstances and legal systems, and in cooperation with States of origin, take appropriate measures to promote, in coordination with normal education, teaching of the mother tongue and culture of the country of origin for the children referred to in Article 1.

Article 4. The Member States shall take the necessary measures to comply with this Directive within four years of its notification and shall forthwith inform the Commission thereof.

The Member States shall also inform the Commission of all laws, regulations and administrative or other provisions which they adopt in the field governed by this Directive.

Article 5. The Member States shall forward to the Commission within five years of the notification of this Directive, and subsequently at regular intervals at the request of the Commission, all relevant information to enable the Commission to report to the Council on the application of this Directive.

Article 6. This Directive is addressed to the Member States.

[Final provisions omitted.]

The Right of Establishment and the Freedom to Provide Services

General Programme for the abolition of restrictions on freedom of establishment[1]

The Council of the European Economic Community,
    Having regard to the provisions of the Treaty, and in particular Arts. 54 and 132 (5) thereof;

[Recitals omitted.]

TITLE I. BENEFICIARIES

Subject to any decisions taken by the Council under the second sub-paragraph of Art. 227 (2) of the Treaty and without prejudice to subsequent provisions laying down association arrangements between the European Economic Community and the overseas countries and territories having attained independence after the entry into force of the Treaty, the persons entitled to benefit from the abolition of restrictions on freedom of establishment as set out in this General Programme are:

– nationals of Member States or of the overseas countries and territories, and
– companies and firms formed under the law of a Member State or of an overseas country or territory and having either the seat prescribed by their statutes, or their centre of administration, or their main establishment situated within the Community or in an overseas country or territory,

who wish to establish themselves in order to pursue activities as self-employed persons in a Member State; and

– nationals of Member States or of the overseas countries and territories who are established in a Member State or in an overseas country or territory, and
– companies and firms as above, provided that, where only the seat prescribed by their statutes is situated within the Community or in an overseas country or territory, their activity shows a real and continuous link with the economy of a Member State or of an overseas country or territory; such link shall not be one of nationality, whether of the

---

[1] OJ, Sp. Ed., Second Series, IX, p. 7.

members of the company or firm, or of the persons holding managerial or supervisory posts therein, or of the holders of the capital,

who wish to set up agencies, branches or subsidiaries in a Member State.

[Provisions omitted.]

TITLE III. RESTRICTIONS

Subject to the exceptions or special provisions laid down in the Treaty
and in particular to:

- Art. 55 concerning activities which are connected with the exercise of
  official authority in a Member State; and to
- Art. 56 concerning provisions on special treatment for foreign nationals
  on grounds of public policy, public security or public health.

the following restrictions are to be eliminated. . .

A. Any measure which, pursuant to any provisions laid down by law,
regulation or administrative action in a Member State, or as the result
of the application of such a provision, or of administrative practices,
prohibits or hinders nationals of other Member States in their pursuit
of an activity as a self-employed person by treating nationals of other
Member States differently from nationals of the country concerned.

Such restrictive provisions and practices are in particular those which,
in respect of foreign nationals only:

(a) prohibit the taking up or pursuit of an activity as a self-employed
    person;
(b) make the taking up or pursuit of an activity as a self-employed per-
    son subject to an authorisation or to the issue of a document such as
    a foreign trader's permit;
(c) impose additional conditions in respect of the granting of any autho-
    risation required for the taking up or pursuit of an activity as a self-
    employed person;
(d) make the taking up or pursuit of an activity as a self-employed per-
    son subject to a period of prior residence or training in the host
    country;
(e) make the taking up or pursuit of an activity as a self-employed per-
    son more costly through taxation or other financial burdens, such as
    a requirement that the person concerned shall lodge a deposit or pro-
    vide security in the host country;
(f) limit or hinder, by making it more costly or more difficult access to
    sources of supply or to distribution outlets;
(g) prohibit or hinder access to any vocational training which is neces-
    sary or useful for the pursuit of an activity as a self-employed person;

(h) prohibit foreign nationals from becoming members of companies or firms, or restrict their rights as members, in particular as regards the functions which they may perform within the company or firm;

(i) deny or restrict the right to participate in social security schemes, in particular sickness, accident, invalidity or old age insurance schemes, or the right to receive family allowances;

(j) grant less favourable treatment in the event of nationalisation, expropriation or requisition.

The like shall apply to provisions and practices which, in respect of foreign nationals only, exclude, limit or impose conditions on the power to exercise rights normally attaching to an activity as a self-employed person, and in particular the power:

(a) to enter into contracts, in particular contracts for work, business or agricultural tenancies, and contracts of employment, and to enjoy all rights arising under such contracts;

(b) to submit tenders for or to act directly as a party or as a subcontractor in contracts with the State or with any other legal person governed by public law;

(c) to obtain licences or authorisations issued by the State or by any other legal person governed by public law;

(d) to acquire, use or dispose of movable or immovable property or rights therein;

(e) to acquire, use or dispose of intellectual property and all rights deriving therefrom;

(f) to borrow, and in particular to have access to the various forms of credit;

(g) to receive aids granted by the State, whether direct or indirect;

(h) to be a party to legal or administrative proceedings;

(i) to join professional or trade organisations;

where the professional or trade activities of the person concerned necessarily involve the exercise of such power.

Furthermore, included among the above-mentioned provisions and practices are those which limit or impair the freedom of personnel belonging to the main establishment in one Member State to take up managerial or supervisory posts in agencies, branches or subsidiaries in another Member State.

B. Any requirements imposed, pursuant to any provisions laid down by law, regulation or administrative action or in consequence of any administrative practice, in respect of the taking up or pursuit of an activity as a self-employed person where, although applicable irrespective of nationality, their effect is exclusively or principally, to hinder the taking up or pursuit of such activity by foreign nationals.

[Provisions omitted.]

TITLE V. MUTUAL RECOGNITION OF DIPLOMAS AND OTHER EVIDENCE OF FORMAL QUALIFICATIONS — CO-ORDINATION

[Provisions omitted.]

Pending such mutual recognition of diplomas, or such co-ordination, and in order to facilitate the taking up and pursuit of activities as self-employed persons and to avoid distortions, a transitional system may be applied; such system may where appropriate include provision for the production of a certificate establishing that the activity in question was actually and lawfully carried on in the country of origin.

[Remainder of General Programme omitted.]

General Programme for the abolition of restrictions of freedom to provide services[2]

The Council of the European Economic Community,
  Having regard to the provisions of the Treaty, and in particular Arts. 63, 106 and 227 (2) thereof;

[Recitals omitted.]

TITLE I. BENEFICIARIES

The persons entitled to benefit from the abolition of restrictions on freedom to provide services as set out in this General Programme are:

– nationals of Member States who are established within the Community;
– companies or firms formed under the law of a Member State and having the seat prescribed by their statutes, or their centre of administration, or their main establishment situated within the Community, provided that where only that seat is situated within the Community their activity shows a real and continuous link with the economy of a Member State; such link shall not be one of nationality, whether of the members of the company or firm, or of the persons holding managerial or supervisory posts therein, or of the holders of the capital;

subject to the condition that the service is carried out either personally by the person contracting to provide it or by one of his agencies or branches established in the Community.

[Provisions omitted.]

[2] OJ, Sp. Ed., Second Series, IX, p. 3.

TITLE III. RESTRICTIONS

Subject to the exceptions or special provisions laid down in the Treaty, and in particular to:

- Art. 55 concerning activities which are connected with the exercise of official authority in a Member State;
- Art. 56 concerning provisions on special treatment for foreign nationals on grounds of public policy, public security or public health;
- Art. 61, which provides that freedom to provide services in the field of transport is to be governed by the provisions of the Title relating to transport; and to
- the provisions concerning the free movement of goods, capital and persons, and those concerning taxation systems:

the following restrictions are to be eliminated . . . whether they affect the person providing the services directly, or indirectly through the recipient of the service or through the service itself;

A. Any measure which, pursuant to any provision laid down by law, regulation or administrative action in a Member State, or as a result of the application of such a provision, or of administrative practices, prohibits or hinders the person providing services in his pursuit of an activity as a self-employed person by treating him differently from nationals of the State concerned.

Such restrictive provisions and practices are in particular those which, in respect of foreign nationals only:

(a) prohibit the provision of services;
(b) make the provision of services subject to an authorisation or to the issue of a document such as a foreign trader's permit;
(c) impose additional conditions in respect of the granting of any authorisation required for the provision of services;
(d) make the provision of services subject to a period of prior residence or training in the host country;
(e) make the provision of services more costly through taxation or other financial burdens, such as a requirement that the person concerned must lodge a deposit or provide security in the host country;
(f) limit or hinder, by making it more costly or more difficult, access to sources of supply or to distribution outlets;
(g) deny or restrict the right to participate in social security schemes, in particular, in sickness, accident, invalidity or old age insurance schemes, or the right to receive family allowances;
(h) grant less favourable treatment in the event of nationalisation, expropriation or requisition.

The like shall apply to provisions and practices which, in respect of foreign nationals only, exclude, limit or impose conditions on the power to exercise rights normally attaching to the provision of services and in particular the power:

(a) to enter into contracts, in particular contracts for work, contracts of hire and contracts of employment, and to enjoy all rights arising under such contracts;

(b) to submit tenders for or to act directly as a party or a subcontractor in contracts with the State or with any other legal person governed by public law;

(c) to obtain licences or authorisations issued by the State or by any other legal person governed by public law;

(d) to acquire, use or dispose of movable or immovable property or rights therein;

(c) to acquire, use or dispose of intellectual property and all rights deriving therefrom;

(d) to borrow, and in particular to have access to the various forms of credit;

(e) to receive aids granted by the State, whether direct or indirect;

(f) to be a party to legal or administrative proceedings;

where the professional or trade activities of the person concerned necessarily involve the exercise of such power.

Furthermore, any requirements imposed, pursuant to any provision laid down by law, regulation or administrative action or in consequence of any administrative practice, in respect of the provision of services are also to be regarded as restrictions where, although applicable irrespective of nationality, their effect is exclusively or principally to hinder the provision of services by foreign nationals.

B. Any prohibition of, or hindrance to, the movement of the item to be supplied in the course of the service or of the materials comprising such item or of the tools, machinery equipment and other means to be employed in the provision of the service.

C. Any prohibition of, or impediment to, the transfer of the funds needed to perform the service.

D. Any prohibition of, or hindrance to, payments for services, where the provision of such services between the Member States is limited only by restrictions in respect of the payments therefor.

However, in respect of the provisions referred to in paragraphs C and D, Member States shall retain the right to verify the nature and genuineness of transfer of funds and of payments and to take all necessary measures in order to prevent contravention of their laws and regulations, in particular as regards the issue of foreign currency to tourists.

[Provisions omitted.]

B. TRANSFER OF FUNDS. PAYMENT

[Provisions omitted.]

. . . limits on foreign currency allowances for tourists may be maintained in force during the transitional period, but they are to be progressively raised from the end of the first stage.

[Provisions omitted.]

TITLE VI. MUTUAL RECOGNITION OF DIPLOMAS AND OTHER EVIDENCE OF FORMAL QUALIFICATIONS – CO-ORDINATION

[Provisions omitted.]

Pending such mutual recognition of diplomas, or such co-ordination, and in order to facilitate the provision of services and to avoid distortions, a transitional system may be applied; such system may where appropriate include provision for the production of a certificate establishing that the activity in question was actually and lawfully carried on in the country of origin.

[Final provisions omitted.]

Council Directive of 21 May 1973 on the abolition of restrictions on movement and residence within the Community for nationals of Member States with regard to establishment and the provision of services (73/148/EEC)[3]

The Council of the European Communities,
    Having regard to the Treaty establishing the European Economic Community, and in particular Art. 54 (2) and Art. 63 (2) thereof;
    Having regard to the General Programmes for the abolition of restrictions on freedom of establishment and freedom to provide services, and in particular Title II thereof;

[Recitals omitted.]

    Has adopted this Directive:

[3] OJ 1973 L 172/14.

Article 1. 1. The Member States shall, acting as provided in this Directive, abolish restrictions on the movement and residence of:

(a) nationals of a Member State who are established or who wish to establish themselves in another Member State in order to pursue activities as self-employed persons, or who wish to provide services in that State;

(b) nationals of Member States wishing to go to another Member State as recipients of services;

(c) the spouse and the children under twenty-one years of age of such nationals, irrespective of their nationality;

(d) the relatives in the ascending and descending lines of such nationals and of the spouse of such nationals, which relatives are dependent on them, irrespective of their nationality.

2. Member States shall favour the admission of any other member of the family of a national referred to in paragraph 1 (a) or (b) or of the spouse of that national, which member is dependent on that national or spouse of that national or who in the country of origin was living under the same roof.

Article 2. 1. Member States shall grant the persons referred to in Art. 1 the right to leave their territory. Such right shall be exercised simply on production of a valid identity card or passport. Members of the family shall enjoy the same right as the national on whom they are dependent.

2. Member States shall, acting in accordance with their laws, issue to their nationals, or renew, an identity card or passport, which shall state in particular the holder's nationality.

3. The passport must be valid at least for all Member States and for countries through which the holder must pass when travelling between Member States. Where a passport is the only document on which the holder may lawfully leave the country, its period of validity shall be not less than five years.

4. Member States may not demand from the persons referred to in Art. 1 any exit visa or any equivalent requirement.

Article 3. 1. Member States shall grant to the persons referred to in Art. 1 the right to enter their territory merely on production of a valid identity card or passport.

2. No entry visa or equivalent requirement may be demanded save in respect of members of the family who do not have the nationaity of a Member State. Member States shall afford to such persons every facility for obtaining any necessary visas.

Article 4.   1. Each Member State shall grant the right of permanent residence to nationals of other Member States who establish themselves within its territory in order to pursue activities as self-employed persons, when the restrictions on these activities have been abolished pursuant to the Treaty.

As proof of the right of residence, a document entitled 'Residence Permit for a National of a Member State of the European Communiuties' shall be issued. This document shall be valid for not less than five years from the date of issue and shall be automatically renewable.

Breaks in residence not exceeding six consecutive months and absence on military service shall not affect the validity of a residence permit.

A valid residence permit may not be withdrawn from a national referred to in Art. 1 (1) (a) solely on the grounds that he is no longer in employment because he is temporarily incapable of work as a result of illness or accident.

Any national of a Member State who is not specified in the first subparagraph but who is authorised under the laws of another Member State to pursue an activity within its territory shall be granted a right of abode for a period not less than that of the authorisation granted for the pursuit of the activity in question.

However, any national referred to in subparagraph 1 and to whom the provisions of the preceding subparagraph apply as a result of a change of employment shall retain his residence permit until the date on which it expires.

2. The right of residence for persons providing and receiving services shall be of equal duration with the period during which the services are provided.

Where such period exceeds three months, the Member State in the territory of which the services are performed shall issue a right of abode as proof of the right of residence.

Where the period does not exceed three months, the identity card or passport with which the person concerned entered the territory shall be sufficient to cover his stay. The Member State may, however, require the person concerned to report his presence in the territory.

3. A member of the family who is not a national of a Member State shall be issued with a residence document which shall have the same validity as that issued to the national on whom he is dependent.

Article 5.   The right of residence shall be effective throughout the territory of the Member State concerned.

Article 6.   An applicant for a residence permit or right of abode shall not be required by a Member State to produce anything other than the following, namely:

(a) the identity card or passport with which he or she entered its territory;
(b) proof that he or she comes within one of the classes of person referred to in Arts. 1 and 4.

Article 7. 1. The residence documents granted to nationals of a Member State shall be issued and renewed free of charge or on payment of an amount not exceeding the dues and taxes charged for the issue of identity cards to nationals. These provisions shall also apply to documents and certificates required for the issue and renewal of such residence documents.

2. The visas referred to in Art. 3 (2) shall be free of charge.

3. Member States shall take the necessary steps to simplify as much as possible the formalities and the procedure for obtaining the documents mentioned in paragraph 1.

Article 8. Member States shall not derogate from the provisions of this Directive save on grounds of public policy, public security or public health.

[The remainder of the Directive is omitted.]

Council Directive of 17 December 1974 concerning
the right of nationals of a Member State to remain
in the territory of another Member State after
having pursued therein an activity in a
self-employed capacity (75/34/EEC)[4]

The Council of the European Communities,
   Having regard to the Treaty establishing the European Economic Community, and in particular Art. 235 thereof;
   Having regard to the General Programme for the abolition of restrictions on freedom of establishment, and in particular Title II thereof;

[Recitals omitted.]

   Whereas pursuant to Council Directive No 73/148/EEC of 21 May 1973 on the abolition of restrictions on movement and residence within

---

[4] OJ 1975 L 14/10.

the Community for nationals of Member States with regard to establishment and the provision of services, each Member State grants the right of permanent residence to nationals of other Member States who establish themselves within its territory in order to pursue activities as self-employed persons, when the restrictions on these activities have been abolished pursuant to the Treaty;

Whereas it is normal for a person to prolong a period of permanent residence in the territory of a Member State by remaining there after having pursued an activity there; whereas the absence of a right so to remain in such circumstances is an obstacle to the attainment of freedom of establishment; whereas, as regards employed persons, the conditions under which such a right may be exercised have already been laid down by Regulation (EEC) No 1251/70;

Whereas Art. 48 (3) (d) of the Treaty recognises the right of workers to remain in the territory of a Member State after having been employed in that State; whereas Art. 54 (2) does not expressly provide a similar right for self-employed persons; whereas, nevertheless, the nature of establishment, together with attachments formed to the countries in which they have pursued their activities, means that such persons have a definite interest in enjoying the same right to remain as that granted to workers; whereas in justification of this measure reference should be made to the Treaty provision enabling it to be taken;

[Recitals omitted.]

Has adopted this Directive:

Article 1.   Member States shall, under the conditions laid down in this Directive, abolish restrictions on the right to remain in their territory in favour of nationals of another Member State who have pursued activities as self-employed persons in their territory, and members of their families, as defined in Art. 1 of Directive No 73/148/EEC.

Article 2.   1. Each Member State shall recognise the right to remain permanently in its territory of:

(a) any person who, at the time of termination of his activity, has reached the age laid down by the law of that State for entitlement to an old-age pension and who has pursued his activity in that State for at least the previous twelve months and has resided there continuously for more than three years.

   Where the law of that Member State does not grant the right to an old-age pension to certain categories of self-employed workers, the age requirement shall be considered as satisfied when the beneficiary reaches 65 years of age;

(b) any person who, having resided continuously in the territory of that State for more than two years, ceases to pursue his activity there as a result of permanent incapacity to work.

If such incapacity is the result of an accident at work or an occupational illness entitling him to a pension which is payable in whole or in part by an institution of that State no condition shall be imposed as to length of residence;

(c) any person who, after three years' continuous activity and residence in the territory of that State, pursues his activity in the territory of another Member State, while retaining his residence in the territory of the first State, to which he returns, as a rule, each day or at least once a week.

Periods of activity so completed in the territory of the other Member State shall, for the purposes of entitlement to the rights referred to in (a) and (b), be considered as having been completed in the territory of the State of residence.

2. The conditions as to length of residence and activity laid down in paragraph 1 (a) and the condition as to length of residence laid down in paragraph 1 (b) shall not apply if the spouse of the self-employed person is a national of the Member State concerned or has lost the nationality of that State by marriage to that person.

Article 3. 1. Each Member State shall recognise the right of the members of the self-employed person's family referred to in Art. 1 who are residing with him in the territory of that State to remain there permanently, if the person concerned has acquired the right to remain in the territory of that State in accordance with Art. 2. This provision shall continue to apply even after the death of the person concerned.

2. If, however, the self-employed person dies during his working life and before having acquired the right to remain in the territory of the State concerned, that State shall recognise the right of the members of his family to remain there permanently on condition that:

- the person concerned, on the date of his decease, had resided continuously in its territory for at least two years; or
- his death resulted from an accident at work or an occupational illness; or
- the surviving spouse is a national of that State or lost such nationality by marriage to the person concerned.

Article 4. 1. Continuity of residence as provided for in Arts. 2 (1) and 3 (2) may be attested by any means of proof in use in the country of residence. It may not be affected by temporary absences not exceeding a total of three months per year, nor by longer absences due to compliance with the obligations of military service.

2. Periods of inactivity due to circumstances outside the control of the person concerned or of inactivity owing to illness or accident must be considered as periods of activity within the meaning of Art. 2 (1).

Article 5. 1. Member States shall allow the person entitled to the right to remain to exercise such right within two years from the time of becoming entitled thereto pursuant to Art. 2 (1) (a) and (b) and Art. 3. During this period the beneficiary must be able to leave the territory of the Member State without adversely affecting such right.

2. Member States shall not require the person concerned to comply with any particular formality in order to exercise the right to remain.

Article 6. 1. Member States shall recognise the right of persons having the right to remain in their territory to a residence permit, which must:

(a) be issued and renewed free of charge or on payment of a sum not exceeding the dues and taxes payable by nationals for the issue or renewal of identity cards;
(b) be valid throughout the territory of the Member State issuing it;
  be valid for five years and renewable automatically.

2. Periods of non-residence not exceeding six consecutive months and longer absences due to compliance with the obligations of military service may not affect the validity of a residence permit.

Article 7. Member States shall apply to persons having the right to remain in their territory the right of equality of treatment recognised by the Council Directives on the abolition of restrictions on freedom of establishment pursuant to Title III of the General Programme which provides for such abolition.

Article 8. 1. This Directive shall not affect any provisions laid down by law, regulation or administrative action of any Member State which would be more favourable to nationals of other Member States.

2. Member States shall facilitate re-admission to their territories of self-employed persons who left those territories after having resided there permanently for a long period while pursuing an activity there and who wish to return when they have reached retirement age as defined in Art. 2 (1) (a) or are permanently incapacitated for work.

Article 9. Member States may not derogate from the provisions of this Directive save on grounds of public policy, public security or public health.

[Final provisions omitted.]

Council Directive of 21 December 1988 on a general system for the recognition of higher-education diplomas awarded on completion of professional education and training of at least three years' duration (89/48/EEC)[5]

The Council of the European Communities,

Having regard to the Treaty establishing the European Economic Community, and in particular Arts. 49, 57 (1) and 66 thereof,

[Recitals omitted.]

Whereas, pursuant to Art. 3 (c) of the Treaty the abolition, as between Member States, of obstacles to freedom of movement for persons and services constitutes one of the objectives of the Community; whereas, for nationals of the Member States, this means in particular the possibility of pursuing a profession, whether in a self-employed or employed capacity, in a Member State other than that in which they acquired their professional qualifications;

Whereas the provisions so far adopted by the Council, and pursuant to which Member States recognise mutually and for professional purposes higher-education diplomas issued within their territory, concern only a few professions; whereas the level and duration of the education and training governing access to those professions have been regulated in a similar fashion in all the Member States or have been the subject of the minimal harmonisation needed to establish sectoral systems for the mutual recognition of diplomas;

Whereas, in order to provide a rapid response to the expectations of nationals of Community countries who hold higher-education diplomas awarded on completion of professional education and training issued in a Member State other than that in which they wish to pursue their profession, another method of recognition of such diplomas should also be put in place such as to enable those concerned to pursue all those professional activities which in a host Member State are dependent on the completion of post-secondary education and training provided they hold such a diploma preparing them for those activities awarded on completion of a course of studies lasting at least three years and issued in another Member State;

Whereas this objective can be achieved by the introduction of a general system for the recognition of higher-education diplomas awarded on completion of professional education and training of at least three years' duration;

[5] OJ 1989 L 19/16.

Whereas, for those professions for the pursuit of which the Community has not laid down the necessary minimum level of qualification, Member States reserve the option of fixing such a level with a view to guaranteeing the quality of services provided in their territory; whereas, however, they may not, without infringing their obligations laid down in Art. 5 of the Treaty, require a national of a Member State to obtain those qualifications which in general they determine only by reference to diplomas issued under their own national education systems, where the person concerned has already acquired all or part of those qualifications in another Member State; whereas, as a result, any host Member State in which a profession is regulated is required to take account of qualifications acquired in another Member State and to determine whether those qualifications correspond to the qualifications which the Member State concerned requires;

Whereas collaboration between the Member States is appropriate in order to facilitate their compliance with those obligations; whereas, therefore, the means of organising such collaboration should be established;

Whereas the term 'regulated professional activity' should be defined so as to take account of differing national sociological situations; whereas the term should cover not only professional activities access to which is subject, in a Member State, to the possession of a diploma, but also professional activities, access to which is unrestricted when they are practised under a professional title reserved for the holders of certain qualifications; whereas the professional associations and organisations which confer such titles on their members and are recognised by the public authorities cannot invoke their private status to avoid application of the system provided for by this Directive;

Whereas it is also necessary to determine the characteristics of the professional experience or adaptation period which the host Member State may require of the person concerned in addition to the higher-education diploma, where the person's qualifications do not correspond to those laid down by national provisions;

Whereas an aptitude test may also be introduced in place of the adaptation period; whereas the effect of both will be to improve the existing situation with regard to the mutual recognition of diplomas between Member States and therefore to facilitate the free movement of persons within the Community; whereas their function is to assess the ability of the migrant, who is a person who has already received his professional training in another Member State, to adapt to this new professional environment; whereas, from the migrant's point of view, an aptitude test will have the advantage of reducing the length of the practice period; whereas, in principle, the choice between the adaptation period and the aptitude test should be made by the migrant; whereas, however, the nature of certain professions is such that Member States must be allowed to prescribe, under certain conditions, either the adaptation period or the test; whereas, in particular, the differences between the legal systems of the Member States, whilst they may vary in extent from one Member State to another, warrant special provisions since, as a rule, the education or training attested by the diploma, certificate or other evidence of formal qualifications in a field of law in the Member State of origin does not cover the legal knowledge required in the host Member State with respect to the corresponding legal field;

Whereas, moreover, the general system for the recognition of higher-education diplomas is intended neither to amend the rules, including those relating to professional ethics, applicable to any person pursuing a profession in the territory of a Member State nor to exclude migrants from the application of those rules; whereas that system is confined to laying down appropriate arrangements to ensure that migrants comply with the professional rules of the host Member State;

Whereas Arts. 49, 57 (1) and 66 of the Treaty empower the Community to adopt provisions necessary for the introduction and operation of such a system;

Whereas the general system for the recognition of higher-education diplomas is entirely without prejudice to the application of Art. 48 (4) and Art. 55 of the Treaty;

Whereas such a system, by strengthening the right of a Community national to use his professional skills in any Member State, supplements and reinforces his right to acquire such skills wherever he wishes;

Whereas this system should be evaluated, after being in force for a certain time, to determine how efficiently it operates and in particular how it can be improved or its field of application extended.

Has adopted this Directive:

Article 1. For the purposes of this Directive the following definitions shall apply:

(a) diploma: any diploma, certificate or other evidence of formal qualifications or any set of such diplomas, certificates or other evidence:

- which has been awarded by a competent authority in a Member State, designated in accordance with its own laws, regulations or administrative provisions;
- which shows that the holder has successfully completed a post-secondary course of at least three years' duration, or of an equivalent duration part-time, at a university or establishment of higher education or another establishment of similar level and, where

appropriate, that he has successfully completed the professional training required in addition to the post-secondary course, and
– which shows that the holder has the professional qualifications required for the taking up or pursuit of a regulated profession in that Member State,

provided that the education and training attested by the diploma, certificate or other evidence of formal qualifications were received mainly in the Community, or the holder thereof has three years' professional experience certified by the Member State which recognised a third-country diploma, certificate or other evidence of formal qualifications.

The following shall be treated in the same way as a diploma, within the meaning of the first subparagraph: any diploma, certificate or other evidence of formal qualifications or any set of such diplomas, certificates or other evidence awarded by a competent authority in a Member State if it is awarded on the successful completion of education and training received in the Community and recognised by a competent authority in that Member State as being of an equivalent level and if it confers the same rights in respect of the taking up and pursuit of a regulated profession in that Member State;

(b) host Member State: any Member State in which a national of a Member State applies to pursue a profession subject to regulation in that Member State, other than the State in which he obtained his diploma or first pursued the profession in question;

(c) a regulated profession: the regulated professional activity or range of activities which constitute this profession in a Member State;

(d) regulated professional activity: a professional activity, in so far as the taking up or pursuit of such activity or one of its modes of pursuit in a Member State is subject, directly or indirectly by virtue of laws, regulations or administrative provisions, to the possession of a diploma. The following in particular shall constitute a mode of pursuit of a regulated professional activity:

– pursuit of an activity under a professional title, in so far as the use of such a title is reserved to the holders of a diploma governed by laws, regulations or administrative provisions,
– pursuit of a professional activity relating to health, in so far as remuneration and/or reimbursement for such an activity is subject by virtue of national social security arrangements to the possession of a diploma.

Where the first subparagraph does not apply, a professional activity shall be deemed to be a regulated professional activity if it is pursued by the members of an association or organisation the purpose of which is, in particular, to promote and maintain a high standard in the professional field concerned and which, to achieve that purpose, is recognised in a special form by a Member State and:

- awards a diploma to its members,
- ensures that its members respect the rules of professional conduct which it prescribes, and
- confers on them the right to use a title or designatory letters, or to benefit from a status corresponding to that diploma.

A non-exhaustive list of associations or organisations which, when this Directive is adopted, satisfy the conditions of the second subparagraph is contained in the Annex. Whenever a Member State grants the recognition referred to in the second subparagraph to an association or organisation, it shall inform the Commission thereof, which shall publish this information in the *Official Journal of the European Communities.*

(e) professional experience: the actual and lawful pursuit of the profession concerned in a Member State;

(f) adaptation period: the pursuit of a regulated profession in the host Member State under the responsibility of a qualified member of that profession, such period of supervised practice possibly being accompanied by further training. This period of supervised practice shall be the subject of an assessment. The detailed rules governing the adaptation period and its assessment as well as the status of a migrant person under supervision shall be laid down by the competent authority in the host Member States;

(g) aptitude test: a test limited to the professional knowledge of the applicant, made by the competent authorities of the host Member State with the aim of assessing the ability of the applicant to pursue a regulated profession in that Member State.

In order to permit this test to be carried out, the competent authorities shall draw up a list of subjects which, on the basis of a comparison of the education and training required in the Member State and that received by the applicant, are not covered by the diploma or other evidence of formal qualifications possessed by the applicant.

The aptitude test must take account of the fact that the applicant is a qualified professional in the Member State of origin or the Member State from which he comes. It shall cover subjects to be selected from those on the list, knowledge of which is essential in order to be able to exercise the profession in the host Member State. The test may also include knowledge of the professional rules applicable to the activities in question in the host Member State. The detailed application of the aptitude test shall be determined by the competent authorities of that State with due regard to the rules of Community law.

The status, in the host Member State, of the applicant who wishes to prepare himself for the aptitude test in that State shall be determined by the competent authorities in that State.

Article 2. This Directive shall apply to any national of a Member State wishing to pursue a regulated profession in a host Member State in a self-employed capacity or as an employed person.

This Directive shall not apply to professions which are the subject of a separate Directive establishing arrangements for the mutual recognition of diplomas by Member States.

Article 3. Where, in a host Member State, the taking up or pursuit of a regulated profession is subject to possession of a diploma, the competent authority may not, on the grounds of inadequate qualifications, refuse to authorise a national of a Member State to take up or pursue that profession on the same conditions as apply to its own nationals:

(a) if the applicant holds the diploma required in another Member State for the taking up or pursuit of the profession in question in its territory, such diploma having been awarded in a Member State; or

(b) if the applicant has pursued the profession in question full-time for two years during the previous ten years in another Member State which does not regulate that profession, within the meaning of Art. 1 (c) and the first subparagraph of Art. 1 (d), and possesses evidence of one or more formal qualifications:

– which have been awarded by a competent authority in a Member State, designated in accordance with the laws, regulations or administrative provisions of such State,

– which show that the holder has successfully completed a post-secondary course of at least three years' duration, or of an equivalent duration part-time, at a university or establishment of higher education or another establishment of similar level of a Member State and, where appropriate, that he has successfully completed the professional training required in addition to the post-secondary course and

– which have prepared the holder for the pursuit of his profession.

The following shall be treated in the same way as the evidence of formal qualifications referred to in the first subparagraph: any formal qualifications or any set of such formal qualifications awarded by a competent authority in a Member State if it is awarded on the successful completion of training received in the Community and is recognised by that Member State as being of an equivalent level, provided that the other Member States and the Commission have been notified of this recognition.

Article 4. 1. Notwithstanding Art. 3, the host Member State may also require the applicant:

(a) to provide evidence of professional experience, where the duration of the education and training adduced in support of his application, as laid down in Art. 3 (a) and (b), is at least one year less than that required in the host Member State. In this event, the period of professional experience required:

    – may not exceed twice the shortfall in duration of education and training where the shortfall relates to post-secondary studies and/or to a period of probationary practice carried out under the control of a supervising professional person and ending with an examination,

    – may not exceed the shortfall where the shortfall relates to professional practice acquired with the assistance of a qualified member of the profession.

In the case of diplomas within the meaning of the last subparagraph of Art. 1 (a), the duration of education and training recognised as being of an equivalent level shall be determined as for the education and training defined in the first subparagraph of Art. 1 (a).

When applying these provisions, account must be taken of the professional experience referred to in Art. 3 (b).

At all events, the professional experience required may not exceed four years;

(b) to complete an adaptation period not exceeding three years or take an aptitude test:

    – where the matters covered by the education and training he has received as laid down in Art. 3 (a) and (b), differ substantially from those covered by the diploma required in the host Member State, or

    – where, in the case referred to in Art. 3 (a), the profession regulated in the host Member State comprises one or more regulated professional activities which are not in the profession regulated in the Member State from which the applicant originates or comes and that difference corresponds to specific education and training required in the host Member State and covers matters which differ substantially from those covered by the diploma adduced by the applicant, or

    – where, in the case referred to in Art. 3 (b), the profession regulated in the host Member State comprises one or more regulated professional activities which are not in the profession pursued by the applicant in the Member State from which he originates or comes, and that difference corresponds to specific education and training required in the host Member State and covers matters which differ substantially from those covered by the evidence of formal qualifications adduced by the applicant.

Should the host Member State make use of this possibility, it must give the applicant the right to choose between an adaptation period and an aptitude test. By way of derogation from this principle, for professions whose practice requires precise knowledge of national law and in respect of which the provision of advice and/or assistance concerning national law is an essential and constant aspect of the professional activity, the host Member State may stipulate either an adaptation period or an aptitude test. Where the host Member State intends to introduce derogations for other professions as regards an applicant's right to choose, the procedure laid down in Art. 10 shall apply.

2.   However, the host Member State may not apply the provisions of paragraph 1 (a) and (b) cumulatively.

Article 5.   Without prejudice to Arts. 3 and 4, a host Member State may allow the applicant, with a view to improving his possibilities of adapting to the professional environment in that State, to undergo there, on the basis of equivalence, that part of his professional education and training represented by professional practice, acquired with the assistance of a qualified member of the profession, which he has not undergone in his Member State of origin or the Member State from which he has come.

Article 6.   1. Where the competent authority of a host Member State requires of persons wishing to take up a regulated profession proof that they are of good character or repute or that they have not been declared bankrupt, or suspends or prohibits the pursuit of that profession in the event of serious professional misconduct or a criminal offence, that State shall accept as sufficient evidence, in respect of nationals of Member States wishing to pursue that profession in its territory, the production of documents issued by competent authorities in the Member State of origin or the Member State from which the foreign national comes showing that those requirements are met.

Where the competent authorities of the Member State of origin or of the Member State from which the foreign national comes do not issue the documents referred to in the first subparagraph, such documents shall be replaced by a declaration on oath – or, in States where there is no provision for declaration on oath, by a solemn declaration – made by the person concerned before a competent judicial or administrative authority or, where appropriate, a notary or qualified professional body of the Member State of origin or the Member State from which the person comes; such authority or notary shall issue a certificate attesting the authenticity of the declaration on oath or solemn declaration.

2. Where the competent authority of a host Member State requires of nationals of that Member State wishing to take up or pursue a regulated profession a certificate of physical or mental health, that authority shall accept as sufficient evidence in this respect the production of the document required in the Member State of origin or the Member State from which the foreign national comes.

Where the Member State of origin or the Member State from which the foreign national comes does not impose any requirements of this nature on those wishing to take up or pursue the profession in question, the host Member State shall accept from such nationals a certificate issued by a competent authority in that State corresponding to the certificates issued in the host Member State.

3. The competent authorities of host Member States may require that the documents and certificates referred to in paragraphs 1 and 2 are presented no more than three months after their date of issue.

4. Where the competent authority of a host Member State requires nationals of that Member State wishing to take up or pursue a regulated profession to take an oath or make a solemn declaration and where the form of such oath or declaration cannot be used by nationals of other Member States, that authority shall ensure that an appropriate and equivalent form of oath or declaration is offered to the person concerned.

Article 7. 1. The competent authorities of host Member States shall recognise the right of nationals of Member States who fulfil the conditions for the taking up and pursuit of a regulated profession in their territory to use the professional title of the host Member State corresponding to that profession.

2. The competent authorities of host Member States shall recognise the right of nationals of Member States who fulfil the conditions for the taking up and pursuit of a regulated profession in their territory to use their lawful academic title and, where appropriate, the abbreviation thereof deriving from their Member State of origin or the Member State from which they come, in the language of that State. Host Member State may require this title to be followed by the name and location of the establishment or examining board which awarded it.

3. Where a profession is regulated in the host Member State by an association or organisation referred to in Art. 1 (d), nationals of Member States shall only be entitled to use the professional title or designatory

letters conferred by that organisation or association on proof of membership.

Where the association or organisation makes membership subject to certain qualification requirements, it may apply these to nationals of other Member States who are in possession of a diploma within the meaning of Art. 1 (a) or a formal qualification within the meaning of Art. 3 (b) only in accordance with this Directive, in particular Arts. 3 and 4.

Article 8.   1. The host Member State shall accept as proof that the conditions laid down in Arts. 3 and 4 are satisfied the certificates and documents issued by the competent authorities in the Member States, which the person concerned shall submit in support of his application to pursue the profession concerned.

2. The procedure for examining an application to pursue a regulated profession shall be completed as soon as possible and the outcome communicated in a reasoned decision of the competent authority in the host Member State not later than four months after presentation of all the documents relating to the person concerned. A remedy shall be available against this decision, or the absence thereof, before a court or tribunal in accordance with the provisions of national law.

Article 9.   1. Member States shall designate, within the period provided for in Art. 12, the competent authorities empowered to receive the applications and take the decisions referred to in this Directive.
They shall communicate this information to the other Member States and to the Commission.

2. Each Member State shall designate a person responsible for coordinating the activities of the authorities referred to in paragraph 1 and shall inform the other Member States and the Commission to that effect. His role shall be to promote uniform application of this Directive to all the professions concerned. A coordinating group shall be set up under the aegis of the Commission, composed of the coordinators appointed by each Member State or their deputies and chaired by a representative of the Commission.
The task of this group shall be:
– to facilitate the implementation of this Directive,
– to collect all useful information for its application in the Member States.
The group may be consulted by the Commission on any changes to the existing system that may be contemplated.

3. Member States shall take measures to provide the necessary information on the recognition of diplomas within the framework of this

Directive. They may be assisted in this task by the information centre on the academic recognition of diplomas and periods of study established by the Member States within the framework of the Resolution of the Council and the Ministers of Education meeting within the Council of 9 February 1976,[6] and, where appropriate, the relevant professional associations or organisations. The Commission shall take the necessary initiatives to ensure the development and co-ordination of the communication of the necessary information.

Article 10.   1. If, pursuant to the third sentence of the second subparagraph of Art. 4 (1) (b), a Member State proposes not to grant applicants the right to choose between an adaptation period and an aptitude test in respect of a profession within the meaning of this Directive, it shall immediately communicate to the Commission the corresponding draft provision. It shall at the same time notify the Commission of the grounds which make the enactment of such a provision necessary.

The Commission shall immediately notify the other Member States of any draft it has received; it may also consult the coordinating group referred to in Art. 9 (2) of the draft.

2. Without prejudice to the possibility for the Commission and the other Member States of making comments on the draft, the Member State may adopt the provision only if the Commission has not taken a decision to the contrary within three months.

3. At the request of a Member State or the Commission, Member States shall communicate to them, without delay, the definitive text of a provision arising from the application of this Article.

Article 11.   Following the expiry of the period provided for in Art. 12, Member States shall communicate to the Commission, every two years, a report on the application of the system introduced.
In addition to general remarks, this report shall contain a statistical summary of the decisions taken and a description of the main problems arising from application of the Directive.

Article 12.   Member States shall take the measures necessary to comply with this Directive within two years of its notification.[7] They shall forthwith inform the Commission thereof.

Member States shall communicate to the Commission the texts of the main provisions of national law which they adopt in the field governed by this Directive.

Article 13.   Five years at the latest following the date specified in Art.

---

[6] OJ 1976, C38/1.   [7] This Directive was notified to Member States on 4 January 1989.

12, the Commission shall report to the European Parliament and the Council on the state of application of the general system for the recognition of higher-education diplomas awarded on completion of professional education and training of at least three years' duration.

After conducting all necessary consultations, the Commission shall, on this occasion, present its conclusions as to any changes that need to be made to the system as it stands. At the same time the Commission shall, where appropriate, submit proposals for improvements in the present system in the interest of further facilitating the freedom of movement, right of establishment and freedom to provide services of the persons covered by this Directive.

[Final provisions omitted.]

ANNEX

List of professional associations or organizations which satisfy the conditions of the second subparagraph of Art. 1 (d)

IRELAND[8]
1. The Institute of Chartered Accountants in Ireland[9]
2. The Institute of Certified Public Accountants in Ireland[9]
3. The Association of Certified Accountants[9]
4. Institution of Engineers of Ireland
5. Irish Planning Institute

UNITED KINGDOM
1. Institute of Chartered Accountants in England and Wales
2. Institute of Chartered Accountants of Scotland
3. Institute of Chartered Accountants in Ireland
4. Chartered Association of Certified Accountants
5. Chartered Institute of Loss Adjusters

---

[8] Irish nationals are also members of the following United Kingdom chartered bodies:
Institute of Chartered Accountants in England and Wales
Institute of Chartered Accountants in Scotland
Institute of Actuaries
Faculty of Actuaries
The Chartered Institute of Management Accountants
Institute of Chartered Secretaries and Administrators
Royal Town Planning Institute
Royal Institution of Chartered Surveyors
Chartered Institute of Building.
[9] For the purposes of the activity of auditing only.

6. Chartered Institute of Management Accountants
7. Institute of Chartered Secretaries and Administrators
8. Chartered Insurance Institute
9. Institute of Actuaries
10. Faculty of Actuaries
11. Chartered Institute of Bankers
12. Institute of Bankers in Scotland
13. Royal Institution of Chartered Surveyors
14. Royal Town Planning Institute
15. Chartered Society of Physiotherapy
16. Royal Society of Chemistry
17. British Psychological Society
18. Library Association
19. Institute of Chartered Foresters
20. Chartered Institute of Building
21. Engineering Council
22. Institute of Energy
23. Institution of Structural Engineers
24. Institution of Civil Engineers
25. Institution of Mining Engineers
26. Institution of Mining and Metallurgy
27. Institution of Electrical Engineers
28. Institution of Gas Engineers
29. Institution of Mechanical Engineers
30. Institution of Chemical Engineers
31. Institution of Production Engineers
32. Institution of Marine Engineers
33. Royal Institution of Naval Architects
34. Royal Aeronautical Society
35. Institute of Metals
36. Chartered Institution of Building Services Engineers
37. Institute of Measurement and Control
38. British Computer Society

Statement by the Council and the Commission

Re Article 9 (1)

'The Council and the Commission agree that professional bodies and higher-education establishments should be consulted or be involved in an appropriate way in the decision-making process.'

Council Recommendation 21 December 1988
concerning nationals of Member States who
hold a diploma conferred in a third State (89/49/EEC)[10]

The Council of The European Communities,
   Approving Council Directive 89/48/EEC of 21 December 1988 on a
general system for the recognition of higher-education diplomas awarded
on completion of professional education and training of at least three
years' duration;
   Noting that this Directive refers only to diplomas, certificates and other
evidence of formal qualifications awarded in Member States to nationals
of Member States;
   Anxious, however, to take account of the special position of nationals
of Member States who hold diplomas, certificates or other evidence of
formal qualifications awarded in third States and who are thus in a position comparable to one of those described in Art. 3 of the Directive,
hereby recommends:

that the Governments of the Member States should allow the persons
referred to above to take up and pursue regulated professions within the
Community by recognising these diplomas, certificates and other evidence
of formal qualifications in their territories.

[Final provisions omitted.]

Council Directive of 22 March 1977 to facilitate
the effective exercise by lawyers of freedom to
provide services (77/249/EEC)[11]

The Council of the European Communities,
   Having regard to the Treaty establishing the European Economic
Community, and in particular Arts. 57 and 66 thereof,
   Having regard to the proposal from the Commission,
   Having regard to the opinion of the European Parliament,
   Having regard to the opinion of the Economic and Social Committee,
   Whereas, pursuant to the Treaty, any restriction on the provision of
services which is based on nationality or on conditions of residence has
been prohibited since the end of the transitional period;

[10] OJ 1989 L 19/24.
[11] OJ 1977 L 78/17. As last amended by the 1985 Act of Accession.

Whereas this Directive deals only with measures to facilitate the effective pursuit of the activities of lawyers by way of provision of services; whereas more detailed measures will be necessary to facilitate the effective exercise of the right of establishment;

Whereas if lawyers are to exercise effectively the freedom to provide services host Member States must recognise as lawyers those persons practising the profession in the various Member States;

Whereas, since this Directive solely concerns provision of services and does not contain provisions on the mutual recognition of diplomas, a person to whom the Directive applies must adopt the professional title used in the Member State in which he is established, hereinafter referred to as 'the Member State from which he comes'.

Has adopted this Directive:

Article 1. 1. This Directive shall apply, within the limits and under the conditions laid down herein, to the activities of lawyers pursued by way of provision of services.

Notwithstanding anything contained in this Directive, Member States may reserve to prescribed categories of lawyers the preparation of formal documents for obtaining title to administer estates of deceased persons, and the drafting of formal documents creating or transferring interests in land.

2. 'Lawyer' means any person entitled to pursue his professional activities under one of the following designations:

Belgium:	Avocat – Advocaat
Denmark:	Advokat
Germany:	Rechtsanwalt
Greece	[dikigoros]
France:	Avocat
Ireland	Barrister
	Solicitor
Italy:	Avvocato
Luxembourg:	Avocat-avoué
Netherlands:	Advocaat
Portugal:	Advogado
Spain:	Abogado
United Kingdom:	Advocate
	Barrister
	Solicitor.

Article 2. Each Member State shall recognise as a lawyer for the purpose of pursuing the activities specified in Art. 1 (1) any person listed in paragraph 2 of that Article.

Article 3.   A person referred to in Art. 1 shall adopt the professional title used in the Member State from which he comes, expressed in the language or one of the languages, of that State, with an indication of the professional organisation by which he is authorised to practise or the court of law before which he is entitled to practise pursuant to the laws of that State.

Article 4.   1. Activities relating to the representation of a client in legal proceedings or before public authorities shall be pursued in each host Member State under the conditions laid down for lawyers established in that State, with the exception of any conditions requiring residence, or registration with a professional organisation, in that State.

2. A lawyer pursuing these activities shall observe the rules of professional conduct of the host Member State, without prejudice to his obligations in the Member State from which he comes.

3. When these activities are pursued in the United Kingdom, 'rules of professional conduct of the host Member State' means the rules of professional conduct applicable to solicitors, where such activities are not reserved for barristers and advocates. Otherwise the rules of professional conduct applicable to the latter shall apply. However, barristers from Ireland shall always be subject to the rules of professional conduct applicable in the United Kingdom to barristers and advocates.

When these activities are pursued in Ireland 'rules of professional conduct of the host Member State' means, in so far as they govern the oral presentation of a case in court, the rules of professional conduct applicable to barristers. In all other cases the rules of professional conduct applicable to solicitors shall apply. However, barristers and advocates from the United Kingdom shall always be subject to the rules of professional conduct applicable in Irelands to barristers.

4. A lawyer pursuing activities other than those referred to in paragraph 1 shall remain subject to the conditions and rules of professional conduct of the Member State from which he comes without prejudice to respect for the rules, whatever their source, which govern the profession in the host Member State, especially those concerning the incompatibility of the exercise of the activities of a lawyer with the exercise of other activities in that State, professional secrecy, relations with other lawyers, the prohibition on the same lawyer acting for parties with mutually conflicting interests, and publicity. The latter rules are applicable only if they are capable of being observed by a lawyer who is not established in the host Member State and to the extent to which their observance is objectively justified to ensure, in that State, the proper exercise of a lawyer's activities, the standing of the profession and respect for the rules concerning incompatibility.

Article 5. For the pursuit of activities relating to the representation of a client in legal proceedings, a Member State may require lawyers to whom Art. 1 applies:

- to be introduced, in accordance with local rules or customs, to the presiding judge and, where appropriate, to the President of the relevant Bar in the host Member State;
- to work in conjunction with a lawyer who practises before the judicial authority in question and who would, where necessary, be answerable to that authority, or with an 'avoué' or 'procuratore' practising before it.

Article 6. Any Member State may exclude lawyers who are in the salaried employment of a public or private undertaking from pursuing activities relating to the representation of that undertaking in legal proceedings in so far as lawyers established in that State are not permitted to pursue those activities.

Article 7. 1. The competent authority of the host Member State may request the person providing the services to establish his qualifications as a lawyer.

2. In the event of non-compliance with the obligations referred to in Art. 4 and in force in the host Member State, the competent authority of the latter shall determine in accordance with its own rules and procedures the consequences of such non-compliance, and to this end may obtain any appropriate professional information concerning the person providing services. It shall notify the competent authority of the Member State from which the person comes of any decision taken. Such exchanges shall not affect the confidential nature of the information supplied.

[Final provisions omitted.]

Council Directive of 17 December 1974 extending
the scope of Directive No 64/221/EEC on the
co-ordination of special measures concerning the
movement and residence of foreign nationals which
are justified on grounds of public policy, public
security or public health to include nationals of a
Member State who exercise the right to remain in
the territory of another Member State after having
pursued therein an activity in a self-employed
capacity (75/35/EEC)[12]

[Note: Art. 1 of Dir. 64/221 provides that that Directive applies to any national
of a Member State who resides in or travels to another Member State, either in
order to pursue an activity as a self-employed person, or as a recipient of services,
see above at p. 182]

The Council of the European Communities,
    Having regard to the Treaty establishing the European Economic
Community, and in particular Art. 56 (2) and Art. 235 thereof;
    Having regard to the proposal from the Commission;
    Having regard to the Opinion of the European Parliament;
    Having regard to the Opinion of the Economic and Social Committee;
    Whereas Directive No 64/221/EEC co-ordinated special measures con-
cerning the movement and residence of foreign nationals which are
justified on grounds of public policy, public security or public health and
whereas Directive No 75/34/EEC laid down conditions for the exercise of
the right of nationals of a Member State to remain in the territory of
another Member State after having pursued therein an activity in a self-
employed capacity;
    Whereas Directive No 64/221/EEC should therefore apply to persons to
whom Directive No 75/34/EEC applies,
    Has adopted this Directive:

Article 1.   Directive No 64/221/EEC shall apply to nationals of Member
States and members of their families who have the right to remain in the
territory of a Member State pursuant to Directive No 75/34/EEC.

[Final provisions omitted.]

[12] OJ 1975 L 14/14.

First Council Directive of 12 December 1977 on the co-ordination of laws, regulations and administrative provisions relating to the taking up and pursuit of the business of credit institutions (77/780/EEC)[13]

The Council of the European Communities,

Having regard to the Treaty establishing the European Economic Community, and in particular Art. 57 thereof,

[Recitals omitted.]

Whereas, pursuant to the Treaty, any discriminatory treatment with regard to establishment and to the provision of services, based either on nationality or on the fact that an undertaking is not established in the Member States where the services are provided, is prohibited from the end of the transitional period;

Whereas, in order to make it easier to take up and pursue the business of credit institutions, it is necessary to eliminate the most obstructive differences between the laws of the Member States as regards the rules to which these institutions are subject;

Whereas, however, given the extent of these differences, the conditions required for a common market for credit institutions cannot be created by means of a single Directive; whereas it is therefore necessary to proceed by successive stages; whereas the result of this process should be to provide for overall supervision of a credit institution operating in several Member States by the competent authorities in the Member State where it has its head office, in consultation, as appropriate, with the competent authorities of the other Member States concerned;

Whereas measures to co-ordinate credit institutions must, both in order to protect savings and to create equal conditions of competition between these institutions, apply to all of them; whereas due regard must be had, where applicable, to the objective differences in their statutes and their proper aims as laid down by national laws;

Whereas the scope of those measures should therefore be as broad as possible, covering all institutions whose business is to receive repayable funds from the public whether in the form of deposits or in other forms such as the continuing issue of bonds and other comparable securities and to grant credits for their own account; whereas exceptions must be provided for in the case of certain credit institutions to which this Directive cannot apply;

---

[13] OJ 1977 L 322/30. As last amended by Dir. 89/646, OJ 1989 L 386/1

Whereas the provisions of this Directive shall not prejudice the application of national laws which provide for special supplementary authorisations permitting credit institutions to carry on specific activities or undertake specific kinds of operations;

Whereas the same system of supervision cannot always be applied to all types of credit institution; whereas provision should therefore be made for application of this Directive to be deferred in the case of certain groups or types of credit institutions to which its immediate application might cause technical problems; whereas more specific provisions for such institutions may prove necessary in the future; whereas these specific provisions should nonetheless be based on a number of common principles;

Whereas the eventual aim is to introduce uniform authorisation requirements throughout the Community for comparable types of credit institution; whereas at the initial stage it is necessary, however, to specify only certain minimum requirements to be imposed by all Member States;

Whereas this aim can be achieved only if the particularly wide discretionary powers which certain supervisory authorities have for authorising credit establishments are progressively reduced; whereas the requirement that a programme of operations must be produced should therefore be seen merely as a factor enabling the competent authorities to decide on the basis of more precise information using objective criteria;

Whereas the purpose of co-ordination is to achieve a system whereby credit institutions having their head office in one of the Member States are exempt from any national authorisation requirement when setting up branches in other Member States;

Whereas a measure of flexibility may nonetheless be possible in the initial stage as regards the requirements on the legal form of credit institutions and the protection of banking names;

Whereas equivalent financial requirements for credit institutions will be necessary to ensure similar safeguards for savers and fair conditions of competition between comparable groups of credit institutions; whereas, pending further co-ordination, appropriate structural ratios should be formulated that will make it possible within the framework of co-operation between national authorities to observe, in accordance with standard methods, the position of comparable types of credit institutions; whereas this procedure should help to bring about the gradual approximation of the systems of coefficients established and applied by the Member States; whereas it is necessary, however, to make a distinction between co-efficients intended to ensure the sound management of credit institutions an those established for the purposes of economic and monetary policy; whereas, for the purpose of formulating structural ratios and of more general co-operation between supervisory authorities, standardisation of the layout of credit institutions' accounts will have to begin as soon as possible;

Whereas the rules governing branches of credit institutions having their head office outside the Community should be analogous in all Member States; whereas it is important at the present time to provide that such rules may not be more favourable than those for branches of institutions from another Member State; whereas it should be specified that the Community may conclude agreements with third countries providing for the application of rules which accord such branches the same treatment throughout its territory, account being taken of the principle of reciprocity;

Whereas the examination of problems connected with matters covered by Council Directives on the business of credit institutions requires co-operation between the competent authorities and the Commission within an Advisory Committee, particularly when conducted with a view to closer co-ordination;

Whereas the establishment of an Advisory Committee of the competent authorities of the Member States does not rule out other forms of co-operation between authorities which supervise the taking up and pursuit of the business of credit institutions and, in particular, co-operation within the Contact Committee set up between the banking supervisory authorities,

Has adopted this Directive:

TITLE I. DEFINITIONS AND SCOPE

Article 1. For the purposes of this Directive:

- 'credit institution' means an undertaking whose business is to receive deposits or other repayable funds from the pubic and to grant credits for its own account,
- 'authorisation' means an instrument issued in any form by the authorities by which the right to carry on the business of a credit institution is granted,
- 'branch' means a place of business which forms a legally dependent part of a credit institution and which conducts directly all or some of the operations inherent in the business of credit institutions; any number of branches set up in the same Member State by a credit institution having its head office in another Member State shall be regarded as a single branch, without prejudice to Art. 4 (1),
- 'own funds' means the credit institution's own capital, including items which may be treated as capital under national rules.

Article 2. 1. This Directive shall apply to the taking up and pursuit of the business of credit institutions.

2. It shall not apply to:

- the central banks of Member States;
- post office giro institutions;
- in Belgium, the 'Institut de Réescompte et de Garantie – Herdisconter-ing – en Waarborginstituut', the 'sociétés nationale et régionales d'investissement – national en gewestelijke investeringsmaatschappijen', the regional development companies ('sociétés développement régionales – gewestelijke ontwikkelingsmaatschappijen'), the 'Société Nationale du Logement – Nationale Maatschappij voor de Huisvesting' and its authorised companies and the 'Société Nationale Terrienne – Nationale Landmaatschappij' and its authorised companies;
- in Denmark, the 'Dansk Eksportfinansieringsfond', 'Danmarks Skibs-kreditfond', 'Industriens Realkreditfond' and 'Dank Landbrugs Realkreditfond';
- in Germany, the 'Kreditanstalt für Wiederaufbau', undertakings which are recognised under the 'Wohnungsgemeinnützigkeitsgesetz' as bodies of State housing policy and are not mainly engaged in banking transactions and undertakings recognised under that law as non-profit housing undertaking;
- in Greece, the 'Ελληνικη Τραπεζα Βιομηχανικης Αναπτυξεως', the 'Ταμειο Παρακαταϑηκων και Δανειων', the 'Τραπεζα Υποϑηκων', the 'Ταχυδρομικο Ταμειευτηριο' and the 'Ελληνικαι Εξαγωγαι ΑΕ';
- in Spain, the 'Instituto de Crédito Oficial', with the exception of its subsidiaries;
- in France, the 'Caisse de dépôts et consignations';
- in Ireland, credit unions and the friendly societies;
- in Italy, the 'Cassa Depositi et Prestiti';
- in the Netherlands, the 'NV Export-Financieringsmaatschappij', the 'Nederlandse Financieringsmaatschappij voor Ontwikkelingslanden NV', the 'Nederlandse Investeringsbank voor Ontwikkelingslanden NV', the 'Nederlandse Waterschapsbank NV', the 'Financierings-maatschappij Industrieel Garantiefonds Amsterdam NV', the 'Financeringsmaatschappij Industrieel Garantiefonds 's-Gravenhage NV', the 'NV Noordelijke Ontwikkelings maatschappij', the 'NV Industriebank Limburgs Instituut voor ontwikkeling en financiering' and the 'Overijsselse Ontwikkelingsmaatschappij NV';
- in Portugal, Caixas EconMmicas existing on 1 January 1986 which are not incorporated as limited companies;
- in the United Kingdom, the National Savings Bank, the Commonwealth Development Finance Company Ltd, the Agricultural Mortgage Corporation Ltd, the Scottish Agricultural Scurities Corporation Ltd, the Crown Agents for overseas governments and administrations, credit unions, and municipal banks.

3. The Council, acting on a proposal from the Commission, which for this purpose, shall consult the Committee referred to in Art. 11 (hereinafter referred to as 'the Advisory Committee') shall decide on any amendments to the list in paragraph 2.

4. (a) Credit institutions existing in the same Member State at the time of the notification of this Directive and permanently affiliated at that time to a central body which supervises them and which is established in that same Member State, may be exempted from the requirements listed in the first, second and third indents of the first subparagraph of Art. 3 (2), the second subparagraph of Art. 3 (2), Art. 3 (4) and Art. 6, if no later than the date when the national authorities take the measures necessary to translate this Directive into national law, that law provides that:

the commitments of the central body and affiliated institutions are joint and several liabilities or the commitments of its affiliated institutions are entirely guaranteed by the central body,
- the solvency and liquidity of the central body and of all the affiliated institutions are monitored as a whole on the basis of consolidated accounts,
- the management of the central body is empowered to issue instructions to the management of the affiliated institutions.

(b) Credit institutions operating locally which are affiliated, subsequent to notification of this Directive, to a central body within the meaning of subparagraph (a) may benefit from the conditions laid down in subparagraph (a) if they constitute normal additions to the network belonging to that central body.

(c) In the case of credit institutions other than those which are set up in areas newly reclaimed from the sea or have resulted from scission or mergers of existing institutions dependent or answerable to the central body, the Council, acting on a proposal from the Commission, which shall, for this purpose, consult the Advisory Committee, may lay down additional rules for the application of subparagraph (b) including the repeal of exemptions provided for in subparagraph (a), where it is of the opinion that the affiliation of new institutions benefiting from the arrangements laid down in subparagraph (b) might have an adverse effect on competition. The Council shall decide by a qualified majority.

5. Member States may defer in whole or in part the application of this Directive to certain types or groups of credit institutions where such immediate application would cause technical problems which cannot be overcome in the short-term. The problems may result either from

the fact that these institutions are subject to supervision by an authority different from that normally responsible for the supervision of banks, or from the fact that they are subject to a special system of supervision. In any event, such deferment cannot be justified by the public law statutes, by the smallness of size or by the limited scope of activity of the particular institutions concerned.

Deferment can apply only to groups or types of institutions already existing at the time of notification of this Directive.

6. Pursuant to paragraph 5, a Member State may decide to defer application of this Directive for a maximum period of five years from the notification thereof and, after consulting the Advisory Committee may extend deferment once only for a maximum period of three years.

The Member State shall inform the Commission of its decision and the reasons therefor not later than six months following the notification of this Directive. It shall also notify the Commission of any extension or repeal of this decision. The Commission shall publish any decision regarding deferment in the *Official Journal of the European Communities*.

Not later than seven years following the notification of this Directive, the Commission shall, after consulting the Advisory Committee, submit a report to the Council on the situation regarding deferment. Where appropriate, the Commission shall submit to the Council, not later than six months following the submission of its report, proposals for either the inclusion of the institutions in question in the list in paragraph 2 or for the authorisation of a further extension of deferment. The Council shall act on these proposals not later than six months after their submission.

TITLE II.

CREDIT INSTITUTIONS HAVING THEIR HEAD OFFICE IN A MEMBER STATE AND THEIR BRANCHES IN OTHER MEMBER STATES

Article 3. 1. Member States shall require credit institutions subject to this Directive to obtain authorisation before commencing their activities. They shall lay down the requirements for such authorisation subject to paragraphs 2, 3 and 4 and notify them to both the Commission and the Advisory Committee.

2. Without prejudice to other conditions of general application laid down by national laws, the competent authorities shall grant authorisation only when the following conditions are complied with:

- the credit institution must possess separate own funds,
- the credit institution must possess adequate minimum own funds,
- there shall be at least two persons who effectively direct the business of the credit institution.

Moreover, the authorities concerned shall not grant authorisation if the persons referred to in the third indent of the first paragraph are not of sufficiently good repute or lack sufficient experience to perform such duties.

3. (a) The provisions referred to in paragraphs 1 and 2 may not require the application for authorisation to be examined in terms of the economic needs of the market.

   (b) Where the laws, regulations or administrative provisions of a Member State provide, at the time of notification of the present Directive, that the economic needs of the market shall be a condition of authorisation and where technical or structural difficulties in its banking system do not allow it to give up the criterion within the period laid down in Art. 14 (1), the State in question may continue to apply the criterion for a period of seven years from notification.

   It shall notify its decision and the reasons therefor to the Commission within six months of notification.

   The Hellenic Republic may continue to apply the criterion of economic need. On a request from the Hellenic Republic, the Commission shall, if appropriate, submit to the Council by 15 June 1989 proposals authorising the Hellenic Republic to continue to apply the criterion of economic need until 15 December 1992.

   The Council shall act within six months of the submission of those proposals.

   (c) Within six years of the notification of this Directive the Commission shall submit to the Council, after consulting the Advisory Committee, a report on the application of the criterion of economic need. If appropriate, the Commission shall submit to the Council proposals to terminate the application of that criterion. The period referred to in subparagraph (b) shall be extended for one further period of five years, unless, in the meantime, the Council, acting unanimously on proposals from the Commission, adopts a Decision to terminate the application of that criterion.

   (d) The criterion of economic need shall be applied only on the basis of general predetermined criteria, published and notified to both the Commission and the Advisory Committee and aimed at promoting:

- security of savings,
- higher productivity in the banking system
- greater uniformity of competition between the various banking networks,
- a broader range of banking services in relation to population and economic activity.

Specification of the above objectives shall be determined within the Advisory Committee, which shall begin its work as from its initial meetings.

4. Member States shall also require applications for authorisation to be accompanied by a programme of operations setting out *inter alia* the types of business envisaged and the structural organisation of the institution.

5. The Advisory Committee shall examine the content given by the competent authorities to requirements listed in paragraph 2, any other requirements which the Member States apply and the information which must be included in the programme of operations, and shall, where appropriate, make suggestions to the Commission with a view to a more detailed co-ordination.

6. Reasons shall be given whenever an authorisation is refused and the applicant shall be notified thereof within six months of receipt of the application or, should the latter be incomplete, within six months of the applicant's sending the information required for the decision. A decision shall, in any case, be taken within 12 months of the receipt of the application.

7. Every authorisation shall be notified to the Commission. Each credit institution shall be entered in a list which the Commission shall publish in the *Official Journal of the European Communities* and shall keep up to date.

Article 4. 1. Member States may make the commencement of business in their territory by branches of credit institutions covered by this Directive which have their head office in another Member State subject to authorisation according to the law and procedure applicable to credit institutions established on their territory.

2. However, authorisation may not be refused to a branch of a credit institution on the sole ground that it is established in another Member State in a legal form which is not allowed in the case of a credit institution carrying out similar activities in the host country. This provision shall not apply, however, to credit institutions which possess no separate own funds.

3. The competent authorities shall inform the Commission of any authorisations which they grant to the branches referred to in paragraph 1.

4. This Article shall not affect the rules applied by Member States to branches set up on their territory by credit institutions which have their head office there. Notwithstanding the second part of the third indent of Art. 1, the laws of Member States requiring a separate authorisation for each branch of a credit institution having its head office in their territory shall apply equally to the branches of credit institutions the head offices of which are in other Member States.

Article 5. For the purpose of exercising their activities, credit institutions to which this Directive applies may, notwithstanding any provisions concerning the use of the words 'bank', 'saving bank' or other banking names which may exist in the host Member State, use throughout the territory of the Community the same name as they use in the Member States in which their head office is situated. In the event of there being any danger of confusion, the host Member State may, for the purposes of clarification, require that the name be accompanied by certain explanatory particulars.

Article 6. 1. Pending subsequent co-ordination, the competent authorities shall, for the purposes of observation and, if necessary, in addition to such coefficients as may be applied by them, establish ratios between the various assets and/or liabilities of credit institutions with a view to monitoring their solvency and liquidity and the other measures which may serve to ensure that savings are protected.

To this end, the Advisory Committee shall decide on the content of the various factors of the observation ratios referred to in the first subparagraph and lay down the method to be applied in calculating them.

Where appropriate, the Advisory Committee shall be guided by technical consultations between the supervisory authorities of the categories of institutions concerned.

2. The observation ratios established in pursuance of paragraph 1 shall be calculated at least every six months.

3. The Advisory Committee shall examine the results of analyses carried out by the supervisory authorities referred to in the third subparagraph of paragraph 1 on the basis of the calculations referred to in paragraph 2.

4. The Advisory Committee make make suggestions to the Commission with a view to co-ordinating the coefficients applicable in the Member States.

Article 7. 1. The competent authorities of the Member States concerned shall collaborate closely in order to supervise the activities of credit institutions operating, in particular by having established branches there, in one or more Member States other than that in which their head offices are situated. They shall supply one another with all information concerning the management and ownership of such credit institutions that is likely to facilitate their supervision and the examination of the conditions for their authorisation and all information likely to facilitate the monitoring such institutions, in particular with regard to liquidity, solvency, deposit guarantees, the limiting of large exposures, administrative and accounting procedures and internal control mechanisms.

2. The competent authorities may also, for the purposes and within the meaning of Art. 6, lay down ratios applicable to the branches referred to in this Article by reference to the factors laid down in Art. 6.

3. The Advisory Committee shall take account of the adjustments necessitated by the specific situation of the branches in relation to national regulations.

Article 8.   1. The competent authorities may withdraw the authorisation issued to a credit institution subject to this Directive or to a branch authorised under Art. 4 only where such an institution or branch:

(a) does not make use of the authorisation within 12 months, expressly renounces the authorisation or has ceased to engage in business for more than six months, if the Member State concerned has made no provision for the authorisation to lapse in such cases;

(b) has obtained the authorisation through false statements or any other irregular means;

(c) no longer fulfils the conditions under which authorisation was granted, with the exception of those in respect of own funds;

(d) no longer possesses sufficient own funds or can no longer be relied upon to fulfil its obligations towards its creditors, and in particular no longer provides security for the assets entrusted to it;

(e) falls within one of the other cases where national law provides for withdrawal of authorisation.

2. In addition, the authorisation issued to a branch under Art. 4 shall be withdrawn if the competent authority of the country in which the credit institution which established the branch has its head office has withdrawn authorisation from that institution.

3. Member States which grant the authorisations referred to in Arts. 3 (1) and 4 (1) only if, economically, the market situation requires it may not invoke the disappearance of such a need as grounds for withdrawing such authorisations.

4. Before withdrawal from a branch of an authorisation granted under Art. 4, the competent authority of the Member State in which its head office is situated shall be consulted. Where immediate action is called for,

notification may take the place of such consultation. The same procedure shall be followed, by analogy, in cases of withdrawal of authorisation from a credit institution which has branches in other Member States.

5. Reasons must be given for any withdrawal of authorisation and those concerned informed thereof; such withdrawal shall be notified to the Commission.

TITLE III.

BRANCHES OF CREDIT INSTITUTIONS HAVING THEIR HEAD OFFICES OUTSIDE THE COMMUNITY

Article 9. 1. Member States shall not apply to branches of credit institutions having their head office outside the Community, when commencing or carrying on their business, provisions which result in more favourable treatment than that accorded to branches of credit institutions having their head office in the Community.

2. The competent authorities shall notify the Commission and the Advisory Committee of all authorisations for branches granted to credit institutions having their head office outside the Community.

3. Without prejudice to paragraph 1, the Community may, through agreements concluded in accordance with the Treaty with one or more third countries, agree to apply provisions which, on the basis of the principle of reciprocity, accord to branches of a credit institution having its head office outside the Community identical treatment throughout the territory of the Community.

TITLE IV.

GENERAL AND TRANSITIONAL PROVISIONS

Article 10. 1. Credit institutions subject to this Directive, which took up their business in accordance with the provisions of the Member States in which they have their head offices before the entry into force of the provisions implementing this Directive shall be deemed to be authorised. They shall be subject to the provisions of this Directive concerning the carrying on of the business of credit institutions and to the requirements set out in the first and third indents of the first subparagraph and in the second subparagraph of Art. 3 (2).

Member States may allow credit institutions which at the time of notification of this Directive do not comply with the requirement laid down in the third indent of the first subparagraph of Art. 3 (2), no more than five years in which to do so.

Member States may decide that undertakings which do not fulfil the requirements set out in the first indent of the first subparagraph of Art. 3 (2) and which are in existence at the time this Directive enters into force may continue to carry on their business. They may exempt such undertakings from complying with the requirement contained in the third indent of the first subparagraph of Art. 3 (2).

2. All the credit institutions referred to in paragraph 1 shall be given in the list referred to in Art. 3 (7).

3. If a credit institution deemed to be authorised under paragraph 1 has not undergone any authorisation procedure prior to commencing business, a prohibition on the carrying on of its business shall take the place of withdrawal of authorisation.

Subject to the first subparagraph, Art. 8 shall apply by analogy.

4. By way of derogation from paragraph 1, credit institutions established in a Member State without having undergone an authorisation procedure in that Member State prior to commencing business may be required to obtain authorisation from the competent authorities of the Member State concerned in accordance with the provisions implementing this Directive. Such institutions may be required to comply with the requirement in the second indent of Art. 3 (2) and with such other conditions of general application as may be laid down by the Member State concerned.

Article 11. 1. An 'Advisory Committee of the Competent Authorities of the Member States of the European Economic Community' shall be set up alongside the Commission.

2. The tasks of the Advisory Committee shall be to assist the Commission in ensuring the proper implementation of both this Directive and Council Directive 73/183/EEC of 28 June 1973 on the abolition of restrictions on freedom of establishment and freedom to provide services in respect of self-employed activities of banks and other financial institutions[14] in so far as it relates to credit institutions. Further it shall carry out the other tasks prescribed by this Directive and shall assist the Commission in the preparation of new proposals to the Council concerning further co-ordination in the sphere of credit institutions.

3. The Advisory Committee shall not concern itself with concrete problems relating to individual credit institutions.

4. The Advisory Committee shall be composed of not more than three representatives from each Member State and from the Commission. These representatives may be accompanied by advisers from time[15] and

---

[14] OJ 1973, L 1941.
[15] Presumably this should read 'from time to time'; the French text says 'occasionnellement'.

subject to the prior agreement of the Committee. The Committee may also invite qualified persons and experts to participate in its meetings. The secretariat shall be provided by the Commission.

5. The first meeting of the Advisory Committee shall be convened by the Commission under the chairmanship of one of its representatives. The Advisory Committee shall then adopt its rules of procedure and shall elect a chairman from among the representatives of Member States. Thereafter it shall meet at regular intervals and whenever the situation demands. The Commission may ask the Committee to hold an emergency meeting if it considers that the situation so requires.

6. The Advisory Committee's discussions and the outcome thereof shall be confidential except when the Committee decides otherwise.

Article 12. 1. The Member States shall provide that all persons working or who have worked for the competent authorities, as well as auditors or experts acting on behalf of the competent authorities, shall be bound by the obligation of professional secrecy. This means that no confidential information which they may receive in the course of their duties may be divulged to any person or authority whatsoever, except in summary or collective form, such that individual institutions cannot be identified, without prejudice to cases covered by criminal law.

Nevertheless, where a credit institution has been declared bankrupt or is being compulsorily wound up, confidential information which does not concern third parties involved in attempts to rescue that credit institution may be divulged in civil or commercial proceedings.

2. Paragraph 1 shall not prevent the competent authorities of the various Member States from exchanging information in accordance with the Directives applicable to credit institutions. That information shall be subject to the conditions of professional secrecy indicated in paragraph 1.

3. Member States may conclude co-operation agreements, providing for exchanges of information with the competent authorities of third countries only if the information disclosed is subject to guarantees of professional secrecy at least equivalent to those referred to in this Article.

4. Competent authorities receiving confidential information under paragraphs 1 or 2 may use it only in the course of their duties:

– to check that the conditions governing the taking-up of the business of credit institutions are met and to facilitate monitoring, on a non-consolidated or consolidated basis, of the conduct of such business especially with regard to the monitoring of liquidity, solvency, large exposures, and administrative and accounting procedures and internal contramechanisms, or
– to impose sanctions, or

– in an administrative appeal against a decision of the competent authority, or
– in court proceedings initiated pursuant to Art. 13 or to special provisions provided for in the Directives adopted in the field of credit institutions.

5. Paragraphs 1 and 4 shall not preclude the exchange of information within a Member State, where there are two or more competent authorities in the same Member State, or between Member States, between competent authorities and:

– authorities entrusted with the public duty of supervising other financial organisations and insurance companies and the authorities responsible for the supervision of financial markets,
– bodies involved in the liquidation and bankruptcy of credit institutions and in other similar procedures,
– persons responsible for carrying out statutory audits of the accounts of credit institutions and other financial institutions,

in the discharge of their supervisory functions, and the disclosure to bodies which administer deposit-guarantee schemes of information necessary to the exercise of their functions. The information received shall be subject to the conditions of professional secrecy indicated in paragraph 1.

6. Nor shall the provisions of this Article preclude a competent authority from disclosing to those central banks which do not supervise credit institutions individually such information as they may need to act as monetary authorities. Information received in this context shall be subject to the conditions of professional secrecy indicated in paragraph 1.

7. In addition, notwithstanding the provisions referred to in paragraphs 1 and 4, the Member States may, by virtue of provisions laid down by law, authorise the disclosure of certain information to other departments of their central government administrations responsible for legislation on the supervision of credit institutions, financial institutions, investment services and insurance companies and to inspectors acting on behalf of those departments.

However, such disclosures may be made only where necessary for reasons of prudential control.

However, the Member States shall provide that information received under paragraphs 2 and 5 and that obtained by means of the on-the-spot verification referred to in Art. 15 (1) and (2) of Directive 89/646/EEC[16] may never be disclosed in the cases referred to in this paragraph except with the express consent of the competent authorities which disclosed the information or of the competent authorities of the Member State in which on-the-spot verification was carried out.

[16] OJ 1982 L 386/1.

Article 13. Member States shall ensure that decisions taken in respect of a credit institution in pursuance of laws, regulations and administrative provisions adopted in accordance with this Directive may be subject to the right to apply to the courts. The same shall apply where no decision is taken within six months of its submission in respect of an application for authorisation which contains all the information required under the provisions in force.

[Final provisions omitted.]

Second Council Directive of 15 December 1989 on the co-ordination of laws, regulations and administrative provisions relating to the taking up and pursuit of the business of credit institutions and amending Directive 77/780/EEC (89/646/EEC)[17]

The Council of the European Communities,

Having regard to the Treaty establishing the European Economic Community, and in particular the first and third sentences of Art. 57 (2) thereof,

[provisions omitted]

Whereas this Directive is to constitute the essential instrument for the achievement of the internal market, a course determined by the Single European Act and set out in timetable form in the Commission's White Paper, from the point of view of both the freedom of establishment and the freedom to provide financial services, in the field of credit institutions;

Whereas this Directive will join the body of Community legislation already enacted, in particular the first Council Directive 77/780/EEC of 12 December 1977 on the co-ordination of laws, regulation is and administrative provisions relating to the taking up and pursuit of the business of credit institutions,[18] as last amended by Directive 86/524/EEC,[19] Council Directive 83/350/EEC of 13 June 1983 on the supervision of credit institutions on a consolidated basis,[20] Council Directive 86/635/EEC of 8 December 1986 on the annual and consolidated

---

[17] OJ 1989 L 386/1. As last amended by Dir. 92/30, OJ 1992 L 110/52.
[18] OJ No 1977 L 322/30. supra, p. 341.
[19] OJ No 1986 L 309/15. See now Dir. 92/30, note 16.
[20] OJ No 1983 L 193/18.

accounts of banks and other financial institutions[21] and Council Directive 89/299/EEC of 17 April 1989 on the own funds of credit institutions;[22]

Whereas the Commission has adopted recommendations 87/62/EEC on large exposures of credit institutions[23] and 87/63/EEC concerning the introduction of deposit-guarantee schemes;[24]

Whereas the approach which has been adopted is to achieve only the essential harmonisation necessary and sufficient to secure the mutual recognition of authorisation and of prudential supervision systems, making possible the granting of a single licence recognised throughout the Community and the application of the principle of home Member State prudential supervision;

Whereas, in this context, this Directive can be implemented only simultaneously with specific Community legislation dealing with the additional harmonisation of technical matters relating to own funds and solvency ratios;

Whereas, moreover, the harmonisation of the conditions relating to the reorganisation and winding-up of credit institutions is also proceeding;

Whereas the arrangements necessary for the supervision of the liquidity, market, interest-rate and foreign-exchange risks run by credit institutions will also have to be harmonised;

Whereas the principles of mutual recognition and of home Member State control require the competent authorities of each Member State not to grant authorisation or to withdraw it where factors such as the activities programme, the geographical distribution or the activities actually carried on make it quite clear that a credit institution has opted for the legal system of one Member State for the purpose of evading the stricter standards in force in another Member State in which it intends to carry on or carries on the greater part of its activities; whereas, for the purposes of this Directive, a credit institution shall be deemed to be situated in the Member State in which it has its registered office; whereas the Member States must require that the head office be situated in the same Member State as the registered office;

Whereas the home Member State may also establish rules stricter than those laid down in Arts. 4, 5, 11, 12 and 16 for institutions authorised by its competent authorities;

Whereas responsibility for supervising the financial soundness of a credit institution, and in particular its solvency, will rest with the competent authorities of its home Member State; whereas the host Member State's competent authorities will retain responsibility for the supervision of liquidity and monetary policy; whereas the supervision of market risk

---

[21] OJ No 1986 L 372/1.   [22] OJ 1989 L 124/16.
[23] OJ 1987 L 33/10.   [24] OJ 1987 L 33/16.

must be the subject of close co-operation between the competent authorities of the home and host Member States;

Whereas the harmonisation of certain financial and investment services will be effected, where the need exists, by specific Community instruments, with the intention, in particular, of protecting consumers and investors; whereas the Commission has proposed measures for the harmonisation of mortgage credit in order, *inter alia*, to allow mutual recognition of the financial techniques peculiar to that sphere;

Whereas, by virtue of mutual recognition, the approach chosen permits credit institutions authorised in their home Member States to carry on, throughout the Community, any or all of the activities listed in the Annex by establishing branches or by providing services;

Whereas the carrying-on of activities not listed in the Annex shall enjoy the right of establishment and the freedom to provide services under the general provisions of the Treaty;

Whereas it is appropriate, however, to extend mutual recognition to the activities listed in the Annex when they are carried on by financial institutions which are subsidiaries of credit institutions, provided that such subsidiaries are covered by the consolidated supervision of their parent undertakings and meet certain strict conditions;

Whereas the host Member State may, in connection with the exercise of the right of establishment and the freedom to provide services, require compliance with specific provisions of its own national laws or regulations on the part of institutions not authorised as credit institutions in their home Member States and with regard to activities not listed in the Annex provided that, on the one hand, such provisions are compatible with Community law and are intended to protect the general good and that, on the other hand, such institutions or such activities are not subject to equivalent rules under the legislation or regulations of their home Member States;

Whereas the Member States must ensure that there are no obstacles to carrying on activities receiving mutual recognition in the same manner as in the home Member State, as long as the latter do not conflict with legal provisions protecting the general good in the host Member State;

Whereas the abolition of the authorisation requirement with respect to the branches of Community credit institutions once the harmonisation in progress has been completed necessitates the abolition of endowment capital; whereas Art. 6 (2) constitutes a first transitional step in this direction, but does not, however, affect the Kingdom of Spain or the Portuguese Republic, as provided for in the Act concerning the conditions of those States' accession to the Community;

Whereas there is a necessary link between the objective of this Directive and the liberalisation of capital movements being brought about by other Community legislation; whereas in any case the measures regarding the liberalisation of banking services must be in harmony with the measures liberalising capital movements; whereas where the Member States may, by virtue of Council Directive 88/361/EEC of 24 June 1988 for the implementation of Art. 67 of the Treaty,[25] invoke safeguard clauses in respect of capital movements, they may suspend the provision of banking services to the extent necessary for the implementation of the abovementioned safeguard clauses;

Whereas the procedures established in Directive 77/780/EEC, in particular with regard to the authorisation of branches of credit institutions authorised in third countries, will continue to apply to such institutions; whereas those branches will not enjoy the freedom to provide services under the second paragraph of Art. 59 of the Treaty or the freedom of establishment in Member States other than those in which they are established; whereas, however, requests for the authorisation of subsidiaries or of the acquisition of holdings made by undertakings governed by the laws of third countries are subject to a procedure intended to ensure that Community credit institutions receive reciprocal treatment in the third countries in question;

Whereas the authorisations granted to credit institutions by the competent national authorities pursuant to this Directive will have Community-wide and no longer merely nationwide, application, and whereas existing reciprocity clauses will henceforth have no effect; whereas a flexible procedure is therefore needed to make it possible to assess reciprocity on a Community basis; whereas the aim of this procedure is not to close the Community's financial markets but rather, as the Community intends to keep its financial markets open to the rest of the world, to improve the liberalisation of the global financial markets in other third countries; whereas, to that end, this Directive provides for procedures for negotiating with third countries and, as a last resort, for the possibility of taking measures involving the suspension of new applications for authorisation or the restriction of new authorisations;

Whereas the smooth operation of the internal banking market will require not only legal rules but also close and regular co-operation between the competent authorities of the Member States; whereas for the consideration of problems concerning individual credit institutions the Contact Committee set up between the banking supervisory authorities, referred to in the final recital of Directive 77/780/EEC, remains the most appropriate forum; whereas that Committee is a suitable body for the mutual exchange of information provided for in Art. 7 of that Directive;

Whereas that mutual information procedure will not in any case

[25] OJ 1988 L 178/5.

replace the bilateral collaboration established by Art. 7 of Directive 77/780/EEC; whereas the competent host Member State authorities can, without prejudice to their powers of control proper, continue either, in an emergency, on their own initiative or following the initiative of the competent home Member State authorities to verify that the activities of a credit institution established within their territories comply with the relevant laws and with the principles of sound administrative and accounting procedures and adequate internal control;

Whereas technical modifications to the detailed rules laid down in this Directive may from time to time be necessary to take account of new developments in the banking sector; whereas the Commission shall accordingly make such modifications as are necessary, after consulting the Banking Advisory Committee, within the limits of the implementing powers conferred on the Commission by the Treaty; whereas that Committee shall act as a 'Regulatory' Committee, according to the rules of procedure laid down in Art. 2, procedure III, variant (b), of Council Decision 87/373/EEC of 13 July 1987 laying down the procedures for the exercise of implementing powers conferred on the Commission,[26]

Has adopted this Directive:

TITLE I. DEFINITIONS AND SCOPE

Article 1. For the purpose of this Directive:

1. 'credit institution' shall mean a credit institution as defined in the first indent of Art. 1 of Directive 77/780/EEC;
2. 'authorisation' shall mean authorisation as defined in the second indent of Art. 1 of Directive 77/780/EEC;
3. 'branch' shall mean a place of business which forms a legally dependent part of a credit institution and which carries out directly all or some of the transactions inherent in the business of credit institutions; any number of places of business set up in the same Member State by a credit institution with headquarters in another Member State shall be regarded as a single branch;
4. 'own funds' shall mean own funds as defined in Directive 89/299/EEC;
5. 'competent authorities' shall mean the national authorities which are empowered by law or regulation to supervise credit institutions;
6. 'financial institution' shall mean an undertaking other than a credit institution the principal activity of which is to acquire holdings or to carry on one or more of the activities listed in points 2 to 12 in the Annex;

[26] OJ 1987 L 197/33.

7. 'home Member State' shall mean the Member State in which a credit institution has been authorised in accordance with Art. 3 of Directive 77/780/EEC;

8. 'host Member State' shall mean the Member State in which a credit institution has a branch or in which it provides services;

9. 'control' shall mean the relationship between a parent undertaking and a subsidiary, as defined in Art. 1 of Directive 83/349/EEC,[27] or a similar relationship between any natural or legal person and an undertaking;

10. 'qualifying holding' shall mean a direct or indirect holding in an undertaking which represents 10% or more of the capital or of the voting rights or which makes it possible to exercise a significant influence over the management of the undertaking in which a holding subsists.

    For the purposes of this definition, in the context of Arts. 5 and 11 and of the other levels of holding referred to in Art. 11, the voting rights referred to in Art. 7 of Directive 88/627/EEC[28] shall be taken into consideration;

11. 'initial capital' shall mean capital as defined in Art. 2 (1) (1) and (2) of Directive 89/299/EEC;

12. 'parent undertaking' shall mean a parent undertaking as defined in Arts. 1 and 2 of Directive 83/349/EEC;

13. 'subsidiary' shall mean a subsidiary undertaking as defined in Arts. 1 and 2 of Directive 83/349/EEC; any subsidiary of a subsidiary undertaking shall also be regarded as a subsidiary of the parent undertaking which is at the head of those undertakings;

14. 'solvency ratio' shall mean the solvency coefficient of credit institutions calculated in accordance with Directive 89/647/EEC.[29]

Article 2.   1. This Directive shall apply to all credit institutions.

2. It shall not apply to the institutions referred to in Art. 2 (2) of Directive 77/780/EEC.

3. A credit institution which, as defined in Art. 2 (4) (a) of Directive 77/780/EEC, is affiliated to a central body in the same Member State may be exempted from the provisions of Arts. 4, 10 and 12 of this Directive provided that, without prejudice to the application of those provisions to the central body, the whole as constituted by the central body together with its affiliated institutions is subject to the abovementioned provisions on a consolidated basis.

In cases of exemption, Arts. 6 and 18 to 21 shall apply to the whole as constituted by the central body together with its affiliated institutions.

---

[27] OJ 1983 L 193/1.   [28] OJ 1988 L 348/62.   [29] OJ 1989 L 386/14.

Article 3. The Member States shall prohibit persons or undertakings that are not credit institutions from carrying on the business of taking deposits or other repayable funds from the public. This prohibition shall not apply to the taking of deposits or other funds repayable by a Member State or by a Member State's regional or local authorities or by public international bodies of which one or more Member States are members or to cases expressly covered by national or Community legislation, provided that those activities are subject to regulations and controls intended to protect depositors and investors and applicable to those cases.

TITLE II. HARMONISATION OF AUTHORISATION CONDITIONS

Article 4 1. The competent authorities shall not grant authorisation in cases where initial capital is less than ECU 5 million.

2. The Member States shall, however, have the option of granting authorisation to particular categories of credit institutions the initial capital of which is less than that prescribed in paragraph 1. In such cases:

(a) the initial capital shall not be less than ECU 1 million;
(b) the Member States concerned must notify the Commission of their reasons for making use of the option provided for in this paragraph;
(c) when the list referred to in Art. 3 (7) of Directive 77/780/EEC is published, the name of each credit institution that does not have the minimum capital prescribed in paragraph 1 shall be annotated to that effect;
(d) within five years of the date referred to in Art. 24 (1), the Commission shall draw up a report on the application of this paragraph in the Member States, for the attention of the Banking Advisory Committee referred to in Art. 11 of Directive 77/780/EEC.

Article 5. The competent authorities shall not grant authorisation for the taking-up of the business of credit institutions before they have been informed of the identities of the shareholders or members, whether direct or indirect, natural or legal persons, that have qualifying holdings, and of the amounts of those holdings.

The competent authorities shall refuse authorisation if, taking into account the need to ensure the sound and prudent management of a credit institution, they are not satisfied as to the suitability of the above-mentioned shareholders or members.

Article 6. 1. Host Member States may no longer require authorisation, as provided for in Art. 4 of Directive 77/780/EEC, or endowment capital for branches of credit institutions authorised in other Member States. The establishment and supervision of such branches shall be effected as pre-scribed in Arts. 13, 19 and 21 of this Directive.

2. Until the entry into force of the provisions implementing paragraph 1, host Member States may not, as a condition of the authorisation of branches of credit institutions, authorised in other Member States, require initial endowment capital exceeding 50% of the initial capital required by national rules for the authorisation of credit institutions of the same nature.

3. Credit institutions shall be entitled to the free use of the funds no longer required pursuant to paragraphs 1 and 2.

Article 7. There must be prior consultation with the competent authori-ties of the other Member State involved on the authorisation of a credit institution which is:

– a subsidiary of a credit institution authorised in another Member State, or
– a subsidiary of the parent undertaking of a credit institution authorised in another Member State, or
– controlled by the same persons, whether natural or legal, as control a credit institution authorised in another Member State.

TITLE III. RELATIONS WITH THIRD COUNTRIES

Article 8. The competent authorities of the Member States shall inform the Commission:

(a) of any authorisation of a direct or indirect subsidiary one or more parent undertakings of which are governed by the laws of a third country. The Commission shall inform the Banking Advisory Committee accordingly;
(b) whenever such a parent undertaking acquires a holding in a Community credit institution such that the latter would become its subsidiary. The Commission shall inform the Banking Advisory Committee accordingly.

When authorisation is granted to the direct or indirect subsidiary of one or more parent undertakings governed by the law of third countries, the structure of the group shall be specified in the notification which the competent authorities shall address to the Commission in accordance with Art. 3 (7) of Directive 77/780/EEC.

Article 9. 1. The Member States shall inform the Commission of any general difficulties encountered by their credit institutions in establishing themselves or carrying on banking activities in a third country.

2. Initially no later than six months before the application of this Directive and thereafter periodically, the Commission shall draw up a report examining the treatment accorded to Community credit institutions in third countries, in the terms referred to in paragraphs 3 and 4, as regards establishment and the carrying-on of banking activities, and the acquisition of holdings in third-country credit institutions. The Commission shall submit those reports to the Council, together with any appropriate proposals.

3. Whenever it appears to the Commission, either on the basis of the reports referred to in paragraph 2 or on the basis of other information, that a third country is not granting Community credit institutions effective market access comparable to that granted by the Community to credit institutions from that third country, the Commission may submit proposals to the Council for the appropriate mandate for negotiation with a view to obtaining comparable competitive opportunities for Community credit institutions. The Council shall decide by a qualified majority.

4. Whenever it appears to the Commission, either on the basis of the reports referred to in paragraph 2 or on the basis of other information that Community credit institutions in a third country do not receive national treatment offering the same competitive opportunities as are available to domestic credit institutions and the conditions of effective market access are not fulfilled, the Commissions may initiate negotiations in order to remedy the situation.

In the circumstances described in the first subparagraph, it may also be decided at any time, and in addition to initiating negotiations, in accordance with the procedure laid down in Art. 22 (2), that the competent authorities of the Member States must limit or suspend their decisions regarding requests pending at the moment of the decision or future requests for authorisations and the acquisition of holdings by direct or indirect parent undertakings governed by the laws of the third country in question. The duration of the measures referred to may not exceed three months.

Before the end of that three-month period, and in the light of the results of the negotiations, the Council may, acting on a proposal from the Commission, decide by a qualified majority whether the measures shall be continued.

Such limitations or suspension may not apply to the setting up of subsidiaries by credit institutions or their subsidiaries duly authorised in the Community, or to the acquisition of holdings in Community credit institutions by such institutions or subsidiaries.

5. Whenever it appears to the Commission that one of the situations described in paragraphs 3 and 4 obtains, the Member States shall inform it at its request:

(a) of any request for the authorisation of a direct or indirect subsidiary one or more parent undertakings of which are governed by the laws of the third country in question;

(b) whenever they are informed in accordance with Art. 11 that such an undertaking proposes to acquire a holding in a Community credit institution such that the latter would become its subsidiary.

This obligation to provide information shall lapse whenever an agreement is reached with the third country referred to in paragraph 3 or 4 or when the measures referred to in the second and third subparagraphs of paragraph 4 cease to apply.

6. Measures taken pursuant to this Article shall comply with the Community's obligations under any international agreements, bilateral and multilateral, governing the taking-up and pursuit of the business of credit institutions.

TITLE IV. HARMONISATION OF THE CONDITIONS GOVERNING PURSUIT OF THE BUSINESS OF CREDIT INSTITUTIONS

Article 10. 1. A credit institution's own funds may not fall below the amount of initial capital required pursuant to Art. 4 at the time of its authorisation.

2. The Member States may decide that credit institutions already in existence when the Directive is implemented, the own funds of which do not attain the levels prescribed for initial capital in Art. 4, may continue to carry on their activities. In that event, their own funds may not fall below the highest level reached after the date of the notification of this Directive.

3. If control of a credit institution falling within the category referred to in paragraph 2 is taken by a natural or legal person other than the person who controlled the institution previously, the own funds of that institution must attain at least the level prescribed for initial capital in Art. 4.

4. However, in certain specific circumstances and with the consent of the competent authorities, where there is a merger of two or more credit institutions falling within the category referred to in paragraph 2, the own funds of the institution resulting from the merger may not fall below the total own funds of the merged institutions at the time of the merger, as long as the appropriate levels pursuant to Art. 4 have not been attained.

5. However, if, in the cases referred to in paragraphs 1, 2 and 4, the own funds should be reduced, the competent authorities may, where the circumstances justify it, allow an institution a limited period in which to rectify its situation or cease its activities.

Article 11. 1. The Member States shall require any natural or legal person who proposes to acquire, directly or indirectly a qualifying holding in a credit institution first to inform the competent authorities, telling them of the size of the intended holding. Such a person must likewise inform the competent authorities if he proposes to increase his qualifying holding so that the proportion of the voting rights or of the capital held by him would reach or exceed 20%, 33% or 50% or so that the credit institution would become his subsidiary.

Without prejudice to the provisions of paragraph 2 the competent authorities shall have a maximum of three months from the date of the notification provided for in the first subparagraph to oppose such a plan if, in view of the need to ensure sound and prudent management of the credit institution, they are not satisfied as to the suitability of the person referred to in the first subparagraph. If they do not oppose the plan referred to in the first subparagraph, they may fix a maximum period for its implementation.

2. If the acquirer of the holdings referred to in paragraph 1 is a credit institution authorised in another Member State or the parent undertaking of a credit institution authorised in another Member State or a natural or legal person controlling a credit institution authorized in another Member State and if, as a result of that acquisition, the institution in which the acquirer proposes to acquire a holding would become a subsidiary or subject to the control of the acquirer, the assessment of the acquisition must be the subject of the prior consultation referred to in Art. 7.

3. The Member States shall require any natural or legal person who proposes to dispose, directly or indirectly, of a qualifying holding in a credit institution first to inform the competent authorities, telling them of the size of his intended holding. Such a person must likewise inform the competent authorities if he proposes to reduce his qualifying holding so that the proportion of the voting rights or of the capital held by him would fall below 20%, 33% or 50% or so that the credit institution would cease to be his subsidiary.

4. On becoming aware of them, credit institutions shall inform the competent authorities of any acquisitions or disposals of holdings in their capital that cause holdings to exceed or fall below one of the thresholds referred to in paragraphs 1 and 3.

They shall also, at least once a year, inform them of the names of shareholders and members possessing qualifying holdings and the sizes of such holdings as shown, for example, by the information received at the annual general meetings of shareholders and members or as a result of compliance with the regulations relating to companies listed on stock exchanges.

5. The Member States shall require that, where the influence exercised

by the persons referred to in paragraph 1 is likely to operate to the detriment of the prudent and sound management of the institution, the competent authorities shall take appropriate measures to put an end to that situation. Such measures may consist for example in injunctions, sanctions against directors and managers, or the suspension of the exercise of the voting rights attaching to the shares held by the shareholders or members in question.

Similar measures shall apply to natural or legal persons failing to comply with the obligation to provide prior information, as laid down in paragraph 1. If a holding is acquired despite the opposition of the competent authorities, the Member States shall, regardless of any other sanctions to be adopted, provide either for exercise of the corresponding voting rights to be suspended, or for the nullity of votes cast or for the possibility of their annulment.

Article 12. 1. No credit institution may have a qualifying holding the amount of which exceeds 15% of its own funds in an undertaking which is neither a credit institution, nor a financial institution, nor an undertaking carrying on an activity referred to in the second subparagraph of Art. 43 (2) (f) of Directive 86/635/EEC.

2. The total amount of a credit institution's qualifying holdings in undertakings other than credit institutions, financial institutions or undertakings carrying on activities referred to in the second subparagraph of Art. 43 (2) (f) of Directive 86/635/EEC may not exceed 60% of its own funds.

3. The Member States need not apply the limits laid down in paragraphs 1 and 2 to holdings in insurance companies as defined in Directive 73/239/EEC,[30] as last amended by Directive 88/357/EEC,[31] and Directive 79/267/EEC,[32] as last amended by the Act of Accession of 1985.

4. Shares held temporarily during a financial reconstruction or rescue operation or during the normal course of underwriting or in an institution's own name on behalf of others shall not be counted as qualifying holdings for the purpose of calculating the limits laid down in paragraphs 1 and 2. Shares which are not financial fixed assets as defined in Art. 35 (2) of Directive 86/635/EEC shall not be included.

5. The limits laid down in paragraphs 1 and 2 may be exceeded only in exceptional circumstances. In such cases, however, the competent authorities shall require a credit institution either to increase its own funds or to take other equivalent measures.

6. Compliance with the limits laid down in paragraphs 1 and 2 shall be ensured by means of supervision and monitoring on a consolidated basis in accordance with Directive 92/30/EEC.

[30] OJ 1973 L 228/3.   [31] OJ 1988 L 172/1.   [32] OJ 1979 L 63/1.

7. Credit institutions which, on the date of entry into force of the provisions implementing this Directive, exceed the limits laid down in paragraphs 1 and 2 shall have a period of 10 years from that date in which to comply with them.

8. The Member States may provide that the competent authorities shall not apply the limits laid down in paragraph 1 and 2 if they provide that 100% of the amounts by which a credit institution's qualifying holdings exceed those limits must be covered by own funds and that the latter shall not be included in the calculation of the solvency ratio. If both the limits laid down in paragraphs 1 and 2 are exceeded, the amount to be covered by own funds shall be the greater of the excess amounts.

Article 13. 1. The prudential supervision of a credit institution, including that of the activities it carries on in accordance with Art 18, shall be the responsibility of the competent authorities of the home Member State, without prejudice to those provisions of this Directive which give responsibility to the authorities of the host Member State.

2. Home Member State competent authorities shall require that every credit institution have sound administrative and accounting procedures and adequate internal control mechanisms.

3. Paragraphs 1 and 2 shall not prevent supervision on a consolidated basis pursuant to Directive 92/30/EEC.

Article 14. 1. [Amends Art. 7 (2) of Dir. 77/780.]

2. Host Member States shall retain responsibility in co-operation with the competent authorities of the home Member State for the supervision of the liquidity of the branches of credit institutions pending further co-ordination. Without prejudice to the measures necessary for the reinforcement of the European Monetary System, host Member States shall retain complete responsibility for the measures resulting from the implementation of their monetary policies. Such measures may not provide for discriminatory or restrictive treatment based on the fact that a credit institution is authorised in another Member State.

3. Without prejudice to further co-ordination of the measures designed to supervise the risks arising out of open positions on markets, where such risks result from transactions carried out on the financial markets of other Member States, the competent authorities of the latter shall collaborate with the competent authorities of the home Member State to ensure that the institutions concerned take steps to cover those risks.

Article 15. 1. Host Member States shall provide that, where a credit institution authorised in another Member State carries on its activities through a branch, the competent authorities of the home Member State may, after having first informed the competent authorities of the host Member State, carry out themselves or through the intermediary of persons they appoint for that purpose on-the-spot verification of the information referred to in Art. 7 (1) of Directive 77/780/EEC.

2. The competent authorities of the home Member State may, also, for purposes of the verification of branches, have recourse to one of the other procedures laid down in Art. 5 (4) of Directive 92/30/EEC.

3. This Article shall not affect the right of the competent authorities of the host Member State to carry out, in the discharge of their responsibilities under this Directive, on-the-spot verifications of branches established within their territory.

Article 16. [Replaces Art. 12 of Dir. 77/780.]

Article 17. Without prejudice to the procedures for the withdrawal of authorisations and the provisions of criminal law, the Member States shall provide that their respective competent authorities may, as against credit institutions or those who effectively control the business of credit institutions which breach laws, regulations or administrative provisions concerning the supervision or pursuit of their activities, adopt or impose in respect of them penalties or measures aimed specifically at ending observed breaches or the causes of such breaches.

TITLE V. PROVISIONS RELATING TO THE FREEDOM OF ESTABLISHMENT AND THE FREEDOM TO PROVIDE SERVICES

Article 18. 1. The Member States shall provide that the activities listed in the Annex may be carried on within their territories, in accordance with Arts. 19 to 21, either by the establishment of a branch or by way of the provision of services, by any credit institution authorised and supervised by the competent authorities of another Member State, in accordance with this Directive, provided that such activities are covered by the authorisation.

2. The Member States shall also provide that the activities listed in the Annex may be carried on within their territories, in accordance with Arts. 19 to 21, either by the establishment of a branch or by way of the provision of services, by any financial institution from another Member State, whether a subsidiary of a credit institution or the jointly-owned subsidiary of two or more credit institutions, the memorandum and articles of association of which permit the carrying on of those activities and which fulfils each of the following conditions:

– the parent undertaking or undertakings must be authorised as credit institutions in the Member State by the law of which the subsidiary is governed,

- the activities in question must actually be carried on within the territory of the same Member State,
- the parent undertaking or undertakings must hold 90% or more of the voting rights attaching to shares in the capital of the subsidiary,
- the parent undertaking or undertakings must satisfy the competent authorities regarding the prudent management of the subsidiary and must have declared, with the consent of the relevant home Member State competent authorities, that they jointly and severally guarantee the commitments entered into by the subsidiary,
- the subsidiary must be effectively included, for the activities in question in particular, in the consolidated supervision of the parent undertaking, or of each of the parent undertakings, in accordance with Directive 83/350/EEC, in particular for the calculation of the solvency ratio, for the control of large exposures and for purposes of the limitation of holdings provided for in Art. 12 of this Directive.

Compliance with these conditions must be verified by the competent authorities of the home Member State and the latter must supply the subsidiary with a certificate of compliance which must form part of the notification referred to in Arts. 19 and 20.

The competent authorities of the home Member State shall ensure the supervision of the subsidiary in accordance with Arts. 10 (1), 11, 13, 14 (1), 15 and 17 of this Directive and Arts. 7 (1) and 12 of Directive 77/780/EEC.

The provisions mentioned in this paragraph shall be applicable to subsidiaries, subject to the necessary modifications. In particular, the words 'credit institution' should be read as 'financial institution fulfilling the conditions laid down in Art. 18 (2)' and the word 'authorisation' as 'memorandum and articles of association'.

The second subparagraph of Art. 19 (3) shall read:

'The home Member State competent authorities shall also communicate the amount of own funds of the subsidiary financial institution and the consolidated solvency ratio of the credit institution which is its parent undertaking.'

If a financial institution eligible under this paragraph should cease to fulfil any of the conditions imposed, the home Member State shall notify the competent authorities of the host Member State and the activities carried on by that institution in the host Member State shall become subject to the legislation of the host Member State.

Article 19. 1. A credit institution wishing to establish a branch within the territory of another Member State shall notify the competent authorities of its home Member State.

2. The Member State shall require every credit institution wishing to establish a branch in another Member State to provide the following information when effecting the notification referred to in paragraph 1:

(a) the Member State within the territory of which it plans to establish a branch;
(b) a programme of operations setting out *inter alia* the types of business envisaged and the structural organisation of the branch;
(c) the address in the host Member State from which documents may be obtained;
(d) the names of those responsible for the management of the branch.

3. Unless the competent authorities of the home Member State have reason to doubt the adequacy of the administrative structure or the financial situation of the credit institution, taking into account the activities envisaged, they shall within three months of receipt of the information referred to in paragraph 2 communicate that information to the competent authorities of the host Member State and shall inform the institution concerned accordingly.

The home Member State competent authorities shall also communicate the amount of own funds and the solvency ratio of the credit institution and, pending subsequent co-ordination, details of any deposit-guarantee scheme which is intended to ensure the protection of depositors in the branch.

Where the competent authorities of the home Member State refuse to communicate the information referred to in paragraph 2 to the competent authorities of the host Member State, they shall give reasons for their refusal to the institution concerned within three months of receipt of all the information. That refusal or failure to reply shall be subject to a right to apply to the courts in the home Member State.

4. Before the branch of a credit institution commences its activities the competent authorities of the host Member State shall, within two months of receiving the information mentioned in paragraph 3, prepare for the supervision of the credit institution in accordance with Art. 21 and if necessary indicate the conditions under which, in the interest of the general good, those activities must be carried on in the host Member State.

5. On receipt of a communication from the competent authorities of the host Member State, or in the event of the expiry of the period provided for in paragraph 4 without receipt of any communication from the latter, the branch may be established and commence its activities.

6. In the event of a change in any of the particulars communicated pursuant to paragraph 2 (b), (c) or (d) or in the deposit-guarantee scheme referred to in paragraph 3 a credit institution shall give written notice of the change in question to the competent authorities of the home and host Member States at least one month before making the change so as to

enable the competent authorities of the home Member State to take a decision pursuant to paragraph 3 and the competent authorities of the host Member State to take a decision on the change pursuant to paragraph 4.

Article 20. 1. Any credit institution wishing to exercise the freedom to provide services by carrying on its activities within the territory of another Member State for the first time shall notify the competent authorities of the home Member State of the activities on the list in the Annex which it intends to carry on.

2. The competent authorities of the home Member State shall, within one month of receipt of the notification mentioned in paragraph 1, send that notification to the competent authorities of the host Member State.

Article 21. 1 Host Member States may, for statistical purposes, require that all credit institutions having branches within their territories shall report periodically on their activities in those host Member States to the competent authorities of those host Member States.

In discharging the responsibilities imposed on them in Art. 14 (2) and (3), host Member States may require that branches of credit institutions from other Member States provide the same information as they require from national credit institutions for that purpose.

2. Where the competent authorities of a host Member State ascertain that an institution having a branch or providing services within its territory is not complying with the legal provisions adopted in that State pursuant to the provisions of this Directive involving powers of the host Member State competent authorities, those authorities shall require the institution concerned to put an end to that irregular situation.

3. If the institution concerned fails to take the necessary steps, the competent authorities of the host Member State shall inform the competent authorities of the home Member State accordingly. The competent authorities of the home Member State shall, at the earliest opportunity, take all appropriate measures to ensure that the institution concerned puts an end to that irregular situation. The nature of those measures shall be communicated to the competent authorities of the host Member State.

4. If, despite the measures taken by the home Member State or because such measures prove inadequate or are not available in the Member State in question, the institution persists in violating the legal rules referred to in paragraph 2 in force in the host Member State, the latter State may, after informing the competent authorities of the home Member State, take appropriate measures to prevent or to punish further irregularities and, insofar as is necessary, to prevent that institution from initiating further transactions within its territory. The Member States

shall ensure that within their territories it is possible to serve the legal documents necessary for these measures on credit institutions.

5. The foregoing provisions shall not affect the power of host Member States to take appropriate measures to prevent or to punish irregularities committed within their territories which are contrary to the legal rules they have adopted in the interest of the general good. This shall include the possibility of preventing offending institutions from initiating any further transactions within their territories.

6. Any measure adopted pursuant to paragraphs 3, 4 and 5 involving penalties or restrictions on the exercise of the freedom to provide services must be properly justified and communicated to the institution concerned. Every such measure shall be subject to a right of appeal to the courts in the Member State the authorities of which adopted it.

7. Before following the procedure provided for in paragraphs 2 to 4, the competent authorities of the host Member State may, in emergencies, take any precautionary measures necessary to protect the interests of depositors, investors and others to whom services are provided. The Commission and the competent authorities of the other Member States concerned must be informed of such measures at the earliest opportunity.
The Commission may, after consulting the competent authorities of the Member States concerned, decide that the Member State in question must amend or abolish those measures.

8. Host Member States may exercise the powers conferred on them under this Directive by taking appropriate measures to prevent or to punish irregularities committed within their territories. This shall include the possibility of preventing institutions from initiating further transactions within their territories.

9. In the event of the withdrawal of authorisation the competent authorities of the host Member State shall be informed and shall take appropriate measures to prevent the institution concerned from initiating further transactions within its territory and to safeguard the interests of depositors. Every two years the Commission shall submit a report on such cases to the Banking Advisory Committee.

10. The Member States shall inform the Commission of the number and type of cases in which there has been a refusal pursuant to Art. 19 or in which measures have been taken in accordance with paragraph 4. Every two years the Commission shall submit a report on such cases to the Banking Advisory Committee.

11. Nothing this Article shall prevent credit institutions with head offices in other Member States from advertising their services through all available means of communication in the host Member State, subject to any rules governing the form and the content of such advertising adopted in the interest of the general good.

TITLE VI. FINAL PROVISIONS

Article 22. 1. The technical adaptations to be made to this Directive in the following areas shall be adopted in accordance with the procedure laid down in paragraph 2:
- expansion of the content of the list referred to in Art. 18 and set out in the Annex or adaptation of the terminology used in that list to take account of developments on financial markets,
- alteration of the amount of initial capital prescribed in Art. 4 to take account of developments in the economic and monetary field,
- the areas in which the competent authorities must exchange information as listed in art. 7 (1) of Directive 77/780/EEC,
- clarification of the definitions in order to ensure uniform application of this Directive throughout the Community,
  clarification of the definitions in order to take account of the implementation of this Directive of developments on financial markets,
- the alignment of terminology on and the framing of definitions in accordance with subsequent acts on credit institutions and related matters.

2. The Commission shall be assisted by a committee composed of representatives of the Member States and chaired by a representative of the Commission.

The Commission representative shall submit to the committee a draft of the measures to be taken. The committee shall deliver its opinion on the draft within a time limit which the chairman may lay down according to the urgency of the matter. The opinion shall be delivered by the majority laid down in Art. 148 (2) of the Treaty in the case of decisions which the Council is required to adopt on a proposal from the Commission. The votes of the representatives of the Member States in the committee shall be weighted in the manner set out in that Article. The chairman shall not vote.

The Commission shall adopt the measures envisaged if they are in accordance with the opinion of the committee.

If the measures envisaged are not in accordance with the opinion of the committee, or if no opinion is delivered, the Commission shall, without delay, submit to the Council a proposal concerning the measures to be taken. The Council shall act by a qualified majority.

If the Council does not act within three months of the referral to it the Commission shall adopt the measures proposed, unless the Council has decided against those measures by a simple majority.

Article 23. 1. Branches which have commenced their activities, in accordance with the provisions in force in their host Member States, before the entry into force of the provisions adopted in implementation of this

Directive shall be presumed to have been subject to the procedure laid down in Art. 19 (1) to (5). They shall be governed, from the date of that entry into force, by Arts. 15, 18, 19 (6) and 21. They shall benefit pursuant to Art. 6 (3).

2. Art. 20 shall not affect rights acquired by credit institutions providing services before the entry into force of the provisions adopted in implementation of this Directive.

Article 24.   1. Subject to paragraph 2, the Member States shall bring into force the laws, regulations and administrative provisions necessary for them to comply with this Directive by the later of the two dates laid down for the adoption of measures to comply with Directives 89/299/EEC and 89/647/EEC and at the latest by 1 January 1993. They shall forthwith inform the Commission thereof.

2. The Member States shall adopt the measures necessary for them to comply with Art. 6 (2) by 1 January 1990.

3. The Member States shall communicate to the Commission the texts of the main provisions of national law which they adopt in the field covered by this Directive.

[Final provisions omitted.]

ANNEX

LIST OF ACTIVITIES SUBJECT TO MUTUAL RECOGNITION

1. Acceptance of deposits and other repayable funds from the public.
2. Lending.[33]
3. Financial leasing.
4. Money transmission services.
5. Issuing and administering means of payment (e.g. credit cards, travellers' cheques and bankers' drafts).
6. Guarantees and commitments.
7. Trading for own account or for account of customers in:
    (a) money market instruments (cheques, bills, CDs, etc.);
    (b) foreign exchange;
    (c) financial futures and options;

---

[33] Including inter alia:
   − consumer credit,
   − mortgage credit,
   − factoring, with or without recourse,
   − financing of commercial transactions (including forfaiting).

(d) exchange and interest rate instruments;

(e) transferable securities.

8. Participation in share issues and the provision of services related to such issues.

9. Advice to undertakings on capital structure, industrial strategy and related questions and advice and services relating to mergers and the purchase of undertakings.

10. Money broking.

11. Portfolio management and advice.

12. Safekeeping and administration of securities.

13. Credit reference services.

14. Safe custody services.

Social Security for Migrants

Regulation (EEC) No 1408/71 of the Council of 14 June 1971 on the application of social security schemes to employed persons, to self-employed persons and to members of their families moving within the Community[1]

[Recitals omitted.]

TITLE I. GENERAL PROVISIONS

Article 1. Definitions

For the purpose of this Regulation:

(a) 'employed person' and 'self-employed person' mean respectively:
  (i) any person who is insured, compulsorily or on an optional continued basis, for one or more of the contingencies covered by the branches of a social security scheme for employed or self-employed persons;
  (ii) any person who is complsorily insured for one or more of the contingencies covered by the branches of social security dealt with in this Regulation, under a social secrity scheme for all residents or for the whole working population, if such person:
    – can be identified as an employed or self-employed person by virtue of the manner in which such scheme is administered or financed, or,
    – failing such criteria, is insured for some other contingency specified in Annex I under a scheme for employed or self-employed persons, or under a scheme referred to in (iii), either compulsorily or on an optional continued basis, or, where no such scheme exists in the Member State concerned, complies with the definition given in Annex I; any person who is compulsorily insured for several of the contingencies covered by the branches dealt with in this Regulation, under a standard social security scheme for the whole rural population in accordance with the criteria laid down in Annex I;
  (iii) any person who is voluntarily insured for one or more of the contingencies covered by the branches dealt with in this

[1] OJ sp. Ed. 1971 (II), p. 416. As amended and up-dated (and in effect consolidated) by Reg. 2001/83, OJ 1983 L 230/6. And as last amended by Reg. 1249/92 OJ 1992 L 136/28.

Regulation, under a standard social security scheme for the whole rural population in accordance with the criteria laid down in Annex I;

    (iv) any person who is voluntarily insured for one or more of the contingencies covered by the branches dealt with in this Regulation, under a social security cheme of a Member State for employed or self-employed persons or for all residents or for certain categories of residents:

        – if such person carried out an activity as an employed or self-employed person, or

        – if such person has previously been compulsorily insured for the same contingency under a scheme for employed or self-employed persons of the same Member State;

(b) 'frontier worker' means any employed or self employed person who pursues his occupation in the territory of a Member State and resides in the territory of another Member State to which he returns as a rule daily or at least once a week; however, a frontier worker who is posted elsewhere in the territory of the same or another Member State by the undertaking to which he is normally attached, or who engages in the provision of services elsewhere in the territory of the same or another Member State, shall retain the status of frontier worker for a period not exceeding four months, even if he is prevented, during that period, from returning daily or at least once a week to the place where he resides;

(c) 'seasonal worker' means any employed person who goes to the territory of a Member State other than the one in which he is resident to do work there of a seasonal nature for an undertaking or an employer of that State for a period which may on no account exceed eight months, and who stays in the territory of the said State for the duration of his work; work of a seasonal nature shall be taken to mean work which, being dependent on the succession of the seasons, automatically recurs each year;

(d) 'refugee' shall have the meaning assigned to it in Art. 1 of the Convention on the Status of Refugees, signed at Geneva on 28 July 1951;

(e) 'stateless person' shall have the meaning assigned to it in Art. 1 of the Convention on the Status of Stateless Persons, signed in New York on 28 September 1954;

(f) (i) 'member of the family' means any person defined or recognised as a member of the family or designated as a member of the household by the legislation under which benefits are provided or, in the cases referred to in Arts. 22 (1) (a) and 31, by the legislation of the Member State in whose territory such person resides;

where, however, the said legislations regard as a member of the family or a member of the household only a person living under the same roof as the employed or self-employed person, this condition shall be considered satisfied if the person in question is mainly dependent on that person. Where the legislation of a Member State on sickness or maternity benefits in kind does not enable members of the family to be distinguished from the other persons to whom it applies, the term 'member of the family' shall have the meaning given to it in Annex I;

(ii) where, however, the benefits concerned are benefits for disabled persons granted under the legislation of a Member State to all nationals of that State who fulfil the prescribed conditions, the term 'member of the family' means at least the spouse of an employed or self-employed person and the children of such person who are either minors or who are dependent upon such person.

(g) 'survivor' means any person defined or recognised as such by the legislation under which the benefits are granted; where, however, the said legislation regards as a survivor only a person who was living under the same roof as the deceased, this condition shall be considered satisfied if such person was mainly dependent on the deceased;

(h) 'residence' means habitual residence;

(i) 'stay' means temporary residence;

(j) 'legislation' means in respect of each Member State statutes, regulations and other provisions and all other implementing measures, present or future, relating to the branches and schemes of social security covered by Art. 4 (1) and (2) or those special non-contributory benefits covered by Art. 4 (2) (a).

The term excludes provisions of existing or future industrial agreements, whether or not they have been the subject of a decision by the authorities rendering them compulsory or extending their scope. However, in so far as such provisions:

(i) serve to put into effect compulsory insurance imposed by the laws and regulations referred to in the preceding subparagraph; or

(ii) set up a scheme administered by the same institution as that which administers the schemes set up by the laws and regulations referred to in the preceding subparagraph,

the limitation on the term may at any time be lifted by a declaration of the Member State concerned specifying the schemes of such a kind to which this Regulation applies. Such a declaration shall be notified and published in accordance with the provisions of Art. 97.

The provisions of the preceding subparagraph shall not have the effect of exempting from the application of this Regulation the schemes to which Regulation No. 3 applied.

The term 'legislation' also excludes provisions governing special schemes for self-employed persons the creation of which is left to the initiatives of those concerned or which apply only to a part of the territory of the Member State concerned, irrespective of whether or not the authorities decided to make them compulsory or extend their scope. The special schemes in question are specified in Annex II;

[Provisions omitted.]

(l) 'competent authority' means, in respect of each Member State, the Minister, Ministers or other equivalent authority responsible for social security schemes throughout or in any part of the territory of the State in question;

[Provisions omitted.]

(m) 'institution' means, in respect of each Member State, the body or authority responsible for administering all or part of the legislation;

(o) 'competent institution' means:

(i) the institution with which the person concerned is insured at the time of the application for benefit; or

(ii) the institution from which the person concerned is entitled or would be entitled to benefits if he or a member or members of his family were resident in the territory of the Member State in which the institution is situated, or

(iii) the institution designated by the competent authority of the Member State concerned, or

(iv) in the case of a scheme relating to an employer's liability in respect of the benefits set out in Art. 4 (1), either the employer or the insurer involved or, in default thereof, a body or authority designated by the competent authority of the Member State concerned;

(p) 'institution of the place of residence' and 'institution of the place of stay' mean respectively the institution which is competent to provide benefits in the place where the person concerned resides and the institution which is competent to provide benefits in the place where the person concerned is staying, under the legislation administered by that institution or, where no such institution exists, the institution designated by the competent authority of the Member State in question;

(q) 'competent State' means the Member State in whose territory the competent institution is situated;

(r) 'periods of insurance' means periods of contribution or periods of employment or self-employment as defined or recognised as periods of insurance by the legislation under which they were completed or considered as completed, and all periods treated as such, where they are regarded by the said legislation as equivalent to periods of insurance;

(s) 'periods of employment' and 'periods of self-employment' means periods so defined or recognised as such by the legislation under which they were completed, and all periods treated as such, where they are regarded by the said legislation as equivalent to periods of employment or self-employment;

(a) 'periods of residence' means periods of residence as defined or recognised as such by the legislation under which they were completed or are deemed to have been completed.

(t) 'benefits' and 'pensions' mean all benefits and pensions, including all elements thereof payable out of public funds, revalorisation increases and supplementary allowances, subject to the provisions of Title III, as also lump-sum benefits which may be paid in lieu of pensions, and payments made by way of reimbursement of contributions;

[Provisions omitted.]

Article 2. Persons covered.

1. This Regulation shall apply to employed or self-employed persons who are or have been subject to the legislation of one or more Member States and who are nationals of one of the Member States or who are stateless persons or refugees residing within the territory of one of the Member States, as also to the members of their families and their survivors.

2. In addition, this Regulation shall apply to the survivors of employed or self-employed persons who have been subject to the legislation of one or more Member States, irrespective of the nationality of such employed or self-employed persons, where their survivors are nationals of one of the Member States, or stateless persons or refugees residing within the territory of one of the Member States.

3. This Regulation shall apply to civil servants and to persons who, in accordance with the legislation applicable, are treated as such, where they are or have been subject to the legislation of a Member State to which this Regulation applies.

Article 3. Equality of treatment

1. Subject to the special provisions of this Regulation, persons resident in the territory of one of the Member States to whom this Regulation applies shall be subject to the same obligations and enjoy the same benefits under the legislation of any Member State as the nationals of that State.

2. The provisions of paragraph 1 shall apply to the right to elect members of the organs of social security institutions or to participate in their

nomination, but shall not affect the legislative provisions of any Member Stte relating to eligibility or methods of nomination of persons concerned to those organs.

3. Save as provided in Annex III, the provisions of social security conventions which remain in force pursuant to Art. 7 (2) (c) and the provisions of conventions concluded pursuant to Art. 8 (1), shall apply to all persons to whom this Regulation applies.

Article 4.   Matters covered

1. This Regulation shall apply to all legislation concerning the following branches of social security;

(a) sickness and maternity benefits;
(b) invalidity benefits, including those intended for the maintenance or improvement of earning capacity;
(c) old-age benefits;
(d) survivors' benefits;
(e) benefits in respect of accidents at work and occupational diseases;
(f) death grants;
(g) unemployment benefits;
(h) family benefits.

2. This Regulation shall apply to all general and special social security schemes, whether contributory or non-contributory, and to schemes concerning the liability of an employer or shipowner in respect of the benefits referred to in paragraph 1.

2a.[2] This Regulation shall also apply to special non-contributory benefits which are provided under a legislation or schemes other than those referred to in paragraph 1 or excluded by virtue of paragraph 4, where such benefits are intended:

(a) either to provide supplementary, substitute or ancillary cover against the risks covered by the branches of social security referred to in paragraph 1 (a) to (h), or
(b) solely as specific protection for the disabled.

2b. Tlhis Regulation shall not apply to the provisions in the legislation of a Member State concerning special non-contributory benefits, referred to in Annex II, Section III, the validity of which is confined to part of the territory.

3. The provisions of Title III of this Regulation shall not, however, affect the legislative provisions of any Member State concerning a shipowner's liability.

---

[2] For temporal effects see Art. 2 of Reg. 1247/92, OJ 1992 L 136/1.

4. This Regulation shall not apply to social and medical assistance, to benefit schemes for victims of war or its consequences, or to special schemes for civil servants and persons treated as such.

[Provisions omitted.]

Article 9. Admission to voluntary or optional continued insurance

1. The provisions of the legislation of any Member State which make admission to voluntary or optional continued insurance conditional upon residence in the territory of that State shall not apply to persons resident in the territory of another Member State, provided that at some time in their past working life they were subject to the legislation of the first State as employed or as self-employed persons.

2. Where, under the legislation of a Member State, admission to voluntary or optional continued insurance is conditional upon completion of periods of insurance, the periods of insurance or residence completed under the legislation of another Member State shall be taken into account, to the extent required, as if they were completed under the legislation of the first State.

Article 9a.[2] Prolongation of the reference period

Where, under the legislation of a Member State, recognition of entitlement to a benefit is conditional upon completion of a minimum period of insurance during a specific period preceding the contingency insured against (reference period) and where the aforementioned legislation provides that the periods during which the benefits have been granted under the legislation of that Member State or periods devoted to the upbringing of children in the territory of that Member State shall give rise to prolongation of the reference period, periods during which invalidity pensions or old-age pensions or sickness benefits, unemployment benefits or benefits for accidents at work (except for pensions) have been awarded under the legislation of another Member State and periods devoted to the upbringing of children in the territory of another Member State shall likewise give rise to prolongation of the aforesaid reference period.

Article 10. Waiving of residence clauses—Effect of compulsory insurance on reimbursement of contributions

1. Save as otherwise provided in this Regulation, invalidity, old-age or survivors' cash benefits, pensions for accidents at work or occupational diseases and death grants acquired under the legislation of one or more Member States shall not be subject to any reduction, modification, suspension, withdrawal or confiscation by reason of the fact that the recipient resides in the territory of a Member State other than that in which the institution responsible for payment is situated.

The preceding subparagraph shall also apply to lump-sum benefits granted in cases of remarriage of a surviving spouse who was entitled to a survivor's pension.

2. Where under the legislation of a Member State reimbursement of contributions is conditional upon the person concerned having ceased to be subject to compulsory insurance, this condition shall not be considered satisfied as long as the person concerned is subject to compulsory insurance as an employed or self-employed person under the legislation of another Member State.

Article 10a.[3] Special non-contributory benefits

1. Notwithstanding the provisions of Art. 10 and the Title III, persons to whom this Regulation applies shall be granted special non-contributory cash benefits as referred to in Art. 4 (2a) exclusively in territory of the Member State in which they reside, in accordance with the legislation of that State, provided that such benefits are listed in Annex IIa. Such benefits shall be granted by and at the expense of the institution of the place of residence.

2. The institution of a Member State whose legislation entitlement to benefits covered by paragraph 1 subject to the completion of periods of employment, self-employment or residence shall regard, to the extent necessary, periods of employment, self-employment or residence completed in the territory of any other Member State as periods completed in the territory of the first Member State.

3. Where the entitlement to a benefit covered by paragraph paragraph 1 but granted in the form of a supplement is subject, under the legislation of a Member State, to receipt of a benefit coming within the scope of Art. 4 (1) (a) to (h), and no such benefit is due under that legislation, any corresponding benefit granted under the legislation of any other Member State shall be treated as a benefit granted under the legislation of the first Member State for the purposes of entitlement to the supplement.

4. Where the granting of a disability or invalidity benefit covered by paragraph 1 is subject, under the legislation of a Member State, to the condition that the disability or invalidity should be diagnosed for the first time in the territory of that Member State, this condition shall be deemed to be fulfilled where such diagnosis is made for the first time in the territory of another Member State.

Article 11. Revalorisation of benefits

Rules for revalorisation provided by the legislation of a Member State shall apply to benefits due under that legislation by taking into account the provisions of this Regulation.

[3] For temporal effects see Art. 2 of Reg. 1247/92, OJ 1992 L 136/1.

Article 12.   Prevention of overlapping of benefits

1. This Regulation can neither confer nor maintain the right to several benefits of the same kind for one and the same period of compulsory insurance. However, this provision shall not apply to benefits in respect of invalidity, old age, death (pensions) or occupational disease which are awarded by the institutions of two or more Member States, in accordance with the provisions of Arts. 41, 43 (2) and (3), 46, 50 and 51 or 60 (1) (b).

2. Save as otherwise provided in this Regulation, the provisions of the legislation of a Member State governing the reduction, suspension or withdrawal of benefits in cases of overlapping with other social security benefits or any other form of income may be invoked even where such benefits were acquired under the legislation of another Member State or where such income was acquired in the territory of another Member State.

3. The provisions of the legislation of a Member State for reduction, suspension or withdrawal of benefit in the case of a person in receipt of invalidity benefits or anticipatory old-age benefits pursuing a professional or trade activity may be invoked against such person even though he is pursuing his activity in the territory of another Member State.

4. An invalidity pension payable under Netherlands legislation shall, in a case where the Netherlands institution is bound under the provisions of Art. 57 (5) or 60 (2) (a) to contribute also to the cost of benefits for occupational disease granted under the legislation of another Member State, be reduced by the amount payable to the institution of the other Member State which is responsible for granting the benefits for occupational disease.

TITLE II. DETERMINATION OF THE LEGISLATION APPLICABLE

Article 13.   General rules

1. Subject to Art. 14 (c), persons to whom this Regulation applies shall be subject to the legislation of a single member State only. That legislation shall be determined in accordance with the provisions of this Title.

2. Subject to Arts. 14 to 17:

(a) a person employed in the territory of one Member State shall be subject to the legislation of that State even if he resides in the territory of another Member State or if the registered office or place of business of the undertaking or individual employing him is situated in the territory of another Member State;

(b) a person who is self-employed in the territory of one Member State shall be subject to the legislation of that State even if he resides in the territory of another Member State;

[Provisions omitted.]

(f) a person to whom the legislation of a Member State ceases to be applicable, without the legislation of another Member State becoming applicable to him in accordance with one of the rules laid down in the aforegoing subparagraphs or in accordance with one of the exceptions or special provisions laid down in Arts. 14 to 17 shall be subject to the legislation of the Member State in whose territory he resides in accordance with the provisions of that legislation alone.

Article 14. Special rules . . .

Art. 13 (2) (a) shall apply subject to the following exceptions and circumstances:

1. (a) A person employed in the territory of a Member State by an undertaking to which he is normally attached who is posted by that undertaking to the territory of another Member State to perform work there for that undertaking shall continue to be subject to the legislation of the first Member State, provided that the anticipated duration of that work does not exceed twelve months and that he is not sent to replace another worker who has completed his term of posting;

    (b) if the duration of the work to be done extends beyond the duration originally anticipated, owing to unforeseeable circumstances, and exceeds twelve months, the legislation of the first State shall continue to apply until the completion of such work, provided that the competent authority of the Member State in whose territory the person concerned is posted or the body designated by that authority gives its consent; such consent must be requested before the end of the initial 12 month period. Such consent cannot, however, be given for a period exceeding 12 months.

2. A person normally employed in the territory of two or more Member States shall be subject to the legislation determined as follows:

(a) [Travelling or flying personnel.]

[Text omitted.]

(b) a person other than that referred to in (a) shall be subject:

    (i) to the legislation of the Member State in whose territory he resides, if he pursues his activity partly in that territory or if he is attached to several undertakings or several employers who have their registered offices or places of business in the territory of different Member States;

(ii) to the legislation of the Member State in whose territory is situated the registered office or place of business of the undertaking or individual employing him, if he does not reside in the territory of any of the Member States where he is pursuing his activity.

3. A person who is employed in the territory of one Member State by an undertaking which has its registered office or place of business in the territory of another Member State and which straddles the common frontier of these States shall be subject to the legislation of the Member State in whose territory the undertaking has its registered office or place of business.

Article 14a. Special rules applicable to persons, other than mariners, who are self-employed.

Art. 13 (2) (b) shall apply subject to the following exceptions and circumstances:

1. (a) A person normally self-employed in the territory of a Member State and who performs work in the territory of another Member State shall continue to be subject to the legislation of the first Member State, provided that the anticipated duration of the work does not exceed 12 months.
   (b) If the duration of the work to be done extends beyond the duration originally anticipated, owing to unforeseeable circumstances, and exceeds 12 months, the legislation of the first Member State shall continue to apply until the completion of such work, provided that the competent authority of the Member State in whose territory the person concerned has entered to perform the work in question or the body appointed by that authority gives its consent; such consent must be requested before the end of the initial 12-month period. Such consent cannot, however, be given for a period exceeding 12 months.
2. A person normally self-employed in the territory of two or more Member States shall be subject to the legislation of the Member State in whose territory he resides if he pursues any part of his activity in the territory of that Member State. If he does not pursue any activity in the territory of the Member State in which he resides, he shall be subject to the legislation of the Member State in whose territory he pursues his main activity. The criteria used to determine the principal activity are laid down in the Regulation referred to in Art. 98.
3. A person who is self-employed in an undertaking which has its registered office or place of business in the territory of one Member State and which straddles the common frontier of two Member States shall be subject to the legislation of the Member State in whose territory the undertaking has its registered office or place of business.

4. If the legislation to which a person should be subject in accordance with paragraphs 2 or 3 does not enable that person, even on a voluntary basis, to join a pension scheme, the person concerned shall be subject to the legislation of the other Member State which would apply apart from these particular provisions or, should the legislations of two or more Member States apply in this way, he shall be subject to the legislation decided on by common agreement amongst the Member States concerned or their competent authorities.

[Provisions omitted.]

Article 15. Rules concerning voluntary insurance or optional continued insurance

1. Arts. 13 to 14d shall not apply to voluntary insurance or to optional continued insurance unless, in respect of one of the branches referred to in Art. 4 there exists in any Member State only a voluntary scheme of insurance.

2. Where application of the legislations of two or more Member States entails overlapping of insurance:

– under a compulsory insurance scheme and one or more voluntary or optional continued insurance schemes, the person concerned shall be subject exclusively to the compulsory insurance scheme,
– under two or more voluntary or optional continued insurance schemes, the person concerned may join only the voluntary or optional continued insurance scheme for which he has opted

3. However, in respect of invalidity, old age and death (pensions), the person concerned may join the voluntary or optional continued insurance scheme of a Member State, even if he is compulsorily subject to the legislation of another Member State, to the extent that such overlapping is explicitly or implicitly admitted in the first Member State.

[Provisions omitted.]

TITLE III. SPECIAL PROVISIONS RELATING TO THE VARIOUS CATEGORIES OF BENEFITS

CHAPTER I. SICKNESS AND MATERNITY

Section 1. Common provisions

Article 18. Aggregation of periods of insurance, employment or residence

1. The competent institution of a Member State whose legislation

makes the acquisition, retention or recovery of the right to benefits conditional upon the completion of periods of insurance, employment or residence shall, to the extent necessary, take account of periods of insurance, employment or residence completed under the legislation of any other Member State as if they were periods completed under the legislation which it administers.

2. The provisions of paragraph 1 shall apply to seasonal workers, even in respect of periods prior to any break in insurance exceeding the period allowed by the legislation of the competent State, provided however that the person concerned has not ceased to be insured for a period exceeding four months.

Section 2. Employed and self-employed persons and members of their families

Article 19. Residence in a member state other than the competent State—General Rules

1. An employed or self-employed person residing in the territory of a Member State other than the competent State, who satisfies the conditions of the legislation of the competent State for entitlement to benefits, taking account where appropriate of the provisions of Art. 18, shall receive in the State in which he is resident:

(a) benefits in kind provided on behalf of the competent institution by. the institution of the place of residence in accordance with the provisions of the legislation administered by that institution as though he were insured with it;

(b) cash benefits provided by the competent institution in accordance with the legislation which it administers. However, by agreement between the competent institution and the institution of the place of residence, such benefits may be provided by the latter institution on behalf of the former, in accordance with the legislation of the competent State.

2. The provisions of paragraph 1 shall apply by analogy to members of the family who reside in the territory of a Member State other than the competent State in so far as they are not entitled to such benefits under the legislation of the State in whose territory they reside.

Where the members of the family reside in the territory of a Member State under whose legislation the right to receive benefits in kinds is not subject to conditions of insurance or employment, benefits in kind which they receive shall be considered as being on behalf of the institution with which the employed or self-employed person is insured, unless the spouse or the person looking after the children exercises a professional or trade activity in the territory of the said Member State.

Article 20. Frontier workers and members of their families - Special rules

A frontier worker may also obtain benefits in the territory of the competent State. Such benefits shall be provided by the competent institution in accordance with the provisions of the legislation of that State, as though the person concerned were resident in that State. Members of his family may receive benefits under the same conditions; however, receipt of such benefits shall, except in urgent cases, be conditional upon an agreement between the States concerned or between the competent authorities of those States or, in its absence, on prior authorisation by the competent institution.

Article 21. Stay in or transfer of residence to the competent State

1. The employed or self-employed person referred to in Art. 19 (1) who is staying in the territory of the competent State shall receive benefits in accordance with the provisions of the legislation of that State as though he were resident there, even if he has already received benefits for the same case of sickness or maternity before his stay.

2. Paragraph 1 shall apply by analogy to the members of the family referred to in Art. 19 (2).

However, where the latter reside in the territory of a Member State other than the one in whose territory the employed or self-employed person resides, benefits in kind shall be provided by the institution of the place of stay on behalf of the institution of the place of residence of the persons concerned.

3. Paragraphs 1 and 2 shall not apply to frontier workers and the members of their families.

4. An employed or self-employed person and members of his family referred to in Art. 19 who transfer their residence to the territory of the competent State shall receive benefits in accordance with the provisions of the legislation of that State even if they have already received benefits for the same case of sickness or maternity before transferring their residence.

Article 22. Stay outside the competent State—Return to or transfer of residence to another Member State during sickness or maternity—Need to go to another Member State in order to receive appropriate treatment.

1. An employed or self-employed person who satisfies the conditions of the legislation of the competent State for entitlement to benefits, taking account where appropriate of the provisions of Art. 18, and:

(a) whose condition necessitates immediate benefits during a stay in the territory of another Member State, or
(b) who, having become entitled to benefits chargeable to the competent institution, is authorised by that institution to return to the territory

of the Member State where he resides, or to transfer his residence to the territory of another Member State, or

(c) who is authorised by the competent institution to go to the territory of another Member State to receive there the treatment appropriate to his condition, shall be entitled:

  (i) to benefits in kind provided on behalf of the competent institution by the institution of the place of stay or residence in accordance with the provisions of the legislation which it administers, as though he were insured with it; the length of the period during which benefits are provided shall be governed, however, by the legislation of the competent State;

  (ii) to cash benefits provided by the competent institution in accordance with the provisions of the legislation which it administers. However, by agreement between the competent institution and the institution of the place of stay or residence, such benefits may be provided by the latter institution on behalf of the former, in accordance with the provisions of the legislation of the competent State.

2. The authorisation required under paragraph 1 (b) may be refused only if it is established that movement of the person concerned would be prejudicial to his state of health or the receipt of medical treatment.

The authorisation required under paragraph 1 (c) may not be refused where the treatment in question is among the benefits provided for by the legislation of the Member State on whose territory the person concerned resides and where he cannot be given such treatment within the time normally necessary for obtaining the treatment in question in the Member State of residence taking account of his current state of health and the probable course of the disease.

3. The provisions of paragraphs 1 and 2 shall apply by analogy to members of the family of an employed or self-employed person.

However, for the purpose of applying paragraph 1 (a) and (c) (i) to the members of the family referred to in Art. 19 (2) who reside in the territory of a Member State other than the one in whose territory the employed or self-employed person resides:

(a) benefits in kind shall be provided on behalf of the institution of the Member State in whose territory the members of the family are residing by the institution of the place of stay in accordance with the provisions of the legislation which it administers as if the employed or self-employed person were insured there. The period during which benefits are provided shall, however, be that laid down under the legislation of the Member State in whose territory the members of the family are residing;

(b) the authorisation required under paragraph 1 (c) shall be issued by the institution of the Member State in whose territory the members of the family are residing.

4. The fact that the provisions of paragraph 1 apply to an employed or self-employed person shall not effect the right to benefit of members of his family.

Article 23. Calculation of cash benefits

1. The competent institution of a Member State whose legislation provides that the calculation of cash benefits shall be based on average earnings or an average contributions, shall determine such average earnings or contributions exclusively by reference to earnings or contributions completed under the said legislation.

2. The competent institution of a Member State whose legislation provides that the calculation of cash benefits shall be based on standard earnings, shall take account exclusively of the standard earnings or, where appropriate, of the average of standard earnings for the periods completed under the said legislation.

3. The competent institution of a Member State under whose legislation the amount of cash benefits varies with the number of members of the family, shall also take into account the members of the family of the person concerned who are resident in the territory of another Member State as if they were resident in the territory of the competent State.

Article 24. Substantial benefits in kind

1. Where the right of an employed or self-employed person or a member of his family to a prosthesis, a major appliance or other substantial benefits in kind has been recognised by the institution of a Member State before he becomes insured with the institution of another Member State, the said employed or self-employed person shall receive such benefits at the expense of the first institution, even if they are granted after he becomes insured with the second institution.

2. The Administrative Commission shall draw up the list of benefits to which the provisions of paragraph 1 apply.

[Provisions omitted.]

Section 7. Reimbursement between institutions

Article 36. 1. Without prejudice to the provisions of Art. 32, benefits in kind provided in accordance with the provisions of this Chapter by the institution of one Member State on behalf of the institution of another Member State shall be fully refunded.

2. The refunds referred to in paragraph 1 shall be determined and made in accordance with the procedure provided for by the implementing regulation referred to in Art. 98, either on production of proof of actual expenditure or on the basis of lump-sum payments.

In the latter case, the lump-sum payments shall be such as to ensure that the refund is as close as possible to actual expenditure.

3. Two or more Member States, or the competent authorities of those States, may provide for other methods of reimbursement or may waive all reimbursement between institutions under their jurisdiction.

[Provisions omitted.]

CHAPTER 3. OLD AGE AND DEATH (PENSIONS)[4]

Article 44. General provisions for the award of benefits where an employed or self-employed person has been subject to the legislation of two or more Member States

1. The rights to benefits of an employed or self-employed person who has been subject to the legislation of two or more Member States, or of his survivors, shall be determined in accordance with the provisions of this Chapter.

2. Save as otherwise provided in Art. 49, the processing of a claim for an award submitted by the person concerned shall have regard to all the legislations to which the employed or self-employed person has been subject. Exception shall be made to this rule if the person concerned expressly asks for postponement of the award of old-age benefits to which he would be entitled under the legislation of one or more Member States.

3. This Chapter shall not apply to increases in pensions or to supplements for pensions in respect of children or to orphans' pensions granted in accordance with the provisions of Chapter 8.

Article 45. Consideration of periods of insurance or of residence completed under the legislations to which an employed person or self-employed person was subject, for the acquisition, retention or recovery of the right to benefits

1. Where the legislation of a Member State makes the acquisition, retention or recovery of the right to benefits, under a scheme which is not a special scheme within the meaning of paragraphs 2 or 3, subject to the completion of periods of insurance or of residence, the competent institu-

---

[4] For temporal effects of amendments to pension provisions by Reg 1248/92 OJ 1992 L 136/9 see Art 2(b) of latter Reg. adding Art 95a to Reg. 1408/71.

tion of that Member State shall take account, where necessary, of the periods of insurance or of residence completed under the legislation of any other Member State, be it under a general scheme or under a special scheme and either as an employed person or as a self-employed person. For that purpose, it shall take account of these periods as if they had been completed under its own legislation.

2. Where the legislation of a Member State makes the granting of certain benefits conditional upon the periods of insurance having been completed only in an occupation which is subject to a special scheme for employed persons or, where appropriate, in a specific employment, periods completed under the legislations of other Member States shall be taken into account for the granting of these benefits only if completed under a corresponding scheme or, failing that, in the same occupation or, where appropriate, in the same employment. If, account having been taken of the periods thus completed, the person concerned does not satisfy the conditions for receipt of these benefits, these periods shall be taken into account for the granting of the benefits under the general scheme or, failing that, under the scheme applicable to manual or clerical workers, as the case may be, subject to the condition that the person has been affiliated to one or other of these schemes.

3. Where the legislation of a Member State makes the granting of certain benefits conditional upon the periods of insurance having been completed only in an occupation subject to a special scheme for self-employed persons, periods completed under the legislations of other Member States shall be taken into account for the granting of these benefits only if completed under a corresponding scheme or, failing that, in the same occupation. The special schemes for self-employed persons referred to in this paragraph are listed in Annex IV, part B, for each Member State concerned. If, account having been taken of the periods referred to in this paragraph, the person concerned does not satisfy the conditions for receipt of these benefits, these periods shall be taken into account for the granting of the benefits under the general scheme or, failing this, under the scheme applicable to manual or clerical workers, as the case may be, subject to the condition that the person concerned has been affiliated to one or other of these schemes.

4. The periods of insurance completed under a special scheme of a Member State shall be taken into account under the general scheme or, failing that, under the scheme applicable to manual or clerical workers, as the case may be, of another Member State for the acquisition, retention or recovery of the right to benefits, subject to the condition that the person concerned has been affiliated to one or other of these schemes, even if these periods have already been taken into account in the latter State under a scheme referred to in paragraph 2 or in the first sentence of paragraph 3.

5. Where the legislation of a Member State makes the acquisition, retention or recovery of the right to benefits conditional upon the person concerned being insured at the time of the materialisation of the risk, this condition shall be regarded as having been satisfied in the case of insurance under the legislation of another Member State, in accordance with the procedures provided for in Annex VI for each Member State concerned.

6. A period of full unemployment of a worker to whom Art. 71 (1) (a) (ii) or (b) (ii), first sentence, applies shall be taken into account by the competent institution of the Member State in whose territory the worker concerned resides in accordance with the legislation administered by that institution, as if that legislation applied to him during his last employment.

If the period of full unemployment in the country of residence of the person concerned can be taken into account only if contribution periods have been completed in that country, this condition shall be deemed to be fulfilled if the contribution periods have been completed in another Member State.

Article 46. Award of benefits

1. Where the conditions required by the legislation of a Member State for entitlement to benefits have been satisfied without having to apply Art. 45 or Art. 40 (3), the following rules shall apply:

(a) the competent institution shall calculate the amount of the benefit that would be due:
   (i) on the one hand, only under the provisions of the legislation which it administers;
   (ii) on the other hand, pursuant to paragraph 2;
(b) the competent institution may, however, waive the calculation to be carried out in accordance with (a) (ii) if the result of this calculation, apart from differences arising from the use of round figures, is equal to or lower than the result of the calculation carried out in accordance with (a) (i), in so far as that institution does not apply any legislation containing rules against overlapping as referred to in Arts 46b and 46c or if the aforementioned institution applies a legislation containing rules against overlapping in the case referred to in Art. 46c, provided that the said legislation lays down that benefits of a different kind shall be taken into consideration only on the basis of the relation of the periods of insurance or of residence completed under that legislation alone to the periods of insurance or of residence required by that legislation in order to qualify for full benefit entitlement. Annex IV, part C, lists for each Member State concerned the cases where the two calculations would lead to a result of this kind.

2. Where the conditions required by the legislation of a Member State for entitlement to benefits are satisfied only after application of Art. 45 and/or Art. 40 (3), the following rules shall apply:

(a) the competent institution shall calculate the theoretical amount of the benefit to which the person concerned could lay claim provided all periods of insurance and/or of residence, which have been completed under the legislations of the Member States to which the employed person or self-employed person was subject, have been completed in the State in question under the legislation which it administers on the date of the award of the benefit. If, under this legislation, the amount of the benefit is independent of the duration of the periods completed, the amount shall be regarded as being the theoretical amount referred to in this paragraph;

(b) the competent institution shall subsequently determine the actual amount of the benefit on the basis of the theoretical amount referred to in the preceding paragraph in accordance with the ratio of the duration of the periods of insurance or of residence completed before the materialisation of the risk under the legislation which it administers to the total duration of the periods of insurance and of residence completed before the materialisation of the risk under the legislations of all the Member States concerned.

3. The person concerned shall be entitled to the highest amount calculated in accordance with paragraphs 1 and 2 from the competent institution of each Member State without prejudice to any application of the provisions concerning reduction, suspension or withdrawal provided for by the legislation under which this benefit is due.

Where that is the case, the comparison to be carried out shall relate to the amounts determined after the application of the said provisions.

4. When, in the case of invalidity, old-age or survivor's pensions, the total of the benefits due from the competent institutions of two or more Member States under the provisions of a multilateral social security convention referred to in Art. 6 (b) does not exceed the total which would be due from such Member States under paragraphs 1 to 3, the person concerned shall benefit from the provisions of this Chapter.

Article 46a. General provisions relating to reduction, suspension or withdrawal applicable to benefits in respect of invalidity, old age or survivors under the legislations of the Member States.

1. For the purposes of this Chapter, overlapping of benefits of the same kind shall have the following meaning: all overlapping of benefits in respect of invalidity, old age and survivors calculated or provided on the basis of periods of insurance and/or residence completed by one and the same person.

2. For the purposes of this Chapter, overlapping of benefits of different kinds means all overlapping of benefits that cannot be regarded as being of the same kind within the meaning of paragraph 1.

3. The following rules shall be applicable for the application of provisions on reduction, suspension or withdrawal laid down by the legislation of a Member State in the case of overlapping of a benefit in respect of invalidity, old age or survivors with a benefit of the same kind or a benefit of a different kind or with other income:

(a) account shall be taken of the benefits acquired under the legislation of another Member State or of other income acquired in another Member State only where the legislation of the first Member State provides for the taking into account of benefits or income acquired abroad;

(b) account shall be taken of the amount of benefits to be granted by another Member State before deduction of taxes, social security contributions and other individual levies or deductions;

(c) no account shall be taken of the amount of benefits acquired under the legislation of another Member State which are awarded on the basis of voluntary insurance or continued optional insurance;

(d) where provisions on reduction, suspension or withdrawal are applicable under the legislation of only one Member State on account of the fact that the person concerned receives benefits of a similar or different kind payable under the legislation of other Member States or other income acquired within the territory of other Member States, the benefit payable under the legislation of the first Member State may be reduced only within the limit of the amount of the benefits payable under the legislation or the income acquired within the territory of other Member States.

Article 46b.   Special provisions applicable in the case of overlapping of benefits of the same kind under the legislation of two or more Member States

1. The provisions on reduction, suspension or withdrawal laid down by the legislation of a Member State shall not be applicable to a benefit calculated in accordance with Art. 46 (2).

2. The provisions on reduction, suspension or withdrawal laid down by the legislation of a Member State shall apply to a benefit calculated in accordance with Art. 46 (1) (a) (i) only if the benefit concerned is;

(a) either a benefit, which is referred to in Annex IV, part D, the amount of which does not depend on the length of the periods of insurance or of residence completed, or

(b) a benefit, the amount of which is determined on the basis of a credited period deemed to have been completed between the date on which the risk materialised and a later date. In the latter case, the said provisions shall apply in the case of overlapping of such a benefit:

(i) either with a benefit of the same kind, except where an agreement has been concluded between two or more Member States providing that one and the same credited period may not be taken into account two or more times;

(ii) or with a benefit of the type referred to in (a).

The benefits and agreements referred to in (b) are mentioned in Annex IV, part D.

Article 46c. Special provisions applicable in the case of overlapping of one or more benefits referred to in Art. 46a (1) with one or more benefits of a different kind or with other income, where two or more Member States are concerned

1. If the receipt of benefits of a different kind or other income entails the reduction, suspension or withdrawal of two or more benefits referred to in Art. 46 (1) (a) (i), the amounts which would not be paid in strict application of the provisions concerning reduction, suspension or withdrawal provided for by the legislation of the Member States concerned shall be divided by the number of benefits subject to reduction, suspension or withdrawal.

2. Where the benefit in question is calculated in accordance with Art. 46 (2), the benefit or benefits of a different kind from other Member States or other income and all other elements provided for by the legislation of the Member State for the application of the provisions in respect of reduction, suspension or withdrawal shall be taken into account in proportion to the periods of insurance and/or residence referred to in Art. 46 (2) (b), and shall be used for the calculation of the said benefit.

3. If the receipt of benefits of a different kind or of other income entails the reduction, suspension or withdrawal of one or more benefits referred to in Art. 46 (1) (a) (i), and of one or more benefits referred to in Art. 46 (2), the following rules shall apply:

(a) where in a case of a benefit or benefits referred to in Art. 46 (1) (a) (i), the amounts which would not be paid in strict application of the provisions concerning reduction, suspension or withdrawal provided for by the legislation of the Member States concerned shall be divided by the number of benefits subject to reduction, suspension or withdrawal;

(b) where in a case of a benefit or benefits calculated in accordance with Art. 46 (2), the reduction, suspension or withdrawal shall be carried out in accordance with paragraph 2.

4. Where, in the cases referred to in paragraph 1 and 3(a), the legislation of a Member State provides that, for the application of provisions concerning reduction, suspension or withdrawal, account shall be taken of benefits of a different kind and/or other income and all other elements in proportion to the periods of insurance referred to in Art. 46 (2) (b), the division provided for in the same paragraphs shall not apply in respect of that Member State.

5. All the abovementioned provisions shall apply *mutatis mutandis* where the legislation of one or more Member States provides that the right to a benefit cannot be acquired in the case where the person concerned is in receipt of a benefit of a different kind, payable under the legislation of another Member State, or of other income.

Article 47. Additional provisions for the calculation of benefits

1. For the calculation of the theoretical and pro rata amounts referred to in Art. 46 (2), the following rules shall apply:

(a) where the total length of the periods of insurance and of residence completed before the risk materialised under the legislations of all the Member States concerned is longer than the maximum period required by the legislation of one of these States for receipt of full benefit, the competent institution of that State shall take into consideration this maximum period instead of the total length of the periods completed; this method of calculation must not result in the imposition on that institution of the cost of a benefit greater than the full benefit provided for by the legislation which it administers. This provision shall not apply to benefits, the amount of which does not depend on the length of insurance;

(b) the procedure for taking account of overlapping periods is laid down in the implementing Regulation referred to in Art. 98;

(c) where, under the legislation of a Member State, benefits are calculated on the basis of average earnings, an average contribution, an average increase or on the relation which existed, during the periods of insurance, between the claimant's gross earnings and the average gross earnings of all insured persons other than apprentices, such average figures or relations shall be determined by the competent institution of that State solely on the basis of the periods of insurance completed under the legislation of the said State, or the gross earnings received by the person concerned during those periods only;

(d) where, under the legislation of a Member State, benefits are calculated on the basis of the amount of earnings, contributions or increases, the competent institution of that State shall determine the earnings, contributions and increases to be taken into account in respect of the periods of insurance or residence completed under the legislation of other Member States on the basis of the average earnings, contributions or increases recorded in respect of the periods of insurance completed under the legislation which it administers;

(c) where, under the legislation of a Member State, benefits are calculated on the basis of standard earnings or a fixed amount, the competent institution of that State shall consider the standard earnings or the fixed amount to be taken into account by it in respect of periods of insurance or residence completed under the legislations of other Member States as being equal to the standard earnings or fixed amount or, where appropriate, to the average of the standard earnings or the fixed amount corresponding to the periods of insurance completed under the legislation which it administers;

(f) where, under the legislation of a Member State, benefits are calculated for some periods on the basis of the amount of earnings and, for other periods, on the basis of standard earnings or a fixed amount, the competent institution of that State shall, in respect of periods of insurance or residence completed under the legislations of other Member States, take into account the earnings or fixed amounts determined in accordance with the provisions referred to in (d) or (e) or, as appropriate, the average of these earnings or fixed amounts, where benefits are calculated on the basis of standard earnings or a fixed amount for all the periods completed under the legislation which it administers, the competent institution shall consider the earnings to be taken into account in respect of the periods of insurance or residence completed under the legislations of other Member States as being equal to the national earnings corresponding to the standard earnings or fixed amount;

(g) where, under the legislation of a Member State, benefits are calculated on the basis of average contributions, the competent institution shall determine that average by reference only to those periods of insurance completed under the legislation of the said State.

2. The provisions of the legislation of a Member State concerning the revalorisation of the factors taken into account for the calculation of benefits shall apply, as appropriate, to the factors to be taken into account by the competent institution of that State, in accordance with paragraph 1, in respect of the periods of insurance or residence completed under the legislation of other Member States.

3. If, under the legislation of a Member State, the amount of benefits is determined taking into account the existence of members of the family other than children, the competent institution of that State shall also take into consideration those members of the family of the person concerned who are residing in the territory of another Member State as if they were residing in the territory of the competent State.

4. If the legislation which the competent institution of a Member State administers requires a salary to be taken into account for the calculation of benefits, where the first and second subparagraphs of art. 45 (6) have been applied, and if, in this Member State, only periods of full unemployment with benefit in accordance with Art. 71 (1) (a) (ii) or the first sentence of Art. 71 (1) (b) (ii) are taken into consideration for the payment of pensions, the competent institution of that Member State shall pay the pension on the basis of the salary it used as the reference for providing that unemployment benefit in accordance with the legislation which it administers.

Article 48.   Periods of insurance or of residence of less than one year
   1. Notwithstanding Art. 46 (2), the institution of a Member State shall not be required to award benefits in respect of periods completed under the legislation it administers, which are taken into account when the risk materialises, if:

– the duration of the said periods does not amount to one year, and
– taking only these periods into consideration, no right to benefit is acquired by virtue of the provisions of that legislation.

   2. The competent institution of each of the Member States concerned shall take into account the periods referred to in paragraph 1, for the purposes of applying Art. 46 (2) excepting subparagraph (b).
   3. If the effect of applying paragraph 1 would be to relieve all the institutions of the Member States concerned of their obligations, benefits shall be awarded exclusively under the legislation of the last of those States whose conditions are satisfied, as if all the periods of insurance and residence completed and taken into account in accordance with Art. 45 (1) to (4) had been completed under the legislation of that State.

Article 49.   Calculation of benefits where the person concerned does not simultaneously satisfy the conditions laid down by all the legislations under which periods of insurance or of residence have been completed or when he has expressly requested a postponement of the award of old-age benefits.
   1. If, at a given time, the person concerned does not satisfy the conditions laid down for the provision of benefits by all the legislations of the Member States to which he has been subject, taking into account where appropriate Art. 45 and/or Art. 40 (3), but satisfies the conditions of one or more of them only, the following provisions shall apply:

(a) each of the competent institutions administering a legislation whose conditions are satisfied shall calculate the amount of the benefit due, in accordance with Art. 46;

(b) however:

    (i) if the person concerned satisfies the conditions of at least two legislations without having recourse to periods of insurance or residence completed under the legislations whose conditions are not satisfied, these periods shall not be taken into account for the purposes of Art. 46 (2);

   (ii) if the person concerned satisfies the conditions of only one legislation without having recourse to periods of insurance or residence completed under the legislations whose conditions are not satisfied, the amount of the benefit payable shall be calculated in accordance with the provisions only of that legislation whose conditions are satisfied, taking account of the periods completed under that legislation only.

The provisions of this paragraph shall apply *mutatis mutandis* where the person concerned has expressly requested the postponement of the award of old-age benefits, in accordance with the second sentence of Art. 44 (2).

2. The benefit or benefits awarded under one or more of the legislations in question, in the case referred to in paragraph 1, shall be recalculated automatically in accordance with Art. 46, as and when the conditions required by one or more of the other legislations to which the person concerned has been subject are satisfied, taking into account, where appropriate, Art. 45 and taking into account once again, where appropriate, paragraph 1. This paragraph shall apply *mutatis mutandis* where a person requests the award of old-age benefits acquired under the legislation of one or more Member States which had until then been postponed in accordance with the second sentence of Art. 44 (2).

3. A recalculation shall automatically be made in accordance with paragraph 1, without prejudice to Art. 40 (2), where the conditions required by one or more of the legislations concerned are no longer satisfied.

Article 50. Award of a supplement where the total of benefits payable under the legislations of the various Member States does not amount to the minimum laid down by the legislation of the State in whose territory the recipient resides.

A recipient of benefits to whom this Chapter applies may not, in the State in whose territory he resides and under whose legislation a benefit is payable to him, be awarded a benefit which is less than the minimum benefit fixed by that legislation for a period of insurance or residence equal to all the periods of insurance taken into account for the payment in accordance with the preceding Articles. The competent institution of that State shall, if necessary, pay him throughout the period of his residence in its territory a supplement equal to the difference between the total of the benefits payable under this Chapter and the amount of the minimum benefit.

Article 51. Revalorisation and recalculation of benefits

1. If, by reason of an increase in the cost of living or changes in the level of wages or salaries or other reasons for adjustment, the benefits of the States concerned are altered by a fixed percentage or amount, such percentage or amount must be applied directly to the benefits determined under Art. 46, without the need for a recalculation in accordance with that Article.

2. On the other hand, if the method of determining benefits or the rules for calculating benefits should be altered, a recalculation shall be carried out in accordance with Art. 46.

CHAPTER 6. UNEMPLOYMENT

Section 1. Common provisions

Article 67. Aggregation of periods of insurance or employment

1. The competent institution of a Member State whose legislation makes the acquisition, retention or recovery of the right to benefits subject to the completion periods of insurance shall take into account, to the extent necessary, periods of insurance or employment completed as an employed person under the legislation of any other Member State, as though they were periods of insurance completed under the legislation which it administers, provided, however, that the periods of employment would have been counted as periods of insurance had they been completed under that legislation.

2. The competent institution of a Member State whose legislation makes the acquisition, retention or recovery of the right to benefits subject to the completion of periods of employment shall take into account, to the extent necessary, periods of insurance or employment completed as an employed person under the legislation of any other Member State, as though they were periods of employment completed under the legislation which it administers.

3. Except in the cases referred to in Art. 71 (1) (a) (ii) and (b) (ii)[5], application of the provisions of paragraphs 1 and 2 shall be subject to the condition that the person concerned should have completed lastly:

– in the case of paragraph 1, periods of insurance,
– in the case of paragraph 2, periods of employment,

---

[5] [Referring to certain cases of unemployed persons residing in a Member State other than the competent State during their last employment. Ed.]

in accordance with the provisions of the legislation under which the benefits are claimed.

4. Where the length of the period during which benefits may be granted depends on the length of periods of insurance or employment, the provisions of paragraph 1 or 2 shall apply, as appropriate.

Article 68. Calculation of benefits

1. The competent institution of a Member State whose legislation provides that the calculation of benefits should be based on the amount of the previous wage or salary shall take into account exclusively the wage or salary received by the person concerned in respect of his last employment in the territory of that State. However, if the person concerned had been in his last employment in that territory for less than four weeks, the benefits shall be calculated on the basis of the normal wage or salary corresponding, in the place where the unemployed person is residing or staying, to an equivalent or similar employment to his last employment in the territory of another Member State.

2. The competent institution of a Member State whose legislation provides that the amount of benefits varies with the number of members of the family, shall take into account also members of the family of the person concerned who are residing in the territory of another Member State, as though they were residing in the territory of the competent State. This provision shall not apply if, in the country of residence of the members of the family, another person is entitled to unemployment benefits for the calculation of which the members of the family are taken into consideration.

Section 2. Unemployed persons going to a Member State other than the competent State

Article 69. Conditions and limits for the retention of the right to benefits

1. An employed or self-employed person who is wholly unemployed and who satisfies the conditions of the legislation of a Member State for entitlement to benefits and who goes to one or more other Member States in order to seek employment there shall retain his entitlement to such benefits under the following conditions and within the following limits:

(a) before his departure, he must have been registered as a person seeking work and have remained available to the employment services of the competent State for at least four weeks after becoming unemployed. However, the competent services or institutions may authorise his departure before such time has expired;

(b) he must register as a person seeking work with the employment services of each of the Member States to which he goes and be subject to the control procedure organised therein. This condition shall be considered satisfied for the period before registration if the person concerned registered within seven days of the date when he ceased to be available to the employment services of the State he left. In exceptional cases, this period may be extended by the competent services or institutions;

(c) entitlement to benefits shall continue for a maximum period of three months from the date when the person concerned ceased to be available to the employment services of the State which he left, provided that the total duration of the benefits does not exceed the duration of the period of benefits he was entitled to under the legislation of that State. In the case of a seasonal worker such duration shall, moreover, be limited to the period remaining until the end of the season for which he was engaged.

2. If the person concerned returns to the competent State before the expiry of the period during which he is entitled to benefits under the provisions of paragraph 1 (c), he shall continue to be entitled to benefits under the legislation of that State; he shall lose all entitlement to benefits under the legislation of the competent State if he does not return there before the expiry of that period. In exceptional cases, this time limit may be extended by the competent services or institutions.

3. The provisions of paragraph 1 may be invoked only once between two periods of employment.

4. Where the competent State is Belgium, an unemployed person who returns there after the expiry of the three month period laid down in paragraph 1 (c), shall not requalify for benefits in that country until he has been employed there for at least three months.

Article 70. Provision of benefits and reimbursements

1. In the cases referred to in Art. 69 (1), benefits shall be provided by the institution of each of the States to which an unemployed person goes to seek employment.

The competent institution of the Member State to whose legislation an employed or self-employed person was subject at the time of his last employment shall be obliged to reimburse the amount of such benefits.

2. The reimbursements referred to in paragraph 1 shall be determined and made in accordance with the procedure laid down by the implementing Regulation referred to in Art. 98, on proof of actual expenditure, or by lump-sum payments.

3. Two or more Member States, or the competent authorities of those States, may provide for other methods of reimbursement or payment, or may waive all reimbursement between the institutions coming under their jurisdiction.

[Provisions omitted.]

Article 93. Rights of institutions responsible for benefits against liable third parties

1. If a person receives benefits under the legislation of one Member State in respect of an injury resulting from an occurrence in the territory of another State, any rights of the institution responsible for benefits against a third party bound to compensate for the injury shall be governed by the following rules:

(a) where the institution responsible for benefits is, by virtue of the legislation which is administers, subrogated to the rights which the recipient has against the third party, such subrogation shall be recognised by each Member State;
(b) where the said institution has direct rights against the third party, such rights shall be recognised by each Member State.

2. If a person receives benefits under the legislation of one Member State in respect of an injury resulting from an occurrence in the territory of another Member State, the provisions of the said legislation which determine in which cases the civil liability of employers or of their employees is to be excluded shall apply with regard to the said person or to the competent institution.

The provisions of paragraph 1 shall also apply to any rights of the institution responsible for benefit against an employer or the persons employed by him in cases where their liability is not excluded.

[Remainder of Regulation, and Annexes, omitted.]

Other Rights of Residence

Council Directive of 28 June 1990 on the right of residence for employees and self-employed persons who have ceased their occupational activity (90/365/EEC)[1]

The Council of the European Communities,
Having regard to the Treaty establishing the European Economic Community, and in particular Art. 235 thereof,

[Provisions omitted.]

Whereas Art. 3 (c) of the Treaty provides that the activities of the Community shall include, as provided in the Treaty, the abolition, as between Member States, of obstacles to freedom of movement for persons;
Whereas Art. 8a of the Treaty provides that the internal market must be established by 31 December 1992; whereas the internal market comprises an area without internal frontiers in which the free movement of goods, persons, services and capital is ensured, in accordance with the provisons of the Treaty;
Whereas Arts. 48 and 52 of the Treaty provide for freedom of movement for workers and self-employed persons, which entails the right of residence in the Member States in which they pursue their occupational activity; whereas it is desirable that this right of residence also be granted to persons who have ceased their occupational activity even if they have not exercise their right to freedom of movement during their working life;
Whereas beneficiaries of the right of residence must not become an unreasonable burden on the public finances of the host Member State;
Whereas under Art. 10 of Regulation (EEC) No 1408/71,[2] as amended by Regulation (EEC) No 1390/81,[3] recipients of invalidity or old age cash benefits or pensions for accidents at work or occupational diseases are entitled to continue to receive these benefits and pensions even if they reside in the territory of a Member State other than that in which the institution responsible for payment is situated;
Whereas this right can only be genuinely exercised if it is also granted to members of the family;

[1] OJ 1990 L 180/28.   [2] Sp. Ed. 1971 (II) p. 416, supra at p. 376.   [3] 1981 L 143/1.

Whereas the beneficiaries of this Directive should be covered by administrative arrangements similar to those laid down in particular by Directive 68/360/EEC[4] and Directive 64/221/EEC;[5]

Whereas the Treaty does not provide, for the action concerned, powers other than those of Art. 235,

Has adopted this Directive:

Article 1. 1. Member States shall grant the right of residence to nationals of Member States who have pursued an activity as an employee or self-employed person and to members of their families as defined in paragraph 2, provided that they are recipients of an invalidity or early retirement pension, or old age benefits, or of a pension in respect of an industrial accident or disease of an amount sufficient to avoid becoming a burden on the social security system of the host Member State during their period of residence and provided they are covered by sickness insurance in respect of all risks in the host Member State.

The resources of the applicant shall be deemed sufficient where they are higher than the level of resources below which the host Member State may grant social assistance to its nationals, taking into account the personal circumstances of persons admitted pursuant to paragraph 2.

Where the second subparagraph cannot be applied in a Member State, the resources of the applicant shall be deemed sufficient if they are higher than the level of the minimum social security pension paid by the host Member State.

2. The following shall, irrespective of their nationality, have the right to install themselves in another Member State with the holder of the right of residence:

(a) his or her spouse and their descendants who are dependants;
(b) dependent relatives in the ascending line of the holder of the right of residence and his or her spouse.

Article 2. 1. Exercise of the right of residence shall be evidenced by means of the issue of a document known as a 'Residence permit for a national of a Member State of the EEC', whose validity may be limited to five years on a renewable basis. However, the Member States may, when they deem it to be necessary, require revalidation of the permit at the end of the first two years of residence. Where a member of the family does not hold the nationality of a Member State, he or she shall be issued with a residence document of the same validity as that issued to the national on whom he or she depends.

---

[4] OJ Sp. Ed. 1968 (II), p. 485, supra at p. 295.
[5] OJ Sp. Ed., 1963–4, p. 117, supra at p. 304.

For the purposes of issuing the residence permit or document, the Member State may require only that the applicant present a valid identity card or passport and provide proof that he or she meets the conditions laid down in Art. 1.

2. Arts. 2, 3, 6 (1) (a) and 2 and Art. 9 of Directive 68/360/EEC shall apply *mutatis mutandis* to the beneficiaries of this Directive.

The spouse and the dependent children of a national of a Member State entitled to the right of residence within the territory of a Member State shall be entitled to take up any employed or self-employed activity anywhere within the territory of that Member State, even if they are not nationals of a Member State.

Member States shall not derogate from the provisions of this Directive save on grounds of public policy, public security or public health. In that event, Directive 64/221/EEC shall apply.

3. This Directive shall not affect existing law on the acquisition of second homes.

Article 3. The right of residence shall remain for as long as beneficiaries of that right fulfil the conditions laid down in Art. 1.

Article 4. The Commission shall, not more than three years after the date of implementation of this Directive, and at three-yearly intervals thereafter, draw up a report on the application of this Directive and submit it to the European Parliament and the Council.

[Final provisions omitted.]

Council Directive of 28 June 1990
on the right of residence for students
(90/366/EEC)[6]

The Council of the European Communities,

Having regard to the Treaty establishing the European Economic Community, and in particular Art. 235 thereof,

[Recitals omitted.]

Whereas Art. 3 (c) of the Treaty provides that the activities of the Community shall include, as provided in the Treaty, the abolition, as between Member States, of obstacles to freedom of movement for persons;

[6] OJ 1990 L 180/30 Legal basis of Art. 235 challenged successfully in the Case C-295/90 *Parliament* v. *Council* [1992] ECR I – 4193.

Whereas Art. 8a of the Treaty provides that the internal market must be established by 31 December 1992; whereas the internal market comprises an area without internal frontiers in which the free movement of goods, persons, services and capital is ensured in accordance with the provisions of the Treaty;

Whereas, as the Court of Justice has ruled, Arts. 128 and 7 of the Treaty prohibit any discrimination between nationals of the Member States as regards access to vocational training in the Community;

Whereas the right of residence for students forms part of a set of related measures designed to promote vocational training;

Whereas beneficiaries of the right of residence must not become an unreasonable burden on the public finances of the host Member State;

Whereas, in the present state of Community law, assistance granted to students, as established by the case law of the Court of Justice, does not fall within the scope of the Treaty within the meaning of Art. 7 thereof;

Whereas it is necessary for the Member States to adopt administrative measures to facilitate residence without discrimination;
whereas the right of residence can only be genuinely exercised if it is granted to the spouse and their dependent children;

Whereas the beneficiaries of this Directive should be covered by administrative arrangements similar to those laid down in particular in Directive 68/360/EEC[7] and Directive 64/221/EEC;[8]

Whereas this Directive does not apply to students who enjoy the right of residence by virtue of the fact that they are or have been effectively engaged in economic activities or are members of the family of a migrant worker;

Whereas the Treaty does not provide, for the action concerned, powers other than those of Art. 235,

Has adopted this Directive:

Article 1. Member States shall, in order to facilitate access to vocational training, grant the right of residence to any student who is a national of a Member State and who does not enjoy this right under other provisions of Community law, and to the student's spouse and their dependent children, where the student assures the relevant national authority, by means of a declaration or by such alternative means as the student may choose that are at least equivalent, that he has sufficient resources to avoid becoming a burden on the social assistance system of the host Member State during their period of residence, provided that the student is enrolled in a recognized educational establishment for the principal purpose of following a vocational training course there and that they are

---

[7] See Note 3, supra at p. 406.   [8] See Note 4, supra at p. 407.

covered by sickness insurance in respect of all risks in the host Member State.

Article 2.   1. The right of residence shall be restricted to the duration of the course of studies in question.

The right of residence shall be evidenced by means of the issue of a document known as a 'Residence permit for a national of a Member State of the EEC', the validity of which may be limited to the duration of the course of studies or to one year where the course lasts longer; in the latter event it shall be renewable annually. Where a member of the family does not hold the nationality of a Member State, he or she shall be issued with a residence document of the same validity as that issued to the national on whom he or she depends.

For the purpose of issuing the residence permit or document, the Member State may require only that the applicant present a valid identity card or passport and provide proof that he or she meets the conditions laid down in Art. 1.

2. Arts. 2, 3 and 9 of Directive 68/360/EEC shall apply *mutatis mutandis* to the beneficiaries of this Directive.

The spouse and the dependent children of a national of a Member State entitled to the right of residence within the territory of a Member State shall be entitled to take up any employed or self-employed activity anywhere within the territory of that Member State, even if they are not nationals of a Member State.

Member States shall not derogate from the provisions of this Directive save on grounds of public policy, public security or public health: in that event, Arts. 2 to 9 of Directive 64/221/EEC shall apply.

Article 3. This Directive shall not establish any entitlement to the payment of maintenance grants by the host Member State on the part of students benefiting from the right of residence.

Article 4. The right of residence shall remain for as long as beneficiaries of that right fulfil the conditions laid down in Art. 1.

Article 5. The Commission shall, not more than three years after the date of implementation of this Directive, and at three-yearly intervals thereafter, draw up a report on the application of this Directive and submit it to the European Parliament and the Council.

The Commission shall pay particular attention to any difficulties to which the implementation of Art. 1 might give rise in the Member States; it shall, if appropriate, submit proposals to the Council with the aim of remedying such difficulties.

[Final provisions omitted.]

Council Directive of 28 June 1990
on the right of residence (90/364/EEC)[9]

The Council of the European Communities,

Having regard to the Treaty establishing the European Economic Community, and in particular Art. 235 thereof,

[Recitals omitted.]

Whereas Art. 3 (c) of the Treaty provides that the activities of the Community shall include, as provided in the Treaty, the abolition, as between Member States, of obstacles to freedom of movement for persons;

Whereas Art. 8a of the Treaty provides that the internal market must be established by 31 December 1992; whereas the internal market comprises an area without internal frontiers in which the free movement of goods, persons, services and capital is ensured in accordance with the provisions of the Treaty;

Whereas national provisions on the right of nationals of the Member States to reside in a Member State other than their own must be harmonised to ensure such freedom of movement;

Whereas beneficiaries of the right of residence must not become an unreasonable burden on the public finances of the host Member State;

Whereas this right can only be genuinely exercised if it is also granted to members of the family;

Whereas the beneficiaries of this Directive should be covered by administrative arrangements similar to those laid down in particular in Directive 68/360/EEC[10] and Directive 64/221/EEC;[11]

Whereas the Treaty does not provide, for the action concerned, powers other than those of Art. 235,

Has adopted this Directive:

Article 1. 1. Member States shall grant the right of residence to nationals of Member Sttes who do not enjoy this right under the provisions of Community law and to members of their families as defined in paragraph 2, provided that they themselves and the members of their families are covered by sickness insurance in respect of all risks in the host Member State and have sufficient resources to avoid becoming a burden on the social assistance system of the host Member State during their period of residence.

---

[9] OJ 1990 L 180/26. [10] See Note 3, supra at p. 406.
[11] See Note 4, supra at p. 407

The resources referred to in the first subparagraph shall be deemed sufficient where they are higher than the level of resources below which the host Member State may grant social assistance to its nationals, taking into account the personal circumstances of the applicant and, where appropriate, the personal circumstances of persons admitted pursuant to paragraph 2.

Where the second subparagraph cannot be applied in a Member State, the resources of the applicant shall be deemed sufficient if they are higher than the level of the minimum social security pension paid by the host Member State.

2. The following shall, irrespective of their nationality, have the right to install themselves in another Member State with the holder of the right of residence:

(a) his or her spouse and their descendants who are dependants;
(b) dependent relatives in the ascending line of the holder of the right of residence and his or her spouse.

Article 2.   1. Exercise of the right of residence shall be evidenced by means of the issue of a document known as a 'Residence permit for a national of a Member State of the EEC, the validity of which may be limited to five years on a renewable basis. However, the Member States may, when they deem it to be necessary, require revalidation of the permit at the end of the first two years of residence. Where a member of the family does not hold the nationality of a Member State, he or she shall be issued with a residence document of the same validity as that issued to the national on whom he or she depends.

For the purpose of issuing the residence permit or document, the Member State may require only that the applicant present a valid identity card or passport and provide proof that he or she meets the conditions laid down in Art. 1.

2. Arts. 2, 3, 6 (1) (a) and (2) and Art. 9 of Directive 68/360/EEC shall apply *mutatis mutandis* to the beneficiaries of this Directive.

The spouse and the dependent children of a national of a Member State entitled to the right of residence within the territory of a Member State shall be entitled to take up any employed or self-employed activity anywhere within the territory of that Member State, even if they are not nationals of a Member State.

Member States shall not derogate from the provisions of this Directive save on grounds of public policy, public security or public health. In that event, Directive 64/221/EEC shall apply.

3. This Directive shall not affect existing law on the acquisition of second homes.

Article 3.   The right of residence shall remain for as long as beneficiaries of that right fulfil the conditions laid down in Art. 1.

Article 4. The Commission shall, not more than three years after the date of implementation of this Directive, and at three-yearly intervals thereafter, draw up a report on the application of this Directive and submit it to the European Parliament and the Council.

[Final provisions omitted.]

Public Works Contracts

Council Directive of 26 July 1971
concerning the co-ordination of procedures for the award
of public works contracts (71/305/EEC)[1]

The Council of the European Communities,

Having regard to the Treaty establishing the European Economic Community, and in particular Arts. 57 (2), 66 and 100 thereof;

Having regard to the General Programme for the abolition of restrictions on freedom of establishment,[2] and in particular Title IV B1 thereof,

Having regard to the General Programme for the abolition of restrictions on freedom to provide services,[3] and in particular Title V C (e) 1 thereof;

[Recitals omitted.]

Whereas the simultaneous attainment of freedom of establishment and freedom to provide services in respect of public works contracts awarded in Member States on behalf of the State, or regional or local authorities or other legal persons governed by public law entails not only the abolition of restrictions but also the co-ordination of national procedures for the award of public works contracts;

Whereas such co-ordination should take into account as far as possible the procedures and administrative practices in force in each Member State;

Whereas the Council, in a statement concerning the aforementioned General Programmes, has stressed that co-ordination should be based on the following principles: prohibition of technical specifications that have a discriminatory effect, adequate advertising of contracts, the fixing of objective criteria for participation and the introduction of a procedure of joint supervision to ensure the observation of these principles;

[Recitals omitted.]

Whereas to ensure development of effective competition in the field of public contracts it is necessary that contract notices drawn up by the

---

[1] As last amended by Dir. 92/456, OJ 1990 L 297/1, and as amended in particular by Dir. 89/440, OJ 1989 L 210/1.

[2] OJ No 2, 15. 1. 1962, p. 36/62. Supra, p. 310.

[3] OJ No 2, 15. 1. 1962, p. 32/62. Supra, p. 313.

authorities of Member States awarding contracts be advertised throughout the Community; whereas the information contained in these notices
must enable contractors established in the Community to determine
whether the proposed contracts are of interest to them; whereas, for this
purpose, it is appropriate to give them adequate information about the
services to be provided and the conditions attached thereto; whereas,
more particularly, in restricted procedures advertisement is intended to
enable contractors of Member States to express their interest in contracts
by seeking from the authorities awarding contracts invitations to tender
under the required conditions;

[Recital omitted.]

Has adopted this Directive:

TITLE I. GENERAL PROVISIONS

Article 1. for the purposes of this Directive:

(a) 'public works contracts' are contracts for pecuniary interest concluded
in writing between a contractor and a contracting authority as defined
in (b), which have as their object either the execution, or both the
execution and design, of works related to one of the activities referred
to in Annex II or a work defined in (c) below, or the execution by
whatever means of a work corresponding to the requirements
specified by the contracting authority;

(b) 'contracting authorities' shall be the State, regional or local authorities, bodies governed by public law, associations formed by one or
several of such authorities or bodies governed by public law.

A body governed by public law means any body:

– established for the specific purpose of meeting needs in the general
interest, not having an industrial or commercial character, and
having legal personality, and
– financed, for the most part, by the State, or regional or local
authorities, or other bodies governed by public law; or subject to
management supervision by those bodies; or having an administrative, managerial or supervisory board, more than half of whose
members are appointed by the State, regional or local authorities
or by other bodies governed by public law.

The lists of bodies or of categories of such bodies governed by
public law which fulfil the criteria referred to in the second subparagraph are set out in Annex I. These lists shall be as exhaustive as
possible and may be reviewed in accordance with the procedure laid

down in Art. 30b. To this end, Member States shall periodically notify the Commission of any changes to their lists of bodies and categories of bodies;

(c) a 'work' means the outcome of building or civil engineering works taken as a whole that is sufficient of itself to fulfil an economic and technical function;

(d) 'public works concession' is a contract of the same type as that indicated in (a) except for the fact that the consideration for the works to be carried out consists either solely in the right to exploit the construction or in this right together with payment;

(e) 'open procedures' are those national procedures whereby all interested contractors may submit tenders;

(f) 'restricted procedures' are those national procedures whereby only those contractors invited by the contracting authority may submit tenders;

(g) 'negotiated procedures' are those national procedures whereby contracting authorities consult contractors of their choice and negotiate the terms of the contract with one or more of them;

(h) a contractor who submits a tender shall be designated by the term 'tenderer' and one who has sought an invitation to take part in a restricted and negotiated procedure by the term 'candidate'.

Article 1a. 1. Member States shall take the necessary measures to ensure that the contracting authorities comply or ensure compliance with this Directive where they subsidise directly by more than 50% a works contract awarded by an entity other than themselves.

2. Paragraph 1 shall concern only contracts covered by Class 50, Group 502, of the NACE nomenclature and to contracts relating to building work for hospitals, facilities intended for sports, recreation and leisure, school and university buildings and buildings used for administrative purposes.

Article 1b. 1. Should contracting authorities conclude a public works concession contract as defined in Art. 1 (d), the advertising rules as described in Art. 12 (3), (6), (7) and (9) to (13), and in Art. 15a, shall apply to that contract when its value is not less than ECU 5,000,000.

2. The contracting authority may:

− either require the concessionaire to award contracts representing a minimum of 30% of the total value of the work for which the concession contract is to be awarded, to third parties, at the same time providing the option for candidates to increase this percentage. This minimum percentage shall be specified in the concession contract,

– or request the candidates for concession contracts to specify in their tenders the percentage, if any, of the total value of the work for which the concession contract is to be awarded which they intend to assign to third parties.

3. When the concessionaire is himself one of the authorities awarding contracts within the meaning of Art. 1 (b), he shall comply with the provisions of this Directive in the case of works to be carried out by third parties.

4. Member States shall take the necessary steps to ensure that a concessionaire other than an authority awarding contracts shall apply the advertising rules listed in Art. 12 (4), (6), (7), and (9) to (13), and in Art. 15b, in respect of the contracts which it awards to third parties when the value of the contracts is not less than ECU 5,000,000. Advertising rules shall not be applied where works contracts meet the conditions laid down in Art. 5 (3).

Undertakings which have formed a group in order to obtain the concession contract, or undertakings affiliated to them, shall not be regarded as third parties.

An 'affiliated undertaking' means any undertaking over which the concessionaire may exercise, directly or indirectly, a dominant influence or which may exercise a dominant influence over the concessionaire or which, in common with the concessionaire, is subject to the dominant influence of another undertaking by virtue of ownership, financial participation or the rules which govern it. A dominant influence on the part of an undertaking shall be presumed when, directly or indirectly in relation to another undertaking, it:

– holds the major part of the undertaking's subscribed capital, or
– controls the majority of the votes attaching to shares issued by the undertakings, or
– can appoint more than half of the members of the undertaking's administrative, managerial or supervisory body.

A comprehensive list of these undertakings shall be enclosed with the candidature for the concession. This list shall be brought up to date following any subsequent changes in the relationship between the undertaking.

Article 2. [Repealed]

Article 3. 1. [Repealed]
   2. [Repealed]
   3. [Repealed]
   4. This Directive shall not apply to contracts awarded in the fields

referred to in Arts. 2, 7, 8 and 9 of Council Directive 90/531/EEC of 17 September 1990 on the procurement procedures of entities operating in water, energy, transport and telecommunications sectors[4] or fulfilling the conditions in Art. 6 (2) of the said Directive.

5. [Repealed]

Article 4.   This Directive shall not apply to public contracts governed by different procedural rules and awarded:

(a) in pursuance of an international agreement, concluded in conformity with the EEC Treaty, between a Member State and one or more non-member countries and covering works intended for the joint implementation or exploitation of a project by the signatory States; all agreements shall be communicated to the Commission which may consult the Advisory Committee for Public Contracts set up by Decision 71/306/EEC,[5] as amended by Decision 77/63/EEC;[6]

(b) to undertakings in a Member State or a non-member country in pursuance of an international agreement relating to the stationing of troops;

(c) pursuant to the particular procedure of an international organisation.

Article 4a.   1. The provisions of this Directive shall apply to public works contracts whose estimated value net of VAT is not less than ECU 5,000,000.

2. (a) The value of the threshold in national currencies shall normally be revised every two years with effect from 1 January 1992. The calculation of this value shall be based on the average daily values of these currencies expressed in ecus over the 24 months terminating on the last day of August immediately preceding the 1 January revision. These values shall be published in the *Official Journal of the European Communities* at the beginning of November.

(b) The method of calculation laid down in subparagraph (a) shall be reviewed, on a proposal from the Commission, by the Advisory Committee for Public Contracts in principle two years after its initial application.

3. Where a work is subdivided into several lots, each one the subject of a contract, the value of each lot must be taken into account for the purpose of calculating the amounts referred to in paragraph 1. Where the aggregate value of the lots is not less than the amount referred to in paragraph 1, the provisions of that paragraph shall apply to all lots.

[4] OJ 1990, L 297/1.   [5] OJ No L 185, 16. 8. 1971, p. 15.   [6] OJ No 1977 L 13/15.

Contracting authorities shall be permitted to depart from this provision for lots whose estimated value net of VAT is less than ECU 1,000,000, provided that the total estimated value of all the lots exempted does not, in consequence, exceed 20% of the total estimated value of all lots.

4. No work or contract may be split up with the intention of avoiding the application of the preceding paragraphs.

5. When calculating the amounts referred to in paragraph 1 and in Art. 5, account shall be taken not only of the amount of the public works contracts but also of the estimated value of the supplies needed to carry out the works which are made available to the contractor by the contracting authorities.

Article 5.   1. In awarding public works contracts the contracting authorities shall apply the procedures defined in Art. 1 (e), (f) and (g), adapted to this Directive.

2. The contracting authorities may award their public works contracts by negotiated procedure, with prior publication of a tender notice and after having selected the candidates according to qualitative public criteria, in the following cases:

(a) in the event of irregular tenders in response to an open or restricted procedure or in the event of tenders which are unacceptable under national provisions that are in accordance with the provisions of Title IV, in so far as the original terms of the contract are not substantially altered. The contracting authorities shall not, in these cases, publish a tender notice where they include in such negotiated procedure all the enterprises satisfying the criteria of Arts. 23 to 28 which, during the prior open or restricted procedure, have submitted offers in accordance with the formal requirements of the tendering procedure;

(b) when the works involved are carried out purely for the purpose of research, experiment or development, and not to establish commercial viability or to recover research and development costs;

(c) in exceptional cases, when the nature of the works or the risks attaching thereto do not permit prior overall pricing.

3. The contracting authorities may award their public works contracts by negotiated procedure without prior publication of a tender notice, in the following cases:

(a) in the absence of tenders or of appropriate tenders in response to an open or restricted procedure in so far as the original terms of the contract are not substantially altered and provided that a report is communicated to the Commission at its request;

(b) when, for technical or artistic reasons or for reasons connected with

the protection of exclusive rights, the works may only be carried out
by a particular contractor;

(c) in so far as is strictly necessary when, for reasons of extreme urgency
brought about by events unforeseen by the contracting authorities in
question, the time limit laid down for the open, restricted or negotiated procedures referred to in paragraph 2 above cannot be kept. The
circumstances invoked to justify extreme urgency must not in any
event be attributable for the contracting authorities;

(d) for additional works not included in the project initially considered or
in the contract first concluded but which have, through unforeseen
circumstances, become necessary for the carrying out of the work
described therein, on condition that the award is made to the contractor carrying out such work:

    – when such works cannot be technically or economically separated
from the main contract without great inconvenience to the contracting authorities, or

    – when such works, although separable from the execution of the
original contract, are strictly necessary to its later stages,

however, the aggregate value of contracts awarded for additional
works may not exceed 50% of the amount of the main contract;

(e) for new works consisting of the repetition of similar works entrusted
to the undertaking to which the same contracting authorities awarded
an earlier contract, provided that such works conform to a basic project for which a first contract was awarded according to the procedures referred to in paragraph 4.

As soon as the first project is put up for tender, notice must be
given that this procedure might be adopted and the total estimated
cost of subsequent works shall be taken into consideration by the
contracting authorities when they apply the provisions of Art. 4a.
This procedure may only be applied during the three years following
the conclusion of the original contract.

4. In all other cases, the contracting authorities shall award their public works contracts by the open procedure or by the restricted procedure.

Article 5a   1. The contracting authority shall, within 15 days of the date
on which the request is received, inform any eliminated candidate or tenderer who so requests of the reasons for rejection of his application or his
tender, and, in the case of a tender, the name of the successful tenderer.

2. The contracting authority shall inform candidates or tenderers who
so request of the grounds on which it decided not to award a contract in
respect of which a prior call for competition was made, or to recom-

mence the procedure. It shall also inform the Office for Official Publications of the European Communities of that decision.

3. For each contract awarded the contracting authorities shall draw up a written report which shall include at least the following:

- the name and address of the contracting authority, the subject and value of the contract,
- the names of the candidates or tenderers admitted and the reasons for their selection,
- the names of the candidates or tenderers rejected and the reasons for their rejection,
- the name of the successful tenderer and the reasons for his tender having been selected and, if known, any share of the contract the successful tenderer may intend to subcontract to a third party,
  for negotiated procedures, the circumstances referred to in Art. 5 which justify the use of these procedures.

This report, or the main features of it, shall be communicated to the Community at its request.

Article 6. In the case of contracts relating to the design and construction of a public housing scheme whose size and complexity, and the estimated duration of the work involved, require that planning be based from the outset on close collaboration within a team comprising representatives of the authorities awarding contracts, experts and the contractor to be responsible for carrying out the works, a special award procedure may be adopted for selecting the contractor most suitable for integration into the team.

In particular, authorities awarding contracts shall include in the contract notice as accurate as possible a description of the works to be carried out so as to enable interested contractors to form a valid idea of the project. Furthermore, authorities awarding contracts shall, in accordance with the provisions of Arts. 23 to 28, set out in such contract notice the personal, technical and financial conditions to be fulfilled by candidates. Where such procedure is adopted, authorities awarding contracts shall apply the common advertising rules relating to restricted procedure and to the criteria for qualitative selection.

Article 7. [Repealed]

Article 8. [Repealed]

Article 9. [Repealed.

TITLE II. COMMON RULES IN THE TECHNICAL FIELD

Article 10. 1. The technical specifications defined in Annex III shall be given in the general or contractual documents relating to each contract.

2. Without prejudice to the legally binding national technical rules and in so far as these are compatible with Community law, such technical specifications shall be defined by the contracting authorities by reference to national standards implementing European standards, or by reference to European technical approvals or by reference to common technical specifications.

3. A contracting authority may depart from paragraph 2 if:

(a) the standards, European technical approvals or common technical specifications do not include any provision for establishing conformity, or technical means do not exist for establishing satisfactorily the conformity of a product to these standards, European technical approvals or common technical specifications;

(b) use of these standards, European technical approvals or common technical specifications would oblige the contracting authority to acquire products or materials incompatible with equipment already in use or would entail disproportionate costs or disproportionate technical difficulties, but only as part of a clearly defined and recorded strategy with a view to change-over, within a given period, to European standards, European technical approvals or common technical specifications;

(c) the project concerned is of a genuinely innovative nature for which use of existing European standards, European technical approvals or common technical specifications would not be appropriate.

4. Contracting authorities invoking paragraph 3 shall record, wherever possible, the reasons for doing so in the tender notice published in the *Official Journal of the European Communities* or in the contract documents and in all cases shall record these reasons in their internal documentation and shall supply such information on request to Member States and to the Commission.

5. In the absence of European standards or European technical approvals or common technical specifications, the technical specifications:

(a) shall be defined by reference to the national technical specifications recognised as complying with the basic requirements listed in the Community directives on technical harmonisation, in accordance with the procedures laid down in those directives, and in particular in accordance with the procedures laid down in Council Directive 89/106/EEC of 21 December 1988 on construction products;[7]

[7] OJ 1989 L 40/12.

(b) may be defined by reference to national technical specifications relating to design and method of calculation and execution of works and use of materials;

(c) may be defined by reference to other documents.

In this case, it is appropriate to make reference in order of preference to:

(i) national standards implementing international standards accepted by the country of the contracting authority;

(ii) other national standards and national technical approvals of the country of the contracting authority;

(iii) any other standard.

6. Unless such specifications are justified by the subject of the contract, Member States shall prohibit the introduction into the contractual clauses relating to a given contract of technical specifications which mention products of a specific make or source or of a particular process and which therefore favour or eliminate certain undertakings. In particular, the indication of trade marks, patents, types, or of a specific origin or production shall be prohibited. However, if such indication is accompanied by the words 'or equivalent', it shall be authorised in cases where the authorities awarding contracts are unable to give a description of the subject of the contract using specifications which are sufficiently precise and intelligible to all parties concerned.

Article 11. [Repealed]

TITLE III. COMMON ADVERTISING RULES

Article 12. 1. Contracting authorities shall make known, by means of an indicative notice, the essential characteristics of the works contracts which they intend to award and the estimated value of which is not less than the threshold laid down in Art. 41 (1).

2. Contracting authorities who wish to award a public works contract by open, restricted or negotiated procedure referred to in Art. 5 (2), shall make known their intention by means of a notice.

3. Contracting authorities who wish to award a works concession contract shall make known their intention by means of a notice.

4. Works concessionaires, other than a contracting authority, who wish to award a work contract to be carried out by third parties as defined in Art. 1b (4), shall make known their intention by means of a notice.

5. Contracting authorities who have awarded a contract shall make known the result by means of a notice. However, certain information on contract award may, in certain cases, not be published where release of

such information would impede law enforcement or otherwise be contrary to the public interest, would prejudice the legitimate commercial interests of particular enterprises, public or private, or might prejudice fair competition between contractors.

6. The contracting authorities shall send the notices referred to in the preceding paragraphs as rapidly as possible and by the most appropriate channels to the Office for Official Publications of the European Communities. In the case of the accelerated procedure referred to in Art. 15, the notice shall be sent by telex, telegram or telefax.

(a) The notice referred to in paragraph 1 shall be sent as soon as possible after the decision approving the planning of the works contracts that the contracting authorities intend to award;
(b) the notice referred to in paragraph 5 shall be sent at the latest 48 days after the award of the contract in question.

7. The notices referred to in paragraphs 1, 2, 3, 4 and 5 shall be drawn up in accordance with the models given in Annexes IV, V and VI, and shall specify the information requested in those Annexes.

In open, restricted and negotiated procedures, the contracting authorities may not require any conditions but those specified in Arts. 25 and 26 when requesting information concerning the economic and technical standards which they require of contractors for their selection (point 11 of Annex IV B, point 10 of Annex IV C and point 9 of Annex IV D).

8. The notices referred to in paragraphs 1 and 5 above shall be published in full in the *Official Journal of the European Communities* and in the TED data bank in the official languages of the Communities, the original text alone being authentic.

9. The notices referred to in paragraphs 2, 3 and 4 shall be published in full in the *Official Journal of the European Communities* and in the TED data bank in their original language. A summary of the important elements of each notice shall be published in the other official languages of the Community, the original text alone being authentic.

10. The Office for Official Publications of the European Communities shall publish the notices not later than 12 days after their dispatch. In the case of the accelerated procedure referred to in Art. 15, this period shall be reduced to five days.

11. The notice shall not be published in the official journals or in the press of the country of the contracting authority before the abovementioned date of dispatch, and it shall mention this date. It shall not contain information other than that published in the *Official Journal of the European Communities*.

12. The contracting authorities must be able to supply proof of the date of dispatch.

13. The cost of publication of the notices in the *Official Journal of the European Communities* shall be borne by the Communities. The length of the notice shall not be greater than one page of the Journal, or approximately 650 words. Each edition of the Journal containing one or more notices shall reproduce the model notice or notices on which the published notice or notices are based.

Article 13. 1. In open procedures the time limit for the receipt of tenders shall be fixed by the contracting authorities at not less than 52 days from the date of sending the notice.

2. The time limit for the receipt of tenders provided for in paragraph 1 may be reduced to 36 days where the contracting authorities have published a tender notice, drafted in accordance with the specimen in Annex IV A provided for in Art. 12 (1), in the *Official Journal of the European Communities*.

3. Provided they have been requested in good time, the contract documents and supporting documents must be sent to the contractors by the contracting authorities or competent departments within six days of receiving their application.

4. Provided it has been requested in good time, additional information relating to the contract documents shall be supplied by the contracting authorities not later than six days before the final date fixed for receipt of tenders.

5. Where the contract documents, supporting documents or additional information are too bulky to be supplied within the time limits laid down in paragraph 3 or 4 or where tenders can only be made after a visit to the site or after on-the-spot inspection of the documents supporting the contract documents, the time limits laid down in paragraphs 1 and 2 shall be extended accordingly.

Article 14. 1. In restricted procedures and negotiated procedures as described in Art. 5 (2), the time limit for receipt of requests to participate fixed by the contracting authorities shall be not less than 37 days from the date of dispatch of the notice.

2. The contracting authorities shall simultaneously and in writing invite the selected candidates to submit their tenders. The letter of invitation shall be accompanied by the contract documents and supporting documents. It shall include at least the following information:

(a) where appropriate, the address of the service from which the contract documents and supporting documents can be requested and the final date for making such a request; also the amount and terms of payment of any sum to be paid for such documents;

(b) the final date for receipt of tenders, the address to which they must be sent and the language or languages in which they must be drawn up:

(c) a reference to the contract notice published;

(d) an indication of any documents to be annexed, either to support the verifiable statements furnished by the candidate in accordance with Art. 12 (7), or to supplement the information provided for in that Article under the same conditions as those laid down in Art. 25 and 26;

(e) the criteria for the award of the contract if these are not given in the notice.

3. In restricted procedures, the time limit for receipt of tenders fixed by the contracting authorities may not be less than 40 days from the date of dispatch of the written invitation.

4. The time limit for receipt of tenders laid down in paragraph 3 may be reduced to 26 days where the contracting authorities have published the tender notice, drafted according to the specimen in Annex IV A provided for in Art. 12 (1), in the *Official Journal of the European Communities*.

5. Requests to participate in procedures for the award of contracts may be made by letter, by telegram, telex, telefax or by telephone. If by one of the last four, they must be confirmed by letter dispatched before the end of the period laid down in paragraph 1.

6. Provided it has been requested in good time, additional information relating to the contract documents must be supplied by the contracting authorities not later than six days before the final date fixed for the receipt of tenders.

7. Where tenders can only be made after a visit to the site or after on-the-spot inspection of the documents supporting the contract documents, the time limit laid down in paragraphs 3 and 4 shall be extended accordingly.

Article 15. 1. In cases where urgency renders impracticable the time limits laid down in Art. 14, the contracting authorities may fix the following time limits:

(a) a time limit for receipt of requests to participate which shall be not less than 15 days from the date of dispatch of the notice;

(b) a time limit for the receipt of tenders which shall be not less than 10 days from the date of the invitation to tender.

2. Provided it has been requested in good time, additional information relating to the contract documents must be supplied by the contracting authorities not later than four days before the final date fixed for the receipt of tenders.

3. Requests for participation in contracts and invitations to tender

must be made by the most rapid means of communication possible. When requests to participate are made by telegram, telex, telefax or telephone, they must be confirmed by letter dispatched before the expiry of the time limit referred to in paragraph 1.

Article 15a. Contracting authorities who wish to award a works concession contract as defined in Art. 1 (d) shall fix a time limit for receipt of candidatures for the concession, which shall not be less than 52 days from the date of dispatch of the notice.

Article 15b. In works contracts awarded by a concessionaire of works other than an authority awarding contracts, the time limit for the receipt of requests to participate shall be fixed by the concessionaire at not less than 37 days from the date of dispatch of the notice, and the time limit for the receipt of tenders at not less than 40 days from the date of dispatch of the notice or the invitation to tender.

Article 16. [Repealed]

Article 17. [Repealed]

Article 18. [Repealed]

Article 19. Contracting authorities may arrange for the publication in the *Official Journal of the European Communities* of notices announcing public works contracts which are not subject to the publication requirement laid down in this Directive.

TITLE IV. COMMON RULES ON PARTICIPATION

Article 20. Contracts shall be awarded on the basis of the criteria laid down in Chapter 2 of this Title, taking into account Art. 20a, after the suitability of the contractors not excluded under Art. 23 has been checked by the contracting authorities in accordance with the criteria of economic and financial standing and of technical knowledge or ability referred to in Arts. 25 to 28.

Article 20a. Where the criterion for the award of the contract is that of the most economically advantageous tender, contracting authorities may take account of variants which are submitted by a tenderer and meet the minimum specifications required by the contracting authorities.

The contracting authorities shall state in the contract documents the minimum specifications to be respected by the variants and any specific requirements for their presentation. They shall indicate in the tender notice whether variants will be considered.

Contracting authorities may not reject the submission of a variant on the sole grounds that it has been drawn up with technical specifications defined by reference to national standards transposing European standards, to European technical approvals or to common technical specifications referred to in Art. 10 (2) or again by reference to national technical specifications referred to in Art. 10 (5) (a) and (b).

Article 20b.   In the contract documents, the contracting authority may ask the tenderer to indicate in his tender any share of the contract he may intend to subcontract to third parties.

This indication shall be without prejudice to the question of the principal contractor's responsibility.

Article 21.   Tenders may be submitted by groups of contractors. These groups may not be required to assume a specific legal form in order to submit the tender; however, the group selected may be required to do so when it has been awarded the contract.

Article 22.   1. In restricted and negotiated procedures the contracting authorities shall, on the basis of information given relating to the contractor's personal position as well as to the information and formalities necessary for the evaluation of the minimum conditions of an economic and technical nature to be fulfilled by him, select from among the candidates with the qualifications required by Arts. 23 and 28 those whom they will invite to submit a tender or to negotiate.

2. Where the contracting authorities award a contract by restricted procedure, they may prescribe the range within which the number of undertakings which they intend to invite will fall. In this case the range shall be indicated in the contract notice. The range shall be determined in the light of the nature of the work to be carried out. The range must number at least 5 undertakings and may be up to 20.

In any event, the number of candidates invited to tender shall be sufficient to ensure genuine competition.

3. Where the contracting authorities award a contract by negotiated procedure as referred to in Art. 5 (2), the number of candidates admitted to negotiate may not be less than three provided that there is a sufficient number of suitable candidates.

4. Each Member State shall ensure that contracting authorities issue invitations without discrimination to those nationals of other Member States who satisfy the necessary requirements and under the same conditions as to its own nationals.

Article 22a.   1. The contracting authority may state in the contract documents, or be obliged by a Member State so to do, the authority or authorities from which a tenderer may obtain the appropriate information on the obligations relating to the employment protection provisions and the working conditions which are in force in the Member State, region or locality in which the works are to be executed and which shall be applicable to the works carried out on site during the performance of the contract.

2. The contracting authority which supplies the information referred to in paragraph 1 shall request the tenderers or those participating in the contract procedure to indicate that they have taken account, when drawing up their tender, of the obligations relating to employment protection provisions and the working conditions which are in force in the place where the work is to be carried out. This shall be without prejudice to the application of the provisions of Art. 29 (5) concerning the examination of abnormally low tenders.

CHAPTER 1. CRITERIA FOR QUALITATIVE SELECTION

Article 23. Any contractor may be excluded from participation in the contract who:

(a) is bankrupt or is being wound up, whose affairs are being administered by the court, who has entered into an arrangement with creditors, who has suspended business activities or who is in any analogous situation arising from a similar procedure under national laws and regulations;

(b) is the subject of proceedings for a declaration of bankruptcy, for an order for compulsory winding up or administration by the court or for an arrangement with creditors or of any other similar proceedings under national laws or regulations;

(c) has been convicted of an offence concerning his professional conduct by a judgment which has the force of *res judicata*;

(d) who has been guilty of grave professional misconduct proven by any means which the authorities awarding contracts can justify;

(e) has not fulfilled obligations relating to the payment of social security contributions in accordance with the legal provisions of the country in which he is established or with those of the country of the authority awarding contracts;

(f) has not fulfilled obligations relating to the payment of taxes in accordance with the legal provisions of the country of the authority awarding contracts;

(g) is guilty of serious misrepresentation in supplying the information required under this Chapter.

Where the authority awarding contracts requires of the contractor proof that none of the cases quoted in (a), (b), (c), (e) or (f) applies to him, it shall accept as sufficient evidence:

- for (a), (b) or (c), the production of an extract from the 'judicial record' or, failing this, of an equivalent document issued by a competent judicial or administrative authority in the country of origin or in the country whence that person comes showing that these requirements have been met;
- for (e) or (f), a certificate issued by the competent authority in the Member State concerned.

Where the country concerned does not issue such documents or certificates, they may be replaced by a declaration on oath (or, in Member States where there is no provision for declarations on oath, by a solemn declaration) made by the person concerned before a judicial or administrative authority, a notary or a competent professional or trade body, in the country of origin or in the country whence that person comes.

Member States shall, within the time limit laid down in Art. 32, designate the authorities and bodies competent to issue these documents and shall forthwith inform the other Member States and the Commission thereof.

Article 24. Any contractor wishing to take part in a public works contract may be requested to prove his enrolment in the professional or trade register under the conditions laid down by the laws of the Member State in which he is established:

- in Belgium, the registre du commerce—Handelsregister,
- in Denmark, the Erhvervs- og Selskabsstyrelsen,
- in Germany, the Handelsregister and the Handwerksrolle,
- in Greece, a declaration on the exercise of the profession of public works contractor made on oath before a notary may be required,
- in Spain, the Registro Oficial de Contratistas del Ministerio de Industria y Energia,
- in France, the registre du commerce and the répertoir des métiers,
- in Italy, the Registro della Camera di commercio, industria, agricoltura e artigianato,
- in Luxembourg, the registre aux firmes and the rôle de la Chambre des métiers,
- in the Netherlands, the Handelsregister,
- in Portugal, the Commissão de Alvarás de Empresas de Obras Públicas e Particulares (CAEOPP),
- in the United Kingdom and Ireland, the contractor may be requested to provide a certificate from the Registrar of Companies or the Registrar of Friendly Societies or, if this is not the case, a certificate stating that the person concerned has declared on oath that he is

engaged in the profession in question in the country in which he is established, in a specific place and under a given business name.

Article 25. Proof of the contractor's financial and economic standing may, as a general rule, be furnished by one or more of the following references:

(a) appropriate statements from bankers;
(b) the presentation of the firm's balance sheets or extracts from the balance sheets, where publication of the balance sheet is required under company law in the country in which the contractor is established;
(c) a statement of the firm's overall turnover and the turnover on construction works for the three previous financial years.

The authorities awarding contracts shall specify in the notice or in the invitation to tender which reference or references they have chosen and what references other than those mentioned under (a), (b) or (c) are to be produced.

If, for any valid reason, the contractor is unable to supply the references requested by the authorities awarding contracts, he may prove his economic and financial standing by any other document which the authorities awarding contracts consider appropriate.

Article 26. Proof of the contractor's technical knowledge or ability may be furnished by:

(a) the contractor's educational and professional qualifications and/or those of the firm's managerial staff, and, in particular, those of the person or persons responsible for carrying out the works;
(b) a list of the works carried out over the past five years, accompanied by certificates of satisfactory execution for the most important works. These certificates shall indicate the value, date and site of the works and shall specify whether they were carried out according to the rules of the trade and properly completed. Where necessary, the competent authority shall submit these certificates to the authority awarding contracts direct;
(c) a statement of the tools, plant and technical equipment available to the contractor for carrying out the work;
(d) a statement of the firm's average annual manpower and the number of managerial staff for the last three years;
(e) a statement of the technicians or technical divisions which the contractor can call upon for carrying out the work, whether or not they belong to the firm.

The authorities awarding contracts shall specify in the notice or in the invitation to tender which of these references are to be produced.

Article 27.   The authority awarding contracts may, within the limits of Arts. 23 to 26, invite the contractor to supplement the certificates and documents submitted or to clarify them.

Article 28.   1. Member States who have official lists of recognised contractors must, when this Directive enters into force, adapt them to the provisions of Art. 23 (a) to (d) and (g) and of Arts. 24 to 26.

2. Contractors registered in these lists may, for each contract, submit to the authority awarding contracts a certificate of registration issued by the competent authority. This certificate shall state the references which enabled them to be registered in the list and the classification given in this list.

3. Certified registration in such lists by the competent bodies shall, for the authorities of other Member States awarding contracts, constitute a presumption of suitability for works corresponding to the contractor's classification only as regards Arts. 23 (a) to (d) and (g), 24, 25 (b) and (c) and 26 (b) and (d) and not as regards Arts. 25 (a) and 26 (a), (c) and (e).

Information which can be deduced from registration in official lists may not be questioned. However, with regard to the payment of social security contributions, an additional certificate may be required of any registered contractor whenever a contract is offered.

The authorities of other Member States awarding contracts shall apply the above provisions only in favour of contractors who are established in the country holding the official list.

4. For the registration of contractors of other Member States in such a list, no further proofs and statements may be required other than those requested of nationals and, in any event, only those provided for under Arts. 23 to 26.

5. Member States holding an official list shall communicate to other Member States the address of the body to which requests for registration may be made.

CHAPTER II. CRITERIA FOR THE AWARD OF CONTRACTS

Article 29.   1. The criteria on which the authorities awarding contracts shall base the award of contracts shall be:

– either the lowest price only;
– or, when the award is made to the most economically advantageous tender, various criteria according to the contract: e.g. price, period for completion, running costs, profitability, technical merit.

2. In the latter instance, the authorities awarding contracts shall state in the contract documents or in the contract notice all the criteria they

intend to apply to the award, where possible in descending order of importance.

3. [Repealed]

4. Paragraph 1 shall not apply when a Member State bases the award of contracts on other criteria, within the framework of rules in force at the time of the adoption of this Directive whose aim is to give preference to certain tenderers, on condition that the rules invoked are compatible with the Treaty.

5. If, for a given contract, tenders appear to be abnormally low in relation to the transaction, before it may reject those tenders the contracting authority shall request, in writing, details of the constituent elements of the tender which it considers relevant and shall verify those constituent elements taking account of the explanations received.

The contracting authority may take into consideration explanations which are justified on objective grounds including the economy of the construction method, or the technical solutions chosen, or the exceptionally favourable conditions available to the tenderer for the execution of the work, or the originality of the work proposed by the tenderer.

If the documents relating to the contract provide for its award at the lowest price tendered, the contracting authority must communicate to the Commission the rejection of tenders which it considers to be too low.

However, until the end of 1992, if current national law so permits, the contracting authority may exceptionally, without any discrimination on grounds of nationality, reject tenders which are abnormally low in relation to the transaction, without being obliged to comply with the procedure provided for in the first subparagraph if the number of such tenders for a particular contract is so high that implementation of this procedure would lead to a considerable delay and jeopardize the public interest attaching to the execution of the contract in question. Recourse to this exceptional procedure shall be mentioned in the notice referred to in Art. 12 (5).

TITLE V. FINAL PROVISIONS

Article 29a. 1. Until 31 December 1992, this Directive shall not prevent the application of existing national provisions on the award of public works contracts which have as their objective the reduction of regional disparities and the promotion of job creation in regions whose development is lagging behind and in declining industrial regions, on condition that the provisions concerned are compatible with the Treaty, in particular with the principles of non-discrimination on grounds of nationality, freedom of establishment and freedom to provide services, and with the Community's international obligations.

2. Paragraph 1 shall be without prejudice to Art. 29 (4).

Article 29b.   1. Member States shall inform the Commission of national provisions covered by Art. 29 (4) and Art. 29a and of the rules for applying them.

2. Member States concerned shall forward to the Commission, every year, a report describing the implementation of these provisions. The reports shall be submitted to the Advisory Committee for Public Works Contracts.

Article 30.   The calculation of the time limit for receipt of tenders or requests to participate shall be made in accordance with Council Regulation (EEC, Euratom) No 1182/71 of 3 June 1971 determining the rules applicable to periods, dates and time limits.[8]

Article 30a.   1. In order to permit assessment of the results of applying the Directive, Member States shall forward to the Commission a statistical report on the contracts awarded by contracting authorities by 31 October 1993 at the latest for the preceding year and thereafter by 31 October of every second year.

Nevertheless, for the Hellenic Republic, the Kingdom of Spain and the Portuguese Republic, the date of 31 October 1993 shall be replaced by 31 October 1995.

2. This report shall detail at least the number and value of contracts awarded by each contracting authority or category of contracting authority above the threshold, subdivided as far as possible by procedure, category of work and the nationality of the contractor to whom the contract has been awarded, and in the case of negotiated procedures, subdivided in accordance with Art. 5, listing the number and value of the contracts awarded to each Member State and to third countries.

3. The Commission shall determine the nature of any additional statistical information, which is requested in accordance with the Directive, in consultation with the Advisory Committee for Public Works Contracts.

Article 30b.   1. Annex I to this Directive shall be amended by the Commission when, in particular on the basis of the notifications from the Member States, it is necessary:

(a) to remove from Annex I bodies governed by public law which no longer fulfil the criteria laid down in Art. 1 (b);
(b) to include in that Annex bodies governed by public law which meet those criteria.

2. Amendments to Annex I shall be made by the Commission after consulting the Advisory Committee for Public Works Contracts.

[8] OJ No L 124, 8. 6. 1971, p. 1.

The chairman of the committee shall submit to the committee a draft of any measures to be taken. The committee shall deliver its opinion on the draft, if necessary by taking a vote, within a time limit to be fixed by the chairman in the light of the urgency of the matter.

The opinion shall be recorded in the minutes. In addition, each Member State shall have the right to request that its position be recorded in the minutes.

The Commission shall take the fullest account of the opinion delivered by the committee. It shall inform the committee of the manner in which its opinion has been taken into account.

3. Amended versions of Annex I shall be published in the *Official Journal of the European Communities*.

Article 31. [Repealed]

[Final provisions omitted.]

ANNEX I

LISTS OF BODIES AND CATEGORIES OF BODIES GOVERNED BY PUBLIC LAW REFERRED TO IN ARTICLE I (B)

1. BELGIUM

Bodies
- Archives générales du Royaume et Archives de l'État dans les Provinces—Algemeen Rijksarchief en Rijksarchief in de Provinciën,
- Conseil autonome de l'enseignement communautaire—Autonome Raad van het Gemeenschapsonderwijs,
- Radio et télévision belges, émissions néerlandaises—Belgische Radio en Televisie, Nederlandse uitzendingen,
- Belgisches Rundfunk- und Fernsehzentrum der Deutschsprachigen Gemeinschaft (Centre de radio et télévision belge de la Communauté de langue allemande—Centrum voor Belgische Radio en Televisie voor de Duitstalige Gemeenschap),
- Bibliothèque royale Albert Ier—Koninklijke Bibliotheek Albert I,
- Caisse auxiliaire de paiement des allocations de chômage—Hulpkas voor Werkloosheidsuitkeringen,
- Caisse auxiliaire d'assurance maladie-invalidité—Hulpkas voor Ziekte-en Invaliditeitsverzekeringen,
- Caisse nationale des pensions de retraite et de survie—Rijkskas voor Rust- en Overlevingspensioenen,

- Caisse de secours et de prévoyance en faveur des marins naviguant sous pavillon belge—Hulp- en Voorzorgskas voor Zeevarenden onder Belgische Vlag,
- Caisse nationale des calamités—Nationale Kas voor de Rampenschade,
- Caisse spéciale de compensation pour allocations familiales en faveur des travailleurs de l'industrie diamantaire—Bijzondere Verrekenkas voor Gezinsvergoedingen ten bate van de Arbeiders der Diamantnijverheid,
- Caisse spéciale de compensation pour allocations familiales en faveur des travailleurs de l'industrie du bois—Bijzondere Verrekenkas voor Gezinsvergoedingen ten bate van Arbeiders in de Houtnijverheid,
- Caisse spéciale de compensation pour allocations familiales en faveur des travailleurs occupés dans les entreprises de batellerie—Bijzondere Verrekenkas voor Gezinsvergoedingen ten bate van Arbeiders der Ondernemingen voor Binnenscheepvaaart,
- Caisse spéciale de compensation pour allocations familiales en faveur des travailleurs occupés dans les entreprises de chargement, déchargement et manutention de marchandises dans les ports débarcadères, entropôts et stations (appelée habituellement «Caisse spéciale de compensation pour allocations familiales des régions maritimes»)—Bijzondere Verrekenkas voor Gezinsvergoedingen ten bate van de Arbeiders gebezigd door Ladings- en Lossingsondernemingen en door de Stuwadoors in de Havens, Losplaatsen, Stapelplaatsen en Stations (gewoonlijk genoemd: „Bijzondere Compensatiekas voor kindertoeslagen van de zeevaartgewesten"),
- Centre informatique pour la Région bruxelloise—Centrum voor Informatica voor het Brusselse Gewest,
- Commissariat général de la Communauté flamande pour la coopération internationale—Commissariaat-generaal voor Internationale Samenwerking van de Vlaamse Gemeenschap,
- Commissariat général pour les relations internationales de la Communauté française de Belgique—Commissariaat-generaal bij de Internationale Betrekkingen van de Franse Gemeenschap van België,
- Conseil central de l'économie—Central Raad voor het Bedrijfsleven,
- Conseil économique et social de la Région wallonne—Sociaal-economische Raad van het Waals Gewest,
- Conseil national du travail—Nationale Arbeidsraad,
- Conseil supérieur des classes moyennes—Hoge Raad voor de Middenstand,
- Office pour les travaux d'infrastructure de l'enseignement subsidié—Dienst voor Infrastructuurwerken van het Gesubsidieerd Onderwijs,
- Fondation royale—Koninklijke Schenking,
- Fonds communautaire de garantie des bâtiments scolaires—Gemeenschappelijk Waarborgfonds voor Schoolgebouwen,

- Fonds d'aide médicale urgente—Fonds voor Dringende Geneeskundige Hulp,
- Fonds des accidents du travail—Fonds voor Arbeidsongevallen
- Fonds des maladies professionnelles—Fonds voor Beroepsziekten,
- Fonds des routes—Wegenfonds,
- Fonds d'indemnisation des travailleurs licenciés en cas de fermeture d'entreprises—Fonds tot Vergoeding van de in geval van Sluiting van Ondernemingen Ontslagen Werknemers,
- Fonds national de garantie pour la réparation des dégâts houillers—Nationaal Waarborgfonds inzake Kolenmijnschade,
- Fonds national de retraite des ouvriers mineurs—Nationaal Pensioenfonds voor Mijnwerkers,
- Fonds pour le financement des prêts à des États étrangers—Fonds voor Financiering van de Leningen aan Vreemde Staten,
- Fonds pour la rémunération des mousses enrôlés à bord des bâtiments de pêche—Fonds voor Scheepsjongens aan Boord van Vissersvaartuigen,
- Fonds wallon d'avances pour la réparation des dommages provoqués par des pompages et des prises d'eau souterraine—Waals Fonds van Voorschotten voor het Herstel van de Schade veroorzaakt door Grondwaterzuiveringen en Afpompingen,
- Institut d'aéronomie spatiale—Instituut voor Ruimte-aëronomie,
- Institut belge de normalisation—Belgisch Instituut voor Normalisatie,
- Institut bruxellois de l'environnement—Brussels Instituut voor Milieubeheer,
- Institut d'expertise vétérinaire—Instituut voor Veterinaire Keuring,
- Institut économique et social des classes moyennes—Economisch en Sociaal Instituut voor de Middenstand,
- Institut d'hygiène et d'épidémiologie—Instituut voor Hygiëne en Epidemiologie,
- Institut francophone pour la formation permanente des classes moyennes—Franstalig Instituut voor Permanente Vorming voor de Middenstand,
- Institut géographique national—Nationaal Geografisch Instituut,
- Institut géotechnique de l'État—Rijksinstituut voor Grondmechanica,
- Institut national d'assurance maladie-invalidité—Rijksinstituut voor Ziekte- en Invaliditeitsverzekering,
- Institut national d'assurances sociales pour travailleurs indépendants—Rijksinstituut voor de Sociale Verzekeringen der Zelfstandigen,
- Institut national des industries extractives—Nationaal Instituut voor de Extractiebedrijven,
- Institut national des invalides de guerre, anciens combattants et victimes de guerre—Nationaal Instituut vor Oorlogsinvaliden, Oudstrijders en Oorlogsslachtoffers,

- Institut pour l'amélioration des conditions de travail—Institut voor Verbetering van de Arbeidsvoorwaarden,
- Institut pour l'encouragement de la recherche scientifique dans l'industrie et l'agriculture—Instituut tot Aanmoediging van het Wetenschappelijk Onderzoek in Nijverheid en Landbouw,
- Institut royal belge des sciences naturelles—Koninklijk Belgisch Instituut voor Natuurwetenschappen,
- Institut royal belge du patrimoine artistique—Koninklijk Belgisch Instituut voor het Kunstpatrimonium,
- Institut royal de météorologie—Koninklijk Meteorologisch Instituut,
- Enfance et famille—Kind en Gezin,
- Compagnie des installations maritimes de Bruges—Maatschappij der Brugse Zeevaartinrichtingen,
- Mémorial national du fort de Breendonck—Nationaal Gedenkteken van het Fort van Breendonck,
- Musée royal de l'Afrique centrale—Koninklijk Museum voor Midden-Afrika,
- Musées royaux d'art et d'histoire—Koninklijke Musea voor Kunst en Geschiedenis,
- Musées royaux des beaux-arts de Belgique—Koninklijke Musea voor Schone Kunsten van België,
- Observatoire royal de Belgique—Koninklijke Sterrenwacht van België,
- Office belge de l'économie et de l'agriculture—Belgische Dienst voor Bedrijfsleven en Landbouw,
- Office belge du commerce extérieur—Belgische Dienst voor Buitenlandse Handel,
- Office central d'action sociale et culturelle au profit des membres de la communauté militaire—Central Dienst voor Sociale en Culturele Actie ten behoeve van de Leden van de Militaire Gemeenschap,
- Office de la naissance et de l'enfance—Dienst voor Borelingen en Kinderen,
- Office de la navigation—Dienst voor de Scheepvaart,
- Office de promotion du tourisme de la Communauté française—Dienst voor de Promotie van het Toerisme van de Franse Gemeenschap,
- Office de renseignements et d'aide aux familles des militaires—Hulp- en Informatiebureau voor Gezinnen van Militairen,
- Office de sécurité sociale d'outre-mer—Dienst voor Overzeese Sociale Zekerheid,
- Office national d'allocations familiales pour travailleurs salariés—Rijksdienst voor Kinderbijslag voor Werknemers,
- Office national de l'emploi—Rijksdienst voor de Arbeidsvoorziening,
- Office national des débouchés agricoles et horticoles—Nationale Dienst voor Afzet van Land- en Tuinbouwprodukten,

- Office national de sécurité sociale—Rijksdienst voor Sociale Zekerheid,
- Office national de sécurité sociale des administrations provinciales et locales—Rijksdienst voor Sociale Zekerheid van de Provinciale en Plaatselijke Overheidsdiensten,
- Office national des pensions—Rijksdienst voor Pensionen,
- Office national des vacances annuelles—Rijksdienst voor de Jaarlijkse Vakantie,
- Office national du lait—Nationale Zuiveldienst,
- Office régional bruxellois de l'emploi—Brusselse Gewestelijke Dienst voor Arbeidsbemiddeling,
- Office régional et communautaire de l'emploi et de la formation—Gewestelijke en Gemeenschappelijke Dienst voor Arbeidsvoorziening en Vorming,
- Office régulateur de la navigation intérieure—Dienst voor Regeling der Binnenvaart,
- Société publique des déchets pour la Région flamande—Openbare Afvalstoffenmaatschappij voor het Vlaams Gewest,
- Orchestre national de Belgique—Nationaal Orkest van België,
- Organisme national des déchets radioactifs et des matières fissiles—Nationale Instelling voor Radioactief Afval en Splijtstoffen,
- Palais des beaux-arts—Paleis voor Schone Kunsten,
- Pool des marins de la marine marchande—Pool van de Zeelieden ter Koopvaardij,
- Port autonome de Charleroi—Autonome Haven van Charleroi,
- Port autonome de Liège—Autonome Haven van Luik,
- Port autonome de Namur—Autonome Haven van Namen,
- Radio et télévision belges de la Communauté française—Belgische Radio en Televisie van de Franse Gemeenschap,
- Régie des bâtiments—Regie der Gebouwen,
- Régie des voies aériennes—Regie der Luchtwegen,
- Régie des postes—Regie der Posterijen,
- Régie des télégraphes et des téléphones—Regie van Telegraaf en Telefoon,
- Conseil économique et social pour la Flandre—Sociaal-economische Raad voor Vlaanderen,
- Société anonyme du canal et des installations maritimes de Bruxelles—Naamloze Vennootschap „Zeekanaal en Haveninrichtingen van Brussel",
- Société du logement de la Région bruxelloise et sociétés—Brusselse Gewestelijke Huisvestingsmaatschappij en erkende maatschappijen,
- Société nationale terrienne—Nationale Landmaatschappij,
- Théâtre royal de la Monnaie—De Koninklijke Muntschouwburg,
- Universités relevant de la Communauté flamande—Universiteiten afhangende van de Vlaamse Gemeenschap,

- Universités relevant de la Communauté française—Univertsiteiten afhangende van de Franse Gemeenschap,
- Office flamand de l'emploi et de la formation professionnelle—Vlaamse Dienst voor Arbeidsvoorziening en Beroepsopleiding,
- Fonds flamand de construction d'institutions hospitalières et médico-sociales—Vlaams Fonds voor de Bouw van Ziekenhuizen en Medisch-Sociale Instellingen,
- Société flamande du logement et sociétés agréées—Vlaamse Huisvestingsmaatschappij en erkende maatschappijen,
- Société régionale wallonne du logement et sociétés agréées—Waalse Gewestelijke Maatschappij voor de Huisvesting en erkende maatschappijen,
- Société flamande d'épuration des eaux—Vlaamse Maatschappij voor Waterzuivering,
- Fonds flamand du logement des familles nombreuses—Vlaams Woningfonds van de Grote Gezinnen.

Categories
- les centres publics d'aide sociale (Centros públicos de asistencia social),
- les fabriques d'église (church councils).

II. DENMARK

Bodies
- Københavns Havn,
- Danmarks Radio,
- TV 2/Danmark,
- TV2 Reklame A/S,
- Danmarks Nationalbank,
- A/S Storebæltsforbindelsen,
- A/S Øresundsforbindelsen (alene tilslutningsanlæg i Danmark),
- Københavns Lufthavn A/S,
- Byfornyelsesselskabet København,
- Tele Danmark A/S with subsidiaries:
- Fyns Telefon A/S,
- Jydsk Telefon Aktieselskab A/S,
- Kjøbenhavns Telefon Aktieselskab,
- Tele Sønderjylland A/S,
- Telecom A/S,
- Tele Danmark Mobil A/S.

Categories
- De kommunale havne (municipal ports),
- Andre Forvaltiningssubjekter (other public administrative bodies).

III. GERMANY

1. Legal persons governed by public law

Authority, establishments and foundations governed by public law and created by federal, State or local authorities in particular in the following sectors:

1.1. *Authorities*

- Wissenschaftliche Hochschulen und verfaßte Studentenschaften (universities and established student bodies),
- berufsständige Vereinigungen (Rechtsanwalts-, Notar-, Steuerberater-, Wirtschaftsprüfer-, Architekten-, Ärzte- und Apothekerkammern) (professional associations representing lawyers, notaries, tax consultants, accountants, architects, medical practitioners and pharmacists),
- Wirtschaftsvereinigungen (Landwirtschafts-, Handwerks, Industrie- und Handelskammern, Handwerksinnungen, Handwerkerschaften) (business and trade associations: agricultural and craft associations, chambers of industry and commerce, craftsmen's guilds, tradesmen's associations),
- Sozialversicherungen (Krankenkassen, Unfall- und Rentenversicherungsträger) (social security institutions: health, accident and pension insurance funds),
- kassenärztliche Vereinigungen (associations of panel doctors),
- Genossenschaften und Verbände (cooperatives and other associations).

1.2. *Establishments and foundations*

Non-industrial and non-commercial establishments subject to state control and operating in the general interest, particularly in the following fields:

- Rechtsfähige Bundesanstalten (federal institutions having legal capacity),
- Versorgungsanstalten und Studentenwerke (pension organizations and students' unions),
- Kultur-, Wohlfahrts- und Hilfsstiftungen (cultural, welfare and relief foundations).

2. Legal persons governed by private law

Non-industrial and non-commercial establishments subject to State control and operating in the general interest (including 'kommunale Versorgungsunternehmen'—municipal utilities), particularly in the following fields:

- Gesundheitswesen (Krankenhäuser, Kurmittelbetriebe, medizinische Forschungseinrichtungen, Untersuchungs- und Tierkörperbeseitigungsanstalten) (health: hospitals, health resort estabishments, medical research institutes, testing and carcase-disposal establishments),
- Kultur (öffentliche Bühnen, Orchester, Museen, Bibliotheken, Archive,

zoologische und botanische Gärten) (culture: public theatres, orchestras, museums, libraries, archives, zoological and botanical gardens),

– Soziales (Kindergärten, Kindertagesheime, Erholungseinrichtungen, Kinder- und Jugendheime, Freizeiteinrichtungen, Gemeinschafts- und Bürgerhäuser, Frauenhäuser, Altersheime, Obdachlosenunterkünfte) (social welfare: nursery schools, children's playschools, rest-homes, children's homes, hostels for young people, leisure centres, community and civic centres, homes for battered wives, old people's homes, accommodation for the homeless),

– Sport (Schwimmbäder, Sportanlagen und -einrichtungen) (sport: swimming baths, sports facilities),

– Sicherheit (Feuerwehren, Rettungsdienste) (safety: fire brigades, other emergency services),

– Bildung (Umschulungs-, Aus, Fort- und Weiterbildungseinrichtungen, Volkshochschulen) (education: training, further training and retraining establishments, adult evening classes),

– Wissenschaft, Forschung und Entwicklung (Großforschungseinrichtungen, wissenschaftliche Gesellschaften und Vereine, Wissenschaftsförderung) (science, research and development: large-scale research institutes, scientific societies and associations, bodies promoting science),

– Entsorgung (Straßenreinigung, Abfall- und Abwasserbeseitigung) (refuse and garbage disposal services: street cleaning, waste and sewage disposal),

– Bauwesen und Wohnungswirtschaft (Stadtplanung, Stadtentwicklung, Wohnungsunternehmen, Wohnraumvermittlung) (building, civil engineering and housing: town planning, urban development, housing enterprises, housing agency services),

– Wirtschaft (Wirtschaftsförderungsgesellschaften) (economy: organizations promoting economic development),

– Friedhofs- und Bestattungswesen (cemeteries and burial services),

– Zusammenarbeit mit den Entwicklungsländern (Finanzierung, technische Zusammenarbeit, Entwicklungshilfe, Ausbildung) (cooperation with developing countries: financing, technical cooperation, development aid, training).

IV. GREECE

Categories

Other legal persons governed by public law whose public works contracts are subject to State control.

V. SPAIN

Categories

– Entidades Gestoras y Servicios Comunes de la Seguridad Social (administrative entities and common services of the health and social services)

- Organismos Autónomos de la Administración del Estado (independent bodies of the national administration)
- Organismos Autónomos de las Comunidades Autónomas (independent bodies of the autonomous communities)
- Organismos Autónomos de las Entidades Locales (independent bodies of local authorities)
- Otras entidades sometidas a la legislación de contratos del Estado español (other entities subject to Spanish State legislation on procurement).

VI. FRANCE

Bodies

1. National public bodies:

1.1. with scientific, cultural and professional character:
- Collège de France,
- Conservatoire national des arts et métiers,
- Observatoire de Paris.

1.2 Scientific and technological:
- Centre national de la recherche scientifique (CNRS),
- Institut national de la recherche agronomique,
- Institut national de la santé et de la recherche médicale,
- Institut français de recherche scientifique pour le développement en coopération (ORSTOM).

1.3. with administrative character:
- Agence nationale pour l'emploi,
- Caisse nationale des allocations familiales,
- Caisse nationale d'assurance maladie des travailleurs salariés,
- Caisse nationale d'assurance vieillesse des travailleurs salariés,
- Office national des anciens combattants et victimes de la guerre,
- Agences financières de bassins.

Categories

1. National public bodies:
- universités (universities),
- écoles normales d'instituteurs (teacher training colleges).

2. Administrative public bodies at regional, departmental and local level:
- collèges (secondary schools),
- lycées (secondary schools),
- établissements publics hospitaliers (public hospitals),
- offices publics d'habitations à loyer modéré (OPHLM) (public offices for low-cost housing).

3. Groupings of territorial authorities:
- syndicats de communes (associations of local authorities),

- districts (districts),
- communautés urbaines (municipalities),
- institutions interdépartementales et interrégionales (institutions common to more than one Département and interregional institutions).

VII. IRELAND

Bodies
- Shannon Free Airport Development Company Ltd,
- Local Government Computer Services Board,
- Local Government Staff Negotiations Board,
- Córas Tráchtála (Irish Export Board),
- Industrial Development Authority,
- Irish Goods Council (Promotion of Irish Goods),
- Córas Beostoic agus Feola (CBF) (Irish Meat Board),
- Bord Fáilte Éireann (Irish Tourism Board),
- Údarás na Gaeltachta (Development Authority for Gaeltacht Regions),
- An Bord Pleanála (Irish Planning Board).

Categories
- Third Level Educational Bodies of a Public Character,
- National Training, Cultural or Research Agencies,
- Hospital Boards of a Public Character,
- National Health & Social Agencies of a Public Character,
- Central & Regional Fishery Boards

VIII. ITALY

Bodies
- Agenzia per la promozione dello sviluppo nel Mezzogiorno.

Categories
- Enti portuali e aeroportuali (port and airport authorities),
- Consorzi per le opere idrauliche (consortia for water engineering works),
- Le università statali, gli istituti universitari statali, i consorzi per i lavori interessanti le università (State universities, State university institutes, consortia for university development work),
- Gli istituti superiori scientifici e culturali, gli osservatori astronomici, astrofisici, geofisici o vulcanologici (higher scientific and cultural institutes, astronomical, astrophysical, geophysical or vulcanological observatories),
- Enti di ricerca e sperimentazione (organizations conducting research and experimental work),
- Le istituzioni pubbliche di assistenza e di beneficenza (public welfare and benevolent institutions),
- Enti che gestiscono forme obbligatorie di previdenza e di assistenza

(agencies administering compulsory social security and welfare schemes),
- Consorzi di bonifica (land reclamation consortia),
- Enti di sviluppo o di irrigazione (development or irrigation agencies),
- Consorzi per le aree industriali (associations for industrial areas),
- Comunità montane (groupings of municipalities in mountain areas),
- Enti preposti a servizi di pubblico interesse (organizations providing services in the public interest),
- Enti pubblici preposti ad attività di spettacolo, sportive, turistiche e del tempo libero (public bodies engaged in entertainment, sport, tourism and leisure activities),
- Enti culturali e di promozione artistica (organizations promoting culture and artistic activities)

IX. LUXEMBOURG

Categories
- Les établissements publics de l'État placés sous la surveillance d'un membre du gouvernement (public establishments of the State placed under the supervision of a member of the Government),
- Les établissements publics placés sous la surveillance des communes (public establishments placed under the supervision of the communes),
- Les syndicats de commune créés en vertu de la loi du 14 février 1900 telle qu'elle a été modifiée par la suite (associations of communes created under the law of 14 February 1900 as subsequently modified).

X. THE NETHERLANDS

Bodies
- De Nederlandse Centrale Organisatie voor Toegepast Natuurwetenschappelijk Onderzoek (TNO) en de daaronder ressorterende organisaties.

Categories
- De waterschappen (administration of water engineering works),
- De instellingen van wetenschappelijk onderwijs vermeld in artikel 8 van de Wet op het Wetenschappelijk Onderwijs (1985), de academische ziekenhuizen (Institutions for scientific education, as listed in Article 8 of the Scientific Education Act (1985)) wet op het Wetenschappelijk Onderwijs (1985) (teaching hospitals).

XI. PORTUGAL

Categories
- Estabelecimentos públicos de ensino, investigação científica e saúde (public establishments for education, scientific research and health),
- Institutos públicos sem carácter comercial ou industrial (public institutions without commercial or industrial character),

– Fundações públicas (public foundations),
– Administrações gerais e juntas autonómas (general administration bodies and independent councils).

XII. THE UNITED KINGDOM

Bodies
– Central Blood Laboratories Authority,
– Design Council,
– Health and Safety Executive,
– National Research Development Corporation,
– Public Health Laboratory Services Board,
– Advisory, Conciliation and Arbitration Service,
– Commission for the New Towns,
– Development Board For Rural Wales,
– English Industrial Estates Corporation,
– National Rivers Authority,
– Northern Ireland Housing Executive,
– Scottish Enterprise,
– Scottish Homes,
– Welsh Development Agency.

Categories
– Universities and polytechnics, maintained schools and colleges,
– National Museums and Galleries,
– Research Councils,
– Fire Authorities,
– National Health Service Authorities,
– Police Authorities,
– New Town Development Corporations,
– Urban Development Corporations.

[Annexes II to V omitted.]

Statement concerning Article 5 (4) of Directive 71/305/EEC

The Council and the Commission state that in open and restricted procedures all negotiation with candidates or tenderers on fundamental aspects of contracts, variations in which are likely to distort competition, and in particular on prices, shall be ruled out; however, discussions with candidates or tenderers may be held but only for the purpose of clarifying or supplementing the content of their tenders or the requirements of the contracting authorities and provided this does not involve discrimination.

Council Directive of 21 December 1989 on the co-ordination
of the laws, regulations and administrative provisions relating
to the application of review procedures to the award of
public supply and public works contracts (89/665/EEC)[9]

The Council of the European Communities,

Having regard to the Treaty establishing the European Economic
Community, and in particular Art. 100a thereof,

[Recitals omitted.]

Whereas Community Directives on public procurement, in particular
Council Directive 71/305/EEC of 26 July 1971 concerning the co-ordination of procedures for the award of public works contracts,[10] as last
amended by Directive 89/440/EEC,[11] and Council Directive 77/62/EEC of
21 December 1976 co-ordinating procedures for the award of public supply contracts,[12] as last amended by Directive 88/295/EEC,[13] do not contain any specific provisions ensuring their effective application;

Whereas the existing arrangements at both national and Community
levels for ensuring their application are not always adequate to ensure
compliance with the relevant Community provisions particularly at a
stage when infringements can be corrected;

Whereas the opening-up of public procurement to Community competition necessitates a substantial increase in the guarantees of transparency
and non-discrimination; whereas, for it to have tangible effects, effective
and rapid remedies must be available in the case of infringements of
Community law in the field of public procurement or national rules
implementing that law;

Whereas in certain Member States the absence of effective remedies or
inadequacy of existing remedies deter Community undertakings from submitting tenders in the Member State in which the contracting authority is
established; whereas, therefore, the Member States concerned must remedy this situation;

Whereas, since procedures for the award of public contracts are of such
short duration, competent review bodies must, among other things, be
authorised to take interim measures aimed at suspending such a procedure or the implementation of any decisions which may be taken by the
contracting authority; whereas the short duration of the procedures

[9] OJ 1989 L 395/33.   [10] OJ No L 185, 16. 8. 1971, p. 5.
[11] OJ 1989 L 210/1.   [12] OJ 1977 L 13/1.   [13] OJ 1988 L 127/1.

means that the aforementioned infringements need to be dealt with urgently;

Whereas it is necessary to ensure that adequate procedures exist in all the Member States to permit the setting aside of decisions taken unlawfully and compensation of persons harmed by an infringement;

Whereas, when undertakings do not seek review, certain infringements may not be corrected unless a specific mechanism is put in place;

Whereas, accordingly, the Commission, when it considers that a clear and manifest infringement has been committed during a contract award procedure, should be able to bring it to the attention of the competent authorities of the Member State and of the contracting authority concerned so that appropriate steps are taken for the rapid correction of any alleged infringement;

Whereas the application in practice of the provisions of this Directive should be re-examined within a period of four years of its implementation on the basis of information to be supplied by the Member States concerning the functioning of the national review procedures,

Had adopted this Directive:

Article 1.   1. The Member States shall take the measures necessary to ensure that, as regards contract award procedures falling within the scope of Directives 71/305/EEC and 77/62/EEC, decisions taken by the contracting authorities may be reviewed effectively and, in particular, as rapidly as possible in accordance with the conditions set out in the following Articles, and, in particular, Art. 2 (7) on the grounds that such decisions have infringed Community law in the field of public procurement or national rules implementing that law.

2. Member States shall ensure that there is no discrimination between undertakings claiming injury in the context of a procedure for the award of a contract as a result of the distinction made by this Directive between national rules implementing Community law and other national rules.

3. The Member States shall ensure that the review procedures are available, under detailed rules which the Member States may establish, at least to any person having or having had an interest in obtaining a particular public supply or public works contract and who has been or risks being harmed by an alleged infringement. In particular, the Member States may require that the person seeking the review must have previously notified the contracting authority of the alleged infringement and of his intention to seek review.

Article 2.   1. The Member States shall ensure that the measures taken concerning the review procedures specified in Art. 1 include provision for the powers to:

(a) take, at the earliest opportunity and by way of interlocutory procedures, interim measures with the aim of correcting the alleged infringement or preventing further damage to the interests concerned, including measures to suspend or to ensure the suspension of the procedure for the award of a public contract or the implementation of any decision taken by the contracting authority;

(b) either set aside or ensure the setting aside of decisions taken unlawfully, including the removal of discriminatory technical, economic or financial specifications in the invitation to tender, the contract documents or in any other document relating to the contract award procedure;

(c) award damages to persons harmed by an infringement.

2. The powers specified in paragraph 1 may be conferred on separate bodies responsible for different aspects of the review procedure.

3. Review procedures need not in themselves have an automatic suspensive effect on the contract award procedures to which they relate.

4. The Member States may provide that when considering whether to order interim measures the body responsible may take into account the probable consequences of the measures for all interests likely to be harmed, as well as the public interest, and may decide not to grant such measures where their negative consequences could exceed their benefits. A decision not to grant interim measures shall not prejudice any other claim of the person seeking these measures.

5. The Member States may provide that where damages are claimed on the grounds that a decision was taken unlawfully, the contested decision must first be set aside by a body having the necessary powers.

6. The effects of the exercise of the powers referred to in paragraph 1 on a contract concluded subsequent to its award shall be determined by national law.

Furthermore, except where a decision must be set aside prior to the award of damages, a Member State may provide that, after the conclusion of a contract following its award, the powers of the body responsible for the review procedures shall be limited to awarding damages to any person harmed by an infringement.

7. The Member States shall ensure that decisions taken by bodies responsible for review procedures can be effectively enforced.

8. Where bodies responsible for review procedures are not judicial in character, written reasons for their decisions shall always be given. Furthermore, in such a case, provision must be made to guarantee procedures whereby any allegedly illegal measure taken by the review body or any alleged defect in the exercise of the powers conferred on it can be the subject of judicial review or review by another body which is a court or

tribunal within the meaning of Art. 177 of the EEC Treaty and independent of both the contracting authority and the review body.

The members of such an independent body shall be appointed and leave office under the same conditions as members of the judiciary as regards the authority responsible for their appointment, their period of office, and their removal. At least the President of this independent body shall have the same legal and professional qualifications as members of the judiciary. The independent body shall take its decisions following a procedure in which both sides are heard, and these decisions shall, by means determined by each Member State, be legally binding.

Article 3. 1. The Commission may invoke the procedure for which this Article provides when, prior to a contract being concluded, it considers that a clear and manifest infringement of Community provisions in the field of public procurement has been committed during a contract award procedure falling within the scope of Directives 71/305/EEC and 77/62/EEC.

2. The Commission shall notify the Member State and the contracting authority concerned of the reasons which have led it to conclude that a clear and manifest infringement has been committed and request its correction.

3. Within 21 days of receipt of the notification referred to in paragraph 2, the Member State concerned shall communicate to the Commission:

(a) its confirmation that the infringement has been corrected; or
(b) a reasoned submission as to why no correction has been made; or
(c) a notice to the effect that the contract award procedure has been suspended either by the contracting authority on its own initiative or on the basis of the powers specified in Art. 2 (1) (a).

4. A reasoned submission in accordance with paragraph 3 (b) may rely among other matters on the fact that the alleged infringement is already the subject of judicial or other review proceedings or of a review as referred to in Art. 2 (8). In such a case, the Member State shall inform the Commission of the result of those proceedings as soon as it becomes known.

5. Where notice has been given that a contract award procedure has been suspended in accordance with paragraph 3 (c), the Member State shall notify the Commission when the suspension is lifted or another contract procedure relating in whole or in part to the same subject-matter is begun. That notification shall confirm that the alleged infringement has been corrected or include a reasoned submission as to why no correction has been made.

Article 4.   1. Not later than four years after the implementation of this Directive, the Commission, in consultation with the Advisory Committee for Public Contracts, shall review the manner in which the provisions of this Directive have been implemented and, if necessary, make proposals for amendments.

2. By 1 March each year the Member States shall communicate to the Commission information on the operation of their national review procedures during the preceding calendar year. The nature of the information shall be determined by the Commission in consultation with the Advisory Committee for Public Contracts.

[Final provisions omitted.]

Competition

Regulation No 17
First Regulation implementing Arts. 85 and 86
of the Treaty[1]

The Council of the European Economic Community,

Having regard to the Treaty establishing the European Economic Community, and in particular Art. 87 thereof;

Having regard to the proposal from the Commission;

Having regard to the Opinion of the Economic and Social Committee;

Having regard to the Opinion of the European Parliament;

Whereas, in order to establish a system ensuring that competition shall not be distorted in the common market, it is necessary to provide for balanced application of Arts. 85 and 86 in a uniform manner in the Member States;

Whereas in establishing the rules for applying Art. 85 (3) account must be taken of the need to ensure effective supervision and to simplify administration to the greatest possible extent;

Whereas it is accordingly necessary to make it obligatory, as a general principle, for undertakings which seek application of Art. 85 (3) to notify to the Commission their agreements, decisions and concerted practices;

Whereas, on the one hand, such agreements, decisions and concerted practices are probably very numerous and cannot therefore all be examined at the same time and, on the other hand, some of them have special features which may make them less prejudicial to the development of the common market;

Whereas there is consequently a need to make more flexible arrangements for the time being in respect of certain categories of agreement, decision and concerted practice without prejudging their validity under Art. 85;

Whereas it may be in the interest of undertakings to know whether any agreements, decisions or practices to which they are party, or propose to become party, may lead to action on the part of the Commission pursuant to Art. 85 (1) or Art. 86;

Whereas, in order to secure uniform application of Arts. 85 and 86 in the common market, rules must be made under which the Commission, acting in close and constant liaison with the competent authorities of the

[1] OJ Sp. Ed. 1959–62, p. 87. As last amended by the 1985 Act of Accession.

Member States, may take the requisite measures for applying those Articles;

Whereas for this purpose the Commission must have the co-operation of the competent authorities of the Member States and be empowered, throughout the common market, to require such information to be supplied and to undertake such investigations as are necessary to bring to light any agreement, decision or concerted practice prohibited by Art. 85 (1) or any abuse of a dominant position prohibited by Art. 86;

Whereas, in order to carry out its duty of ensuring that the provisions of the Treaty are applied, the Commission must be empowered to address to undertakings or associations of undertakings recommendations and decisions for the purpose of bringing to an end infringements of Arts. 85 and 86;

Whereas compliance with Arts. 85 and 86 and the fulfilment of obligations imposed on undertakings and associations of undertakings under this Regulation must be enforceable by means of fines and periodic penalty payments;

Whereas undertakings concerned must be accorded the right to be heard by the Commission, third parties whose interests may be affected by a decision must be given the opportunity of submitting their comments beforehand, and it must be ensured that wide publicity is given to decisions taken;

Whereas all decisions taken by the Commission under this Regulation are subject to review by the Court of Justice under the conditions specified in the Treaty; whereas it is moreover desirable to confer upon the Court of Justice, pursuant to Art. 172, unlimited jurisdiction in respect of decisions under which the Commission imposes fines or periodic penalty payments;

Whereas this Regulation may enter into force without prejudice to any other provisions that may hereafter be adopted pursuant to Art. 87; Has adopted this Regulation:

Article 1. Basic provision.
Without prejudice to Arts. 6, 7 and 23 of this Regulation, agreements, decisions and concerted practices of the kind described in Art. 85 (1) of the Treaty and the abuse of a dominant position in the market, within the meaning of Art. 86 of the Treaty, shall be prohibited, no prior decision to that effect being required.

Article 2. Negative clearance.
Upon application by the undertakings or associations of undertakings concerned, the Commission may certify that, on the basis of the facts in its possession, there are no grounds under Art. 85 (1) or Art. 86 of the

Treaty for action on its part in respect of an agreement, decision or practice.

Article 3.   Termination of infringements.
1. Where the Commission, upon application or upon its own initiative, finds that there is infringement of Art. 85 or Art. 86 of the Treaty, it may by decision require the undertakings or associations of undertakings concerned to bring such infringement to an end.
2. Those entitled to make application are:

(a) Member States;
(b) natural or legal persons who claim a legitimate interest.

3. Without prejudice to the other provisions of this Regulation, the Commission may, before taking a decision under paragraph 1, address to the undertakings or associations of undertakings concerned recommendations for termination of the infringement.

Article 4.   Notification of new agreements, decisions and practices.
1. Agreements, decisions and concerted practices of the kind described in Art. 85 (1) of the Treaty which come into existence after the entry into force of this Regulation and in respect of which the parties seek application of Art. 85 (3) must be notified to the Commission. Until they have been notified, no decision in application of Art. 85 (3) may be taken.
2. Paragraph 1 shall not apply to agreements, decisions or concerted practices where:

(1) the only parties thereto are undertakings from one Member State and the agreements, decisions or practices do not relate either to imports or to exports between Member States;
(2) not more than two undertakings are party thereto, and the agreements only:
    (a) restrict the freedom of one party to the contract in determining the prices or conditions of business upon which the goods which he has obtained from the other party to the contract may be resold; or
    (b) impose restrictions on the exercise of the rights of the assignee or user of industrial property rights—in particular patents, utility models, designs or trade marks—or of the person entitled under a contract to the assignment, or grant, of the right to use a method of manufacture or knowledge relating to the use and to the application of industrial processes;
(3) they have as their sole object:
    (a) the development or uniform application of standards or types; or
    (b) joint research and development;

(c) specialisation in the manufacture of products, including agreements necessary for achieving this,
  - where the products which are the subject of specialisation do not, in a substantial part of the common market, represent more than 15% of the volume of business done in identical products or those considered by consumers to be similar by reason of their characteristics, price and use,
    and
  - where the total annual turnover of the participating undertakings does not exceed 200 million units of account.

These agreements, decisions and practices may be notified to the Commission.

Article 5. Notification of existing agreements, decisions and practices.

1. Agreements, decisions and concerted practices of the kind described in Art. 85 (1) of the Treaty which are in existence at the date of entry into force of this Regulation and in respect of which the parties seek application of Art. 85 (3) shall be notified to the Commission before 1 November 1962. However, notwithstanding the foregoing provisions, any agreements, decisions and concerted practices to which not more than two undertakings are party shall be notified before 1 February 1963.

2. Paragraph 1 shall not apply to agreements, decisions or concerted practices falling within Art. 4 (2); these may be notified to the Commission.

Article 6. Decisions pursuant to Art. 85 (3).

1. Whenever the Commission takes a decision pursuant to Art. 85 (3) of the Treaty, it shall specify therein the date from which the decision shall take effect. Such date shall not be earlier than the date of notification.

2. The second sentence of paragraph 1 shall not apply to agreements, decisions or concerted practices falling within Art. 4 (2) and Art. 5 (2), nor to those falling within Art. 5 (1) which have been notified within the time limit specified in Art. 5 (1).

Article 7. Special provisions for existing agreements, decisions and practices.

1. Where agreements, decisions and concerted practices in existence at the date of entry into force of this Regulation and notified within the time limits specified in Art. 5 (1) do not satisfy the requirements of Art. 85 (3) of the Treaty and the undertakings or associations of undertakings concerned cease to give effect to them or modify them in such manner that they no longer fall within the prohibition contained in Art. 85 (1) or

that they satisfy the requirements of Art. 85 (3), the prohibition contained in Art. 85 (1) shall apply only for a period fixed by the Commission. A decision by the Commission pursuant to the foregoing sentence shall not apply as against undertakings and associations of undertakings which did not expressly consent to the notification.

2. Paragraph 1 shall apply to agreements, decisions and concerted practices falling within Art. 4 (2) which are in existence at the date of entry into force of this Regulation if they are notified before 1 January 1967.

Article 8. Duration and revocation of decisions under Art. 85 (3).

1. A decision in application of Art. 85 (3) of the Treaty shall be issued for a specified period and conditions and obligations may be attached thereto.

2. A decision may on application be renewed if the requirements of Art. 85 (3) of the Treaty continue to be satisfied.

3. The Commission may revoke or amend its decision or prohibit specified acts by the parties:

(a) where there has been a change in any of the facts which were basic to the making of the decision;
(b) where the parties commit a breach of any obligation attached to the decision;
(c) where the decision is based on incorrect information or was induced by deceit;
(d) where the parties abuse the exemption from the provisions of Art. 85 (1) of the Treaty granted to them by the decision.

In cases to which subparagraphs (b), (c) or (d) apply, the decision may be revoked with retroactive effect.

Article 9. Powers.

1. Subject to review of its decision by the Court of Justice, the Commission shall have sole power to declare Art. 85 (1) inapplicable pursuant to Art. 85 (3) of the Treaty.

2. The Commission shall have power to apply Art. 85 (1) and Art. 86 of the Treaty; this power may be exercised notwithstanding that the time limits specified in Art. 5 (1) and in Art. 7 (2) relating to notification have not expired.

3. As long as the Commission has not initiated any procedure under Arts. 2, 3 or 6, the authorities of the Member States shall remain competent to apply Art. 85 (1) and Art. 86 in accordance with Art. 88 of the Treaty; they shall remain competent in this respect notwithstanding that the time limits specified in Art. 5 (1) and in Art. 7 (2) relating to notification have not expired.

Article 10. Liaison with the authorities of the Member States.

1. The Commission shall forthwith transmit to the competent authorities of the Member States a copy of the application and notifications together with copies of the most important documents lodged with the Commission for the purpose of establishing the existence of infringements of Arts. 85 or 86 of the Treaty or of obtaining negative clearance or a decision in application of Art. 85 (3).

2. The Commission shall carry out the procedure set out in paragraph 1 in close and constant liaison with the competent authorities of the Member States; such authorities shall have the right to express their views upon that procedure.

3. An Advisory Committee on Restrictive Practices and Monopolies shall be consulted prior to the taking of any decision following upon a procedure under paragraph 1, and of any decision concerning the renewal, amendment or revocation of a decision pursuant to Art. 85 (3) of the Treaty.

4. The Advisory Committee shall be composed of officials competent in the matter of restrictive practices and monopolies. Each Member State shall appoint an official to represent it who, if prevented from attending, may be replaced by another official.

5. The consultation shall take place at a joint meeting convened by the Commission; such meeting shall be held not earlier than fourteen days after dispatch of the notice convening it. The notice shall, in respect of each case to be examined, be accompanied by a summary of the case together with an indication of the most important documents, and a preliminary draft decision.

6. The Advisory Committee may deliver an opinion notwithstanding that some of its members or their alternates are not present. A report of the outcome of the consultative proceedings shall be annexed to the draft decision. It shall not be made public.

Article 11. Request for information.

1. In carrying out the duties assigned to it by Art. 89 and by provisions adopted under Art. 87 of the Treaty, the Commission may obtain all necessary information from the Governments and competent authorities of the Member States and from undertakings and associations of undertakings.

2. When sending a request for information to an undertaking or association of undertakings, the Commission shall at the same time forward a copy of the request to the competent authority of the Member State in whose territory the seat of the undertaking or association of undertakings is situated.

3. In its request the Commission shall state the legal basis and the

purpose of the request and also the penalties provided for in Art. 15 (1) (b) for supplying incorrect information.

4. The owners of the undertakings or their representatives and, in the case of legal persons, companies or firms, or of associations having no legal personality, the persons authorised to represent them by law or by their constitution shall supply the information requested.

5. Where an undertaking or association of undertakings does not supply the information requested within the time limit fixed by the Commission, or supplies incomplete information, the Commission shall by decision require the information to be supplied. The decision shall specify what information is required, fix an appropriate time limit within which it is to be supplied and indicate the penalties provided for in Art. 15 (1) (b) and Art. 16 (1) (c) and the right to have the decision reviewed by the Court of Justice.

6. The Commission shall at the same time forward a copy of its decision to the competent authority of the Member State in whose territory the seat of the undertaking or association of undertakings is situated.

Article 12.   Inquiry into sectors of the economy.

1. If in any sector of the economy the trend of trade between Member States, price movements, inflexibility of prices or other circumstances suggest that in the economic sector concerned competition is being restricted or distorted within the common market, the Commission may decide to conduct a general inquiry into that economic sector and in the course thereof may request undertakings in the sector concerned to supply the information necessary for giving effect to the principles formulated in Arts. 85 and 86 of the Treaty and for carrying out the duties entrusted to the Commission.

2. The Commission may in particular request every undertaking or association of undertakings in the economic sector concerned to communicate to it all agreements, decisions and concerted practices which are exempt from notification by virtue of Art. 4 (2) and Art. 5 (2).

3. When making inquiries pursuant to paragraph 2, the Commission shall also request undertakings or groups of undertakings whose size suggests that they occupy a dominant position within the common market or a substantial part thereof to supply to the Commission such particulars of the structure of the undertakings and of their behaviour as are requisite to an appraisal of their position in the light of Art. 86 of the Treaty.

4. Art. 10 (3) to (6) and Arts. 11, 13, and 14 shall apply correspondingly.

Article 13.   Investigations by the authorities of the Member States.

1. At the request of the Commission, the competent authorities of the

Member States shall undertake the investigations which the Commission considers to be necessary under Art. 14 (1), or which it has ordered by decision pursuant to Art. 14 (3). The officials of the competent authorities of the Member States responsible for conducting these investigations shall exercise their powers upon production of an authorisation in writing issued by the competent authority of the Member State in whose territory the investigation is to be made. Such authorisation shall specify the subject-matter and purpose of the investigation.

2. If so requested by the Commission or by the competent authority of the Member State in whose territory the investigation is to be made, the officials of the Commission may assist the officials of such authorities in carrying out their duties.

Article 14. Investigating powers of the Commission

1. In carrying out the duties assigned to it by Art. 89 and by provisions adopted under Art. 87 of the Treaty, the Commission may undertake all necessary investigations into undertakings and associations of undertakings. To this end the officials authorised by the Commission are empowered:

(a) to examine the books and other business records;
(b) to take copies of or extracts from the books and business records;
(c) to ask for oral explanations on the spot;
(d) to enter any premises, land and means of transport of undertakings.

2. The officials of the Commission authorised for the purpose of these investigations shall exercise their powers upon production of an authorisation in writing specifying the subject-matter and purpose of the investigation and the penalties provided for in Art. 15 (1) (c) in cases where production of the required books or other business records is incomplete. In good time before the investigation, the Commission shall inform the competent authority of the Member State in whose territory the same is to be made of the investigation and of the identity of the authorised officials.

3. Undertakings and associations of undertakings shall submit to investigations ordered by decision of the Commission. The decision shall specify the subject-matter and purpose of the investigation, appoint the date on which it is to begin and indicate the penalties provided for in Art. 15 (1) (c) and Art. 16 (1) (d) and the right to have the decision reviewed by the Court of Justice.

4. The Commission shall take decisions referred to in paragraph 3 after consultation with the competent authority of the Member State in whose territory the investigation is to be made.

5. Officials of the competent authority of the Member State in whose

territory the investigation is to be made may, at the request of such authority or of the Commission, assist the officials of the Commission in carrying out their duties.

6. Where an undertaking opposes an investigation ordered pursuant to this Article, the Member State concerned shall afford the necessary assistance to the officials authorised by the Commission to enable them to make their investigation. Member States shall, after consultation with the Commission, take the necessary measures to this end before 1 October 1962.

Article 15. Fines.

1. The Commission may by decision impose on undertakings or associations of undertakings fines of from 100 to 5000 units of account where, intentionally or negligently:

(a) they supply incorrect or misleading information in an application pursuant to Art. 2 or in a notification pursuant to Arts. 4 or 5; or
(b) they supply incorrect information in response to a request made pursuant to Art. 11 (3) or (5) or to Art. 12, or do not supply information within the time limit fixed by a decision taken under Art. 11 (5); or
(c) they produce the required books or other business records in incomplete form during investigations under Arts. 13 or 14, or refuse to submit to an investigation ordered by decision issued in implementation of Art. 14 (3).

2. The Commission may by decision impose on undertakings or associations of undertakings fines from 1000 to 1 000 000 units of account, or a sum in excess thereof but not exceeding 10% of the turnover in the preceding business year of each of the undertakings participating in the infringement where, either intentionally or negligently:

(a) they infringe Art. 85 (1) or Art. 86 of the Treaty; or
(b) they commit a breach of any obligation imposed pursuant to Art. 8 (1).

In fixing the amount of the fine, regard shall be had both to the gravity and to the duration of the infringement.

3. Art. 10 (3) to (6) shall apply.

4. Decisions taken pursuant to paragraphs 1 and 2 shall not be of a criminal law nature.

5. The fines provided for in paragraph 2 (a) shall not be imposed in respect of acts taking place:

(a) after notification to the Commission and before its decision in application of Art. 85 (3) of the Treaty, provided they fall within the limits of the activity described in the notification;

(b) before notification and in the course of agreements, decisions or concerted practices in existence at the date of entry into force of this Regulation, provided that notification was effected within the time limits specified in Art. 5 (1) and Art. 7 (2).

6. Paragraph 5 shall not have effect where the Commission has informed the undertakings concerned that after preliminary examination it is of opinion that Art. 85 (1) of the Treaty applies and that application of Art. 85 (3) is not justified.

Article 16. Periodic penalty payments.
1. The Commission may by decision impose on undertakings or associations of undertakings periodic penalty payments of from 50 to 1000 units of account per day, calculated from the date appointed by the decision, in order to compel them:

(a) to put an end to an infringement of Arts. 85 or 86 of the Treaty, in accordance with a decision taken pursuant to Art. 3 of this Regulation;
(b) to refrain from any act prohibited under Art. 8 (3);
(c) to supply complete and correct information which it has requested by decision taken pursuant to Art. 11 (5);
(d) to submit to an investigation which it has ordered by decision taken pursuant to Art. 14 (3).

2. Where the undertakings or associations of undertakings have satisfied the obligation which it was the purpose of the periodic penalty payment to enforce, the Commission may fix the total amount of the periodic penalty payment at a lower figure than that which would arise under the original decision.
3. Art. 10 (3) to (6) shall apply.

Article 17. Review by the Court of Justice.
The Court of Justice shall have unlimited jurisdiction within the meaning of Art. 172 of the Treaty to review decisions whereby the Commission has fixed a fine or periodic penalty payment; it may cancel, reduce or increase the fine or periodic penalty payment imposed.

Article 18. Unit of account.
For the purposes of applying Arts. 15 to 17 the unit of account shall be that adopted in drawing up the budget of the Community in accordance with Arts. 207 and 209 of the Treaty.

Article 19. Hearing of the parties and of third persons.
1. Before taking decisions as provided for in Arts. 2, 3, 6, 7, 8, 15 and

16, the Commission shall give the undertakings or associations of undertakings concerned the opportunity of being heard on the matters to which the Commission has taken objection.

2. If the Commission or the competent authorities of the Member States consider it necessary, they may also hear other natural or legal persons. Applications to be heard on the part of such persons shall, where they show a sufficient interest, be granted.

3. Where the Commission intends to give negative clearance pursuant to Art. 2 or take a decision in application of Art. 85 (3) of the Treaty, it shall publish a summary of the relevant application or notification and invite all interested third parties to submit their observations within a time limit which it shall fix being not less than one month. Publication shall have regard to the legitimate interest of undertakings in the protection of their business secrets.

Article 20. Professional secrecy.

1. Information acquired as a result of the application of Arts. 11, 12, 13 and 14 shall be used only for the purpose of the relevant request or investigation.

2. Without prejudice to the provisions of Arts. 19 and 21, the Commission and the competent authorities of the Member States, their officials and other servants shall not disclose information acquired by them as a result of the application of this Regulation and of the kind covered by the obligation of professional secrecy.

3. The provisions of paragraphs 1 and 2 shall not prevent publication of general information or surveys which do not contain information relating to particular undertakings or associations of undertakings.

Article 21. Publication of decisions.

1. The Commission shall publish the decisions which it takes pursuant to Arts. 2, 3, 6, 7, and 8.

2. The publication shall state the names of the parties and the main content of the decision; it shall have regard to the legitimate interest of undertakings in the protection of their business secrets.

Article 22. Special provisions.

1. The Commission shall submit to the Council proposals for making certain categories of agreement, decision and concerted practice falling within Art. 4 (2) or Art. 5 (2) compulsorily notifiable under Art. 4 or 5.

2. Within one year from the date of entry into force of this Regulation, the Council shall examine, on a proposal from the Commission, what special provisions might be made for exempting from the provisions of this Regulation agreements, decisions and concerted practices falling within Art. 4 (2) or Art. 5 (2).

Article 23. Transitional provisions applicable to decisions of authorities of the Member States.

1. Agreements, decisions and concerted practices of the kind described in Art. 85 (1) of the Treaty to which, before the entry into force of this Regulation, the competent authority of a Member State has declared Art. 85 (1) to be inapplicable pursuant to Art. 85 (3) shall not be subject to compulsory notification under Art. 5. The decision of the competent authority of the Member State shall be deemed to be a decision within the meaning of Art. 6; it shall cease to be valid upon expiration of the period fixed by such authority but in any event not more than three years after the entry into force of this Regulation. Art. 8 (3) shall apply.

2. Applications for renewal of decisions of the kind described in paragraph 1 shall be decided upon by the Commission in accordance with Art. 8 (2).

Article 24. Implementing provisions.
The Commission shall have power to adopt implementing provisions concerning the form, content and other details of applications pursuant to Arts. 2 and 3 and of notifications pursuant to Arts. 4 and 5, and concerning hearings pursuant to Art. 19 (1) and (2).

Article 25. 1. As regards agreements, decisions and concerted practices to which Art. 85 of the Treaty applies by virtue of accession, the date of accession shall be substituted for the date of entry into force of this Regulation in every place where reference is made in this Regulation to this latter date.

2. Agreements, decisions and concerted practices existing at the date of accession to which Art. 85 of the Treaty applies by virtue of accession shall be notified pursuant to Art. 5 (1) or Art. 7 (1) and (2) within six months from the date of accession.

3. Fines under Art. 15 (2) (a) shall not be imposed in respect of any act prior to notification of the agreements, decisions and practices to which paragraph 2 applies and which have been notified within the period therein specified.

4. New Member States shall take the measures referred to in Art. 14 (6) within six months from the date of accession after consulting the Commission.

5. The provisions of paragraphs 1 to 4 above shall apply in the same way in the case of the accession of the Hellenic Republic, the Kingdom of Spain and of the Portuguese Republic.

[Final provisions omitted.]

Regulation No 99/63/EEC of the Commission of 25 July 1963 on the hearings provided for in Art. 19 (1) and (2) of Council Regulation No 17[2]

The Commission of the European Economic Community,

Having regard to the Treaty establishing the European Economic Community, and in particular Arts. 87 and 155 thereof;

Having regard to Art. 24 of Council Regulation No 17 of 6 February 1962 (First Regulation implementing Arts. 85 and 86 of the Treaty);

Whereas the Commission has power under Art. 24 of Council Regulation No 17 to lay down implementing provisions concerning the hearings provided for in Art. 19 (1) and (2) of that Regulation;

Whereas in most cases the Commission will in the course of its inquiries already be in close touch with the undertakings or associations of undertakings which are the subject thereof and they will accordingly have the opportunity of making known their views regarding the objections raised against them;

Whereas, however, in accordance with Art. 19 (1) of Regulation No 17 and with the rights of defence, the undertakings and associations of undertakings concerned must have the right on conclusion of the inquiry to submit their comments on the whole of the objections raised against them which the Commission proposes to deal with in its decisions;

Whereas persons other than the undertakings or associations of undertakings which are the subject of the inquiry may have an interest in being heard; whereas, by the second sentence of Art. 19 (2) of Regulation No 17, such persons must have the opportunity of being heard if they apply and show that they have a sufficient interest;

Whereas it is desirable to enable persons who, pursuant to Art. 3 (2) of Regulation No 17, have applied for an infringement to be terminated to submit their comments where the Commission considers that on the basis of the information in its possession there are insufficient grounds for granting the application;

Whereas the various persons entitled to submit comments must do so in writing, both in their own interest and in the interests of good administration, without prejudice to oral procedure where appropriate to supplement the written evidence;

Whereas it is necessary to define the rights of persons who are to be heard, and in particular the conditions upon which they may be represented or assisted and the setting and calculation of time limits;

[2] OJ Sp. Ed. 1963-4, p. 47.

Whereas the Advisory Committee on Restrictive Practices and Monopolies delivers its Opinion on the basis of a preliminary draft decision; whereas it must therefore be consulted concerning a case after the inquiry in respect thereof has been completed; whereas such consultation does not prevent the Commission from re-opening an inquiry if need be;

Has adopted this Regulation:

Article 1. Before consulting the Advisory Committee on Restrictive Practices and Monopolies, the Commission shall hold a hearing pursuant to Art. 19 (1) of Regulation No 17.

Article 2. 1. The Commission shall inform undertakings and associations of undertakings in writing of the objections raised against them. The communication shall be addressed to each of them or to a joint agent appointed by them.

2. The Commission may inform the parties by giving notice in the *Official Journal of the European Communities*, if from the circumstances of the case this appears appropriate, in particular where notice is to be given to a number of undertakings but no joint agent has been appointed. The notice shall have regard to the legitimate interest of the undertakings in the protection of their business secrets.

3. A fine or a periodic penalty payment may be imposed on an undertaking or association of undertakings only if the objections were notified in the manner provided for in paragraph 1.

4. The Commission shall when giving notice of objections fix a time limit up to which the undertakings and associations of undertakings may inform the Commission of their views.

Article 3. 1. Undertakings and associations of undertakings shall, within the appointed time limit, make known in writing their views concerning the objections raised against them.

2. They may in their written comments set out all matters relevant to their defence.

3. They may attach any relevant documents in proof of the facts set out. They may also propose that the Commission hear persons who may corroborate those facts.

Article 4. The Commission shall in its decisions deal only with those objections raised against undertakings and associations of undertakings in respect of which they have been afforded the opportunity of making known their views.

Article 5. If natural or legal persons showing a sufficient interest apply to be heard pursuant to Art. 19 (2) of Regulation No 17, the Commission shall afford them the opportunity of making known their views in writing within such time limit as it shall fix.

Article 6. Where the Commission, having received an application pursuant to Art. 3 (2) of Regulation No 17, considers that on the basis of the information in its possession there are insufficient grounds for granting the application, it shall inform the applicants of its reasons and fix a time limit for them to submit any further comments in writing.

Article 7. 1. The Commission shall afford to persons who have so requested in their written comments the opportunity to put forward their arguments orally, if those persons show a sufficient interest or if the Commission proposes to impose on them a fine or periodic penalty payment.
    2. The Commission may likewise afford to any other person the opportunity of orally expressing his views.

Article 8. 1. The Commission shall summon the persons to be heard to attend on such date as it shall appoint.
    2. It shall forthwith transmit a copy of the summons to the competent authorities of the Member States, who may appoint an official to take part in the hearing.

Article 9. 1. Hearings shall be conducted by the persons appointed by the Commission for that purpose.
    2. Persons summoned to attend shall appear either in person or be represented by legal representatives or by representatives authorised by their constitution. Undertakings and associations of undertakings may moreover be represented by a duly authorised agent appointed from among their permanent staff.
    Persons heard by the Commission may be assisted by lawyers or university teachers who are entitled to plead before the Court of Justice of the European Communities in accordance with Art. 17 of the Protocol on the Statute of the Court, or by other qualified persons.
    3. Hearings shall not be public. Persons shall be heard separately or in the presence of other persons summoned to attend. In the latter case, regard shall be had to the legitimate interest of the undertakings in the protection of their business secrets.
    4. The essential content of the statements made by each persons heard shall be recorded in minutes which shall be read and approved by him.

Article 10. Without prejudice to Art. 2 (2), information and summonses from the Commission shall be sent to the addressees by registered letter with acknowledgement of receipt, or shall be delivered by hand against receipt.

Article 11. 1. In fixing the time limits provided for in Arts. 2, 5 and 6, the Commission shall have regard both to the time required for preparation of comments and to the urgency of the case. The time limit shall be not less than two weeks; it may be extended.

2. Time limits shall run from the day following receipt of a communication or delivery thereof by hand.

3. Written comments must reach the Commission or be dispatched by registered letter before expiry of the time limit. Where the time limit would expire on a Sunday or public holiday, it shall be extended up to the end of the next following working day. For the purpose of calculating this extension, public holidays shall, in cases where the relevant date is the date of receipt of written comments, be those set out in the Annex to this Regulation, and in cases where the relevant date is the date of dispatch, those appointed by law in the country of dispatch.

[Final provisions omitted.]

ANNEX

referred to in the third sentence of Art. 11 (3)
(List of public holidays)

New Year	1 Jan
Good Friday	
Easter Saturday	
Easter Monday	
Labour Day	1 May
Schuman Plan Day	9 May
Ascension Day	
Whit Monday	
Belgian National Day	21 July
Assumption	15 Aug
All Saints	1 Nov
All Souls	2 Nov
Christmas Eve	24 Dec
Christmas Day	25 Dec
The day following Christmas Day	26 Dec
New Year's Eve	31 Dec

Commission Notice Regarding Agreements, Decisions and Concerted Practices in the Field of Co-operation between Enterprises[3]

[EXTRACTS]

The Commission of the European Communities has frequently been asked as to the position it intends to adopt, within the framework of the application of the competition rules in the Treaties of Rome and Paris, on co-operation between enterprises. For this reason, this Notice attempts to furnish enterprises with certain guidance which, while not being exhaustive, should nonetheless provide them with useful tips on the interpretation to be given to the provisions of Art. 85 (1) of the EEC Treaty and Art. 65 (1) of the ECSC Treaty.

I

The Commission is favourably disposed to co-operation between small and medium-sized enterprises to the extent to which they are thereby enabled to work more rationally and to increase their productivity and competitiveness in a larger market. While recognising that its task is to facilitate such co-operation in particular, the Commission recognises that co-operation between large enterprises may also be economically justifiable without giving rise to objections from the point of view of competition policy.

[The text then recites the effect of EEC 85 (1) and ECSC 65 (1).]

The Commission feels it appropriate, and of particular interest to small and medium-sized enterprises, to explain the considerations which it will take into account in the interpretation of EEC 85 (1) and ECSC 65 (1) and in their application to certain co-operation arrangements between enterprises and to indicate which thereof do not, in its opinion, fall under them. This Notice applies to all enterprises, whatever their size.

Forms of co-operation other than those mentioned below may also not be prohibited by EEC 85 (1) or ECSC 65 (1). This applies in particular if the global market position of the co-operating enterprises is too weak to lead, because of the agreement, to appreciable restraint on competition within the common market or, in the context of EEC 85 (1), to affect trade between Member States.

It should also be pointed out that other forms of inter-enterprise co-operation, or agreements containing additional clauses, to which the com-

---

[3] JO 1968 C 75/3 amended C 84 translated by the Editors. The Notice is undated.

petition rules of the Treaties apply, may still be exempted under EEC 85 (3) or authorised under ECSC 65 (2).

The Commission intends, by individual decisions where appropriate, or by general notices, to establish rapidly the status of various types of co-operation in relation to the rules of the Treaties.

At this stage no general guidance can be given on the application of EEC 86 concerning the abuse of a dominant position in the common market or part thereof. The same is true of ECSC 66 (7).

The present Notice should, as a general rule, allay the need to obtain negative clearance for the agreements listed in Regulation 17 Art. 2. Nor should it be necessary to seek clarification of the legal position by a Commission decision on an individual case; there is therefore no need to notify, for that purpose, such agreements. If, however, there is doubt in a particular case, as to whether a co-operation agreement restricts competition, or if other types of inter-enterprise co-operation which, in the opinion of the enterprises, do not restrict competition are not mentioned herein, the enterprises may request negative clearance of EEC 85 (1) or, where ECSC 65 (1) applies, file, as a precaution, an application under ECSC 65 (2).

This Notice does not pre-judge interpretation by the Court of Justice of the European Communities.

II

The Commission considers that the following agreements do not restrict competition.

1. Agreements having as their sole object:

(a) the exchange of opinions or experience,
(b) joint market research,
(c) the joint carrying out of comparative studies of enterprises or industries,
(d) the joint preparation of statistics and calculation models.

Agreements whose sole purpose is the joint acquisition of information necessary to enable the various enterprises to determine their future market behaviour freely and independently or to have individual recourse to a joint advisory body do not have, as their object or effect, the restriction of competition. But such may occur if the enterprises' freedom of action is limited or their market behaviour co-ordinated expressly or through concerted practices. This is particularly the case where concrete recommendations are made or conclusions expressed in such a way as to induce identical market behaviour in at least some of the enterprises.

The exchange of information may take place among the enterprises themselves or through a third party acting as an intermediary body. However, the distinction between information which has no bearing on competition and behaviour in restraint thereof is particularly difficult to draw when such bodies are required to register orders, turnover figures, investments and prices so that, as a general rule, it is impossible, without more, to assume the inapplicability of EEC 85 (1) or ECSC 65 (1). A restriction of competition may occur, in particular, where there is an oligopolist market for homogeneous products.

In the absence of more extensive co-operation between participating enterprises, mere joint market research and comparative studies of enterprises and industries in order to collect information and ascertain facts and market conditions do not of themselves affect competition. Other steps of this type such as, for example, the joint establishment of conjunctural and structural analyses are so obviously untainted that there is no need to give them special mention.

Calculation models containing specific rates of calculation must be considered recommendations which may lead to a restraint of competition.

2. Agreements having as their sole object:

(a) co-operation in accounting matters,
(b) joint credit guarantees,
(c) joint debt-collection offices,
(d) the consultation of joint bodies as to business organisation or tax matters.

These cases involve co-operation in fields which concern neither the supply of goods and services nor economic decisions of enterprises involved so that they cannot lead to any restriction of competition.

Co-operation in accounting matters is neutral from the point of view of competition since it deals only with the technical handling of accounting. Similarly the creation of credit guarantee pools does not come under competition rules since it does not modify the relationship between supply and demand.

Debt-collecting offices which do not limit their activity to collecting payment at the instance and on the instructions of participants, or which fix prices or exercise any influence on price formation, may restrict competition. Application of conditions which are uniform for all participants may constitute a concerted practice, as may joint comparison of prices. In this connection there is no objection to the use of standard forms; their use, however, must not be tied to an agreement or tacit understanding on uniform prices, rebates or conditions of sale.

3. Agreements having as their sole object:

(a) joint research and development projects,
(b) joint allocation of research and development contracts,
(c) the sharing-out of research and development projects among the participants.

Similarly, in the field of research the mere exchange of experience and findings is for information only and does not restrict competition. It does not need special mention.

Agreements made for joint research or the joint development of research results to the stage of their industrial application do not affect the competitive position of the parties. This is equally the case when research fields and development work are shared out provided that the results remain accessible to all participants. But the Treaties' competition rules may be infringed if enterprises contract obligations restricting their own research and development activity or their exploitation of the results of joint work so that, outside the joint project, they are no longer free to carry out research and development for their own account. In the absence of joint research, any contractual obligation or undertaking to give up their own research in full or in part may have the effect of restricting competition.

Specialisation which may restrict competition occurs when research fields are shared out without an agreement providing for reciprocal access to the results.

Competition may also be restricted by the making of agreements, or corresponding concerted practices, as to the practical exploitation of joint research and development work particularly when the participants undertake or agree to manufacture only the products, or type of products, developed jointly or to split future production amongst themselves.

The idea of joint research is that its results be exploited by the participating enterprises in proportion to their participation. If the participation of certain enterprises is limited to a defined field of joint research or to the provision of a fixed financial contribution then—in so far as one can speak here of joint research—there are no restraints on competition merely because the participants have access to the research results only in proportion to their participation. On the other hand, competition may be restricted if certain participants are excluded from exploitation of the results either *in toto* or to an extent incommensurate with their participation.

If the granting of licences to third parties is expressly or tacitly excluded, competition may be restricted; however the pooling of research justifies the obligation not to grant licences to third parties save by common agreement or majority decision.

The legal form taken by joint research and development does not affect any assessment of the compatibility of the agreement with the rules on competition.

4. Agreements whose sole object is the joint use of plant and storage and transport facilities.

These types of co-operation do not restrict competition since they are limited to organisational matters and to the technical use of facilities. There may, however, be restriction of competition if the enterprises involved do not themselves bear the cost of utilising plant and equipment or if agreements are made, or concerted practices applied, regarding joint production or the sharing out of production or the establishment or running of a joint enterprise.

5. Agreements whose sole object is the setting-up of working partnerships for the joint filling of orders when the participating enterprises do not compete with each other as regards the work to be done or where each alone is unable to fill the orders.

Enterprises which do not compete with each other cannot, by setting up temporary associations, restrict competition *inter se*. This is true not only for enterprises belonging to different industries but also for those of the same sector to the extent to which they participate in the working partnership only by providing products or services which the other participants cannot. It matters little that the enterprises compete with each other in other sectors; what matters is to know if, given the concrete circumstances of the particular case, competition in the products or services at issue is possible in the foreseeable future. If the absence of competition between the enterprises and the persistence of this situation rest on agreements or concerted practices there may be a restraint on competition.

Furthermore, even in the case of working partnerships of enterprises which do compete with each other, competition is not restricted when the participants could not alone and by themselves fill a particular order. This is especially so when, because of lack of experience, specialised knowledge, capacity or adequate financial cover, the enterprise by itself is operating with no hope of success or without being able to finish the work on time or bear the financial risk.

Nor is there restriction of competition if the establishment of a working partnership is the only way in which the enterprises can make a tempting offer. Competition may, however, be restricted if the enterprises undertake to operate solely within the framework of a working partnership.

6. Agreements having as their sole object:

(a) joint selling,

(b) joint after-sales and repair services, provided the enterprises participating are not in competition *inter se* for the products or services covered by the agreement.

As already explained in full under section 5, co-operation between enterprises cannot restrict competition if they are not competing with each other.

Very often joint selling carried out by small or medium enterprises does not constitute an appreciable restriction on competition, even when they are in competition *inter se*; it is, however, impossible to lay down in this Notice general criteria or to fix precisely the extent of 'small' or 'medium-sized'.

There is no joint after-sales and repair service if several producers, without acting in concert, entrust the after sales and repair service of their products to the same enterprise which is independent of them.

7. Agreements whose sole object is joint advertising.

Joint advertising aims to draw the buyers' attention to the products of an industry or to a common brand; as such it does not restrict competition between participating enterprises. Competition may, however, be restricted when through an agreement or concerted policy participants are prevented, entirely or in part, from doing their own advertising or when other restrictions are imposed on them.

8. Agreements whose sole object is the use of a common label to denominate products of a certain quality where the label is available to all competitors on the same conditions.

Such labelling associations do not restrict competition if other competitors, whose products meet objectively the required quality standards, may use the label on the same conditions as members. Similarly the obligation to submit to quality control the products bearing the label or to prescribe uniform instructions for use or to use the label for products meeting the quality standards do not constitute a restraint on competition. But there may be restraint on competition if the right to use the label is tied to obligations regarding production, marketing, price formation or other matters as when, for example, the participating enterprises are obliged to manufacture or sell only products of guaranteed quality.

Commission notice of 3 September 1986
on agreements of minor importance which do not
fall under Art. 85 (1) of the Treaty establishing
the European Economic Community[4]

I

1. The Commission considers it important to facilitate co-operation between undertakings where such co-operation is economically desirable without presenting difficulties from the point of view of competition policy, which is particularly true of co-operation between small and medium-sized undertakings. To this end it published the 'Notice concerning agreements, decisions and concerted practices in the field of co-operation between undertakings'[5] listing a number of agreements that by their nature cannot be regarded as restraints of competition. Furthermore, in the Notice concerning its assessment of certain subcontracting agreements[6] the Commission considered that this type of contract which offers opportunities for development, in particular, to small and medium-sized undertakings is not in itself caught by the prohibition in Art. 85 (1). By issuing the present Notice, the Commission is taking a further step towards defining the field of application of Art. 85 (1), in order to facilitate co-operation between small and medium-sized undertakings.

2. In the Commission's opinion, agreements whose effects on trade between Member States or on competition are negligible do not fall under the ban on restrictive agreements contained in Art. 85 (1). Only those agreements are prohibited which have an appreciable impact on market conditions, in that they appreciably alter the market position, in other words the sales or supply possibilities, of third undertakings and of users.

3. In the present Notice the Commission, by setting quantitative criteria and by explaining their application, has given a sufficiently concrete meaning to the concept 'appreciable' for undertakings to be able to judge for themselves whether the agreements they have concluded with other undertakings, being of minor importance, do not fall under Art. 85 (1). The quantitative definition of 'appreciable' given by the Commission is, however, no absolute yardstick; in fact, in individual cases even agreements between undertakings which exceed these limits may still have only a negligible effect on trade between Member States or on competition, and are therefore not caught by Art. 85 (1).

---

[4] OJ 1986 C 231/2. The present Notice replaces the Commission Notice of 19 December 1977, OJ 1977, C 313/3.

[5] JO 1968 C 75/3 corrected by 1968 C 84/14. Supra p. 468.

[6] OJ 1979, C 1/2

4. As a result of this Notice, there should no longer be any point in undertakings obtaining negative clearance, as defined by Art. 2 of Council Regulation No 17,[7] for the agreements covered, nor should it be necessary to have the legal position established through Commission decisions in individual cases; notification with this end in view will no longer be necessary for such agreements. However, if it is doubtful whether in an individual case an agreement appreciably affects trade between Member States or competition, the undertakings are free to apply for negative clearance or to notify the agreement.

5. In cases covered by the present Notice the Commission, as a general rule, will not open proceedings under Regulation No 17, either upon application or upon its own initiative. Where, due to exceptional circumstances, an agreement which is covered by the present Notice nevertheless falls under Art. 85 (1), the Commission will not impose fines. Where undertakings have failed to notify an agreement falling under Art. 85 (1) because they wrongly assumed, owing to a mistake in calculating their market share or aggregate turnover, that the agreement was covered by the present Notice, the Commission will not consider imposing fines unless the mistake was due to negligence.

6. This Notice is without prejudice to the competence of national courts to apply Art. 85 (1) on the basis of their own jurisdiction, although it constitutes a factor which such courts may take into account when deciding a pending case. It is also without prejudice to any interpretation which may be given by the Court of Justice of the European Communities.

II

7. The Commission holds the view that agreements between undertakings engaged in the production or distribution of goods or in the provision of services generally do not fall under the prohibition of Art. 81 (1) if:

– the goods or services which are the subject of the agreement (hereinafter referred to as 'the contract products') together with the participation undertakings' other goods or services which are considered by users to be equivalent in view of their characteristics, price and intended use, do not represent more than 5% of the total market for such goods or services (hereinafter referred to as 'products') in the area of the common market affected by the agreement and
– the aggregate annual turnover of the participating undertakings does not exceed 200 million ECU.

[7] OJ No 13, 21. 2. 1962, p. 204/62.

8. The Commission also holds the view that the said agreements do not fall under the prohibition of Art. 85 (1) if the abovementioned market share or turnover is exceeded by not more than one tenth during two successive financial years.

9. For the purposes of this Notice, participating undertakings are:

(a) undertakings party to the agreement;
(b) undertakings in which a party to the agreement, directly or indirectly,
   - owns more than half the capital or business assets or
   - has the power to exercise more than half the voting rights, or
   - has the power to appoint more than half the members of the supervisory board, board of management or bodies legally representing the undertakings, or
   - has the right to manage the affairs;
(c) undertakings which directly or indirectly have in or over a party to the agreement the rights or powers listed in (b);
(d) undertakings in or over which an undertaking referred to in (c) directly or indirectly has the rights or powers listed in (b).

Undertakings in which several undertakings as referred to in (a) to (d) jointly have, directly or indirectly, the rights or powers set out in (b) shall also be considered to be participating undertakings.

10. In order to calculate the market share, it is necessary to determine the relevant market. This implies the definition of the relevant product market and the relevant geographical market.

11. The relevant product market includes besides the contract products any other products which are identical or equivalent to them. This rule applies to the products of the participating undertakings as well as to the market for such products. The products in question must be interchangeable. Whether or not this is the case must be judged from the vantage point of the user, normally taking the characteristics, price and intended use of the goods together. In certain cases, however, products can form a separate market on the basis of their characteristics, their price or their intended use alone. This is true especially where consumer preferences have developed.

12. Where the contract products are components which are incorporated into another product by the participating undertakings, reference should be made to the market for the latter product, provided that the components represent a significant part of it. Where the contract products are components which are sold to third undertakings, reference should be made to the market for the components. In cases where both conditions apply, both markets should be considered separately.

13. The relevant geographical market is the area within the Community in which the agreement produces its effects. This area will be

the whole common market where the contract products are regularly bought and sold in all Member States. Where the contract products cannot be bought and sold in a part of the common market, or are bought and sold only in limited quantities or at irregular intervals in such a part, that part should be disregarded. ·

14. The relevant geographical market will be narrower than the whole common market in particular where:

— the nature and characteristics of the contract product, e.g. high transport costs in relation to the value of the product, restrict its mobility; or
— movement of the contract product within the common market is hindered by barriers to entry to national markets resulting from State intervention, such as quantitative restrictions, severe taxation differentials and non-tariff barriers, e.g. type approvals or safety standard certifications. In such cases the national territory may have to be considered as the relevant geographical market. However, this will only be justified if the existing barriers to entry cannot be overcome by reasonable effort and at an acceptable cost.

15. Aggregate turnover includes the turnover in all goods and services, excluding tax, achieved during the last financial year by the participating undertaking. In cases where an undertaking has concluded similar agreements with various other undertakings in the relevant market, the turnover of all participating undertakings should be taken together. The aggregate turnover shall not include dealings between participating undertakings.

16. The present Notice shall not apply where in a relevant market competition is restricted by the cumulative effects of parallel networks of similar agreements established by several manufacturers or dealers.

17. The present Notice is likewise applicable to decisions by associations of undertakings and to concerted practices.

Regulation (EEC) No 1983/83 of the Council of 22 June 1983 on the application of Article 85 (3) of the Treaty to categories of exclusive distribution agreements[8]

The Commission of the European Communities,

[Recitals omitted.]

(1) Whereas Regulation No 19/65/EEC empowers the Commission to apply Art. 85 (3) of the Treaty by regulation to certain categories of

[8] OJ 1983 L 173/1.

bilateral exclusive distribution agreements and analogous concerted practices falling within Art. 85 (1);

(2) Whereas experience to date makes it possible to define a category of agreements and concerted practices which can be regarded as normally satisfying the conditions laid down in Art. 85 (3);

(3) Whereas exclusive distribution agreements of the category defined in Art. 1 of this Regulation may fall within the prohibition contained in Art. 85 (1) of the Treaty; whereas this will apply in exceptional cases to exclusive agreements of this kind to which only undertakings from one Member State are party and which concern the resale of goods within that Member State; whereas, however, to the extent that such agreements may affect trade between Member States and also satisfy all the requirements set out in this Regulation there is no reason to withhold from them the benefit of the exemption by category;

(4) Whereas it is not necessary expressly to exclude from the defined category those agreements which do not fulfil the conditions of Art. 85 (1) of the Treaty;

(5) Whereas exclusive distribution agreements lead in general to an improvement in distribution because the undertaking is able to concentrate its sales activities, does not need to maintain numerous business relations with a larger number of dealers and is able, by dealing with only one dealer, to overcome more easily distribution difficulties in international trade resulting from linguistic, legal and other differences;

(6) Whereas exclusive distribution agreements facilitate the promotion of sales of a product and lead to intensive marketing and to continuity of supplies while at the same time rationalising distribution; whereas they stimulate competition between the products of different manufacturers; whereas the appointment of an exclusive distributor who will take over sales promotion, customer services and carrying of stocks is often the most effective way, and sometimes indeed the only way, for the manufacturer to enter a market and compete with other manufacturers already present; whereas this is particularly so in the case of small and medium-sized undertakings; whereas it must be left to the contracting parties to decide whether and to what extent they consider it desirable to incorporate in the agreements terms providing for the promotion of sales;

(7) Whereas, as a rule, such exclusive distribution agreements also allow consumers a fair share of the resulting benefit as they gain directly from the improvement in distribution, and their economic and supply position is improved as they can obtain products manufactured in particular in other countries more quickly and more easily;

(8) Whereas this Regulation must define the obligations restricting competition which may be included in exclusive distribution agreements;

whereas the other restrictions on competition allowed under this Regulation in addition to the exclusive supply obligation produce a clear division of functions between the parties and compel the exclusive distributor to concentrate his sales efforts on the contract goods and the contract territory; whereas they are, where they are agreed only for the duration of the agreement, generally necessary in order to attain the improvement in the distribution of goods sought through exclusive distribution; whereas it may be left to the contracting parties to decide which of these obligations they include in their agreements; whereas further restrictive obligations and in particular those which limit the exclusive distributor's choice of customers or his freedom to determine his prices and conditions of sale cannot be exempted under this Regulation;

(9) Whereas the exemption by category should be reserved for agreements for which it can be assumed with sufficient certainty that they satisfy the conditions of Art. 85 (3) of the Treaty;

(10) Whereas it is not possible, in the absence of a case-by-case examination, to consider that adequate improvements in distribution occur where a manufacturer entrusts the distribution of his goods to another manufacturer with whom he is in competition; whereas such agreements should, therefore, be excluded from the exemption by category; whereas certain derogations from this rule in favour of small and medium-sized undertakings can be allowed;

(11) Whereas consumers will be assured of a fair share of the benefits resulting from exclusive distribution only if parallel imports remain possible; whereas agreements relating to goods which the user can obtain only from the exclusive distributor should therefore be excluded from the exemption by category; whereas the parties cannot be allowed to abuse industrial property rights or other rights in order to create absolute territorial protection; whereas this does not prejudice the relationship between competition law and industrial property rights, since the sole object here is to determine the conditions for exemption by category;

(12) Whereas, since competition at the distribution stage is ensured by the possibility of parallel imports, the exclusive distribution agreements covered by this Regulation will not normally afford any possibility of eliminating competition in respect of a substantial part of the products in question; whereas this is also true of agreements that allot to the exclusive distributor a contract territory covering the whole of the common market;

(13) Whereas, in particular cases in which agreements or concerted practices satisfying the requirements of this Regulation nevertheless have effects incompatible with Art. 85 (3) of the Treaty, the Commission

may withdraw the benefit of the exemption by category from the undertakings party to them;

(14) Whereas agreements and concerted practices which satisfy the conditions set out in this Regulation need not be notified; whereas an undertaking may nonetheless in a particular case where real doubt exists, request the Commission to declare whether its agreements comply with this Regulation;

(15) Whereas this Regulation does not affect the applicability of Commission Regulation (EEC) No 3604/82 of 23 December 1982 on the application of Art. 85 (3) of the Treaty to categories of specialisation agreements, whereas it does not exclude the application of Art. 86 of the Treaty.

Has adopted this regulation:

Article 1.   Pursuant to Art. 85 (3) of the Treaty and subject to the provisions of this Regulation, it is hereby declared that Art. 85 (1) of the Treaty shall not apply to agreements to which only two undertakings are party and whereby one party agrees with the other to supply certain goods for resale within the whole or a defined area of the common market only to that other.

Article 2.   1. Apart from the obligation referred to in Art. 1 no restriction on competition shall be imposed on the supplier other than the obligation not to supply the contract goods to users in the contract territory.

2. No restriction on competition shall be imposed on the exclusive distributor other than:

(a) the obligation not to manufacture or distribute goods which compete with the contract goods;
(b) the obligation to obtain the contract goods for resale only from the other party;
(c) the obligation to refrain, outside the contract territory and in relation to the contract goods, from seeking customers, from establishing any branch, and from maintaining any distribution depot.

3. Art. 1 shall apply notwithstanding that the exclusive distributor undertakes all or any of the following obligations:

(a) to purchase complete ranges of goods or minimum quantities;
(b) to sell the contract goods under trademarks, or packed and present as specified by the other party;
(c) to take measures for promotion of sales, in particular:
  – to advertise,
  – to maintain a sales network or stock of goods,

– to provide customer and guarantee services,
– to employ staff having specialised or technical training.

Article 3.   Art. 1 shall not apply where:

(a) manufacturers of identical goods or of goods which are considered by users as equivalent in view of their characteristics, price and intended use enter into reciprocal exclusive distribution agreements between themselves in respect of such goods;

(b) manufacturers of identical goods or of goods which are considered by users as equivalent in view of their characteristics, price and intended use enter into a non-reciprocal exclusive distribution agreement between themselves in respect of such goods unless at least one of them has a total annual turnover of no more than 100 million ECU;

(c) users can obtain the contract goods in the contract territory only from the exclusive distributor and have no alternative source of supply outside the contract territory;

(d) one or both of the parties makes it difficult for intermediaries or users to obtain the contract goods from other dealers inside the common market or, in so far as no alternative source of supply is available there, from outside the common market, in particular where one or both of them:
   1. exercises industrial property rights so as to prevent dealers or users from obtaining outside, or from selling in, the contract territory properly marked or otherwise properly marketed contract goods;
   2. exercises other rights or take other measures so as to prevent dealers or users from obtaining outside, or from selling in, the contract territory contract goods.

Article 4.   1. Art. 3 (a) and (b) shall also apply where the goods there referred to are manufactured by an undertaking connected with a party to the agreement.

2. Connected undertakings are:

(a) undertakings in which a party to the agreement, directly or indirectly:
   – owns more than half the capital or business assets, or
   – has the power to exercise more than half the voting rights, or
   – has the power to appoint more than half the members of the supervisory board, board of directors or bodies legally representing the undertaking, or
   – has the right to manage the affairs;

(b) undertakings which directly or indirectly have in or over a party to the agreement the rights or powers listed in (a);

(c) undertakings in which an undertaking referred to in (b) directly or indirectly has the rights or powers listed in (a).

3. Undertakings in which the parties to the agreement or undertakings connected with them jointly have the rights or powers set out in paragraph 2 (a) shall be considered to be connected with each of the parties to the agreement.

Article 5. 1. For the purpose of Art. 3 (b), the ECU is the unit of account used for drawing up the budget of the Community pursuant to Arts. 207 and 209 of the Treaty.

2. Article 1 shall remain applicable where during any period of two consecutive financial years the total turnover referred to in Art. 3 (b) is exceeded by no more than 10%.

3. For the purpose of calculating total turnover within the meaning of Art. 3 (b), the turnovers achieved during the last financial year by the party to the agreement and connected undertakings in respect of all goods and services, excluding all taxes and other duties, shall be added together. For this purpose, no account shall be taken of dealings between the parties to the agreement or between these undertakings and undertakings connected with them or between the connected undertakings.

Article 6. The Commission may withdraw the benefit of this Regulation, pursuant to Art. 7 of Regulation No 19/65/EEC, when it finds in a particular case that an agreement which is exempted by this Regulation nevertheless has certain effects which are incompatible with the conditions set out in Art. 85 (3) of the Treaty, and in particular where;

(a) the contract goods are not subject, in the contract territory, to effective competition from identical goods or goods considered by users as equivalent in view of their characteristics, price and intended use;
(b) access by other suppliers to the different stages of distribution within the contract territory is made difficult to a significant extent;
(c) for reasons other than those referred to in Art. 3 (c) and (d) it is not possible for intermediaries or users to obtain supplies of the contract goods from dealers outside the contract territory on the terms there customary;
(d) the exclusive distributor:
    1. without any objectively justified reason refuses to supply in the contract territory categories of purchasers who cannot obtain contract goods elsewhere on suitable terms or applies to them differing prices or conditions of sale;
    2. sells the contract goods at excessively high prices.

Article 7. In the period 1 July 1983 to 31 December 1986, the prohibition in Art. 85 (1) of the Treaty shall not apply to agreements which were in force on 1 July 1983 or entered into force between 1 July and 31

December 1983 and which satisfy the exemption conditions of Regulation No 67/67/EEC.

The provisions of the proceeding paragraph shall apply in the same way to agreements which were in force on the date of accession of the Kingdom of Spain and of the Portuguese Republic and which, as a result of accession fall within the scope of Art. 85 (1) of the Treaty.

Article 8. This Regulation shall not apply to agreements entered into for the resale of drinks in premises used for the sale and consumption of beer or for the resale of petroleum products in service stations.

Article 9. This Regulation shall apply *mutatis mutandis* to concerted practices of the type defined in Art. 1.

Article 10. This Regulation shall enter into force on 1 July 1983. It shall expire on 31 December 1997.

[Final provisions omitted.]

Regulation (EEC) No 1984/83
of the Commission of 22 June 1983
on the application of Article 85 (3) of the
Treaty to categories of exclusive purchasing agreements[9]

The Commission of the European Communities,

[Recitals omitted.]

(1) Whereas Regulation No 19/65/EEC empowers the Commission to apply Art. 85 (3) of the Treaty by regulation to certain categories of bilateral exclusive purchasing agreements entered into for the purpose of the resale of goods and corresponding concerted practices falling within Art. 85;

(2) Whereas experience to date makes it possible to define three categories of agreements and concerted practices which can be regarded as normally satisfying the conditions laid down in Art. 85 (3); whereas the first category comprises exclusive purchasing agreements of short and medium duration in all sectors of the economy; whereas the other two categories comprise long-term exclusive purchasing agreements entered into for the resale of beer in premises used for the sale and consumption (beer supply agreements) and of petroleum products in filling stations (service-station agreements);

[9] OJ 1983 L 173/5.

(3) Whereas exclusive purchasing agreements of the categories defined in this Regulation may fall within the prohibition contained in Art. 85 (1) of the Treaty; whereas this will often be the case with agreements concluded between undertakings from different Member States; whereas an exclusive purchasing agreement to which undertakings from only one Member State are party and which concerns the resale of goods within that Member State may also be caught by the prohibition; whereas this is in particular the case where it is one of a number of similar agreements which together may affect trade between Member States;

(4) Whereas it is not necessary expressly to exclude from the defined categories those agreements which do not fulfil the conditions of Art. 85 (1) of the Treaty;

(5) Whereas the exclusive purchasing agreements defined in this Regulation lead in general to an improvement in distribution; whereas they enable the supplier to plan the sales of his goods with greater precision and for a longer period and ensure that the reseller's requirements will be met on a regular basis for the duration of the agreement; whereas this allows the parties to limit the risk to them of variations in market conditions and to lower distribution costs;

(6) Whereas such agreements also facilitate the promotion of the sales of a product and lead to intensive marketing because the supplier, in consideration for the exclusive purchasing obligation, is as a rule under an obligation to contribute to the improvement of the structure of the distribution network, the quality of the promotional effort or the sales success; whereas, at the same time, they stimulate competition between the products of different manufacturers; whereas the appointment of several resellers, who are bound to purchase exclusively from the manufacturer and who take over sales promotion, customer services and carrying of stock, is often the most effective way, and sometimes the only way, for the manufacturer to penetrate a market and compete with other manufacturers already present; whereas this is particularly so in the case of small and medium-sized undertakings; whereas it must be left to the contracting parties to decide whether and to what extent they consider it desirable to incorporate in their agreements terms concerning the promotion of sales;

(7) Whereas, as a rule, exclusive purchasing agreements between suppliers and resellers also allow consumers a fair share of the resulting benefit as they gain the advantages of regular supply and are able to obtain the contract goods more quickly and more easily;

(8) Whereas this Regulation must define the obligations restricting competition which may be included in an exclusive purchasing agreement; whereas the other restrictions of competition allowed under this

Regulation in addition to the exclusive purchasing obligation lead to a clear division of functions between the parties and compel the reseller to concentrate his sales efforts on the contract goods; whereas they are, where they are agreed only for the duration of the agreement, generally necessary in order to attain the improvement in the distribution of goods sought through exclusive purchasing; whereas further restrictive obligations and in particular those which limit the reseller's choice of customers or his freedom to determine his prices and conditions of sale cannot be exempted under this Regulation;

(9) Whereas the exemption by categories should be reserved for agreements for which it can be assumed with sufficient certainty that they satisfy the conditions of Art. 85 (3) of the Treaty;

(10) Whereas it is not possible, in the absence of a case-by-case examination, to consider that adequate improvements in distribution occur where a manufacturer imposes an exclusive purchasing obligation with respect to his goods on a manufacturer with whom he is in competition; whereas such agreements should, therefore, be excluded from the exemption by categories; whereas certain derogations from this rule in favour of small and medium-sized undertakings can be allowed;

(11) Whereas certain conditions must be attached to the exemption by categories so that access by other undertakings to the different stages of distribution can be ensured; whereas, to this end, limits must be set to the scope and to the duration of the exclusive purchasing obligation; whereas it appears appropriate as a general rule to grant the benefit of a general exemption from the prohibition on restrictive agreements only to exclusive purchasing agreements which are concluded for a specified product or range of products and for not more than five years;

(12) Whereas, in the case of beer supply agreements and service-station agreements, different rules should be laid down which take account of the particularities of the markets in question;

(13) Whereas these agreements are generally distinguished by the fact that, on the one hand, the supplier confers on the reseller special commercial or financial advantages by contributing to his financing, granting him or obtaining for him a loan on favourable terms, equipping him with a site or premises for conducting his business, providing him with equipment or fittings, or undertaking other investments for his benefit and that, on the other hand, the reseller enters into a long-term exclusive purchasing obligation which in most cases is accompanied by a ban on dealing in competing products;

(14) Whereas beer supply and service-station agreements, like the other exclusive purchasing agreements dealt with in this Regulation, normally produce an appreciable improvement in distribution in which consumers are allowed a fair share of the resulting benefit;

(15) Whereas the commercial and financial advantages conferred by the supplier on the reseller make it significantly easier to establish, modernize, maintain and operate premises used for the sale and consumption of drinks and service stations; whereas the exclusive purchasing obligation and the ban on dealing in competing products imposed on the reseller incite the reseller to devote all the resources at his disposal to the sale of the contract goods; whereas such agreements lead to durable cooperation between the parties allowing them to improve or maintain the quality of the contract goods and of the services to the customer and sales efforts of the reseller; whereas they allow long-term planning of sales and consequently a cost effective organisation of production and distribution; whereas the pressure of competition between products of different makes obliges the undertakings involved to determine the number and character of premises used for the sale and consumption of drinks and service stations, in accordance with the wishes of customers;

(16) Whereas consumers benefit from the improvements described, in particular because they are ensured supplies of goods of satisfactory quality at fair prices and conditions while being able to choose between the products of different manufacturers;

(17) Whereas the advantages produced by beer supply agreements and service-station agreements cannot otherwise be secured to the same extent and with the same degree of certainty; whereas the exclusive purchasing obligation on the reseller and the non-competition clause imposed on him are essential components of such agreements and thus usually indispensable for the attainment of these advantages; whereas, however, this is true only as long as the reseller's obligation to purchase from the supplier is confined in the case of premises used for the sale and consumption of drinks to beers and other drinks of the types offered by the supplier, and in the case of service stations to petroleum-based fuel for motor vehicles and other petroleum-based fuels; whereas the exclusive purchasing obligation for lubricants and related petroleum-based products can be accepted only on condition that the supplier provides for the reseller or finances the procurement of specific equipment for the carrying out of lubrication work; whereas this obligation should only relate to products intended for use within the service station;

(18) Whereas, in order to maintain the reseller's commercial freedom and to ensure access to the retail level of distribution on the part of

other suppliers, not only the scope but also the duration of the exclusive purchasing obligation must be limited; whereas it appears appropriate to allow drinks suppliers a choice between a medium-term exclusive purchasing agreement covering a range of drinks and a long-term exclusive purchasing agreement for beer; whereas it is necessary to provide special rules for those premises used for the sale and consumption of drinks which the supplier lets to the reseller; whereas, in this case, the reseller must have the right to obtain, under the conditions specified in this Regulation, other drinks, except beer, supplied under the agreement or of the same type but bearing a different trademark; whereas a uniform maximum duration should be provided for service-station agreements, with the exception of tenancy agreements between the supplier and the reseller, which takes account of the long-term character of the relationship between the parties;

(19) Whereas to the extent that Member States provide, by law or administrative measures, for the same upper limit of duration for the exclusive purchasing obligation upon the reseller as in service-station agreements laid down in this Regulation but provide for a permissible duration which varies in proportion to the consideration provided by the supplier or generally provide for a shorter duration than that permitted by this Regulation, such laws or measures are not contrary to the objectives of this Regulation which, in this respect, merely sets an upper limit to the duration of service-station agreements; whereas the application and enforcement of such national laws or measures must therefore be regarded as compatible with the provisions of this Regulation;

(20) Whereas the limitations and conditions provided for in this Regulation are such as to guarantee effective competition on the markets in question; whereas, therefore, the agreements to which the exemption by category applies do not normally enable the participating undertakings to eliminate competition for a substantial part of the products in question;

(21) Whereas, in particular cases in which agreements or concerted practices satisfying the conditions of this Regulation nevertheless have effects incompatible with Art. 85 (3) of the Treaty, the Commission may withdraw the benefit of the exemption by category from the undertakings party thereto;

(22) Whereas agreements and concerted practices which satisfy the conditions set out in this Regulation need not be notified; whereas an undertaking may nonetheless, in a particular case where real doubt exists, request the Commission to declare whether its agreements comply with this Regulation;

(23) Whereas this Regulation does not affect the applicability of Commission Regulation (EEC) No 3604/82 of 23 December 1982 on the application of Art. 85 (3) of the Treaty to categories of specialisation agreements; whereas it does not exclude the application of Art. 86 of the Treaty;

Has adopted this regulation:

TITLE I. GENERAL PROVISIONS

Article 1.   Pursuant to Art. 85 (3) of the Treaty, and subject to the conditions set out in Arts. 2 to 5 of this Regulation, it is hereby declared that Art. 85 (1) of the Treaty shall not apply to agreements to which only two undertakings are party and whereby one party, the reseller, agrees with the other, the supplier, to purchase certain goods specified in the agreement for resale only from the supplier or from a connected undertaking or from another undertaking which the supplier has entrusted with the sale of his goods.

Article 2.   1. No other restriction of competition shall be imposed on the supplier than the obligation not to distribute the contract goods or goods which compete with the contract goods in the reseller's principal sales area and at the reseller's level of distribution.

2. Apart from the obligation described in Art. 1, no other restriction of competition shall be imposed on the reseller than the obligation not to manufacture or distribute goods which compete with the contract goods.

3. Art. 1 shall apply notwithstanding that the reseller undertakes any or all of the following obligations:

(a) to purchase complete ranges of goods;
(b) to purchase minimum quantities of goods which are subject to the exclusive purchasing obligation;
(c) to sell the contract goods under trademarks, or packed and presented as specified by the supplier;
(d) to take measures for the promotion of sales, in particular:
 – to advertise,
 – to maintain a sales network or stock of goods,
 – to provide customer and guarantee services,
 – to employ staff having specialised or technical training.

Article 3.   Art. 1 shall not apply where:

(a) manufacturers of identical goods or of goods which are considered by users as equivalent in view of their characteristics, price and intended use enter into reciprocal exclusive purchasing agreements between themselves in respect of such goods;

(b) manufacturers of identical goods or of goods which are considered by users as equivalent in view of their characteristics, price and intended use enter into a non-reciprocal exclusive purchasing agreement between themselves in respect of such goods, unless at least one of them has a total annual turnover of no more than 100 million ECU;

(c) the exclusive purchasing obligation is agreed for more than one type of goods where these are neither by their nature nor according to commercial usage connected to each other;

(d) the agreement is concluded for an indefinite duration or for a period of more than five years.

Article 4.   1. Art. 3 (a) and (b) shall also apply where the goods there referred to are manufactured by an undertaking connected with a party to the agreement.

2. Connected undertakings are:

(a) undertakings in which a party to the agreement, directly or indirectly:
  owns more than half the capital or business assets, or
  – has the power to exercise more than half the voting rights, or
  – has the power to appoint more than half the members of the supervisory board, board of directors or bodies legally representing the undertaking, or
  – has the right to manage the affairs;

(b) undertakings which directly or indirectly have in or over a party to the agreement the rights or powers listed in (a);

(c) undertakings in which an undertaking referred to in (b) directly or indirectly has the rights or powers listed in (a).

3. Undertakings in which the parties to the agreement or undertakings connected with them jointly have the rights or powers set out in paragraph 2 (a) shall be considered to be connected with each of the parties to the agreement.

Article 5.   1. For the purpose of Art. 3 (b), the ECU is the unit of account used for drawing up the budget of the Community pursuant to Arts. 207 and 209 of the Treaty.

2. Art. 1 shall remain applicable where during any period of two consecutive financial years the total turnover referred to in Art. 3 (b) is exceeded by no more than 10%.

3. For the purpose of calculating total turnover within the meaning of Art. 3 (b), the turnovers achieved during the last financial year by the party to the agreement and connected undertakings in respect of all goods and services, excluding all taxes and other duties, shall be added together. For this purpose, no account shall be taken of dealings between

the parties to the agreement or between these undertakings and undertakings connected with them or between the connected undertakings.

TITLE II. SPECIAL PROVISIONS FOR BEER SUPPLY AGREEMENTS

Article 6. 1. Pursuant to Art. 85 (3) of the Treaty, and subject to Arts. 7 to 9 of this Regulation, it is hereby declared that Art. 85 (1) of the Treaty shall not apply to agreements to which only two undertakings are party and whereby one party, the reseller, agrees with the other, the supplier, in consideration for according special commercial or financial advantages, to purchase only from the supplier, an undertaking connected with the supplier or another undertaking entrusted by the supplier with the distribution of his goods, certain beers, or certain beers and certain other drinks, specified in the agreement for resale in premises used for the sale and consumption of drinks and designated in the agreement.

2. The declaration in paragraph 1 shall also apply where exclusive purchasing obligations of the kind described in paragraph 1 are imposed on the reseller in favour of the supplier by another undertaking which is itself not a supplier.

Article 7. 1. Apart from the obligation referred to in Art. 6, no restriction on competition shall be imposed on the reseller other than:

(a) the obligation not to sell beers and other drinks which are supplied by other undertakings and which are of the same type as the beers or other drinks supplied under the agreement in the premises designated in the agreement;

(b) the obligation, in the event that the reseller sells in the premises designated in the agreement beers which are supplied by other undertakings and which are of a different type from the beers supplied under the agreement, to sell such beers only in bottles, cans or other small packages, unless the sale of such beers in draught form is customary or is necessary to satisfy a sufficient demand from consumers;

(c) the obligation to advertise goods supplied by other undertakings within or outside the premises designated in the agreement only in proportion to the share of these goods in the total turnover realised in the premises.

2. Beers or other drinks of the same type are those which are not clearly distinguishable in view of their composition, appearance and taste.

Article 8. 1. Art. 6 shall not apply where:

(a) the supplier or a connected undertaking imposes on the reseller exclusive purchasing obligations for goods other than drinks or for services;

(b) the supplier restricts the freedom of the reseller to obtain from an undertaking of his choice either services or goods for which neither an exclusive purchasing obligation nor a ban on dealing in competing products may be imposed;

(c) the agreement is concluded for an indefinite duration or for a period of more than five years and the exclusive purchasing obligation relates to specified beers and other drinks;

(d) the agreement is concluded for an indefinite duration or for a period of more than 10 years and the exclusive purchasing obligation relates only to specified beers;

(e) the supplier obliges the reseller to impose the exclusive purchasing obligation on his successor for a longer period than the reseller would himself remain tied to the supplier.

4. Where the agreement relates to premises which the supplier lets to the reseller or allows the reseller to occupy on some other basis in law or in fact, the following provisions shall also apply:

(a) notwithstanding paragraphs (1) (c) and (d), the exclusive purchasing obligations and bans on dealing in competing products specified in this Title may be imposed on the reseller for the whole period for which the reseller in fact operates the premises;

(b) the agreement must provide for the reseller to have the right to obtain:
  – drinks, except beer, supplied under the agreement from other undertakings where these undertakings offer them on more favourable conditions which the supplier does not meet,
  – drinks, except beer, which are of the same type as those supplied under the agreement but which bear different trade marks, from other undertakings where the supplier does not offer them.

Article 9. Arts. 2 (1) and (3), 3 (a) and (b), 4 and 5 shall apply *mutatis mutandis.*

TITLE III. SPECIAL PROVISIONS FOR SERVICE-STATION AGREEMENTS

Article 10. Pursuant to Art. 85 (3) of the Treaty and subject to Arts. 11 to 13 of this Regulation, it is hereby declared that Art. 85 (1) of the Treaty shall not apply to agreements to which only two undertakings are party and whereby one party, the reseller, agrees with the other, the supplier, in consideration for the according of special commercial or financial advantages, to purchase only from the supplier, an undertaking connected with the supplier or another undertaking entrusted by the supplier with the distribution of his goods, certain petroleum-based motor-vehicle fuels or certain petroleum-based motor-vehicle and other fuels specified in the agreement for resale in a service station designated in the agreement.

Article 11. Apart from the obligation referred to in Art. 10, no restriction on competition shall be imposed on the reseller other than:

(a) the obligation not to sell motor-vehicle fuel and other fuels which are supplied by other undertakings in the service station designated in the agreement;

(b) the obligation not to use lubricants or related petroleum-based products which are supplied by other undertakings within the service station designated in the agreement where the supplier or a connected undertaking has made available to the reseller, or financed, a lubrication bay or other motor-vehicle lubrication equipment;

(c) the obligation to advertise goods supplied by other undertakings within or outside the service station designated in the agreement only in proportion to the share of these goods in the total turnover realised in the service station;

(d) the obligation to have equipment owned by the supplier or a connected undertaking or financed by the supplier or a connected undertaking serviced by the supplier or an undertaking designated by him.

Article 12. 1. Art. 10 shall not apply where:

(a) the supplier or a connected undertaking imposes on the reseller exclusive purchasing obligations for goods other than motor-vehicle and other fuels or for services, except in the case of the obligations referred to in Art. 11 (b) and (d);

(b) the supplier restricts the freedom of the reseller to obtain, from an undertaking of his choice, goods or services, for which under the provisions of this Title neither an exclusive purchasing obligation nor a ban on dealing in competing products may be imposed;

(c) the agreement is concluded for an indefinite duration or for a period of more than 10 years;

(d) the supplier obliges the reseller to impose the exclusive purchasing obligation on his successor for a longer period than the reseller would himself remain tied to the supplier.

2. Where the agreement relates to a service station which the supplier lets to the reseller, or allows the reseller to occupy on some other basis, in law or in facts, exclusive purchasing obligations or prohibitions of competition indicated in this Title may, notwithstanding paragraph 1 (c), be imposed on the reseller for the whole period for which the reseller in fact operates the premises.

Article 13. Arts. 2 (1) and (3), 3 (a) and (b), 4 and 5 of this Regulation shall apply *mutatis mutandis.*

TITLE IV. MISCELLANEOUS PROVISIONS

Article 14. The Commission may withdraw the benefit of this Regulation, pursuant to Art. 7 of Regulation No 19/65/EEC, when it finds in a particular case that an agreement which is exempted by this Regulation nevertheless has certain effects which are incompatible with the conditions set out in Art. 85 (3) of the Treaty, and in particular where:

(a) the contract goods are not subject, in a substantial part of the common market, to effective competition from identical goods or goods considered by users as equivalent in view of their characteristics, price and intended use;
(b) access by other suppliers to the different stages of distribution in a substantial part of the common market is made difficult to a significant extent;
(c) the supplier without any objectively justified reason:
    1. refuses to supply categories of resellers who cannot obtain the contract goods elsewhere on suitable terms or applies to them differing prices or conditions of sale;
    2. applies less favourable prices or conditions of sale to resellers bound by an exclusive purchasing obligation as compared with other resellers at the same level of distribution.

Article 15. 1. In the period 1 July 1983 to 31 December 1986, the prohibition in Art. 85 (1) of the Treaty shall not apply to agreements of the kind described in Art. 1 which either were in force on 1 July 1983 or entered into force between 1 July and 31 December 1983 and which satisfy the exemption conditions under Regulation No 67/67/EEC.

2. In the period 1 July 1983 to 31 December 1988, the prohibition in Art. 85 (1) of the Treaty shall not apply to agreements of the kinds described in Arts. 6 and 10 which either were in force on 1 July 1983 or entered into force between 1 July and 31 December 1983 and which satisfy the exemption conditions of Regulation No 67/67/EEC.

3. In the case of agreements of the kinds described in Arts. 6 and 10, which were in force on 1 July 1983 and which expire after 31 December 1988, the prohibition in Art. 85 (1) of the Treaty shall not apply in the period from 1 January 1989 to the expiry of the agreement but at the latest to the expiry of this Regulation to the extent that the supplier releases the reseller, before 1 January 1989, from all obligations which would prevent the application of the exemption under Titles II and III.

4. The provisions of the preceding paragraphs shall apply in the same way to the agreements referred to respectively in those paragraphs, which were in force on the date of accession of the Kingdom of Spain and of the Portuguese Republic and which, as a result of accession, fall within the scope of Art. 85 (1) of the Treaty.

Article 16.   This Regulation shall not apply to agreements by which the supplier undertakes with the reseller to supply only to the reseller certain goods for resale, in the whole or in a defined part of the Community, and the reseller undertakes with the supplier to purchase these goods only from the supplier.

Article 17.   This Regulation shall not apply where the parties or connected undertakings, for the purpose of resale in one and the same premises used for the sale and consumption of drinks or service station, enter into agreements both of the kind referred to in Title I and of a kind referred to in Title II or III.

Article 18.   This Regulation shall apply *mutatis mutandis* to the categories of concerted practices defined in Arts. 1, 6 and 10.

Article 19.   This Regulation shall enter into force on 1 July 1983.
   It shall expire on 31 December 1997.

[Final provisions omitted.]

Regulation (EEC) No 2349/84 of the Commission of 23 July 1984 on the application of Article 85 (3) of the Treaty to certain categories of patent licensing agreements[10]

The Commission of the European Communities,

[Recitals omitted.]

Whereas:
(1) Regulation No 19/65/EEC empowers the Commission to apply Art. 85 (3) of the Treaty by Regulation to certain categories of agreements and concerted practices falling within the scope of Art. 85 (1) to which only two undertakings are party and which include restrictions imposed in relation to the acquisition or use of industrial property rights, in particular patents, utility models, designs or trade marks, or

[10] OJ 1984 L 219/15 as amended by Reg. 151/93, OJ 1993 L 21/8.

to the rights arising out of contracts for assignment of, or the right to use, a method of manufacture or knowledge relating to the use or application of industrial processes.

(2) Patent licensing agreements are agreements whereby one undertaking, the holder of a patent (the licensor), permits another undertaking (the licensee) to exploit the patented invention by one or more of the means of exploitation afforded by patent law, in particular manufacture, use or putting on the market.

(3) In the light of experience acquired so far, it is possible to define a category of patent licensing agreements which are capable of falling within the scope of Art. 85 (1), but which can normally be regarded as satisfying the conditions laid down in Art. 85 (3). To the extent that patent licensing agreements to which undertakings in only one Member State are party and which concern only one or more patents for that Member State are capable of affecting trade between Member States, it is appropriate to include them in the exempted category.

(4) The present Regulation applies to licences issued in respect of national patents of the Member States, Community patents,[11] or European patents[12] granted for Member States, licences in respect of utility models or 'certificats d'utilité' issued in the Member States, and licences in respect of inventions for which a patent application is made within one year. Where such patent licensing agreements contain obligations relating not only to territories within the common market but also obligations relating to non-member countries, the presence of the latter does not prevent the present Regulation from applying to the obligations relating to territories within the common market.

(5) However, where licensing agreements for non-member countries or for territories which extend beyond the frontiers of the Community have effects within the common market which may fall within the scope of Art. 85 (1), such agreements should be covered by the Regulation to the same extent as would agreements for territories within the common market.

(6) The Regulation should also apply to agreements concerning the assignment and acquisition of the rights referred to in point 4 above where the risk associated with exploitation remains with the assignor, patent licensing agreements in which the licensor is not the patentee but is authorised by the patentee to grant the licence (as in the case of sub-licences) and patent licensing agreements in which the parties' rights or obligations are assumed by connected undertakings.

(7) The Regulation does not apply to agreements concerning sales alone,

[11] Convention for the European patent for the common market (Community Patent Convention) of 15 December 1975 (OJ 1976, L 17/1).
[12] Convention on the grant of European patents of 5 October 1973.

which are governed by the provisions of Commission Regulation (EEC) No 1983/83 of 22 June 1983 concerning the application of Art. 85 (3) of the Treaty to categories of exclusive distribution agreements.

(8) Since the experience so far acquired is inadequate, it is not appropriate to include within the scope of the Regulation patent pools, licensing agreements entered into in connection with joint ventures, reciprocal licensing or distribution agreements, or licensing agreements in respect of plant breeder's rights. Reciprocal agreements which do not involve any territorial restrictions within the common market should, however, be so included.

(9) On the other hand, it is appropriate to extend the scope of the Regulation to patent licensing agreements which also contain provisions assigning, or granting the right to use, non-patented technical knowledge, since such mixed agreements are commonly concluded in order to allow the transfer of a complex technology containing both patented and non-patented elements. Such agreements can only be regarded as fulfilling the conditions of Art. 85 (3) for the purposes of this Regulation where the communicated technical knowledge is secret and permits a better exploitation of the licensed patents (know-how). Provisions concerning the provision of know-how are covered by the Regulation only in so far as the licensed patents are necessary for achieving the objects of the licensed technology and as long as at least one of the licensed patents remains in force.

(10) It is also appropriate to extend the scope of the Regulation to patent licensing agreements containing ancillary provisions relating to trade marks, subject to ensuring that the trade mark licence is not used to extend the effects of the patent licence beyond the life of the patents. For the purpose it is necessary to allow the licensee to identify himself within the 'licensed territory' i.e. the territory covering all or part of the common market where the licensor holds patents which the licensee is authorised to exploit, as the manufacturer of the 'licensed product', i.e. the product which is the subject-matter of the licensed patent or which has been obtained directly from the process which is the subject-matter of the licensed patent, to avoid his having to enter into a new trade-mark agreement with the licensor when the licensed patents expire in order not to lose the goodwill attaching to the licensed product.

(11) Exclusive licensing agreements, i.e. agreements in which the licensor undertakes not to exploit the 'licensed invention', i.e. the licensed patented invention and any know-how communicated to the licensee, in the licensed territory himself or to grant further licences there, are not in themselves incompatible with Art. 85 (1) where they are concerned with the introduction and protection of a new tech-

nology in the licensed territory, by reason of the scale of the research which has been undertaken and of the risk that is involved in manufacturing and marketing a product which is unfamiliar to users in the licensed territory at the time the agreement is made. This may also be the case where the agreements are concerned with the introduction and protection of a new process for manufacturing a product which is already known. In so far as in other cases agreements of this kind may fall within the scope of Art. 85 (1) it is useful for the purposes of legal certainty to include them in Art. 1, in order that they may also benefit from the exemption. However, the exemption of exclusive licensing agreements and certain export bans imposed on the licensor and the licensees is without prejudice to subsequent developments in the case law of the Court of Justice regarding the status of such agreements under Art. 85 (1)

(12) The obligations listed in Art. 1 generally contribute to improving the production of goods and to promoting technical progress; they make patentees more willing to grant licenses and licensees more inclined to undertake the investment required to manufacture, use and put on the market a new product or to use a new process, so that undertakings other than the patentee acquire the possibility of manufacturing their products with the aid of the latest techniques and of developing those techniques further. The result is that the number of production facilities and the quantity and quality of goods produced in the common market are increased. This is true, in particular, of obligations on the licensor and on the licensee not to exploit the licensed invention in, and in particular not to export the licensed product into, the licensed territory in the case of the licensor and the 'territories reserved for the licensor', that is to say, territories within the common market in which the licensor has patent protection and has not granted any licenses, in the case of the licensee. This is also true both of the obligation of the licensee not to conduct an active policy of putting the product on the market (i.e. a prohibition of active competition as defined in Art. 1 (1) (5)) in the territories of other licensees for a period which may equal the duration of the licence and also the obligation of the licensee not to put the licensed product on the market in the territories of other licensees for a limited period of a few years (i.e. a prohibition not only of active competition but also of 'passive competition' whereby the licensee of a territory simply responds to requests which he has not solicited from users or resellers established in the territories of other licensees—Art. 1 (1) (6)). However, such obligations may be permitted under the Regulation only in respect of territories in which the licensed product is protected by 'parallel patents', that is to say, patents covering the same invention, within

the meaning of the case law of the Court of Justice, and as long as the patents remain in force.

(13) Consumers will as a rule be allowed a fair share of the benefit resulting from this improvement in the supply of goods on the market. To safeguard this effect, however, it is right to exclude from the application of Art. 1 cases where the parties agree to refuse to meet demand from users or resellers within their respective territories who would resell for export, or to take other steps to impede parallel imports, or where the licensee is obliged to refuse to meet unsolicited demand from the territory of other licensees (passive sales). The same applies where such action is the result of a concerted practice between the licensor and the licensee.

(14) The obligations referred to above thus do not impose restrictions which are not indispensable to the attainment of the abovementioned objectives.

(15) Competition at the distribution stage is safeguarded by the possibility of parallel imports and passive sales. The exclusivity obligations covered by the Regulation thus do not normally entail the possibility of eliminating competition in respect of a substantial part of the products in question. This is so even in the case of agreements which grant exclusive licences for a territory covering the whole of the common market.

(16) To the extent that in their agreements the parties undertake obligations of the type referred to in Arts. 1 and 2 but which are of more limited scope and thus less restrictive of competition than is permitted by those Arts., it is appropriate that these obligations should also benefit under the exemptions provided for in the Regulation.

(17) If in a particular case an agreement covered by this Regulation is found to have effects which are incompatible with the provisions of Art. 85 (3) of the Treaty, the Commission may withdraw the benefit of the block exemption from the undertakings concerned, in accordance with Art. 7 of Regulation No 19/65/EEC.

(18) It is not necessary expressly to exclude from the category defined in the Regulation agreements which do not fulfil the conditions of Art. 85 (1). Nevertheless it is advisable in the interests of legal certainty for the undertakings concerned, to list in Art. 2 a number of obligations which are not normally restrictive of competition, so that these also may benefit from the exemption in the event that, because of particular economic or legal circumstances, they should exceptionally fall within the scope of Art. 85 (1). The list of such obligations given in Art. 2 is not exhaustive.

(19) The Regulation must also specify what restrictions or provisions may not be included in patent licensing agreements if these are to

benefit from the block exemption. The restrictions listed in Art. 3 may fall under the prohibition of Art. 85 (1); in these cases there can be no general presumption that they will lead to the positive effects required by Art. 85 (3), as would be necessary for the granting of a block exemption.

(20) Such restrictions include those which deny the licensee the right enjoyed by any third party to challenge the validity of the patent or which automatically prolong the agreement by the life of any new patent granted during the life of the licensed patents which are in existence at the time the agreement is entered into. Nevertheless, the parties are free to extend their contractual relationship by entering into new agreements concerning such new patents, or to agree the payment of royalties for as long as the licensee continues to use know-how communicated by the licensor which has not entered into the public domain, regardless of the duration of the original patents and of any new patents that are licensed.

(21) They also include restrictions on the freedom of one party to compete with the other and in particular to involve himself in techniques other than those licensed, since such restrictions impede technical and economic progress. The prohibition of such restrictions should however be reconciled with the legitimate interest of the licensor in having his patented invention exploited to the full and to this end to require the licensee to use his best endeavours to manufacture and market the licensed product.

(22) Such restrictions include, further, an obligation on the licensee to continue to pay royalties after all the licensed patents have expired and the communicated know-how has entered into the public domain, since such an obligation would place the licensee at a disadvantage by comparison with his competitors, unless it is established that this obligation results from arrangements for spreading payments in respect of previous use of the licensed invention.

(23) They also include restrictions imposed on the parties regarding prices, customers or marketing of the licensed products or regarding the quantities to be manufactured or sold, especially since restrictions of the latter type may have the same effect as export bans.

(24) Finally, they include restrictions to which the licensee submits at the time the agreement is made because he wishes to obtain the licence, but which give the licensor an unjustified competitive advantage, such as an obligation to assign to the licensor any improvements the licensee may make to the invention, or to accept other licences or goods and services that the licensee does not want from the licensor.

(25) It is appropriate to offer to parties to patent licensing agreements containing obligations which do not come within the terms of Arts

1 and 2 and yet do not entail any of the effects restrictive of competition referred to in Art. 3 a simplified means of benefiting, upon notification, from the legal certainty provided by the block exemption (Art. 4). This procedure should at the same time allow the Commission to ensure effective supervision as well as simplifying the administrative control of agreements.

(26) The Regulation should apply with retroactive effect to patent licensing agreements in existence when the Regulation comes into force where such agreements already fulfil the conditions for application of the Regulation or are modified to do so (Arts. 6 to 8). Under Art. 4 (3) of Regulation No 19/65/EEC, the benefit of these provisions may not be claimed in actions pending at the date of entry into force of this Regulation, nor may it be relied on as grounds for claims for damages against third parties.

(27) Agreements which come within the terms of Arts. 1 and 2 and which have neither the object nor the effect of restricting competition in any other way need no longer be notified. Nevertheless, undertakings will still have the right to apply in individual cases for negative clearance under Art. 2 of Council Regulation No 17 or for exemption under Art. 85 (3).

Has adopted this regulation:

Article 1. 1. Pursuant to Art. 85 (3) of the Treaty and subject to the provisions of this Regulation, it is hereby declared that Art. 85 (1) of the Treaty shall not apply to patent licensing agreements, and agreements combining the licensing of patents and the communication of know-how, to which only two undertakings are party and which include one or more of the following obligations:

1. an obligation on the licensor not to license other undertakings to exploit the licensed invention in the licensed territory, covering all or part of the common market, in so far and as long as one of the licensed patents remains in force;
2. an obligation on the licensor not to exploit the licensed invention in the licensed territory himself in so far and as long as one of the licensed patents remains in force;
3. an obligation on the licensee not to exploit the licensed invention in territories within the common market which are reserved for the licensor, in so far and as long as the patented product is protected in those territories by parallel patents;
4. an obligation on the licensee not to manufacture or use the licensed product, or use the patented process or the communicated know-how, in territories within the common market which are licensed to other

licensees, in so far and as long as the licensed product is protected in those territories by parallel patents;

5. an obligation on the licensee not to pursue an active policy of putting the licensed product on the market in the territories within the common market which are licensed to other licensees, and in particular not to engage in advertising specifically aimed at those territories or to establish any branch or maintain any distribution depot there, in so far and as long as the licensed product is protected in those territories by parallel patents;

6. an obligation on the licensee not to put the licensed product on the market in the territories licensed to other licensees within the common market for a period not exceeding five years from the date when the product is first put on the market within the common market by the licensor or one of his licensees, in so far as and for as long as the product is protected in those territories by parallel patents;

7. an obligation on the licensee to use only the licensor's trade mark or the get-up determined by the licensor to distinguish the licensed product, provided that the licensee is not prevented from identifying himself as the manufacturer of the licensed product.

2. The exemption of restrictions on putting the licensed product on the market resulting from the obligations referred to in paragraph 1 (2), (3), (5) and (6) shall apply only if the licensee manufactures the licensed product himself or has it manufactured by a connected undertaking or by a subcontractor.

3. The exemption provided for in paragraph 1 shall also apply where in a particular agreement the parties undertake obligations of the types referred to in that paragraph but with a more limited scope than is permitted by the paragraph.

Article 2. 1. Art. 1 shall apply notwithstanding the presence in particular of any of the following obligations, which are generally not restrictive of competition:

1. an obligation on the licensee to procure goods or services from the licensor or from an undertaking designated by the licensor, in so far as such products or services are necessary for a technically satisfactory exploitation of the licensed invention;

2. an obligation on the licensee to pay a minimum royalty or to produce a minimum quantity of the licensed product or to carry out a minimum number of operations exploiting the licensed invention;

3. an obligation on the licensee to restrict his exploitation of the licensed invention to one or more technical fields of application covered by the licensed patent;

4. an obligation on the licensee not to exploit the patent after termination of the agreement in so far as the patent is still in force;

5. an obligation on the licensee not to grant sub-licences or assign the licence;

6. an obligation on the licensee to mark the licensed product with an indication of the patentee's name, the licensed patent or the patent licensing agreement;

7. an obligation on the licensee not to divulge know-how communicated by the licensor; the licensee may be held to this obligation after the agreement has expired;

8. obligations:
   (a) to inform the licensor of infringements of the patent,
   (b) to take legal action against an infringer,
   (c) to assist the licensor in any legal action against an infringer,
   provided that these obligations are without prejudice to the licensee's right to challenge the validity of the licensed patent;

9. an obligation on the licensee to observe specifications concerning the minimum quality of the licensed product, provided that such specifications are necessary for a technically satisfactory exploitation of the licensed invention, and to allow the licensor to carry out related checks;

10. an obligation on the parties to communicate to one another any experience gained in exploiting the licensed invention and to grant one another a licence in respect of inventions relating to improvements and new applications, provided that such communication or licence is non-exclusive;

11. an obligation on the licensor to grant the licensee any more favourable terms that the licensor may grant to another undertaking after the agreement is entered into.

2. In the event that, because of particular circumstances, the obligations referred to in paragraph 1 fall within the scope of Art. 85 (1), they shall also be exempted even if they are not accompanied by any of the obligations exempted by Art. 1.

The exemption provided for in this paragraph shall also apply where in an agreement the parties undertake obligations of the types referred to in paragraph 1 but with a more limited scope than is permitted by that paragraph.

Article 3. Arts. 1 and 2 (2) shall not apply where:

1. the licensee is prohibited from challenging the validity of licensed patents or other industrial or commercial property rights within the common market belonging to the licensor or undertakings connected

with him, without prejudice to the right of the licensor to terminate the licensing agreement in the event of such a challenge;

2. the duration of the licensing agreement is automatically prolonged beyond the expiry of the licensed patents existing at the time the agreement was entered into by the inclusion in it of any new patent obtained by the licensor, unless the agreement provides each party with the right to terminate the agreement at least annually after the expiry of the licensed patents existing at the time the agreement was entered into, without prejudice to the right of the licensor to charge royalties for the full period during which the licensee continues to use know-how communicated by the licensor which has not entered into the public domain, even if that period exceeds the life of the patents;

3. one party is restricted from competing with the other party, with undertakings connected with the other party or with other undertakings within the common market in respect of research and development, manufacture, use or sales, save as provided in Art. 1 and without prejudice to an obligation on the licensee to use his best endeavours to exploit the licensed invention;

4. the licensee is charged royalties on products which are not entirely or partially patented or manufactured by means of a patented process, or for the use of know-how which has entered into the public domain otherwise than by the fault of the licensee or an undertaking connected with him, without prejudice to arrangements whereby, in order to facilitate payment by the licensee, the royalty payments for the use of a licensed invention are spread over a period extending beyond the life of the licensed patents or the entry of the know-how into the public domain;

5. the quantity of licensed products one party may manufacture or sell or the number of operations exploiting the licensed invention he may carry out are subject to limitations;

6. one party is restricted in the determination of prices, components of prices or discounts for the licensed products;

7. one party is restricted as to the customers he may serve, in particular by being prohibited from supplying certain classes of user, employing certain forms of distribution or, with the aim of sharing customers, using certain types of packaging for the products, save as provided in Art. 1 (1) (7) and Art. 2 (1) (3);

8. the licensee is obliged to assign wholly or in part to the licensor rights in or to patents for improvements or for new applications of the licensed patents;

9. the licensee is induced at the time the agreement is entered into to accept further licences which he does not want or to agree to use patents, goods or services which he does not want, unless such patents,

products or services are necessary for a technically satisfactory exploitation of the licensed invention;

10. without prejudice to Art. 1 (1) (5), the license is required, for a period exceeding that permitted under Art. 1 (1) (6), not to put the licensed product on the market in territories licensed to other licensees within the common market or does not do so as a result of a concerted practice between the parties;

11. one or both of the parties are required:

(a) to refuse without any objectively justified reason to meet demand from users or resellers in their respective territories who would market products in other territories within the common market;

(b) to make it difficult for users or resellers to obtain the products from other resellers within the common market, and in particular to exercise industrial or commercial property rights or take measures so as to prevent users or resellers from obtaining outside, or from putting on the market in, the licensed territory products which have been lawfully put on the market within the common market by the patentee or with his consent;

or do so as a result of a concerted practice between them.

Article 4. 1. The exemption provided for in Arts. 1 and 2 shall also apply to agreements containing obligations restrictive of competition which are not covered by those Arts. and do not fall within the scope of Art. 3, on condition that the agreements in question are notified to the Commission in accordance with the provisions of Commission Regulation No 27,[13] as last amended by Regulation (EEC) No 1699/75,[14] and that the Commission does not oppose such exemption within a period of six months.

2. The period of six months shall run from the date on which the notification is received by the Commission. Where, however, the notification is made by registered post, the period shall run from the date shown on the postmark of the place of posting.

3. Paragraph 1 shall apply only if:

(a) express reference is made to this Article in the notification or in a communication accompanying it; and

(b) the information furnished with the notification is complete and in accordance with the facts.

4. The benefit of paragraph 1 may be claimed for agreements notified before the entry into force of this Regulation by submitting a communication to the Commission referring expressly to this Article and to the notification. Paragraphs 2 and 3 (b) shall apply *mutatis mutandis.*

---

[13] OJ No 35, 10. 5. 1962, p. 1118/62.   [14] OJ 1975 L 172/11.

5. The Commission may oppose the exemption. It shall oppose exemption if it receives a request to do so from a Member State within three months of the transmission to the Member State of the notification referred to in paragraph 1 or of the communication referred to in paragraph 4. This request must be justified on the basis of considerations relating to the competition rules of the Treaty.

6. The Commission may withdraw the opposition to the exemption at any time. However, where the opposition was raised at the request of a Member State and this request is maintained, it may be withdrawn only after consultation of the Advisory Committee on Restrictive Practices and Dominant Positions.

7. If the opposition is withdrawn because the undertakings concerned have shown that the conditions of Art. 85 (3) are fulfilled, the exemption shall apply from the date of notification

8. If the opposition is withdrawn because the undertakings concerned have amended the agreement so that the conditions of Art. 85 (3) are fulfilled, the exemption shall apply from the date on which the amendments take effect.

9. If the Commission opposes exemption and the opposition is not withdrawn, the effects of the notification shall be governed by the provisions of Regulation No 17.

Article 5. 1. This Regulation shall not apply:

1. to agreements between members of a patent pool which relate to the pooled patents;
2. to patent licensing agreements between competitors who hold interests in a joint venture or between one of them and the joint venture, if the licensing agreements relate to the activities of the joint venture;
3. to agreements under which the parties, albeit in separate agreements or through connected undertakings, grant each other reciprocal patent or trade-mark licences or reciprocal sales rights for unprotected products or exchange know-how, where the parties are competitors in relation to the products covered by those agreements;
4. to licensing agreements in respect of plant breeder's rights.

2. This Regulation shall nevertheless apply:

(a) to agreements to which paragraph 1 (2) applies, under which a parent undertaking grants the joint venture a patent licence, provided that the contract products and the other products of the participating undertakings which are considered by users to be equivalent in view of their characteristics, price and intended use represent:
 – in case of a licence limited to production not more than 20%,

 – in case of a licence covering production and distribution not more than 10%,

of the market for all such products in the common market or a substantial part thereof;

(b) to reciprocal licences within the meaning of point 3 of paragraph 1, provided that the parties are not subject to any territorial restriction within the common market with regard to the manufacture, use or putting on the market of the contract products or on the use of the licensed processes.

3. This Regulation shall continue to apply where the market shares referred to in point (a) of paragraph 2 are exceeded during any period of two consecutive financial years by not more than one-tenth.

Where this latter limit is also exceeded, this Regulation shall continue to apply for a period of six months following the end of the financial year during which it was exceeded.

Article 6. 1. As regards agreements existing on 13 March 1962 and notified before 1 February 1963 and agreements, whether notified or not, to which Art. 4 (2) (2) (b) of Regulation No 17 applies, the declaration of inapplicability of Art. 85 (1) of the Treaty contained in this Regulation shall have retroactive effect from the time at which the conditions for application of this Regulation were fulfilled.

2. As regards all other agreements notified before this Regulation entered into force, the declaration of inapplicability of Art. 85 (1) of the Treaty contained in this Regulation shall have retroactive effect from the time at which the conditions for application of this Regulation were fulfilled, or from the date of notification, whichever is the later.

Article 7. If agreements existing on 13 March 1962 and notified before 1 February 1963 or agreements to which Art. 4 (2) (2) (b) of Regulation No 17 applies and notified before 1 January 1967 are amended before 1 April 1985 so as to fulfil the conditions for application of this Regulation, and if the amendment is communicated to the Commission before 1 July 1985 the prohibition in Art. 85 (1) of the Treaty shall not apply in respect of the period prior to the amendment. The communication shall take effect from the time of its receipt by the Commission. Where the communication is sent by registered post, it shall take effect from the date shown on the postmark of the place of posting.

Article 8. 1. As regards agreements to which Art. 85 of the Treaty applies as a result of the accession of the United Kingdom, Ireland and Denmark, Arts. 6 and 7 shall apply except that the relevant dates shall be

1 January 1973 instead of 13 March 1962 and 1 July 1973 instead of 1 February 1963 and 1 January 1967.

2. As regards agreements to which Art. 85 of the Treaty applies as a result of the accession of Greece, Arts. 6 and 7 shall apply except that the relevant dates shall be 1 January 1981 instead of 13 March 1962 and 1 July 1981 instead of 1 February 1963 and 1 January 1967.

3. As regards agreements to which Art. 85 of the Treaty applies as a result of the accession of the Kingdom of Spain and of the Portuguese Republic, Arts. 6 and 7 shall apply except that the relevant dates shall be 1 January 1986 instead of 13 March 1962 and 1 July 1986 instead of 1 February 1963, 1 January 1967 and 1 April 1985. The amendment made to these agreements in accordance with Art. 7 need not be notified to the Commission.

Article 9. The Commission may withdraw the benefit of this Regulation, pursuant to Art. 7 of Regulation No 19/65/EEC, where it finds in a particular case that an agreement exempted by this Regulation nevertheless has certain effects which are incompatible with the conditions laid down in Art. 85 (3) of the Treaty, and in particular where:

1. such effects arise from an arbitration award;
2. the licensed products or the services provided using a licensed process are not exposed to effective competition in the licensed territory from identical products or services or products or services considered by users as equivalent in view of their characteristics, price and intended use;
3. the licensor does not have the right to terminate the exclusivity granted to the licensee at the latest five years from the date the agreement was entered into and at least annually thereafter if, without legitimate reason, the licensee fails to exploit the patent or to do so adequately;
4. without prejudice to Art. 1 (1) (6), the licensee refuses, without objectively valid reason, to meet unsolicited demand from users or resellers in the territory of other licensees;
5. one or both of the parties:
   (a) without any objectively justified reason, refuse to meet demand from users or resellers in their respective territories who would market the products in other territories within the common market; or
   (b) make it difficult for users or resellers to obtain the products from other resellers within the common market, and in particular where they exercise industrial or commercial property rights or take measures so as to prevent resellers or users from obtaining outside, or from putting on the market in, the licensed territory products

which have been lawfully put on the market within the common market by the patentee or with his consent.

Article 10.   1. This Regulation shall apply to:

(a) patent applications;
(b) utility models;
(c) applications for registration of utility models;
(d) 'certificats d'utilité' and 'certificats d'addition' under French law; and
(e) applications for 'certificats d'utilité' and 'certificats d'addition' under French law;

equally as it applies to patents.

2. This Regulation shall also apply to agreements relating to the exploitation of an invention if an application within the meaning of paragraph 1 is made in respect of the invention for the licensed territory within one year from the date when the agreement was entered into.

Article 11.   This Regulation shall also apply to:

1. patent licensing agreements where the licensor is not the patentee but is authorised by the patentee to grant a licence or a sub-licence;
2. assignments of a patent or of a right to a patent where the sum payable in consideration of the assignment is dependent upon the turnover attained by the assignee in respect of the patented products, the quantity of such products manufactured or the number of operations carried out employing the patented invention;
3. patent licensing agreements in which rights or obligations of the licensor or the licensee are assumed by undertakings connected with them.

Article 12.   1. 'Connected undertakings' for the purposes of this Regulation means:

(a) undertakings in which a party to the agreement, directly or indirectly:
   – owns more than half the capital or business assets, or
   – has the power to exercise more than half the voting rights, or
   – has the power to appoint more than half the members of the supervisory board, board of directors or bodies legally representing the undertaking, or
   – has the right to manage the affairs of the undertaking;
(b) undertakings which directly or indirectly have in or over a party to the agreement the rights or powers listed in (a);
(c) undertakings in which an undertaking referred to in (b) directly or indirectly has the rights or powers listed in (a).

2. Undertakings in which the parties to the agreement or undertakings connected with them jointly have the rights or powers set out in para-

graph 1 (a) shall be considered to be connected with each of the parties to the agreement.

Article 13. 1. Information acquired pursuant to Art. 4 shall be used only for the purposes of this Regulation.

2. The Commission and the authorities of the Member States, their officials and other servants shall not disclose information acquired by them pursuant to this Regulation of the kind covered by the obligation of professional secrecy.

3. The provisions of paragraphs 1 and 2 shall not prevent publication of general information or surveys which do not contain information relating to particular undertakings or associations of undertakings.

Article 14. This Regulation shall enter into force on 1 January 1985. It shall apply until 31 December 1994.

[Final provisions omitted.]

Regulation (EEC) No 123/85 of the Commission of 12 December 1984 on the application of Article 85 (3) of the Treaty to certain categories of motor vehicle distribution and servicing agreements[15]

The Commission of the European Communities,

[Recitals omitted.]

Whereas:

(1) Under Art. 1 (1) (a) of Regulation No 19/65/EEC the Commission is empowered to declare by means of a Regulation that Art. 85 (3) of the Treaty applies to certain categories of agreements falling within Art. 85 (1) to which only two undertakings are party and by which one party agrees with the other to supply only to that undertaking other certain goods for resale within a defined territory of the common market. In the light of experience since Commission Decision 75/73/EEC and of the many motor vehicle distribution and servicing agreements which have been notified to the Commission pursuant to Arts. 4 and 5 of Council Regulation No 17, as last amended by Regulation (EEC) No 2821/71, a category of agreements can be defined as satisfying the conditions laid down in Regulation No 19/65/EEC. They are agreements, for a definite or an indefinite

---

[15] OJ 1984 L 15/16

period, by which the supplying party entrusts to the reselling party the task of promoting the distribution and servicing of certain products of the motor vehicle industry in a defined area and by which the supplier undertakes to supply contract goods for resale only to the dealer, or only to a limited number of undertakings within the distribution network besides the dealer, within the contract territory.

A list of definitions for the purpose of this Regulation is set out in Art. 13.

(2) Notwithstanding that the obligations imposed by distribution and servicing agreements which are listed in Arts. 1, 2 and 3 of this Regulation normally have as their object or effect the prevention, restriction or distortion of competition within the common market and are normally apt to affect trade between Member States, the prohibition in Art. 85 (1) of the Treaty may nevertheless be declared inapplicable to these agreements by virtue of Art. 85 (3), albeit only under certain restrictive conditions.

(3) The applicability of Art. 85 (1) of the Treaty to distribution and servicing agreements in the motor vehicle industry stems in particular from the fact that restrictions on competition and the obligations connected with the distribution system listed in Arts. 1 to 4 of this Regulation are regularly imposed in the same or similar form throughout the common market for the products supplied within the distribution system of a particular manufacturer. The motor vehicle manufacturers cover the whole common market or substantial parts of it by means of a cluster of agreements involving similar restrictions on competition and affect in this way not only distribution and servicing within Member States but also trade between them.

(4) The exclusive and selective distribution clauses can be regarded as indispensable measures of rationalisation in the motor vehicle industry because motor vehicles are consumer durables which at both regular and irregular intervals require expert maintenance and repair, not always in the same place. Motor vehicle manufacturers cooperate with the selected dealers and repairers in order to provide specialised servicing for the product. On grounds of capacity and efficiency alone, such a form of cooperation cannot be extended to an unlimited number of dealers and repairers. The linking of servicing and distribution must be regarded as more efficient than a separation between a distribution organisation for new vehicles on the one hand and a servicing organisation which would also distribute spare parts on the other, particularly as, before a new vehicle is delivered to the final consumer, the undertaking within the distribution system must give it a technical inspection according to the manufacturer's specification.

(5) However, obligatory recourse to the authorised network is not in all

respects indispensable for efficient distribution. The exceptions to the block exemption provide that the supply of contract goods to resellers may not be prohibited where they:
- belong to the same distribution system (Art. 3, point 10 (a)), or
- purchase spare parts for their own use in effecting repairs or maintenance (Art. 3, point 10 (b)).

Measures taken by a manufacturer or by undertakings within the distribution system with the object of protecting the selective distribution system are compatible with the exemption under this Regulation. This applies in particular to a dealer's obligation to sell vehicles to a final consumer using the services of an intermediary only where that consumer has authorised that intermediary to act as his agent (Art. 3, point 11).

(6) It should be possible to bar wholesalers not belonging to the distribution system from reselling parts originating from motor vehicle manufacturers. It may be supposed that the system of rapid availability of spare parts across the whole contract programme, including those with a low turnover, which is beneficial to the consumer, could not be maintained without obligatory recourse to the authorised network.

(7) The ban on dealing in competing products and that on dealing in other vehicles at stated premises may in principle be exempted, because they contribute to concentration by the undertakings in the distribution network of their efforts on the products supplied by the manufacturer or with his consent, and thus ensure distribution and servicing appropriate for the vehicles (Art. 3, point 3). Such obligations provide an incentive for the dealer to develop sales and servicing of contract goods and thus promotes competition in the supply of those products as well as between those products and competing products.

(8) However, bans on dealing in competing products cannot be regarded as indispensable in all circumstances to efficient distribution. Dealers must be free to obtain from third parties supplies of parts which match the quality of those offered by the manufacturer, for example where the parts are produced by a sub-contract manufacturer who also supplies the motor vehicle manufacturer, and to use and sell them. They must also keep their freedom to choose parts which are usable in motor vehicles within the contract programme and which not only match but exceed the quality standard. Such a limit on the ban on dealing in competing products takes account of the importance of vehicle safety and of the maintenance of effective competition (Art. 3, point 4 and Art. 4 (1), points 6 and 7).

(9) The restrictions imposed on the dealer's activities outside the allotted area lead to more intensive distribution and servicing efforts in an easily supervised contract territory, to knowledge of the market based on closer contact with consumers, and to more demand-orientated

supply (Art. 3, points 8 and 9). However, demand for contract goods must remain flexible and should not be limited on a regional basis. Dealers must not be confined to satisfying the demand for contract goods within their contract territories, but must also be able to meet demand from persons and undertakings in other areas of the common market. Dealers' advertising in a medium which is directed to customers in the contract territory but also covers a wider area should not be prevented, because it does not run counter to the obligation to promote sales within the contract territory.

(10) The obligations listed in Art. 4 (1) are directly related to the obligations in Arts. 1, 2 and 3, and influence their restrictive effect. These obligations, which might in individual cases be caught by the prohibition in Art. 85 (1) of the Treaty, may also be exempted because of their direct relationship with one or more of the obligations exempted by Arts. 1, 2 and 3 (Art. 4 (2)).

(11) According to Art. 1 (2) (b) of Regulation No 19/65/EEC, conditions which must be satisfied if the declaration of inapplicability is to take effect must be specified.

(12) Under Art. 5 (1), points 1 (a) and (b) it is a condition of exemption that the undertaking should honour the minimum guarantee and provide the minimum free servicing and vehicle recall work laid down by the manufacturer, irrespective of where in the common market the vehicle was purchased. These provisions are intended to prevent the consumer's freedom to buy anywhere in the common market from being limited.

(13) Art. 5 (1), point 2 (a) is intended to allow the manufacturer to build up a coordinated distribution system, but without hindering the relationship of confidence between dealers and sub-dealers. Accordingly, if the supplier reserves the right to approve appointments of sub-dealers by the dealer, he must not be allowed to withhold approval arbitrarily.

(14) Art. 5 (1), point 2 (b) obliges the supplier not to impose on a dealer within the distribution system requirements, as defined in Art. 4 (1), which are discriminatory or inequitable.

(15) Art. 5 (1), point 2 (c) is intended to counter the concentration of the dealer's demand on the supplier which might follow from cumulation of discounts. The purpose of this provision is to allow spare-parts suppliers which do not offer as wide a range of goods as the manufacturer to compete on equal terms.

(16) Art. 5 (1), point 2 (d) makes exemption subject to the conditions that the dealer must be able to purchase for customers in the common market volume-produced passenger cars with the specifications appropriate for their place of residence or where the vehicle is to be

registered, in so far as the corresponding model is also supplied by the manufacturer through undertakings within the distribution system in that place (Art. 13, point 10). This provision obviates the danger that the manufacturer and undertakings within the distribution network might make use of product differentiation as between parts of the common market to partition the market.

(17) Art. 5 (2) makes the exemption of the no-competition clause and of the ban on dealing in other makes of vehicle subject to further threshold conditions. This is to prevent the dealer from becoming economically overdependent on the supplier because of such obligations, and abandoning the competitive activity which is nominally open to him, because to pursue it would be against the interests of the manufacturer or other undertakings within the distribution network.

(18) Under Art. 5 (2), point 1 (a), the dealer may, where there are exceptional reasons, oppose application of excessive obligations covered by Art. 3, point 3 or 5.

(19) The supplier may reserve the right to appoint further distribution and servicing undertakings in the contract territory or to alter the territory, but only if he can show that there are exceptional reasons for doing so (Art. 5 (2), point 1 (b) and Art. 5 (3)). This is, for example, the case where there would otherwise be reason to apprehend a serious deterioration in the distribution or servicing of contract goods.

(20) Art. 5 (2), points 2 and 3 lay down minimum requirements for exemption which concern the duration and termination of the distribution and servicing agreement; the combined effect of a no-competition clause or a ban on dealing in other makes of vehicle, the investments the dealer makes in order to improve the distribution and servicing of contract goods and a short-term agreement or one terminable at short notice is greatly to increase the dealer's dependence on the supplier.

(21) In accordance with Art. 1 (2) (a) of Regulation No 19/65/EEC, restrictions or provisions which must not be contained in the agreements, if the declaration of inapplicability of Art. 85 (1) by this Regulation is to take effect, are to be specified.

(22) Agreements under which one motor vehicle manufacturer entrusts the distribution of its products to another must be excluded from the block exemption under this Regulation because of their far-reaching impact on competition (Art. 6, point 1).

(23) An obligation to apply minimum resale prices or maximum trade discounts precludes exemption under this Regulation (Art. 6, point 2).

(24) The exemption does not apply where the parties agree between themselves obligations concerning goods covered by this Regulation

which would be acceptable in the combination of obligations which is exempted by Commission Regulations (EEC) No 1983/83 or (EEC) No 1984/83 on the application of Art. 85 (3) of the Treaty to categories of exclusive distribution agreements and exclusive purchasing agreements respectively, but which go beyond the scope of the obligations exempted by this Regulation (Art. 6, point 3).

(25) Distribution and servicing agreements can be exempted, subject to the conditions laid down in Arts. 5 and 6, so long as the application of obligations covered by Arts. 1 to 4 of this Regulation brings about an improvement in distribution and servicing to the benefit of the consumer and effective competition exists, not only between manufacturers' distribution systems but also to a certain extent within each system within the common market. As regards the categories of products set out in Art. 1 of this Regulation, the conditions necessary for effective competition, including competition in trade between Member States, may be taken to exist at present, so that European consumers may be considered in general to take an equitable share in the benefit from the operation of such competition.

(26) Arts. 7, 8 and 9, concerning the retroactive effect of the exemption, are based on Arts. 3 and 4 of Regulation No 19/65/EEC and Arts. 4 to 7 of Regulation No 17. Art. 10 embodies the Commission's powers under Art. 7 of Regulation No 19/65/EEC to withdraw the benefit of its exemption or to alter its scope in individual cases, and lists several important examples of such cases.

(27) In view of the extensive effect of this Regulation on the persons it concerns, it is appropriate that it should not enter into force until 1 July 1985. In accordance with Art. 2 (1) of Regulation No 19/65/EEC, the exemption may be made applicable for a definite period. A period extending until 30 June 1995 is appropriate, because overall distribution schemes in the motor vehicle sector must be planned several years in advance.

(28) Agreements which fulfil the conditions set out in this Regulation need not be notified.

(29) This Regulation does not affect the application of Regulations (EEC) No 1983/83 or (EEC) No 1984/83 or of Commission Regulation (EEC) No 3604/82 of 23 December 1982 on the application of Art. 85 (3) of the Treaty to categories of specialisation agreements, or the right to request a Commission decision in an individual case pursuant to Council Regulation No 17. It is without prejudice to laws and administrative measures of the Member States by which the latter, having regard to particular circumstances, prohibit or declare unenforceable particular restrictive obligations

contained in an agreement exempted under this Regulation; the foregoing cannot, however, affect the primacy of Community law,

Has adopted this regulation:

Article 1. Pursuant to Art. 85 (3) of the Treaty it is hereby declared that
subject to the conditions laid down in this Regulation Art. 85 (1) 8 shall
not apply to agreements to which only two undertakings are party and in
which one contracting party agrees to supply within a defined territory of
the common market

— only to the other party, or
— only to the other party and to a specified number of other undertakings within the distribution system, for the purpose of resale certain
  motor vehicles intended for use on public roads and having three or
  more road wheels, together with spare parts therefor.

Article 2. The exemption under Art. 85 (3) of the Treaty shall also
apply where the obligation referred to in Art. 1 is combined with an
obligation on the supplier neither to sell contract goods to final consumers nor to provide them with servicing for contract goods in the contract territory.

Article 3. The exemption under Art. 85 (3) of the Treaty shall also apply
where the obligation referred to in Art. 1 is combined with an obligation
on the dealer:

1. not, without the supplier's consent, to modify contract goods or corresponding goods, unless such modification is the subject of a contract with a final consumer and concerns a particular motor vehicle
   within the contract programme purchased by that final consumer;
2. not to manufacture products which compete with contract goods;
3. neither to sell new motor vehicles which compete with contract goods
   nor to sell, at the premises used for the distribution of contract
   goods, new motor vehicles other than those offered for supply by the
   manufacturer;
4. neither to sell spare parts which compete with contract goods and do
   not match the quality of contract goods nor to use them for repair or
   maintenance of contract goods or corresponding goods;
5. not to conclude with third parties distribution or servicing agreements
   for goods which compete with contract goods;
6. without the supplier's consent, neither to conclude distribution or servicing agreements with undertakings operating in the contract territory for contract goods or corresponding goods nor to alter or
   terminate such agreements;

7. to impose upon undertakings with which the dealer has concluded agreements in accordance with point 6 obligations corresponding to those which the dealer has accepted in relation to the supplier and which are covered by Arts. 1 to 4 and are in conformity with Arts. 5 and 6;

8. outside the contract territory
    (a) not to maintain branches or depots for the distribution of contract goods or corresponding goods,
    (b) not to seek customers for contract goods or corresponding goods;

9. not to entrust third parties with the distribution or servicing of contract goods or corresponding goods outside the contract territory;

10. to supply to a reseller:
    (a) contract goods or corresponding goods only where the reseller is an undertaking within the distribution system, or
    (b) spare parts within the contract programme only where they are for the purposes of repair or maintenance of a motor vehicle by the reseller;

11. to sell motor vehicles within the contract programme or corresponding goods to final consumers using the services of an intermediary only if that intermediary has prior written authority to purchase a specified motor vehicle and, as the case may be, to accept delivery thereof on their behalf;

12. to observe the obligations referred to in points 1 and 6 to 11 for a maximum period of one year after termination or expiry of the agreement.

Article 4. 1. Arts. 1, 2 and 3 shall apply notwithstanding any obligation imposed on the dealer to:

(1) observe, for distribution and servicing, minimum standards which relate in particular to:
    (a) the equipment of the business premises and of the technical facilities for servicing;
    (b) the specialised and technical training of staff;
    (c) advertising;
    (d) the collection, storage and delivery to customers of contract goods or corresponding goods and servicing relating to them;
    (e) the repair and maintenance of contract goods and corresponding goods, particularly as concerns the safe and reliable functioning of motor vehicles;

(2) order contract goods from the supplier only at certain times or within certain periods, provided that the interval between ordering dates does not exceed three months;

(3) endeavour to sell, within the contract territory and within a specified

period, such minimum quantity of contract goods as may be determined by agreement between the parties or, in the absence of such agreement, by the supplier on the basis of estimates of the dealer's potential sales;

(4) keep in stock such quantity of contract goods as may be determined by agreement between the parties or, in the absence of such agreement, by the supplier on the basis of estimates of the dealer's potential sales of contract goods within the contract territory and within a specified period;

(5) keep such demonstration vehicles within the contract programme, or such number thereof, as may be determined by agreement between the parties or, in the absence of such agreement, by the supplier on the basis of estimates of the dealer's potential sales of motor vehicles within the contract programme;

(6) perform guarantee work, free servicing and vehicle recall work for contract goods and corresponding goods;

(7) use only spare parts within the contract programme or corresponding goods for guarantee work, free servicing and vehicle recall work in respect of contract goods or corresponding goods;

(8) inform customers, in a general manner, of the extent to which spare parts from other sources might be used for the repair or maintenance of contract goods or corresponding goods;

(9) inform customers whenever spare parts from other sources have been used for the repair or maintenance of contract goods or corresponding goods for which spare parts within the contract programme or corresponding goods, bearing a mark of the manufacturer, were also available.

2. The exemption under Art. 85 (3) of the Treaty shall also apply where the obligation referred to in Art. 1 is combined with obligations referred to in paragraph 1 above and such obligations fall in individual cases under the prohibition contained in Art. 85 (1).

Article 5. 1. Arts. 1, 2 and 3 and Art. 4 (2) shall apply provided that:

(1) the dealer undertakes
   (a) in respect of motor vehicles within the contract programme or corresponding thereto which have been supplied in the common market by another undertaking within the distribution network, to honour guarantees and to perform free servicing and vehicle recall work to an extent which corresponds to the dealer's obligation covered by point 6 of Art. 4 (1) but which need not exceed that imposed upon the undertaking within the distribution system

or accepted by the manufacturer when supplying such motor vehicles;

(b) to impose upon the undertakings operating within the contract territory with which the dealer has concluded distribution and servicing agreements as provided for in point 6 of Art. 3 an obligation to honour guarantees and to perform free servicing and vehicle recall work at least to the extent to which the dealer himself is so obliged;

(2) the supplier

(a) shall not without objectively valid reasons withhold consent to conclude, alter or terminate sub-agreements referred to in Art. 3, point 6;

(b) shall not apply, in relation to the dealer's obligations referred to in Art. 4 (1), minimum requirements or criteria for estimates such that the dealer is subject to discrimination without objectively valid reasons or is treated inequitably;

(c) shall, in any scheme for aggregating quantities or values of goods obtained by the dealer from the supplier and from connected undertakings within a specified period for the purpose of calculating discounts, at least distinguish between supplies of
   – motor vehicles within the contract programme,
   – spare parts within the contract programme, for supplies of which the dealer is dependent on undertakings within the distribution network, and
   – other goods;

(d) shall also supply to the dealer, for the purpose of performance of a contract of sale concluded between the dealer and a final customer in the common market, any passenger car which corresponds to a model within the contract programme and which is marketed by the manufacturer or with the manufacturer's consent in the Member State in which the vehicle is to be registered.

2. In so far as the dealer has, in accordance with Art. 5 (1), assumed obligations for the improvement of distribution and servicing structures, the exemption referred to in Art. 3, points 3 and 5 shall apply to the obligation not to sell new motor vehicles other than those within the contract programme or not to make such vehicles the subject of a distribution and servicing agreement, provided that

(1) the parties

(a) agree that the supplier shall release the dealer from the obligations referred to in Art. 3, points 3 and 5 where the dealer shows that there are objectively valid reasons for doing so;

(b) agree that the supplier reserves the right to conclude distribution and servicing agreements for contract goods with specified further undertakings operating within the contract territory or to alter the contract territory only where the supplier shows that there are objectively valid reasons for doing so;

(2) the agreement is for a period of at least four years or, if for an indefinite period, the period of notice for regular termination of the agreement is at least one year for both parties, unless
   – the supplier is obliged by law or by special agreement to pay appropriate compensation on termination of the agreement, or
   – the dealer is a new entrant to the distribution system and the period of the agreement or the period of notice for regular termination of the agreement, is the first agreed by that dealer.

(3) each party undertakes to give the other at least six months' prior notice of intention not to renew an agreement concluded for a definite period.

3. A party may only invoke particular objectively valid grounds within the meaning of this Art. which have been exemplified in the agreement if such grounds are applied without discrimination to undertakings within the distribution system in comparable cases.

4. The conditions for exemption laid down in this Article shall not affect the right of a party to terminate the agreement for cause.

Article 6. Arts. 1, 2 and 3 and Art. 4 (2) shall not apply where:

1. both parties to the agreement or their connected undertakings are motor vehicle manufacturers; or
2. the manufacturer, the supplier or another undertaking within the distribution system obliges the dealer not to resell contract goods or corresponding goods below stated prices or not to exceed stated rates of trade discount; or
3. the parties make agreements or engage in concerted practices concerning motor vehicles having three or more road wheels or spare parts therefor which are exempted from the prohibition in Art. 85 (1) of the Treaty under Regulations (EEC) No 1983/83, or (EEC) No 1984/83 to an extent exceeding the scope of this Regulation.

Article 7. 1. As regards agreements existing on 13 March 1962 and notified before 1 February 1963 and agreements, whether notified or not, falling under Art. 4 (2), point 1 of Regulation No 17, the declaration of inapplicability of Art. 85 (1) of the Treaty contained in this Regulation shall apply with retroactive effect from the time at which the conditions of this Regulation were fulfilled.

2. As regards all other agreements notified before this Regulation entered into force, the declaration of inapplicability of Art. 85 (1) of the Treaty contained in this Regulation shall apply from the time at which the conditions of this Regulation were fulfilled, or from the date of notification, whichever is the later.

Article 8. If agreements existing on 13 March 1962 and notified before 1 February 1963 or agreements to which Art. 4 (2), point 1 of Regulation No 17 applies and which were notified before 1 January 1967 are amended before 1 October 1985 so as to fulfil the conditions for application of this Regulation, and if the amendment is communicated to the Commission before 31 December 1985, the prohibition in Art. 85 (1) of the Treaty shall not apply in respect of the period prior to the amendment. The communication shall take effect from the time of its receipt by the Commission. Where the communication is sent by registered post, it shall take effect from the date shown on the postmark of the place of posting.

Article 9. 1. As regards agreements to which Art. 85 of the Treaty applies as a result of the accession of the United Kingdom, Ireland and Denmark, Arts. 7 and 8 shall apply except that the relevant dates shall be 1 January 1973 instead of 13 March 1962 and 1 July 1973 instead of 1 February 1963 and 1 January 1967.

2. As regards agreements to which Art. 85 of the Treaty applies as a result of the accession of Greece, Arts. 7 and 8 shall apply except that the relevant dates shall be 1 January 1981 instead of 13 March 1962 and 1 July 1981 instead of 1 February 1963 and 1 January 1967.

3. As regards agreements to which Art. 85 of the Treaty applies as a result of the accession of the Kingdom of Spain and of the Portuguese Republic, Arts. 7 and 8 shall apply except that the relevant dates shall be 1 January 1986 instead of 13 March 1962 and 1 July 1986 instead of 1 February 1963, 1 January 1967 and 1 October 1985. The amendment made to the agreements in accordance with Art. 8 need not be notified to the Commission.

Article 10. The Commission may withdraw the benefit of the application of this Regulation, pursuant to Art. 7 of Regulation No 19/65/EEC, where it finds that in an individual case an agreement which falls within the scope of this Regulation nevertheless has effects which are incompatible with the provisions of Art. 85 (3) of the Treaty, and in particular:

1. where, in the common market or a substantial part thereof, contract goods or corresponding goods are not subject to competition from products considered by consumers as similar by reason of their characteristics, price and intended use;

2. where the manufacturer or an undertaking within the distribution system continuously or systematically, and by means not exempted by this Regulation, makes it difficult for final consumers or other undertakings within the distribution system to obtain contract goods or corresponding goods, or to obtain servicing for such goods, within the common market;

3. where, over a considerable period, prices or conditions of supply for contract goods or for corresponding goods are applied which differ substantially as between Member States, and such substantial differences are chiefly due to obligations exempted by this Regulation;

4. where, in agreements concerning the supply to the dealer of passenger cars which correspond to a model within the contract programme, prices or conditions which are not objectively justifiable are applied, with the object or the effect of partitioning the common market.

Article 11.   The provisions of this Regulation shall also apply in so far as the obligations referred to in Arts. 1 to 4 apply to undertakings which are connected with a party to an agreement.

Article 12.   This Regulation shall apply *mutatis mutandis* to concerted practices of the types defined in Arts. 1 to 4.

Article 13.   For the purposes of this Regulation the following terms shall have the following meanings.

1. 'Distribution and servicing agreements' are framework agreements between two undertakings, for a definite or indefinite period, whereby the party supplying goods entrusts to the other the distribution and servicing of those goods.

2. 'Parties' are the undertakings which are party to an agreement within the meaning of Art. 1: 'the supplier' being the undertaking which supplies the contract goods, and 'the dealer', the undertaking entrusted by the supplier with the distribution and servicing of contract goods.

3. The 'contract territory' is the defined territory of the common market to which the obligation of exclusive supply in the meaning of Art. 1 applies.

4. 'Contract goods' are motor vehicles intended for use on public roads and having three or more road wheels, and spare parts therefor, which are the subject of an agreement within the meaning of Art. 1.

5. The 'contract programme' refers to the totality of the contract goods.

6. 'Spare parts' are parts which are to be installed in or upon a motor vehicle so as to replace components of that vehicle. They are to be distinguished from other parts and accessories according to customary usage in the trade.

7. The 'manufacturer' is the undertaking
   (a) which manufactures or procures the manufacture of the motor vehicles in the contract programme, or
   (b) which is connected with an undertaking described at (a).
8. 'Connected undertakings' are:
   (a) undertakings one of which directly or indirectly
      - holds more than half of the capital or business assets of the other, or
      - has the power to exercise more than half the voting rights in the other, or
      - has the power to appoint more than half the members of the supervisory board, board of directors or bodies legally representing the other, or
      - has the right to manage the affairs of the other;
   (b) undertakings in relation to which a third undertaking is able directly or indirectly to exercise such rights or powers as are mentioned in (a) above.
9. 'Undertakings within the distribution system' are, besides the parties to the agreement, the manufacturer and undertakings which are entrusted by the manufacturer or with the manufacturer's consent with the distribution or servicing of contract goods or corresponding goods.
10. A 'passenger car which corresponds to a model within the contract programme' is a passenger car
    - manufactured or assembled in volume by the manufacturer, and
    - identical as to body style, drive-line, chassis, and type of motor with a passenger car within the contract programme.
11. 'Corresponding goods', 'corresponding motor vehicles' and 'corresponding parts' are those which are similar in kind to those in the contract programme, are distributed by the manufacturer or with the manufacturer's consent, and are the subject of a distribution or servicing agreement with an undertaking within the distribution system.
12. 'Distribute' and 'sell' include other forms of supply such as leasing.

Article 14. This Regulation shall enter into force on 1 July 1985.
   It shall remain in force until 30 June 1995.

[Final provisions omitted.]

Regulation (EEC) No 417/85 of the Commission of 19 December 1984 on the application of Article 85 (3) of the Treaty to categories of specialisation agreements[16]

The Commission of the European Communities,

[Recitals omitted.]

Whereas:

(1) Regulation (EEC) No 2821/71 empowers the Commission to apply Art. 85 (3) of the Treaty by Regulation to certain categories of agreements, decisions and concerted practices falling within the scope of Art. 85 (1) which relate to specialisation, including agreements necessary for achieving it.

(2) Agreements on specialisation in present or future production may fall within the scope of Art. 85 (1).

(3) Agreements on specialisation in production generally contribute to improving the production or distribution of goods, because undertakings concerned can concentrate on the manufacture of certain products and thus operate more efficiently and supply the products more cheaply. It is likely that, given effective competition, consumers will receive a fair share of the resulting benefit.

(4) Such advantages can arise equally from agreements whereby each participant gives up the manufacture of certain products in favour of another participant and from agreements whereby the participants undertake to manufacture certain products or have them manufactured only jointly.

(5) The Regulation must specify what restrictions of competition may be included in specialisation agreements. The restrictions of competition that are permitted in the Regulation in addition to reciprocal obligations to give up manufacture are normally essential for the making and implementation of such agreements. These restrictions are therefore, in general, indispensable for the attainment of the desired advantages for the participating undertakings and consumers. It may be left to the parties to decide which of these provisions they include in their agreements.

(6) The exemption must be limited to agreements which do not give rise to the possibility of eliminating competition in respect of a substantial part of the products in question. The Regulation must therefore apply only as long as the market share and turnover of the participating undertakings do not exceed a certain limit.

[16] OJ 1985 L 53/1, as amended by Reg. 151/93, OJ 1993 L 21/8.

(7) It is, however, appropriate to offer undertakings which exceed the turnover limit set in the Regulation a simplified means of obtaining the legal certainty provided by the block exemption. This must allow the Commission to exercise effective supervision as well as simplifying its administration of such agreements.

(8) In order to facilitate the conclusion of long-term specialisation agreements, which can have a bearing on the structure of the participating undertakings, it is appropriate to fix the period of validity of the Regulation at 13 years. If the circumstances on the basis of which the Regulation was adopted should change significantly within this period, the Commission will make the necessary amendments.

(9) Agreements, decisions and concerted practices which are automatically exempted pursuant to this Regulation need not be notified. Undertakings may none the less in an individual case request a decision pursuant to Council Regulation No 17, as last amended by the Act of Accession of Greece,

Has adopted this regulation:

Article 1. Pursuant to Art. 85 (3) of the Treaty and subject to the provisions of this Regulation, it is hereby declared that Art. 85 (1) of the Treaty shall not apply to agreements on specialisation whereby, for the duration of the agreement, undertakings accept reciprocal obligations:

(a) not to manufacture certain products or to have them manufactured, but to leave it to other parties to manufacture the products or have them manufactured; or

(b) to manufacture certain products or have them manufactured only jointly.

Article 2. 1. Article 1 shall also apply to the following restrictions of competition:

(a) an obligation not to conclude with third parties specialisation agreements relating to identical products or to products considered by users to be equivalent in view of their characteristics, price and intended use;

(b) an obligation to procure products which are the subject of the specialisation exclusively from another party, a joint undertaking or an undertaking jointly charged with their manufacture, except where they are obtainable on more favourable terms elsewhere and the other party, the joint undertaking or the undertaking charged with manufacture is not prepared to offer the same terms;

(c) an obligation to grant other parties the exclusive right, within the whole or a defined areas of the common market, to distribute prod-

ucts which are the subject of the specialisation provided that intermediaries and users can also obtain the products from other suppliers
and the parties do not render it difficult for intermediaries or users
thus to obtain the products.

(d) an obligation to grant one of the parties the exclusive right to distribute products which are the subject of the specialisation provided that
the party does not distribute products of a third undertaking which
compete with the contract products;

(e) an obligation to grant the exclusive right to distribute products which
are the subject of the specialisation to a joint undertaking or to a
third undertaking, provided that the joint undertaking or third undertaking does not manufacture or distribute products which compete
with the contract products;

(f) an obligation to grant the exclusive right to distribute within the
whole or a defined area of the common market the products which
are the subject of the specialisation to joint undertakings or third
undertakings which do not manufacture or distribute products which
compete with the contract products, provided that users and intermediaries can also obtain the contract products from other suppliers
and that neither the parties nor the joint undertakings or third undertakings entrusted with the exclusive distribution of the contract products render it difficult for users and intermediaries to thus obtain the
contract products.

2a. Article 1 shall not apply if restrictions of competition other than
those set out in paragraphs 1 and 2 are imposed upon the parties by
agreement, decision or concerted practice;

2. Art. 1 shall also apply where the parties undertake obligations of
the types referred to in paragraph 1 but with a more limited scope than is
permitted by that paragraph.

3. Art. 1 shall apply notwithstanding that any of the following obligations, in particular, are imposed:

(a) an obligation to supply other parties with products which are the
subject of the specialisation and in so doing to observe minimum
standards of quality;

(b) an obligation to maintain minimum stocks of products which are the
subject of the specialisation and of replacement parts for them;

(c) an obligation to provide customer and guarantee services for products
which are the subject of the specialisation.

Article 3. 1. Art. 1 shall apply only if:

(a) the products which are the subject of the specialisation together with
the participating undertakings' other products which are considered

by users to be equivalent in view of their characteristics, price and intended use do not represent more than 20% of the market for all such products in the common market or a substantial part thereof; and

(b) the aggregate turnover of all the participating undertakings does not exceed ECU 1000 million.

2. If pursuant to point (d), (e) or (f) of Article 2 (1), one of the parties, a joint undertaking, a third undertaking or more than one joint undertaking or third undertaking are entrusted with the distribution of the products which are the subject of the specialisation, Article 1 shall apply only if:

(a) the products which are the subject of the specialisation together with the participating undertakings' other products which are considered by users to be equivalent in view of their characteristics, price and intended use do not represent more than 10% of the market for all such products in the common market or a substantial part thereof; and

(b) the aggregate annual turnover of all the participating undertakings does not exceed ECU 1000 million.

3. Article 1 shall continue to apply if the market shares and turnover referred to in paragraphs 1 and 2 are exceeded during any period of two consecutive financial years by not more than one-tenth.

4. Where the limits laid down in paragraphs 3 are also exceeded, Art. 1 shall continue to apply for a period of six months following the end of the financial year during which it was exceeded.

Article 4. 1. The exemption provided for in Art. 1 shall also apply to agreements involving participating undertakings whose aggregate turnover exceeds the limits laid down in Art. 3 (1) (b), 2(b) and (3), on condition that the agreements in question are notified to the Commission in accordance with the provisions of Commission Regulation No 27, and that the Commission does not oppose such exemption within a period of six months.

2. The period of six months shall run from the date on which the notification is received by the Commission. Where, however, the notification is made by registered post, the period shall run from the date shown on the postmark of the place of posting.

3. Paragraph 1 shall apply only if:

(a) express reference is made to this Article in the notification or in a communication accompanying it; and

(b) the information furnished with the notification is complete and in accordance with the facts.

4. The benefit of paragraph 1 may be claimed for agreements notified before the entry into force of this Regulation by submitting a communication to the Commission referring expressly to this Art. and to the notification. Paragraphs 2 and 3 (b) shall apply *mutatis mutandis*.

5. The Commission may oppose the exemption. It shall oppose exemption if it receives a request to do so from a Member State within three months of the forwarding to the Member State of the notification referred to in paragraph 1 or of the communication referred to in paragraph 4. This request must be justified on the basis of considerations relating to the competition rules of the Treaty.

6. The Commission may withdraw the opposition to the exemption at any time. However, where the opposition was raised at the request of a Member State and this request is maintained, it may be withdrawn only after consultation of the Advisory Committee on Restrictive Practices and Dominant Positions.

7. If the opposition is withdrawn because the undertakings concerned have shown that the conditions of Art. 85 (3) are fulfilled, the exemption shall apply from the date of notification.

8. If the opposition is withdrawn because the undertakings concerned have amended the agreement so that the conditions of Art. 85 (3) are fulfilled, the exemption shall apply from the date on which the amendments take effect.

9. If the Commission opposes exemption and the opposition is not withdrawn, the effects of the notification shall be governed by the provisions of Regulation No 17.

Article 5. 1. Information acquired pursuant to Art. 4 shall be used only for the purposes of this Regulation.

2. The Commission and the authorities of the Member States, their officials and other servants shall not disclose information acquired by them pursuant to this Regulation of a kind that is covered by the obligation of professional secrecy.

3. Paragraphs 1 and 2 shall not prevent publication of general information or surveys which do not contain information relating to particular undertakings or associations of undertakings.

Article 6. For the purpose of calculating total annual turnover within the meaning of Art. 3 (1)(b) and (2)(b), the turnovers achieved during the last financial year by the participating undertakings in respect of all goods and services excluding tax shall be added together. For this purpose, no account shall be taken of dealings between the participating undertakings or between these undertakings and a third undertaking jointly charged with manufacture or sale.

Article 7. 1. For the purposes of Art. 3 (1) and (2) and Art. 6, participating undertakings are:

(a) undertakings party to the agreement;
(b) undertakings in which a party to the agreement, directly or indirectly:
 – owns more than half the capital or business assets,
 – has the power to exercise more than half the voting rights,
 – has the power to appoint at least half the members of the supervisory board, board of management or bodies legally representing the undertakings, or
 – has the right to manage the affairs;
(c) undertakings which directly or indirectly have in or over a party to the agreement the rights or powers listed in (b);
(d) undertakings in or over which an undertaking referred to in (c) directly or indirectly has the rights or powers listed in (b).

2. Undertakings in which the undertakings referred to in paragraph 1 (a) to (d) directly or indirectly jointly have the rights or powers set out in paragraph 1 (b) shall also be considered to be participating undertakings.

Article 8. The Commission may withdraw the benefit of this Regulation, pursuant to Art. 7 of Regulation (EEC) No 2821/71, where it finds in a particular case that an agreement exempted by this Regulation nevertheless has effects which are incompatible with the conditions set out in Art. 85 (3) of the Treaty, and in particular where:

(a) the agreement is not yielding significant results in terms of rationalisation or consumers are not receiving a fair share of the resulting benefit; or
(b) the products which are the subject of the specialisation are not subject in the common market or a substantial part thereof to effective competition from identical products or products considered by users to be equivalent in view of their characteristics, price and intended use.

Article 9. This Regulation shall apply *mutatis mutandis* to decisions of associations of undertakings and concerted practices.

Article 9a. The prohibition in Art. 85 (1) of the Treaty shall not apply to the specialisation agreements which were in existence at the date of the accession of the Kingdom of Spain and of the Portuguese Republic and which, by reason of this accession, fall within the scope of Art. 85 (1), if, before 1 July 1986, they are so amended that they comply with the conditions laid down in this Regulation.

Article 10.   1. This Regulation shall enter into force on 1 March 1985. It shall apply until 31 December 1997.

2. Commission Regulation (EEC) No 3604/82 is hereby repealed.

[Final provisions omitted.]

Regulation (EEC) No 418/85 of the Commission of 19 December 1984 on the application of Article 85 (3) of the Treaty to categories of research and development agreements[17]

The Commission of the European Communities,

[Recitals omitted.]

Whereas:

(1) Regulation (EEC) No 2821/71 empowers the Commission to apply Art. 85 (3) of the Treaty by Regulation to certain categories of agreements, decisions and concerted practices falling within the scope of Art. 85 (1) which have as their object the research and development of products or processes up to the stage of industrial application, and exploitation of the results, including provisions regarding industrial property rights and confidential technical knowledge.

(2) As stated in the Commission's 1968 notice concerning agreements, decisions and concerted practices in the field of cooperation between enterprises, agreements on the joint execution of research work or the joint development of the results of the research, up to but not including the stage of industrial application, generally do not fall within the scope of Art. 85 (1) of the Treaty. In certain circumstances, however, such as where the parties agree not to carry out other research and development in the same field, thereby forgoing the opportunity of gaining competitive advantages over the other parties, such agreements may fall within Art. 85 (1) and should therefore not be excluded from this Regulation.

(3) Agreements providing for both joint research and development and joint exploitation of the results may fall within Art. 85 (1) because the parties jointly determine how the products developed are manufactured or the processes developed are applied or how related intellectual property rights or know-how are exploited.

(4) Cooperation in research and development and in the exploitation of the results generally promotes technical and economic progress by increasing the dissemination of technical knowledge between the

[17] OJ 1985 L 53/5, as amended by Reg. 151/93, OJ 1993 L 21/8

parties and avoiding duplication of research and development work, by stimulating new advances through the exchange of complementary technical knowledge, and by rationalising the manufacture of the products or application of the processes arising out of the research and development. These aims can be achieved only where the research and development programme and its objectives are clearly defined and each of the parties is given the opportunity of exploiting any of the results of the programme that interest it; where universities or research institutes participate and are not interested in the industrial exploitation of the results, however, it may be agreed that they may use the said results solely for the purpose of further research.

(5) Consumers can generally be expected to benefit from the increased volume and effectiveness of research and development through the introduction of new or improved products or services or the reduction of prices brought about by new or improved processes.

(6) This Regulation must specify the restrictions of competition which may be included in the exempted agreements. The purpose of the permitted restrictions is to concentrate the research activities of the parties in order to improve their chances of success, and to facilitate the introduction of new products and services onto the market. These restrictions are generally necessary to secure the desired benefits for the parties and consumers.

(7) The joint exploitation of results can be considered as the natural consequence of joint research and development. It can take different forms ranging from manufacture to the exploitation of intellectual property rights or know-how that substantially contributes to technical or economic progress. In order to attain the benefits and objectives described above and to justify the restrictions of competition which are exempted, the joint exploitation must relate to products or processes for which the use of the results of the research and development is decisive. Joint exploitation is not therefore justified where it relates to improvements which were not made within the framework of a joint research and development programme but under an agreement having some other principal objective, such as the licensing of intellectual property rights, joint manufacture or specialisation, and merely containing ancillary provisions on joint research and development.

(8) The exemption granted under the Regulation must be limited to agreements which do not afford the undertakings the possibility of eliminating competition in respect of a substantial part of the products in question. In order to guarantee that several independent poles of research can exist in the common market in any economic sector,

it is necessary to exclude from the block exemption agreements between competitors whose combined share of the market for products capable of being improved or replaced by the results of the research and development exceeds a certain level at the time the agreement is entered into.

(9) In order to guarantee the maintenance of effective competition during joint exploitation of the results, it is necessary to provide that the block exemption will cease to apply if the parties' combined shares of the market for the products arising out of the joint research and development become too great. However, it should be provided that the exemption will continue to apply, irrespective of the parties' market shares, for a certain period after the commencement of joint exploitation, so as to await stabilisation of their market shares, particularly after the introduction of an entirely new product, and to guarantee a minimum period of return on the generally substantial investments involved.

(10) Agreements between undertakings which do not fulfil the market share conditions laid down in the Regulation may, in appropriate cases, be granted an exemption by individual decision, which will in particular take account of world competition and the particular circumstances prevailing in the manufacture of high technology products.

(11) It is desirable to list in the Regulation a number of obligations that are commonly found in research and development agreements but that are normally not restrictive of competition and to provide that, in the event that, because of the particular economic or legal circumstances, they should fall within Art. 85 (1), they also would be covered by the exemption. This list is not exhaustive.

(12) The Regulation must specify what provisions may not be included in agreements if these are to benefit from the block exemption by virtue of the fact that such provisions are restrictions falling within Art. 85 (1) for which there can be no general presumption that they will lead to the positive effects required by Art. 85 (3).

(13) Agreements which are not automatically covered by the exemption because they include provisions that are not expressly exempted by the Regulation and are not expressly excluded from exemption are none the less capable of benefiting from the general presumption of compatibility with Art. 85 (3) on which the block exemption is based. It will be possible for the Commission rapidly to establish whether this is the case for a particular agreement. Such an agreement should therefore be deemed to be covered by the exemption provided for in this Regulation where it is notified to the Commission and the Commission does not oppose the application of the exemption within a specified period of time.

(14) Agreements covered by this Regulation may also take advantage of provisions contained in other block exemption Regulations of the Commission, and in particular Regulation (EEC) No 417/85 on specialisation agreements, Regulation (EEC) No 1983/83 on exclusive distribution agreements, Regulation (EEC) No 1984/83, on exclusive purchasing agreements and Regulation (EEC) No 2349/84 on patent licensing agreements, if they fulfil the conditions set out in these Regulations. The provisions of the aforementioned Regulations are, however, not applicable in so far as this Regulation contains specific rules.

(15) If individual agreements exempted by this Regulation nevertheless have effects which are incompatible with Art. 85 (3), the Commission may withdraw the benefit of the block exemption.

(16) The Regulation should apply with retroactive effect to agreements in existence when the Regulation comes into force where such agreements already fulfil its conditions or are modified to do so. The benefit of these provisions may not be claimed in actions pending at the date of entry into force of this Regulation, nor may it be relied on as grounds for claims for damages against third parties.

(17) Since research and development cooperation agreements are often of a long-term nature, especially where the cooperation extends to the exploitation of the results, it is appropriate to fix the period of validity of the Regulation at 13 years. If the circumstances on the basis of which the Regulation was adopted should change significantly within this period, the Commission will make the necessary amendments.

(18) Agreements which are automatically exempted pursuant to this Regulation need not be notified. Undertakings may nevertheless in a particular case request a decision pursuant to Council Regulation No 17, as last amended by the Act of Accession of Greece,

Has adopted this Regulation:

Article 1. 1. Pursuant to Art. 85 (3) of the Treaty and subject to the provisions of this Regulation, it is hereby declared that Art. 85 (1) of the Treaty shall not apply to agreements entered into between undertakings for the purpose of:

(a) joint research and development of products or processes and joint exploitation of the results of that research and development;

(b) joint exploitation of the results of research and development of products or processes jointly carried out pursuant to a prior agreement between the same undertakings; or

(c) joint research and development of products or processes excluding joint exploitation of the results, in so far as such agreements fall within the scope of Art. 85 (1).

2. For the purposes of this Regulation:

(a) *research and development of products or processes* means the acquisition of technical knowledge and the carrying out of theoretical analysis, systematic study or experimentation, including experimental production, technical testing of products or processes, the establishment of the necessary facilities and the obtaining of intellectual property rights for the results;

(b) *contract processes* means processes arising out of the research and development;

(c) *contract products* means products or services arising out of the research and development or manufactured or provided applying the contract processes;

(d) *exploitation of the results* means the manufacture of the contract products or the application of the contract processes or the assignment or licensing of intellectual property rights or the communication of know-how required for such manufacture or application;

(e) *technical knowledge* means technical knowledge which is either protected by an intellectual property right or is secret (know-how).

3. Research and development of the exploitation of the results are carried out *jointly* where:

(a) the work involved is:
   – carried out by a joint team, organisation or undertaking,
   – jointly entrusted to a third party, or
   – allocated between the parties by way of specialisation in research, development or production;

(b) the parties collaborate in any way in the assignment or the licensing of intellectual property rights or the communication of know-how, within the meaning of paragraph 2 (d), to third parties.

Article 2. The exemption provided for in Art. 1 shall apply on condition that:

(a) the joint research and development work is carried out within the framework of a programme defining the objectives of the work and the field in which it is to be carried out;

(b) all the parties have access to the results of the work;

(c) where the agreement provides only for joint research and development, each party is free to exploit the results of the joint research and development and any pre-existing technical knowledge necessary therefor independently;

(d) the joint exploitation relates only to results which are protected by intellectual property rights or constitute know-how which substantially contributes to technical or economic progress and that the results are decisive for the manufacture of the contract products or the application of the contract processes;

(f) undertakings charged with manufacture by way of specialisation in production are required to fulfil orders for supplies from all the parties.

Article 3. 1. Where the parties are not competing manufacturers of products capable of being improved or replaced by the contract products, the exemption provided for in Article 1 shall apply for the duration of the research and development programme and, where the results are jointly exploited, for five years from the time the contract products are first put on the market within the common market.

2. Where two or more of the parties are competing manufacturers within the meaning of paragraph 1, the exemption provided for in Art. 1 shall apply for the period specified in paragraph 1 only if, at the time the agreement is entered into, the parties' combined production of the products capable of being improved or replaced by the contract products does not exceed 20% of the market for such products in the common market or a substantial part thereof.

3. After the end of the period referred to in paragraph 1, the exemption provided for in Art. 1 shall continue to apply as long as the production of the contract products together with the parties' combined production of other products which are considered by users to be equivalent in view of their characteristics, price and intended use does not exceed 20% of the total market for such products in the common market or a substantial part thereof. Where contract products are components used by the parties of the manufacture of other products, reference shall be made to the markets for such of those latter products for which the components represent a significant part.

3a. Where one of the parties, a joint undertaking, a third undertaking or more than one joint undertaking or third undertaking are entrusted with the distribution of the products which are the subject of the agreement under Article 4(1)(fa), (fb) or (fc), the exemption provided for in Article 1 shall apply only if the parties production of the products referred to in paragraphs 2 and 3 does not exceed 10% of the market for all such products in the common market or a substantial part thereof.

4. The exemption provided for in Article 1 shall continue to apply where the market shares referred to in paragraph 3 and 4 is exceeded during any period of two consecutive financial years by not more than one-tenth.

5. Where the limits laid down in paragraph 5 are also exceeded, the exemption provided for in Article 1 shall continue to apply for a period of six months following the end of the financial year during which they were exceeded.

Article 4. 1. The exemption provided for in Art. 1 shall also apply to the following restrictions of competition imposed on the parties:

(a) an obligation not to carry out independently research and development in the field to which the programme relates or in a closely connected field during the execution of the programme;

(b) an obligation not to enter into agreements with third parties on research and development in the field to which the programme relates or in a closely connected field during the execution of the programme;

(c) an obligation to procure the contract products exclusively from parties, joint organisations or undertakings or third parties, jointly charged with their manufacture;

(d) an obligation not to manufacture the contract products or apply the contract processes in territories reserved for other parties;

(e) an obligation to restrict the manufacture of the contract products or application of the contract processes to one or more technical fields of application, except where two or more of the parties are competitors within the meaning of Art. 3 at the time the agreement is entered into;

(f) an obligation not to pursue, for a period of five years from the time the contract products are first put on the market within the common market, an active policy of putting the products on the market in territories reserved for other parties, and in particular not to engage in advertising specifically aimed at such territories or to establish any branch or maintain any distribution depot there for the distribution of the products, provided that users and intermediaries can obtain the contract products from other suppliers and the parties do not render it difficult for intermediaries and users to thus obtain the products;

(fa) an obligation to grant one of the parties the exclusive right to distribute the contract products, provided that that party does not distribute products manufactured by a third producer which compete with the contract products;

(fb) an obligation to grant the exclusive right to distribute the contract products to a joint undertaking or a third undertaking, provided that the joint undertaking or third undertaking does not manufacture or distribute products which compete with the contract products;

(fc) an obligation to grant the exclusive right to distribute the contract products in the whole or defined area of the common market to joint undertakings or third undertakings which do not manufacture or distribute products which compete with the contract products, provided that users and intermediaries are also able to obtain the contract products from other suppliers and neither the parties nor the joint undertakings or third undertakings entrusted with the exclusive distribution of the contract products render it difficult for users and intermediaries to thus obtain the contract products.

(g) an obligation on the parties to communicate to each other any experience they may gain in exploiting the results and to grant each other non-exclusive licences for inventions relating to improvements or new applications.

2. The exemption provided for in Art. 1 shall also apply where in a particular agreement the parties undertake obligations of the types referred to in paragraph 1 but with a more limited scope than is permitted by that paragraph.

Article 5. 1. Art. 1 shall apply notwithstanding that any of the following obligations, in particular, are imposed on the parties during the currency of the agreement:

(a) an obligation to communicate patented or non-patented technical knowledge necessary for the carrying out of the research and development programme for the exploitation of its results;

(b) an obligation not to use any know-how received from another party for purposes other than carrying out the research and development programme and the exploitation of its results;

(c) an obligation to obtain and maintain in force intellectual property rights for the contract products or processes;

(d) an obligation to preserve the confidentiality of any know-how received or jointly developed under the research and development programme; this obligation may be imposed even after the expiry of the agreement;

(e) an obligation:
   (i) to inform other parties of infringements of their intellectual property rights,
   (ii) to take legal action against infringers, and
   (iii) to assist in any such legal action or share with the other parties in the cost thereof;

(f) an obligation to pay royalties or render services to other parties to compensate for unequal contributions to the joint research and development or unequal exploitation of its results;

(g) an obligation to share royalties received from third parties with other parties;

(h) an obligation to supply other parties with minimum quantities of contract products and to observe minimum standards of quality.

2. In the event that, because of particular circumstances, the obligations referred to in paragraph 1 fall within the scope of Art. 85 (1), they also shall be covered by the exemption. The exemption provided for in this paragraph shall also apply where in a particular agreement the parties undertake obligations of the types referred to in paragraph 1 but with a more limited scope than is permitted by that paragraph.

Article 6.   The exemption provided for in Art. 1 shall not apply where the parties, by agreement, decision or concerted practice:

(a) are restricted in their freedom to carry out research and development independently or in cooperation with third parties in a field unconnected with that to which the programme relates or, after its completion, in the field to which the programme relates or in a connected field;
(b) are prohibited after completion of the research and development programme from challenging the validity of intellectual property rights which the parties hold in the common market and which are relevant to the programme or, after the expiry of the agreement, from challenging the validity of intellectual property rights which the parties hold in the common market and which protect the results of the research and development;
(c) are restricted as to the quantity of the contract products they may manufacture or sell or as to the number of operations employing the contract process they may carry out;
(d) are restricted in their determination of prices, components of prices or discounts when selling the contract products to third parties;
(e) are restricted as to the customers they may serve, without prejudice to Art. 4 (1) (e);
(f) are prohibited from putting the contract products on the market or pursuing an active sales policy for them in territories within the common market that are reserved for other parties after the end of the period referred to in Art. 4 (1) (f);
(g) are required not to grant licences to third parties to manufacture the contract products or to apply the contract processes even though the exploitation by the parties themselves of the results of the joint research and development is not provided for or does not take place;
(h) are required:
   – to refuse without any objectively justified reason to meet demand from users or dealers established in their respective territories who would market the contract products in other territories within the common market, or

– to make it difficult for users or dealers to obtain the contract products from other dealers within the common market, and in particular to exercise intellectual property rights or take measures so as to prevent users or dealers from obtaining, or from putting on the market within the common market, products which have been lawfully put on the market within the common market by another party or with its consent.

Article 7. 1. The exemption provided for in this Regulation shall also apply to agreements of the kinds described in Art. 1 which fulfil the conditions laid down in Arts. 2 and 3 and which contain obligations restrictive of competition which are not covered by Arts. 4 and 5 and do not fall within the scope of Art. 6, on condition that the agreements in question are notified to the Commission in accordance with the provisions of Commission Regulation No 27, and that the Commission does not oppose such exemption within a period of six months.

2. The period of six months shall run from the date on which the notification is received by the Commission. Where, however, the notification is made by registered post, the period shall run from the date shown on the postmark of the place of posting.

3. Paragraph 1 shall apply only if:

(a) express reference is made to this Article in the notification or in a communication accompanying it, and
(b) the information furnished with the notification is complete and in accordance with the facts.

4. The benefit of paragraph 1 may be claimed for agreements notified before the entry into force of this Regulation by submitting a communication to the Commission referring expressly to this Article and to the notification. Paragraphs 2 and 3 (b) shall apply *mutatis mutandis*.

5. The Commission may oppose the exemption. It shall oppose exemption if it receives a request to do so from a Member State within three months of the forwarding to the Member State of the notification referred to in paragraph 1 or of the communication referred to in paragraph 4. This request must be justified on the basis of considerations relating to the competition rules of the Treaty.

6. The Commission may withdraw the opposition to the exemption at any time. However, where the opposition was raised at the request of a Member State and this request is maintained, it may be withdrawn only after consultation of the Advisory Committee on Restrictive Practices and Dominant Positions.

7. If the opposition is withdrawn because the undertakings concerned have shown that the conditions of Art. 85 (3) are fulfilled, the exemption shall apply from the date of notification.

8. If the opposition is withdrawn because the undertakings concerned have amended the agreement so that the conditions of Art. 85 (3) are fulfilled, the exemption shall apply from the date on which the amendments take effect.

9. If the Commission opposes exemption and the opposition is not withdrawn, the effects of the notification shall be governed by the provisions of Regulation No 17.

Article 8. 1. Information acquired pursuant to Art. 7 shall be used only for the purposes of this Regulation.

2. The Commission and the authorities of the Member States, their officials and other servants shall not disclose information acquired by them pursuant to this Regulation of a kind that is covered by the obligation of professional secrecy.

3. Paragraphs 1 and 2 shall not prevent publication of general information or surveys which do not contain information relating to particular undertakings or associations of undertakings.

Article 9. 1. The provisions of this Regulation shall also apply to rights and obligations which the parties create for undertakings connected with them. The market shares held and the actions and measures taken by connected undertakings shall be treated as those of the parties themselves.

2. Connected undertakings for the purposes of this Regulation are:

(a) undertakings in which a party to the agreement, directly or indirectly:
  – owns more than half the capital or business assets,
  – has the power to exercise more than half the voting rights,
  – has the power to appoint more than half the members of the supervisory board, board of directors or bodies legally representing the undertakings, or
  – has the right to manage the affairs;
(b) undertakings which directly have in or over a party to the agreement the rights or powers listed in (a);
(c) undertakings in or over which an undertaking referred to in (b) directly or indirectly has the rights or powers listed in (a);

3. Undertakings in which the parties to the agreement or undertakings connected with them jointly have, directly or indirectly, the rights or powers set out in paragraph 2 (a) shall be considered to be connected with each of the parties to the agreement.

Article 10. The Commission may withdraw the benefit of this Regulation, pursuant to Art. 7 of Regulation (EEC) No 2821/71, where it finds in a particular case that an agreement exempted by this Regulation nevertheless has certain effects which are incompatible with the conditions laid down in Art. 85 (3) of the Treaty, and in particular where:

(a) the existence of the agreement substantially restricts the scope for third parties to carry out research and development in the relevant field because of the limited research capacity available elsewhere;

(b) because of the particular structure of supply, the existence of the agreement substantially restricts the access of third parties to the market for the contract products;

(c) without any objectively valid reason, the parties do not exploit the results of the joint research and development;

(d) the contract products are not subject in the whole or a substantial part of the common market to effective competition from identical products or products considered by users as equivalent in view of their characteristics, price and intended use.

Article 11. 1. In the case of agreements notified to the Commission before 1 March 1985, the exemption provided for in Art. 1 shall have retroactive effect from the time at which the conditions for application of this Regulation were fulfilled or, where the agreement does not fall within Art. 4 (2) (3) (b) of Regulation No 17, not earlier than the date of notification.

2. In the case of agreements existing on 13 March 1962 and notified to the Commission before 1 February 1963, the exemption shall have retroactive effect from the time at which the conditions for application of this Regulation were fulfilled.

3. Where agreements which were in existence on 13 March 1962 and which were notified to the Commission before 1 February 1963, or which are covered by Art. 4 (2) (3) (b) of Regulation No 17 and were notified to the Commission before 1 January 1967, are amended before 1 September 1985 so as to fulfil the conditions for application of this Regulation, such amendment being communicated to the Commission before 1 October 1985, the prohibition laid down in Art. 85 (1) of the Treaty shall not apply in respect of the period prior to the amendment. The communication of amendments shall take effect from the date of their receipt by the Commission. Where the communication is sent by registered post, it shall take effect from the date shown on the postmark of the place of posting.

4. In the case of agreements to which Art. 85 of the Treaty applies as a result of the accession of the United Kingdom, Ireland and Denmark, paragraphs 1 to 3 shall apply except that the relevant dates shall be 1 January 1973 instead of 13 March 1962 and 1 July 1973 instead of 1 February 1963 and 1 January 1967.

5. In the case of agreements to which Art. 85 of the Treaty applies as a result of the accession of Greece, paragraphs 1 to 3 shall apply except

that the relevant dates shall be 1 January 1981 instead of 13 March 1962 and 1 July 1981 instead of 1 February 1963 and 1 January 1967.

6. As regards agreements to which Art. 85 of the Treaty applies as a result of the accession of the Kingdom of Spain and of the Portuguese Republic, paragraphs 1- to 3 shall apply except that the relevant dates should be 1 January 1986 instead of 13 March 1962 and 1 July 1986 instead of 1 February 1963, 1 January 1967, 1 March 1985 and 1 September 1985. The amendments made to the agreements in accordance with the provisions of paragraph 3 need not be notified to the Commission.

Article 12. This Regulation shall apply *mutatis mutandis* to decisions of associations of undertakings.

Article 13 This Regulation shall enter into force on 1 March 1985.
It shall apply until 31 December 1997.

[Final provisions omitted.]

Commission Regulation (EEC) No 4087/88 of 30 November 1988 on the application of Article 85 (3) of the Treaty to categories of franchise agreements[18]

The Commission of the European Communities,

Having regard to the Treaty establishing the European Economic Community,
Having regard to Council Regulation No 19/65/EEC of 2 March 1965 on the application of Art. 85 (3) of the Treaty to certain categories of agreements and concerted practices,[19] as last amended by the Act of Accession of Spain and Portugal, and in particular Art. 1 thereof,
Having published a draft of this Regulation,[20]
Having consulted the Advisory Committee on Restrictive Practices and Dominant Positions,
Whereas:

(1) Regulation No 19/65/EEC empowers the Commission to apply Art. 85 (3) of the Treaty by Regulation to certain categories of bilateral exclusive agreements falling within the scope of Art. 85 (1) which either have as their object the exclusive distribution or exclusive purchase of goods, or include restrictions imposed in relation to the assignment or use of industrial property rights.

[18] OJ 1988 L 359/46.   [19] OJ No 36, 6. 3. 1965, p. 533/65.   [20] OJ 1987 C 229/3.

(2) Franchise agreements consist essentially of licences of industrial or intellectual property rights relating to trade marks or signs and know-how, which can be combined with restrictions relating to supply or purchase of goods.

(3) Several types of franchise can be distinguished according to their object: industrial franchise concerns the manufacturing of goods, distribution franchise concerns the sale of goods, and service franchise concerns the supply of services.

(4) It is possible on the basis of the experience of the Commission to define categories of franchise agreements which fall under Art. 85 (1) but can normally be regarded as satisfying the conditions laid down in Art. 85 (3). This is the case for franchise agreements whereby one of the parties supplies goods or provides services to end users. On the other hand, industrial franchise agreements should not be covered by this Regulation. Such agreements, which usually govern relationships between producers, present different characteristics than the other types of franchise. They consist of manufacturing licences based on patents and/or technical know-how, combined with trade-mark licences. Some of them may benefit from other block exemptions if they fulfil the necessary conditions.

(5) This Regulation covers franchise agreements between two undertakings, the franchisor and the franchisee, for the retailing of goods or the provision of services to end users, or a combination of these activities, such as the processing or adaptation of goods to fit specific needs of their customers. It also covers cases where the relationship between franchisor and franchisees is made through a third undertaking, the master franchisee. It does not cover wholesale franchise agreements because of the lack of experience of the Commission in that field.

(6) Franchise agreements as defined in this Regulation can fall under Art. 85 (1). They may in particular affect intra-Community trade where they are concluded between undertakings from different Member States or where they form the basis of a network which extends beyond the boundaries of a single Member State.

(7) Franchise agreements as defined in this Regulation normally improve the distribution of goods and/or the provision of services as they give franchisors the possibility of establishing a uniform network with limited investments, which may assist the entry of new competitors on the market, particularly in the case of small and medium-sized undertakings, thus increasing interbrand competition. They also allow independent traders to set up outlets more rapidly and with higher chance of success than if they had to do so without the franchisor's experience and assistance. They have therefore the possibility of competing more efficiently with large distribution undertakings.

(8) As a rule, franchise agreements also allow consumers and other end users a fair share of the resulting benefit, as they combine the advantage of a uniform network with the existence of traders personally interested in the efficient operation of their business. The homogeneity of the network and the constant cooperation between the franchisor and the franchisees ensures a constant quality of the products and services. The favourable effect of franchising on interbrand competition and the fact that consumers are free to deal with any franchisee in the network guarantees that a reasonable part of the resulting benefits will be passed on to the consumers.

(9) This Regulation must define the obligations restrictive of competition which may be included in franchise agreements. This is the case in particular for the granting of an exclusive territory to the franchisees combined with the prohibition on actively seeking customers outside that territory, which allows them to concentrate their efforts on their allotted territory. The same applies to the granting of an exclusive territory to a master franchisee combined with the obligation not to conclude franchise agreements with third parties outside that territory. Where the franchisees sell or use in the process of providing services, goods manufactured by the franchisor or according to its instructions and/or bearing its trade mark, an obligation on the franchisees not to sell, or use in the process of the provision of services, competing goods, makes it possible to establish a coherent network which is identified with the franchised goods. However, this obligation should only be accepted with respect to the goods which form the essential subject-matter of the franchise. It should notably not relate to accessories or spare parts for these goods.

(10) The obligations referred to above thus do not impose restrictions which are not necessary for the attainment of the abovementioned objectives. In particular, the limited territorial protection granted to the franchisees is indispensable to protect their investment.

(11) It is desirable to list in the Regulation a number of obligations that are commonly found in franchise agreements and are normally not restrictive of competition and to provide that if, because of the particular economic or legal circumstances, they fall under Art. 85 (1), they are also covered by the exemption. This list, which is not exhaustive, includes in particular clauses which are essential either to preserve the common identity and reputation of the network or to prevent the know-how made available and the assistance given by the franchisor from benefiting competitors.

(12) The Regulation must specify the conditions which must be satisfied for the exemption to apply. To guarantee that competition is not eliminated for a substantial part of the goods which are the subject

of the franchise, it is necessary that parallel imports remain possible. Therefore, cross deliveries between franchisees should always be possible. Furthermore, where a franchise network is combined with another distribution system, franchisees should be free to obtain supplies from authorised distributors. To better inform consumers, thereby helping to ensure that they receive a fair share of the resulting benefits, it must be provided that the franchisee shall be obliged to indicate its status as an independent undertaking, by any appropriate means which does not jeopardize the common identity of the franchised network. Furthermore, where the franchisees have to honour guarantees for the franchisor's goods, this obligation should also apply to goods supplied by the franchisor, other franchisees or other agreed dealers.

(13) The Regulation must also specify restrictions which may not be included in franchise agreements if these are to benefit from the exemption granted by the Regulation, by virtue of the fact that such provisions are restrictions falling under Art. 85 (1) for which there is no general presumption that they will lead to the positive effects required by Art. 85 (3). This applies in particular to market sharing between competing manufacturers, to clauses unduly limiting the franchisee's choice of suppliers or customers, and to cases where the franchisee is restricted in determining its prices. However, the franchisor should be free to recommend prices to the franchisees, where it is not prohibited by national laws and to the extent that it does not lead to concerted practices for the effective application of these prices.

(14) Agreements which are not automatically covered by the exemption because they contain provisions that are not expressly exempted by the Regulation and not expressly excluded from exemption may nonetheless generally be presumed to be eligible for application of Art. 85 (3). It will be possible for the Commission rapidly to establish whether this is the case for a particular agreement. Such agreements should therefore be deemed to be covered by the exemption provided for in this Regulation where they are notified to the Commission and the Commission does not oppose the application of the exemption within a specified period of time.

(15) If individual agreements exempted by this Regulation nevertheless have effects which are incompatible with Art. 85 (3), in particular as interpreted by the administrative practice of the Commission and the case law of the Court of Justice, the Commission may withdraw the benefit of the block exemption. This applies in particular where competition is significantly restricted because of the structure of the relevant market.

(16) Agreements which are automatically exempted pursuant to this Regulation need not be notified. Undertakings may nevertheless in a particular case request a decision pursuant to Council Regulation No 17[21] as last amended by the Act of Accession of Spain and Portugal.

(17) Agreements may benefit from the provisions either of this Regulation or of another Regulation, according to their particular nature and provided that they fulfil the necessary conditions of application. They may not benefit from a combination of the provisions of this Regulation with those of another block exemption Regulation,

Has adopted this Regulation:

Article 1. 1. Pursuant to Art. 85 (3) of the Treaty and subject to the provisions of this Regulation, it is hereby declared that Art. 85 (1) of the Treaty shall not apply to franchise agreements to which two undertakings are party, which include one or more of the restrictions listed in Art. 2.

2. The exemption provided for in paragraph 1 shall also apply to master franchise agreements to which two undertakings are party. Where applicable, the provisions of this Regulation concerning the relationship between franchisor and franchisee shall apply *mutatis mutandis* to the relationship between franchisor and master franchisee and between master franchisee and franchisee.

3. For the purposes of this Regulation:

(a) 'franchise' means a package of industrial or intellectual property rights relating to trade marks, trade names, shop signs, utility models, designs, copyrights, know-how or patents, to be exploited for the resale of goods or the provision of services to end users;

(b) 'franchise agreement' means an agreement whereby one undertaking, the franchisor, grants the other, the franchisee, in exchange for direct or indirect financial consideration, the right to exploit a franchise for the purposes of marketing specified types of goods and/or services; it includes at least obligations relating to:

- the use of a common name or shop sign and a uniform presentation of contract premises and/or means of transport,
- the communication by the franchisor to the franchisee of know-how,
- the continuing provision by the franchisor to the franchisee of commercial or technical assistance during the life of the agreement;

[21] OJ No 13, 21. 2. 1962, p. 204/62.

(c) 'master franchise agreement' means an agreement whereby one under-taking, the franchisor, grants the other, the master franchisee, in exchange for direct or indirect financial consideration, the right to exploit a franchise for the purposes of concluding franchise agree-ments with third parties, the franchisees;

(d) 'franchisor's goods' means goods produced by the franchisor or according to its instructions, and/or bearing the franchisor's name or trade mark;

(e) 'contract premises' means the premises used for the exploitation of the franchise or, when the franchise is exploited outside those premises, the base from which the franchisee operates the means of transport used for the exploitation of the franchise (contract means of transport);

(f) 'know-how' means a package of non-patented practical information, resulting from experience and testing by the franchisor, which is secret, substantial and identified;

(g) 'secret' means that the know-how, as a body or in the precise configuration and assembly of its components, is not generally known or easily accessible; it is not limited in the narrow sense that each individual component of the know-how should be totally unknown or unobtainable outside the franchisor's business;

(h) 'substantial' means that the know-how includes information which is of importance for the sale of goods or the provision of services to end users, and in particular for the presentation of goods for sale, the processing of goods in connection with the provision of services, methods of dealing with customers, and administration and financial management; the know-how must be useful for the franchisee by being capable, at the date of conclusion of the agreement, of improv-ing the competitive position of the franchisee, in particular by improving the franchisee's performance or helping it to enter a new market;

(i) 'identified' means that the know-how must be described in a sufficiently comprehensive manner so as to make it possible to verify that it fulfils the criteria of secrecy and substantiality; the description of the know-how can either be set out in the franchise agreement or in a separate document or recorded in any other appropriate form.

Article 2. The exemption provided for in Art. 1 shall apply to the fol-lowing restrictions of competition:

(a) an obligation on the franchisor, in a defined area of the common market, the contract territory, not to:
  – grant the right to exploit all or part of the franchise to third par-ties,

- itself exploit the franchise, or itself market the goods or services which are the subject-matter of the franchise under a similar formula,
- itself supply the franchisor's goods to third parties;

(b) an obligation on the master franchisee not to conclude franchise agreements with third parties outside its contract territory;

(c) an obligation on the franchisee to exploit the franchise only from the contract premises;

(d) an obligation on the franchisee to refrain, outside the contract territory, from seeking customers for the goods or the services which are the subject-matter of the franchise;

(e) an obligation on the franchisee not to manufacture, sell or use in the course of the provision of services, goods competing with the franchisor's goods which are the subject-matter of the franchise; where the subject-matter of the franchise is the sale or use in the course of the provision of services both certain types of goods and spare parts or accessories therefor, that obligation may not be imposed in respect of these spare parts or accessories.

Article 3. 1. Art. 1 shall apply notwithstanding the presence of any of the following obligations on the franchisee, in so far as they are necessary to protect the franchisor's industrial or intellectual property rights or to maintain the common identity and reputation of the franchised network:

(a) to sell, or use in the course of the provision of services, exclusively goods matching minimum objective quality specifications laid down by the franchisor;

(b) to sell, or use in the course of the provision of services, goods which are manufactured only by the franchisor or by third parties designed by it, where it is impracticable, owing to the nature of the goods which are the subject-matter of the franchise, to apply objective quality specifications;

(b) not to engage, directly or indirectly, in any similar business in a territory where it would compete with a member of the franchised network, including the franchisor; the franchisee may be held to this obligation after termination of the agreement, for a reasonable period which may not exceed one year, in the territory where it has exploited the franchise;

(d) not to acquire financial interests in the capital of a competing undertaking, which would give the franchisee the power to influence the economic conduct of such undertaking;

(e) to sell the goods which are the subject-matter of the franchise only to end users, to other franchisees and to resellers within other channels of distribution supplied by the manufacturer of these goods or with its consent;

(f) to use is best endeavours to sell the goods or provide the services that are the subject-matter of the franchise; to offer for sale a minimum range of goods, achieve a minimum turnover, plan its orders in advance, keep minimum stocks and provide customer and warranty services;

(g) to pay to the franchisor a specified proportion of its revenue for advertising and itself carry out advertising for the nature of which it shall obtain the franchisor's approval.

2. Art. 1 shall apply notwithstanding the presence of any of the following obligations on the franchisee:

(a) not to disclose to third parties the know-how provided by the franchisor; the franchisee may be held to this obligation after termination of the agreement;

(b) to communicate to the franchisor any experience gained in exploiting the franchise and to grant it, and other franchisees, a non-exclusive licence for the know-how resulting from that experience;

(c) to inform the franchisor of infringements of licensed industrial or intellectual property rights, to take legal action against infringers or to assist the franchisor in any legal action against infringers:

(d) not to use know-how licensed by the franchisor for purposes other than the exploitation of the franchise; the franchisee may be held to this obligation after termination of the agreement;

(e) to attend or have its staff attend training courses arranged by the franchisor;

(f) to apply the commercial methods devised by the franchisor, including any subsequent modification thereof, and use the licensed industrial or intellectual property rights;

(g) to comply with the franchisor's standards for the equipment and presentation of the contract premises and/or means of transport;

(h) to allow the franchisor to carry out checks of the contract premises and/or means of transport, including the goods sold and the services provided, and the inventory and accounts of the franchisee;

(i) not without the franchisor's consent to change the location of the contract premises;

(j) not without the franchisor's consent to assign the rights and obligations under the franchise agreement.

3. In the event that, because of particular circumstances, obligations referred to in paragraph 2 fall within the scope of Art. 85 (1), they shall also be exempted even if they are not accompanied by any of the obligations exempted by Art. 1.

Article 4. The exemption provided for in Art. 1 shall apply on condition that:

(a) the franchisee is free to obtain the goods that are the subject-matter of the franchise from other franchisees; where such goods are also distributed through another network of authorised distributors, the franchisee must be free to obtain the goods from the latter;

(b) where the franchisor obliges the franchisee to honour guarantees for the franchisor's goods, that obligation shall apply in respect of such goods supplied by any member of the franchised network or other distributors which give a similar guarantee, in the common market;

(c) the franchisee is obliged to indicate its status as an independent undertaking; this indication shall however not interfere with the common identity of the franchised network resulting in particular from the common name or shop sign and uniform appearance of the contract premises and/or means of transport.

Article 5. The exemption granted by Art. 1 shall not apply where:

(a) undertakings producing goods or providing services which are identical or are considered by users as equivalent in view of their characteristics, price and intended use, enter into franchise agreements in respect of such goods or services;

(b) without prejudice to Art. 2 (e) and Art. 3 (1) (b), the franchisee is prevented from obtaining supplies of goods of a quality equivalent to those offered by the franchisor;

(c) without prejudice to Art. 2 (e), the franchisee is obliged to sell, or use in the process of providing services, goods manufactured by the franchisor or third parties designated by the franchisor and the franchisor refuses, for reasons other than protecting the franchisor's industrial or intellectual property rights, or maintaining the common identity and reputation of the franchised network, to designate as authorised manufacturers third parties proposed by the franchisee;

(d) the franchisee is prevented from continuing to use the licensed know-how after termination of the agreement where the know-how has become generally known or easily accessible, other than by breach of an obligation by the franchisee;

(e) the franchisee is restricted by the franchisor, directly or indirectly, in the determination of sale prices for the goods or services which are the subject-matter of the franchise, without prejudice to the possibility for the franchisor of recommending sale prices;

(f) the franchisor prohibits the franchisee from challenging the validity of the industrial or intellectual property rights which form part of the franchise, without prejudice to the possibility for the franchisor of terminating the agreement in such a case;

(g) franchisees are obliged not to supply within the common market the goods or services which are the subject-matter of the franchise to end users because of their place of residence.

Article 6. 1. The exemption provided for in Art. 1 shall also apply to franchise agreements which fulfil the conditions laid down in Art. 4 and include obligations restrictive of competition which are not covered by Arts. 2 and 3 (3) and do not fall within the scope of Art. 5, on condition that the agreements in question are notified to the Commission in accordance with the provisions of Commission Regulation No 27[22] and that the Commission does not oppose such exemption within a period of six months.

2. The period of six months shall run from the date on which the notification is received by the Commission. Where, however, the notification is made by registered post, the period shall run from the date shown on the postmark of the place of posting.

3. Paragraph 1 shall apply only if:

(a) express reference is made to this Article in the notification or in a communication accompanying it; and
(b) the information furnished with the notification is complete and in accordance with the facts.

4. The benefit of paragraph 1 can be claimed for agreements notified before the entry into force of this Regulation by submitting a communication to the Commission referring expressly to this Article and to the notification. Paragraphs 2 and 3 (b) shall apply *mutatis mutandis.*

5. The Commission may oppose exemption. It shall oppose exemption if it receives a request to do so from a Member State within three months of the forwarding to the Member State of the notification referred to in paragraph 1 or the communication referred to in paragraph 4. This request must be justified on the basis of considerations relating to the competition rules of the Treaty.

6. The Commission may withdraw its opposition to the exemption at any time. However, where that opposition was raised at the request of a Member State, it may be withdrawn only after consultation of the advisory Committee on Restrictive Practices and Dominant Positions.

7. If the opposition is withdrawn because the undertakings concerned have shown that the conditions of Art. 85 (3) are fulfilled, the exemption shall apply from the date of the notification.

8. If the opposition is withdrawn because the undertakings concerned have amended the agreement so that the conditions of Art. 85 (3) are fulfilled, the exemption shall apply from the date on which the amendments take effect.

9. If the Commission opposes exemption and its opposition is not withdrawn, the effects of the notification shall be governed by the provisions of Regulation No 17.

Article 7. 1. Information acquired pursuant to Art. 6 shall be used only for the purposes of this Regulation.

2. The Commission and the authorities of the Member States, their officials and other servants shall not disclose information acquired by them pursuant to this Regulation of a kind that is covered by the obligation of professional secrecy.

3. Paragraphs 1 and 2 shall not prevent publication of general information or surveys which do not contain information relating to particular undertakings or associations of undertakings.

Article 8. The Commission may withdraw the benefit of this Regulation, pursuant to Art. 7 of Regulation No 19/65/EEC, where it finds in a particular case that an agreement exempted by this Regulation nevertheless has certain effects which are incompatible with the conditions laid down in Art. 85 (3) of the EEC Treaty, and in particular where territorial protection is awarded to the franchisee and:

(a) access to the relevant market or competition therein is significantly restricted by the cumulative effect of parallel networks of similar agreements established by competing manufacturers or distributors;

(b) the goods or services which are the subject-matter of the franchise do not face, in a substantial part of the common market, effective competition from goods or services which are identical or considered by users as equivalent in view of their characteristics, price and intended use;

(c) the parties, or one of them, prevent end users, because of their place of residence, from obtaining, directly or through intermediaries, the goods or services which are the subject-matter of the franchise within the common market, or use differences in specifications concerning those goods or services in different Member States, to isolate markets;

(d) franchisees engage in concerted practices relating to the sale prices of the goods or services which are the subject-matter of the franchise;

(e) the franchisor uses its right to check the contract premises and means of transport, or refuses its agreement to requests by the franchisee to move the contract premises or assign its rights and obligations under the franchise agreement, for reasons other than protecting the franchisor's industrial or intellectual property rights, maintaining the common identity and reputation of the franchised network or verifying that the franchisee abides by its obligations under the agreement.

Article 9. This Regulation shall enter into force on 1 February 1989. It shall remain in force until 31 December 1999.

[Final provisions omitted.]

Council Regulation (EEC) No 4064/89 of 21 December 1989 on the control of concentrations between undertakings[23]

The Council of the European Communities,

Having regard to the Treaty establishing the European Economic Community, and in particular Arts. 87 and 235 thereof,

(1) Whereas, for the achievement of the aims of the Treaty establishing the European Economic Community, Art. 3 (f) gives the Community the objective of instituting 'a system ensuring that competition in the common market is not distorted';

(2) Whereas this system is essential for the achievement of the internal market by 1992 and its further development;

(3) Whereas the dismantling of internal frontiers is resulting and will continue to result in major corporate reorganisations in the Community, particularly in the form of concentrations;

(4) Whereas such a development must be welcomed as being in line with the requirements of dynamic competition and capable of increasing the competitiveness of European industry, improving the conditions of growth and raising the standard of living in the Community;

(5) Whereas, however, it must be ensured that the process of reorganisation does not result in lasting damage to competition; whereas Community law must therefore include provisions governing those concentrations which may significantly impede effective competition in the common market or in a substantial part of it;

(6) Whereas Arts. 85 and 86, while applicable, according to the case-law of the Court of Justice, to certain concentrations, are not, however, sufficient to control all operations which may prove to be incompatible with the system of undistorted competition envisaged in the Treaty;

(7) Whereas a new legal instrument should therefore be created in the form of a Regulation to permit effective control of all concentrations from the point of view of their effect on the structure of competition in the Community and to be the only instrument applicable to such concentrations;

(8) Whereas this Regulation should therefore be based not only on Art.

---

[23] OJ 1990 L 257/14 (corrigendum to OJ 1989 L 395/1).

87 but, principally, on Art. 235 of the Treaty, under which the Community may give itself the additional powers of action necessary for the attainment of its objectives, including with regard to concentrations on the markets for agricultural products listed in Annex II to the Treaty;

(9) Whereas the provisions to be adopted in this Regulation should apply to significant structural changes the impact of which on the market goes beyond the national borders of any one Member State;

(10) Whereas the scope of application of this Regulation should therefore be defined according to the geographical area of activity of the undertakings concerned and be limited by quantitative thresholds in order to cover those concentrations which have a Community dimension; whereas, at the end of an initial phase of the application of this Regulation, these thresholds should be reviewed in the light of the experience gained;

(11) Whereas a concentration with a Community dimension exists where the combined aggregate turnover of the undertakings concerned exceeds given levels worldwide and within the Community and where at least two of the undertakings concerned have their sole or main fields of activities in different Member States or where, although the undertakings in question act mainly in one and the same Member State, at least one of them has substantial operations in at least one other Member State; whereas that is also the case where the concentrations are effected by undertakings which do not have their principal fields of activities in the Community but which have substantial operations there;

(12) Whereas the arrangements to be introduced for the control of concentrations should, without prejudice to Art. 90 (2) of the Treaty, respect the principle of non-discrimination between the public and the private sectors; whereas, in the public sector, calculation of the turnover of an undertaking concerned in a concentration needs, therefore, to take account of undertakings making up an economic unit with an independent power of decision, irrespective of the way in which their capital is held or of the rules of administrative supervision applicable to them;

(13) Whereas it is necessary to establish whether concentrations with a Community dimension are compatible or not with the common market from the point of view of the need to maintain and develop effective competition in the common market; whereas, in so doing, the Commission must place its appraisal within the general framework of the achievement of the fundamental objectives referred to in Art. 2 of the Treaty, including that of strengthening the Community's economic and social cohesion, referred to in Art. 130a;

(14) Whereas this Regulation should establish the principle that a concentration with a Community dimension which creates or strengthens a position as a result of which effective competition in the common market or in a substantial part of it is significantly impeded is to be declared incompatible with the common market;

(15) Whereas concentrations which, by reason of the limited market share of the undertakings concerned, are not liable to impede effective competition may be presumed to be compatible with the common market; whereas, without prejudice to Arts. 85 and 86 of the Treaty, an indication to this effect exists, in particular, where the market share of the undertakings concerned does not exceed 25% either in the common market or in a substantial part of it;

(16) Whereas the Commission should have the task of taking all the decisions necessary to establish whether or not concentrations with a Community dimension are compatible with the common market, as well as decisions designed to restore effective competition;

(17) Whereas to ensure effective control undertakings should be obliged to give prior notification of concentrations with a Community dimension and provision should be made for the suspension of concentrations for a limited period, and for the possibility of extending or waiving a suspension where necessary; whereas in the interests of legal certainty the validity of transactions must nevertheless be protected as much as necessary;

(18) Whereas a period within which the Commission must initiate proceedings in respect of a notified concentration and periods within which it must give a final decision on the compatibility or incompatibility with the common market of a notified concentration should be laid down;

(19) Whereas the undertakings concerned must be afforded the right to be heard by the Commission when proceedings have been initiated; whereas the members of the management and supervisory bodies and the recognised representatives of the employees of the undertakings concerned, and third parties showing a legitimate interest, must also be given the opportunity to be heard;

(20) Whereas the Commission should act in close and constant liaison with the competent authorities of the Member States from which it obtains comments and information;

(21) Whereas, for the purposes of this Regulation, and in accordance with the case-law of the Court of Justice, the Commission must be afforded the assistance of the Member States and must also be empowered to require information to be given and to carry out the necessary investigations in order to appraise concentrations;

(22) Whereas compliance with this Regulation must be enforceable by

means of fines and periodic penalty payments; whereas the Court of Justice should be given unlimited jurisdiction in that regard pursuant to Art. 172 of the Treaty;

(23) Whereas it is appropriate to define the concept of concentration in such a manner as to cover only operations bringing about a lasting change in the structure of the undertakings concerned; whereas it is therefore necessary to exclude from the scope of this Regulation those operations which have as their object or effect the coordination of the competitive behaviour of undertakings which remain independent, since such operations fall to be examined under the appropriate provisions of the Regulations implementing Arts. 85 and 86 of the Treaty; whereas it is appropriate to make this distinction specifically in the case of the creation of joint ventures,

(24) Whereas there is no coordination of competitive behaviour within the meaning of this Regulation where two or more undertakings agree to acquire jointly control of one or more other undertakings with the object and effect of sharing amongst themselves such undertakings or their assets;

(25) Whereas this Regulation should still apply where the undertakings concerned accept restrictions directly related and necessary to the implementation of the concentration;

(26) Whereas the Commission should be given exclusive competence to apply this Regulation, subject to review by the Court of Justice;

(27) Whereas the Member States may not apply their national legislation on competition to concentrations with a Community dimension, unless this Regulation makes provision therefor; whereas the relevant powers of national authorities should be limited to cases where, failing intervention by the Commission, effective competition is likely to be significantly impeded within the territory of a Member State and where the competition interests of that Member State cannot be sufficiently protected otherwise by this Regulation; whereas the Member States concerned must act promptly in such cases; whereas this Regulation cannot, because of the diversity of national law, fix a single deadline for the adoption of remedies;

(28) Whereas, furthermore, the exclusive application of this Regulation to concentrations with a Community dimension is without prejudice to Art. 223 of the Treaty, and does not prevent the Member States from taking appropriate measures to protect legitimate interests other than those pursued by this Regulation, provided that such measures are compatible with the general principles and other provisions of Community law;

(29) Whereas concentrations not covered by this Regulation come, in principle, within the jurisdiction of the Member States; whereas,

however, the Commission should have the power to act, at the request of a Member State concerned, in cases where effective competition could be significantly impeded within that Member State's territory;

(30) Whereas the conditions in which concentrations involving Community undertakings are carried out in non-member countries should be observed, and provision should be made for the possibility of the Council giving the Commission an appropriate mandate for negotiation with a view to obtaining non-discriminatory treatment for Community undertakings;

(31) Whereas this Regulation in no way detracts from the collective rights of employees as recognised in the undertakings concerned,

Has adopted this Regulation:

Article 1. Scope.

1. Without prejudice to Art. 22 this Regulation shall apply to all concentrations with a Community dimension as defined in paragraph 2.

2. For the purposes of this Regulation, a concentration has a Community dimension where:

(a) the combined aggregate worldwide turnover of all the undertakings concerned is more than ECU 5000 million; and

(b) the aggregate Community-wide turnover of each of at least two of the undertakings concerned is more than ECU 250 million,

unless each of the undertakings concerned achieves more than two-thirds of its aggregate Community-wide turnover within one and the same Member State.

3. The thresholds laid down in paragraph 2 will be reviewed before the end of the fourth year following that of the adoption of this Regulation by the Council acting by a qualified majority on a proposal from the Commission.

Article 2. Appraisal of concentrations.

1. Concentrations within the scope of this Regulation shall be appraised in accordance with the following provisions with a view to establishing whether or not they are compatible with the common market.

In making this appraisal, the Commission shall take into account:

(a) the need to maintain and develop effective competition within the common market in view of, among other things, the structure of all the markets concerned and the actual or potential competition from undertakings located either within or outwith the Community;

(b) the market position of the undertakings concerned and their economic and financial power, the alternatives available to suppliers and users, their access to supplies or markets, any legal or other barriers to entry, supply and demand trends for the relevant goods and services, the interests of the intermediate and ultimate consumers, and the development of technical and economic progress provided that it is to consumers' advantage and does not form an obstacle to competition.

2. A concentration which does not create or strengthen a dominant position as a result of which effective competition would be significantly impeded in the common market or in a substantial part of it shall be declared compatible with the common market.

3. A concentration which creates or strengthens a dominant position as a result of which effective competition would be significantly impeded in the common market or in a substantial part of it shall be declared incompatible with the common market.

Article 3. Definition of concentration.

1. A concentration shall be deemed to arise where:

(a) two or more previously independent undertakings merge, or
(b) – one or more persons already controlling at least one undertaking, or
   – one or more undertakings

acquire, whether by purchase of securities or assets, by contract or by any other means, direct or indirect control of the whole or parts of one or more other undertakings.

2. An operation, including the creation of a joint venture, which has as its object or effect the coordination of the competitive behaviour of undertakings which remain independent shall not constitute a concentration within the meaning of paragraph 1 (b).

The creation of a joint venture performing on a lasting basis all the functions of an autonomous economic entity, which does not give rise to coordination of the competitive behaviour of the parties amongst themselves or between them and the joint venture, shall constitute a concentration within the meaning of paragraph 1 (b).

3. For the purposes of this Regulation, control shall be constituted by rights, contracts or any other means which, either separately or in combination and having regard to the considerations of fact or law involved, confer the possibility of exercising decisive influence on an undertaking, in particular by:

(a) ownership or the right to use all or part of the assets of an undertaking;

(b) rights or contracts which confer decisive influence on the composition, voting or decisions of the organs of an undertaking.

4. Control is acquired by persons or undertakings which:

(a) are holders of the rights or entitled to rights under the contracts concerned; or
(b) while not being holders of such rights or entitled to rights under such contracts, have the power to exercise the rights deriving therefrom.

5. A concentration shall not be deemed to arise where:

(a) credit institutions or other financial institutions or insurance companies, the normal activities of which include transactions and dealing in securities for their own account or for the account of others, hold on a temporary basis securities which they have acquired in an undertaking with a view to reselling them, provided that they do not exercise voting rights in respect of those securities with a view to determining the competitive behaviour of that undertaking or provided that they exercise such voting rights only with a view to preparing the disposal of all or part of that undertaking or of its assets or the disposal of those securities and that any such disposal takes place within one year of the date of acquisition; that period may be extended by the Commission on request where such institutions or companies can show that the disposal was not reasonably possible within the period set;
(b) control is acquired by an office-holder according to the law of a Member State relating to liquidation, winding up, insolvency, cessation of payments, compositions or analogous proceedings;
(c) the operations referred to in paragraph 1 (b) are carried out by the financial holding companies referred to in Art. 5 (3) of the Fourth Council Directive 78/660/EEC of 25 July 1978 on the annual accounts of certain types of companies,[24] as last amended by Directive 84/569/EEC,[25] provided however that the voting rights in respect of the holding are exercised, in particular in relation to the appointment of members of the management and supervisory bodies of the undertakings in which they have holdings, only to maintain the full value of those investments and not to determine directly or indirectly the competitive conduct of those undertakings.

Article 4. Prior notification of concentrations.
1. Concentrations with a Community dimension defined in this Regulation shall be notified to the Commission not more than one week

[24] OJ 1978 L 222/11.   [25] OJ 1984 L 314/28.

after the conclusion of the agreement, or the announcement of the public bid, or the acquisition of a controlling interest. That week shall begin when the first of those events occurs.

2. A concentration which consists of a merger within the meaning of Art. 3 (1) (a) or in the acquisition of joint control within the meaning of Art. 3 (1) (b) shall be notified jointly by the parties to the merger or by those acquiring joint control as the case may be. In all other cases, the notification shall be effected by the person or undertaking acquiring control of the whole or parts of one or more undertakings.

3. Where the Commission finds that a notified concentration falls within the scope of this Regulation, it shall publish the fact of the notification, at the same time indicating the names of the parties, the nature of the concentration and the economic sectors involved. The Commission shall take account of the legitimate interest of undertakings in the protection of their business secrets.

Article 5. Calculation of turnover.

1. Aggregate turnover within the meaning of Art. 1 (2) shall comprise the amounts derived by the undertakings concerned in the preceding financial year from the sale of products and the provision of services falling within the undertakings' ordinary activities after deduction of sales rebates and of value added tax and other taxes directly related to turnover. The aggregate turnover of an undertaking concerned shall not include the sale of products or the provision of services between any of the undertakings referred to in paragraph 4.

Turnover, in the Community or in a Member State, shall comprise products sold and services provided to undertakings or consumers, in the Community or in that Member State as the case may be.

2. By way of derogation from paragraph 1, where the concentration consists in the acquisition of parts, whether or not constituted as legal entities, of one or more undertakings, only the turnover relating to the parts which are the subject of the transaction shall be taken into account with regard to the seller or sellers.

However, two or more transactions within the meaning of the first sub-paragraph which take place within a two-year period between the same persons or undertakings shall be treated as one and the same concentration arising on the date of the last transaction.

3. In place of turnover the following shall be used:

(a) for credit institutions and other financial institutions, as regards Art. 1 (2) (a), one-tenth of their total assets.

   As regards Art. 1 (2) (b) and the final part of Art. 1 (2), total Community-wide turnover shall be replaced by one-tenth of total assets multiplied by the ratio between loans and advances to credit institutions and customers in transactions with Community residents and the total sum of those loans and advances.

As regards the final part of Art. 1 (2), total turnover within one Member State shall be replaced by one-tenth of total assets multiplied by the ratio between loans and advances to credit institutions and customers in transactions with residents of that Member State and the total sum of those loans and advances;

(b) for insurance undertakings, the value of gross premiums written which shall comprise all amounts received and receivable in respect of insurance contracts issued by or on behalf of the insurance undertakings, including also outgoing reinsurance premiums, and after deduction of taxes and parafiscal contributions or levies charged by reference to the amounts of individual premiums or the total volume of premiums; as regards Art. 1 (2) (b) and the final part of Art. 1 (2), gross premiums received from Community residents and from residents of one Member State respectively shall be taken into account.

4. Without prejudice to paragraph 2, the aggregate turnover of an undertaking concerned within the meaning of Art. 1 (2) shall be calculated by adding together the respective turnovers of the following:

(a) the undertaking concerned;
(b) those undertakings in which the undertaking concerned, directly or indirectly:
   – owns more than half the capital or business assets, or
   – has the power to exercise more than half the voting rights, or
   – has the power to appoint more than half the members of the supervisory board, the administrative board or bodies legally representing the undertakings, or
   – has the right to manage the undertakings' affairs;
(c) those undertakings which have in the undertaking concerned the rights or powers listed in (b);
(d) those undertakings in which an undertaking as referred to in (c) has the rights or powers listed in (b);
(e) those undertakings in which two or more undertakings as referred to in (a) to (d) jointly have the rights or powers listed in (b).

5. Where undertakings concerned by the concentration jointly have the rights or powers listed in paragraph 4 (b), in calculating the aggregate turnover of the undertakings concerned for the purposes of Art. 1 (2):

(a) no account shall be taken of the turnover resulting from the sale of products or the provision of services between the joint undertaking and each of the undertakings concerned or any other undertaking connected with any one of them, as set out in paragraph 4 (b) to (e);
(b) account shall be taken of the turnover resulting from the sale of

products and the provision of services between the joint undertaking and any third undertakings. This turnover shall be apportioned equally amongst the undertakings concerned.

Article 6. Examination of the notification and initiation of proceedings.

1. The Commission shall examine the notification as soon as it is received.

(a) Where it concludes that the concentration notified does not fall within the scope of this Regulation, it shall record that finding by means of a decision.

(b) Where it finds that the concentration notified, although falling within the scope of this Regulation, does not raise serious doubts as to its compatibility with the common market, it shall decide not to oppose it and shall declare that it is compatible with the common market.

(c) If, on the other hand, it finds that the concentration notified falls within the scope of this Regulation and raises serious doubts as to its compatibility with the common market, it shall decide to initiate proceedings.

2. The Commission shall notify its decision to the undertakings concerned and the competent authorities of the Member States without delay.

Article 7. Suspension of concentrations.

1. For the purposes of paragraph 2 a concentration as defined in Art. 1 shall not be put into effect either before its notification or within the first three weeks following its notification.

2. Where the Commission, following a preliminary examination of the notification within the period provided for in paragraph 1, finds it necessary in order to ensure the full effectiveness of any decision taken later pursuant to Art. 8 (3) and (4), it may decide on its own initiative to continue the suspension of a concentration in whole or in part until it takes a final decision, or to take other interim measures to that effect.

3. Paragraphs 1 and 2 shall not prevent the implementation of a public bid which has been notified to the Commission in accordance with Art. 4 (1), provided that the acquirer does not exercise the voting rights attached to the securities in question or does so only to maintain the full value of those investments and on the basis of a derogation granted by the Commission under paragraph 4.

4. The Commission may, on request, grant a derogation from the obligations imposed in paragraphs 1, 2 or 3 in order to prevent serious damage to one or more undertakings concerned by a concentration or to a third party. That derogation may be made subject to conditions and

obligations in order to ensure conditions of effective competition. A derogation may be applied for and granted at any time, even before notification or after the transaction.

5. The validity of any transaction carried out in contravention of paragraph 1 or 2 shall be dependent on a decision pursuant to Art. 6 (1) (b) or Art. 8 (2) or (3) or on a presumption pursuant to Art. 10 (6).

This Article shall, however, have no effect on the validity of transactions in securities including those convertible into other securities admitted to trading on a market which is regulated and supervised by authorities recognised by public bodies, operates regularly and is accessible directly or indirectly to the public, unless the buyer and seller knew or ought to have known that the transaction was carried out in contravention of paragraph 1 or 2.

Article 8. Powers of decision of the Commission.

1. Without prejudice to Art. 9, all proceedings initiated pursuant to Art. 6 (1) (c) shall be closed by means of a decision as provided for in paragraphs 2 to 5.

2. Where the Commission finds that, following modification by the undertakings concerned if necessary, a notified concentration fulfils the criterion laid down in Art. 2 (2), it shall issue a decision declaring the concentration compatible with the common market.

It may attach to its decision conditions and obligations intended to ensure that the undertakings concerned comply with the commitments they have entered into *vis-à-vis* the Commission with a view to modifying the original concentration plan. The decision declaring the concentration compatible shall also cover restrictions directly related and necessary to the implementation of the concentration.

3. Where the Commission finds that a concentration fulfils the criterion laid down in Art. 2 (3), it shall issue a decision declaring that the concentration is incompatible with the common market.

4. Where a concentration has already been implemented, the Commission may, in a decision pursuant to paragraph 3 or by separate decision, require the undertakings or assets brought together to be separated or the cessation of joint control or any other action that may be appropriate in order to restore conditions of effective competition.

5. The Commission may revoke the decision it has taken pursuant to paragraph 2 where:

(a) the declaration of compatibility is based on incorrect information for which one of the undertakings is responsible or where it has been obtained by deceit; or
(b) the undertakings concerned commit a breach of an obligation attached to the decision.

6. In the cases referred to in paragraph 5, the Commission may take a decision under paragraph 3, without being bound by the deadline referred to in Art. 10 (3).

Article 9. Referral to the competent authorities of the Member States.

1. The Commission may, by means of a decision notified without delay to the undertakings concerned and the competent authorities of the other Member States, refer a notified concentration to the competent authorities of the Member State concerned in the following circumstances.

2. Within three weeks of the date of receipt of the copy of the notification a Member State may inform the Commission, which shall inform the undertakings concerned, that a concentration threatens to create or to strengthen a dominant position as a result of which effective competition would be significantly impeded on a market, within that Member State, which presents all the characteristics of a distinct market, be it a substantial part of the common market or not.

3. If the Commission considers that, having regard to the market for the products or services in question and the geographical reference market within the meaning of paragraph 7, there is such a distinct market and that such a threat exists, either:

(a) it shall itself deal with the case in order to maintain or restore effective competition on the market concerned; or

(b) it shall refer the case to the competent authorities of the Member State concerned with a view to the application of that State's national competition law.

If, however, the Commission considers that such a distinct market or threat does not exist it shall adopt a decision to that effect which it shall address to the Member State concerned.

4. A decision to refer or not to refer pursuant to paragraph 3 shall be taken:

(a) as a general rule within the six-week period provided for in Art. 10 (1), second subparagraph, where the Commission, pursuant to Art. 6 (1) (b), has not initiated proceedings; or

(b) within three months at most of the notification of the concentration concerned where the Commission has initiated proceedings under Art 6 (1) (c), without taking the preparatory steps in order to adopt the necessary measures under Art. 8 (2), second subparagraph, (3) or (4) to maintain or restore effective competition on the market concerned.

5. If within the three months referred to in paragraph 4 (b) the Commission, despite a reminder from the Member State concerned, has not taken a decision on referral in accordance with paragraph 3 nor has

taken the preparatory steps referred to in paragraph 4 (b), it shall be deemed to have taken a decision to refer the case to the Member State concerned in accordance with paragraph 3 (b).

6. The publication of any report or the announcement of the findings of the examination of the concentration by the competent authority of the Member State concerned shall be effected not more than four months after the Commission's referral.

7. The geographical reference market shall consist of the area in which the undertakings concerned are involved in the supply and demand of products or services, in which the conditions of competition are sufficiently homogeneous and which can be distinguished from neighbouring areas because, in particular, conditions of competition are appreciably different in those areas. This assessment should take account in particular of the nature and characteristics of the products or services concerned, of the existence of entry barriers or of consumer preferences, of appreciable differences of the undertakings' market shares between the area concerned and neighbouring areas or of substantial price differences.

8. In applying the provisions of this Article, the Member State concerned may take only the measures strictly necessary to safeguard or restore effective competition on the market concerned.

9. In accordance with the relevant provisions of the Treaty, any Member State may appeal to the Court of Justice, and in particular request the application of Art. 186, for the purpose of applying its national competition law.

10. This Article will be reviewed before the end of the fourth year following that of the adoption of this Regulation.

Article 10.   Time limits for initiating proceedings and for decisions.

1. The decisions referred to in Art. 6 (1) must be taken within one month at most. That period shall begin on the day following that of the receipt of a notification or, if the information to be supplied with the notification is incomplete, on the day following that of the receipt of the complete information.

That period shall be increased to six weeks if the Commission receives a request from a Member State in accordance with Art. 9 (2).

2. Decisions taken pursuant to Art. 8 (2) concerning notified concentrations must be taken as soon as it appears that the serious doubts referred to in Art. 6 (1) (c) have been removed, particularly as a result of modifications made by the undertakings concerned, and at the latest by the deadline laid down in paragraph 3.

3. Without prejudice to Art. 8 (6), decisions taken pursuant to Art. 8 (3) concerning notified concentrations must be taken within not more than four months of the date on which proceedings are initiated.

4. The period set by paragraph 3 shall exceptionally be suspended where, owing to circumstances for which one of the undertakings involved in the concentration is responsible, the Commission has had to request information by decision pursuant to Art. 11 or to order an investigation by decision pursuant to Art. 13.

5. Where the Court of Justice gives a Judgement which annuls the whole or part of a Commission decision taken under this Regulation, the periods laid down in this Regulation shall start again from the date of the Judgement.

6. Where the Commission has not taken a decision in accordance with Art. 6 (1) (b) or (c) or Art. 8 (2) or (3) within the deadlines set in paragraphs 1 and 3 respectively, the concentration shall be deemed to have been declared compatible with the common market, without prejudice to Art. 9.

Article 11. Requests for information.

1. In carrying out the duties assigned to it by this Regulation, the Commission may obtain all necessary information from the Governments and competent authorities of the Member States, from the persons referred to in Art. 3 (1) (b), and from undertakings and associations of undertakings.

2. When sending a request for information to a person, an undertaking or an association of undertakings, the Commission shall at the same time send a copy of the request to the competent authority of the Member State within the territory of which the residence of the person or the seat of the undertaking or association of undertakings is situated.

3. In its request the Commission shall state the legal basis and the purpose of the request and also the penalties provided for in Art. 14 (1) (c) for supplying incorrect information.

4. The information requested shall be provided, in the case of undertakings, by their owners or their representatives and, in the case of legal persons, companies or firms, or of associations having no legal personality, by the persons authorised to represent them by law or by their statutes.

5. Where a person, an undertaking or an association of undertakings does not provide the information requested within the period fixed by the Commission or provides incomplete information, the Commission shall by decision require the information to be provided. The decision shall specify what information is required, fix an appropriate period within which it is to be supplied and state the penalties provided for in Arts. 14 (1) (c) and 15 (1) (a) and the right to have the decision reviewed by the Court of Justice.

6. The Commission shall at the same time send a copy of its decision

to the competent authority of the Member State within the territory of which the residence of the person or the seat of the undertaking or association of undertakings is situated.

Article 12.   Investigations by the authorities of the Member States.

1. At the request of the Commission, the competent authorities of the Member States shall undertake the investigations which the Commission considers to be necessary under Art. 13 (1), or which it has ordered by decision pursuant to Art. 13 (3). The officials of the competent authorities of the Member States responsible for conducting those investigations shall exercise their powers upon production of an authorisation in writing issued by the competent authority of the Member State within the territory of which the investigation is to be carried out. Such authorisation shall specify the subject-matter and purpose of the investigation.

2. If so requested by the Commission or by the competent authority of the Member State within the territory of which the investigation is to be carried out, officials of the Commission may assist the officials of that authority in carrying out their duties.

Article 13.   Investigative powers of the Commission.

1. In carrying out the duties assigned to it by this Regulation, the Commission may undertake all necessary investigations into undertakings and associations of undertakings.

To that end the officials authorised by the Commission shall be empowered:

(a) to examine the books and other business records;
(b) to take or demand copies of or extracts from the books and business records;
(c) to ask for oral explanations on the spot;
(d) to enter any premises, land and means of transport of undertakings.

2. The officials of the Commission authorised to carry out the investigations shall exercise their powers on production of an authorisation in writing specifying the subject-matter and purpose of the investigation and the penalties provided for in Art. 14 (1) (d) in cases where production of the required books or other business records is incomplete. In good time before the investigation, the Commission shall inform, in writing, the competent authority of the Member State within the territory of which the investigation is to be carried out of the investigation and of the identities of the authorised officials.

3. Undertakings and associations of undertakings shall submit to investigations ordered by decision of the Commission. The decision shall specify the subject-matter and purpose of the investigation, appoint the

date on which it shall begin and state the penalties provided for in Arts. 14 (1) (d) and 15 (1) (b) and the right to have the decision reviewed by the Court of Justice.

4. The Commission shall in good time and in writing inform the competent authority of the Member State within the territory of which the investigation is to be carried out of its intention of taking a decision pursuant to paragraph 3. It shall hear the competent authority before taking its decision.

5. Officials of the competent authority of the Member State within the territory of which the investigation is to be carried out may, at the request of that authority or of the Commission, assist the officials of the Commission in carrying out their duties.

6. Where an undertaking or association of undertakings opposes an investigation ordered pursuant to this Article, the Member State concerned shall afford the necessary assistance to the officials authorised by the Commission to enable them to carry out their investigation. To this end the Member States shall, after consulting the Commission, take the necessary measures within one year of the entry into force of this Regulation.

Article 14. Fines.

1. The Commission may by decision impose on the persons referred to in Art. 3 (1) (b), undertakings or associations of undertakings fines of from ECU 1000 to 50 000 where intentionally or negligently:

(a) they fail to notify a concentration in accordance with Art. 4;
(b) they supply incorrect or misleading information in a notification pursuant to Art. 4;
(c) they supply incorrect information in response to a request made pursuant to Art. 11 or fail to supply information within the period fixed by a decision taken pursuant to Art. 11;
(d) they produce the required books or other business records in incomplete form during investigations under Arts. 12 or 13, or refuse to submit to an investigation ordered by decision taken pursuant to Art. 13.

2. The Commission may by decision impose fines not exceeding 10% of the aggregate turnover of the undertakings concerned within the meaning of Art. 5 on the persons or undertakings concerned where, either intentionally or negligently, they:

(a) fail to comply with an obligation imposed by decision pursuant to Art. 7 (4) or 8 (2), second subparagraph;
(b) put into effect a concentration in breach of Art. 7 (1) or disregard a decision taken pursuant to Art. 7 (2);

(c) put into effect a concentration declared incompatible with the common market by decision pursuant to Art. 8 (3) or do not take the measures ordered by decision pursuant to Art. 8 (4).

3. In setting the amount of a fine, regard shall be had to the nature and gravity of the infringement.

4. Decisions taken pursuant to paragraphs 1 and 2 shall not be of criminal law nature.

Article 15. Periodic penalty payments.

1. The Commission may by decision impose on the persons referred to in Art. 3 (1) (b), undertakings or associations of undertakings concerned periodic penalty payments of up to ECU 25 000 for each day of delay calculated from the date set in the decision, in order to compel them:

(a) to supply complete and correct information which it has requested by decision pursuant to Art. 11;
(b) to submit to an investigation which it has ordered by decision pursuant to Art. 13.

2. The Commission may by decision impose on the persons referred to in Art. 3 (1) (b) or on undertakings periodic penalty payments of up to ECU 100 000 for each day of delay calculated from the date set in the decision, in order to compel them:

(a) to comply with an obligation imposed by decision pursuant to Art. 7 (4) or Art. 8 (2), second subparagraph, or
(b) to apply the measures ordered by decision pursuant to Art. 8 (4).

3. Where the persons referred to in Art. 3 (1) (b), undertakings or associations of undertakings have satisfied the obligation which it was the purpose of the periodic penalty payment to enforce, the Commission may set the total amount of the periodic penalty payments at a lower figure than that which would arise under the original decision.

Article 16. Review by the Court of Justice.

The Court of Justice shall have unlimited jurisdiction within the meaning of Art. 172 of the Treaty to review decisions whereby the Commission has fixed a fine or periodic penalty payments; it may cancel, reduce or increase the fine or periodic penalty payments imposed.

Article 17. Professional secrecy.

1. Information acquired as a result of the application of Arts. 11, 12, 13 and 18 shall be used only for the purposes of the relevant request, investigation or hearing.

2. Without prejudice to Arts. 4 (3), 18 and 20, the Commission and the competent authorities of the Member States, their officials and other servants shall not disclose information they have acquired through the application of this Regulation of the kind covered by the obligation of professional secrecy.

3. Paragraphs 1 and 2 shall not prevent publication of general information or of surveys which do not contain information relating to particular undertakings or associations of undertakings.

Article 18. Hearing of the parties and of third persons.

1. Before taking any decision provided for in Arts. 7 (2) and (4), Art. 8 (2), second subparagraph, and (3) to (5) and Arts. 14 and 15, the Commission shall give the persons, undertakings and associations of undertakings concerned the opportunity, at every stage of the procedure up to the consultation of the Advisory Committee, of making known their views on the objections against them.

2. By way of derogation from paragraph 1, a decision to continue the suspension of a concentration or to grant a derogation from suspension as referred to in Art. 7 (2) or (4) may be taken provisionally, without the persons, undertakings or associations of undertakings concerned being given the opportunity to make known their views beforehand, provided that the Commission gives them that opportunity as soon as possible after having taken its decision.

3. The Commission shall base its decision only on objections on which the parties have been able to submit their observations. The rights of the defence shall be fully respected in the proceedings. Access to the file shall be open at least to the parties directly involved, subject to the legitimate interest of undertakings in the protection of their business secrets.

4. In so far as the Commission or the competent authorities of the Member States deem it necessary, they may also hear other natural or legal persons. Natural or legal persons showing a sufficient interest and especially members of the administrative or management bodies of the undertakings concerned or the recognised representatives of their employees shall be entitled, upon application, to be heard.

Article 19. Liaison with the authorities of the Member States.

1. The Commission shall transmit to the competent authorities of the Member States copies of notifications within three working days and, as soon as possible, copies of the most important documents lodged with or issued by the Commission pursuant to this Regulation.

2. The Commission shall carry out the procedures set out in this Regulation in close and constant liaison with the competent authorities of the Member States, which may express their views upon those

procedures. For the purposes of Art. 9 it shall obtain information from the competent authority of the Member State as referred to in paragraph 2 of that Article and give it the opportunity to make known its views at every stage of the procedure up to the adoption of a decision pursuant to paragraph 3 of that Article; to that end it shall give it access to the file.

3. An Advisory Committee on concentrations shall be consulted before any decision is taken pursuant to Art. 8 (2) to (5), 14 or 15, or any provisions are adopted pursuant to Art. 23.

4. The Advisory Committee shall consist of representatives of the authorities of the Member States. Each Member State shall appoint one or two representatives; if unable to attend, they may be replaced by other representatives. At least one of the representatives of a Member State shall be competent in matters of restrictive practices and dominant positions.

5. Consultation shall take place at a joint meeting convened at the invitation of and chaired by the Commission. A summary of the case, together with an indication of the most important documents and a preliminary draft of the decision to be taken for each case considered, shall be sent with the invitation. The meeting shall take place not less than 14 days after the invitation has been sent. The Commission may in exceptional cases shorten that period as appropriate in order to avoid serious harm to one or more of the undertakings concerned by a concentration.

6. The Advisory Committee shall deliver an opinion on the Commission's draft decision, if necessary by taking a vote. The Advisory Committee may deliver an opinion even if some members are absent and unrepresented. The opinion shall be delivered in writing and appended to the draft decision. The Commission shall take the utmost account of the opinion delivered by the Committee. It shall inform the Committee of the manner in which its opinion has been taken into account.

7. The Advisory Committee may recommend publication of the opinion. The Commission may carry out such publication. The decision to publish shall take due account of the legitimate interest of undertakings in the protection of their business secrets and of the interest of the undertakings concerned in such publication's taking place.

Article 20. Publication of decisions.

1. The Commission shall publish the decisions which it takes pursuant to Art. 8 (2) to (5) in the *Official Journal of the European Communities.*

2. The publication shall state the names of the parties and the main content of the decision; it shall have regard to the legitimate interest of undertakings in the protection of their business secrets.

Article 21. Jurisdiction.

1. Subject to review by the Court of Justice, the Commission shall have sole jurisdiction to take the decisions provided for in this Regulation.

2. No Member State shall apply its national legislation on competition to any consideration that has a Community dimension.

The first subparagraph shall be without prejudice to any Member State's power to carry out any enquiries necessary for the application of Art. 9 (2) or after referral, pursuant to Art. 9 (3), first subparagraph, indent (b), or (5), to take the measures strictly necessary for the application of Art. 9 (8).

3. Notwithstanding paragraphs 1 and 2, Member States may take appropriate measures to protect legitimate interests other than those taken into consideration by this Regulation and compatible with the general principles and other provisions of Community law.

Public security, plurality of the media and prudential rules shall be regarded as legitimate interests within the meaning of the first subparagraph.

Any other public interest must be communicated to the Commission by the Member State concerned and shall be recognised by the Commission after an assessment of its compatibility with the general principles and other provisions of Community law before the measures referred to above may be taken. The Commission shall inform the Member State concerned of its decision within one month of that communication.

Article 22. Application of the Regulation.

1. This Regulation alone shall apply to concentrations as defined in Art. 3.

2. Regulations No 17,[26] (EEC) No 1017/68,[27] (EEC) No 4056/86[28] and (EEC) No 3975/87[29] shall not apply to concentrations as defined in Art. 3.

3. If the Commission finds, at the request of a Member State, that a concentration as defined in Art. 3 that has no Community dimension within the meaning of Art. 1 creates or strengthens a dominant position as a result of which effective competition would be significantly impeded within the territory of the Member State concerned it may, in so far as the concentration affects trade between Member States, adopt the decisions provided for in Art. 8 (2), second subparagraph, (3) and (4).

4. Arts. 2 (1) (a) and (b), 5, 6, 8 and 10 to 20 shall apply. The period within which proceedings may be initiated pursuant to Art. 10 (1) shall begin on the date of the receipt of the request from the Member State. The request must be made within one month at most of the date on which the concentration was made known to the Member State or effected. This period shall begin on the date of the first of those events.

[26] OJ No 13, 21. 2. 1962, p. 204/62.
[27] OJ No L 175. 23. 7. 1968, p. 1.
[28] OJ 1986 L 378/4.
[29] OJ 1987 L 374/1.

5. Pursuant to paragraph 3 the Commission shall take only the measures strictly necessary to maintain or store effective competition within the territory of the Member State at the request of which it intervenes.

6. Paragraphs 3 to 5 shall continue to apply until the thresholds referred to in Art. 1 (2) have been reviewed.

Article 23.   Implementing provisions.

The Commission shall have the power to adopt implementing provisions concerning the form, content and other details of notifications pursuant to Art. 4, time limits pursuant to Art. 10, and hearings pursuant to Art. 18.

Article 24.   Relations with non-member countries.

1. The Member States shall inform the Commission of any general difficulties encountered by their undertakings with concentrations as defined in Art. 3 in a non-member country.

2. Initially not more than one year after the entry into force of this Regulation and thereafter periodically the Commission shall draw up a report examining the treatment accorded to Community undertakings, in the terms referred to in paragraphs 3 and 4, as regards concentrations in non-member countries. The Commission shall submit those reports to the Council, together with any recommendations.

3. Whenever it appears to the Commission, either on the basis of the reports referred to in paragraph 2 or on the basis of other information, that a non-member country does not grant Community undertakings treatment comparable to that granted by the Community to undertakings from that non-member country, the Commission may submit proposals to the Council for an appropriate mandate for negotiation with a view to obtaining comparable treatment for Community undertakings.

4. Measures taken under this Article shall comply with the obligations of the Community or of the Member States, without prejudice to Art. 234 of the Treaty, under international agreements, whether bilateral or multilateral.

Article 25.   Entry into force.

1. This Regulation shall enter into force on 21 September 1990.

2. This Regulation shall not apply to any concentration which was the subject of an agreement or announcement or where control was acquired within the meaning of Art. 4 (1) before the date of this Regulation's entry into force and it shall not in any circumstances apply to any concentration in respect of which proceedings were initiated before that date by a Member State's authority with responsibility for competition.

[Final provisions omitted.]

Commission Regulation (EEC) No 2367/90 of 25 July 1990 on the notifications, time limits and hearings provided for in Council Regulation (EEC) No 4064/89 on the control of concentrations between undertakings[30]

The Commission of the European Communities,

Having regard to the Treaty establishing the European Economic Community,

Having regard to Council Regulation (EEC) No 4064/89 of 21 December 1989 on the control of concentrations between undertakings,[31] and in particular Art. 23 thereof,

Having regard to Council Regulation No 17 of 6 February 1962, First Regulation implementing Arts. 85 and 86 of the Treaty,[32] as last amended by the Act of Accession of Spain and Portugal, and in particular Art. 24 thereof,

Having regard to Council Regulation (EEC) No 1017/68 of 19 July 1968 applying rules of competition to transport by rail, road and inland waterway,[33] as last amended by the Act of Accession of Spain and Portugal, and in particular Art. 29 thereof,

Having regard to Council Regulation (EEC) No 4056/86 of 22 December 1986 laying down detailed rules for the application of Arts. 85 and 86 of the Treaty to maritime transport,[34] and in particular Art. 26 thereof,

Having regard to Council Regulation (EEC) No 3975/87 of 14 December 1987 laying down detailed rules for the application of the competition rules to undertakings in air transport,[35] and in particular Art. 19 thereof,

Having consulted the Advisory Committee on Concentrations, as well as the Advisory Committees on Restrictive Practices and Monopolies in the Transport Industry, in Maritime Transport and in Air Transport,

1. Whereas Art. 23 of Regulation (EEC) No 4064/89 empowers the Commission to adopt implementing provisions concerning the form, content and other details of notifications pursuant to Art. 4, time limits pursuant to Art. 10, and hearings pursuant to Art. 18;

2. Whereas Regulation (EEC) No 4064/89 is based on the principle of compulsory notification of concentrations before they are put into effect; whereas, on the one hand, a notification has important legal consequences which are favourable to the parties, while, on the other

---

[30] OJ 1990 L 219/5. [31] OJ 1989 L 395/1. [32] OJ No 13, 21. 2. 1962, p. 204/62.
[33] OJ No L 175, 23. 7. 1968, p. 1. [34] OJ 1986 L 378/4. [35] OJ 1987 L 374/1.

hand, failure to comply with the obligation to notify renders the parties liable to a fine and may also entail civil law disadvantages for them; whereas it is therefore necessary in the interests of legal certainty to define precisely the subject-matter and content of the information to be provided in the notification;

3. Whereas it is for the parties concerned to make full and honest disclosure to the Commission of the facts and circumstances which are relevant for taking a decision on the notified concentration;

4. Whereas in order to simplify and expedite examination of the notification it is desirable to prescribe that a form be used;

5. Whereas since notification sets in motion legal time limits for initiating proceedings and for decisions, the conditions governing such time limits and the time when they become effective must also be determined;

6. Whereas rules must be laid down in the interests of legal certainty for calculating the time limits provided for in Regulation (EEC) No 4064/89; whereas in particular the beginning and end of the period and the circumstances suspending the running of the period must be determined; whereas the provisions should be based on the principles of Regulation (EEC, Euratom) No 1182/71 of 3 June 1971 determining the rules applicable to periods, dates and time limits,[36] subject to certain adaptations made necessary by the exceptionally short legal time limits referred to above;

7. Whereas the provisions relating to the Commission's procedure must be framed in such way as to safeguard fully the right to be heard and the rights of defence;

8. Whereas the Commission will give the parties concerned, if they so request, an opportunity before notification to discuss the intended concentration informally and in strict confidence; whereas in addition it will, after notification, maintain close contact with the parties concerned to the extent necessary to discuss with them any practical or legal problems which it discovers on a first examination of the case and if possible to remove such problems by mutual agreement;

9. Whereas in accordance with the principle of the right to be heard, the parties concerned must be given the opportunity to submit their comments on all the objections which the Commission proposes to take into account in its decisions;

10. Whereas third parties having sufficient interest must also be given the opportunity of expressing their views where they make a written application;

11. Whereas the various persons entitled to submit comments should do so in writing, both in their own interest and in the interest of good

[36] JO No L 124, 8.6.1971, p. 1.

administration, without prejudice to their right to request an oral hearing where appropriate to supplement the written procedure; whereas in urgent cases, however, the Commission must be able to proceed immediately to oral hearings of the parties concerned or third parties; whereas in such cases the persons to be heard must have the right to confirm their oral statements in writing;

12. Whereas it is necessary to define the rights of persons who are to be heard, to what extent they should be granted access to the Commission's file and on what conditions they may be represented or assisted;

13. Whereas it is also necessary to define the rules for fixing and calculating the time limits for reply fixed by the Commission;

14. Whereas the Advisory Committee on Concentrations shall deliver its opinion on the basis of a preliminary draft decision; whereas it must therefore be consulted on a case after the inquiry into that case has been completed; whereas such consultation does not, however, prevent the Commission from re-opening an inquiry if need be,

Has adopted this Regulation:

SECTION I. NOTIFICATIONS

Article 1. Persons entitled to submit notifications.

1. Notifications shall be submitted by the persons or undertakings referred to in Art. 4 (2) of Regulation (EEC) No 4064/89.

2. Where notifications are signed by representatives of persons or of undertakings, such representatives shall produce written proof that they are authorised to act.

3. Joint notifications should be submitted by a joint representative who is authorised to transmit and to receive documents on behalf of all notifying parties.

Article 2. Submission of notifications.

1. Notifications shall be submitted in the manner prescribed by form CO as shown in Annex I. Joint notifications shall be submitted on a single form.

2. Twenty copies of each notification and fifteen copies of the supporting documents shall be submitted to the Commission at the address indicated in form CO.

3. The supporting documents shall be either originals or copies of the originals; in the latter case the notifying parties shall confirm that they are true and complete.

4. Notifications shall be in one of the official languages of the

Community. This language shall also be the language of the proceeding for the notifying parties. Supporting documents shall be submitted in their original language. Where the original language is not one of the official languages, a translation into the language of the proceeding shall be attached.

Article 3. Information to be provided.

1. Notifications shall contain the information requested by form CO. The information must be correct and complete.

2. Material changes in the facts specified in the notification which the notifying parties know or ought to have known must be communicated to the Commission voluntarily and without delay.

3. Incorrect or misleading information shall be deemed to be incomplete information.

Article 4. Effective date of notifications.

1. Subject to paragraph 2 notifications shall become effective on the date on which they are received by the Commission.

2. Subject to paragraph 3, where the information contained in the notification is incomplete in a material respect, the Commission shall without delay inform the notifying parties or the joint representative in writing and shall fix an appropriate time limit for the completion of the information; in such cases, the notification shall become effective on the date on which the complete information is received by the Commission.

3. The Commission may dispense with the obligation to provide any particular information requested by form CO where the Commission considers that such information is not necessary for the examination of the case.

4. The Commission shall without delay acknowledge in writing to the notifying parties or the joint representative receipt of the notification and of any reply to a letter sent by the Commission pursuant to paragraph 2 above.

Article 5. Conversion of notifications.

1. Where the Commission finds that the operation notified does not constitute a concentration within the meaning of Art. 3 of Regulation (EEC) No 4064/89 it shall inform the notifying parties or the joint representative in writing. In such a case, the Commission may, if requested by the notifying parties, as appropriate and subject to paragraph 2 below, treat the notification as an application within the meaning of Art. 2 or a notification within the meaning of Art. 4 of Regulation No 17, as an application within the meaning of Art. 12 or a notification within the meaning of Art. 14 of Regulation (EEC) No 1017/68, as an application

within the meaning of Art. 12 of Regulation (EEC) No 4056/86 or as an application within the meaning of Art. 3 (2) or of Art. 5 of Regulation (EEC) No 3975/87.

2. In cases referred to in paragraph 1, second sentence, the Commission may require that the information given in the notification be supplemented within an appropriate time limit fixed by it in so far as this is necessary for assessing the operation on the basis of the abovementioned Regulations. The application or notification shall be deemed to fulfil the requirements of such Regulations from the date of the original notification where the additional information is received by the Commission within the time limit fixed.

SECTION II. TIME LIMITS FOR INITIATING PROCEEDINGS AND FOR DECISIONS

Article 6. Beginning of the time limit.

1. The periods referred to in Art. 10 (1) of Regulation (EEC) No 4064/89 shall start at the beginning of the day following the effective date of the notification, within the meaning of Art. 4 (1) and (2) of this Regulation.

2. The period referred to in Art. 10 (3) of Regulation (EEC) No 4064/89 shall start at the beginning of the day following the day on which proceedings were initiated.

3. Where the first day of a period is not a working day within the meaning of Art. 19, the period shall start at the beginning of the following working day.

Article 7. End of the time limit.

1. The period referred to in the first subparagraph of Art. 10 (1) of Regulation (EEC) No 4064/89 shall end with the expiry of the day which in the month following that in which the period began falls on the same date as the day from which the period runs. Where such a day does not occur in that month, the period shall end with the expiry of the last day of that month.

2. The period referred to in the second sub-paragraph of Art. 10 (1) of Regulation (EEC) No 4064/89 shall end with the expiry of the day which in the sixth week following that in which the period began is the same day of the week as the day from which the period runs.

3. The period referred to in Art. 10 (3) of Regulation (EEC) No 4064/89 shall end with the expiry of the day which in the fourth month following that in which the period began falls on the same date as the day from which the period runs. Where such a day does not occur in that month, the period shall end with the expiry of the last day of that month.

4. Where the last day of the period is not a working day within the meaning of Art. 19, the period shall end with the expiry of the following working day.

5. Paragraphs 2 to 4 above shall be subject to the provisions of Art. 8.

Article 8.   Addition of holidays.

Where public holidays or other holidays of the Commission as defined in Art. 19 fall within the periods referred to in Art. 10 (1) and in Art. 10 (3) of Regulation (EEC) No 4064/89, these periods shall be extended by a corresponding number of days.

Article 9.   Suspension of the time limit.

1. The period referred to in Art. 10 (3) of Regulation (EEC) No 4064/89 shall be suspended where the Commission, pursuant to Arts. 11 (5) or 13 (3) of the same Regulation, has to take a decision because:

(a) Information which the Commission has requested pursuant to Art. 11 (2) of Regulation (EEC) No 4064/89 from an undertaking involved in a concentration is not provided or not provided in full within the time limit fixed by the Commission;

(b) an undertaking involved in the concentration has refused to submit to an investigation deemed necessary by the Commission on the basis of Art. 13 (1) of Regulation (EEC) No 4064/89 or to cooperate in the carrying out of such an investigation in accordance with the above-mentioned provision;

(c) the notifying parties have failed to inform the Commission of material changes in the facts specified in the notification.

2. The period referred to in Art. 10 (3) of Regulation (EEC) No 4064/89 shall be suspended:

(a) in the cases referred to in subparagraph 1 (a) above, for the period between the end of the time limit fixed in the request for information and the receipt of the complete and correct information required by decision,

(b) in the cases referred to in subparagraph 1 (b) above, for the period between the unsuccessful attempt to carry out the investigation and the completion of the investigation ordered by decision;

(c) in the cases referred to in subparagraph 1 (c) above, for the period between the occurrence of the change in the facts referred to therein and the receipt of the complete and correct information requested by decision or the completion of the investigation ordered by decision.

3. The suspension of the time limit shall begin on the day following that on which the event causing the suspension occurred. It shall end with

the expiry of the day on which the reason for suspension is removed. Where such day is not a working day within the meaning of Art. 19, the suspension of the time limit shall end with the expiry of the following working day.

Article 10.   Compliance with the time limit.
The time limits referred to in Art. 10 (1) and (3) of Regulation (EEC) No 4064/89 shall be met where the Commission has taken the relevant decision before the end of the period. Notification of the decision to the undertakings concerned must follow without delay.

SECTION III. HEARING OF THE PARTIES AND OF THIRD PARTIES

Article 11.   Decisions on the suspension of concentrations.
  1. Where the Commission intends to take a decision under Art. 7 (2) of Regulation (EEC) No 4064/89 or a decision under Art. 7 (4) of that Regulation which adversely affects the parties, it shall, pursuant to Art. 18 (1) of that Regulation, inform the parties concerned in writing of its objections and shall fix a time limit within which they may make known their views.
  2. Where the Commission pursuant to Art. 18 (2) of Regulation (EEC) No 4064/89 has taken a decision referred to in paragraph 1 provisionally without having given the parties concerned the opportunity to make known their views, it shall without delay and in any event before the expiry of the suspension send them the text of the provisional decision and shall fix a time limit within which they may make known their views.
  Once the parties concerned have made known their views, the Commission shall take a final decision annulling, amending or confirming the provisional decision. Where the parties concerned have not made known their view within the time limit fixed, the Commission's provisional decision shall become final with the expiry of that period.
  3. The parties concerned shall make known their views in writing or orally within the time limit fixed. They may confirm their oral statements in writing.

Article 12.   Decisions on the substance of the case.
  1. Where the Commission intends to take a decision pursuant to Art. 8 (2), second subparagraph, Art. 8 (3), (4) and (5), Art. 14 or Art. 15 of Regulation (EEC) No 4064/89, it shall, before consulting the Advisory Committee on Concentrations, hold a hearing of the parties concerned pursuant to Art. 18 of that Regulation.
  2. The Commission shall inform the parties concerned in writing of its

objections. The communication shall be addressed to the notifying parties or to the joint representative. The Commission shall, when giving notice of objections, fix a time limit within which the parties concerned may inform the Commission of their views.

3. Having informed the parties of its objections, the Commission shall upon request give the parties concerned access to the file for the purposes of preparing their observations. Documents shall not be accessible in so far as they contain business secrets of other parties concerned or of third parties, or other confidential information including sensitive commercial information the disclosure of which would have a significant adverse effect on the supplier of such information or where they are internal documents of the authorities.

4. The parties concerned shall, within the time limit fixed, make known in writing their views on the Commission's objections. They may in their written comments set out all matters relevant to the case and may attach any relevant documents in proof of the facts set out. They may also propose that the Commission hear persons who may corroborate those facts.

Article 13. Oral hearings.

1. The Commission shall afford parties concerned who have so requested in their written comments the opportunity to put forward their arguments orally, if those persons show a sufficient interest or if the Commission proposes to impose a fine or periodic penalty payment on them. It may also in other cases afford the parties concerned the opportunity of expressing their views orally.

2. The Commission shall summon the persons to be heard to attend on such date as it shall appoint.

3. It shall forthwith transmit a copy of the summons to the competent authorities of the Member States, who may appoint an official to take part in the hearing.

Article 14. Hearings.

1. Hearings shall be conducted by persons appointed by the Commission for that purpose.

2. Persons summoned to attend shall either appear in person or be represented by legal representatives or representatives authorised by their constitution. Undertakings and associations of undertakings may be represented by a duly authorised agent appointed from among their permanent staff.

3. Persons heard by the Commission may be assisted by lawyers or university teachers who are entitled to plead before the Court of Justice of the European Communities in accordance with Art. 17 of the Protocol on the Statute (EEC) of the Court of Justice, or by other qualified persons.

4. Hearings shall not be public. Persons shall be heard separately or in the presence of other persons summoned to attend. In the latter case, regard shall be had to the legitimate interest of the undertakings in the protection of their business secrets.

5. The statements made by each person heard shall be recorded.

Article 15. Hearing of third parties.

1. If natural or legal persons showing a sufficient interest, and especially members of the administrative or management organs of the undertakings concerned or recognised workers' representatives of those undertakings, apply in writing to be heard pursuant to the second sentence of Art. 18 (4) of Regulation (EEC) No 4064/89, the Commission shall inform them in writing of the nature and subject-matter of the procedure and shall fix a time limit within which they may make known their views.

2. The third parties referred to in paragraph 1 above shall make known their views in writing or orally within the time limit fixed. They may confirm their oral statements in writing.

3. The Commission may likewise afford to any other third parties the opportunity of expressing their views.

SECTION IV. MISCELLANEOUS PROVISIONS

Article 16. Transmission of documents.

1. Transmission of documents and summonses from the Commission to the addressees may be effected in any of the following ways:

(a) delivery by hand against receipt;
(b) registered letter with acknowledgement of receipt;
(c) telefax with a request for acknowledgement of receipt;
(d) telex.

2. Subject to Art. 18 (1), paragraph 1 above also applies to the transmission of documents from the parties concerned or from third parties to the Commission.

3. Where a document is sent by telex or by telefax, it shall be presumed that it has been received by the addressee on the day on which it was sent.

Article 17. Setting of time limits.

1. In fixing the time limits provided for in Arts. 4 (2), 5 (2), 11 (1) and (2), 12 (2) and 15 (1), the Commission shall have regard to the time required for preparation of statements and to the urgency of the case. It shall also take account of public holidays in the country of receipt of the Commission's communication.

2. The day on which the addressee received a communication shall not be taken into account for the purpose of fixing time limits.

Article 18.   Receipt of documents by the Commission.

1. Subject to Art. 4 (1), notifications must be delivered to the Commission at the address indicated in form CO or have been dispatched by registered letter before expiry of the period referred to in Art. 4 (1) of Regulation (EEC) No 4064/89. Additional information requested to complete notifications pursuant to Art. 4 (2) or to supplement notifications pursuant to Art. 5 (2) of this Regulation must reach the Commission at the aforesaid or have been dispatched by registered letter before the expiry of the time limit fixed in each case. Written comments on Commission communications pursuant to Arts. 11 (1) and (2), 12 (2) and 15 (1) must be delivered to the Commission at the aforesaid address before the time limit fixed in each case.

2. Where the last day of a period referred to in paragraph 1 is a day by which documents must be received and that day is not a working day within the meaning of Art. 19, the period shall end with the expiry of the following working day.

3. Where the last day of a period referred to in paragraph 1 is a day by which documents must be dispatched and that day is a Saturday, Sunday or public holiday in the country of dispatch, the period shall end with the expiry of the following working day in that country.

Article 19.   Definition of Commission working days.
The term 'working days' in Arts. 6 (3), 7 (4), 9 (3) and 18 (2) means all days other than Saturdays, Sundays, public holidays set out in Annex II and other holidays as determined by the Commission and published in the *Official Journal of the European Communities* before the beginning of each year.

Article 20.   Entry into force.
This Regulation shall enter into force on 21 September 1990.

[Final provisions omitted.]

Product Liability

Council Directive of 25 July 1985 on the approximation of the laws, regulations and administrative provisions of the Member States concerning liability for defective products (85/374/EEC)[1]

The Council of the European Communities,

Having regard to the Treaty establishing the European Economic Community, and in particular Art. 100 thereof,

[Recitals omitted.]

Whereas approximation of the laws of the Member States concerning the liability of the producer for damage caused by the defectiveness of his products is necessary because the existing divergences may distort competition and affect the movement of goods within the common market and entail a differing degree of protection of the consumer against damage caused by a defective product to his health or property;

Whereas liability without fault on the part of the producer is the sole means of adequately solving the problem, peculiar to our age of increasing technicality, of a fair apportionment of the risks inherent in modern technological production;

Whereas liability without fault should apply only to movables which have been industrially produced; whereas, as a result, it is appropriate to exclude liability for agricultural products and game, except where they have undergone a processing of an industrial nature which could cause a defect in these products; whereas the liability provided for in this Directive should also apply to movables which are used in the construction of immovables or are installed in immovables;

Whereas protection of the consumer requires that all producers involved in the production process should be made liable, in so far as their finished product, component part or any raw material supplied by them was defective; whereas, for the same reason, liability should extend to importers of products into the Community and to persons who present themselves as producers by affixing their name, trade mark or other distinguishing feature or who supply a product the producer of which cannot be identified;

Whereas, in situations where several persons are liable for the same damage, the protection of the consumer requires that the injured person

[1] OJ 1985 L 210/29.

should be able to claim full compensation for the damage from any one of them;

Whereas, to protect the physical well-being and property of the consumer, the defectiveness of the product should be determined by reference not to its fitness for use but to the lack of the safety which the public at large is entitled to expect; whereas the safety is assessed by excluding any misuse of the product not reasonable under the circumstances;

Whereas a fair apportionment of risk between the injured person and the producer implies that the producer should be able to free himself from liability if he furnishes proof as to the existence of certain exonerating circumstances;

Whereas the protection of the consumer requires that the liability of the producer remains unaffected by acts or omissions of other persons having contributed to cause the damage; whereas, however, the contributory negligence of the injured person may be taken into account to reduce or disallow such liability;

Whereas the protection of the consumer requires compensation for death and personal injury as well as compensation for damage to property; whereas the latter should nevertheless be limited to goods for private use or consumption and be subject to a deduction of a lower threshold of a fixed amount in order to avoid litigation in an excessive number of cases; whereas this Directive should not prejudice compensation for pain and suffering and other non-material damages payable, where appropriate, under the law applicable to the case;

Whereas a uniform period of limitation for the bringing of action for compensation is in the interests both of the injured person and of the producer;

Whereas products age in the course of time, higher safety standards are developed and the state of science and technology progresses; whereas, therefore, it would not be reasonable to make the producer liable for an unlimited period for the defectiveness of his product; whereas, therefore, liability should expire after a reasonable length of time, without prejudice to claims pending at law;

Whereas, to achieve effective protection of consumers, no contractual derogation should be permitted as regards the liability of the producer in relation to the injured person;

Whereas under the legal systems of the Member States an injured party may have a claim for damages based on grounds of contractual liability or on grounds of non-contractual liability other than that provided for in this Directive; in so far as these provisions also serve to attain the objective of effective protection of consumers, they should remain unaffected by this Directive; whereas, in so far as effective protection of consumers in the sector of pharmaceutical products is already also attained in a

Member State under a special liability system, claims based on this system should similarly remain possible;

Whereas, to the extent that liability for nuclear injury or damage is already covered in all Member States by adequate special rules, it has been possible to exclude damage of this type from the scope of this Directive;

Whereas, since the exclusion of primary agricultural products and game from the scope of this Directive may be felt, in certain Member States, in view of what is expected for the protection of consumers, to restrict unduly such protection, it should be possible for a Member State to extend liability to such products;

Whereas, for similar reasons, the possibility offered to a producer to free himself from liability if he proves that the state of scientific and technical knowledge at the time when he put the product into circulation was not such as to enable the existence of a defect to be discovered may be felt in certain Member States to restrict unduly the protection of the consumer; whereas it should therefore be possible for a Member State to maintain in its legislation or to provide by new legislation that this exonerating circumstance is not admitted; whereas, in the case of new legislation, making use of this derogation should, however, be subject to a Community stand-still procedure, in order to raise, if possible, the level of protection in a uniform manner throughout the Community;

Whereas, taking into account the legal traditions in most of the Member States, it is inappropriate to set any financial ceiling on the producer's liability without fault; whereas, in so far as there are, however, differing traditions, it seems possible to admit that a Member State may derogate from the principle of unlimited liability by providing a limit for the total liability of the producer for damage resulting from a death or personal injury and caused by identical items with the same defect, provided that this limit is established at a level sufficiently high to guarantee adequate protection of the consumer and the correct functioning of the common market;

Whereas the harmonisation resulting from this cannot be total at the present stage, but opens the way towards greater harmonisation; whereas it is therefore necessary that the Council receive at regular intervals, reports from the Commission on the application of this Directive, accompanied, as the case may be, by appropriate proposals;

Whereas it is particularly important in this respect that a re-examination be carried out of those parts of the Directive relating to the derogations open to the Member States, at the expiry of a period of sufficient length to gather practical experience on the effects of these derogations on the protection of consumers and on the functioning of the common market,

Has adopted this Directive:

Article 1. The producer shall be liable for damage caused by a defect in his product.

Article 2. For the purpose of this Directive 'product' means all movables, with the exception of primary agricultural products and game, even though incorporated into another movable or into an immovable. 'Primary agricultural products' means the products of the soil, of stock-farming and of fisheries, excluding products which have undergone initial processing. 'Product' includes electricity.

Article 3. 1. 'Producer' means the manufacturer of a finished product, the producer of any raw material or the manufacturer of a component part and any person who, by putting his name, trade mark or other distinguishing feature on the product presents himself as its producer.

2. Without prejudice to the liability of the producer, any person who imports into the Community a product for sale, hire, leasing or any form of distribution in the course of his business shall be deemed to be a producer within the meaning of this Directive and shall be responsible as a producer.

3. Where the producer of the product cannot be identified, each supplier of the product shall be treated as its producer unless he informs the injured person, within a reasonable time, of the identity of the producer or of the person who supplied him with the product. The same shall apply, in the case of an imported product, if this product does not indicate the identity of the importer referred to in paragraph 2, even if the name of the producer is indicated.

Article 4. The injured person shall be required to prove the damage, the defect and the causal relationship between defect and damage.

Article 5. Where, as a result of the provisions of this Directive, two or more persons are liable for the same damage, they shall be liable jointly and severally, without prejudice to the provisions of national law concerning the rights of contribution or recourse.

Article 6. 1. A product is defective when it does not provide the safety which a person is entitled to expect, taking all circumstances into account, including:

(a) the presentation of the product;
(b) the use to which it could reasonably be expected that the product would be put;
(c) the time when the product was put into circulation.

2. A product shall not be considered defective for the sole reason that a better product is subsequently put into circulation.

Article 7. The producer shall not be liable as a result of this Directive if he proves:

(a) that he did not put the product into circulation; or
(b) that, having regard to the circumstances, it is probable that the defect which caused the damage did not exist at the time when the product was put into circulation by him or that this defect came into being afterwards; or
(c) that the product was neither manufactured by him for sale or any form of distribution for economic purpose nor manufactured or distributed by him in the course of his business; or
(d) that the defect is due to compliance of the product with mandatory regulations issued by the public authorities; or
(e) that the state of scientific and technical knowledge at the time when he put the product into circulation was not such as to enable the existence of the defect to be discovered; or
(f) in the case of a manufacturer of a component, that the defect is attributable to the design of the product in which the component has been fitted or to the instructions given by the manufacturer of the product.

Article 8. 1. Without prejudice to the provisions of national law concerning the right of contribution or recourse, the liability of the producer shall not be reduced when the damage is caused both by a defect in product and by the act or omission of a third party.

2. The liability of the producer may be reduced or disallowed when, having regard to all the circumstances, the damage is caused both by a defect in the product and by the fault of the injured person or any person for whom the injured person is responsible.

Article 9. For the purpose of Art. 1, 'damage' means:

(a) damage caused by death or by personal injuries;
(b) damage to, or destruction of, any item of property other than the defective product itself, with a lower threshold of 500 ECU, provided that the item of property:
  (i) is of a type ordinarily intended for private use or consumption, and
  (ii) was used by the injured person mainly for his own private use or consumption.

This Article shall be without prejudice to national provisions relating to non-material damage.

Article 10. 1. Member States shall provide in their legislation that a limitation period of three years shall apply to proceedings for the recovery of damages as provided for in this Directive. The limitation period shall begin to run from the day on which the plaintiff became aware, or should reasonably have become aware, of the damage, the defect and the identity of the producer.

2. The laws of Member States regulating suspension or interruption of the limitation period shall not be affected by this Directive.

Article 11. Member States shall provide in their legislation that the rights conferred upon the injured person pursuant to this Directive shall be extinguished upon the expiry of a period of 10 years from the date on which the producer put into circulation the actual product which caused the damage, unless the injured person has in the meantime instituted proceedings against the producer.

Article 12. The liability of the producer arising from this Directive may not, in relation to the injured person, be limited or excluded by a provision limiting his liability or exempting him from liability.

Article 13. This Directive shall not affect any rights which an injured person may have according to the rules of the law of contractual or non-contractual liability or a special liability system existing at the moment when this Directive is notified.

Article 14. This Directive shall not apply to injury or damage arising from nuclear accidents and covered by international conventions ratified by the Member States.

Article 15. 1. Each Member State may:

(a) by way of derogation from Art. 2, provide in its legislation that within the meaning of Art. 1 of this Directive 'product' also means primary agricultural products and game;
(b) by way of derogation from Art. 7 (e), maintain or, subject to the procedure set out in paragraph 2 of this Article, provide in this legislation that the producer shall be liable even if he proves that the state of scientific and technical knowledge at the time when he put the product into circulation was not such as to enable the existence of a defect to be discovered.

2. A Member State wishing to introduce the measure specified in paragraph 1 (b) shall communicate the text of the proposed measure to the Commission. The Commission shall inform the other Member States thereof.

The Member State concerned shall hold the proposed measure in abeyance for nine months after the Commission is informed and provided that in the meantime the Commission has not submitted to the Council a proposal amending this Directive on the relevant matter. However, if within three months of receiving the said information, the Commission does not advise the Member State concerned that it intends submitting such a proposal to the Council, the Member State may take the proposed measure immediately.

If the Commission does submit to the Council such a proposal amending this Directive within the aforementioned nine months, the Member State concerned shall hold the proposed measure in abeyance for a further period of 18 months from the date on which the proposal is submitted.

3. Ten years after the date of notification of this Directive, the Commission shall submit to the Council a report on the effect that rulings by the courts as to the application of Art. 7 (e) and of paragraph 1 (b) of this Article have on consumer protection and the functioning of the common market. In the light of this report the Council, acting on a proposal from the Commission and pursuant to the terms of Art. 100 of the Treaty, shall decide whether to repeal Art. 7 (e).

Article 16. 1. Any Member State may provide that a producer's total liability for damage resulting from a death or personal injury and caused by identical items with the same defect shall be limited to an amount which may not be less than 70 million ECU.

2. Ten years after the date of notification of this Directive, the Commission shall submit to the Council a report on the effect on consumer protection and the functioning of the common market of the implementation of the financial limit on liability by those Member States which have used the option provided for in paragraph 1. In the light of this report the Council, acting on a proposal from the Commission and pursuant to the terms of Art. 100 of the Treaty, shall decide whether to repeal paragraph 1.

Article 17. This Directive shall not apply to products put into circulation before the date on which the provisions referred to in Art. 19 enter into force.

Article 18. 1. For the purposes of this Directive, the ECU shall be that defined by Regulation (EEC) No 3180/78,[2] as amended by Regulation (EEC) No 2626/84.[3] The equivalent in national currency shall initially be calculated at the rate obtaining on the date of adoption of this Directive.

[2] OJ 1978 L 379/1.   [3] OJ 1984 L 247/1.

2. Every five years the Council, acting on a proposal from the Commission, shall examine and, if need be, revise the amounts in this Directive, in the light of economic and monetary trends in the Community.

Article 19. 1. Member States shall bring into force, not later than three years from the date of notification of this Directive, the laws, regulations and administrative provisions necessary to comply with this Directive. They shall forthwith inform the Commission thereof.[4]

2. The procedure set out in Art. 15 (2) shall apply from the date of notification of this Directive.

Article 20. Member States shall communicate to the Commission the texts of the main provisions of national law which they subsequently adopt in the field governed by this Directive.

Article 21. Every five years the Commission shall present a report to the Council on the application of this Directive and, if necessary, shall submit appropriate proposals to it.

Article 22. This Directive is addressed to the Member States.

[Final provisions omitted.]

---

[4] This Directive was notified to the Member States on 30 July 1985.

Social Policy

Council Directive of 10 February 1975 on the approximation of the laws of the Member States relating to the application of the principle of equal pay for men and women (75/117/EEC)[1]

The Council of the European Communities,

Having regard to the Treaty establishing the European Economic Community, and in particular Art. 100 thereof;

Having regard to the proposal from the Commission;

Having regard to the Opinion of the European Parliament;

Having regard to the Opinion of the Economic and Social Committee;

Whereas implementation of the principle that men and women should receive equal pay contained in Art. 119 of the Treaty is an integral part of the establishment and functioning of the common market;

Whereas it is primarily the responsibility of the Member States to ensure the application of this principle by means of appropriate laws, regulations and administrative provisions;

Whereas the Council resolution of 21 January 1974 concerning a social action programme aimed at making it possible to harmonise living and working conditions while the improvement is being maintained and at achieving a balanced social and economic development of the Community, recognised that priority should be given to action taken on behalf of women as regards access to employment and vocational training and advancement, and as regards working conditions, including pay;

Whereas it is desirable to reinforce the basic laws by standards aimed at facilitating the practical application of the principle of equality in such a way that all employees in the Community can be protected in these matters;

Whereas differences continue to exist in the various Member States despite the efforts made to apply the resolution of the conference of the Member States of 30 December 1961 on equal pay for men and women and whereas, therefore, the national provisions should be approximated as regards application of the principle of equal pay,

Has adopted this Directive:

Article 1. The principle of equal pay for men and women outlined in Art. 119 of the Treaty, hereinafter called 'principle of equal pay', means,

[1] OJ 1975 L 45/19.

for the same work or for work to which equal value is attributed, the elimination of all discrimination on grounds of sex with regard to all aspects and conditions of remuneration.

In particular, where a job classification system is used for determining pay, it must be based on the same criteria for both men and women and so drawn up as to exclude any discrimination on grounds of sex.

Article 2. Member States shall introduce into their national legal systems such measures as are necessary to enable all employees who consider themselves wronged by failure to apply the principle of equal pay to pursue their claims by judicial process after possible recourse to other competent authorities.

Article 3. Member States shall abolish all discrimination between men and women arising from laws, regulations or administrative provisions which is contrary to the principle of equal pay.

Article 4. Member States shall take the necessary measures to ensure that provisions appearing in collective agreements, wage scales, wage agreements or individual contracts of employment which are contrary to the principle of equal pay shall be, or may be declared, null and void or may be amended.

Article 5. Member States shall take the necessary measures to protect employees against dismissal by the employer as a reaction to a complaint within the undertaking or to any legal proceedings aimed at enforcing compliance with the principle of equal pay.

Article 6. Member States shall, in accordance with their national circumstances and legal systems, take the measures necessary to ensure that the principle of equal pay is applied. They shall see that effective means are available to take care that this principle is observed.

Article 7. Member States shall take care that the provisions adopted pursuant to this Directive, together with the relevant provisions already in force, are brought to the attention of employees by all appropriate means, for example at their place of employment.

[Final provisions omitted.]

Council Directive of 9 February 1976 on the implementation of the principle of equal treatment for men and women as regards access to employment, vocational training and promotion, and working conditions (76/207/EEC)[2]

The Council of the European Communities,

Having regard to the Treaty establishing the European Economic Community, and in particular Art. 235 thereof,

Having regard to the proposal from the Commission,

Having regard to the opinion of the European Parliament,

Having regard to the opinion of the Economic and Social Committee,

Whereas the Council, in its resolution of 21 January 1974 concerning a social action programme, included among the priorities action for the purpose of achieving equality between men and women as regards access to employment and vocational training and promotion and as regards working conditions, including pay;

Whereas, with regard to pay, the Council adopted on 10 February 1975 Directive 75/117/EEC on the approximation of the laws of the Member States relating to the application of the principle of equal pay for men and women;

Whereas Community action to achieve the principle of equal treatment for men and women in respect of access to employment and vocational training and promotion and in respect of other working conditions also appears to be necessary; whereas equal treatment for male and female workers constitutes one of the objectives of the Community, in so far as the harmonisation of living and working conditions while maintaining their improvement are *inter alia* to be furthered; whereas the Treaty does not confer the necessary specific powers for this purpose;

Whereas the definition and progressive implementation of the principle of equal treatment in matters of social security should be ensured by means of subsequent instruments,

Has adopted this Directive:

Article 1. 1. The purpose of this Directive is to put into effect in the Member States the principle of equal treatment for men and women as regards access to employment, including promotion, and to vocational training and as regards working conditions and, on the conditions referred to in paragraph 2, social security. This principle is hereinafter referred to as 'the principle of equal treatment'.

[2] OJ 1976 L 39/40.

2. With a view to ensuring the progressive implementation of the principle of equal treatment in matters of social security, the Council, acting on a proposal from the Commission, will adopt provisions defining its substance, its scope and the arrangements for its application.

Article 2. 1. For the purposes of the following provisions, the principle of equal treatment shall mean that there shall be no discrimination whatsoever on grounds of sex either directly or indirectly by reference in particular to marital or family status.

2. This Directive shall be without prejudice to the right of Member States to exclude from its field of application those occupational activities and, where appropriate, the training leading thereto, for which, by reason of their nature or the context in which they are carried out, the sex of the worker constitutes a determining factor.

3. This Directive shall be without prejudice to provisions concerning the protection of women, particularly as regards pregnancy and maternity.

4. This Directive shall be without prejudice to measures to promote equal opportunity for men and women, in particular by removing existing inequalities which affect women's opportunities in the areas referred to in Art. 1 (1).

Article 3. 1. Application of the principle of equal treatment means that there shall be no discrimination whatsoever on grounds of sex in the conditions, including selection criteria, for access to all jobs or posts, whatever the sector or branch of activity, and to all levels of the occupational hierarchy.

2. To this end, Member States shall take the measures necessary to ensure that:

(a) any laws, regulations and administrative provisions contrary to the principle of equal treatment shall be abolished;
(b) any provisions contrary to the principle of equal treatment which are included in collective agreements, individual contracts of employment, internal rules of undertakings or in rules governing the independent occupations and professions shall be, or may be declared, null and void or may be amended;
(c) those laws, regulations and administrative provisions contrary to the principle of equal treatment when the concern for protection which originally inspired them is no longer well founded shall be revised; and that where similar provisions are included in collective agreements labour and management shall be requested to undertake the desired revision.

Article 4. Application of the principle of equal treatment with regard to access to all types and to all levels, of vocational guidance, vocational training, advanced vocational training and retraining, means that Member States shall take all necessary measures to ensure that:

(a) any laws, regulations and administrative provisions contrary to the principle of equal treatment shall be abolished;

(b) any provisions contrary to the principle of equal treatment which are included in collective agreements, individual contracts of employment, internal rules of undertakings or in rules governing the independent occupations and professions shall be, or may be declared, null and void or may be amended;

(c) without prejudice to the freedom granted in certain Member States to certain private training establishments, vocational guidance, vocational training, advanced vocational training and retraining shall be accessible on the basis of the same criteria and at the same levels without any discrimination on grounds of sex.

Article 5. 1. Application of the principle of equal treatment with regard to working conditions, including the conditions governing dismissal, means that men and women shall be guaranteed the same conditions without discrimination on grounds of sex.

2. To this end, Member States shall take the measures necessary to ensure that:

(a) any laws, regulations and administrative provisions contrary to the principle of equal treatment shall be abolished;

(b) any provisions contrary to the principle of equal treatment which are included in collective agreements, individual contracts of employment, internal rules of undertakings or in rules governing the independent occupations and professions shall be, or may be declared, null and void or may be amended;

(c) those laws, regulations and administrative provisions contrary to the principle of equal treatment when the concern for protection which originally inspired them is no longer well founded shall be revised; and that where similar provisions are included in collective agreements labour and management shall be requested to undertake the desired revision.

Article 6. Member States shall introduce into their national legal systems such measures as are necessary to enable all persons who consider themselves wronged by failure to apply to them the principle of equal treatment within the meaning of Arts. 3, 4 and 5 to pursue their claims by judicial process after possible recourse to other competent authorities.

Article 7. Member States shall take the necessary measures to protect employees against dismissal by the employer as a reaction to a complaint within the undertaking or to any legal proceedings aimed at enforcing compliance with the principle of equal treatment.

Article 8. Member States shall take care that the provisions adopted pursuant to this Directive, together with the relevant provisions already in force, are brought to the attention of employees by all appropriate means, for example at their place of employment.

Article 9. 1. Member States shall put into force the laws, regulations and administrative provisions necessary in order to comply with this Directive within 30 months of its notification and shall immediately inform the Commission thereof.

However, as regards the first part of Art. 3 (2) (c) and the first part of Art. 5 (2) (c), Member States shall carry out a first examination and if necessary a first revision of the laws, regulations and administrative provisions referred to therein within four years of notification of this Directive.

2. Member States shall periodically assess the occupational activities referred to in Art. 2 (2) in order to decide, in the light of social developments, whether there is justification for maintaining the exclusions concerned. They shall notify the Commission of the results of this assessment.

3. Member States shall also communicate to the Commission the texts of laws, regulations and administrative provisions which they adopt in the field covered by this Directive.

[Final provisions omitted.]

Council Directive of 19 December 1978 on the progressive implementation of the principle of equal treatment for men and women in matters of social security (79/7/EEC)[3]

The Council of the European Communities,
Having regard to the Treaty establishing the European Economic Community, and in particular Art. 235 thereof,
Having regard to the proposal from the Commission,
Having regard to the opinion of the European Parliament,
Having regard to the opinion of the Economic and Social Committee,
Whereas Art. 1 (2) of Council Directive 76/207/EEC of 9 February

[3] OJ 1979 L 6/24.

1976 on the implementation of the principle of equal treatment for men and women as regards access to employment, vocational training and promotion, and working conditions provides that, with a view to ensuring the progressive implementation of the principle of equal treatment in matters of social security, the Council, acting on a proposal from the Commission, will adopt provisions defining its substance, its scope and the arrangements for its application; whereas the Treaty does not confer the specific powers required for this purpose;

Whereas the principle of equal treatment in matters of social security should be implemented in the first place in the statutory schemes which provide protection against the risks of sickness, invalidity, old age, accidents at work, occupational diseases and unemployment, and in social assistance in so far as it is intended to supplement or replace the above-mentioned schemes;

Whereas the implementation of the principle of equal treatment in matters of social security does not prejudice the provisions relating to the protection of women on the ground of maternity; whereas, in this respect, Member States may adopt specific provisions for women to remove existing instances of unequal treatment,

Has adopted this Directive:

Article 1. The purpose of this Directive is the progressive implementation, in the field of social security and other elements of social protection provided for in Art. 3, of the principle of equal treatment for men and women in matters of social security, hereinafter referred to as 'the principle of equal treatment'.

Article 2. This Directive shall apply to the working population—including self-employed persons, workers and self-employed persons whose activity is interrupted by illness, accident or involuntary unemployment and persons seeking employment—and to retired or invalided workers and self-employed persons.

Article 3. 1. This Directive shall apply to:

(a) statutory schemes which provide protection against the following risks:
 – sickness,
 – invalidity,
 – old age,
 – accidents at work and occupational diseases,
 – unemployment;
(b) social assistance, in so far as it is intended to supplement or replace the schemes referred to in (a).

2. This Directive shall not apply to the provisions concerning survivors' benefits nor to those concerning family benefits, except in the case of family benefits granted by way of increases of benefits due in respect of the risks referred to in paragraph 1 (a).

3. With a view to ensuring implementation of the principle of equal treatment in occupational schemes, the Council, acting on a proposal from the Commission, will adopt provisions defining its substance, its scope and the arrangements for its application.

Article 4. 1. The principle of equal treatment means that there shall be no discrimination whatsoever on ground of sex either directly, or indirectly by reference in particular to marital or family status, in particular as concerns:

– the scope of the schemes and the conditions of access thereto,
– the obligation to contribute and the calculation of contributions,
– the calculation of benefits including increases due in respect of a spouse and for dependants and the conditions governing the duration and retention of entitlement to benefits.

2. The principle of equal treatment shall be without prejudice to the provisions relating to the protection of women on the grounds of maternity.

Article 5. Member States shall take the measures necessary to ensure that any laws, regulations and administrative provisions contrary to the principle of equal treatment are abolished.

Article 6. Member States shall introduce into their national legal systems such measures as are necessary to enable all persons who consider themselves wronged by failure to apply the principle of equal treatment to pursue their claims by judicial process, possibly after recourse to other competent authorities.

Article 7. 1. This Directive shall be without prejudice to the right of Member States to exclude from its scope:

(a) the determination of pensionable age for the purposes of granting old-age and retirement pensions and the possible consequences thereof for other benefits;
(b) advantages in respect of old-age pension schemes granted to persons who have brought up children; the acquisition of benefit entitlements following periods of interruption of employment due to the bringing up of children;
(c) the granting of old-age or invalidity benefit entitlements by virtue of the derived entitlements of a wife;

(d) the granting of increases of long-term invalidity, old-age, accidents at work and occupational disease benefits for a dependent wife;

(e) the consequences of the exercise, before the adoption of this Directive, of a right of option not to acquire rights or incur obligations under a statutory scheme.

2. Member States shall periodically examine matters excluded under paragraph 1 in order to ascertain, in the light of social developments in the matter concerned, whether there is justification for maintaining the exclusions concerned.

Article 8. 1. Member States shall bring into force the laws, regulations and administrative provisions necessary to comply with this Directive within six years of its notification. They shall immediately inform the Commission thereof.

2. Member States shall communicate to the Commission the text of laws, regulations and administrative provisions which they adopt in the field covered by this Directive, including measures adopted pursuant to Art. 7 (2).

They shall inform the Commission of their reasons for maintaining any existing provisions on the matters referred to in Art. 7 (1) and of the possibilities for reviewing them at a later date.

Article 9. Within seven years of notification of this Directive, Member States shall forward all information necessary to the Commission to enable it to draw up a report on the application of this Directive for submission to the Council and to propose such further measures as may be required for the implementation of the principle of equal treatment.

[Final provisions omitted.]

Council Directive of 24 July 1986 on the implementation of the principle of equal treatment for men and women in occupational social security schemes (86/378/EEC)[4]

The Council of the European Communities,

Having regard to the Treaty establishing the European Economic Community, and in particular Arts. 100 and 235 thereof,

[Recitals omitted.]

[4] OJ 1986 L 225/40.

Whereas the Treaty provides that each Member State shall ensure the application of the principle that men and women should receive equal pay for equal work; whereas 'pay' should be taken to mean the ordinary basic or minimum wage or salary and any other consideration, whether in cash or in kind, which the worker receives, directly or indirectly, from his employer in respect of his employment;

Whereas, although the principle of equal pay does indeed apply directly in cases where discrimination can be determined solely on the basis of the criteria of equal treatment and equal pay, there are also situations in which implementation of this principle implies the adoption of additional measures which more clearly define its scope;

Whereas Art. 1 (2) of Council Directive 76/207/EEC of 9 February 1976 on the implementation of the principle of equal treatment for men and women as regards access to employment, vocational training and promotion, and working conditions[5] provides that, with a view to ensuring the progressive implementation of the principle of equal treatment in matters of social security, the Council, acting on a proposal from the Commission, will adopt provisions defining its substance, its scope and the arrangements for its application; whereas the Council adopted to this end Directive 79/7/EEC of 19 December 1978 on the progressive implementation of the principle of equal treatment for men and women in matters of social security;[6]

Whereas Art. 3 (3) of Directive 79/7/EEC provides that, with a view to ensuring implementation of the principle of equal treatment in occupational schemes, the Council, acting on a proposal from the Commission, will adopt provisions defining its substance, its scope and the arrangements for its application;

Whereas the principle of equal treatment should be implemented in occupational social security schemes which provide protection against the risks specified in Art. 3 (1) of Directive 79/7/EEC as well as those which provide employees with any other consideration in cash or in kind within the meaning of the Treaty;

Whereas implementation of the principle of equal treatment does not prejudice the provisions relating to the protection of women by reason of maternity,

Has adopted this Directive:

Article 1. The object of this Directive is to implement, in occupational social security schemes, the principle of equal treatment for men and women, hereinafter referred to as 'the principle of equal treatment'.

[5] OJ 1976 L 39/40.　　[6] OJ 1979 L 6/24.

Article 2. 1. 'Occupational social security schemes' means schemes not governed by Directive 79/7/EEC whose purpose is to provide workers, whether employees or self-employed, in an undertaking or group of undertakings, area of economic activity or occupational sector or group of such sectors with benefits intended to supplement the benefits provided by statutory social security schemes or to replace them, whether membership of such schemes is compulsory or optional.

2. This Directive does not apply to:

(a) individual contracts,
(b) schemes having only one member,
(c) in the case of salaried workers, insurance schemes offered to participants individually to guarantee them:
    – either additional benefits, or
    – a choice of date on which the normal benefits will start, or a choice between several benefits.

Article 3. This Directive shall apply to members of the working population including self-employed persons, persons whose activity is interrupted by illness, maternity, accident or involuntary unemployment and persons seeking employment, and to retired and disabled workers.

Article 4. This Directive shall apply to:

(a) occupational schemes which provide protection against the following risks:
    – sickness,
    – invalidity,
    – old age, including early retirement,
    – industrial accidents and occupational diseases,
    – unemployment;
(b) occupational schemes which provide for other social benefits, in cash or in kind, and in particular survivors' benefits and family allowances, if such benefits are accorded to employed persons and thus constitute a consideration paid by the employer to the worker by reason of the latter's employment.

Article 5. 1. Under the conditions laid down in the following provisions, the principle of equal treatment implies that there shall be no discrimination on the basis of sex, either directly or indirectly, by reference in particular to marital or family status, especially as regards:

– the scope of the schemes and the conditions of access to them;
– the obligation to contribute and the calculation of contributions;
– the calculation of benefits, including supplementary benefits due in

respect of a spouse or dependants, and the conditions governing the duration and retention of entitlement to benefits.

2. The principle of equal treatment shall not prejudice the provisions relating to the protection of women by reason of maternity.

Article 6. 1. Provisions contrary to the principle of equal treatment shall include those based on sex, either directly or indirectly, in particular by reference to marital or family for:

(a) determining the persons who may participate in an occupational scheme;

(b) fixing the compulsory or optional nature of participation in an occupational scheme;

(c) laying down different rules as regards the age of entry into the scheme or the minimum period of employment or membership of the scheme required to obtain the benefits thereof;

(d) laying down different rules, except as provided for in subparagraphs (h) and (i), for the reimbursement of contributions where a worker leaves a scheme without having fulfilled the conditions guaranteeing him a deferred right to long-term benefits;

(e) setting different conditions for the granting of benefits or restricting such benefits to workers of one or other of the sexes;

(f) fixing different retirement ages;

(g) suspending the retention or acquisition of rights during periods of maternity leave or leave for family reasons which are granted by law or agreement and are paid by the employer;

(h) setting different levels of benefit, except insofar as may be necessary to take account of actuarial calculation factors which differ according to sex in the case of benefits designated as contribution-defined;

(i) setting different levels of worker contribution;

   setting different levels of employer contribution in the case of benefits designated as contribution-defined, except with a view to making the amount of those benefits more nearly equal;

(j) laying down different standards or standards applicable only to workers of a specified sex, except as provided for in subparagraphs (h) and (i), as regards the guarantee or retention of entitlement to deferred benefits when a worker leaves a scheme.

2. Where the granting of benefits within the scope of this Directive is left to the discretion of the scheme's management bodies, the latter must take account of the principle of equal treatment.

Article 7. Member States shall take all necessary steps to ensure that:

(a) provisions contrary to the principle of equal treatment in legally compulsory collective agreements, staff rules of undertakings or any other arrangements relating to occupational schemes are null and void, or may be declared null and void or amended;

(b) schemes containing such provisions may not be approved or extended by administrative measures.

Article 8. 1. Member States shall take all necessary steps to ensure that the provisions of occupational schemes contrary to the principle of equal treatment are revised by 1 January 1993.

2. This Directive shall not preclude rights and obligations relating to a period of membership of an occupational scheme prior to revision of that scheme from remaining subject to the provisions of the scheme in force during that period.

Article 9. Member States may defer compulsory application of the principle of equal treatment with regard to:

(a) determination of pensionable age for the purposes of granting old-age or retirement pensions, and the possible implications for other benefits:
  – either until the date on which such equality is achieved in statutory schemes,
  – or, at the latest, until such equality is required by a directive.

(b) survivors' pensions until a directive requires the principle of equal treatment in statutory social security schemes in that regard;

(c) the application of the first subparagraph of Art. 6 (1) (i) to take account of the different actuarial calculation factors, at the latest until the expiry of a thirteen-year period as from the notification of this Directive.

Article 10. Member States shall introduce into their national legal systems such measures as are necessary to enable all persons who consider themselves injured by failure to apply the principle of equal treatment to pursue their claims before the courts, possibly after bringing the matters before other competent authorities.

Article 11. Member States shall take all the necessary steps to protect workers against dismissal where this constitutes a response on the part of the employer to a complaint made at undertaking level or to the institution of legal proceedings aimed at enforcing compliance with the principle of equal treatment.

[Final provisions omitted.]

Council Directive of 11 December 1986 on the application of the principle of equal treatment between men and women engaged in an activity, including agriculture, in a self-employed capacity, and on the protection of self-employed women during pregnancy and motherhood (86/613/EEC)[7]

The Council of the European Communities,

Having regard to the Treaty establishing the European Economic Community, and in particular Arts. 100 and 235 thereof,

[Recitals omitted.]

Has adopted this Directive:

SECTION I. AIMS AND SCOPE

Article 1. The purpose of this Directive is to ensure, in accordance with the following provisions, application in the Member States of the principle of equal treatment as between men and women engaged in an activity in a self-employed capacity, or contributing to the pursuit of such an activity, as regards those aspects not covered by Directives 76/207/EEC and 79/7/EEC.

Article 2. This Directive covers:

(a) self-employed workers, i.e. all persons pursuing a gainful activity for their own account, under the conditions laid down by national law, including farmers and members of the liberal professions;

(b) their spouses, not being employees or partners, where they habitually, under the conditions laid down by national law, participate in the activities of the self-employed worker and perform the same tasks or ancillary tasks.

Article 3. For the purposes of this Directive the principle of equal treatment implies the absence of all discrimination on grounds of sex, either directly or indirectly, by reference in particular to marital or family status.

---

[7] OJ 1986 L 359/56.

SECTION II. EQUAL TREATMENT BETWEEN SELF-EMPLOYED MALE AND FEMALE WORKERS—POSITION OF THE SPOUSES WITHOUT PROFESSIONAL STATUS OF SELF-EMPLOYED WORKERS—PROTECTION OF SELF-EMPLOYED WORKERS OR WIVES OF SELF-EMPLOYED WORKERS DURING PREGNANCY AND MOTHERHOOD

Article 4. As regards self-employed persons, Member States shall take the measures necessary to ensure the elimination of all provisions which are contrary to the principle of equal treatment as defined in Directive 76/207/EEC, especially in respect of the establishment, equipment or extension of a business or the launching or extension of any other form of self-employed activity including financial facilities.

Article 5. Without prejudice to the specific conditions for access to certain activities which apply equally to both sexes, Member States shall take the measures necessary to ensure that the conditions for the formation of a company between spouses are not more restrictive than the conditions for the formation of a company between unmarried persons.

Article 6. Where a contributory social security system for self-employed workers exists in a Member State, that Member State shall take the necessary measures to enable the spouses referred to in Art. 2 (b) who are not protected under the self-employed worker's social security scheme to join a contributory social security scheme voluntarily.

Article 7. Member States shall undertake to examine under what conditions recognition of the work of the spouses referred to in Art. 2 (b) may be encouraged and, in the light of such examination, consider any appropriate steps for encouraging such recognition.

Article 8. Member States shall undertake to examine whether, and under what conditions, female self-employed workers and the wives of self-employed workers may, during interruptions in their occupational activity owing to pregnancy or motherhood,

– have access to services supplying temporary replacements or existing national social services, or
– be entitled to cash benefits under a social security scheme or under any other public social protection system.

SECTION III. GENERAL AND FINAL PROVISIONS

Article 9. Member States shall introduce into their national legal systems such measures as are necessary to enable all persons who consider themselves wronged by failure to apply the principle of equal treatment in self-employed activities to pursue their claims by judicial process, possibly after recourse to other competent authorities.

Article 10. Member States shall ensure that the measures adopted pursuant to this Directive, together with the relevant provisions already in force, are brought to the attention of bodies representing self-employed workers and vocational training centres.

Article 11. The Council shall review this Directive, on a proposal from the Commission, before 1 July 1993.

[Final provisions omitted.]

Council Directive of 14 February 1977 on the approximation of the laws of the Member States relating to the safeguarding of employees' rights in the event of transfers of undertakings, businesses or parts of businesses (77/187/EEC)[8]

The Council of the European Communities,
  Having regard to the Treaty establishing the European Economic Community, and in particular Art. 100 thereof,

[Recitals omitted.]

Whereas economic trends are bringing in their wake, at both national and Community level, changes in the structure of undertakings, through transfers of undertakings, businesses or parts of businesses to other employers as a result of legal transfers or mergers;
  Whereas it is necessary to provide for the protection of employees in the event of a change of employer, in particular, to ensure that their rights are safeguarded;
  Whereas differences still remain in the Member States as regards the extent of the protection of employees in this respect and these differences should be reduced;
  Whereas these differences can have a direct effect on the functioning of the common market;

[8] OJ 1977 L 61/26.

Whereas it is therefore necessary to promote the approximation of laws in this field while maintaining the improvement described in Art. 117 of the Treaty,

Has adopted this Directive:

SECTION I. SCOPE AND DEFINITIONS

Article 1. 1. This Directive shall apply to the transfer of an undertaking, business or part of a business to another employer as a result of a legal transfer or merger.

2. This Directive shall apply where and in so far as the undertaking, business or part of the business to be transferred is situated within the territorial scope of the Treaty.

3. This Directive shall not apply to sea-going vessels.

Article 2. For the purposes of this Directive:

(a) 'transferor' means any natural or legal person who, by reason of a transfer within the meaning of Art. 1 (1), ceases to be the employer in respect of the undertaking, business or part of the business;
(b) 'transferee' means any natural or legal person who, by reason of a transfer within the meaning of Art. 1 (1), becomes the employer in respect of the undertaking, business or part of the business;
(c) 'representatives of the employees' means the representatives of the employees provided for by the laws or practice of the Member States, with the exception of members of administrative, governing or supervisory bodies of companies who represent employees on such bodies in certain Member States.

SECTION II. SAFEGUARDING OF EMPLOYEES' RIGHTS

Article 3. 1. The transferor's rights and obligations arising from a contract of employment or from an employment relationship existing on the date of a transfer within the meaning of Art. 1 (1) shall, by reason of such transfer, be transferred to the transferee.

Member States may provide that, after the date of transfer within the meaning of Art. 1 (1) and in addition to the transferee, the transferor shall continue to be liable in respect of obligations which arose from a contract of employment or an employment relationship.

2. Following the transfer within the meaning of Art. 1 (1), the transferee shall continue to observe the terms and conditions agreed in any collective agreement on the same terms applicable to the transferor under that agreement, until the date of termination or expiry of the collective

agreement or the entry into force or application of another collective agreement.

Member States may limit the period for observing such terms and conditions, with the proviso that it shall not be less than one year.

3. Paragraphs 1 and 2 shall not cover employees' rights to old-age, invalidity or survivors' benefits under supplementary company or intercompany pension schemes outside the statutory social security schemes in Member States.

Member States shall adopt the measures necessary to protect the interests of employees and of persons no longer employed in the transferor's business at the time of the transfer within the meaning of Art. 1 (1) in respect of rights conferring on them immediate or prospective entitlement to old-age benefits, including survivors' benefits, under supplementary schemes referred to in the first subparagraph.

Article 4. 1. The transfer of an undertaking, business or part of a business shall not in itself constitute grounds for dismissal by the transferor or the transferee. This provision shall not stand in the way of dismissals that may take place for economic, technical or organisational reasons entailing changes in the work-force.

Member States may provide that the first subparagraph shall not apply to certain specific categories of employees who are not covered by the laws or practice of the Member States in respect of protection against dismissal.

2. If the contract of employment or the employment relationship is terminated because the transfer within the meaning of Art. 1 (1) involves a substantial change in working conditions to the detriment of the employee, the employer shall be regarded as having been responsible for termination of the contract of employment or of the employment relationship.

Article 5. 1. If the business preserves its autonomy, the status and function, as laid down by the laws, regulations or administrative provisions of the Member States, of the representatives or of the representation of the employees affected by the transfer within the meaning of Art. 1 (1) shall be preserved.

The first subparagraph shall not apply if, under the laws, regulations, administrative provisions or practice of the Member States, the conditions necessary for the re-appointment of the representatives of the employees or for the reconstitution of the representation of the employees are fulfilled.

2. If the term of office of the representatives of the employees affected by a transfer within the meaning of Art. 1 (1) expires as a result of the

transfer, the representatives shall continue to enjoy the protection provided by the laws, regulations, administrative provisions or practice of the Member States.

SECTION III. INFORMATION AND CONSULTATION

Article 6. 1. The transferor and the transferee shall be required to inform the representatives of their respective employees affected by a transfer within the meaning of Art. 1 (1) of the following:

— the reasons for the transfer,
— the legal, economic and social implications of the transfer for the employees,
— measures envisaged in relation to the employees.

The transferor must give such information to the representatives of his employees in good time before the transfer is carried out.

The transferee must give such information to the representatives of his employees in good time, and in any event before his employees are directly affected by the transfer as regards their conditions of work and employment.

2. If the transferor or the transferee envisages measures in relation to his employees, he shall consult his representatives of the employees in good time on such measures with a view to seeking agreement.

3. Member States whose laws, regulations or administrative provisions provide that representatives of the employees may have recourse to an arbitration board to obtain a decision on the measures to be taken in relation to employees may limit the obligations laid down in paragraphs 1 and 2 to cases where the transfer carried out gives rise to a change in the business likely to entail serious disadvantages for a considerable number of the employees.

The information and consultations shall cover at least the measures envisaged in relation to the employees.

The information must be provided and consultations take place in good time before the change in the business as referred to in the first subparagraph is effected.

4. Member States may limit the obligations laid down in paragraphs 1, 2 and 3 to undertakings or businesses which, in respect of the number of employees, fulfil the conditions for the election or designation of a collegiate body representing the employees.

5. Member States may provide that where there are no representatives of the employees in an undertaking or business, the employees concerned must be informed in advance when a transfer within the meaning of Art. 1 (1) is about to take place.

SECTION IV. FINAL PROVISIONS

Article 7. This Directive shall not affect the right of Member States to apply or introduce laws, regulations or administrative provisions which are more favourable to employees.

[Final provisions omitted.]

Community Charter of the Fundamental Social Rights of Workers

The Heads of State or Government of the Member States of the European Community meeting at Strasbourg on 9 December 1989[1]

Whereas, under the terms of Art. 117 of the EEC Treaty, the Member States have agreed on the need to promote improved living and working conditions for workers so as to make possible their harmonisation while the improvement is being maintained;

Whereas following on from the conclusions of the European Councils of Hanover and Rhodes the European Council of Madrid considered that, in the context of the establishment of the single European market, the same importance must be attached to the social aspects as to the economic aspects and whereas, therefore, they must be developed in a balanced manner;

Having regard to the Resolutions of the European Parliament of 15 March 1989, 14 September 1989 and 22 November 1989, and to the Opinion of the Economic and Social Committee of 22 February 1989;

Whereas the completion of the internal market is the most effective means of creating employment and ensuring maximum well-being in the Community; whereas employment development and creation must be given first priority in the completion of the internal market; whereas it is for the Community to take up the challenges of the future with regard to economic competitiveness, taking into account, in particular, regional imbalances;

Whereas the social consensus contributes to the strengthening of the competitiveness of undertakings, of the economy as a whole and to the creation of employment; whereas in this respect it is an essential condition for ensuring sustained economic development;

Whereas the completion of the internal market must favour the approximation of improvements in living and working conditions, as well as economic and social cohesion within the European Community while avoiding distortions of competition;

Whereas the completion of the internal market must offer improvements in the social field for workers of the European Community, especially in terms of freedom of movement, living and working conditions, health and safety at work, social protection, education and training;

---

[1] Text adopted by the Heads of State or Government of 11 Member States.

Whereas, in order to ensure equal treatment, it is important to combat every form of discrimination, including discrimination on grounds of sex, colour, race, opinions and beliefs, and whereas, in a spirit of solidarity, it is important to combat social exclusion;

Whereas it is for Member States to guarantee that workers from non-member countries and members of their families who are legally resident in a Member State of the European Community are able to enjoy, as regards their living and working conditions, treatment comparable to that enjoyed by workers who are nationals of the Member State concerned;

Whereas inspiration should be drawn from the Conventions of the International Labour Organisation and from the European Social Charter of the Council of Europe;

Whereas the Treaty, as amended by the Single European Act, contains provisions laying down the powers of the Community relating *inter alia* to the freedom of movement of workers (Arts. 7, 48 to 51), the right of establishment (Arts. 52 to 58), the social field under the conditions laid down in Arts. 117 to 122—in particular as regards the improvement of health and safety in the working environment (Art. 118a), the development of the dialogue between management and labour at European level (Art. 118b), equal pay for men and women for equal work (Art. 119)—the general principles for implementing a common vocational training policy (Art. 128), economic and social cohesion (Art. 130a to 130e) and, more generally, the approximation of legislation (Arts. 100, 100a and 235); whereas the implementation of the Charter must not entail an extension of the Community's powers as defined by the Treaties;

Whereas the aim of the present Charter is on the one hand to consolidate the progress made in the social field, through action by the Member States, the two sides of industry and the Community;

Whereas its aim is on the other hand to declare solemnly that the implementation of the Single European Act must take full account of the social dimension of the Community and that it is necessary in this context to ensure at appropriate levels the development of the social rights of workers of the European Community, especially employed workers and self-employed persons;

Whereas, in accordance with the conclusions of the Madrid European Council, the respective roles of Community rules, national legislation and collective agreements must be clearly established;

Whereas, by virtue of the principle of subsidiarity, responsibility for the initiatives to be taken with regard to the implementation of these social rights lies with the Member States or their constituent parts and, within the limits of its powers, with the European Community; whereas such implementation may take the form of laws, collective agreements or existing practices at the various appropriate levels and whereas it requires in many spheres the active involvement of the two sides of industry;

Whereas the solemn proclamation of fundamental social rights at European Community level may not, when implemented, provide grounds for any retrogression compared with the situation currently existing in each Member State,

Have adopted the following declaration constituting the 'Community charter of the fundamental social rights of workers':

TITLE I. FUNDAMENTAL SOCIAL RIGHTS OF WORKERS

Freedom of movement

1. Every worker of the European Community shall have the right to freedom of movement throughout the territory of the Community, subject to restrictions justified on grounds of public order, public safety or public health.

2. The right to freedom of movement shall enable any worker to engage in any occupation or profession in the Community in accordance with the principles of equal treatment as regards access to employment, working conditions and social protection in the host country.

3. The right of freedom of movement shall also imply:

- harmonisation of conditions of residence in all Member States, particularly those concerning family reunification;
- elimination of obstacles arising from the non-recognition of diplomas or equivalent occupational qualifications;
- improvement of the living and working conditions of frontier workers.

Employment and remuneration

4. Every individual shall be free to choose and engage in an occupation according to the regulations governing each occupation.

5. All employment shall be fairly remunerated.

To this end, in accordance with arrangements applying in each country:

- workers shall be assured of an equitable wage, i.e. a wage sufficient to enable them to have a decent standard of living;
- workers subject to terms of employment other than an open-ended full-time contract shall benefit from an equitable reference wage;
- wages may be withheld, seized or transferred only in accordance with national law; such provisions should entail measures enabling the worker concerned to continue to enjoy the necessary means of subsistence for him or herself and his or her family.

6. Every individual must be able to have access to public placement services free of charge.

Improvement of living and working conditions

7. The completion of the internal market must lead to an improvement in the living and working conditions of workers in the European Community. This process must result from an approximation of these conditions while the improvement is being maintained, as regards in particular the duration and organisation of working time and forms of employment other than open-ended contracts, such as fixed-term contracts, part-time working, temporary work and seasonal work.

The improvement must cover, where necessary, the development of certain aspects of employment regulations such as procedures for collective redundancies and those regarding bankruptcies.

8. Every worker of the European Community shall have a right to a weekly rest period and to annual paid leave, the duration of which must be progressively harmonised in accordance with national practices.

9. The conditions of employment of every worker of the European Community shall be stipulated in laws, a collective agreement or a contract of employment, according to arrangements applying in each country.

Social protection

According to the arrangements applying in each country:

10. Every worker of the European Community shall have a right to adequate social protection and shall, whatever his status and whatever the size of the undertaking in which he is employed, enjoy an adequate level of social security benefits.

Persons who have been unable either to enter or re-enter the labour market and have no means of subsistence must be able to receive sufficient resources and social assistance in keeping with their particular situation.

Freedom of association and collective bargaining

11. Employers and workers of the European Community shall have the right of association in order to constitute professional organisations or trade unions of their choice for the defence of their economic and social interests.

Every employer and every worker shall have the freedom to join or not to join such organisations without any personal or occupational damage being thereby suffered by him.

12. Employers or employers' organisations, on the one hand, and workers' organisations, on the other, shall have the right to negotiate and conclude collective agreements under the conditions laid down by national legislation and practice.

The dialogue between the two sides of industry at European level which must be developed, may, if the parties deem it desirable, result in contractual relations in particular at inter-occupational and sectoral level.

13. The right to resort to collective action in the event of a conflict of interests shall include the right to strike, subject to the obligations arising under national regulations and collective agreements.

In order to facilitate the settlement of industrial disputes the establishment and utilization at the appropriate levels of conciliation, mediation and arbitration procedures should be encouraged in accordance with national practice.

14. The internal legal order of the Member States shall determine under which conditions and to what extent the rights provided for in Articles 11 to 13 apply to the armed forces, the police and the civil service.

Vocational training

15. Every worker of the European Community must be able to have access to vocational training and to benefit therefrom throughout his working life. In the conditions governing access to such training there may be no discrimination on grounds of nationality.

The competent public authorities, undertakings or the two sides of industry, each within their own sphere of competence, should set up continuing and permanent training systems enabling every person to undergo retraining more especially through leave for training purposes, to improve his skills or to acquire new skills, particularly in the light of technical developments.

Equal treatment for men and women

16. Equal treatment for men and women must be assured. Equal opportunities for men and women must be developed.

To this end, action should be intensified to ensure the implementation of the principle of equality between men and women as regards in particular access to employment, remuneration, working conditions, social protection, education, vocational training and career development.

Measures should also be developed enabling men and women to reconcile their occupational and family obligations.

Information, consultation and participation for workers

17. Information, consultation and participation for workers must be developed along appropriate lines, taking account of the practices in force in the various Member States.

This shall apply especially in companies or groups of companies having establishments or companies in two or more Member States of the European Community.

18. Such information, consultation and participation must be implemented in due time, particularly in the following cases:

- when technological changes which, from the point of view of working conditions and work organisation, have major implications for the work-force, are introduced into undertakings;
- in connection with restructuring operations in undertakings or in cases of mergers having an impact on the employment of workers;
- in cases of collective redundancy procedures;
- when transfrontier workers in particular are affected by employment policies pursued by the undertaking where they are employed.

Health protection and safety at the workplace

19. Every worker must enjoy satisfactory health and safety conditions in his working environment. Appropriate measures must be taken in order to achieve further harmonisation of conditions in this area while maintaining the improvements made.

These measures shall take account, in particular, of the need for the training, information, consultation and balanced participation of workers as regards the risks incurred and the steps taken to eliminate or reduce them.

The provisions regarding implementation of the internal market shall help to ensure such protection.

Protection of children and adolescents

20. Without prejudice to such rules as may be more favourable to young people, in particular those ensuring their preparation for work through vocational training, and subject to derogations limited to certain light work, the minimum employment age must not be lower than the minimum school-leaving age and, in any case, not lower than 15 years.

21. Young people who are in gainful employment must receive equitable remuneration in accordance with national practice.

22. Appropriate measures must be taken to adjust labour regulations applicable to young workers so that their specific development and vocational training and access to employment needs are met.

The duration of work must, in particular, be limited—without it being possible to circumvent this limitation through recourse to overtime—and night work prohibited in the case of workers of under 18 years of age, save in the case of certain jobs laid down in national legislation or regulations.

23. Following the end of compulsory education, young people must be entitled to receive initial vocational training of a sufficient duration to enable them to adapt to the requirements of their future working life; for young workers, such training should take place during working hours.

Elderly persons

According to the arrangements applying in each country:

24. Every worker of the European Community must, at the time of retirement, be able to enjoy resources affording him or her a decent standard of living.

25. Any person who has reached retirement age but who is not entitled to a pension or who does not have other means of subsistence, must be entitled to sufficient resources and to medical and social assistance specifically suited to his needs.

Disabled persons

26. All disabled persons, whatever the origin and nature of their disablement, must be entitled to additional concrete measures aimed at improving their social and professional integration.

These measures must concern, in particular, according to the capacities of the beneficiaries, vocational training, ergonomics, accessibility, mobility, means of transport and housing.

TITLE II. IMPLEMENTATION OF THE CHARTER

27. It is more particularly the responsibility of the Member States, in accordance with national practices, notably through legislative measures or collective agreements, to guarantee the fundamental social rights in this Charter and to implement the social measures indispensable to the smooth operation of the internal market as part of a strategy of economic and social cohesion.

28. The European Council invites the Commission to submit as soon as possible initiatives which fall within its powers, as provided for in the Treaties, with a view to the adoption of legal instruments for the effective implementation, as and when the internal market is completed, of those rights which come within the Community's area of competence.

29. The Commission shall establish each year, during the last three months, a report on the application of the Charter by the Member States and by the European Community.

30. The report of the Commission shall be forwarded to the European Council, the European Parliament and the Economic and Social Committee.

PART III
UK SOURCES

European Communities Act 1972
(as amended)

[EXTRACTS]

An Act to make provision in connection with the enlargement of the European Communities to include the United Kingdom, together with (for certain purposes) the Channel Islands, the Isle of Man and Gibraltar. Be it enacted by the Queen's most Excellent Majesty, by and with the advice and consent of the Lords Spiritual and Temporal, and Commons, in this present Parliament assembled, and by the authority of the same, as follows:–

PART I. GENERAL PROVISIONS

1. *Short Title and interpretation*
    (1) This Act may be cited as the European Communities Act 1972.
    (2) In this Act 'the Communities' means the European Economic Community, the European Coal and Steel Community and the European Atomic Energy Community;
    'the Treaties' or 'the Community Treaties' means, subject to subsection 3 below, the pre-accession treaties, that is to say, those described in Part I of Schedule 1 to this Act, taken with:

(a) the treaty relating to the accession of the United Kingdom to the European Economic Community and to the European Atomic Energy Community, signed at Brussels on 22 January 1972; and

(b) the decision, of the same date, of the Council of the European Communities relating to the accession of the United Kingdom to the European Coal and Steel Community; and

(c) the treaty relating to the accession of the Hellenic Republic to the European Economic Community and to the European Atomic Energy Community, signed at Athens on 28 May 1979; and

(d) the decision, of 24 May 1979, of the Council relating to the accession of the Hellenic Republic to the European Coal and Steel Community;

(e) the decisions, of 7th May 1985 and of 24th June 1988, of the Council on the Communities' system of own resources; and

(f) the undertaking made by the Representatives of the Governments of the Member States, as confirmed at their meeting within the Council in June 1988 in Luxembourg, to make payments to finance the Communities' general budget for the financial year 1988; and

(g) the Treaty relating to the accession of the Kingdom of Spain and the

Portuguese Republic to the European Economic Community and the European Atomic Energy Community, signed at Lisbon and Madrid on 12th June 1985; and

(h) the decision, of 11th June 1985, of the Council relating to the accession of the Kingdom of Spain and the Portuguese Republic to the European Coal and Steel Community; and

(j) the following provisions of the Single European Act signed at Luxembourg and the Hague on 17th and 28th February 1986, namely Title II (amendment of the treaties establishing the Communities) and, so far as they relate to any of the Communities or any Community institution, the preamble and Titles I (common provisions) and IV (general and final provisions);

and any other treaty entered into by any of the Communities, with or without any of the Member States, or entered into, as a treaty ancillary to any of the Treaties, by the United Kingdom;

and any expression defined in Schedule 1 to this Act has the meaning there given to it.

(3) If Her Majesty by Order in Council declares that a treaty specified in the Order is to be regarded as one of the Community Treaties as herein defined, the Order shall be conclusive that it is to be so regarded; but a treaty entered into by the United Kingdom after 22 January 1972, other than a pre-accession treaty to which the United Kingdom accedes on terms settled on or before that date, shall not be so regarded unless it is so specified, nor be so specified unless a draft of the Order in Council has been approved by resolution of each House of Parliament.

(4) For purposes of subsections (2) and (3) above, 'treaty' includes any international agreement, and any protocol or annex to a treaty or international agreement.

2. *General implementation of Treaties*

(1) All such rights, powers, liabilities, obligations and restrictions from time to time created or arising by or under the Treaties, and all such remedies and procedures from time to time provided for by or under the Treaties, as in accordance with the Treaties are without further enactment to be given legal effect or used in the United Kingdom shall be recognised and available in law, and be enforced, allowed and followed accordingly; and the expression 'enforceable Community right' and similar expressions shall be read as referring to one to which this subsection applies.

(2) Subject to Schedule 2 of this Act, at any time after its passing Her Majesty may by Order in Council, and any designated Minister or department may by regulations, make provision:

(a) for the purpose of implementing any Community obligation of the United Kingdom, or of enabling any rights enjoyed or to be enjoyed by the United Kingdom under or by virtue of the Treaties to be exercised; or

(b) for the purpose of dealing with matters arising out of or related to any such obligation or rights or the coming into force, or the operation from time to time, of subsection (1) above;

and in the exercise of any statutory power or duty, including any power to give directions or to legislate by means of orders, rules, regulations or other subordinate instrument, the person entrusted with the power or duty may have regard to the objects of the Communities and to any such obligation or rights as aforesaid.

In this subsection 'designated Minister or department' means such Minister of the Crown or government department as may from time to time be designated by Order in Council in relation to any matter or for any purpose, but subject to such restrictions or conditions (if any) as may be specified by the Order in Council.

(3) There shall be charged on and issued out of the Consolidated Fund or, if so determined by the Treasury, the National Loans Fund the amounts required to meet any Community obligation to make payments to any of the Communities or Member States, or any Community obligation in respect of contributions to the capital or reserves of the European Investment Bank or in respect of loans to the Bank, or to redeem any notes or obligations issued or created in respect of any such Community obligation; and, except as otherwise provided by or under any enactment:

(a) any other expenses incurred under or by virtue of the Treaties or this Act by any Minister of the Crown or government department may be paid out of moneys provided by Parliament; and

(b) any sums received under or by virtue of the Treaties or this Act by any Minister of the Crown or government department, save for such sums as may be required for disbursements permitted by any other enactment, shall be paid into the Consolidated Fund or, if so determined by the Treasury, the National Loans Fund.

(4) The provision that may be made under subsection (2) above includes, subject to Schedule 2 to this Act, any such provision (of any such extent) as might be made by Act of Parliament, and any enactment passed or to be passed, other than one contained in this Part of this Act, shall be construed and have effect subject to the foregoing provisions of this section; but, except as may be provided by any Act passed after this Act, Schedule 2 shall have effect in connection with the powers conferred by this and the following sections of this Act to make Orders in Council and regulations.

(5) and the references in that subsection to a Minister of the Crown or government department and to a statutory power or duty shall include a Minister or department of the Government of Northern Ireland and a power or duty arising under or by virtue of an Act of the Parliament of Northern Ireland.

(6) A law passed by the legislature of any of the Channel Islands or of the Isle of Man, or a colonial law (within the meaning of the Colonial Laws Validity Act 1865) passed or made for Gibraltar, if expressed to be passed or made in the implementation of the Treaties and of the obligations of the United Kingdom thereunder, shall not be void or inoperative by reason of any inconsistency with or repugnancy to an Act of Parliament, passed or to be passed, that extends to the Island or Gibraltar or any provision having the force and effect of an Act there (but not including this section), nor by reason of its having some operation outside the Island or Gibraltar; and any such Act or provision that extends to the Island or Gibraltar shall be construed and have effect subject to the provisions of any such law.

3. *Decisions on, and proof of, Treaties and Community instruments etc.*

(1) For the purposes of all legal proceedings any question as to the meaning or effect of any of the Treaties, or as to the validity, meaning or effect of any Community instrument, shall be treated as a question of law (and, if not referred to the European Court, be for determination as such in accordance with the principles laid down by and any relevant decision of the European Court or any court attached thereto).

(2) Judicial notice shall be taken of the Treaties, of the *Official Journal of the Communities* and of any decision of, or expression of opinion by, the European Court or any court attached thereto on any such question as aforesaid; and the *Official Journal* shall be admissible as evidence of any instrument or other act thereby communicated of any of the Communities or of any Community institution.

(3) Evidence of any instrument issued by a Community institution, including any judgment or order of the European Court or any court attached thereto, or of any document in the custody of a Community institution, or any entry in or extract from such a document, may be given in any legal proceedings by production of a copy certified as a true copy by an official of that institution; and any document purporting to be such a copy shall be received in evidence without proof of the official position or handwriting of the person signing the certificate.

(4) Evidence of any Community instrument may also be given in any legal proceedings:

(a) by production of a copy purporting to be printed by the Queen's Printer;

(b) where the instrument is in the custody of a government department (including a department of the Government of Northern Ireland), by production of a copy certified on behalf of the department to be a true copy by an officer of the department generally or specially authorised so to do;

and any document purporting to be such a copy as is mentioned in paragraph (b) above of an instrument in the custody of a department shall be received in evidence without proof of the official position or handwriting of the person signing the certificate, or of his authority to do so, or of the document being in the custody of the department.

(5) In any legal proceedings in Scotland evidence of any matter given in a manner authorised by this section shall be sufficient evidence of it.

[Sections 4–12 and schedules 1, 3 and 4 are omitted.]

Schedule 2. Provisions as to Subordinate Legislation

I

(1) The powers conferred by section 2 (2) of this Act to make provision for the purposes mentioned in section 2 (2) (a) and (b) shall not include power:

(a) to make any provision imposing or increasing taxation; or
(b) to make any provision taking effect from a date earlier than that of the making of the instrument containing the provision; or
(c) to confer any power to legislate by means of orders, rules, regulations or other subordinate instrument, other than rules of procedure for any court or tribunal; or
(d) to create any new criminal offence punishable with imprisonment for more than two years or punishable on summary conviction with imprisonment for more than three months or with a fine of more than level 5 on the standard scale (if not calculated on a daily basis) or with a fine of more than £100 a day.

(2) Subparagraph (1) (c) above shall not be taken to preclude the modification of a power to legislate conferred otherwise than under section 2 (2), or the extension of any such power to purposes of the like nature as those for which it was conferred; and a power to give directions as to matters of administration is not to be regarded as a power to legislate within the meaning of subparagraph (1) (c).

2

(1) Subject to paragraph 3 below, where a provision contained in any section of this Act confers power to make regulations (otherwise than by modification or extension of an existing power), the power shall be exercisable by statutory instrument.

(2) Any statutory instrument containing an Order in Council or regulations made in the exercise of a power so conferred, if made without a draft having been approved by resolution of each House of Parliament, shall be subject to annulment in pursuance of a resolution of either House.

3

Nothing in paragraph 2 above shall apply to any Order in Council made by the Governor of Northern Ireland or to any regulations made by a Minister or department of the Government of Northern Ireland; but where a provision contained in any section of this Act confers power to make such an Order in Council or regulations, then any Order in Council or regulations made in the exercise of that power, if made without a draft having been approved by resolution of each House of the Parliament of Northern Ireland, shall be subject to negative resolution within the meaning of section 41 (6) of the Interpretation Act (Northern Ireland) 1954 as if the Order or regulations were a statutory instrument within the meaning of that Act.

European Parliamentary Elections Act 1978
(as amended)

[EXTRACTS]

An Act to make provision for and in connection with the election of representatives to the Parliament of the European Communities, and to prevent any treaty providing for any increase in the powers of the Parliament from being ratified by the United Kingdom unless approved by Act of Parliament.

Be it enacted by the Queen's most Excellent Majesty, by and with the advice and consent of the Lords Spiritual and Temporal, and Commons, in this present Parliament assembled, and by the authority of the same, as follows:–

1. *Election of Representatives to the European Assembly*

The representatives of the people of the United Kingdom in the Parliament of the European Communities shall be elected in accordance with this Act.

2. *Number of Representatives*

The number of representatives to the European Parliament to be elected in the United Kingdom shall be 81; and of those representatives:

(a) 66 shall be elected in England;
(b) 8 shall be elected in Scotland;
(c) 4 shall be elected in Wales; and
(d) 3 shall be elected in Northern Ireland.

3. *Method of election*

European Parliamentary elections shall be held and conducted in accordance with the provisions of Schedule 1 to this Act (with Schedule 2) under the simple majority system (for Great Britain) and the single transferable vote system (for Northern Ireland).

[Sections 4 and 5 are omitted.]

6. *Parliamentary approval of Treaties increasing Parliament's powers*

(1) No treaty which provides for any increase in the powers of the Parliament shall be ratified by the United Kingdom unless it has been approved by an Act of Parliament.

(2) In this section 'treaty' includes any international agreement, and any protocol or annex to a treaty or international agreement.

[Sections 7–9 and the Schedules are omitted.]

Rules of the Supreme Court. Order 114.
(Added by R.S.C. (Amendment No. 3) 1972
(S.I. 1972 No. 1899)).

REFERENCES TO THE EUROPEAN COURT

1. *Interpretation*

In this Order:
'the Court' means the court by which an order is made and includes the Court of Appeal;

'the European Court' means the Court of Justice of the European Communities; and

'order' means an order referring a question to the European Court for a preliminary ruling under Art. 177 of the Treaty establishing the European Economic Community, Art. 150 of the Treaty establishing the European Atomic Energy Community or Art. 41 of the Treaty establishing the European Coal and Steel Community or for a ruling on the interpretation of any of the instruments referred to in s. 1 (1) of the Civil Jurisdiction and Judgments Act 1982 or in s. 1 of the Contracts (Applicable Law Act) 1990.

2. *Making of order*

(1) An order may be made by the Court of its own motion at any stage in a cause or matter, or on application by a party before or at the trial or hearing thereof.

(2) Where an application is made before the trial or hearing, it shall be made by motion.

(3) In the High Court no order shall be made except by a judge in person.

3. *Schedule to order to set out request for ruling*

An order shall set out in a schedule the request for the preliminary ruling of the European Court, and the Court may give directions as to the manner and form in which the schedule is to be prepared.

4. *Stay of proceedings pending ruling*

The proceedings in which an order is made shall, unless the Court otherwise orders, be stayed until the European Court has given a preliminary ruling on the question referred to it.

5. *Transmission of order to the European Court*

When an order has been made, the Senior Master shall send a copy thereof to the Registrar of the European Court; but in the case of an order made by the High Court, he shall not do so, unless the Court otherwise orders, until the time for appealing against the order has expired or, if an appeal is entered within that time, until the appeal has been determined or otherwise disposed of.

6. *Appeals from orders made by High Court*

An order made by the High Court shall be deemed to be a final decision, and accordingly an appeal against it shall lie to the Court of Appeal without leave; but the period within which a notice of appeal must be served under O. 59, r. 4 (1), shall be 14 days.

European Communities Amendment Bill 1993 as amended
(A Bill to make provision consequential on the Treaty on European Union signed at Maastricht on 7th February 1992.)

Be it enacted . . . as follows:–

1. (1) In section 1(2) of the European Communities Act 1972, in the definition of 'the Treaties' and 'the Community Treaties', after paragraph (j) (inserted by the European Communities (Amendment) Act 1986) there shall be inserted the words 'and
   (k) Titles II, III and IV of the Treaty on European Union signed at Maastricht on 7th February 1992, together with the other provisions of the Treaty so far as they relate to those Titles, and the Protocols adopted at Maastricht on that date and annexed to the Treaty establishing the European Community with the exception of the Protocol on Social Policy on page 117 of Cm 1934'.
   (2) For the purpose of section 6 of the European Parliamentary Elections Act 1978 (approval of treaties increasing the Parliament's powers) the Treaty on European Union signed at Maastricht on 7th February 1992 is approved.

2. No notification shall be given to the Council of the European Communities that the United Kingdom intends to move to the third stage of economic and monetary union (in accordance with the Protocol on certain provisions relating to the United Kingdom adopted at Maastricht on 7th February 1992) unless a draft of the notification has first been approved by Act of Parliament and unless Her Majesty's Government has reported to Parliament on its proposals for the co-ordination of economic policies, its role in the European Council of Finance Ministers (ECOFIN) in pursuit of the objectives of Article 2 of the Treaty establishing the European Community as provided for in Articles 103 and 102a, and the work of the European Monetary Institute in preparation for economic and monetary union.

3. In implementing Article 108 of the Treaty establishing the European Community, and ensuring compatibility of the statutes of the national central bank, Her Majesty's Government shall, by order, make provision for the Governor of the Bank of England to make an annual report to Parliament, which shall be subject to approval by a Resolution of each House of Parliament.

4. In implementing the provisions of Article 103(3) of the Treaty establishing the European Community, information shall be submitted to the Commission from the United Kingdom indicating performance on

economic growth, industrial investment, employment and balance of trade, together with comparisons with those items of performance from other member States.

5. Before submitting the information required in implementing Article 103(3) of the Treaty establishing the European Community, Her Majesty's Government shall report to Parliament for its approval an assessment of the medium term economic and budgetary position in relation to public investment expenditure and to the social, economic and environmental goals set out in Article 2, which report shall form the basis of any submission to the Council and Commission in pursuit of their responsibilities under Articles 103 and 104c.

6. A person may be proposed as a member or alternate member for the United Kingdom of the Committee of the Regions constituted under Article 198a of the Treaty establishing the European Community only if, at the time of the proposal, he is an elected member of a local authority.

7. This Act shall come into force only when each House of Parliament has come to a Resolution on a motion tabled by a Minister of the Crown considering the question of adopting the Protocol on Social Policy.

8. This Act may be cited as the European Communities (Amendment) Act 1993.